T0202855

Lecture Notes in Computer Science 11589

Commenced Publication in 1973
Founding and Former Series Editors:
Gerhard Goos, Juris Hartmanis, and Jan van Leeuwen

More information about this series at http://www.springer.com/series/7409

Fiona Fui-Hoon Nah · Keng Siau (Eds.)

HCI in Business, Government and Organizations

Information Systems and Analytics

6th International Conference, HCIBGO 2019
Held as Part of the 21st HCI International Conference, HCII 2019
Orlando, FL, USA, July 26–31, 2019
Proceedings, Part II

 Springer

Editors
Fiona Fui-Hoon Nah
Missouri University of Science
and Technology
Rolla, MO, USA

Keng Siau
Missouri University of Science
and Technology
Rolla, MO, USA

ISSN 0302-9743   ISSN 1611-3349 (electronic)
Lecture Notes in Computer Science
ISBN 978-3-030-22337-3   ISBN 978-3-030-22338-0 (eBook)
https://doi.org/10.1007/978-3-030-22338-0

LNCS Sublibrary: SL3 – Information Systems and Applications, incl. Internet/Web, and HCI

This Springer imprint is published by the registered company Springer Nature Switzerland AG
The registered company address is: Gewerbestrasse 11, 6330 Cham, Switzerland

Foreword

The 21st International Conference on Human-Computer Interaction, HCI International 2019, was held in Orlando, FL, USA, during July 26–31, 2019. The event incorporated the 18 thematic areas and affiliated conferences listed on the following page.

A total of 5,029 individuals from academia, research institutes, industry, and governmental agencies from 73 countries submitted contributions, and 1,274 papers and 209 posters were included in the pre-conference proceedings. These contributions address the latest research and development efforts and highlight the human aspects of design and use of computing systems. The contributions thoroughly cover the entire field of human-computer interaction, addressing major advances in knowledge and effective use of computers in a variety of application areas. The volumes constituting the full set of the pre-conference proceedings are listed in the following pages.

This year the HCI International (HCII) conference introduced the new option of "late-breaking work." This applies both for papers and posters and the corresponding volume(s) of the proceedings will be published just after the conference. Full papers will be included in the *HCII 2019 Late-Breaking Work Papers Proceedings* volume of the proceedings to be published in the Springer LNCS series, while poster extended abstracts will be included as short papers in the HCII 2019 *Late-Breaking Work Poster Extended Abstracts* volume to be published in the Springer CCIS series.

I would like to thank the program board chairs and the members of the program boards of all thematic areas and affiliated conferences for their contribution to the highest scientific quality and the overall success of the HCI International 2019 conference.

This conference would not have been possible without the continuous and unwavering support and advice of the founder, Conference General Chair Emeritus and Conference Scientific Advisor Prof. Gavriel Salvendy. For his outstanding efforts, I would like to express my appreciation to the communications chair and editor of *HCI International News*, Dr. Abbas Moallem.

July 2019   Constantine Stephanidis

HCI International 2019 Thematic Areas
and Affiliated Conferences

Thematic areas:

- HCI 2019: Human-Computer Interaction
- HIMI 2019: Human Interface and the Management of Information

Affiliated conferences:

- EPCE 2019: 16th International Conference on Engineering Psychology and Cognitive Ergonomics
- UAHCI 2019: 13th International Conference on Universal Access in Human-Computer Interaction
- VAMR 2019: 11th International Conference on Virtual, Augmented and Mixed Reality
- CCD 2019: 11th International Conference on Cross-Cultural Design
- SCSM 2019: 11th International Conference on Social Computing and Social Media
- AC 2019: 13th International Conference on Augmented Cognition
- DHM 2019: 10th International Conference on Digital Human Modeling and Applications in Health, Safety, Ergonomics and Risk Management
- DUXU 2019: 8th International Conference on Design, User Experience, and Usability
- DAPI 2019: 7th International Conference on Distributed, Ambient and Pervasive Interactions
- HCIBGO 2019: 6th International Conference on HCI in Business, Government and Organizations
- LCT 2019: 6th International Conference on Learning and Collaboration Technologies
- ITAP 2019: 5th International Conference on Human Aspects of IT for the Aged Population
- HCI-CPT 2019: First International Conference on HCI for Cybersecurity, Privacy and Trust
- HCI-Games 2019: First International Conference on HCI in Games
- MobiTAS 2019: First International Conference on HCI in Mobility, Transport, and Automotive Systems
- AIS 2019: First International Conference on Adaptive Instructional Systems

Pre-conference Proceedings Volumes Full List

1. LNCS 11566, Human-Computer Interaction: Perspectives on Design (Part I), edited by Masaaki Kurosu
2. LNCS 11567, Human-Computer Interaction: Recognition and Interaction Technologies (Part II), edited by Masaaki Kurosu
3. LNCS 11568, Human-Computer Interaction: Design Practice in Contemporary Societies (Part III), edited by Masaaki Kurosu
4. LNCS 11569, Human Interface and the Management of Information: Visual Information and Knowledge Management (Part I), edited by Sakae Yamamoto and Hirohiko Mori
5. LNCS 11570, Human Interface and the Management of Information: Information in Intelligent Systems (Part II), edited by Sakae Yamamoto and Hirohiko Mori
6. LNAI 11571, Engineering Psychology and Cognitive Ergonomics, edited by Don Harris
7. LNCS 11572, Universal Access in Human-Computer Interaction: Theory, Methods and Tools (Part I), edited by Margherita Antona and Constantine Stephanidis
8. LNCS 11573, Universal Access in Human-Computer Interaction: Multimodality and Assistive Environments (Part II), edited by Margherita Antona and Constantine Stephanidis
9. LNCS 11574, Virtual, Augmented and Mixed Reality: Multimodal Interaction (Part I), edited by Jessie Y. C. Chen and Gino Fragomeni
10. LNCS 11575, Virtual, Augmented and Mixed Reality: Applications and Case Studies (Part II), edited by Jessie Y. C. Chen and Gino Fragomeni
11. LNCS 11576, Cross-Cultural Design: Methods, Tools and User Experience (Part I), edited by P. L. Patrick Rau
12. LNCS 11577, Cross-Cultural Design: Culture and Society (Part II), edited by P. L. Patrick Rau
13. LNCS 11578, Social Computing and Social Media: Design, Human Behavior and Analytics (Part I), edited by Gabriele Meiselwitz
14. LNCS 11579, Social Computing and Social Media: Communication and Social Communities (Part II), edited by Gabriele Meiselwitz
15. LNAI 11580, Augmented Cognition, edited by Dylan D. Schmorrow and Cali M. Fidopiastis
16. LNCS 11581, Digital Human Modeling and Applications in Health, Safety, Ergonomics and Risk Management: Human Body and Motion (Part I), edited by Vincent G. Duffy

34. CCIS 1033, HCI International 2019 - Posters (Part II), edited by Constantine Stephanidis
35. CCIS 1034, HCI International 2019 - Posters (Part III), edited by Constantine Stephanidis

http://2019.hci.international/proceedings

6th International Conference on HCI in Business, Government and Organizations (HCIBGO 2019)

Program Board Chair(s): **Fiona Fui-Hoon Nah**
and Keng Siau, *USA*

- Kaveh Abhari, USA
- Miguel Aguirre-Urreta, USA
- Andreas Auinger, Austria
- Michel Avital, Denmark
- Dinko Bacic, USA
- Denise Baker, USA
- Gaurav Bansal, USA
- Valerie Bartelt, USA
- Langtao Chen, USA
- Constantinos Coursaris, USA
- Soussan Djamasbi, USA
- Brenda Eschenbrenner, USA
- Ann Fruhling, USA
- JM Goh, Canada
- Richard H. Hall, USA
- Milena Head, Canada
- Netta Iivari, Finland
- Qiqi Jiang, Denmark
- Richard Johnson, USA
- Mala Kaul, USA
- Yi-Cheng Ku, Taiwan
- Nanda Kumar, USA
- Eleanor Loiacono, USA
- Murad Moqbel, USA
- Robbie Nakatsu, USA
- Chee Wei Phang, P.R. China
- Eran Rubin, USA
- Roozmehr Safi, USA
- Hamed Sarbazhosseini, Australia
- Norman Shaw, Canada
- Yani Shi, P.R. China
- Choon Ling Sia, Hong Kong, SAR China
- Austin Silva, USA
- Martin Stabauer, Austria
- Chee-Wee Tan, Denmark
- Deliang Wang, Singapore
- Werner Wetzlinger, Austria
- I-Chin Wu, Taiwan
- Dezhi Wu, USA
- Shuang Xu, USA
- Cheng Yi, P.R. China
- Dezhi Yin, USA
- Jie YU, P.R. China
- Dongsong Zhang, USA

The full list with the Program Board Chairs and the members of the Program Boards of all thematic areas and affiliated conferences is available online at:

http://www.hci.international/board-members-2019.php

HCI International 2020

The 22nd International Conference on Human-Computer Interaction, HCI International 2020, will be held jointly with the affiliated conferences in Copenhagen, Denmark, at the Bella Center Copenhagen, July 19–24, 2020. It will cover a broad spectrum of themes related to HCI, including theoretical issues, methods, tools, processes, and case studies in HCI design, as well as novel interaction techniques, interfaces, and applications. The proceedings will be published by Springer. More information will be available on the conference website: http://2020.hci.international/.

General Chair
Prof. Constantine Stephanidis
University of Crete and ICS-FORTH
Heraklion, Crete, Greece
E-mail: general_chair@hcii2020.org

http://2020.hci.international/

Contents – Part II

Social Media and Big Data Analytics in Business

Contents – Part I

Consumer Behaviour

Business Information Systems, Dashboards and Visualization

Prohibiting Bring Your Own Device (BYOD) in Companies: Effectiveness and Efficiency vs. Satisfaction

Andreas Auinger[✉] and Werner Wetzlinger

Digital Business, School of Management,
University of Applied Sciences Upper Austria, Steyr, Austria
{andreas.auinger,werner.wetzlinger}@fh-steyr.at

Abstract. Smartphones are the most relevant digital companions that we employ on a daily basis and increasingly used by employees to perform business tasks. However, some companies do not allow the use of personal devices to access their IT infrastructure (BYOD) due to security concerns or for other organizational reasons; thus these employees have to use a smartphone provided by the company. Hence, employees may be confronted with unfamiliar operating systems or applications and which may influence their satisfaction and performance. We analyzed these effects by conducting a usability study that measured efficiency, effectiveness, and satisfaction of iOS and Android users when required to use a company provided device (CPD) in the form of a Nokia Lumia Windows Phone compared to their own device when executing the same tasks on their own device. The study used a within-subjects design and three measurement points, each of which consisted of multiple typical business tasks. The study used a within-subjects design and three measurement points each, which consisted of multiple typical business tasks. Results show that users become accustomed to the Company Provides Devices fast, since efficiency and effectiveness improve rapidly. The satisfaction level also improves, but remains below the personal devices.

Keywords: Bring Your Own Device (BYOD) · IT consumerization · IT adoption · Mobile devices · Usability evaluation

1 Introduction

Due to size, weight, portability, connectivity, built-in sensors, and diversity of applications, mobile devices are now ubiquitous. In addition to tablets, smartphones in particular have achieved a high level of market penetration, and sales continue to grow [1]. However, the broad ubiquity of mobile devices is not limited to the consumer market. Businesses have also recognized the potential of mobile devices for supporting the engagement of business customers, suppliers and employees [2]. For employees, mobile devices provide the opportunity for new mobile work styles that shift work to the most convenient location and time [3]. By supporting these state-of-the-art styles, organizations can increase flexibility, optimize operational performance, enhance employee productivity, improve customer service, and attract and retain employees

© Springer Nature Switzerland AG 2019
F. F.-H. Nah and K. Siau (Eds.): HCII 2019, LNCS 11589, pp. 3–21, 2019.
https://doi.org/10.1007/978-3-030-22338-0_1

[3–7]. Benefits for mobile workers include better utilization of downtime, reduced travel time, access to data while on the move, enhanced situational and activity awareness, improved knowledge sharing tools, and support for multiple communication channels [3, 8–10].

As a result of these benefits, the percentage of "anytime, anywhere information workers" in the USA and Europe has risen and continues to do so. Overall, about 48% of employees use smartphones on a regular basis in a work context [11]. In many cases companies do not provide smartphones and therefore allow employees to use their personal devices (PD) due to the expected mutually beneficial effects. This concept of using a private device at work to undertake business tasks is called bring your own device (BYOD) [12].

BYOD was initiated by employees. The "bring your own" phenomenon has risen significantly among employees with direct client-contact [13]. Since users are typically very familiar with their PD, 61% of smartphone users want to use just one device for both work and personal activities [11]. Gartner estimated in 2013 that more than one third of employers worldwide no longer provide employees with mobile devices and that by 2018, 70% of mobile users will manage significant parts of their workload on personal smart devices [14]. In fact, 59% of organizations allowed employees to use their own devices for work purposes in 2017. Another 13% had planned to allow use within a year [15].

In this situation, organizations have to consider that when restrictions are imposed on personal activities, employees try to avoid such employers [16] or it may lead to work-life blurring [17, 18]. Removing such constraints by providing BYOD services therefore generally improves employee satisfaction; moreover, it can serve as a cost reduction and cost avoidance mechanism for companies [14]. However, in bypassing the IT department, employees seize the power to decide which IT tool fits their job needs best. Junglas [19] conducted a study, which defined and explicated the concept of IT empowerment, i.e., the level of authority an employee assumes in utilizing IT to control or improve aspects of his/her job, and tested this concept in the context of IT consumerization. Overall, the results demonstrated that employees can no longer be viewed only as passive consumers of technology as they now voluntarily accept responsibility for deciding which tech tool best fits their job needs, and thus, shift some of the fundamental tenets of IT governance.

Consequently, organizations have to scrutinize BYOD concepts and manage the associated risks in order to enable this business transformation by protecting and securing networks and data regardless of how workers access them [20]. To manage these risks, possible security issues and challenges have been [21, 22] and basic mitigation strategies have been assigned [23–26]. Additionally technical security frameworks have been developed [27], and wider organizational security frameworks (including people, policy management as well as technology) have been established [28]. Accordingly, successful BYOD deployment requires a comprehensive approach [29].

When facing these challenges, many organizations reject BYOD because they do not want to open up internal networks or provide access to information systems using unknown devices due to security and privacy concerns [30, 31]. Instead these organizations provide employees with a specific mobile device integrated into the organization's IT infrastructure (here is your own device - HYOD) or even let them choose from a set of devices (choose your own device - CYOD) [24].

These business devices can contain discernible differences compared to the employee's PD, which may include the operating system, software, screen size, or other hardware specifications like the processor or memory. Currently, four main mobile operating systems exist on the market, while two in particular were dominant during the period of this study (2015/2016: Android 82.8%, iOS 13.9%, Windows Phone 2.6%, BlackBerry OS 0.3%) (IDC, 2017). While iOS and Android dominate the consumer market, many organizations provided their employees with devices containing the mobile operating system Windows Phone since they wanted to keep the number of supported operating systems low and avoid BYOD due to security concerns, legal issues, technical complexity, administrative overheads, and high costs [7, 32]. In recent years, the overall share of new Windows phone devices on the market has decreased and therefore most users are unfamiliar with it. For this reason, we choose Windows phone devices as company provided devices (CPD) for this study.

Consequently, if employees are required to use a certain device for business activities, they may be confronted with an operating system and applications with which they are not familiar. Since the main benefits of BYOD are greater employee productivity and satisfaction, revoking BYOD may lead to lower results in these categories (PAC, 2013). Therefore, we conducted a usability study that assessed these constructs after users performed typical business tasks on their PD and on a device they were unfamiliar with (CPD - company provided device).

The remainder of this paper is structured as follows: in Sect. 2 we present related work; the methodology is described in Sect. 3; Sect. 4 includes all results based on the three metrics: effectiveness, efficiency, and satisfaction; and we discuss the limitations of this study in Sect. 4. Finally, we provide a discussion of the results and conclusions in Sect. 5.

2   Related Work

To increase work progress, users need to learn how to access systems and their data and how to leverage the information they provide to perform their daily tasks as effectively as possible [33]. To assess the work progress, multiple qualitative and quantitative methods like interviews, surveys, or tests can be used. When asked, employees indicated they would perform better with their PD. De Kok et al. found that in companies that implement a CYOD program, and despite the fact that 70% of employees stated they can perform their work well on the device provided, a majority (52%) believed their performance would improve further if they could choose a device themselves [34]. Similarly, a study by Harris revealed employees think that using their PD would enable them to complete more tasks on time (49%), be more innovative (50%), and be happier (53%) [25]. Additionally, in a meta-analysis, Niehaves et al. [35] and Pillet et al. [36] established that, of all positive aspects of IT consumerization, employee satisfaction was mentioned the most.

Based on such surveys, various theoretical models and frameworks have been developed that suggest correlations between BYOD and employee performance and satisfaction. Niehaves et al. [37] expect the use of consumer IT devices for business purposes to contribute to work performance of employees via more highly perceived autonomy and competence. Additionally, Giddens and Tripp [63] theorize that the increased perceived competence is influenced by device self-efficacy and device innovativeness, and that BYOD may increase job satisfaction due to higher job autonomy and job performance. Köffer et al. [38] suggest that part of the increase in job performance is due to increased work satisfaction when using PDs. Additionally, Ostermann et al. detail decision factors such as the inconvenience of handling two devices, work life conflict concerns, perceived privacy risk and perceived financial risk in a multi-item scale to measure the influence of business use and private use of company owned devices in comparison to private devices (BYOD) [39].

Consequently, several contributions suggest that BYOD is generally associated with higher productivity and higher job satisfaction. However, these contributions are based on self-reported data in surveys (e.g. [7, 25, 32, 34]. In a literature review, no study could be identified which utilizes an experimental usability evaluation setting measuring performance by efficiency, effectiveness, and satisfaction as a methodological approach to investigate these effects; yet, there are usability studies that investigate related problems.

In usability testing of mobile devices perceived usability can be influenced by the hardware, the operating system, and the application used. Therefore, evaluating the usability of devices may include one or more of these layers. Some studies investigate hardware issues such as the battery life [40] or the impact of mobile phone screen size on user comprehension [41, 42]. However, general conclusions for the leading platforms (iOS, Android and Windows Phone) are not possible due to the variety of different devices with varying hardware configurations.

Several empirical studies compare the usability of operating systems by focusing on specific features such as virtual keyboards of different mobile platforms [43], tactile feedback from touch screens while entering text [44], text input methods on smartphones (ITU-T, Swype, Swiftkey, Thick Buttons, Keypurr) [45], or the position of virtual keyboards [46].

Moreover, some studies have compared the usability of different smartphones like Nokia (Symbian), HTC (Windows Phone), and Palm Treo (Palm OS). Results showed significant differences in the usability for some functions (e.g. searching for information on a website using an internet browser, making a call); however, these results are based on outdated hardware and software [47].

A more recent study compared the usability of the different device types, e.g. tablets and smartphones (iPad 2, iPhone 4S, Huawei Impulse 4G, HTC status), for accessing health-related information via different applications (web browser, mobile apps). It found significantly different results in task completion time for devices and applications [48]. One important difference, though, is that this study used only one metric and did not consider possible learning effects based on previous experience with devices or operating systems.

A study in 2014 identified usability issues by applying a qualitative approach, using a task-based test setting, observation, and thinking aloud to compare three smartphones (Apple iPhone 4 s - iOS 5, Samsung Galaxy Nexus - Android 4.0, Nokia Lumia 800 - Windows 7.5). It concluded that for efficient and effective device operation, the user experience (UX) must consider three different layers: hardware, operating system, and application [49].

Additionally, coherence between OS characteristics and the UX assessments of devices has been investigated. It was found that certain characteristics of operating systems (Windows Phone 8, iOS 6, Android 4.2) lead to satisfactory or unsatisfactory UX assessments. For example, iOS 6 and Android 4.2, provide a satisfactory support architecture whereas Windows Phone 8 devices were deemed to be difficult to use, saddled with inadequate graphic user interface (GUI) support, and complicated to learn [50].

Galetta [51] illustrates a methodology for a task set to evaluate smart phone platforms with regard to ease of learning and ease of use. Results provide preliminary evidence which indicates significant differences concerning these two constructs among the leading smartphone platforms (Android, iOS, Windows and Blackberry), especially between novice and expert users. Furthermore, the adaptation to new interaction styles has been investigated. It was found that users do not have significant difficulties when transferring to an unfamiliar mobile phone model [52].

Thus, to the best of our knowledge, to date there is no study that investigates users' adaptation process to an unfamiliar smartphone and assesses it through usability tests that measure the performance and satisfaction of users. Therefore, we conducted a usability evaluation comparing how iOS and Android users rate their PD (used for BYOD) in comparison to a Windows Phone device (CPD) when performing typical business tasks.

3 Methodology

The study was based on a within-subjects design. At multiple measurement points a triangulation of complementary usability methods was used. Every measurement point included a usability test, a standardized usability questionnaire, and a qualitative survey. The usability tests assessed the usability of the devices using the ISO 9241-11 definition. It defines usability as "the extent to which a product can be used by specified users to achieve specified goals with effectiveness, efficiency and satisfaction in a specified context of use" [53]. Effectiveness and efficiency were measured by a usability test and satisfaction was determined by the standardized questionnaire PSSUQ (Post-Study System Usability Questionnaire) [54]. Additionally, qualitative questions were asked to gather information on potential reasons for the evaluation results. The study comprised twenty participants and included three iterated evaluation points to measure effects on the performance and to assess the potential change in satisfaction over time. Further details on tasks, metrics, participants, procedure, and used devices are presented in the following sections.

3.1 Tasks

We wanted to test tasks that cover typical business activities. Because we tested smartphones, we selected the four business-related tasks most executed on smartphones based on the Forrester research [29]. The results of this study indicate that (i) reading or viewing documents, spreadsheets, or presentations; (ii) accessing employee intranet/portal; (iii) accessing email and/or calendar applications; and (iv) taking work-related photos and/or videos are the most relevant tasks carried out with smart devices to be considered within our research.

Based on this selection we identified suitable actions involving these tasks. In some cases, the complexity of the tasks was increased by further activities to avoid a trivial level (e.g. accessing and reading a document) and to ensure that the data would express measurable differences between the analyzed devices. This approach led to the selection of the following tasks:

- *Task 1 - Taking a Photo:* Participants had to take an arbitrary photo, create a new folder called work, move the picture into this folder, and check whether it was successfully moved in the respective default media database (iOS: Photos; Android: Gallery; Windows Phone: Photos).
- *Task 2 - Writing an Email*: This task was not limited to accessing emails but also included writing an email. Participants had to open the standard email client, create a new email, insert a specific subject, address it to a pre-defined email address, type a specific text, assign the priority high, and include the photo from Task 1.
- *Task 3 - Creating a Calendar Entry*: This task was not limited to accessing a calendar but also included creating a new calendar entry. Participants had to open the default calendar app, create a new appointment, and enter a specific name, date, time, location, and duration, as well as a reminder. After saving the appointment, participants had to change to the monthly view. Finally, participants had to move the appointment to another day and add a specific text note.
- *Task 4 - Searching for a Document*: This task was supposed to mimic the search for documents in an intranet portal. It combined activities for searching, accessing, reading, and saving a document. Consequently, participants had to open the standard web browser, type in a specific search term, open a specific PDF file, save the URL as a bookmark, copy the URL, and save it as a separate note.

3.2   Metrics and Measurement

Since the study was based on the ISO 9241 definition of usability [53], we used established metrics for effectiveness, efficiency, and satisfaction. Because the tasks were somewhat complex, we decided to combine metrics for effectiveness and efficiency in a composite score metric.

Efficiency. Efficiency is defined as the "resources expended in relation to the accuracy and completeness with which users achieve goals" [53]. It is typically measured by the effort needed to successfully execute a task. In our study, efficiency was measured by the time needed to complete a task measured in seconds (task completion time). Task completion time is widely accepted as a valid metric in usability tests [55].

Effectiveness. Effectiveness is defined as the "accuracy and completeness with which users achieve specified goals" [53]. Two commonly used ways to measure effectiveness are "completion rate" and "number of errors" [56].

- Task completion was assessed based on three levels; whether the user could finish the task (i) without help or, (ii) with help/support, or (iii) did not finish/gave up. The need for help was an especially important metric for economic reasons because the human desire to communicate with other employees when performing one's own tasks reduces the other employees' productivity since they are prevented from executing their own tasks [57]. A task was considered successfully completed if all assigned activities were performed.
- The number of errors was incorporated by counting the attempts needed to finish the task, considering the levels at (i) the first attempt and (ii) multiple attempts.

Additionally, we deemed tasks not to have been successfully completed if users were unable to complete them within a given time frame. To compare the efficiency of task completion, the primary time frame (180 s) was based on the mean time taken to complete each task [58]. We defined time frames as: (i) primary time frame, within the defined time frame of 180 s; (ii) secondary time frame, max. 90 s outside of the primary time frame; and (iii) exceeding the time frame of 270 s in total. Support was only provided when participants actively requested it and was only provided within the primary and secondary time frame. Combining these levels, we defined five task execution success levels, as shown in Table 1.

Table 1. Task execution success levels

Task execution success level	Task completion level (Help needed/not needed)	Number of errors (Attempts needed)	Time frame
Level 1	without help	at first attempt	primary time frame > 180 s
Level 2	without help	multiple attempts	primary time frame > 180 s
Level 3	without help	at first attempt or multiple attempts	secondary time frame: between 180 and 270 s
Level 4	with help/support	at first attempt or multiple attempts	secondary time frame: between 180 and 270 s
Level 5	did not finish/gave up		exceeding time frame of 270 s

Satisfaction. Satisfaction is the "freedom from discomfort and positive attitudes towards the use of the product" [53]. Among the numerous standardized questionnaires (e.g. QUIS, SUMI, SUS, UMUX,) the PSSUQ was chosen [59]. The PSSUQ is a post-study questionnaire for assessing users' perceived satisfaction with the usability of a system in scenario-based usability evaluations. Studies proved the reliability and validity of the PSSUQ and provided evidence of significant generalizability for the questionnaire [54]. We chose the PSSUQ because of its brevity and manageability, and it has been proven to be highly reliable (Cronbach's alpha = .96) [54]). It also includes subscales, which provided us with the opportunity to compare the smartphones also based on system quality, information quality, and interface quality.

We used the 19-item version of the PSSUQ. Each item was rated on a 7-point Likert-scale from 1 (totally agree) to 7 (totally disagree). There was also the possibility to not answer the question (no answer). The PSSUQ contains the following scales:

- OVERALL (items 1–19): The scale OVERALL represents the aggregate satisfaction score of a system including the items 1–18, which are also used to calculate the other scales and the control item 19.
- SYSUSE (items 1–8): The subscale SYSUSE (system usefulness) measures how easy it is to use and learn a system to effectively complete tasks and quickly become productive.
- INFOQUAL (items 9–15): The sub-scale INFOQUAL (information quality) measures the quality of the system feedback by assessing whether it is easy to understand and effectively helps users. This includes error messages, online help, onscreen messages, and documentation.
- INTERQUAL (items 16–18): The sub-scale INTERQUAL (interface quality) measures how pleasant the user's experience is by assessing whether the system provides the expected functionality and capability.

In our study, participants had to complete the PSSUQ after performing all tasks with a certain device. Devices were compared using the arithmetic mean of all Likert-scale ratings.

3.3 Survey

Additionally, every participant was asked five questions after performing all tasks of a particular measurement point to obtain qualitative insights into and arguments about the experience they had when executing the tasks on the different devices. These questions were:

- What are the advantages and disadvantages of using the Nokia Lumia or your own smartphone in performing the tasks?
- What are the specific differences in using the Nokia Lumia to perform the tasks compared to the last measurement point?
- Was the task execution easier than at the last measurement point?
- Would you consider using the Nokia Lumia in a business context?
- Would you consider using the Nokia Lumia as your personal device?

3.4 Participants

The study involved 20 participants (13 female/7 male) aged 21–51 (7 participants younger than 30 years, 13 participants aged 30 years or older; mean = 29.55, sd = 7.38). Ten participants were Android users while 10 were iOS users. The number of participants was chosen based on an argument by Nielsen, who claims using 20 participants typically offers a reasonably tight confidence interval collecting quantitative usability metrics [60]. The 20 participants had to meet the following requirements to join the study:

- They had to have used the respective operating systems (iOS or Android) and devices (versions did not matter) for at least three months.
- They had to consider themselves as advanced users with good knowledge and skills in handling the device and operating system.
- They had to be regular users of the standard email client and calendar app on the respective device and operating system.
- They had to lack any experience in handling smartphones with the Windows Phone operating system, as this was the provided benchmark device for the study.

3.5 Procedure

Every participant was tested three times. At the first measurement point they had to perform the tasks with their PD and with the Windows Phone device. Participants received a short introduction to the Windows Phone device and were allowed to use it for three minutes. To reduce carryover effects at the first measurement point based on order [61] and practice [62] due to carrying out the same tasks twice, half of the participants first used their own device and the other half first used the Windows Phone device.

At the two following measurement points participants used just the Windows Phone device. Using this multi-staged approach we wanted to examine the learning and practice effects as well as the change of effectiveness, efficiency, and satisfaction over time.

Before every task, the participants were provided with written instructions, which included the overall goal to be performed, a list of applications to be used, the state to be achieved, and a time limit. Before each particular task the participants had as much time as they wanted to read the task instructions and were given the opportunity to ask questions to clarify each task prior to attempting its performance.

- After completing all four tasks using a particular device, participants had to complete the PSSUQ and were asked qualitative open questions. Table 2 summarizes this multi-stage evaluation procedure.

Table 2. Multi-stage evaluation (PD = personal device, CPD = company provided device)

Measurement point	Day	Used methods
Baseline measure (0)	Day 0	Tasks with PD & PSSUQ
First measure CPD (1)	Day 0	Tasks with CPD & PSSUQ qualitative questions
Second measure CPD (2)	2–7 days after first measure CPD (1)	Tasks with CPD & PSSUQ qualitative questions
Second measure CPD (3)	2–7 days after second measure CPD (2)	Tasks with CPD & PSSUQ qualitative questions

3.6 Devices

The PDs of participants differed, including various Apple iPhone models, and Android devices from Samsung, HTC, and even Alcatel. The only condition for these devices was that they had the standard email, calendar, and photo gallery apps installed. Other specifications were not relevant for the evaluation settings. The Windows Phone device used was the Nokia Lumia 630 (Windows Phone 8.1, 4.5 inch display, 1.2 GHz quad core processor, 512 MB RAM).

4 Results

4.1 Effectiveness and Efficiency

Effectiveness was measured using the cumulative percentage of participants that reached the task goals in the defined levels of effectiveness (see Table 1). Figure 1 shows the effectiveness of all tasks. It includes the results for the PD (personal smartphone) at the first measurement point and the results for the CPD (Windows Phone Nokia Lumia) at all three measurement points.

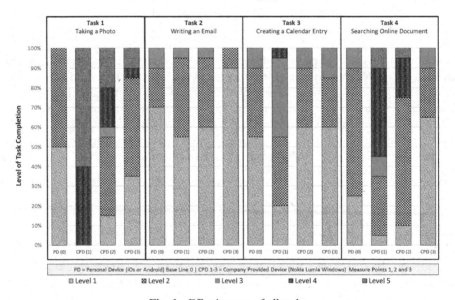

Fig. 1. Effectiveness of all tasks

Efficiency was measured by the task completion time in seconds using the geometric mean, standard deviation, and range (see Sect. 3.2). Less time for task completion and subsequently a lower time range indicates more effective task completion. Table 3 includes these metrics for all four tasks and three evaluation points.

Table 3. Efficiency metrics - task completion in seconds

Task		PD (0)	CPD (1)	CPD (2)	CPD (3)
Task 1	Mean	62	203	130	101
Taking a Picture	Std. Dev	43	29	62	35
	Range	20–150	147–238	53–266	43–212
Task 2	Mean	100	96	82	71
Writing an Email	Std. Dev	41	30	30	18
	Range	45–213	58–194	50–194	49–107
Task 3	Mean	126	166	121	118
Creating a Calendar Entry	Std. Dev	34	49	33	41
	Range	69–188	100–270	80–194	59–218
Task 4	Mean	137	178	135	105
Searching for an Online Document	Std. Dev	34	45	39	37
	Range	90–219	118–270	88–234	56–194

Figure 2 illustrates these results using a diagram. The bars represent the mean values, while the whiskers show the 95% confidence interval. As already mentioned, this data only includes successfully finished tasks. Since Task 1 on the CPD (Windows Phone Nokia Lumia) at the first attempt led to a high number of failed tasks (60%), the resulting data is skewed. Using data from all participants and calculating the time spent until participants gave up would lead to much higher values (mean: 247; std. dev: 51, max: 370). The next two attempts with the CPD in Task 1 also led to unfinished tasks (attempt 2: 20%, attempt 3: 10%). Participants also had problems with Task 4 where Attempt 1, 10%, and Attempt 2, 5%, failed to finish the task.

Results for Single Tasks

- *Task 1 (Taking a Photo).* This task was very difficult for the participants with the CPD. 60% were not able to finish at the first attempt, while the rest required assistance. Even, at the third measurement point (CPD3) some participants still were not able to finish the task. Post hoc tests using the Bonferroni correction revealed that Attempts 1 and 2 on the CPD led to significantly lower effectiveness levels ($p = .000$) when compared with the PD. Attempt 3 also led to a lower effectiveness level, but not on a significant level ($p = .547$). Consequently, the time spent on the first attempt was very high; however, task completion time decreased significantly at the following two attempts. Post hoc tests revealed that the results of the first two measurement points on the CPD were slower in comparison to the PD (measurement point 1 and 2: $p = .000$; measurement point 3: $p = .07$).

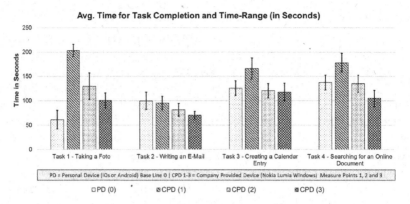

Fig. 2. Efficiency of all four tasks using the mean time of successfully finished tasks

- *Task 2 (Writing an Email).* The results for Task 2 show an entirely different picture in comparison to Task 1 (see Fig. 1), which indicates that the task is a relevant moderating variable, as participants had already had a similar success rate with the CPD at the first attempt rather than with their PD. In the course of the evaluation, all participants managed to finish the task without help in the given time frame (level 1 and 2). Post hoc tests using the Bonferroni correction led to no significant differences in the effectiveness level. These results are supported by the data for efficiency; i.e. participants were slightly faster even on the first attempt with the CPD. This led up to a significantly faster performance in Attempt 3 on the CPD compared to the PD (p = .006). Answers on post-study questions showed that participants liked the Outlook style of the CPD email app, and therefore were very comfortable with using it.
- *Task 3 (Creating a Calendar Entry).* Task 3 seemed to be difficult for the participants, though they quickly adapted to the situation. Using the CPD, the participants struggled at the first attempt but improved significantly in Attempt 2, reaching a similar level as with their PD. Interestingly, there was no significant improvement at Measurement Point 3. Post hoc tests using the Bonferroni correction revealed that only Attempt 1 on the CPD led to a significant lower effectiveness level (p = .014). Concerning efficiency, Task 3 was performed significantly more slowly with the CPD at Measurement Point 1 (p = .008), though performance improved so strongly in Measurement Points 2 and 3 that no significant difference could be observed. This led to a similar task completion time of the PD and the CPD at Measurement Point 3.
- *Task 4 (Searching for an Online Document).* The task again shows very interesting results for the PD and the CPD. At the first measurement point, over 50% of the participants needed assistance or failed completely. However, they evidently learned very quickly, and effectiveness improved considerably for the next two attempts, leading to a better result than with their own device at Measurement Point 3. Post hoc tests using the Bonferroni correction revealed that only Attempt 1 on the CPD led to a significantly lower effectiveness level (p = .000). In terms of efficiency, Task 4 was performed significantly more slowly with the CPD only at

Measurement Point 1 (p = .002). However, the performance showed a progressive improvement of the participant's efficiency, leading to an even faster task completion at Measurement Point 3 in comparison with the PD.

4.2 Satisfaction

Satisfaction was measured using the PSSUQ [59], which had to be filled out by the subjects after completing the four tasks with a particular device. The 19 items were rated on a 7-point Likert-scale from 1 (totally agree) to 7 (totally disagree). Based on the order of the response categories, low values correspond to high satisfaction ratings. Responses were analyzed using the arithmetic mean for the 4 PSSUQ scales OVER-ALL, SYSUSE, INFOQUAL and INTERQUAL (interface quality).

Figure 3 illustrates the means of all four scales and measurement points. The whiskers represent the 95% confidence interval. Results show that participants rated their PD (iOS or Android devices) better than the company provided CPD Nokia Lumia Windows Phone in all scales and at all measurement points.

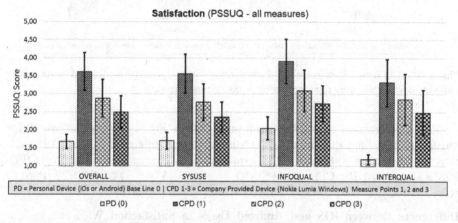

Fig. 3. Satisfaction measured by PSSUQ based on [59]

Post hoc tests using the Bonferroni correction revealed that using the CPD led to significantly lower satisfaction ratings (high PSSUQ score) after Measuring Points 1 and 2, but not after Measuring Point 3 in the scales OVERALL (1) p = .000, (2) p = .002; (3) p = .079; SYSUSE (1) p = .000, (2) p = .007, (3) p = .256; and INFOQUAL (1) p = .000, (2) p = .038, (3) p = .384.

The INTERQUAL scale shows the biggest differences between the PD and the CPD. Compared to the PD, the ratings after all attempts with the CPD are significantly worse (Bonferroni correction: p = .000; p = .001; p = .016). This sub-scale incorporates items 16–18, which are represented by the following statements:

16. The interface of this system was pleasant.
17. I liked using the interface of this system.
18. This system has all the functions and capabilities I expected it to have.

Participants' answers to the post-study questions stated that this difference was caused by the way the CPD structures the home screen using animations and the starting of apps using an alphabetical list rather than icon grids, as used in iOS and Android. Participants considered these representations to be unusual, unclear, and confusing.

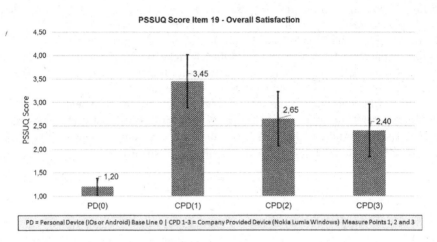

Fig. 4. PSSUQ item 19 - average satisfaction ratings of the personal device and the company provided device (whiskers represent the 95% confidence interval)

Item 19 (Overall, I am satisfied with this system – Fig. 4) reveals that overall the satisfaction rate for CPD improves over time; but, the difference to the PD remains large as satisfaction with the CPD is significantly lower after all three attempts (PD: PSSUQ score = 1.20; CPD (1): PSSUQ score = 3,45 p = .000; CPD(2): PSSUQ score = 2.65, p = .001; CPD(3): PSSUQ score = 2.40, p = .010).

Differences Between iOS and Android Users in Satisfaction When we look at differences between iOS and Android users there is a significant mismatch in the PSSUQ score (see Fig. 5). The users of iOS were more satisfied overall with their PD, and the rating of the CPD did not increase as strongly as the satisfaction ratings of Android users. Compared to the PD, iOS users rated the CPD significantly lower after the first two measurement points (Bonferroni correction: (1) p = .00; (2) p = .014; (3) p = .067).

Overall, the satisfaction rating of Android users after Measurement Point 3 was 1.99, which was already close to their PD score at the beginning of the study (1.81). Therefore, ratings were only significantly lower after the first measurement point (Bonferroni correction: (1) p = .000; (2) p = .206; (3) p = 1.000).

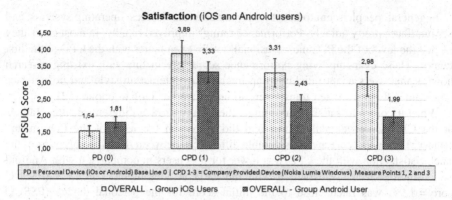

Fig. 5. OVERALL satisfaction ratings of the CPD (Nokia Lumia Windows Phone) by iOS and Android users (whiskers represent the 95% confidence interval)

5 Discussion and Conclusion

The paper examined the user adaptation process to a new smartphone platform using usability tests to simulate an adoption process of private devices (PD – in the form of iOS and Android phones) for a possible BYOD setting in comparison to a company provided device (CPD – in the form of Nokia Lumia Windows Phone). The tests used a summative usability evaluation approach to measure effectiveness, efficiency, and satisfaction at three different measurement points. The results will be discussed separately at first before final conclusions are drawn.

With regard to effectiveness, the study shows mixed results. Taking a photo (Task 1) and searching for an online document (Task 4) led to significant difficulties at the first and second measurement point. When performing strongly business-related tasks, such as writing an email (Task 2) and creating a calendar entry (Task 3), the results indicated a reasonable adaptation process for the CPD due to its similar style of the apps with Microsoft Outlook, with which most participants were familiar.

The analysis of data for efficiency showed that participants were even faster in writing an email (Task 2) with the CPD in comparison to their own device, even at the first attempt. In comparison to that, taking a photo (Task 1) was executed much faster on the PD, and at the third measurement point, participants were still substantially slower on the CPD. Creating a calendar entry (Task 3) and searching for an online document (Task 4) were initially executed more slowly on the CPD, but after repeated use, the participants executed these tasks faster than with their PD at the third attempt.

Consequently, we can conclude that there is a positive tendency for the performance indicators of efficiency and effectiveness, for all tasks except for taking a picture. Qualitative statements from the post hoc survey stated that this was particularly different on the CPD as opposed to the participants' own device. Furthermore, the ratings for both efficiency and effectiveness show that the selected tasks significantly moderated the results of the study (e.g. email and calendar apps of the CPD scored well, since their interfaces replicate the desktop Outlook experience well).

In general, people seem to adapt to new or different devices, operating systems, and user interfaces pretty quickly. Performance ratings improved rapidly, in most cases they reached the level of the PD, and occasionally were even better with the CPD at the first attempt. These ever-improving performance scores are in line with existing research showing that users adapt quickly to an interface or interaction style and do not face significant difficulties when transferring to an unfamiliar mobile phone [52].

When it comes to satisfaction ratings, the results show a different picture. Ratings for the CPD were generally lower and did not reach the level of the PDs in any instance. However, there are considerable differences between the two subgroups of the panel. Satisfaction with the CPD was lower for iOS users in comparison with Android users. Android users' satisfaction with the CPD at Measurement Point 3 (PSSUQ score = 1.99) was rated close to the initial score for the personal device (PSSUQ score = 1.81) at the beginning of the study.

In summary, these results indicate that employees are likely to be equally effective and efficient after a short adaption phase with a CPD. On the other hand, the level of satisfaction when using CPDs will be presumably lower in comparison to their own devices. In our study, this effect was mainly observable in iOS users whose satisfaction rating of the PD was twice as high as for the CPD (PSSUQ score iOS = 1.54, CPD = 2.98). Ultimately, companies will have to decide for or against BYOD based on strategic and company culture considerations. Hence, future research could either focus particularly on how the satisfaction of the users could be measured and improved with, for example, additional training for CPD, or how to securely integrate PDs into companies' IT infrastructure.

Acknowledgement. We would like to thank Eva-Maria Gaumberger from Engel Austria for her supportive work during the evaluation phase in the course of her master thesis in Digital Business Management.

References

1. Gartner, I.: Gartner Says Worldwide Sales of Smartphones Recorded First Ever Decline During the Fourth Quarter of 2017. https://www.gartner.com/newsroom/id/3859963
2. Schadler, T., McCarthy, J.C.: Mobile Is the New Face of Engagement – CIOs Must Plan Now for New Systems of Engagement. https://www.forrester.com/report/Mobile+Is+The+New+Face+Of+Engagement/-/E-RES60544
3. Citrix: Workshifting: a global market research report. https://www.citrix.com/content/dam/citrix/en_us/documents/news/workshifting-a-global-market-research-report.pdf
4. Nah, F.F.-H., Siau, K., Sheng, H.: The value of mobile applications. Commun. ACM **48**, 85–90 (2005)
5. Vuolle, M.: Intangible benefits of mobile business services. IJLIC **8**, 50 (2011)
6. York, J., Pendharkar, P.C.: Human–computer interaction issues for mobile computing in a variable work context. Int. J. Hum Comput Stud. **60**, 771–797 (2004)
7. Citrix: Workplace of the Future - a global market research report. https://www.citrix.com/content/dam/citrix/en_us/documents/products-solutions/workplace-of-the-future-a-global-market-research-report.pdf

8. Pascoe, J., Ryan, N., Morse, D.: Using while moving: HCI issues in fieldwork environments. ACM Trans. Comput.-Hum. Interact. **7**, 417–437 (2000)
9. Streefkerk, J.W., van Esch-Bussemakers, M.P., Neerincx, M.A.: Field evaluation of a mobile location-based notification system for police officers. In: ter Hofte, G.H., Mulder, I., de Ruyter, B.E.R. (eds.) 10th International Conference on Human Computer Interaction with Mobile Devices and Services, pp. 101–108. Amsterdam, Netherlands (2008)
10. Vuolle, M.: Productivity impacts of mobile office service. IJSTM **14**, 326 (2010)
11. Schadler, T.: 2013 Mobile Workforce Adoption Trends. https://www.forrester.com/report/2013+Mobile+Workforce+Adoption+Trends/-/E-RES89442
12. Disterer, G., Kleiner, C.: BYOD Bring Your Own Device. Procedia Technol. **9**, 43–53 (2013)
13. McConnell, J.: Tracking the Trends in Bringing Our Own Devices to Work. https://hbr.org/2016/05/tracking-the-trends-in-bringing-our-own-devices-to-work
14. Willis, D.A.: Bring Your Own Device: The Facts and the Future. https://www.gartner.com/newsroom/id/2466615
15. Lazar, M.: BYOD Statistics Provide Snapshot of Future. https://www.insight.com/en_US/learn/content/2017/01182017-byod-statistics-provide-snapshot-of-future.html
16. Bradley, J., Loucks, J., Macaulay, J., Medcalf, R., Buckalew, L.: BYOD: A Global Perspective
17. Köffer, S., Anlauf, L., Ortbach, K., Niehaves, B.: The intensified blurring of boundaries between work and private life though IT consumerisation. In: European Conference on Information Systems, Paper 108, Münster, Germany (2015)
18. Ostermann, U., Wiewiorra, L.: Bring it on(e)! personal preferences and traits as influencing factors to participate in BYOD programs. In: Twenty-Fourth European Conference on Information Systems, Research Paper 47 (2016)
19. Junglas, I., Goel, L., Ives, B., Harris, J.G.: Consumer IT at work: development and test of an IT empowerment model. In: Proceedings of the International Conference on Information Systems, Auckland, New Zealand (2014)
20. Thomson, G.: BYOD: enabling the chaos. Netw. Secur. **2012**, 5–8 (2012)
21. Olalere, M., Abdullah, M.T., Mahmod, R., Abdullah, A.: A review of Bring Your Own Device on security issues. SAGE Open **5**, 1–11 (2015)
22. Wang, Y., Wei, J., Vangury, K.: Bring your own device security issues and challenges. In: Proceedings of the 11th Consumer Communications and Networking Conference (CCNC), Las Vegas, NV, USA, pp. 80–85 (2014)
23. Eslahi, M., Naseri, M.V., Hashim, H., Tahir, N.M., Saad, E.H.M.: BYOD: current state and security challenges. In: Proceedings of the Symposium on Computer Applications & Industrial Electronics (ISCAIE), Penang, Malaysia, pp. 189–192 (2014)
24. Gajar, P.K., Ghosh, A., Rai, S.: Bring your own device (BYOD): security risks and mitigating strategies. J. Glob. Res. Comput. Sci. **4**, 62–70 (2013)
25. Harris, J., Ives, B., Junglas, I.: IT consumerization: when gadgets turn into enterprise IT tools. MIS Q. Executive **11**, 99–112 (2012)
26. Jaramillo, D., Katz, N., Bodin, B., Tworek, W., Smart, R., Cook, T.: Cooperative solutions for Bring Your Own Device (BYOD). IBM J. Res. Dev. **57**, 5:1–5:11 (2013)
27. Armando, A., Costa, G., Verderame, L., Merlo, A.: Securing the "Bring Your Own Device" Paradigm. Computer **47**, 48–56 (2014)
28. Zahadat, N., Blessner, P., Blackburn, T., Olson, B.A.: BYOD security engineering: a framework and its analysis. Comput. Secur. **55**, 81–99 (2015)
29. Forrester Research: The Expanding Role of Mobility in the Workplace
30. Miller, K.W., Voas, J., Hurlburt, G.F.: BYOD: security and privacy considerations. IT Prof. **14**, 53–55 (2012)

31. Miller, J., Katz, I., Mack, R., Marks, L., Muller, M.J., McClard, A.: Validating an extension to participatory heuristic evaluation. In: Conference Companion, pp. 115–116

32. PAC: Mobile Device & Application Management in Germany, France, the UK, and Switzerland. https://www.pac-online.com/download/7215/121178

33. Gnewuch, U., Haake, P., Mueller, B., Mädche, A.: The effect of learning on the effective use of enterprise systems. In: Proceedings of the International Conference on Information Systems, Dublin, Ireland (2016)

34. de Kok, A., Lubbers, Y., Helms, R.W.: Mobility and security in the new way of working: employee satisfaction in a Choose Your Own Device (CYOD) environment. In: Proceedings of the 9th Mediterranean Conference on Information Systems (MCIS), Paper 31, Samos, Greece (2015)

35. Niehaves, B., Köffer, S., Ortbach, K.: IT consumerization – a theory and practice review. In: Proceedings of the 18th Americas Conference on Information Systems (AMCIS), Paper 18, Seattle, Washington, USA (2012)

36. Pillet, J.-C., Pigni, F., Vitari, C.: Learning about ambiguous technologies. Conceptualization and research agenda. In: 25th European Conference on Information Systems, Guimaraes, Portugal (2017)

37. Niehaves, B., Köffer, S., Ortbach, K.: The effect of private IT use on work performance - towards an IT consumerization theory. In: Proceedings of the 11th International Conference on Wirtschaftsinformatik, Leipzig, Germany, pp. 39–53 (2013)

38. Köffer, S., Ortbach, K.C., Niehaves, B.: Exploring the relationship between IT consumerization and job performance: a theoretical framework for future research. Commun. Assoc. Inf. Syst. **35**, Article 14 (2014)

39. Ostermann, U., Wiewiorra, L., Franzmann, D.: One of two or two for one? - Analyzing employees' decisions to dual use devices. In: Thirty Eighth International Conference on Information Systems (2017)

40. Ferreira, D., Dey, A.K., Kostakos, V.: Understanding human-smartphone concerns: a study of battery life. In: Lyons, K., Hightower, J., Huang, E.M. (eds.) Pervasive 2011. LNCS, vol. 6696, pp. 19–33. Springer, Heidelberg (2011). https://doi.org/10.1007/978-3-642-21726-5_2

41. Alghamdi, E., Yunus, F., Househ, M.S.: The impact of mobile phone screen size on user comprehension of health information. In: Mantas, J., Hasman, A. (eds.) Informatics, Management and Technology in Healthcare, pp. 154–156. IOS Press, Amsterdam (2013). Athens, Greece, 5–7 July 2013

42. Alghamdi, E., Yunus, F., Househ, M.S.: Revisiting the impact of mobile phone screen size on user comprehension of health information. In: Mantas, J., Househ, M.S., Hasman, A. (eds.) Integrating Information Technology and Management for Quality of Care, pp. 217–220. IOS Press, Amsterdam (2014)

43. Schaub, F., Deyhle, R., Weber, M.: Password entry usability and shoulder surfing susceptibility on different smartphone platforms. In: Rukzio, E. (ed.) 11th International Conference on Mobile and Ubiquitous Multimedia, Ulm, Germany, pp. 1–10 (2012)

44. Hoggan, E., Brewster, S.A., Johnston, J.: Investigating the effectiveness of tactile feedback for mobile touchscreens. In: Czerwinski, M., Lund, A., Tan, D. (eds.) Proceedings of the SIGCHI Conference on Human Factors in Computing Systems, Florence, Italy, pp. 1573–1582

45. Page, T.: Usability of text input interfaces in smartphones. J. Des. Res. **11**, 39–56 (2013)

46. Nakagawa, T., Uwano, H.: Usability differential in positions of software keyboard on smartphone. In: 2012 IEEE 1st Global Conference on Consumer Electronics (GCCE), Tokyo, Japan, pp. 304–308 (2012)

47. Keijzers, J., den Ouden, E., Lu, Y.: Usability benchmark study of commercially available smart phones: cell phone type platform, PDA type platform and PC type platform. In: ter Hofte, H., Mulder, I. (eds.) Proceedings of the 10th International Conference on Human Computer Interaction with Mobile Devices and Services, Amsterdam, Netherlands, pp. 265–272 (2008)

48. Sheehan, B., Lee, Y., Rodriguez, M., Tiase, V., Schnall, R.: A comparison of usability factors of four mobile devices for accessing healthcare information by adolescents. Appl. Clin. Inform. **3**, 356–366 (2012)

49. Alshehri, F., Freeman, M.: User experience of mobile devices: a three layer method of evaluation. In: Proceedings of the 25th Australasian Conference on Information Systems, Auckland, New Zealand, pp. 1–10 (2014)

50. Chien, C.-F., Lin, K.-Y., Yu, A.P.-I.: User-experience of tablet operating system: an experimental investigation of Windows 8, iOS 6, and Android 4.2. Comput. Ind. Eng. **73**, 75–84 (2014)

51. Galletta, D.F., Dunn, B.K.: Assessing smartphone ease of use and learning from the perspective of novice and expert users: development and illustration of mobile benchmark tasks. AIS Trans. Hum.-Comput. Interact. **6**, 74–91 (2014)

52. Kiljander, H.: Evolution and usability of mobile phone interaction styles. Helsinki University of Technology, Espoo (2004)

53. ISO: Ergonomics of Human–System Interaction - Part 210: Human-Centred Design for Interactive Systems. ISO, Geneva (2010)

54. Lewis, J.R.: Psychometric evaluation of the PSSUQ using data from five years of usability studies. Int. J. Hum.-Comput. Interact. **14**, 463–488 (2002)

55. Sauro, J., Lewis, J.R.: Correlations among prototypical usability metrics. In: Proceedings of the SIGCHI Conference on Human Factors in Computing Systems, Boston, MA, USA, pp. 1609–1618 (2009)

56. Sauro, J., Lewis, J.R.: Quantifying the User Experience. Practical Statistics for User Research. Elsevier/Morgan Kaufmann, Amsterdam (2012)

57. Leger, P.-M., Riedl, R., Vom Brocke, J.: Emotions and ERP information sourcing. The moderating role of expertise. Industr Manag. Data Syst. **114**, 456–471 (2014)

58. ISO/IEC: Software engineering – Software product Quality Requirements and Evaluation (SQuaRE) – Common Industry Format (CIF) for usability test reports (2006)

59. Lewis, J.R.: IBM computer usability satisfaction questionnaires: Psychometric evaluation and instructions for use. Int. J. Hum.-Comput. Interact. **7**, 57–78 (1995)

60. Nielsen, J.: Quantitative Studies: How Many Users to Test? https://www.nngroup.com/articles/quantitative-studies-how-many-users/

61. Cozby, P.C.: Methods in behavioral research. McGraw-Hill Higher Education, Boston (2009)

62. Heiman, G.W.: Research Methods in Psychology. Houghton Mifflin Co., Boston (2002)

63. Giddens, L., Tripp, J.: It's my tool, i know how to use it: a theory of the impact of IT consumerization on device competence and job satisfaction. In: Proceedings of the 20th Americas Conference on Information Systems, Savannah, Georgia, USA (2014)

Multi-sided Platforms: A Business Model for BIM Adoption in Built Environment SMEs

Saeed Banihashemi[1]([⊠]) ⓘ, Hamed Sarbazhosseini[1], Sisira Adikari[1],
Farshid Hosseini[1], and M. Reza Hosseini[2] ⓘ

[1] University of Canberra, Bruce, ACT 2601, Australia
Saeed.Banihashemi@Canberra.edu.au
[2] Deakin University, Geelong, VIC 3220, Australia

Abstract. It has been cogently acknowledged that employing BIM in the built environment companies has delivered remarkable benefits such as enhanced HCI, superior visualization, precise documentation, integrated design, construction and project management processes. Yet, the Architecture, Engineering and Construction (AEC) enterprises involved are still lagging behind in embracing BIM into core practices of their projects. This is particularly evident in the case of Small and Medium Sized Enterprises (SMEs) where higher levels of BIM implementation need to be scrutinized. There is little evidence on how these SMEs perceive the role of BIM management, and to some extent, they apply this process in their projects. The limited financial and human resources of these SMEs make it difficult to keep up with such BIM adoption processes. Therefore, to address these challenges, this paper is to shed light on the potentials of applying the business strategy of Multi-Sided Platform (MSP) in the construction industry and adapting its conceptual model for managing BIM implementation in construction SMEs. Positioning BIM professional services in MSP model can enable these firms to focus on their core businesses while benefiting from the senior talents which offer immediate access to BIM industry best practices. The study contributes to the field by providing succinct information on MSP implementation and its adoption in AEC SMEs. The study contributes to the body of knowledge through positioning BIM management platform in a rather overlooked context namely SMEs. Practically, policy makers and stakeholders would also benefit from the findings in order to promote BIM adoption.

Keywords: BIM · SMEs · MSP · Construction · Built environment · Conceptual model

1 Introduction

One of the major responsibilities of a project management team in construction industry is to finish the project within the budget, time and quality stipulated in the contract documents [1]. As the time goes by, the construction process gets more complicated and requires superior Human-Computer Interaction (HCI), hence controlling all aspects of a project lies in a bird's eye view over its life cycle. Although the fundamental tenet in the success of this end is having an efficient and organized system of management, monitoring, implementation, collection and dissemination of

© Springer Nature Switzerland AG 2019
F. F.-H. Nah and K. Siau (Eds.): HCII 2019, LNCS 11589, pp. 22–32, 2019.
https://doi.org/10.1007/978-3-030-22338-0_2

information from the project to the parties involved, the dominance of the CAD as the traditional representative of HCI's in the built environment have overshadowed this momentum [2]. Such shortcoming is particularly intensified in Small and Medium-sized Enterprises (SMEs) where low productivity, high-level of waste, recurrent cost overruns and chronic delays in completion of construction projects are still major issues [3]. The common project management method applied in most construction firms today is document based approach in which individuals are assigned to obtain data from different parties involved in the construction stage [4]. As a consequence, a wide range of construction data is typically collected in the field and in a fragmented nature without taking their holistic implications into account toward managing the construction process efficiently [5].

In recent years, Building Information Modeling (BIM) has emerged as a comprehensive concept of process and tools which integrates all projects required data and information [6]. BIM supports new information workflows and integrates them more closely with existing simulation and analysis tools used by consultants and contractors [7]. It provides higher levels of user experience, better interaction with designers and drafters and greater HCI compared to outdated CAD. Since most processes in BIM are automated, and the involvement of human resources is minimized, it is claimed that by using BIM, the efficiency of monitoring, controlling and managing in construction projects life cycle is enhanced remarkably [8]. But, in spite of the proven advantages of BIM employment in the construction projects and observed trend in its adoption worldwide, the rate of BIM implementation is far below the current potentials in the construction industry and SMEs, particularly [9]. The reason for this fact might lie in the silence of literature on the studies toward the research and development on BIM management platforms in the Architecture. Engineering and Construction (AEC) SMEs and developing enhanced HCI for AEC users.

Lower BIM adoption is deemed as a challenge in small businesses [10], while studies on BIM adoption are mostly concentrated on large-sized companies and large-scale projects [11]. Therefore, the effective methods in better BIM adoption within SMEs have remained underrepresented in the existing literature [12]. Despite such scant attention devoted to BIM in SMEs, this area is of outmost importance for the construction industry in view of the fact that "...smaller firms will continue to dominate the construction industry landscape far into the future" [13].

Progressively, AEC sectors have realized how important and productive it is to implement BIM and its managerial packages [14]. Developing the best and error-free design is what attracts customers and brings in new business. Even so, in the meanwhile, we cannot efficiently deliver the design and construction projects without solid BIM processes in place [15]. In fact, if valuable employees of the design teams are solely devoted to managing BIM, fewer human resources would be left to apply in the project [16]. On the other hand, if fundamental elements of BIM workflows such as BIM templates and guidelines or deployment of key software updates get ignored, the team will be hindered from working quickly and professionally [17].

This problem is certainly intensified where SMEs are to implement BIM in their digital design and construction workflows [18]. The limited financial and human resources of these SMEs make it difficult to keep up with such BIM adoption process [19]. Therefore, new business strategies should be analyzed and applied in order to facilitate BIM implementation activities in the meantime of minimizing the costs incurred and providing improved HCI experience for AEC experts. Multi-Sided Platforms (MSP) are among the emerging business strategies which have caught significant attention in recent years and remarkably changed the professional services methods. In fact, "professional service firms are moving away from pure vertically integrated models in which all client services are provided by their employees (e.g. traditional consulting firms), and towards the MSP model, in which they enable independent contractors or professionals to deal directly with clients" [20]. Developing an online and outsourced BIM management based on MSP can enable these firms to focus on their core businesses while benefiting from the senior talents which offer immediate access to BIM industry best practices. Through this achievement, the whole built environment industry can benefit from BIM adoption and application in a more efficient and easier integration. However, no research hitherto has been conducted on positioning BIM management in MSP and for AEC SMEs.

There is a conspicuous lack of studies on the identification of potential areas of MSP utilization in the construction industry and its associations with BIM management platforms. Against this backdrop, mathematical expression of the trade-offs among clients, consultants and third parties involved in BIM management and their interactions can be a significant achievement for construction project practitioners, policymakers and BIM advocates.

2   Background

2.1   Building Information Modelling (BIM)

Since the conventional 2D CAD system requires investing large amounts of time for construction projects operation, BIM expedites this process and provides the opportunity of testing and assessing different design and construction alternatives and their impacts on buildings [21]. "BIM is a digital representation of physical and functional characteristics of a facility" [7]. According to BS1192, "it is the management of information through the whole life cycle of a built asset, from initial design all the way through to construction, maintaining and finally de-commissioning, through the use of digital modelling" [22]. Thus, decisions that are made in the early stages of design play a significant role in the level of projects throughout the lifecycle of buildings. The ability to pinpoint the weaknesses of the design and implementing changes based on the available alternatives helps the construction industry mitigate the adversarial impact of construction errors and enhance the digital integration of buildings [23].

BIM involves collating, applying and maintaining an integral digital representation of all building information for different phases of the project life cycle in the form of a data repository [24]. It provides a comprehensive concept as an umbrella for the processes and tools, which integrate all projects required data through containing information needed in particular phases of a building's life-cycle (scheduling, analysis, cost evaluation, etc.) [7]. Yet, BIM is much more than a data container for the building model; it is an object-oriented building design and construction-specific model to assist the progress of the exchange and interoperability of data in the digital format [25].

A major benefit of utilizing BIM in the design and construction phase of a project is obviously coming through its ability to 'model' and test the constructability of the design within the model prior to setting foot on the project site.

As a management paradigm, BIM can be implemented through chains of ICT (Information and Communication Technologies) including BIM authoring tools such as Revit, ArchiCAD, Microstation and Navisworks [26]. Implementing BIM helps avoid errors alongside improving the productivity, scheduling, safety, cost and quality of construction projects [27]. BIM is a fast and effective process by which information pertaining to one project can be updated at any stage of the project from any department or unit (e.g. engineering department) [28]. Accordingly, because of its efficiency in adopting and propagating changes in the model, editing objects and reloading updated links, the entire project model will be updated based on the changes on one aspect of the project [15]. It is asserted that BIM is capable of enhancing the performance within the industry along with overcoming the problems stemmed from the fragmented structure dominating the industry [29]. Serving a catalyst of change for the construction industry, BIM encompasses a radical HCI reorientation of 2D to 3D modelling and a recent shift to 4D (project scheduling integrated), 5D (project cost integrated) and 6D (facility management integrated), exploiting more intelligent data analysis techniques in order to achieve a superior performance in delivering an As-Built BIM [16].

2.2 Small and Medium-Sized Enterprises (SMEs)

SMEs as the backbone of projects implementation in the construction industry are usually characterized by the number of employees in the business world [30]. Henceforth, a summary of available definitions is given in Table 1 to put it into the context of various countries. In the US, a small business is defined by having less than 99 staff, and a medium business ranges from 100 to 499 people. However, in Australia, SME Association of Australia [31] defines a micro business as having less than 4 employees and labels companies between 5 and 20 employees as a small business. In addition, a medium-sized business is determined to have staff between 20 up to 200 people. In the case of Canada, financial turnover is also considered in addition to the number of employees. In terms of the number, Canadian SMEs are featured as the same as American ones but, as to the financial index, companies are "small" subject to the less than $1 million and "medium" if ranging up to $5 million. In line with these definitions, SMEs represent more than 90% of the construction sector with similar percentages applicable to countries, e.g. the US, the UK, Australia, Asia [10] and Canada [12].

SMEs play a key role in developing prosperous economic and social structures around the world [31]. However, these companies are disadvantaged in preserving their competitiveness due to the dearth of benefitting from sufficient human resources; which is the mainstay of the built environment industry [32]. It is generally contended in construction literature that SMEs are typically lagging behind large-sized firms in embracing innovation and technological advancements [13, 30]. This is the BIM scenario as well [10, 12, 33] due to the number of issues such as the lack of knowledge and awareness, initial costs and lack of skilled personnel.

Table 1. SMEs definitions in various countries (Adapted from [19])

Country	Number of employees	Annual turnover	Source
Australia	0 < Micro < 4	N/A	[31]
	5 < Small < 20		
	21 < Medium < 200		
USA	Small < 99	N/A	[34]
	100 < Medium < 499		
Canada	Small < 99	Small < $1 million	[35, 36]
	100 < Medium < 499	$1 million < Medium < $5 million	

2.3 Multi-sided Platform (MSP)

The two-sided market is an intermediary platform which includes at least two specific user groups providing network benefits for them. The organization, association or firm that develops such platform via facilitating direct interactions between two (or more) specific types of affiliated users is regarded as the MSP [20]. This is grounded upon the notion of linking both sides of customers who are in need of each other. MSP exists because there is a need of intermediary in order to match both parts of the platform in a more efficient way. In fact, this intermediary will minimize the overall cost by avoiding duplication and minimizing transaction costs. It will further create possible exchanges that could be impossible without the platform and bring value for both sides. These platforms, by playing an intermediary role, generate values for all parties involved that are interconnected through it, and hence, those sides (parties) could be considered as customers.

In general, MSPs are recognized by three key elements [37]:

- A multi-product business exists including a platform to provide specific services to two or more sides of the market.
- Cross-network effects are facilitated. Experts benefit from mutual participation on both sides of the market.
- Platforms are financially tweaked by bilateral price setters on both sides of the market.

In light of the network effects, prosperous platforms benefit from rising returns to scale. Users are inclined to pay more for access to a bigger network, and as a result, margins increase because user bases grow. So, network platforms are differentiated from traditional service businesses. In traditional businesses, growth beyond some point generally causes a decrease in returns since new customers' acquisition gets harder as fewer people find it competitive. Furthermore, the idea of increasing returns makes the competition fierce in MSPs. Therefore, platform leaders should invest more in research and development in order to improve their competitive edge, reduce the prices and leverage their higher margins to defeat weaker rivals. As a result, mature MSPs are often run by larger platforms [38].

3   Research Method

The methodology adopted for this study is based on Design Thinking (DT) process integrated with qualitative method and inductive analysis of literature. Design Thinking is a human-centered creative problem-solving approach to come up with feasible solutions that meet customer needs with added business value. The integration of DT processes into qualitative research delivers new and deeper levels of insights. The DT process employed in this research is shown in Fig. 1 [39]. It includes five iterative activities with specific deliverables highlighted in yellow.

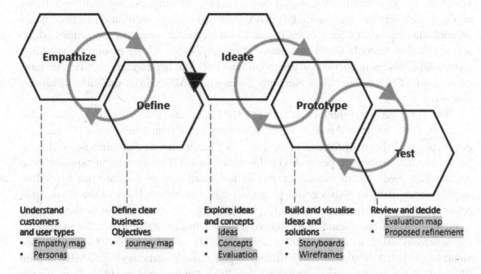

Understand customers and user types	Define clear business Objectives	Explore ideas and concepts	Build and visualise Ideas and solutions	Review and decide
• Empathy map • Personas	• Journey map	• Ideas • Concepts • Evaluation	• Storyboards • Wireframes	• Evaluation map • Proposed refinement

Fig. 1. Design thinking process with main activities and deliverables [39] (Color figure online)

Specifically, empathy maps, personas, and journey maps were extensively used to develop ideas and concepts which were represented in storyboards and wireframes for evaluations. The integrated method is recommended for all stages of research including the case of this paper. By applying the integrated qualitative method, the design emerges as the study unfolds in which the data is in the form of words, ideas, concepts, pictures or objects. Subsequently, the inductive logic is used to deduce patterns and frameworks from observations to know the variables and constraints and hypothetical relationships. This leads to developing a conceptual model to represents the researcher's synthesis of literature on how to explain a phenomenon. It illustrates what is expected to find through the research, including how the variables might relate to each other and how the characteristics of the model are mapped [40].

4 Conceptual Model

In view of the arguments on the lower adoption of BIM in SMEs and the emergence of MSP as the pioneering business strategy, a theoretical model is developed to conceptualize the interactions between AEC SMEs, BIM adopters and the role of platform amongst (see Fig. 2). The platform here hosts BIM adopters and SMEs as two distinct sides of the business in which they directly interact together and are affiliated with the platform. Direct interaction means that these two sides maintain the control on the key terms of their interactions rather being fully controlled via the intermediary. As evident, the nature of the interaction is to provide BIM adoption services to AEC SMEs. However, the key terms of the interaction involve marketing, pricing and the delivery of the traded services and its quality assurance and control. Affiliation in this model denotes the conscious efforts of each side to invest in platform-specific actions which are essential to provide direct interaction with each other. Using resources, spending money on developing required APIs to connect and subscription fees can be the items of investment to affiliate. Such elements differentiate MSPs from traditional business models.

Providing the direct interaction between BIM adopters and SMEs distinguishes this model from the traditional type in which SMEs need to recruit a full-time BIM manager or procure a BIM consultant and spend large overheads on that. Furthermore, affiliation by all relevant customer types (sides) helps distinguish MSPs from input suppliers who are not "adopted" by all sides. Because of the small size of projects run by SMEs, implementing BIM in SMEs could be greatly effective which leads to the remarkable return on investment and productivity [11, 12, 41]. The bottom line is that smaller groups of project participants and shorter project duration make it simpler to achieve the benefits of BIM, its adoption in higher levels [42] and possible swift organizational changes [43]. It is revealed that different organizational structures of SMEs require different skills, training and equipment for BIM implementation [44]. It is further identified that the cost of BIM implementation in SMEs are higher than that of in large counterparts due to the demerits of software acquisitions. In fact, due to the limited resources available for SMEs, implementing BIM takes considerable risk [41] (Fig. 2).

Hosseini et al. [19] theorized the barriers of BIM adoption in SMEs into three main clusters of the supply chain, organizational and project barriers. Supply chain barriers comprise industry and institutional issues in which the former group indicates the barriers stemmed from the location, market and lack of demand from stakeholders and proximity to markets where BIM is flourishing, and the latter denotes the policies, practices, knowledge and procedures implemented by the various parties involved in the construction supply chain surrounding the organization [45]. Organization context covers intentions, support and commitments of management and personnel with regard to BIM adoption, strategic objectives, resource allocation and addressing training needs. In light of adapting MSP to overcome these challenges, there are three key factors including innovate, offering and consume which are internalized in MSP and linked to the sides of the business. The service providers, BIM managers and adopters, in this case, should strive for creating innovative solutions in order to offer their BIM services through the platform and make it available and accessible.

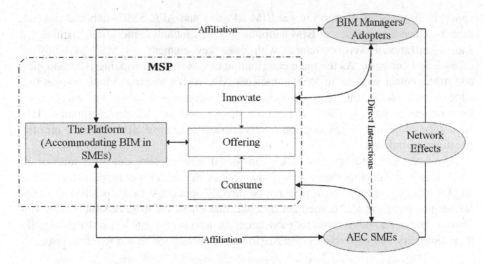

Fig. 2. Conceptual business model of MSP for BIM adoption in AEC SMEs

The innovation campaign, handled by service providers, could focus on alleviating the industry-based barriers by getting stakeholders familiar with BIM adoption benefits, sharing knowledge and expertise, lowering the adoption costs and providing accessible and affordable BIM services. According to the model, consume is another internalized factor of MSP which is bilaterally linked to the customer side; AEC SMEs. This connection could be exerted to resolve the organizational barriers by facilitating the connection of management and staff of SMEs with the service providers and platform and motivate them to invest in the affiliation. The offering is the third internal factor of MSP which is exclusively managed by the platform and refers to the regulatory role of MSP in balancing the model. Among the BIM adoption barriers discussed, it is in the equivalence relation with the institutional barriers and its policy and procedure elements. In fact, the platform is responsible for regulating and tweaking how the model works in order to maximize its efficiency and competitiveness. Eventually, the whole model is positively influenced by the network effect. This is the virtue which affects the model on two levels. In the lower level, the number of AEC SMEs and BIM adopters as customers and service providers increase in light of the network-based function of the platform leading to a more prosperous market for BIM adoption in the construction industry. Likewise, in the upper level, this effect enhances the platform popularity, value and its competitive edge resulting in expanding MSPs in the built environment.

5 Conclusion

This study is a point of departure for putting forward remedial solutions for BIM implementation in SMEs by outlining the insight toward the application of MSP as a cutting-edge approach in business and marketing. As the first study in its kind, BIM adoption in AEC SMEs was grounded upon the business model and the MSP was conceptualized as the platform to get BIM adopters and AEC SMEs onboard and link them together. The barriers of BIM adoption in SMEs including industrial, institutional and organizational were correlated with three key elements of MSP as innovate, offering and consume. As the main contribution of this study, theorizing BIM adoption and management services in MSP empowers AEC SMEs to expand their competitive edge on and enhance their core businesses in the meantime of achieving benefits from the best service providers which offer immediate access to BIM implementation. This advantage could lower the adoption overheads and maximize BIM diffusion into the construction industry.

However, the findings should be considered with caution due to a number of limitations in conducting the present study. That is, the model is conceptual and still in its preliminary stage and so, it may not be directly applicable to the practice. It needs further improvement and refinement by collecting empirical evidence and model validation. Moreover, other business models can be also investigated in order to identify their similarity and discrepancy and feasibility in application to the research issue.

References

1. Hosseini, M.R., Banihashemi, S., Martek, I., Golizadeh, H., Ghodoosi, F.: Sustainable delivery of megaprojects in Iran: Integrated model of contextual factors. J. Manag. Eng. **34**, 05017011 (2017)
2. Banihashemi, S., Hassanabadi, M.S., Tahmasebi, M.M.: Applications of PRC (PDA, RFID, camera) in construction monitoring. In: Six International Conference on Construction in the 21st Century (CITC-VI) "Construction Challenges in the New Decade" (2011)
3. Ghoddousi, P., Poorafshar, O., Chileshe, N., Hosseini, M.R.: Labour productivity in Iranian construction projects: perceptions of chief executive officers. Int. J. Prod. Perform. Manag. **64**, 811–830 (2015)
4. Banihashemi, S., Tabadkani, A., Hosseini, M.R.: Integration of parametric design into modular coordination: a construction waste reduction workflow. Autom. Constr. **88**, 1–12 (2018)
5. Banihashemi, S., Hosseini, M.R., Golizadeh, H., Sankaran, S.: Critical success factors (CSFs) for integration of sustainability into construction project management practices in developing countries. Int. J. Project Manag. **35**, 1103–1119 (2017)
6. Hosseini, M.R., Banihashemi, S., Zaeri, F., Adibfar, A.: Advanced ICT Methodologies (AIM) in the Construction Industry. Encyclopedia of Information Science and Technology. IGI Global, Hershey (2017)
7. Eastman, C., Eastman, C.M., Teicholz, P., Sacks, R.: BIM Handbook: A Guide to Building Information Modeling for Owners, Managers, Designers, Engineers and Contractors. Wiley, Hoboken (2011)
8. Golizadeh, H., Banihashemi, S., Sadeghifam, A.N., Preece, C.: Automated estimation of completion time for dam projects. Int. J. Constr. Manag. **17**, 197–209 (2017)
9. Hosseini, M.R., Azari, E., Tivendale, L., Banihashemi, S., Chileshe, N.: Building information modeling (BIM) in Iran: an exploratory study. J. Eng. Project Prod. Manag. **6**, 78–89 (2016)
10. Forsythe, P.: The case for BIM uptake among small construction contracting businesses. In: Proceedings of the 31st International Symposium on Automation and Robotics in Construction and Mining. University of Technology Sydney (2014)

11. Rodgers, C., Hosseini, M.R., Chileshe, N., Rameezdeen, R.: BIM within the Australian construction related small and medium sized enterprises: awareness, practices and drivers. In: Raidén, A., Aboagye-Nimo, E. (eds.) Proceedings of the 31st Annual ARCOM Conference, vol. 691, p. 700. Association of Researchers in Construction Management, Lincoln (2015)
12. Poirier, E., Staub-French, S., Forgues, D.: Embedded contexts of innovation: BIM adoption and implementation for a specialty contracting SME. Constr. Innov. **15**, 42–65 (2015)
13. Shelton, J., Martek, I., Chen, C.: Implementation of innovative technologies in small-scale construction firms: five Australian case studies. Eng. Constr. Architect. Manag. **23**, 177–191 (2016)
14. Banihashemi, S.: The Integration of Industrialized Building System (IBS) with BIM: A concept and Theory to Improve Construction Industry Productivity. LAP Lambert Academic Publishing, Saarbrucken (2012)
15. Shourangiz, E., Mohamad, M.I., Hassanabadi, M.S., Banihashemi, S.: Flexibility of BIM towards design change. In: 2nd International Conference on Construction and Project Management, IPEDR, pp. 79–83. ACSIT Press, Singapore (2011)
16. Oraee, M., Hosseini, M.R., Banihashemi, S., Merschbrock, C.: Where the gaps lie: ten years of research into collaboration on BIM-enabled construction projects. Constr. Econ. Build. **17**, 121–139 (2017)
17. Hardin, B., McCool, D.: BIM and Construction Management: Proven Tools, Methods, and Workflows. Wiley, Hoboken (2015)
18. Banihashemi, S., Meynagh, M.M., Vahed, Y.K.: Developing IFC standards for implementing industrialized building system components into BIM applications. In: Proceedings of 2012 International Conference on Construction and Project Management, ICCPM 2012 (2012)
19. Hosseini, M.R., et al.: BIM adoption within Australian small and medium-sized enterprises (SMEs): an innovation diffusion model. Constr. Econ. Build. **16**, 71–86 (2016)
20. Hagiu, A., Wright, J.: Multi-sided platforms. Int. J. Ind. Organ. **43**, 162–174 (2015)
21. Khanzadi, M., Sheikhkhoshkar, M., Banihashemi, S.: BIM applications toward key performance indicators of construction projects in Iran. Int. J. Constr. Manag., 1–17 (2018)
22. BSI: BS 1192: 2007+ A2: 2016. Collaborative production of architectural, engineering and construction information. Code of practice. BSI, London, UK (2008)
23. Banihashemi, S., Ding, G., Wang, J.: Identification of BIM-compatible variables for energy optimization of buildings – a Delphi study. In: 40th AUBEA 2016 (Radical Innovation in the Built Environment), Cairns, Queensland, Australia, pp. 281–291 (2016)
24. Azhar, S.: Building information modeling (BIM): trends, benefits, risks, and challenges for the AEC industry. Leadersh. Manag. Eng. **11**, 241–252 (2011)
25. Babič, N.Č., Podbreznik, P., Rebolj, D.: Integrating resource production and construction using BIM. Autom. Constr. **19**, 539–543 (2010)
26. Banihashemi, S., Ding, G., Wang, J.: Developing an artificial intelligence-based decision making tool for energy optimization of residential buildings in BIM. In: RICS COBRA AUBEA 2015 (2015)
27. Zuppa, D., Issa, R.R., Suermann, P.C.: BIM's impact on the success measures of construction projects. Comput. Civil Eng., 503–512 (2009)
28. Hosseini, M.R., Martek, I., Papadonikolaki, E., Sheikhkhoshkar, M., Banihashemi, S.: Viability of the BIM manager enduring as a distinct role: association rule mining of job advertisements. Constr. Eng. Manag. **144**, 1–11 (2018)
29. Succar, B.: Building information modelling framework: a research and delivery foundation for industry stakeholders. Autom. Constr. **18**, 357–375 (2009)

30. Acar, E., Koçak, I., Sey, Y., Arditi, D.: Use of information and communication technologies by small and medium-sized enterprises (SMEs) in building construction. Constr. Manag. Econ. **23**, 713–722 (2005)

31. SMEAA: SME infographic illustrates vital role of sector in Australian economy. SME Association of Australia (SMEAA) (2011). http://www.smea.org.au/

32. Saridakis, G., Muñoz Torres, R., Johnstone, S.: Do human resource practices enhance organizational commitment in SMEs with low employee satisfaction? Br. J. Manag. **24**, 445–458 (2013)

33. McGraw Hill: The Business Value of BIM in Australia and New Zealand: how Building Information Modelling Is Transforming the Design and Construction Industry. McGraw Hill Construction, Bedford (2014)

34. USCB: Economic Census of the United States. The United States Census Bureau (American Fact Finder) (2016)

35. Gibson, B., Rispoli, L., Leung, D.: Small, medium-sized and large businesses in the Canadian economy: measuring their contribution to gross domestic product in 2005. Statistics Canada, Analytical Studies Branch (2011)

36. Seens, D.: SME Operating Performance. Industry Canada (2015)

37. Weyl, E.G.: A price theory of multi-sided platforms. Am. Econ. Rev. **100**, 1642–1672 (2010)

38. Eisenmann, T., Parker, G., Van Alstyne, M.W.: Strategies for two-sided markets. Harvard Bus. Rev. **84**, 92 (2006)

39. Ling, D.: Complete Design Thinking Guide for Successful Professionals. Emerge Creatives Group, Singapore (2015)

40. Creswell, J.W., Creswell, J.D.: Research Design: Qualitative, Quantitative, and Mixed Methods Approaches. Sage, Thousand Oaks (2017)

41. Poirier, E.A., Staub-French, S., Forgues, D.: Assessing the performance of the building information modeling (BIM) implementation process within a small specialty contracting enterprise. Can. J. Civ. Eng. **42**, 766–778 (2015)

42. https://www.engineersaustralia.org.au/news/driving-building-information-modelling-bim-uptake

43. Arayici, Y., Coates, P., Koskela, L., Kagioglou, M., Usher, C., O'Reilly, K.: BIM adoption and implementation for architectural practices. Struct. Surv. **29**, 7–25 (2011)

44. Wood, G., Davis, P., Olatunji, O.A.: Modelling the costs of corporate implementation of building information modelling. J. Financ. Manag. Property Constr. **16**, 211–231 (2011)

45. Hosseini, M.R., Namzadi, M., Rameezdeen, R., Banihashemi, S., Chileshe, N.: Barriers to BIM adoption: perceptions from Australian Small And Medium-Sized Enterprises (SMEs). In: 40th AUBEA 2016 (Radical Innovation in the Built Environment), pp. 271–280 (2016)

An Investigation to the Impacts of Information Systems Flexibility on Information Systems Strategy Implementation

Si Chen[✉], Jiaqi Yan, and Qing Ke

Nanjing University, Nanjing 210023, China
{si.chen, jiaqiyan, keqing}@nju.edu.cn

Abstract. The utilization of information technology has altered the basic nature of industry. Information technology also changed its traditional role from back office to a strategic role. The strategic use of information technology has been realized as a fundamental issue for business. The fast information technology development and its adoption in the business organization in recent years, for examples, the use of blockchain, or Internet of Things in business has brought an information systems strategic change in the organizations. This paper explores the impacts of information systems flexibility on information systems strategy implementation in a Chinese multinational State-owned Enterprise. The research design for the study follows a rigorous grounded theory approach, which consisted of 41 semi-structured interviews in 7 different company branches in China. Based on the study, we propose five main categories of information systems flexibility impacts on the information systems strategy implementation. Our study contributes to the new information technology adoption literature and provides implications for information technology adoption in practice.

Keywords: Information systems flexibility · Information systems strategy · Strategy implementation

1 Introduction

Under a more dynamic and changing marketplace environment, companies are facing increased complexity and economic uncertainty (Ness 2005). Information technology (IT) has taken a prominent role in the organizations, to achieve not only operational efficiencies but also competitive advantages in the dynamic and changing environment. Many studies have paid attention to the role of IT in sustaining competitive advantages of companies (Kim et al. 2011; Joshi et al. 2011). Moreover, examining IT capabilities as dynamic capabilities is emphasized in prior research (Mikalef and Pateli 2016; Chung et al. 2003). However, the investigation to the role of IT in maintaining competitive advantages mainly focuses on if IT has a positive or negative role on competitive advantages formulation. Few studies paid attention to how IT influences competitive advantages of companies, especially, how IT impacts the strategy implementation. This paper explores the role of IT in strategy implementation rather than strategy formulation in a changing environment.

© Springer Nature Switzerland AG 2019
F. F.-H. Nah and K. Siau (Eds.): HCII 2019, LNCS 11589, pp. 33–41, 2019.
https://doi.org/10.1007/978-3-030-22338-0_3

2 Literature Review

2.1 Information Systems Strategy

Information systems strategy is inconsistently defined and has heterogeneous inter-pretations in literature (Teubner 2013; Chen et al. 2010). In a broader understanding, information systems strategy is concerned with long-term strategic thinking and planning which aim to achieve effective management and best impact from all forms of information such as information systems, information technology or telecommunica-tions (Ward and Peppard 2005). Some researchers argue the information systems strategy is considered with a close integration with business strategy (Ward and Pep-pard 2005). For instance, Chaffey and Wood (2005: 275) stated that information systems strategy is "the formulation of approaches and planning needed to deploy information systems resources to support organisational strategy". Furthermore, they pointed out one of the purposes of planning an information systems strategy is to combine the business aims of the organisation with an understanding of information and systems applications to determine the computer systems which should be imple-mented in the organisation (Chaffey and Wood 2005). Ward and Peppard (2005) claimed through highly aligning with the business strategy, information systems strategy is better placed to develop organisational advantages compared to competitors. On the other hand, Chen et al. (2010) stated IS strategy should be examined inde-pendently from business strategy since it is argued business and IS strategies can support and lead each other mutually. They defined IS strategy as "an organizational perspective on the investment in, deployment, use, and management of information systems." In addition, some researchers equates IS strategy with existing IS application portfolios (Chan et al. 1997). For example, Lederer and Sethi (1988) argued infor-mation systems strategy considers the objectives of the computing process and the applications the organisation should implement (Lederer and Sethi 1988).

Normally, information systems environment includes the business application environment, desktop environment, server environment, network environment, telecommunications environment and data centre environment (Cassidy 2006). To investigate the IS environment implies a need to understand the business strategy. It means to determine the opportunities, threats and to recognise the strengths and weakness of the business, and therefore determine the business requirements for information systems and information systems operations (Ward and Peppard 2005). Based on the information systems environment, the current information systems situ-ation is analysed through identifying the trends of the information systems industry and competitors (Cassidy 2006). Finally, in the last phase, the direction phase, information systems visions, mission, goals and strategies are developed (Cassidy 2006).

It is argued research on IS strategy content is limited while considerable research focuses on IS strategy process issues (Teubner 2013; Sabherwal and Chan 2001). To exploring the reason to this, Teubner (2013) stated it might be expected that IS strategy itself as the outcome of strategic information systems planning, which should also be an issue of academic investigation. Especially, the evolution of IS planning is sum-marised (Teubner 2013; Ward and Peppard 2002), which shows the emerging of business-IT alignment concept. In the 1960s, IS/IT is in the data processing era, the aim of IS planning was to develop efficient systems to automate standardized data processing. During this time, IS planning was independent from business planning, without any direct relationship with strategic business planning (Teubner 2013). During 1970s, it became known as the era of management information systems (Ward and Peppard 2002). IS deployment grew significantly, especially in the domain of management. New methods for IS planning were developed and applied to assist IS provide extensive management information (Teubner 2013). During 1980s, companies began to realize the strategic value of IT, which is defined as strategic information systems era. During this time IS planning started to focus on the competitive advantage (Teubner 2013). In the 1990s, it entered the "strategic alignment" ear, IS planning aimed at a mutual aligning of business and IS strategy (Teubner 2013). The concept of business-IT alignment starts to be developed from 1980–1990, which is discussed in the next section.

2.2   IT Flexibility

IT flexibility is defined as "the extent to which key IT resources can scale and adapt for different purpose" (Tallon and Pinsonneault 2011; Byrd and Turner 2000). It is argued in the literatures one dimension of IT flexibility is modularity, which means the ability to reconfigure the technology components easily (Duncan 1995; Chung 2003). Prior research has confirmed the positive correlation between IT flexibility and information systems strategy implementation (Ness 2005; Tallon 2003; Chung 2003). Furthermore, it is also argued that increased IT flexibility can enable the strategic alignment and a dynamic state of strategic alignment (Ness 2005; Tallon 2003). IT strategy needs to be tightly aligned with organizational strategy in order to facilitate the organizational responses to dynamic environments, which require the IT flexibility (Chung 2003).

3   Methodology

3.1   Combination of Grounded Theory and Case Study

A combination of case study and grounded theory strategies is used in the research. Allan (2003) argued that there are certain tensions between use of case study and grounded theory. To be specific, Allan (2003) stated that, according to Yin (1994: 13), the case study approach "benefits from the prior development of theoretical propositions to guide data collection and analysis"; however, Glaser and Strauss argued that grounded theory should start without preconceived ideas or hypothesis. To avoid this potential conflict, Saunders et al. (2003: 99) argued that, as one of the advantages of employing multi-methods in the research, different methods can be used to fulfil different requirements in the study. This point is able to address Allan's concerns. In this study, case study is used as a support tool to provide a social context for the adoption of grounded theory. Grounded theory is the main strategy used in the data collection and data analysis processes in the study. Furthermore, every research method or strategy has its own weaknesses and strengths that influence the research to some extent. To adopt a combination of different methods may reduce these effects so as to lead to better conclusions (Saunders et al. 2003: 99). Grounded theory aims to investigate the actualities in the real world and build theory from discovering the concepts grounded in the data. The adoption of grounded theory needs context, and case study provides the context for using grounded theory.

3.2 Case Study Illustration

This study selected Chinese State-Owned Enterprises as the case study site, which is composed of seven enterprises which are alumina and primary aluminium producers and one research institute when it was established in 2001. As it is claimed on the official website, the aluminium business is still the core business in the corporation. This study focused on the headquarters in Beijing which is mainly responsible of management and original seven manufacturing branches since the research institute has no producing function. These seven branches are geographically dispersed in six provinces including Shanxi, Shandong, Henan, Guizhou, Guangxi and Qinghai in China.

3.3 Data Collection and Data Analysis

Data collection adopted semi-structured interviews as the tool. In this project, a total number of 41 interviews were conducted following the theoretical sampling strategy. The data collection and data analysis were conducted concurrently. Participants were approached individually in groups of three or four, based on the need for theory formulation reflected by the data analysis. After each set of interviews, the interview data were immediately transcribed and a brief analysis was conducted. The analysis results were used to revise the interview script and to guide the further sampling. The data collection was stopped when it is perceived that the theoretical saturation has achieved.

Coding is used for the data analysis with grounded theory approach. There are three types of coding adopted in data analysis with Strauss and Corbin (1998) approach, including open coding, axial coding and selective coding. There are four supporting tools used to support the data analysis practice, including data analysis software (Nvivo10), code definition table, quotation list, and concept map.

4 Findings

4.1 Business Strategy Change

The case SOE includes headquarters in Beijing, and seven other main manufacturing branches located in different cities in China. Business strategy has changed since 2002, when the corporation became the listed companies it has remained as, up to the present. There are two main obvious changes of business strategy. Firstly, the business in the corporation has experienced a product diversification process, from the single product aluminium to multi-products, including different types of aluminium, the product Gallium, and so on.

"In 2010 we had an important restructuring adjustment. The corporation proposed a new strategy." "It indicated that we have a single business sector previously, which means we just have one business. Now we are involved in ten business sectors. The business scope has changed." (No40 Manager IT H)

"Now we are trying to achieve product diversification and sustainable development. Our strategy is to develop diversified products on the base of mines. Previously we only had alumina. Now, as well as alumina, aluminium hydroxide, we have Metal gallium… We are developing diversification." (N13 Manager Function)

To summarise the quotations above, the corporation now has many more business sectors than previously and a long term sustainable development plan.

Secondly, a centralized control was undertaken when the corporation started to be listed companies while changing to strategic control along with the development.

"When ERP was built there was only aluminium business and at that time the management idea was centralized control." "The idea was raised in 2002. At that time, the corporation needed restructuring in order to be listed on the stock market. The first goal for restructuring is to withdraw the branches and institute unified management." (N40 Manager IT H)

Moreover, the contents of business strategy were mentioned in interviews: for instance, a functional manager stated:

"When branches started to implement ERP systems, it was based on management ideas, and management requirements to set the configurations of ERP. It refers to our strategy requirements, and strategy requirements in headquarters, such as financial centralized management, centralized management of funds, investment centralized management and centralized management of purchasing and sales." (N28 Manager Function)

As reflected in the quotation, there are five main requirements for centralized control in business strategy, including "financial centralized management", "centralized management of funds", "investment centralized management" and "centralized management of purchasing and sales". For these five perspectives of the centralized management, the manager in the headquarters argued that "we do not mention them anymore" (N40 Manager IT). Furthermore, the roles branches play in the SOE group under centralized management are similar to manufacturing plants:

"We are actually a factory. It means headquarters consider the strategy. We are just a cost centre for them or a production plant." (N14 Manager Function)

To summarise, under the centralized management, finance, funds, investment, purchasing and sales were all managed and controlled at headquarters, while branches were just in charge of production. However, along with market-oriented reforms and market development, the SOE group is growing, and the business strategy has changed from centralized management to "strategic control" (N40 Manager IT H), as one of the interviewees stated:

"The SOE group is developing. However, there was only several hundred staff at headquarters. It is impossible for them to manage so many staff in branches. You must allow branches to adapt to the markets themselves. So we use strategic control now. There is a huge change in management ideas." (N40 Manager IT H)

As shown in the quotation, headquarters use strategic control to manage the branches now, which means "the headquarters manage the branches at a strategic level without considering the business operations specifically", "headquarters formulate the strategic objectives and performance assessment objectives" (N40 Manager IT H), and all the branches "self-manage the business" (N41 Manager IT H). The business strategy has changed in this large SOE group with the development of enterprises and markets. It is realised that centralised management is not suitable to manage different branches located in various cities in large area of China. Strategic control is used instead in order to activate the enthusiasm of the branches.

4.2   IS Strategy Change

Correspondingly, there was an IS strategy change along with the business strategy change at headquarters. Previously, the IS strategy was produced there, which provides an overall IS management thinking, while branches implemented the IS strategy with a few developments for some special IS projects, based on individual requirements, as IT staff stated:

> "We all comply with the strategy command in headquarters. We must not deviate from it since there is a master plan. It means our plan is an implementation under on overall plan in headquarters." (N8 Manager IT)
> "The IS strategy for the SOE group are made in IT department in Beijing. We made IS strategy in Henan. Subject to standards in Beijing, called 'five unified plan', we made ours in Henan, considering our characteristics". (N7 Manager IT)

To explain the process to put the IS plan into action in the branches, he stated further:

> "Our plan is made according to the standards in Beijing, including 'unified planning and construction, unified investment, unified management and maintenance'. Based on this five point unified plan, we refer to our Henan branch. For instance, we are considering IS built in mining part, including exploration, mining, and digital mine. Or including all the other branches, we are considering communications, such kinds of things, for further implementation. Project implementation is our further consideration. This kind of implementation refers to a cost, if above one million or two millions, we should report to headquarters for approval. If the project needs a large investment, it is organized in Beijing." (N7 Manager IT)

As reflected in the quotations above, the IS strategy is made at headquarters. In branches, the "IS strategy in Henan" is actually given some considerations on IS projects based on business requirements, showing a lack of an overall planning referring to business strategy. As another IT manager stated:

> "IS strategy is not involved in our job. The reason for saying this is the IS strategy is generated at headquarters." (N11 Manager IT)

To summarise, headquarters are responsible for generating an IS strategy while branches are implementing IS strategy in enterprises. However, it is not realised that there was an IS strategy change in 2010. As mentioned, a new business strategy was proposed in 2010. In the same year, IT department in headquarters made the new IS strategy to support the business strategy.

> "It was in 2010 when we made the plan because in China there is planning every five years. We made further development plans for the next five years. So the current strategy is consistent with the strategy. The IS strategy is consistent with the business one." (N40 Manager IT H)

As reflected in the quotation, new IS strategy was produced in the same year of the new business strategy, 2010. IT managers argue that the current IS strategy "is consistent with the business one". To be specific, the process of new IS strategy formulation refers to the business and management development objectives in the corporation.

"Firstly, you need to understand the corporation itself, its development direction, which means the main business. [To understand] whether the future development emphasizes the main business or if there are any strategic adjustments, such as new business being involved. According to this development direction... the IT department created an IS development plan based on the requirements." (N40 Manager IT H)

As shown in the quotation, the new IS strategy is made according to the new business development direction. In addition, since the business strategy has changed to strategic control, which means the branches need to manage the business themselves, the branches also need to consider the IS development plan themselves, as headquarters do not generate IS plans for them in this situation.

"The current operation mode in the corporation is self-management, which means that whatever the business branches want to do, they take responsibility themselves. What they are going to do for IS development, actually we did not participate at all, we did not manage or plan......We were in charge of the budget in branches. In terms of what they are going to build, we are not helping". (N41 Manager IT H)

As reflected from the quotations above, headquarters no longer participate in decision-making on the IS development plan in headquarters. Branches need to consider the IS construction and development plan themselves. However, headquarters take responsibility of the IS development budget. It is perceived that it will influence the strategic and creative thinking of IS development in branches if there is a lack of good communication between headquarters and branches.

4.3   Misalignment of Systems Operations and Business Processes

It is found that the functions and operations of current systems do not match with the business functions and processes from three perspectives. Firstly, ERP operations do not match with the business processes in reality. For instance, one of the interviewees stated:

"I think ERP is under the ideal processes... but different from reality. In real operations, it is not possible to be ideal." "In ERP, when you receive the products, you settle the account in the same month. But we can't make it like this now. We need a period for quality acceptance check... as delays in the pricing system means they don't reflect the real price". (N4 Manager Function)

As reflected here, the business processes in reality are not the same as the ones set in the IS. There are some business processes which are not considered with the systems. Furthermore, for some business functions or business requirements, there is a lack of function in IS to support or fulfil the requirements.

"I think there are differences between the IS and their requirements." "For example, I think for many people, when they need systems support, maybe there it is not available. For instance, previously I learnt contract approval... They need IS applications to facilitate the fast delivery and joint check and approval. These were not available and they have to do it by hand." (N11 Manager IT)

As reflected in the quotations, some business work is still finished by hand. The existing IS applications did not support all the business work. It is also worth noting those misalignments between business processes and systems processes caused by organizational change.

> "The production situation changes very quickly. This system is relatively fixed. It is not able to change whenever you change. It is very difficult to make changes on systems" "For instance, last year, at the beginning, there were two alumina producing plants, and then these two were merged together. After merging, the costing in the systems should have been modified. It was very difficult when we made changes. (N20 Manager Function)
> "For instance, the financial system has recently been abandoned... because the financial system is SAP, as decided by headquarters. After implementation, no changes were made to it, such as... data measures and the control department; it has disappeared. The electrolysis plant disappeared and production management units disappeared. But in SAP, these cost centres are still there. Although these departments do not exist in reality, the costings still need to be issued here, even after merger. Now the system has peeled off, and operates with great difficulty... If the information does not change along with the management, information is dead." (N11 Manager IT)

As reflected in the quotations, when there are organizational changes, IS applications are not able to change in time, therefore the operation processes in systems do not match with the real business process. As a result, the IS use brings troubles to business work.

4.4   Frequent Reforms and Low IS/IT Flexibility

As mentioned in previous sections, enterprises are not in a good business situation now, therefore there are frequent reforms made in order to reduce the cost and increase efficiency.

> "Because now the situations of enterprise are not well, it's always in reforms. Maybe there were reforms last year and then other reforms this year. This is not suitable." (N20 Manager Function)

As reflected in the quotation, when there are frequent reforms, the IS applications are not suitable to the business structure or processes well. The low IS/IT flexibility has been discussed in the previous section.

5   Discussions

In this research, the deferred IS application change when business strategy and organizational change cause the strategic implementation problems both in structural and operational levels. When there are business strategy and organizational changes, the management activities and business processes are different. IS applications are not flexible to change along to fulfil the new requirements, which turns to be information systems strategy implementation barriers in both structural and operational levels. In structural level, a low IT flexibility leads to insufficient IS support to management when business strategy and management hierarchies change in headquarters and branches.

In operational level, low IT flexibility results in misaligns of business processes and systems operations when there is organizational changing. IT flexibility is important factor that influences the IS strategy implementation in the organizations.

References

Allan, G.: A critique of using grounded theory as a research method. Electron. J. Bus. Res. Methods 2(1), 1–10 (2003)

Chaffey, D., Wood, S.: Business Information Management: Improving Performance Using Information Systems. Financial Times Prentice Hall, Harlow (2005)

Chan, Y.E., Huff, S.L.: Strategy: an information systems research perspective. J. Strateg. Inf. Syst. 1(4), 191–204 (1992)

Lederer, A.L., Sethi, V.: The implementation of strategic information systems planning methodologies. MIS Q. 12, 445–461 (1988)

Sabherwal, R., Chan, Y.E.: Alignment between business and IS strategies: a study of prospectors, analyzers, and defenders. Inf. Syst. Res. 12(1), 11–33 (2001)

Saunders, M., et al.: Research Methods for Business Students, 3rd edn. Pearson Education Limited, London (2003)

Strauss, A., Corbin, J.: Basics of Qualitative Research: Techniques and Procedures for Developing Grounded Theory. Sage publications, Thousand Oaks (1998)

Tallon, P.P., Pinsonneault, A.: Competing perspectives on the link between strategic information technology alignment and organizational agility: insights from a mediation model. MIS Q. 35 (2), 463–486 (2011)

Teubner, A.: Information systems strategy - theory, practice, and challenges for future research. Bus. Inf. Syst. Eng. 5(4), 243–257 (2013)

Ward, J., Peppard, J.: Strategic Planning for Information Systems, 3rd edn. Wiley, Chichester (2005)

Upstream, Downstream or Competitor? Detecting Company Relations for Commercial Activities

Yi-Pei Chen, Ting-Lun Hsu$^{(\boxtimes)}$, Wen-Kai Chung, Shih-Chieh Dai, and Lun-Wei Ku

Institute of Information Science, Academia Sinica, Taipei, Taiwan
{ypc,hsutingl,wkchung,sjdai,lwku}@iis.sinica.edu.tw

Abstract. Due to intricate network in industry business and high cost of supervision, financial institutions usually focus on supervising core enterprises in a supply chain instead of all corporations, which indirectly lower the strength and efficiency of financial institutions as a role of capital supervisor and credit-risk transformer. Furthermore, banks require these corporations to provide correct information by themselves, which lacks of the objectivity of the source information and increases the supervision cost for these banks. Thus, we summarize a company relation detection task in hope to exposing more information about companies to investors and banks by learning a system from public available datasets. We regard this task as an classification problem, and our system can predict relations between any two companies by learning on both structured and unstructured data. To the best of our knowledge, it's the first time to implement deep learning technique to this task. A F1 score 0.769 is achieved from our system.

Keywords: Business dashboards · Commercial activity ·
Company relation detection · Knowledge graph ·
Multi-relational graph embedding · Deep learning application

1 Introduction

Traditionally, suppliers and buyers in a supply chain have competing financial interests: while buyers want to pay as late as possible, suppliers want to receive money as early as possible. Supply chain finance (SCF) is a solution to bridge these conflicting interests. By transforming risks from upstream suppliers and downstream buyers to professional finance institutions, these experts such as banks can supervise all players in the chain, thus providing short-term credit for optimizing working capital for both sides.

Nonetheless, a typical SCF can be very large and complicated. Therefore, banks usually focus on supervising core enterprises and related business instead

---

Y.-P. Chen, T.-L. Hsu, W.-K. Chung and S.-C. Dai—Equal contribution.

of all companies in the same chain due to the difficulty and expensive cost of information collection. To alleviate this problem and expose more information of companies to banks and investors, we focus on predicting the relation between any two given companies by leveraging news articles and public-available dataset (datasets are detailed in the section Dataset).

Generally speaking, while we know the high level concept about who are suppliers and buyers in a specific industry chain, we cannot know this kind of information for a specific company: who are indeed the suppliers and clients of a particular company. Take the semiconductor industry as example, we know that IC design companies should be upstream suppliers of IC manufacturing companies, but given any two specific companies in this industry, we don't know if they really have relationship with each other.

Thus, by using public available datasets such as news data and government released data, we hope to predict the relations between two given company entities. We simplify the task as a classification problem and tries to predict the following four types of relations: upstream supplier, downstream retailer, competitor and no relation.

The task is separated into two part. First, we utilize the datasets to learn embeddings for companies, which can encode the information from both news and government released data. Thereafter, we build a classifier to predict the relationship between any two given companies.

In the following, Sect. 2 introduces the background of related work; Sect. 3 describes the dataset we use; Sect. 4 details the proposed system; Sect. 5 puts experiment; followed by result and analysis in Sect. 6, and finally Sect. 7 gives summary of this paper.

2   Background

In real world, companies that are traded at stock exchange or over-the-counter markets are required by law to report financial statements. Despite this, information about suppliers and clients of a company are not compulsory, and most of the time companies regard such information as secrets from their potential competitors, which makes it more impenetrable to the public. Thereafter, past researches usually pre-assumed upstream, downstream and competitor relations of companies based on the industry they belong to and the products they make.

Hsieh et al. [1] predefined upstream and downstream groups based on industry chain and applied data mining technique to trading data in order to find stock price relations between these groups.

3   Dataset

To train our system, we crawl both structured and unstructured data. For the unstructured data, the financial news data is crawled. And for the structured data, Taiwan company corpus and relation data between companies are crawled. Following details each of the above datasets.

Table 1. A segment of an article from Economic Daily News. It is originally written in Chinese. Here we translate the article to English for demonstration purpose.

The Release of iPhone X

The new model iPhoneX was released yesterday. Highlight of this phone includes wireless charging, face recognition and Augmented Reality. All these functions should have a big influence on the cellphone market, which should also benefit the related manufactures in Taiwan. Though manufactures in Taiwan are not the main suppliers of chips, TSMC, Pegatron, Largan Precision, and Foxconn still play important roles in the market. (...skip...) However, the problems of face recognition still exist: the high cost and low yield rate. As a result, iPhone 8 and iPhone 8+ keep the original home button for fingerprint recognition

---

First, financial news data is crawled from a local media Economic Daily News[1] in Taiwan. An article from Economic Daily News is shown in Table 1 for illustration. The dataset contains 22,400 news from year 2016 to 2017 containing 352,470 Chinese and English words and numbers. To parse Chinese language, we use CKIP parser [2] to segment news data into word tokens. The number of total unique words (vocab size), including English words and numbers, is 38,372. Next, We crawl the company corpus from Taiwan Stock Exchange (TWSE) (both listed equities and TPEx equities)[2] to identify company entities in our news dataset. 1,704 companies can be found in total.

Thirdly, the relation data between companies, the ground truth data in our task, is crawled from Money Link website[3], which gives upstream, downstream, and competitor relation information of companies. Table 2 shows some statistics about our ground truth data. Since it doesn't contain "no-relation" data, we do negative sampling to train our system, as described in the section Experiments. After that, we then construct triples in order to build a knowledge graph. Formal definition is given below.

Given two companies A and B, we construct the ordered triple as

- (A, B, upstream), if A is an upstream supplier of B,
- (A, B, downstream), if A is a downstream client of B,
- (A, B, competitor), if A is a competitor of B,
- (A, B, no-relation), if A has no relation with B.

Notice that (A, B, upstream) holds if and only if (B, A, downstream), (A, B, competitor) holds if and only if (B, A, competitor), and (A, B, no-relation) holds if and only if (B, A, no-relation). Consequently, we construct all possible triples as long as they hold. Fro example, if (B, A, downstream) exists in the dataset while (B, A, downstream) does not, we will add (B, A, downstream) to the dataset.

---

[1] https://money.udn.com/money/index.
[2] http://www.twse.com.tw/en/page/products/stock_code.html.
[3] https://ww2.money-link.com.tw.

Table 2. The table shows the size of our ground truth data, the relations between two companies. Since upstream and downstream relations are conceptually inverse with each other, they have the same number of pairs. Unique company size in Money Link: 1608

Dataset	relation type			
	# of pairs	Competitor	Upstream	Downstream
Money Link	19,150	9,496	4,827	4,827

All information described in the above is then used to train the embeddings for companies. These embeddings can be put into our classifier for relation prediction between any two given companies. Notice that, although we conduct experiments on Taiwan markets, our system can indeed be applied on other markets as long as datasets are prepared. Details about how we exactly train the embeddings for company are elaborated in the next section.

4 System Overview

There are two main steps in our system: (1) embeddings training for companies, and (2) classifier training for companies' relation detection by leveraging embeddings trained by (1).

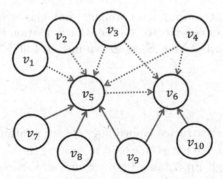

Fig. 1. Sample multi-relational directed graph. Directed arrows show directed links. The two relations in this graph are presented as solid and dashed lines, respectively. When predicting v_5, linked vertices v_1 to v_4 and v_7 to v_9 are used as the l's in Eq. 1; when predicting v_6, linked vertices v_3, v_4, v_5, v_9 and v_{10} are used as the l's. Embeddings will be generated for all vertices except v_6, whose links are all inlinks.

4.1 Embedding Training Stage

Because our datasets contain unstructured data (news) and structured data (relation information between companies), we develop a multi-relational graph embedding to encode both kinds of information. We will first introduce how our multi-relational graph embedding works, followed by how we utilize this to build embeddings for companies.

Multi-relational Graph Embedding. To encode the graph structure by embeddings, we predict a vertex given its linked vertices, where different relation vertices are mapped to the same space through different relation transform matrices. Formally, given a graph with k multi-relations $r_1, r_2, \ldots, r_k$, and the vertices to be predicted O, the objective function is to maximize the average probability

$$\frac{1}{|O|} \sum_{o_i \in O} \sum_{r_j \in R} \log p\left(o_i | l_{j,1}, l_{j,2}, \ldots, l_{j,|l_j|}\right) \tag{1}$$

where R is the set of all relations, and $l_{j,1}, l_{j,2}, \ldots, l_{j,|l_j|}$ are the linked vertices of o_i with the relation r_j. As shown in Eq. 2, for each vertex o_i, we use one multiclass classifier with softmax to obtain the conditional probabilities, and it is repeated for each relation.

$$p\left(o_i | l_{j,1}, l_{j,2}, \ldots, l_{j,|l_j|}\right) = \frac{e^{y_{o_i}}}{\sum_s e^{y_s}} \tag{2}$$

Each of y_s is the unnormalized probability to each output vertex o_s, computed as

$$y = Uh(l_{j,1}, l_{j,2}, \ldots, l_{j,|l_j|}; E) + b \tag{3}$$

where U and b are the output layer weights and bias, respectively; h is the output of a hidden layer constructed by the transformation for relation r_j of the embeddings of l_j extracted from E, as shown in Eqs. 4 and 5:

$$h = t_j \cdot h_j \tag{4}$$

$$h_j = [v_{l_{j,1}}, v_{l_{j,2}}, \ldots, v_{l_{j,|l_j|}}] \cdot E \tag{5}$$

where t_j transforms the extracted embeddings of each relation to the same space, and $v_{l_{j,n}} \in \mathbb{R}^{1 \times |l_j|}$ is a one-hot vector used to retrieve the corresponding embeddings of l_j, n. Although Eq. 3 takes into account all vertices for prediction, in practice, we train E, U, and b using each of the linked vertices in l_j as the sample to predict the vertex o_i. Therefore, unlike some intuitive methods which treat each relation as a separate graph and then concatenate the generated embeddings, we encoded through t_j, places all relations on the same graph for consideration when generating embeddings.

It is noticed that in this framework, only vertices in l (i.e., those who have outlinks) learn embeddings. Vertices with only inlinks are not embedded, since they are only predicted by other vertices. Figure 1 illustrates an example.

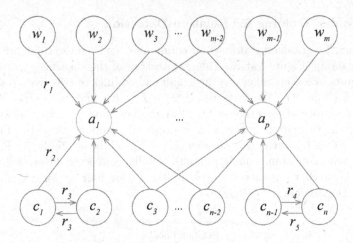

Fig. 2. Multi-relational graph: Assume m words, n companies, and p articles exist in the dataset. Moreover, c_1 and c_2 are competitor while c_{n-1} is c_n's upstream supplier and c_n is c_{n-1}'s downstream retailer.

Embedding Training for Companies. To apply our multi-relational graph embedding to the relation classification task, we first construct a graph representing the entities and relations in the experimental datasets. Engaged entities include the articles, the article content words, and the companies exist in articles. The steps to construct this graph are as follows:

1. Entity: each article, each company, and all distinct words in the dataset are vertices.
2. Word-inclusion relation (r1): if a word belongs to the article, create a directed link from the word vertex to the article vertex.
3. Company-engagement relation(r2): if a company exists in the article, create a directed link from the company vertex to the article vertex.
4. Competitor relation(r3): if company A is company B's competitor, create a directed link from vertex company A to vertex company B.
5. Upstream relation(r4): if company A is company B's upstream supplier, create a directed link from vertex company A to vertex company B.
6. Downstream relation(r5): if company A is company B's downstream retailer, create a directed link from vertex company A to vertex company B.

Figure 2 is an illustration of the constructed graph. Note that even there is no link between words and companies, the words in this graph would still affect the embeddings of companies due to the universal weights U and bias b in Eq. 3. During the back-propagation in the training process, the weights U and bias b will be influenced by the words, thus influence the embedding of companies.

4.2   Classifier Training for Relation Detection

After getting the graph embeddings for companies, we then use them for relation classifier training. Figure 3 shows the architecture of the classifier.

The inputs of the classifier are the graph embeddings of two given companies A and B: E_A and E_B. We first concatenate E_A, E_B and $E_A - E_B$. We do a element-wise subtraction because there might be some patterns between two embeddings in the latent space. For example, if company A is B's upstream supplier and C is D's upstream supplier, $E_A - E_B$ might be similar to $E_C - E_D$. Thereafter, the concatenation is put into a fully connected layer, followed by a softmax layer that outputs the probability of each four options: Competitor, Upstream, Downstream, No-Relation.

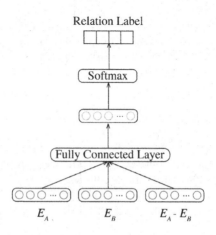

Fig. 3. An illustration of classifier

After training, we can put any two companies into our system, and the system will predict the relation between the input company pair.

5   Experiments

To train this classifier, we use the ground truth from Money Link website. There are three types of relation contained in the dataset: upstream supplier, downstream retailer, and competitor. We also generate the negative samples, which means no relation between two companies. There are 9,496 competitors, 4,827 upstream, 4,827 downstream, and 6,432 negative samples.

The upstream and downstream are the reverse concept of each other. That is, (A, B, upstream) if and only if (B, A, downstream). Hence, to make our experiment more reliable, we require that both the upstream and its reverse downstream sample should be categorized into the same set when splitting data into train/val/test set. Moreover, because (A, B, Competitor) also means (B, A,

Competitor), as well as No-relation. As the result, the pairs should also be split into same train/val/test set. The split ratio is 0.8/0.1/0.1.

In order to know how well our graph embedding method utilizes the information from different datasets, we have three variation during the graph embeddings training stage.

1. Both Economic Daily News in Taiwan and the relation pairs between companies (upstream, downstream, competitor) in training and validation set from Money Link website are put into the graph embedding training.
2. Only Economic Daily News are put into the graph embedding training.
3. Only relation pairs in training and validation set are put into the graph embedding training.

Moreover, we use Glove from Pennington et al. [3] to train word and company embeddings on the Economic Daily News. Glove uses unsupervised learning algorithm to obtain vector representation for each token in the corpus. During Glove's training process, it considers both the local context windows and global word-word co-occurrence probability from the corpus. As a result, it should be a good baseline to measure whether our model captures the semantic information in the news.

In the end, we generate randomly initialized embeddings for sanity check that both our graph embedding and Glove actually utilize the information from the news for classification task.

To train the classifier, we use one of the optimizer: Adadelta [4], Adam [5], RMSprop [6], SGD [7,8] with momentum [9], with cross entropy loss and apply dropout [10] and L2 regularization [11]. We do the grid search on the validation set to pick the best hyperparameters and optimizer. Thereafter, we put training and validation set together, train it with the best hyperparameters and the picked optimizer, and test the result on the test set. To better understand the effectiveness of embeddings training stage, we do experiment on both finetuning and not finetuning the embeddings. The finetuning means that we dynamically update the embeddings during training the classifier.

6   Results

We measure each of the setting's precision, recall, and macro F1 score. The result is showed in Table 3. From Table 3, we can see that if we dynamically update the embeddings during the classifier training, the performance of all the settings except *Random* are pretty similar. However, even for the best setting, *News + Relation*, it only outperforms *Random* by 2.1% F1 score. This result is not expected because *Random* does not utilize any information in the embedding training stage. In only updates its company embeddings when training the classifier, but it could still achieve F1 score of 0.748.

To further investigate what the model actually learns during the training of embeddings, we do an experiment that do not allow the dynamically updating embeddings when we train the classifier. The performance of *Random* drops

Table 3. The metric result for each class and the total performance. The scores in overall are calculated by macro averaging each measure of the listed four classes

		Finetune			No-Finetune		
		Precison	Recall	F1 score	Precison	Recall	F1 score
News + Relation	Competitor	0.876	0.831	0.853	0.684	0.828	0.749
	Upstream	0.778	0.714	0.745	0.701	0.578	0.634
	Downstream	0.739	0.729	0.734	0.733	0.581	0.649
	No-relation	0.697	0.800	0.745	0.619	0.584	0.601
	Overall	0.772	0.768	0.769	0.685	0.643	0.658
News	Competitor	0.870	0.830	0.849	0.546	0.633	0.586
	Upstream	0.723	0.727	0.725	0.606	0.470	0.530
	Downstream	0.727	0.711	0.719	0.598	0.485	0.535
	No-relation	0.706	0.764	0.734	0.396	0.413	0.404
	Overall	0.756	0.758	0.757	0.536	0.500	0.514
Relation	Competitor	0.837	0.842	0.839	0.766	0.828	0.796
	Upstream	0.771	0.712	0.741	0.706	0.558	0.623
	Downstream	0.743	0.720	0.732	0.680	0.599	0.637
	No-relation	0.713	0.761	0.736	0.639	0.707	0.671
	Overall	0.766	0.759	0.762	0.698	0.673	0.682
Glove	Competitor	0.837	0.865	0.851	0.545	0.654	0.594
	Upstream	0.733	0.730	0.731	0.637	0.536	0.582
	Downstream	0.745	0.727	0.736	0.543	0.520	0.531
	No-relation	0.744	0.720	0.732	0.388	0.321	0.351
	Overall	0.765	0.760	0.762	0.528	0.508	0.515
Random	Competitor	0.858	0.795	0.825	0.484	0.687	0.568
	Upstream	0.722	0.725	0.724	0.464	0.527	0.494
	Downstream	0.694	0.744	0.718	0.543	0.392	0.455
	No-relation	0.706	0.748	0.726	0.264	0.118	0.163
	Overall	0.745	0.753	0.748	0.439	0.431	0.420

dramatically to F1 score of 0.420, while others' performance drops some extent, but do much better than *Random*. In detail, *Relation* does the best, *News + Relation* second, followed by *Glove* and *News*. Previously, *News + Relation* outperforms the *Relation*, but here *Relation* outperforms the *News + Relation*. We guess this is because a large portion of information in the news is not related to the relation classification for companies, but those words that contain noise are still linked to the articles and being optimized when we train our graph embedding. If we do not finetune embeddings in the classifier, those noise cannot be filtered out, thus hurt the performance of the classifier. On the other hand, despite the noise contained in the news, the news still provides certain amount of information for the classifier because *Glove* and *News* outperform *Random* by almost 10%.

Based on the observation that (1) The F1 score of all the settings in Finetune are silimar. (2) All the other settings' performance is much better than *Random* in No-Finetune. We can know that the news actually provides some information for the relation classification task. However, most the information extracted from the news are actually included in the relation pairs that we used to train the classifier.

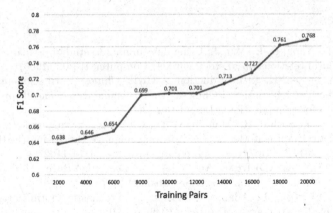

Fig. 4. F1 score with respect to the number of training relation pairs used in the classifier.

To measure how the amount of training data used in the classifier influences the performance, we do an experiment on the embeddings from the best setting, Finetune *News+Relation*. We use different amount of data to train the classifier, and the result is showed in Fig. 4. We have two observation here: (1) The more the training data, the better the performance. (2) When we use only 2000 training relation pairs, which is 1/10 of all the training relation pairs, the performance does not drop a lot. This means that the effectiveness of embeddings will emerge when the training data is not a lot.

Lastly, by comparing *News* and *Glove*, our graph embedding has the competing ability to capture the semantic information from News data. Moreover, our model can utilize both the structured data(relation pairs) and unstructured data(News) while Glove embedding can only be trained on word corpus.

7   Conclusion

In this paper, we propose a system which can utilize the data from both News dataset and relation pairs dataset to detect relation between companies. In the meantime, we also propose a method to train multi-relational graph embedding, which can encode information from varies kinds of data as long as a graph is constructed. The graph embedding is used to capture the information from our datasets, thus helping the training of relation classifier. After training, our system can provide the relation between companies. This kind of information should be helpful for the current complex financial market. Although improvements can be made on our static method such as adding time into consideration to be dynamic prediction or by search for more related dataset, we believe this method has shown its possibility to help exposing more information hidden in industry business and it is a worth-trying direction. Furthermore, the current approach is not restricted to Taiwan market, which can be applied to any other markets as long as the related data is available.

References

1. Hsieh, Y.L., Yang, D.-L., Wu, J.: Using data mining to study upstream and downstream causal relationship in stock market. Computer **1**, F02 (2005)
2. Ma, W.-Y., Chen, K.-J.: Introduction to CKIP Chinese word segmentation system for the first international Chinese Word Segmentation Bakeoff, pp. 168–171. Association for Computational Linguistics (2003)
3. Pennington, J., Socher, R., Manning, C.D.: GloVe: global vectors for word representation. In: Empirical Methods in Natural Language Processing (EMNLP), pp. 1532–1543 (2014). http://www.aclweb.org/anthology/D14-1162
4. Zeiler, M.D.: ADADELTA: An Adaptive Learning Rate Method. CoRR abs/1212.5701 (2012). http://arxiv.org/abs/1212.5701
5. Kingma, D.P., Ba, J.: Adam: A Method for Stochastic Optimization. CoRR abs/1412.6980 http://arxiv.org/abs/1412.6980 (2014)
6. Hinton, G.: Neural networks for machine learning - lecture 6a - overview of mini-batch gradient descent (2012)
7. Robbins, H., Monro, S.: A stochastic approximation method. Ann. Math. Statist. **22**(3), 400–407 (1951). https://doi.org/10.1214/aoms/1177729586. https://projecteuclid.org/euclid.aoms/1177729586
8. Kiefer, J., Wolfowitz, J.: Stochastic estimation of the maximum of a regression function. Ann. Math. Statist. **23**(3), 462–466 (1952). https://doi.org/10.1214/aoms/1177729392. https://projecteuclid.org/euclid.aoms/1177729392
9. Qian, N.: On the momentum term in gradient descent learning algorithms. Neural Netw. **12**(1), 145–151 (1999). http://www.sciencedirect.com/science/article/pii/S0893608098001166
10. Srivastava, N., Hinton, G., Krizhevsky, A., Sutskever, I., Salakhutdinov, R.: Dropout: a simple way to prevent neural networks from overfitting. J. Mach. Learn. Res. **15**, 1929–1958 (2014). http://jmlr.org/papers/v15/srivastava14a.html
11. Ng, A.Y.: Feature selection, L1 vs. L2 regularization, and rotational invariance. In: Proceedings of the Twenty-First International Conference on Machine Learning, ICML 2004, Banff, Alberta, Canada, p. 78. ACM, New York (2004). http://doi.acm.org/10.1145/1015330.1015435

Exploring Errors in Reading a Visualization via Eye Tracking Models Using Stochastic Geometry

Michael G. Hilgers[(✉)] and Aaron Burke

Missouri University of Science and Technology, Rolla, MO 65409, USA
hilgers@mst.edu

Abstract. Information visualizations of quantitative data are rapidly becoming more complex as the dimension and volume of data increases. Critical to modern applications, an information visualization is used to communicate numeric data using objects such as lines, rectangles, bars, circles, and so forth. Via visual inspection, the viewer assigns numbers to these objects using their geometric properties of size and shape. Any difference between this estimation and the desired numeric value we call the "visual measurement error". The research objective of this paper is to propose models of the visual measure error utilizing stochastic geometry. The fundamental technique in building our models is the conceptualization of eye fixation points as might be determined by an eye-tracking experiment of viewers estimating size and shape of a visualization's object configurations. The fixation points are first considered as a stochastic point process whose characteristics require comment before proceeding to the statistical shape analysis of the visualization. Once clarified the fixation points are reinterpreted as a sampling of the shape and size of the landmark configurations of geometric landmarks on the visualization. The ultimate end of these models is to find optimal shape and size parameters leading to minimum visual measurement error.

Keywords: Information visualization · Reading error · Stochastic shape analysis

1 Introduction

Information visualizations of quantitative data are rapidly becoming more complex as the dimension and volume of data increases [1]. Critical to modern applications, an information visualization is used to communicate numeric data using objects such as lines, rectangles, bars, circles, and so forth. Via visual inspection, the viewer assigns numbers to these objects using their geometric properties of size and shape [2]. Any difference between this estimation and the desired numeric value we call the "visual measurement error". The research objective of this paper is to propose models of the visual measurement error utilizing stochastic geometry. The fundamental technique in building these models is to abstract the accumulation of eye fixation points produced during an eye-tracking experiment [3]. Participants will be asked to "measure" the size of objects with the visualization configuration. The fixation points are first viewed as a spatial point pattern of a spatial stochastic point process. We will look at its properties and see various shortcomings when applied to the analysis of the structure of

© Springer Nature Switzerland AG 2019
F. F.-H. Nah and K. Siau (Eds.): HCII 2019, LNCS 11589, pp. 53–71, 2019.
https://doi.org/10.1007/978-3-030-22338-0_5

information visualization. At this point, the research takes a novel turn. The fixation points are reinterpreted as a sampling of the landmark configuration of a visualization construct. The study of visualization measurement error will utilize Bookstein's analysis of the size and shape of a triangle. An error model will be given under strongly simplifying assumptions.

2 Eye Tracking Analysis of Information Visualization

We pose the following abstract usability experiment. A group of people is shown the simple bar chart seen in Fig. 1. They are given the task of measuring bar A against the ruler and estimate it's "height" according to the ruler's scale. (We will use the term height as if the scale where in inches.). While doing so they are monitored using an eye tracker. Previous related research [22] showed the fixation points of the search appeared as in the right-hand side of Fig. 1. Of course, the striking feature is the formation of three clustered regions. To understand the information stored in these clusters, it is necessary to build a mathematical framework to describe the experiment. We will follow the lines of development and definitions used in [4] and [5].

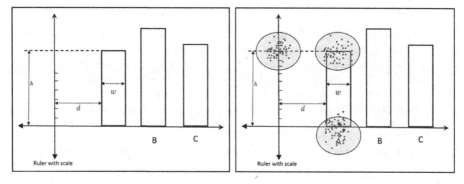

Fig. 1. The left picture shows the visualization. The right picture shows the fixation points from the eye tracking data.

Denote $\tilde{S}$ as a set of fixation points in $\mathbb{R}^2$. Mathematically, it is viewed as a spatial point pattern.

Definition 1: A *spatial point pattern* is a set of points in the plane denoted as:

$$\{\mathbf{x}_1, \mathbf{x}_2, \ldots, \mathbf{x}_k\} \tag{1}$$

where

$$\mathbf{x}_j = \begin{bmatrix} x_j \\ y_j \end{bmatrix}.$$

Each person in the experiment will compare the Bar A to the axis to the left as shown in Fig. 1 then report the bar's height they observed, $\hat{h}$. Meanwhile, we collected the data produced by the eye tracker. In an idealized sense, we have captured the formation of a spatial point pattern $\hat{S}$ during the measurement process. For each test subject, we obtain the pairing $(\hat{S}, \hat{h})$. If there are n participants in the experiment, we collect a set of information of the form

$$\{(\tilde{S}_1, \tilde{h}_1), (\tilde{S}_2, \tilde{h}_2), \ldots, (\tilde{S}_n, \tilde{h}_n)\}. \tag{2}$$

2.1 Addressing Error

Error is the difference between h and $\tilde{h}$. The determination of the measurement $\tilde{h}$ is the result of a complex system of interactions between the eye, brain, and visualization. Identifying every possible physiological and cognitive effect leading to $\tilde{h}$ is beyond our current level of understanding [2]. However, it is the hope of usability research that many of these complexities are encapsulated in the eye's motion during the measurement process [6, 7]. Eye tracking can be view then as an indirect sampling of unobservable processes. Unless the measurement of $\tilde{h}$ is the result of a completely random process, it seems reasonable any underlying process could be influenced by observable factors such as lengths, widths, and areas. Expressing this influence will occupy the rest of this paper.

3 Modeling

The purpose of this research is to propose models of visual measurement error. Some models we will simply offer for future consideration. For other models, we will discuss their reasonableness. Since we are using eye-tracking experiments as our inspirational gateway into this topic, all of our models begin with a spatial point pattern. Based on this, our models can be divided into approaches: spatial point processes and spatial shape processes. Introductory ideas, including motivation, and some basic results will be included in this section. The details of more involved models will be deferred to the particular application. (We assume the reader is familiar with basic probabilities theory a little measure theory.)

4 Stochastic Point Processes

4.1 Basic Premises

For beginners, the mathematical definition of a point process is surprising complex (see [8] or [9]). To simplify our situation as much as possible, we will consider a **point process** a random mechanism whose outcomes are spatial point patterns. Believing there are only a finite number of fixation points on a visualization, we restrict attention to finite point processes; bringing us to the following definition [4]:

Definition 2: A *finite point process* **X is a random mechanism for which,**

1. Every possible outcome is a spatial point pattern with a finite number of points,
2. For all test sets (closed and bounded) subsets B of $\mathbb{R}^2$, the number of points of **X** in B is finite, denoted as $N(\mathbf{X} \cap B)$, is a well-defined random variable.

In considering spatial point pattern realizations of the underlying point process, people seek answers to standards questions. Is the density (number of points per area) constant? Are the points distributed "evenly" or "uniformly" across some region? Are there voids (empty regions)? Has the data clustered? Is there evidence of point or area interaction? What is the distribution function of the random processes at play? We continue by following the presentation of Baddeley, Rubak, and Turner in their excellent book [4].

4.2   Complete Spatial Randomness

Our first objective is to define *complete spatial randomness* (*CSR*). This is important because our approach to building models is inspired by eye tracking. It is reasonable to believe seemingly random motion of the eye demonstrates a certain lack of understanding or interest on the part of the viewer and will provide little insight into geometric structure.

Formulating CSR requires several characteristics of the finite point distribution. We want the spatial pattern to have no preferred location so they the points appear to be distributed uniformly. This introduces the concept of a spatial probability density. To comply with Definition 2 part (2), we will need the probability distribution of the count functions $N(X \cap B)$.

We begin with the notion of a spatial pattern being uniformly distributed. To keep things simple, we begin considering how to place a point in a window set W uniformly. First, suppose that location of the single point (u_1, u_2) in Fig. 2 is expressed by random variables U_1 and U_2 with joint probability distribution $\lambda(u_1, u_2)$. The probability that $U = (U_1, U_2)$ lies in the so-called test set B is

$$\mathbb{P}(U \in B) = \int_B \lambda(u_1, u_2) du_1 du_2. \tag{3}$$

Since the Lebesgue measure is non-atomic, Eq. (3) is different than

$$\mathbb{P}((U_1, U_2) = (u_1, u_2)) = 0 \tag{4}$$

If we require the probability density function $\lambda(u_1, u_2)$ to be a bivariate uniform distribution on W, we have

$$\lambda(u_1, u_2) = \begin{cases} 1/|W| & (u_1, u_2) \in W \\ 0 & \text{otherwise} \end{cases} \tag{5}$$

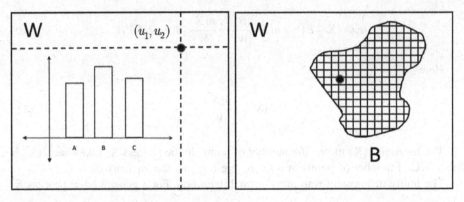

Fig. 2. Uniformly distributed random points. Right: point is in a test set. left: point is given coordinates as realization of random variables

Here and elsewhere $|W|$ is the two-dimensional Lebesgue measure of W, which is its area. Using Eq. (5) in Eq. (3),

$$\mathbb{P}(U \in B) = \int_B \lambda(u_1, u_2) du_1 du_2 = \frac{1}{W} \int_B 1 du_1 du_2 = \frac{|B|}{|W|}. \tag{6}$$

This is intuitively pleasing as the probability a spatial point "hits" the test set is the proportion of area it occupies. Let us call this probability $p(B)$.

Suppose now that we wish to place n points uniformly in W. To this end, we define a finite point process $\mathbf{X} = \{U_1, U_2, \ldots, U_n\}$ where each U_j is a uniformly distribution random point as per the proceeding the paragraph. Let B be a test set. If we associate a "hit" with a "success", we are counting the number of successes out of n trials. If we suppose that each trial is independent of the others but share the same probability of hitting B, we have from Eq. (6)

$$\mathbb{P}(U_j \in B) = |B|/|W| = p(B) \text{ for } i = 1, 2, \ldots, n. \tag{7}$$

From this, we quickly recognize that $N(\mathbf{X} \cap B)$ has the binomial distribution [10]

$$\mathbb{P}(N(\mathbf{X} \cap B) = k) = \frac{n!}{k!(n-k)!} p(B)^k (1 - p(B))^{n-k}. \tag{8}$$

The expected value of a binomial process [10] is

$$\mathbb{E}[N(\mathbf{X} \cap B)] = np(B). \tag{9}$$

From Eq. (6),

$$\mathbb{E}[N(\mathbf{X} \cap B)] = n(\mathbf{X}) \frac{|B|}{|W|} = \frac{n(\mathbf{X})}{|W|} |B| = \hat{\lambda}(\mathbf{X})|B|. \tag{10}$$

Here

$$\hat{\lambda}(\mathbf{X}) = \frac{n(\mathbf{X})}{|W|}. \tag{11}$$

The notation $n(\mathbf{X})$ means the number of points in the process $\mathbf{X}$. Likewise, $\hat{\lambda}(\mathbf{X})$ is the expected number of points in a set B. We call this the *intensity* of $\mathbf{X}$.

The utility of intensity warrants a formal definition. For a general point process $\mathbf{X}$,

$$\mathbb{E}[N(\mathbf{X} \cap B)] = \int_B \lambda(u)du \tag{12}$$

If it exists, $\lambda(u)$ is called the *intensity function*. We call a process *homogeneous* if the intensity is constant,

$$\mathbb{E}[N(\mathbf{X} \cap B)] = \lambda|B|. \tag{13}$$

A final issue of primary importance concerns the probability distribution of the random variable $N(\mathbf{X} \cap B)$ as referred to in (2) of Definition 2. Assuming the process is homogeneous; using Eq. (13) it can be shown $N(\mathbf{X} \cap B)$ Poisson distributed [11].

Definition 3: A non-negative integer-valued random variable Y has the *Poisson distribution* [10] (denoted $P(\mu)$) if

$$\mathbb{P}[Y = k] = \mathrm{e}^{-\mu} \frac{\mu^k}{k!} \text{ for } k = 0, 1, 2, \dots \tag{14}$$

An important property of this distribution is

$$\mathbb{E}[\mathbf{Y}] = \mu \text{ and } \mathbb{V}[\mathbf{Y}] = \mu \tag{15}$$

We are now ready to define what it means for process to be spatially random [4].

Definition 4: A *homogenous Poisson Point Process* $\mathbf{X}$ with $\lambda > 0$ has the following properties:

1. *Poisson Counts*: the random variable $N(\mathbf{X} \cap B)$ has a Poisson distribution $P(\mu)$ with

$$\mu(B) = \int_B \lambda(u)du = \lambda|B|; \tag{16}$$

2. *Homogeneous Intensity*: the expected number of points hitting a test set B is

$$\mathbb{E}[N(\mathbf{X} \cap B)] = \lambda |B|; \tag{17}$$

3. *Independence*: if $B_1, B_2, \ldots$ are disjoint regions of the plane, then $N(\mathbf{X} \cap B_1), N(\mathbf{X} \cap B_2), \ldots$ are independent random variables.

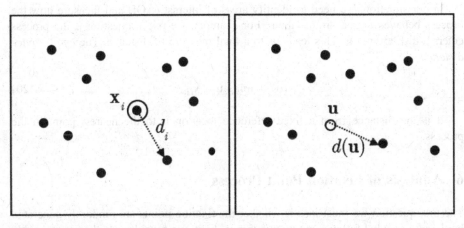

Fig. 3. Right: Shows the nearest neighbor distance is a from point to point in the process. Left: shows the empty-space distance is from a fixed location to a point in the process

5 Point Process Error Models

Returning to the eye tracking experiment, we are asking test subjects to visually measure the height of a bar (h) using a ruler which is d units away. As is suggested in the picture on the right in Fig. 1, the measurement effort leads to the formation of an eye tracking spatial point pattern as a cluster around the point $\mathbf{h}$. (We will use the notation $\mathbf{h} = (0, h)$ when referring to the point in the plane and h for its length.). From out of this cluster, the subject produces a number $\hat{h}_j$ most often different from h leading to a difference ε_j, which we are calling the visual measurement error.

To quantify this, we begin with a spatial point pattern given in Definition 1. In order to specify the magnitude ε_j, we need an appropriate distance measure [4]. A natural approach is the classic Euclidean norm for the plane and use it to define the *pairwise distances*

$$d_{ij} = \left\| \mathbf{x}_i - \mathbf{x}_j \right\| = \sqrt{(x_i - x_j)^2 + (y_i - y_j)^2} \tag{18}$$

This distance is defined independent of the eye tracking behavior, which is a concern, since we are trying to understand the impact of visualization design on the visual measurement error.

We are modelling through the lens of the eye tracking patterns. Therefore, it is reasonable we consider whether there is a characteristic of the pattern that reveals the estimated height. This means we seek a "process specific" distance measure. Choosing a point in the process, say $\mathbf{x}_i$, we define the *nearest neighbor distance* (Fig. 3) as

$$d_i = \min_{j \neq i} d_{ij} \tag{19}$$

In our situation, we need to identify areas of interest (AOI) and measure how the process behaves in and around them. For example, we might question if the process enters a disk around $\mathbf{h}$. This leads us to a final measure of distance. The *empty-space distance*

$$d(\mathbf{u}) = \min_j \|\mathbf{u} - \mathbf{x}_j\|. \tag{20}$$

It is the distance from a fixed reference location $\mathbf{u}$ to the nearest point in the process.

6 Analysis of Fixation Point Process

The first question we must face is whether the fixation points are randomly generated by the eye. In what follows, we do two things. First, we consider whether a reasonable error model derived, assuming the fixation points, satisfies complete spatial randomness (CSR) criteria. Second, we will show that CSR does not provide any of the desired implications of geometric structure.

6.1 Nearest Neighbor

Let us consider the cluster of fixation points about the point $\mathbf{h} = (0, h)$. The experiment asks the test subject is to estimate h. Suppose that $\hat{h}$ is returned. Odds are they are different. We have been calling this the visual measurement error. We have now reached the beginning of the modelling process. The first issue we face is to define the error metric to be used. This is more challenging than it seems. Of course, the distance $|h - \hat{h}|$ is obvious but it contains no information about the point process.

As a starting point, we will suppose fixation points form a homogenous Poisson process called $\mathbf{X}$. To include the point of $\mathbf{X}$ in the measurement process, we could reason as follows. While we do not know how the brain does the visual measurement, it seems safe to believe the points of $\mathbf{X}$ nearest $\mathbf{h}$ contribute the most information. Suppose we place a disk around $\mathbf{h}$ with radius ε. We then increase the radius until the disk makes contact with a point of $\mathbf{X}$. This is the empty space distance discuss above. It is a random variable with a known probability distribution function [9]

$$H_S(r) = 1 - \exp(-\lambda \pi r^2). \tag{21}$$

Using this, we derive the mean empty space distance is

$$m_s = \frac{1}{2\sqrt{\lambda}}. \tag{22}$$

This tells us that the expected difference between the observed and actual height of the bar. Is this a good error model? We note the mean is independent of h. Another feature is the mean is proportional to the inverse square root of the intensity λ. This is curious. If we increase by four the number of points about $\mathbf{h}$, we will reduce the error by only a half. It would seem that increasing the amount of visual activity by so much produced too little.

6.2 Stationary Process

It already seems as though modeling eye tracking as a spatially random point process has issues. We now see another. CSR is stationary or translation invariant [4]. Formally, we say a point process $\mathbf{X}$ stationary if for every vector $\mathbf{v}$, the process $\mathbf{X} + \mathbf{v}$ has the same statistical properties as $\mathbf{X}$.

Suppose that $\mathbf{X}$ is a stationary process associated with an eye tracking experiment. Consider the vector $\mathbf{v} = (d, 0)$ and form the translated process $\mathbf{X}' = \mathbf{X} + \mathbf{v}$. Being stationary $\mathbf{X}'$ has the same properties at (d, h) as $\mathbf{X}$ at $(0, h)$. This would say that the error inherent in measuring the bar height by looking at the ruler is no different than looking at the bar.

Does this seem reasonable? Let us perform a simple analysis. If we think of the eyes as tracing gaze paths generally along $y = h$ from the bar to the ruler, it is seems plausible the paths can be bounded by a triangle[1], as show in Fig. 4. This shows that a small angle error in "shooting" a path from the bar to ruler can result in an error of the form

$$\varepsilon = d \tan(\theta). \tag{23}$$

While not rigorous, it supports a belief the visual measurement error depends on the distance of the bar from the ruler.

---

[1] A more rigorous approach is to consider stochastic paths from the bar to the ruler generated by a Brownian motion. These would be bounded by the famous square root curve opening to the left. This is another interesting research direction to follow, particularly given Kendall's work on diffusion models of Bookstein triangles [12]

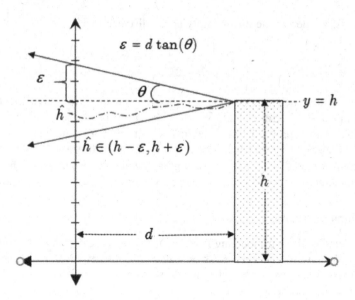

Fig. 4. This suggests that if the eye makes a small error in tracing along the line from the bar to the ruler, then the resulting error grows linearly in the distance.

6.3   Inhomogeneous Processes

Based on the preceding discussion, homogeneous point processes make poor models of visual measurement error. Therefore, our next step along this path is to find a good model with a non-constant intensity. The numerical covariate of the distance from a selected point to say $(0, h)$ might serve as an excellent effect to build into the model. It could represent the challenge/ease one has in concentrating on **h**. This is a good subject to explore in upcoming work.

The most obvious characteristic we have not addressed in our error modeling discussion is that the fixation points cluster around areas critical to measuring the height of bar A. See Fig. 1. Cluster formation is typically modelled in steps similar to growing a forest. First, a process places parent points (trees). Then in a region about the parent, child points (seedlings) are placed according to another distribution. Most of the popular cluster models assign independence to these clusters meaning what happens around one tree does not affect another. (Trees are not interacting with each other.). This confronts another issue. Are the clusters are spatially correlated? Correlation is likely as judging the height of the bar requires looking at both the bar and the ruler.

Gathering our thoughts, a useful cluster model needs the parents to be fixed with clusters forming around them. Consideration needs to be given to how the children in different clusters interact. For example, the eye fixating on a point near the bar might then quickly skip to the ruler. One approach to modeling this skipping behavior is to choose a child in each cluster and connect them by line. The simplest way to connect all three clusters is to build triangles with vertices in each point cluster.

This, then, has led us to statistical shape processes as a reasonable basis for visual measurement error modeling.

7 Stochastic Geometry Processes

We are exploring the relationship between visual measurement error and the geometrical shape of subcomponents of a visualization. In the first part, we viewed the eye as sampling data at points in the picture. We then built models utilizing random point processes. These mechanisms place points "randomly" around the plane based on underlying premises.

We now make a major change of philosophy. While we track fixation points, we suggest that the brain is seeing geometry in our case triangles. As show conceptually in Fig. 5, we propose to consider a mechanism placing triangles randomly on the visualization. To the best of our knowledge, stochastic geometry has yet to be utilized in usability analysis of information visualizations.

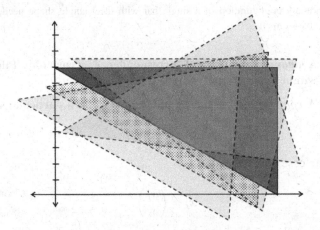

Fig. 5. A random triangle process

To this end, we must introduce the notions of landmark configurations and shape. We follow the approach introduced by Kendall [13]. Herein, we use the presentation by Dryden and Mardia [14].

7.1 Landmark Configurations

Consider a family of bar graphs. Any single bar graph is a collection of rectangles positioned on some (normally unspecified) coordinate system. In order to relate the family of bar graphs to each other, we introduce landmarks [14, 15].

As shown in Fig. 6 the landmarks are chosen as the corners of the bar. The landmarks ensure that a family of bar graphs, which varies the parameters d, w and h, maps the corners correctly. In practice, a heuristic approach is taken to landmark selection [14]. For visualizations of count data, landmarks might be assigned to corners of rectangles, the intersection of lines and so forth.

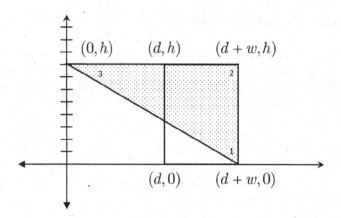

Fig. 6. The landmark configuration of a single bar with the triangle shape needed to capture error in visual measurement

Definition 5: A *landmark* **is a point of correspondence on each object that matches between and within populations**.

Definition 6: A *configuration* **is the set of landmarks on a particular object**:

$$\{x_1, x_2, \ldots, x_k\} \tag{24}$$

For the planar case,

$$x_j = \begin{pmatrix} x_j \\ y_j \end{pmatrix} \tag{25}$$

7.2 Shape and Size

Consider the triangle in Fig. 6. It seems reasonable that where the triangle occurs in the visualization does not affect its intrinsic geometric properties. In most bar graphs, the bar rectangles are either horizontal or vertical. Which one is used will cause the triangle to rotate. Again, one would suspect that rotation does not change the intrinsic properties of the triangle. As a viewer can zoom in or out, the geometric properties should remain unchanged. Translation, rotation, and scaling comprise the so-called Euclidean similarity transformations (see [14] for precise definitions).

With these ideas in mind, Kendall [13] proposed the following definitions of shape and size.

Definition 7: *Shape* **is all of the geometric information that remains after location, scale, and rotational effects are filtered out of an object**.

Definitions require examples. Let us consider the triangle in Fig. 7. If it is translated, the angles do not change. If it is rotated, the angles do not change. If the triangle is dilated, the angles do not change. Hence, the angles invariant under the set of Eucli-dean similarity transformations. Another item to note is that $\alpha + \beta + \gamma = 180°$. Therefore, we need to know only two of the three angles to identify the shape of the triangle. This little observation was made profound by Kendall ([16–18]). In practice however, using all three angles as shape parameters has proven to be problematic particularly in the possibility of a degenerate case of a flat triangle. We will use the shape parameters proposed by Bookstein [15, 19].

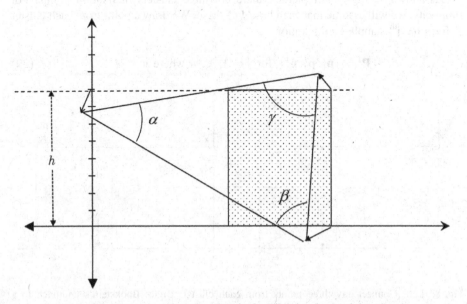

Fig. 7. The internal angles of a triangle describe the shape of the triangle.

Definition 8: The *size-and-shape* is all of the geometric information that remains after location and rotational effects are filtered out of an object.

The notion of the size of an object being is invariant over scaling is odd. It means that size is internal. A common version is the sum of the lengths from a vertex to the centroid. We will introduce another in the next section.

7.3   Bookstein's Approach to Triangles

Rather than continuing this discussion in an abstract sense, let us focus on the case of the triangles in the plane. We will use Bookstein's approach [15, 19] as it illustrate the concept of stochastic triangles fairly well.

We begin the following statistical model:

$$\mathbf{p}_k = \mathbf{z}_k + \mathbf{d}_k \ \text{ for } \ k = 1, 2, 3 \tag{26}$$

We interpret $\mathbf{p}_k$ as the sampling of kth landmark $\mathbf{z}_k$, in which encountered an error of $\mathbf{d}_k$. In coordinate form

$$\begin{bmatrix} x_k \\ y_k \end{bmatrix} = \begin{bmatrix} z_{kx} \\ z_{ky} \end{bmatrix} + \begin{bmatrix} d_{kx} \\ d_{ky} \end{bmatrix} \quad \text{for } k = 1, 2, 3 \tag{27}$$

The error terms are random variables with a normal distribution,

$$d_{kx}, d_{ky} \sim N(0, \sigma_k^2) \tag{28}$$

As shown in Fig. 8 left picture, there are three clusters of fixation points. For simplicity, we will assume that each has M of these. We draw a point from each cluster to form the jth sample configuration

$$\mathbf{P}^j = \{\mathbf{p}_1^j, \mathbf{p}_2^j, \mathbf{p}_3^j\} \quad \text{for } j = 1, \ldots, n \text{ where } n = M^3. \tag{29}$$

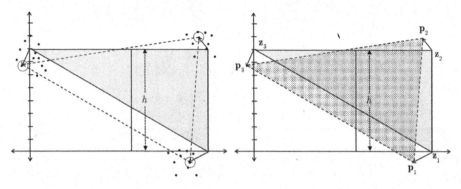

Fig. 8. Left: Connect any three points from each cluster. Right: Bookstein's approach to a random configuration

What can we hope to learn from this information? We will not be able to recover the original landmarks since our data might have been subject to translation, rotation, or scaling changes. Therefore, we must focus on the size and shape parameters. For the purpose of this paper, size characteristics will suffice.

7.4   Configuration Sizes

In our original triangle derived from the eye tracking experiment, we have

$$z_1 = (d + w, 0) \, z_2 = (d + w, h) \, z = (d + w, h) \tag{30}$$

As nothing in what is to follow will distinguish d from w, let us relabel $d + w$ as d. By Eq. (17),

$$d_{12} = \|\mathbf{z}_2 - \mathbf{z}_1\| = h \quad d_{23} = \|\mathbf{z}_3 - \mathbf{z}_2\| = d \quad d_{13} = \|\mathbf{z}_3 - \mathbf{z}_1\| = \sqrt{d^2 + h^2} \quad (31)$$

Using the data from the jth configuration, we estimate the distances with

$$\hat{d}_{12}^j = \|\mathbf{p}_2^j - \mathbf{p}_1^j\| \quad \hat{d}_{23}^j = \|\mathbf{p}_3^j - \mathbf{p}_2^j\| \quad \hat{d}_{13}^j = \|\mathbf{p}_3^j - \mathbf{p}_1^j\| \quad (32)$$

Let us now integrate the stochastic elements. In Fig. 9, we show a simplified calculation of the type in Eq. (32) in which we translated to the origin. By Eq. (28),

$$\eta = d_{2x} - d_{1x}\,\eta \sim N(0,\sigma_{12}^2)$$
$$\xi = d_{2y} - d_{1y}\,\xi \sim N(0,\sigma_{12}^2) \quad (33)$$

With $\sigma_{12}^2 = \sigma_1^2 + \sigma_2^2$

In Fig. 9, we show how an edge of the triangle is calculated based upon the eye tracking fixation points. The edge shown corresponds to the height of the Bar A. The random variable length D represents the measure reported by the test subject so our visual measurement error corresponds to $|h - D|$.

The quantity D/σ_{12}, introduced in Fig. 9, has the non-central Chi-distribution with 2 degrees of freedom and non-centrality parameter $\lambda = h^2/\sigma_{12}^2$ [5]. Its probability density function [20] is

$$\frac{x}{\sigma^2}\exp\left(\frac{-(x^2+h^2)}{2\sigma^2}\right)I_0\left(\frac{xh}{\sigma^2}\right). \quad (34)$$

Here I_0 is the Modified Bessel Function of the First Kind [21] with series expansion

$$1 + \frac{x^2}{4} + \frac{x^4}{64} + \frac{x^6}{2304} + \frac{x^8}{147456} + \frac{x^{10}}{14745600} + O(x^{11}) \quad (35)$$

The mean of the distribution of D [20] as shown in Fig. 9 is

$$\mathbb{E}[D] = \sqrt{\frac{\pi}{2}} * \sigma * L_{1/2}\left(-\frac{h^2}{2\sigma^2}\right) \quad (36)$$

In our notation, $L_{1/2}(x)$ is the generalized Laguerre polynomial [10]. This is

$$L_{1/2}(x) = {}_1F_1\left(-\frac{1}{2};1,x\right) \quad (37)$$

This introduces the Confluent Hypergeometric Functions (Kummer's Functions) [10] into our model. This is equivalent to [10]

$${}_1F_1\left(-\frac{1}{2};1,\left(-\frac{h^2}{2\sigma^2}\right)\right) = \frac{1}{2\sigma^2}e^{-\frac{h^2}{4\sigma^2}}\left(h^2 I_1\left(\frac{h^2}{4\sigma^2}\right) + (h^2+2\sigma^2)I_0\left(\frac{h^2}{4\sigma^2}\right)\right) \qquad (38)$$

Combining the previous three equations, we get

$$\mathbb{E}[D] = \sqrt{\frac{\pi}{8\sigma^2}}e^{-\frac{h^2}{4\sigma^2}}\left(h^2 I_1\left(\frac{h^2}{4\sigma^2}\right) + (h^2+2\sigma^2)I_0\left(\frac{h^2}{4\sigma^2}\right)\right). \qquad (39)$$

Figure 9 on the left shows our conceptual construction of the line segment with length D. A simple means to predicting the expected length would be to believe the two clusters are unrelated and will "average themselves out" regardless of the spread of the fixation points. Hence, we might suspect

$$\mathbb{E}[D] = h. \qquad (40)$$

However, the expression for the expected value in Eq. (39) might cast some doubt on this suspicion. Now we must balance intuition with mathematical analysis.

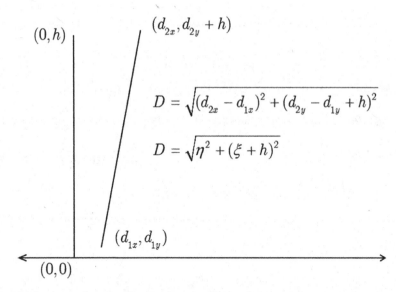

Fig. 9. Approximating the edge length with the distance between sample points

In Fig. 10 we show $|h - \mathbb{E}[D]|$ for different values of the standard deviation of the spatial point pattern (σ). The difference is astounding. If we simply view the point pattern as having a standard normal spatial distribution then the errors are on the size h itself, nearly 100% error. For $\sigma = 5$, the error is so large it is senseless. Now let us go to the other end. If the standard deviations of the fixation point pattern on both ends are small, the expected length of that edge is very close to the actual bar height, particularly for taller bars.

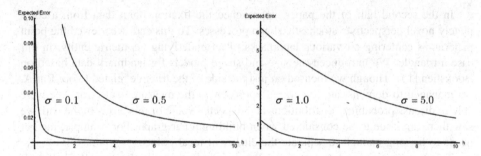

Fig. 10. Notice how the smaller variances in the fixation patterns lead to smaller expected visual measurement error

After some thought, we see that $\lambda = h^2/\sigma^2$ is the critical factor. If $1 \ll \lambda$ then Eq. (40) is approximately true. Hence, there is little visual measurement error on average. However, if $\lambda \approx 1$ then there is significant difference leading to large visual measurement error. In his paper, Bookstein commented that his model needs $1 \ll \lambda$ to be sensible and have reliable statistics. If the spread of the point patterns from both ends of the bar essentially cover the bar, the model allows for large expected lengths of the bar since such long bar lengths can be "drawn" randomly. If we are thinking "point processes", this conversation makes no sense, as we have seen. However, thinking in terms of a triangle process helps us see the issues in visualizing length and not location.

We should also mention, we have not yet discussed the "rest" of the triangle. We can learn several things from the lengths. What can we learn from the shapes? This question is unexplored. Much work remains, but this discussion seems to justify considering stochastic shape processes in modeling eye patterns on information visualizations.

8 Conclusion

Let us summarize what we have discussed in this paper. The problem at hand is visual measurement error encounter in information visualizations. We explored the simplest of all visual tasks: determine the height of a bar relative to a given "ruler". Simple, but we know from experience, answers can vary wildly. As designers of visualizations, we would like to know which qualities of the visualization contribute to the erroneous measurements. It is easy to see that the geometry of the layout of the influences measurement error. Place a bar next to the scale and there is likely to be little error. Move the bar across the page and error would worsen. In modelling error, we need to include geometric factors.

In this paper, we explored the use of eye tracking data to help us understand error models based on the geometry of the figure. In the first half of the paper, we focused on stochastic point processes as a way to model the fixation points. After looking at the qualities of several classical processes, we found they gave no usable information about the error measurement and the underlying geometry.

In the second half of the paper, approached the fixation point data from a completely novel perspective: stochastic shape processes. To this end, we viewed the point patterns as centering on various landmarks of an underlying geometric entity, in our case a triangle. We introduced the size and shape models for landmark data based on Bookstien [15]. Though we focused on just the side of the triangle related to our Bar A, we managed to demonstrate a working approach to the measurement error. We were able to discuss probability distributions and expected value of this error. In the end, we saw there are issue to be considered when building a bar graph. For example, the bar needs to be long enough to separate the cluster of focal points.

This is a new approach to error modeling in information visualization. We believe it has great promise in both experimental design and analytical analysis of visualizations.

References

1. Michalos, M., Tselenti, P., Nalmpantis, S.: Visualization techniques for large datasets. J. Eng. Sci. Technol. Rev. **5**, 72–76 (2012)
2. Cleveland, W.S., McGill, R.: Graphical perception: the visual decoding of quantitative information on graphical displays of data. J. Roy. Stat. Soc. Ser. A (Gen.) **150**, 192–229 (1987)
3. Matzen, Laura E., Haass, Michael J., Divis, Kristin M., Stites, Mallory C.: Patterns of attention: how data visualizations are read. In: Schmorrow, Dylan D., Fidopiastis, Cali M. (eds.) AC 2017. LNCS (LNAI), vol. 10284, pp. 176–191. Springer, Cham (2017). https://doi.org/10.1007/978-3-319-58628-1_15
4. Baddeley, A., Rubak, E., Turner, R.: Spatial Point Patterns: Methodology and Applications with R. Chapman and Hall/CRC (2015)
5. Stoyan, D., Stoyan, H.: Fractals, Random Shapes, and Point Fields: Methods of Geometrical Statistics. Wiley, Hoboken (1994)
6. Jacob, R.J., Karn, K.S.: Eye tracking in human-computer interaction and usability research: ready to deliver the promises. In: The Mind's Eye, pp. 573–605. Elsevier (2003)
7. Manhartsberger, M., Zellhofer, N.: Eye tracking in usability research: what users really see. In: Usability Symposium, pp. 141–152 (2005)
8. Moller, J., Waagepetersen, R.P.: Statistical Inference and Simulation for Spatial Point Processes. Chapman and Hall/CRC (2003)
9. Chiu, S.N., Stoyan, D., Kendall, W.S., Mecke, J.: Stochastic Geometry and Its Applications. Wiley, Hoboken (2013)
10. Johnson, N.L., Kemp, A.W., Kotz, S.: Univariate Discrete Distributions. Wiley, Hoboken (2005)
11. Kingman, J.F.C.: Poisson Processes. Clarendon Press (1992)
12. Kendall, W.S.: A diffusion model for Bookstein triangle shape. Adv. Appl. Probab. **30**, 317–334 (1998)
13. Kendall, D.G.: The diffusion of shape. Adv. Appl. Probab. **9**, 428–430 (1977)
14. Dryden, I., Mardia, K.: Statistical Analysis of Shape. Wiley, Hoboken (1998)
15. Bookstein, F.L.: Size and shape spaces for landmark data in two dimensions. Stat. Sci. **1**, 181–222 (1986)
16. Kendall, D.G.: Shape manifolds, procrustean metrics, and complex projective spaces. Bull. Lond. Math. Soc. **16**, 81–121 (1984)

17. Kendall, D.G.: Exact distributions for shapes of random triangles in convex sets. Adv. Appl. Probab. **17**, 308–329 (1985)
18. Kendall, D.G.: Further developments and applications of the statistical theory of shape. Theor. Probab. Appl. **31**, 407–412 (1987)
19. Bookstein, F.L.: A statistical method for biological shape comparisons. J. Theor. Biol. **107**, 475–520 (1984)
20. Johnson, N.L., Kotz, S., Balakrishnan, N.: Continuous Univariate Distributions, Volume 2 of Wiley Series in Probability and Mathematical Statistics: Applied Probability and Statistics. Wiley, New York (1995)
21. Olver, F.W., Lozier, D.W., Boisvert, R.F., Clark, C.W.: NIST Handbook of Mathematical Functions Hardback and CD-ROM. Cambridge University Press, Cambridge (2010)
22. Bylinskii, Z., Borkin, M.A., Kim, N.W., Pfister, H., Oliva, A.: Eye fixation metrics for large scale evaluation and comparison of information visualizations. In: Burch, M., Chuang, L., Fisher, B., Schmidt, A., Weiskopf, D. (eds.) ETVIS 2015. MATHVISUAL, pp. 235–255. Springer, Cham (2017). https://doi.org/10.1007/978-3-319-47024-5_14

Creating Value with Proto-Research Persona Development

Prateek Jain[1], Soussan Djamasbi[1(✉)], and John Wyatt[2]

[1] Worcester Polytechnic Institute, Worcester, USA
{pjain, djamasbi}@wpi.edu
[2] Oracle, Manchester, USA
john.wyatt@oracle.com

Abstract. To stay competitive in marketplace, companies have to design compelling products that are successfully adopted by their intended users. To achieve this goal, companies must establish and validate a shared understanding of their customer base. In this paper we propose a persona development process for creating value in an organization. This process, which can be conducted relatively quickly and cost-effectively, provides a roadmap for continual assessment of organizational understanding of customer base. It creates value for companies by allowing them (1) to build consensus internally around their customers' needs, goals, and preferences, and (2) to validate/test the accuracy of the assumptions they make about their customers. We tested this process in a fortune 500 company. Our results suggest that our process is both effective and efficient in establishing a shared understanding of the customer base and in testing the accuracy of assumptions made by organizations about their customers.

Keywords: User experience · Persona development · Design decisions · Business value of design

1 Introduction

Understanding customers and what their needs are is paramount to the success of any organization. These insights are the first step in enabling the framing and development of products and services that achieve product market fit. However, despite the foundational importance of this understanding and empathy towards market base, many organizations fail to develop these insights due to significant resource and/or logistical challenges. Keeping track of current and anticipated needs of every single current or future customer can be a challenging task. Depending on the size of the organization, the customer base can range from few hundreds to millions. One way to make this challenging task manageable is by organizing the customer base into specific user groups of a product or service and then representing the goals, needs, behavior and other characteristics of each customer group via a fictional but realistic persona [8]. The representation of customer needs, challenges, preferences, and other characteristics via personas can help senior leadership to build consensus about market needs and thus help them to work more effectively together to address opportunities for innovation and

F. F.-H. Nah and K. Siau (Eds.): HCII 2019, LNCS 11589, pp. 72–82, 2019.
https://doi.org/10.1007/978-3-030-22338-0_6

other strategic goals. In addition to improving communication internally through consensus building, personas can also help improve external communication. For example, by providing a deep understanding of customer base, personas can guide sales representatives to better convey to customers how a product can meet their needs.

Personas can help make more effective decisions [1]. For example, human-computer interaction design decisions are often improved when personas are used. By using personas at various stages of development organizations can make sure that their design decisions incorporate the needs of their customers in each design phase [2, 3]. Similarly, organizations can use personas to improve their marketing decisions. For example, personas can help marketing teams to decide which group of customers benefit most from an advertisement and how and where advertisements should be delivered to create the most impact.

Persona development can roughly be divided into two major categories: proto-personas and research personas. As suggested by the name, research personas are developed by conducting user research, for example through observational studies and/or conducting one on one interviews. The patterns identified by observing users and/or during the interviews help capture different aspects of life and work of customers that build the foundation for developing personas [3]. Unlike research personas, proto-personas are developed through indirect interaction with users, that is they are assumption based. These personas are created by members of an organization, usually through a workshop where a group of selected employees are invited to estimate the goals, needs, behavior, and other life and work aspects of their customers [4]. These estimations are then used to provide insight for improving a specific product or service.

The research based approach for persona development provides a rich set of first-hand information from actual users, hence the data gathered through this process is closest to the "truth". However, research persona development process typically takes a longer time to produce, and it tends to be incredibly resource intensive. The proto-persona development process on the other hand is far less resource intensive and can be completed relatively quickly [7]. Another advantage is that the proto-persona development process can serve as an excellent tool for consensus building among senior leadership, which is extremely important for developing successful products and services [4–6]. The drawback of proto-persona development is that it uses an assumption-based approach. If an organization does not have an accurate picture of its customer base, such an assumption-based approach can lead to myopia.

Given the pros and cons of the two approaches, the combination of the two persona development processes offers a comprehensive approach for developing successful products and services. In this paper we discuss a combined proto-research persona development process for design decisions that can be conducted in organizations relatively quickly in a cost-effective way. This process, which can afford senior leaders in an organization the opportunity to build consensus about and a deeper understanding of their customers, not only facilitates a roadmap for meeting the needs of current and future markets but also lends itself as a useful tool to assess the accuracy of organizational assumptions about customers. Our proposed approach involves consensus and empathy building thorough a relatively short workshop that aims at developing proto-personas of current customers. Then, our approach assesses the correctness of the assumptions that were made about customers via a relatively efficient user research. We implemented our proposed persona development process in a fortune 500 company. Our results show that our approach can help organizations to build relatively quickly consensus around assumptions they make about user needs and to verify their assumptions effectively and efficiently.

2   Developing Personas for Design Decisions

By developing a common understanding of a certain group of users, personas help the design teams to focus their efforts around an agreed upon set of characteristics, desires, and behaviors that need to be considered during the design decision making process. In particular, personas help design teams to prioritize implementation, e.g., which features to implement next so that they can provide a more effective, useful, and enjoyable experience for users.

Personas are typically visualized through templates that have several sections summarizing background information (e.g., age, gender, occupation) as well as information about user needs, challenges, concerns, goals, and other characteristics that can impact design decisions. Depending on project needs, persona templates can have various formats and elements [9]. However, within the same project the template for different personas must have a consistent format (i.e., include the same sections) and their content must be clear and concise. Figure 1 displays an example of a basic structure for a persona template.

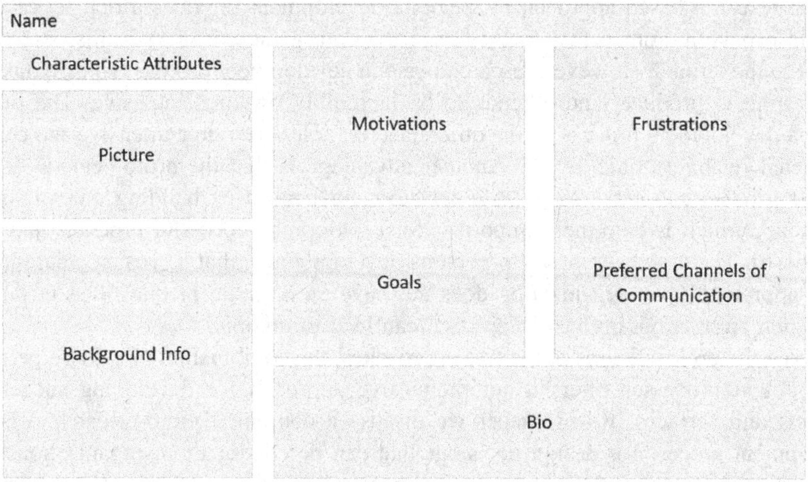

Fig. 1. Example of a basic structure for a persona template

In the following sections we provide a brief review of common practices for conducting proto and user persona development projects. We then discuss a combined approach that can be conducted in organizations. The efficiency of our proposed process is particularly important in organizational settings because to be effective our proposed process needs to be repeated in regular basis. To stay competitive and maintain or grow their market share, companies need to repeatedly assess the accuracy of their assumptions against the evolving changes in their user base.

2.1 Proto-Persona Development

Compared to research personas, proto-personas can be developed relatively quickly and inexpensively. The efficiency and cost-effectiveness of proto persona development makes them particularly helpful to startup companies and/or those companies that wish to experiment with persona development. To build consensus among senior leadership, key representatives from multiple departments that are stake holders in the design of a specific product are typically invited to participate in the proto-persona development via a workshop [4–6]. Figure 2 displays the major steps in a proto-persona development process that are typically completed in such a workshop. Participants are first provided with a brief explanation of the purpose of the workshop which includes a brief discussion of the proto persona template that will be used in the workshop. Next, participants which are divided into cross-departmental groups, are engaged in a brain storming session that requires them to identify key characteristics of consumers that can affect design decisions for a specific product or service. In this step, each group is tasked with creating as many different personas as they can. Next the groups are asked to map each of their personas on a set of spectrums that are relevant and important to the project. Spectrums refer to non-binary characteristics that provide a meaningful differentiation between personas for a specific project. For example, a customer's level of technology savviness may serve as a suitable spectrum for designing products and services that can target novice to experienced users. Once all the personas are mapped on multiple spectrums, distinct patterns are identified by participating groups. Based on these patterns, groups will decide if personas with similar characteristics should be merged. After finalizing the personas, groups will then decide which personas have the highest priority in design decisions that meet their business strategy.

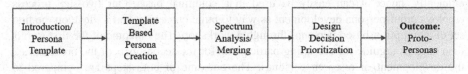

Fig. 2. Major steps in proto-persona development process

2.2 Research-Persona Development

Contrary to proto-persona development, research persona development is time and resource intensive. The first step in developing research personas is to decide which users should be recruited to participate in the study. For example, should participants be recruited from the existing customer base or should participants be recruited from the pool of prospective customers using products or services of competitors. Or, should participants be recruited based on their user roles (e.g., whether they use the product as a technical user or as a business oriented user). The business strategy of the organization or project stake holders can help to decide the type and range of participants to recruit for the research persona study [10–12]. The next step is to design a detailed interview process to capture information for personas. This typically semi structured interview process aims at documenting the information that users provide about different aspects of experience with the product, their needs and goals, the challenges they face and their motivation to use the product or service to meet needs or accomplish goals. The interview data is then analyzed for patterns, for example, the types of behaviors that leads a user to adopt the product or patterns of needs and goals that motivate a user pay for the service. These patterns are then merged into a finalized set of personas, which in turn are prioritized based on strategic goals. Major steps in a typical research persona development process is shown in Fig. 3.

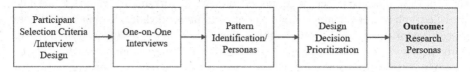

Fig. 3. Major steps in research-persona development process

3   Proposed Process

Persona development process, which is invaluable in consensus building and understanding user needs, is most effective in improving market needs if it is repeated periodically. This is because personas represent a snapshot of the market, they represent customers in a specific context at a specific period of time. To stay in touch with evolving customer needs organizations have to repeatedly engage in persona development process. For this reason, the persona development process must be efficient. Our proposed process provides an effective way to capture user needs and preferences efficiently, hence it can easily be used in a continual basis. Our two-step process employs proto-persona development as way to build consensus and to develop the first set of assumption-based personas through a workshop. The outcome of the first step is then used as a guide for recruiting participants for the second part of the process, i.e., the development of research personas. The outcome of both steps are compared to examine the level of disparity between the assumption-based and the research-based personas. This examination can serve as a great tool for assessing the alignment between organizational assumptions about the market and the market reality. The analysis also provides information for correcting and/or refining assumption as well as insight for the timeline and context of the next iteration of the process. The periodic repetition of the process not only helps to effectively maintain the alignment between assumption and reality but also helps the process to becomes more efficient overtime.

Our proposed two-part process is outlined in Fig. 4. The first part, which focuses on developing proto personas, starts by gathering information from key representatives of various departments that are the major stakeholders of the project. This information, which can be collected through an online survey, captures defining characteristics of the customers. Because these characteristics are based on the input from various stake holders in different departments they tend to provide a more comprehensive picture of product users. This information can also provide additional insight for the format of the persona templates, which are created prior to workshop based on project goals. The responses are also analyzed for identifying relevant spectrums to be used in the workshop.

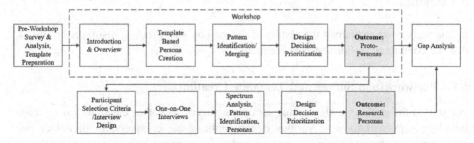

Fig. 4. Our proposed process for persona development

The workshop starts with a brief discussion of personas and a brief overview of the workshop. Participants are then formed into groups; they are encouraged to use the provided templates to create as many personas as they can. The personas are mapped along the spectrum to identify patterns which help merge personas into a final set. The workshop ends by ranking personas to prioritize implementation.

The second part of our proposed process focuses on developing research personas, driven by proto-personas created in first part. That is, we use the information obtained in the first part of the process as criteria for recruiting participants and conducting one-on-one interviews. The data that is obtained from individual interviews is carefully reviewed and organized into groups. The summarization of differences and similarities within and between groups not only helps to refine the groups but also helps to identify a set of spectrums that are relevant to the project. The patterns and clusters revealed by the spectrum analysis are then merged into a finalized set of personas. Next, personas are prioritized based on strategic goals.

The final step in our proposed process compares the differences between the obtained proto-personas and research personas with a gap analysis. The alignment (or its lack) between the two sets of personas provides insight for improving the consensus about and the accuracy of the assumptions. The gap analysis also provides insight for making the subsequent design and business decisions. The repetition of the proposed process not only documents the evolution of user needs but also serves as a suitable organizational assessment for assumption accuracy.

4   Method

We implemented the proposed process (see Fig. 4) at a Fortune 500 company. We were able to complete the study with a total of 25 participants. We recruited 11 senior stakeholders from critical departments to participate in the proto-persona workshop.

We then used an online tool to recruit and screen participants for the research persona portion of our study. In order to keep the process efficient, we selected a small representative sample for the first round of one-on-one semi structured interviews, which took approximately an hour for each participant.

5   Results

In this section we explained the results of the step by step process, displayed in Fig. 4, that we conducted at Fortune 500 company.

5.1   Pre-workshop Survey and Template Creation

We started the process with creating an online survey to gather customer information from key representatives of various departments of the company. In particular, we asked participants to tell us what they wished to know about customers, how often and what assumptions they made about the customers, what challenges did they face in understanding customers, and how confident they were in their understanding of customers. We also asked them to tell us the job title and type of customers they interacted with. To gather information for developing and conducting spectrum analysis during the workshop we asked participants to tell us what they thought were the defining characteristics of their customers. We also asked what they hoped to get out of the workshop (we used the responses to this question to make the workshop more effective). This survey along with a brief description about the project was sent to key representatives that accepted to participate in the workshop.

Based on responses that we received at this part of the process, we created a basic persona template and 5 spectrums. Our persona template included general information (name, job title, job roles), narrative, behaviors and beliefs, needs and goals, challenges or pain points, key initiatives and success metrics, and some specific elements (such as device preferences, services and features used) that were relevant to the project.

5.2   Proto-Persona Workshop

Eleven key representatives from departments representing, Customer Success, Customer Support, Outbound and Inbound Product Marketing, Digital Go-to-Market Experience, Product Management and Product Experience Design participated in our 2-hour proto-persona workshop. We divided the workshop participants into 3 groups comprised of individuals from diverse departments. We asked each group to brainstorm about their customers. Each group was required to use the persona template that was handed to them to come up with as many personas as they could in the allocated time. Once this step was completed, all personas were mapped through a collective discussion on the set of 5 spectrums that were developed based on pre-workshop survey data. After mapping each persona on the 5 spectrums, through directed discussions participants identified patterns and voted to merge similar personas.

This workshop resulted in 6 proto-personas. To prioritize design decisions, these personas were then ranked based on organizational goals and defined business strategies.

5.3   User Sampling and Interview

To conduct the research persona portion of the study we used an online recruitment tool, with which we invited and screened users for one-on-one interviews. We received 117 responses to our invitation. To make the process as efficient as possible we screened the responses and prioritized those that passed our screening criteria based on organization's business strategy. For the first pass, we selected the top 15 responses that represented various types of users (identified as personas in first part of the process) for one hour long online one-on-one interviews. We planned to decide whether we need to collect more interview data after we analyzed the first set of interviews. One participant did not show up for their scheduled time, resulting in 14 completed interviews. All interviews were recorded and transcribed for analysis. The analysis of 14 hours of semi-structured online interviews resulted in visible patterns suitable for developing research personas. This analysis indicated that we had enough data and thus we did not conduct any additional interviews.

5.4   Spectrum and Pattern Identification

A careful review of interviews resulted in grouping the data into different sets. This analysis resulted in identifying 6 spectrums. After mapping the interviews on the identified spectrums we were able to solidify the merging patterns into 8 personas. These personas proved to cover those personas that were developed in the proto-persona workshop and offered additional insight for creating two new personas. We then used IKE, an online persona development group decision support system (GDSS), ike.wpi.edu, to make the data that was generated through this process available for review and further decision making by various stake holders and senior management. IKE, not only provided access to a repository of proto and research personas for decision making, but also made it possible for various departments in the organization to update or refine personas as needed (e.g., through subsequent proto-research persona development process that was discussed in this paper). Additionally, IKE can be used in future repetitions of the process to update personas. IKE can also be used to assess the accuracy of assumptions the organization makes about its consumers.

6   Discussion

Our results showed that our proposed process was effective and efficient in achieving its goals. The results of the workshop showed that the organization had pockets of tribal knowledge around who the customers were and what pain points they were facing. While this tribal knowledge was valuable to individual departments, the shared knowledge that was obtained through consensus building in the first part of our proposed process proved to be far more valuable for making effective design decisions and setting overall business strategies.

We were able to develop our proto-personas effectively with a 2-hour workshop. Proto persona workshops are often conducted via longer workshops. We were able to conduct a shorter workshop effectively because we moved some of the work to pre-workshop process and we were careful to invite a smaller number but strategically highly important representatives and stake holders for the project. Shorter proto-persona workshops at organizations are highly valued because they require senior leadership participation.

In addition to being efficient, the results of proto-persona workshop showed that our proposed process was also effective in involving the senior leadership in an open and honest conversation about what they thought they knew about their customers. Our workshop process made it possible for them to clearly see conflicting viewpoints that existed among various stake holders. This in turn help them to see the need for validating the assumptions they make. Because such a validation can help to align design decisions with market needs, it further supports the business value that can be created through our proposed process.

The proposed process resulted in developing a set of personas that can provide foundation for a long term assessment of organizational performance. As discussed at the beginning of this article, proto persona and research personas provide only a snapshot of customer experience. To maintain an accurate understanding of the markets, personas must be treated as living documents, and as such they need to be validated and/or refined periodically. Thus, to continue their effectiveness for design decisions, personas must be validated or modified over and over again. Our proposed process provides an efficient procedure for periodic assessment of assumption based and research based personas. Our results indicated that research personas were relatively aligned with proto personas that were build based on consensus building during the workshop. While this suggests competitive advantage that can translate into improved design decisions, to maintain this advantage over time the same process must be repeated preferably in a year or before the next major design decision.

The proposed process can also be used to capture new markets. For example, by understanding the needs and pain points of prospective customers who are using competitor's services, companies can make design decisions that can attract unhappy users of competitor products toward their offerings.

7 Limitations

We tested our proposed process in a fortune 500 company for a specific product. To extend the generalizability of our proposed procedure, more tests in companies of different sizes and for different types of products are warranted. Our results so far are encouraging and we are currently conducting our proposed process in another organization.

Our proposed process is particularly time and cost effective if proto-personas are mostly aligned with research personas. Such an alignment reflects an internally unified and accurate picture of the customer base which leads to improved product design and consequently increased market share. To ensure the continuation of such business value, it is essential that our proposed process is repeated periodically.

8 Conclusion

Understanding customer needs is essential in creating compelling products that are successfully adopted by their intended users. This is a challenging task because customer needs and goals can evolve overtime. Both proto and research backed personas can become out of date as soon as they are created because they are representations of the best understanding about a set of customers at a given period of time. To stay up-to-date organization's understanding of their market needs must constantly evolve with the changes in their user base. To achieve this goal companies must treat personas as living documents and validate their assumptions periodically through a systematic and effective process.

In this study we proposed a step by step process for achieving this goal. By harnessing organizational knowledge through proto-persona development and combining it with the higher fidelity understandings achieved through research backed personas, our proposed process facilitates an effective procedure for developing and maintaining accurate picture of consumer market. The proposed process not only provides a road map for keeping customers at the heart of design decisions, it also impacts the design process by improving internal collaborations through shared understanding of customer needs. By facilitating a process for a better understanding of user needs and by developing a common understanding of user needs internally, our proposed process can help companies to develop competitive products and services.

References

1. Junior, P.T.A., Filgueiras, L.V.L.: User modeling with personas. In: Proceedings of the 2005 Latin American Conference on Human-Computer Interaction, pp. 277–282. ACM, October 2005
2. Cooper, A.: The Inmates Are Running the Asylum: Why High-Tech Products Drive Us Crazy and How to Restore the Sanity. Sams, Indianapolis (2004)
3. Cooper, A., Reimann, R.: About Face 2.0 the Essentials of Interaction Design. Wiley, Indianapolis (2003)
4. Gothelf, J.: Using Proto-Personas for Executive Alignment, 1 May 2012. https://uxmag.com/articles/using-proto-personas-for-executive-alignment. Accessed 31 Dec 2018
5. Jacobs, A.: UX: Creating Proto-Personas, 12 September 2016. https://uxdesign.cc/ux-creating-proto-personas-76a1738401a2. Accessed 31 Dec 2018
6. Summers, B.: How to Make Proto-Personas and Get Everyone on the Same Page. https://www.dtelepathy.com/blog/philosophy/how-to-make-proto-pesonas. Accessed 31 Dec 2018
7. McMahon, K.: Proto-Persona's VS Persona's, 18 February 2018. https://medium.com/@karimcmahon/proto-personas-vs-persona-s-db8873a2d2e4. Accessed 31 Dec 2018
8. Harley, A.: Personas Make Users Memorable for Product Team Members, 16 February 2015. https://www.nngroup.com/articles/persona/. Accessed 31 Dec 2018

9. Bloodworth, A., Guerreiro, J.L.: Persona Format, 8 January 2017. https://wiki.fluidproject.org/display/fluid/Persona+Format. Accessed 31 Dec 2018
10. Ogle, D., Bloodworth, A.: Persona Creation, 15 September 2014. https://wiki.fluidproject.org/display/fluid/Persona+Creation. Accessed 31 Dec 2018
11. Goltz, S.: A Closer Look at Personas: A Guide to Developing the Right Ones (Part 2), 13 August 2014. https://www.smashingmagazine.com/2014/08/a-closer-look-at-personas-part-2/. Accessed 31 Dec 2018
12. Brown, D.: Communicating Design: Developing Web Site Documentation for Design and Planning, 2nd edn. New Riders Publishing (2010)

Do Development Strategies Influence the Performance of Mobile Apps? Market Status Matters

Bei Luo[1], Xiaoke Zhang[1(✉)], Lele Kang[1], and Qiqi Jiang[2]

[1] School of Information Management, Nanjing University, Nanjing, China
151070046@smail.nju.edu.cn, 314641740@qq.com,
lelekang@nju.edu.cn
[2] Department of Digitalization, Copenhagen Business School,
Frederiksberg, Denmark
qj.digi@cbs.dk

Abstract. There is substantial academic interest in modeling the determinants of mobile apps' success. However, few relative researches explored the impact of development strategies and market status of mobile apps on their market performance. This paper adopted text mining technique and Boston Consulting Group (BCG) Matrix to measure the divergence of a development strategy and market status, respectively. Furthermore, we construct a multivariable linear regression model of performance of apps using data from five mobile platforms: Mumayi, Baidu mobile assistant, 360 mobile assistant, Eoemarket, and App China. The result shows that apps of Stars require convergent development strategies to attract potential consumers while more generally, the divergent development strategies benefit apps in other quadrants of the BCG Matrix, namely Cash Cows, Problem Children and Dogs.

Keywords: Development strategy · BCG Matrix · Mobile app performance

1 Introduction

Along with the popularity of mobile devices, hundreds of thousands of mobile applications (apps) emerge every single year. The market for mobile apps has been one of the fastest growing segments of mobile technology. Typically, mobile application platforms play a crucial role in app market interactions by collecting software launched by developers and distributing these apps to end-users, which provide a new way for developing, updating and downloading software applications for mobile devices [1]. App, as the main component of mobile platforms, is a form of product based on mobile technology. App developers design and optimize software programs to perform specific functions in an aim to satisfy customers' needs, enhance market influence and gain profits. In fierce competitions, some apps may be in a dominant position whereas others take a weaker position. App developers adopt different strategies to allocate limited resources and optimize the app's overall performance.

Researchers have been trying to understand the inner development patterns of apps and help developers find suitable business strategies. It has already been shown that the

© Springer Nature Switzerland AG 2019
F. F.-H. Nah and K. Siau (Eds.): HCII 2019, LNCS 11589, pp. 83–94, 2019.
https://doi.org/10.1007/978-3-030-22338-0_7

frequency of app updates is positively associated with the capability of the supplier and the developing potentials of the product [2]. Free App offers, high initial ranks, investment in less popular categories, high volume of user reviews can help an app to develop sustainably [3]. Their preliminary findings deliver an important message that development strategies may directly influence the performance of apps.

Development strategy serves as a crucial factor in an app's development since it decides whether an app can attract new customers while maintaining present competitiveness and thus determines its market share and market growth. A development strategy can either be convergent or divergent [4]. The divergent strategy can be interpreted as innovation, which means that the developer exploits new functions and create new needs. At the same time, developers taking convergent strategies learn from present apps and perfect their own apps by adding on functions that others have already had to meet present needs. Both strategies can be useful approaches to enhance competitiveness.

However, the real world is more complicated. The impact of development strategies may be differentiated based on the various market status of the focal apps. For example, an app with an extremely high market share may gain more profit by charging a certain amount of fees since it monopolizes the market while the same may not work for one with low market share. To measure the market status of the apps, we explore patterns in app development more specifically by dividing them into different market status using Boston Consulting Group Matrix (BCG Matrix), which is a widely used tool for portfolio optimization and strategic justification [5]. What our study plans to do is to answer the question which strategy is better in attracting customers for apps in different market status, more specifically in different quadrants of BCG Matrix.

Development strategy can be hard to measure, but in light of text mining technique, we are able to convert text-based app descriptions into text vector and calculate the average vector that represents the general condition of the market. By measuring the distance between every app vector and the average vector, we are able to tell how divergent an app is. Then, it becomes feasible to apply empirical models to explore the relationship between development strategies and download numbers. Furthermore, in practice, a phenomenon is often associated with multiple factors. Multivariable linear regression analysis is created to find an optimal combination of independent variables to estimate or predict the dependent variable. Since the model has been widely applied and achieved significant performance in various fields, it is also adopted in this study. Thereby, we can address our research question of how development strategies interact with market status to influence the performance of an app.

The rest of this manuscript is organized as follows. In Sect. 2, we present the theoretical development of this research, including the text mining technique and the Boston Consulting Group Matrix. In Sect. 3, we present our hypotheses. In Sect. 4, we present our data collection, BCG Matrix distribution, text vectorization and distance calculation process. In Sect. 5, we apply empirical models to examine our hypotheses. In Sect. 6, we discuss this work's contributions, implications and limitations and in Sect. 7, we conclude the study.

2   Theoretical Development

2.1   Text Mining for Convergent and Divergent Development Strategies

Most information of apps lies in the descriptions and update details provided by the operations. By applying text mining, the process of extracting non-trivial patterns or knowledge from text documents [6], to app analysis, we are able to dig out more interesting correlations and patterns from the mobile platforms apart from numerical fields such as downloads or rankings. Much research has been done exploring the texts in the mobile platforms. Maalej and Nabil [7] utilized multiple machine learning algorithms to automatically classify customer reviews into three types, bug report, feature request and simply praise. Finkelstein et al. [8] extracted app features from app descriptions and demonstrated the relationships between customer, business and apps' technical characteristics. Kim et al. [9] adopted keyword vectors in the network analysis of apps.

Nonetheless, little research has been done studying the convergent and divergent development strategies of apps using text mining techniques. According to Gallouj [10], most innovations in digital products are incremental or recombinative. The former took advantage of pre-existing technical characteristics and services whereas the latter developed new features and functions [10]. During the process of developing an app, an operator can either choose to exploit new functions that have not appeared in the market yet or to apply and consummate former functions other apps have al-ready developed to meet market needs. Thus we defined apps with more recombinative features as apps taking convergent development strategies and those with more incremental features as apps taking divergent development strategies [4].

Such development patterns can be examined by text mining techniques like text vectorization. Apps with analogous functions tend to have similar descriptions and update information, which is to say, they may use similar words and expressions. By converting each app description into vectors based on the appearance frequency of words in it and calculate the distance between vectors, we find a way to explain the difference between apps. Research has been done on relevant fields such as Bibliometric and Econometrics. Dias [11] studied 20 million scientific papers over three decades using abstract vectors and found that on average the similarity between disciplines has not changed, but certain areas (e.g. computer science) are becoming increasingly central. Similar methods were applied to analyses product descriptions, which showed that product differentiation significantly improved market gains [12].

2.2   Boston Consulting Group Matrix

The BCG Matrix, developed by the Boston consulting group in the 1970 s, has been used extensively as a portfolio management tool for business. It uses two dimensions namely market growth which represents the extent of industry attractiveness and market share which stands for competitive advantage as a basis for categorizing business units [13]. By dividing products into four quadrants based on the two dimensions, researchers are able to custom specific strategies for them in accordance with their market potentials and competitiveness.

Stars operate in high growth industries and maintain high market share, which indicates that they are both cash generators and cash users. They are the primary units in which the company should invest its money. Cash cows are of high market share and slowly growing market. They are the most profitable brands and should be "milked" to provide as much cash as possible, which can later be invested to stars. Problem Children operate in high growth industries but have low market share. They require much closer consideration since they consume a large amount of cash and incurring losses but have the potential to become stars. Dogs hold low market share in a slowly growing market. In general, they are not worth investing in and should be liquidated. Nevertheless, Hambrick [14] pointed out in his research on the PIMS database that dogs had average net positive cash flow on investment of 3.4%. Thus, it is irrational to merely abandon products in the dog quadrant. Instead, what is needed is creative, positive research and thinking about how dogs can be managed for maximum long term performance [14].

In this study, the BCG matrix is adopted to classify the mobile apps to the four types. The market share and market growth rate are measured by the downloads. Apps of Stars are of high downloads and the downloads are still growing rapidly over time whereas the downloads for apps of cash cows are generally high but stable. Problem children's downloads are low but at the same time growing fast. Downloads for Dogs are low and growing slowly. These four types represent four typical market status and by testing how development strategies influence the performance of an app in different status, we are able to establish a better and more specific understanding of the mobile app market.

3 Hypothesis Development

According to microeconomic theory, the market is classified into four types as perfect competition, monopoly competition, oligopoly and perfect monopoly with the degree of competition and monopoly [15]. This division is based on traditional industry, where competition and monopoly of market present antagonistic relations. However, all of the four types failed to describe network economy because competition and monopoly can reinforce and promote each other there. Enterprise gain and maintain monopoly position via technological innovation competition, which is called by Chinese researchers as Competitive Monopoly [16]. Su et al. [17] concluded Internet market structure as Hierarchical Monopoly and Competition. On the one hand, large Internet enterprises occupy a huge number of user resources, leading to highly concentrated market shares in certain fields. On the other hand, the great success of such enterprises also attracts large quantities of small and medium-sized Internet companies to enter the market or transform from traditional industries to Internet industries. Nonetheless, such entry of enterprises hardly changes the high concentration status of the market and result in withdrawal of quite a few operations. Therefore, high liquidity of small and medium-sized Internet enterprises in and out of the market, together with the relative stability of large Internet enterprises' monopoly status, formed the specific "hierarchical monopoly and competition" market structure.

In the BCG Matrix, apps of Stars show the features of high market share and high market growth. The former symbolizes monopoly status of these apps as Internet market structure demonstrates while the latter implies that they lure consumers continuously. Fast expansion of monopolistic products indicates immaturity of markets they situate in. These products can attract potential customers who have never ever used them or similar products. Therefore, to keep high market growth for apps of Star is to keep attracting possible consumers, which requires developers to design apps in a popular style. The reason refers to customer acceptance of a new product as follows.

Rogers [18] proposed a theoretical framework about what factors affect the diffusion of innovation. He proved that consumers are less likely to accept a new product when perceived product innovation is complicated. Davis [19] provided an understanding of determinants of usage applying to Information Technology as Technology Acceptance Model (TAM), which believed that two factors, namely perceived usefulness and perceived ease of use, predict the attitude towards usage intentions.

Hence, when users who are not attached to any homogeneous apps intend to try a new one, it is more possible for them to use this app if they can know how to operate it quickly. Convergent development strategies, recombining functions developed by both homogeneous and heterogeneous apps help consumers find familiar operation method. Thus we hypothesize the following:

H1: Apps of Stars with convergent development strategies are more likely to achieve better performance.

Apps of Cash Cows present the characteristic of high market share and low market growth. These apps enjoy monopoly status like apps of Stars whereas locating in a mature market. Since transferring potential consumers is hard for them, the major task turns to reduce the loss of customers and converting consumers from competitors.

Jackson [20] defined switching costs as psychological and economic costs of changing supplies, including learning costs, transaction costs and artificial costs imposed by firms, such as repeat-purchase discounts [21]. Before the customers ever purchase one particular product, they have no ties to it since the transaction costs and learning costs are to be the same. However, once they got used to one particular product, the switching costs have been built up and it is less likely for them to use another product with similar functions. Therefore, for cash cows who already own a large number of customers, the crucial thing is to maintain the quantity and increasing the switching cost is a direct way to guarantee it.

The reason for apps of Cash Cows choosing divergent development strategies is that differentiation enhances customer switching costs. By exploiting new functions that have not appeared in the market, monopolistic apps improve customer loyalty and finally maintain monopoly rents. Thus we develop the following hypothesis:

H2: Apps of Cash Cows with convergent development strategies are more likely to achieve better performance.

For decades the debate was dominated by antagonism between a negative 'Schumpeter effect' versus a positive 'Arrow effect' of competition on innovation [22]. A model was proposed by Hashmi [23] to deal with the argument, known as an inverted-U relationship, that if the initial degree of competition is low, the inverted-U predicts a positive impact of rising competition on innovation effort whereas at high levels of initial rivalry, increasing competition reduces the incentives for innovation. Based on Hashmi's model, Zheng et al. conducted a research to examine the relationship between competition and innovation in E-business market, the result of which showed a positive effect between not only competition and innovation but also innovation and performance of companies [24]. As mentioned above that small and medium-sized Internet companies confront fierce competitions, so they need tremendous innovations to stand out. Apps of Problem Children and Dogs have com-mon features of low market share, so we conclude our hypothesis as follows:

H3: Apps in Problem Children and Dogs with divergent development strategies are more likely to achieve better performance.

4   Data Description and Processing

4.1   Sampling and Data Collection

To test our theoretical hypotheses, we examined a dataset containing data collected from five typical Android mobile platforms in China, which are Baidu mobile assistant, 360 mobile assistant. Eoemarket, Mumayi and Appchina. These mobile platforms contain details including introduction, update information, number of downloads, category, and ranking for every single app. Customers will decide whether to download the APK of an app through the platform according to the information provided. The method of conducting empirical studies with second-hand data is widely used in information systems research [25–27].

By implementing a web crawler to collect data of 3000 apps every other week from January 1st 2018 to October 1st 2018 from the five platforms, we managed to obtain high-quality data reflecting basic information and market status of the apps along with its changes over time. We further excluded apps which were withdrawn by the platform during the ten-month collection process or those lacking key attribute fields like introduction or downloads. Eventually, we narrowed our dataset to 1805 apps quanlified for analysis.

4.2   Measuring Convergent and Divergent of Apps

In an aim to explore the impact of divergent and convergent development strategy on apps in different market status, we need to classify the apps into the four quadrants in the Boston Consulting Group Matrix according to their growth rate and market share. In this article, we define an annual growth rate over 10% as a high growth rate and a relative market share of over 20% as a high market share. Let A be the set of all apps in the dataset and P be the set of all mobile platforms. The formulas are as followed.

$$g_i = \frac{final\ download_i - initial\ download_i}{initial\ download_i} \times 100\% \ (i \in A) \tag{1}$$

$$s_{ij} = \frac{download_{ij}}{max\ downloads_j} \times 100\% \ (j \in Pi \in P_j \ \cap A) \tag{2}$$

We utilized the downloads from January 1st to August 1st to calculate the growth rate for each app. Since this time period only covers two-thirds of an entire year, we marked apps with a growth rate more than 6.66% as fast-growing apps. For market share, due largely to the divergence in market size and user numbers, the downloads for each mobile platform are significantly different from one another. For instance, the mean download number for Eoemarket is 451,533 while the average download number in 360 mobile assistant is 13,561,666. It is unreasonable to mark an app with 600,000 downloads in Eoemarket as low-share apps while regarding an app with 1,000,000 downloads in 360 mobile assistant as high-share apps. Taking this problem into consideration, we found the maximum downloads in August 1st for each platform separately as the max downloads and calculated the market share for apps based on the platforms they were in.

4.3 Measuring Convergent and Divergent of Apps

In the text vectorization process, we regarded the description along with all its update information between January 1st and August 1st as the representation of an app. We later used a stable Chinese word segmentation tool in Python called Jieba to segment the texts, eliminated words of low information volume according to the stop-word list provided by Haerbin Institute of Technology and created a dictionary of all terms in the corpus. Every app was then represented in the form of a vector, and each element in the vector was the frequency at which each word in the text appeared. We normalized each vector to unit length so that the result would not be affected by the length of the descriptions. The vectors can be represented as P_i.

Apps belong to different categories (e.g. games, entertainment, music, tools, etc.), in which they have distinct functions and features. Therefore, we calculated the market standardization vector for each category by calculating the average number of each vector component.

The distance was then measured by the Manhattan distance between the app itself and the standardization vector of the category it belongs to. Let $P_i(x_1, x_2, x_3, \ldots, x_n)$ be the vector and $S_i(y_1, y_2, y_3, \ldots, y_n)$ be its standardization vector. The formula is as followed. Generally, the larger the distance is, the more divergent the development strategy of one app is.

$$D_i = \sum_{i=1}^{n} |x_i - y_i| \tag{3}$$

5 Estimation Procedure

In this section, we examine whether convergent or divergent development strategies improve the performance of apps in different market status.

5.1 Measurement

Each of $I = 1, ..., I$ apps possess a certain market status. As mentioned in Sect. 4.2, we identify the position of an app in the BCG matrix by criteria of 10% growth rate and 20% relative market share. We use BCG matrix position dummies to reflect apps' market status. Apps with more than 10% growth rate and 20% relative market are Stars, denoted as $PositionCashCow_i = 0$, $PositionProblemChildren_i = 0$ and $PositionDogs_i = 0$. Similarly, we measure Cash Cow, Problem Children and Dogs apps and denote them as $PositionCashCow_i = 1$, $PositionProblemChildren_i = 1$ and $PositionDogs_i = 1$, respectively.

Using the analytical approach proposed in Sect. 4.3, we use normalized Manhattan distance with regard to the degree of divergence of an app, denoted as $Manhattan_i$. The larger the number $Manhattan_i$ present, the more divergent app_i is. Whereas small $Manhattan_i$ means app_i epitomizes the existing functions in the market.

Our data come from multiple mobile platforms: (1) Mumayi, (2) Baidu mobile assistant, (3) 360 mobile assistant, (4) Eoemarket, and (5) App China. To control the fact that mobile platforms are different from each other due to the difference of subscriber in many ways, including number, preference and so on, we measure platform dummies, called *platforms*.

Apps become more sophisticated when they increase in size, which means consumers need longer time to download and try those new apps. Therefore, we use the file size of an app in megabytes, denoted as *Size*, to control the relationship between file size and performance of an app.

Zhou et al. [2] thought Apps that update at a faster rate are more likely to achieve better performance. Apps fixed issues and provide more features according to update, which means a quick update lead to quick quality improvement. Hence, users are more confident in adopting the updated apps and allocate more time in them. We measure the times that apps update from Jan 1st to Aug 1st as *UpdateCount* to describe the effect.

Consumers tend to choose products that they can get more information. That's to say, the length of an app's description (called *deslen*) may have an effect on its performance. Moreover, the performance of apps at a point of time denoted as $Pref_t$ is followed from the previous performance, denoted as $Pref_{t-1}$, the correlation of which should be eliminated.

5.2 Model

To examine our hypothesis of the effect of development strategy, we estimated the following empirical model:

$$\begin{aligned}
Pref_{it} = &\beta_0 + \beta_1 * PositionCashCow_i + \beta_2 * PositionProblemChildren_i \\
&+ \beta_3 * PositionDogs_i + \beta_4 * Manhattan_i + \beta_5 * PositionCashCow_i \\
&* Manhattan_i + \beta_6 * PositionProblemChildren_i \\
&* Manhattan_i + \beta_7 * PositionDogs_i * Manhattan_i + \beta_8 * Size_i \\
&+ \beta_9 * Pref_{it-1} + \beta_{10} * UpdateCount_i + \beta_{11} * DesLen_i + Platform_i + \varepsilon_i
\end{aligned} \tag{4}$$

where i indexes the apps. The dependent variables, $Pref_{it}$, is the number of download of app indexes i in Oct 1st and $Pref_{it-1}$ is the number of download of app indexes i in Aug 1st, correspondingly.

The model above describes the relationship between performance and development strategy of apps in different market status. The coefficient of $Manhattan_i$ captures the main effect of development strategy on app performance. Then the interaction term of $PositionCashCow_i * Manhattan_i$, $PositionProblemChildren_i * Manhattan_i$, $PositionDogs_i * Manhattan_i$ reflect the moderating role of market status in the effectiveness of development strategy.

5.3   Result

Table 1 reports the parameter estimation of the model above. We discuss the result in four different market status.

Table 1. Estimation result

Development Strategies	$-73.63 * 10^{6***}$
Development Strategies * PositionCashCow	$84.32 * 10^{6***}$
Development Strategies * PositionProblemChildren	$72.24 * 10^{6***}$
Development Strategies * PositionDogs	$73.79 * 10^{6***}$
Preformace_t-1	$1.03***$
Size	196.45^{ns}
UpdateCount	$-10.880 * 10^{3ns}$
Deslen	135.345^{ns}
PositionCash Cow	$-160.80 * 10^{6***}$
PositionProblem Children	$-136.80 * 10^{6***}$
PositionDogs	$-139.90 * 10^{6***}$
Mumayi	$23.6 * 10^{6***}$
Baidu Mobile Assistant	$22.49 * 10^{6***}$
360 Mobile Assistant	$22.73 * 10^{6***}$

For apps in Stars, the development strategy coefficients (β_4) is significant indicating that divergent development strategy has a negative effect on app performance. On the contrary, apps in Star which epitomizes more functions in the market are more likely to obtain better performance. Therefore, H1 is supported.

With regard to the apps in Cash Cow, Fig. 1 reveals the interaction between market status and development strategy. As Table 1 indicates, the parameter estimation of $PositionCashCow_i * Manhattan_i$ suggests that the influence of divergent development strategy for apps in Cash Cow increase 84,320,000 relative to apps in Star. H2 is supported.

Similarly, the parameter estimation of and $PositionDogs_i * Manhattan_i$ in Table 1 implies that the influence of divergent development strategy for apps in Problem Children and Dogs increase 72,240,000 and 73,790,000 relative to apps in Star respectively. H3 is supported.

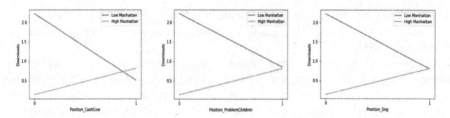

Fig. 1. Downloads of Cash Cows, Problem Children, and Dogs apps under low and high Manhattan distance.

6   Discussion

6.1   Contributions and Managerial Implications

This paper has three contributions to the existing theory. First, this research is a supplement of prior studies of determinants of mobile apps' success. Lee and Raghu [3] proposed that the feature of categories apps belong to is key to the longevity of apps in top charts. Zhou et al. [2] pointed out that update speed is positively associated with the performance of apps based on the ecosystem of the software platform. However, there are not relative researches about development strategies. Our study extended the framework on how to achieve better performance for an app by adding the relationship between development strategies and app performance. Moreover, the division into divergence and convergence using text mining techniques provide a method to measure development strategies.

Second, we introduced the interaction of market status. Supposed that a certain development strategy makes a varying effect on apps in different circumstances, we accepted market status as a typical kind of circumstance and utilized BCG matrix to identify it. The thought, refining the effect of development strategies could be used to improve similar researches such as the influence of update speed on mobile apps' performance.

Third, we found a way to measure the divergence of a development strategy quantitatively using text vectorization techniques, making it possible to take advantage of abundant text information in mobile platforms. Such techniques can be further improved in the future to explore all kinds of relationship in mobile app market.

Forth, we used market structure to explain the relationship between development strategies and performance, which made traditional industry theory migrated to Internet field. Our study made a little contribution to building up the theoretical framework of this new industry.

Prior studies in software management market ignored the fact of apps under different conditions. A general conclusion usually does not suit a certain app. This study made progress to refine result into different market status. So developers in the app market can easier make decisions according to their certain conditions.

6.2 Limitations and Further Directions

The study is subject to several limitations and could also be extended in several ways. First, our data came only from the Android market. Future research may examine whether we can get the same conclusion when it applies to the Apple market since there is a difference of users between the two markets. However, data availability restrictions prevent us from using the number of downloads to measure the performance of mobile apps in the Apple market. We may utilize some different models.

Second, endogeneity is another issue. Although we adopted description length, file size, update frequency, platform and previous performance to control idiosyncratic and time-constant unobserved characteristics associated with each app, the control variables are far from complete. For example, we neglected the divergence of categories and the maturity of apps. We will consider more comprehensive covariates in further study.

Third, we assumed a simple linear connection between development strategies and performance of mobile applications. Further research may include a more complex model to describe the complicity of the mobile app market.

7 Conclusion

In this paper, we empirically evaluate what development strategies most suitable for mobile applications in different market status. To do so, we estimate a multivariable linear regression of the performance of apps, with development strategies and market status. Specifically, we found that apps of Star require convergent development strategies to attract potential consumers. More generally, we demonstrate that divergent development strategies benefit apps in other quadrants of the BCG matrix. The conclusion of this study has certain guiding significance for mobile application developers.

Acknowledgement. The work described in this paper was fully supported by Jiangsu Social Science Foundation (16TQC002).

References

1. Ghose, A., Han, S.: Estimating demand for mobile applications in the new economy. Manag. Sci. **60**(6), 1470–1488 (2014)
2. Zhou, G., Song, P., Wang, Q.: Survival of the fittest: understanding the effectiveness of update speed in the ecosystem of software platforms. J. Organ. Comput. Electron. Commer. **28**(3), 234–251 (2018)
3. Lee, G., Raghu, T.: Determinants of mobile apps' success: evidence from the app store market. J. Manag. Inf. Syst. **31**(2), 133–170 (2014)
4. Kim, J.: Patterns of innovation in digital content services: the case of app store applications. Innov. Manag. Policy Pract. **14**(4), 540–556 (2014)
5. Palia, A., Ryck, J., Mak, W.: Interactive online strategic market planning with the web-based boston consulting group (BCG) matrix graphics package. Dev. Bus. Simul. Exp. Learn. **29**, 140–142 (2002)

6. Tan, A.: Text mining: the state of the art and the challenges. In: Proceedings of the PAKDD (1999)
7. Maalej, W.: Bug report, feature request, or simply praise? On automatically classifying app reviews. In: 2015 IEEE 23rd International Requirements Engineering Conference, pp. 116–125 (2015)
8. Finkelstein, A., et al.: App store analysis: mining app stores for relationships between customer. Business and Technical Characteristics. UCL Res. Note **14**(10), 1–24 (2014)
9. Kim, J., Park, Y., Kim, C.: Mobile application service networks: apple' s App Store. Serv. Bus. **8**(1), 1–27 (2014)
10. Gallouj, F.: Innovation in the Service Economy: The New Wealth of Nations. Edward Elgar Publishing Limited (2002)
11. Dias, L., Gerlach, M., Scharloth, J., Altmann, E.: Using text analysis to quantify the similarity and evolution of scientific disciplines. R. Soc. Open Sci. **5**(1), 171545 (2018)
12. Hoberg, G., Phillips, G.: Product market synergies and competition in mergers and acquisitions: a text-based analysis. Revision Finan. Study **23**(10), 3773–3811 (2010)
13. Mutandwa, E., Kanuma, N.T., Rusatira, E., Mugenzi, P., Govere, I., Foti, R.: Analysis of coffee export marketing in Rwanda: application of the Boston consulting group matrix. Afr. J. Bus. Manag. **2**, 210–219 (2009)
14. Hambrick, D.C., MacMillan, I.C., Day, D.L.: Strategic attributes and performance in the BCG matrix—a PIMS-based analysis of industrial product businesses. Acad. Manag. J. **25**(3), 510–531 (1982)
15. Bowles, S.: Behavior, Institutions, and Evolution, 1st edn. Princeton University Press, New York (2004)
16. Sun, J.M., Qiu, K.: Market problems of competitive monopoly in the internet economy. Business Economy (2013)
17. Su, Z., Jin, W.J., Sun, B.W.: Hierarchical Monopoly and Competition: Characteristics of Internet Industry's Market Structure-Analysis of Internet Platform. Management World (2018)
18. Rogers, E.M.: Diffusion of Innovations, 3rd edn. Free Press, New York (1983)
19. Davis, F.D.: Perceived usefulness, perceived ease of use, and user acceptance of information technology. MIS Q. **82**(6), 319–340 (1996)
20. Jackson, B.: Build customer relationships that last. Harvard Bus. Rev. **11**(12), 78–92 (1985)
21. Klemperer, P.D.: Markets with consumer switching cost. Quart. J. Econ. **102**(2), 375–394 (1987)
22. Peneder, M.: Competition and innovation: revisiting the inverted-U relationship. J. Ind. Compet. Trade **12**(1), 1–5 (2012)
23. Hashmi, R.: Competition and innovation: the inverted-u relationship revisited. Rev. Econ. Stat. **95**(5), 1653–1668 (2013)
24. Zheng, C.D., Wang, Q., Liu, W.X., Ni, L.L., Wu, Y.Z.: Influences of characteristics of e-business market on product innovation: an empirical study. J. Manag. Sci. (2014)
25. Jiang, Q., Tan, C.H., Wei, K.K.: Cross-website navigation behavior and purchase commitment: a pluralistic field research. In: Proceedings of Pacific Asia Conference on Information Systems 2018 (2018)
26. Zhang, W., Kang, L., Jiang, Q., Pei, L.: From buzz to bucks: the impact of social media opinions on the locus of innovation. Electron. Commer. Res. Appl. **30**, 125–137 (2018)
27. Kang, L., Jiang, Q., Tan, C.H.: Remarkable advocates: an investigation of geographic distance and social capital for crowdfunding. Inf. Manag. **54**(3), 336–348 (2017)

Simple Mouse Attribute Analysis

Jennifer Matthiesen and Michael B. Holte[✉]

Department of Architecture, Design and Media Technology,
Aalborg University, Esbjerg, Denmark
jjmatt@outlook.de, mbh@create.aau.dk

Abstract. This work investigates the potential bivariate correlations between selected pattern related mouse attributes and a set of factors for the determination of the satisfaction with the usability. To examine this, a prototype tool for the analyzation and characterization of mouse attributes, Simple Mouse Attribute Analysis (SMATA), within the usage of a cloud-based vertical business software solution for managing soft data, was designed and implemented. A questionnaire was conducted to evaluate the users' satisfaction with the usability. Following, the potential correlation between those properties was investigated. The findings revealed several statistically significant correlations between the factors of satisfaction with the usability and the examined mouse attributes. Mouse attributes like the number of direct movement, the number of long direct movements, the number of made pauses, as well as the covered distance and the total time of the session could be associated with the perception of the system usefulness, the information and interface quality and the overall impression. The objective of this study was to point out a new interesting research direction of using implicit gathered user data from one of the default communication channels in HCI: the computer mouse.

Keywords: Mouse attributes · Mouse behaviour patterns · HCI · Satisfaction · Usability · ECM

1 Introduction

We live in a society, where the digital storage and organisation of data and information gets increasingly important on the everyday life. The use of software to handle the mass of existing data in digital form is omnipresent. The interaction with such software solutions takes mainly place over default communication channel of a computer. These input data within the human-computer interaction (HCI) can give valuable information about the users' working behaviour and the users' performance [1, 2]. Likewise, in this way it might be possible to draw conclusions of the users' satisfaction, based on implicit gained users' input.

Within the HCI, the default communication channels in a normal computer application setup are limited to keyboard and mouse. However, some researchers try to overcome those limitations by using additional sensors for measuring the physical response of the users towards the system [3, 4]. Nevertheless, those sensors cannot be used across the masses. It would be more beneficial to use the default given communication channels to get additional knowledge about the user. A study of [5]

F. F.-H. Nah and K. Siau (Eds.): HCII 2019, LNCS 11589, pp. 95–113, 2019.
https://doi.org/10.1007/978-3-030-22338-0_8

showed, that there are significant correlations between eye and mouse movements during a web-based task. Hence, it can be inferred, that mouse movement analysis is a variable attempt to access information about the user as the perceived user experience or the system usability. [6] estimated that mouse attributes can reflect specific users' behaviour patterns and can be used to model user' behaviour.

Many studies have identified multiple mouse behaviour pattern [1, 5–7] – but their characterisation is generally vague and mainly based on visual interpretation. Mouse patterns are not characterised by quantitative analysis and are hence un-usable for the automatized analysis and auto recognition of users' information.

To overcome the above-described lag within the mouse metrics analysation research, this exploratory study is conducted to research mouse attributes on a quantitative level. The procedure in this study is based on the studies of [2], who examined the correlation pattern related mouse attributes and end-user-behaviour attributes (perceived ease of use, perceived usefulness, self-efficacy, willingness to learn and risk perception). In contrast, this exploratory study will examine the potential association between mouse attributes and factors of the users' satisfaction with the usability.

The initial problem statement of this thesis can be indicated as the lack of knowledge about the specific user of the software solution regarding their interaction on the site and following this an insufficient knowledge base concerning their personal needs and the satisfaction level. The current available software for research and identification in computer mouse analysis has no focus on the utilisation of the pure data of mouse usage. Therefore, a software was developed to analyse this data. The collected measurements could then be used to formulate a hypothesis about the users' satisfaction with the usability based on their mouse metrics data.

This paper is organised as follows. Section 2, visits the related theory of this study. In Sect. 3 and 4 the design and implementation, and the research methodology are detailed, respectively. Section 5, presents the results, which are further discussed in Sect. 6. Finally, conclusive remarks are given in Sect. 7.

2 Theoretical Framework

Zimmermann et al. used an implicit and non-invasive measuring method, using only the parameters from standard input devices (mouse and keyboard) to measure the mood of the user [8]. Multiple researches showed that mouse tracking can be used as a tool to understand web page usability as well as understand user behaviour [1, 9–11]. [10] revealed furthermore, that mouse tracking can not only be used to measure user attention, but also be used to predict the overall experience of the user and contain useful signals about the users' mental state such as struggle and frustration. In this way, they demonstrated that mouse movement patterns can predict whether the experience of a user is perceived as pleasant or not. Thus, it can be hypothesised that mouse movement patters can predict the users' perceived usability factors. Moreover, [10] showed that mouse tracking can reveal the focus of the user's attention. [11] investigated the recognition of self-efficacy, which is in accordance with [12], a key director of user satisfaction via mouse tracking analysis to improve the user's software experience.

2.1 Factors of the Usability

If an application or software is perceived as pleasant or useful, the user will most likely proceed with it. Following [13], usability is not a quality, which exists in neither an absolute nor a real sense. It describes the subject as a 'general quality of the appropriateness to a purpose'.

In related literature, there can be found multiply definitions of the factors of usability. [14] defined usability for example as *"usability is a quality attribute that assesses how easy user interfaces are to use"*. Further, [14] declared five components for the usability: Learnability, Efficiency, Memorability, Errors and Satisfaction. The error component describes i. a. the numbers of errors and can therewith equate with the indicator of effectiveness. The International Organization for Standardization (ISO) in contrast defines just three main points: Effectiveness, efficiency and satisfaction [15].

Effectiveness can be defined as *"accuracy and completeness with which the user fulfils a certain goal or task"* [16]. The information gap theory of Lowenstein explains that a smaller gap will increase curiosity and willingness to learn [17]. In this way the interactivity with the system will increase and the effectiveness will rise. In general, it can further determine, that a smaller knowledge gap, will provoke a higher effectiveness, since the major part of the needed information is already known.

Efficiency describes *"the relation between the accuracy and completeness with which the user fulfils a certain goal or task and the resources expended in achieving them"* [16]. Self-efficiency is according to the self-efficiency theory from [18], the personal judgement of the to-fulfilled action. Following this, self-efficiency require the belief in one's own abilities and can play a major role within the accomplishment of a goal or task. In studies of [19] it is declared that persons with less self-efficiency will be less willing to persist, when the task becomes more challenging. Determining efficiency as a key factor within the task performance can be declared as highly valuable for the perception of the usability. Especially in the area of Enterprise Resource Management (ECM) systems, efficiency is of central importance.

Satisfaction expresses the users' comfort with the use of the system [16]. Satisfaction considers the personal meaning of the user of the system's ease of use [15]. Following the Technology Acceptance Theory from [20] there are two key factors, which will influence the users' attitude towards using the system: Perceived Usefulness and Perceived Ease of Use. Perceived Usefulness is defined by [20] as the subjective perception in which degree the using of a system would improve their performance. According to [12], the perceived usefulness is one of the key directors of the users' satisfaction. The perception of the system is therefore a central element in the determination of the usability.

2.2 Mouse Behaviour Patterns

Like the most web tracking technologies, the main goal of tracking mouse data is to get a better understanding of the user behaviour and the HCI. The focus of this study lies not mainly in the user behaviour, but rather on the satisfaction with the usability expressed by the behaviour. Several researches showed, that mouse tracking can offer a scalable alternative to more expensive methods of eye tracking for the measurement of usability of web pages [21, 22], web browsing behaviour [23] or web searching behaviour [24].

Since the basic character of the tested ECM system (WorkPoint 365) is to have information distributed, but simultaneously multiple accessible, there are diverse possibilities to attain the goal. Therefore, no shortest time toward the target could be defined within the single task. However, it is possible to measure the time difference between defined points of movements (clicks, pauses). This though, was made by a declaration of direct and non-direct movements during the test are calculated through a distance difference parameter. The parameter of time was covered through the calculation of a velocity of movements.

Although it is significantly useful to study user behaviour in an ECM system, mouse movement attributes were not analysed yet in an everyday web-based product for business solutions. In the following, common mouse patterns revealed from literature are described in more detail. Furthermore, attributes are adjusted and complemented referring to the targeted ECM system. There is no focus on a reading pattern, since this was not part of the given tasks.

Straight Pattern. Movements declared as straight patterns [25], are direct movements (in contrast to random movements) towards a specific target. Users move the mouse direct towards a target, once they traced the targeted position. Therefore, such a movement is characterised by a pause before the movement [2, 25]. Due to its characteristic, these straight patterns can be interpreted as a confident move of the user, revealing certainty and task-oriented self-efficiency [5]. [7] defined a direct interaction pattern as "*a direct movement with no big pauses*". It may also reveal that a task was easy, the target was already known or easy to find. All these interpretations following a fast working behaviour and hence a high perceived efficiency as well as ease of use.

Hesitation Pattern. Within literature, two main approaches can be found to interpret a specific mouse movement pattern as hesitation. One view declares a movement between two or more elements as hesitation [7, 21]. Whereas in the application of [26] the pattern of hesitation is defined as "*the average time from the beginning of a mouse hover to the moment of the click*". Hesitation patterns in general are defined in the literature as the reflection of the user's doubt about which (or a specific) option to choose [2]. It was observed by [7], that more hesitation patterns occurred during a task with a higher level of difficulty.

Following this related literature, hesitation patterns can hence be used to determine the users' perceived difficulty and thereby influencing the perceived usability of the interaction with the system.

Random Pattern. *Following the definition of Ferreira, random patterns are "movements without any specific intention, just playing around doing random movements with short pauses or not"* [7, 11]. *In researches of* [2] it revealed that such movements often arise in contrast to straight patterns when the level of difficulty for the task was increased. Following this, random patterns can be an indicator of difficulty and low self-efficacy. In this way, random patterns can also be an indicator for the perceived usability of the system, since it can give a clue about the difficulty level.

Fixed Pattern. [25] defined '*fixed pattern*' as a repose of the cursor and can be likewise found in the paper of [1] and [7]. It describes the phenomena of place the curser on white space mostly on the right side of the page. Users using such a white space area to rest the mouse, avoiding in this way clicking accidently on a link [1, 2]. Fixed patterns are expressed by mouse pauses on a 'blank' area of the website. [2] assumed that the user during this time evaluates the cost and benefits of the particular action to make. Following them, fixed patterns can be used to evaluate the risk-perception as well as the level of usefulness.

Exploring Pattern. Exploring patterns, also referred in literature as '*guide pattern*' [25], are smooth and continuous movements of the cursor. [2] stated that those patterns reveal a correlation between eye and mouse movement. Those patterns give therefore an idea of the users exploring behaviour. Hence, exploring patterns can be used as an indicator for the perceived usefulness and ease of use of the system as well as for the effectiveness.

3 Design and Implementations

3.1 Monitoring Software and Data Extraction

To record the mouse and keyboard data, the JavaScript and PHP-based tool smt2 form Luis Leiva was used [22, 27]. It is available as open source on git hub. The current version is 2.2.0. and was published on the 13. October 2013 (last updated in 2016). Due to this, several changes were made to adapt and modify the software. The modified tool is not event based, but rather coordinate based, saving mouse data in regular intervals (standard is set to 24 frames per second (fps)). For the visualization of the recorded mouse data of the analyzation tool SMATA (Simple Mouse Attribute Analysis) was designed, based on JavaScript. It uses the recorded coordinates and handles all calculation of pattern related mouse attributes on the client side. This was done to reduce traffic between client and database.

The basis for this research of mouse attribute was an online ECM system. The used tool in this study, does not consist of a static web page, but is rather composed of dynamic web pages. Since the tested application enables several possibilities to find or insert information and can be designed in multiple ways, no optimal path for solving the tasks was defined. Instead, the pattern related mouse attributes were examined, so that the results can be transferred to other solution of the application.

Following the researches of [28] and [2] the recorded mouse patterns of each session were likewise separated into multiple mouse attributes in this study. All selected mouse attributes were then examined separately to see which of them are significantly correlated with the factors of the satisfaction with the usability. Hence the main research goal is to examine the bivariate potential correlations between the pattern related mouse attributes and the factors of the satisfaction with the usability (system usefulness/ease of use, information quality, interface quality). For this purpose, further sub-research questions are defined.

1. *Which direct-movements (straight pattern) attributes can be associated with the satisfaction of the usability?*
2. *Which non-direct-movements (random pattern) attributes can be associated with the satisfaction of the usability?*
3. *Which hesitation pattern attributes can be associated with the satisfaction of the usability?*
4. *Which fixed pattern attributes can be associated with the satisfaction of the usability?*
5. *Which attributes of mouse activity can be associated with the satisfaction of the usability?*

Movements are separated by specific points, including the starting point, pauses, clicks and the end point. Double entries are prevented. A movement must be at least 3.5 pixels long [2]. In addition, pauses are prioritized before clicks since they have a start and an end. A new movement is measured from the end of a pause. To find factors for the definition of a straight pattern, a curved pattern, as well as fast and slow movements, several pre-tests were made beforehand to find a factor for each of them. The procedure will be explained in more detail in the respective paragraph.

3.2 Pattern Attributes

Straight Pattern Attributes. Straight pattern can be following [28] expressed through direct movements that may not include a pause. It is further mentioned that those movements are often targeted oriented and end by a mouse click. In this research, straight pattern may also end on a pause, since the given task included to find and target information. Therefore, the examined mouse attributes for investigating straight patterns include the following:

- *Direct movements*
- *Average time between straight movements*

For the determination of a direct movement a pre-study test was fulfilled to define a factor, which should define the percentage derived from the Euclidian distance between two points. The pre-study test included the targeting of several buttons arranged on a screen within a straight line. 25 iterations were conducted in which each button was tested several times. In this way, a direct movement is defined as in Eq. (1).

$$|x_1 - x_0| \geq x_e * a \tag{1}$$

Where a describes the degree of the derivation of the Euclidian distance x_e.

Hesitation Pattern Attributes. Hesitation patterns are defined in related literature as the *"average time from the beginning of a mouse hover to the moment of the mouse click"* [29], a pause before the click [2] or a movement between two elements [7, 21]. Therefore, following mouse attributes are examined regarding the hesitation pattern:

- *Hovers that turned into clicks*

- *Average Time of pauses that turn into clicks*
- *Total number of all hovers*

To measure the hovers before clicks, all clicks are examined if the cursor stayed longer than 0.2 s on the same position (±2px, due to natural hand movements [30]).

Random Pattern Attributes. In contrast to straight patterns, random patterns are not directly targeted and do not follow a specific intention [7]. Such non-direct movements are examined by following mouse attributes:

- *Number of non-direct movements*
- *Total number of movements (following [2] a large number of mouse movements could point out a high percentage of movements without intention)*
- *Total mouse distance (since it likewise could determine long movements without intentions)*

Fixed Pattern Attributes. Fixed patterns encompass pauses and refer to the position where the cursor is being reposed [25]. Due to the quite height accuracy of the mouse tracking (24 frames per second), not every single pause is also perceived as a pause from humans. In different studies there can be found diverse definitions for the characterization of a pause. In [31] a single pause was considered if it was longer than 0.5 s. In the research of [30] a definition of 200 ms was set. This value was also used in the researches of [2]. Due to more recent studies, pauses are considered in this study as such, if they are longer than 0.2 s. Long Pauses are defined as such, if over 4 s as underlined in the related literature [2, 30].

Within this research there is no focus on the cursor position of the pause in relation to the displayed objects on the site. However, the cursor coordinates are logged to define further attributes and set the pause in relation to the recorded patterns. The examined attributes are therefore as follows:

- *Number of pauses*
- *Number of long Pauses (>4 s)*
- *Average time of pauses*
- *Average time of long pauses*

Mouse Attributes of Activity. Besides the above-described patterns, further mouse attributes are examined regarding the activity of the mouse. The activity level is defined here as the relation between the movement of the cursor and the duration of the task session. Additionally, the following attributes are examined:

- *The total amount of the covered distance during the tasks*
- *Average velocity during the task*
- *Total time of the task*
- *Activity Level (covered distance/time of task)*
- *The number of slow movements*

Besides the activity level and the belonging attributes, the number of slow movements is examined, since a large number could imply an exploratory or searching behaviour [2].

Since no clear definition of the perception of a slow movement was found within related work, a pre-study test was conducted. 14 participants between the age of 19 and 60 volunteered. The study included two buttons (a start and an end button), which should be clicked after each other. The test was split into two sub-tests: one for horizontal and one for vertical movements. All buttons were placed with 35% distance towards the screen edge. Each session included an iteration with a no given assignment of velocity, a fast and a slow iteration. The average velocity of fast movements for horizontal movements (hm) was ~750.25 px/sec while it was ~589.26 px/sec on vertical movements. The average velocity of slow movements for horizontal movements was ~305.18 px/sec while it was ~216.17 px/sec on vertical movements (vm). Since the standard deviation for all four cases was quite high (hm.-fast: ~128.708; hm.-slow: ~143.896; vm-fast: ~133.431; vm-slow: ~54.709) it was decided to set the slowest of the as fast perceived movement as a limit to characterised slow movements, which in this study, was at 360 px/sec. However, it should be mentioned that the conducted study supported the Fitts' law of movement which stated that a bigger and closer object (to the cursor), is easier to move to [32]. The average time for a fast-perceived movement was for both directions around one second (hm-fast: ~1.055 s; vm-fast: ~1.109 s) and for a slow-perceived movement around 3.2 s (hm-fast: ~3.314 s; vm-fast: ~3.175 s), even if the distance for a horizontal movement was longer than the vertical movement (due to the rectangular orientation of the screen) (Fig. 1).

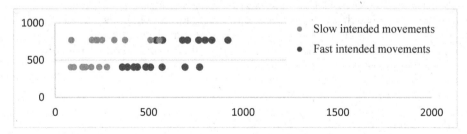

Fig. 1. Diagram of the velocity in pixel/s (x-axis) for each participant for different distances (y-axis).

4   Research Methodology

This part will present the steps for the examination of the potential correlations between the pattern related mouse attributes and the factors of the satisfaction with the usability in a cloud-based ECM software solution based on Microsoft SharePoint. First, the algorithms for the calculation of the pattern related mouse attributes will be explained. Afterwards, follows a description of the conducted field test, including the volunteered participants, the given task and test procedure, assessment and performance measurement, the questionnaires and the calculation of the selected mouse attributes. Finally, the data analysis process will be presented.

4.1 Mouse Attribute Analysis

Table 1 describes all examined mouse attributes as presented in Sect. 3 with their type and characterization. In addition, all created objects for the storage of multiple events of an attribute are listed with their corresponding interface.

Table 1. Examined mouse attributes and calculated variables.

Attribute	Type	Meaning
numMov	Count (units)	Number of movements in the assignment (>3.5 pixel)[c]
numDirMov	Count (units)	Number of direct movements (<4,33% of Euclidian distance; >3.5 pixel)[a,c]
numNonDirMov	Count (units)	Number of non-direct movements (>4,33% of Euclidian distance; >3.5 pixel)[a,c]
numLongDirMov	Count (units)	Number of long direct movements (>a fourth of the screen diagonal)
numSlowMov	Count (units)	Number of slow movements (<360 pixel/sec)[a]
pausesBfrClick	Count (units)	Number of pause before clicks
numClicks	Count (units)	Number of clicks
pausesBfrClickArray	Array [{ index: number; length: time (sec)}]	Array with information about pauses done before clicks (pauses >0.2 s)[b]
numHover	Count (units)	Number of hovers
numPauses	Count (units)	Number of pauses (>0.2 s)[b]
numLongPauses	Count (units)	Number of long pauses (>4 s)[c]
avgPause	Time (sec)	Ratio of average time of all pauses
avgLongPause	Time (sec)	Ratio of average time of long pauses
pauses	Array [{ length: time(sec); xcoord: number; ycoord: number; startIndex: number; endIndex: number}]	Array for all pauses (>0.2 s)[b] made during the test session It encompasses, the length of the pauses, index, x- and y-coordinate for each pause
pointsOfMov	Array [{ index: number; xcoord: number; ycoord: number; evt: string}]	Points for the movements calculation. Movements are separated by start point, pauses (>0,2 s)[b], clicks (of coordinates are not already in array unless the index distance is >=10)
covDist	Distance (pixel)	The covered distance in the assignment
eucDist	Distance (pixel)	The shortest possible distance between two points of movements

(continued)

Table 1. (*continued*)

Attribute	Type	Meaning
actLevel	Number (pixel/sec)	Activity level for the mouse movements
velocity	Number (pixel/sec)	Velocity for every single movement
avgVelocity	Number (pixel/sec)	Ratio of average velocity from all movements (so pauses will be excluded)
sessTime	Time (sec)	The time of the assignment

[a]Determined by pre-study test (see Sect. 3).
[b][30].
[c][11].

4.2 Field Test

A study was conducted to answer the research questions presented in the introduction. The objective was to reveal potential correlations between the pattern-related mouse attributes and the factors of the users' satisfaction with the usability. The participants were given two tasks, which they had to try to fulfil with the help of the given WorkPoint solution. For this purpose, every participant was further given the same laptop and the same mouse. The test was conducted within the companies of the participants and at WorkPoint A/S in Esbjerg. Besides the data recording, there was also a screen recording for backup-tracking and a video recording of every test session for documentation. However, the participants were at no point informed about the recording of mouse metrics, since this could possibly cause a behaviour change. To ensure a relative constant starting point for the mouse cursor, an alert box, including a button for starting the record, was implemented. This should make the sessions of the participants more comparable.

Pilot Test and Cooperation Work. A pilot test was conducted with the employees of WorkPoint A/S, to ensure a proper operation and quality of the used solutions as well as to verify the adequacy of the given tasks. During this procedure, the solutions were adapted to the respective participant to fit their current knowledge point [33]. Further, the procedure of the test has been improved through these pilot tests by adapting the given tasks, using another screen recording software for backup-tracking and the improvement of the conduction of the test session.

Participants. The experiment was conducted with customers of the software solution. During the study, 10 participants between the age of 19 and 55 years volunteered. The participants were chosen regarding to their experience. All of them had middle to high computer and web-experiences, but middle to less programming experiences. The WorkPoint experience was ranged from middle to high (2 to 5) and was Normal distributed. This was ensured by a pre-experiment questionnaire, collecting personal information (working position, age, sex) and experience level of web-usage, databases, programming, computer and WorkPoint experiences. Their experience level was measured on a 5-point scale, where 1 corresponds to no experience at all and 5 equals to "very high" experience. The mean value of the participants' programming experiences was 1.43 and 2.14 for database experience, which shows that they can be considered as non-experts users in programming and database development. In addition, the mean value for the web-experience was 3.43 and the mean value for the web-experience 3.86 (see Table 2). This validated the participants fitting into the target group (non-experienced programmer; limited database experience, but familiar with web-technology, especially with the software).

Table 2. Descriptive statistics of the pre-questionnaire about the participants' experience level.

Measured item	Mean (1–5)	St. derivation	St. error
Computer experience	3.86	0.832	0.340
Web experience	3.43	0.728	0.297
Database experience	2.14	1.124	0.459
Programming experience	1.43	0.495	0.202
WorkPoint 365 experience	3.86	0.990	0.404

Assessment and Performance Measurement. The requirements for the test task were that it should be small enough to be understood and conducted by the participants in a limited amount of time. Further, the task had to be executable with as little loading time as possible, to not affect the collected mouse data. Forms and structure of the software system were familiar to all participants. The first task given to the participant was to find specific information, while the second one includes the creation of a task within the found case of task one. Each information and subtask were assigned to an estimated difficulty level included in the calculation of the user performance. After completing both tasks, a post-task questionnaire was conducted to identify the satisfaction with the usability using the Computer System Usability Questionnaire (CSUQ) [34].

Questionnaire. Since the uses system is a B2B software, the CSUQ was chosen for the post-session explicit usability measurement. The questionnaire was developed by Lewis in 1995 and was designed for a study of IBM. Therefore, the questionnaire has a strong focus on business and is very suitable for business applications. It encompasses 19 statements, which have to be evaluated by the participant. Each statement will be evaluated using a 7-point Likert scale with 1 = 'strongly agree' and 7 'strongly disagree'. In this way, low scores are better than high scores [34]. It identifies the following factors:

- SYSUSE (system usefulness): items 1 through 8
- INFOQUAL (information quality): items 9 through 15
- INTERQUAL (interface quality): items 16 through 18
- OVERALL (overall satisfaction score): all items

Data Analysis. As mentioned in Sect. 3, the for this study, the designed tool SMATA was used for calculating the single mouse attributes. Further data analyzation took place with statistic tools. For the analyzation, the sample data was characterised. Therefore, a Normal distribution test was conducted. A Shapiro-Wilk's test and a visual inspection of the Quantile-quantile plots showed that the value for the system usefulness, information quality, interface quality as well as the overall satisfaction scores are normally distributed. All mouse attributes except the covered mouse distance are normal distributed. To inspect the bivariate correlation between the measured variables, the Spearman correlation (S) analysis (for the correlation between the covered mouse distance and the attributes of usability) as well as the Pearson correlation (P) analysis were performed. These analyses expose the strength of the association between each two variables.

5   Results

In this section the results of the usability questionnaire and the correlation analysis are presented. The pre-estimated coefficient alpha for the determination of the reliability exceeded 0.89 (0.93 for SYSUSE, 0.91 for INFOQUAL, 0.89 for INTERQUAL, and 0.95 for the OVERALL), calculated in a research of Lewis [34]. This result could be confirmed in this study. The calculated Cronbach's alpha coefficient for the executed questionnaire was for all values above 0.9789.

Table 3 shows an overview of the items of the satisfaction with the usability, measured by the questionnaire.

Table 3. Descriptive statistic of the factors of the CSUQ.

Measured item	Mean (1–7)	St. derivation	St. error
SYSUSE	2.940	1.818	0.642
INFOQUAL	3.031	1.498	0.530
INTERQUAL	2.722	1.082	0.382
OVERALL	2.927	1.481	0.523

Figure 2 shows the average value from the single measured mouse attributes from all participants. The average value is used for the variables *avgPause*, *avgLongPause*, *avgVelocity* and the sum of all visited pages is used for the variable *numMov*, *numDirMov*, *numNonDirMov*, *numLongDirMov*, *numSlowMov*, *numClicks*, *pauseBfrClick*, *numPauses*, *numLongPauses*, *sessTime*, *numHovers* and *covDistance*.

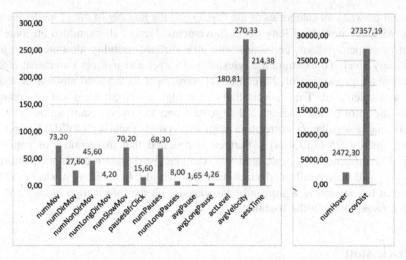

Fig. 2. Diagram of the examined mouse attribute values of the participants.

Table 4 shows the correlation analysis between every single examined mouse attribute and the items of the satisfaction with the usability. The result shows that there can be identified several highly significant (p < 0.01) and significant (p < 0.05) correlations. The result of the Pearson correlation analysis showed a highly statistical

Table 4. Correlation analysis between the examined mouse attributes and the factors of satisfaction with the usability.

Pattern category	Mouse attribute	Correlation	SYSUSE	INFOQUAL	INTERQUAL	OVERALL
Straight patterns	numDirMov	(P)	−0.708*	−0.852**	−0.770**	−0.797**
	numLongDirMov	(P)	−0.871**	−0.819**	−0.799**	−0.882**
Hesitation pattern	pausesBfrClick	(P)	−0.078	−0.005	0.103	−0.02
	numHover	(P)	0.334	0.263	0.406	0.341
Random pattern	numMov	(P)	0.347	0.339	0.29	0.355
	percentNumNonDirMov	(P)	0.739*	0.813**	0.670*	0.787**
	numNonDirMov	(P)	0.581	0.625	0.549	0.621
Fixed pattern	numPauses	(P)	0.747*	0.699*	0.592	0.741*
	numLongPauses	(P)	0.187	0.324	0.119	0.229
	avgPause	(P)	−0.134	0.146	−0.077	−0.041
	avgLongPause	(P)	−0.311	−0.356	−0.639*	−0.398
Mouse attributes of activity	numSlowMov	(P)	0.324	0.305	0.302	0.334
	numClicks	(P)	−0.080	0.048	0.207	0.014
	covDist	(S)	0.48	0.345	0.492	0.467
	actLevel	(P)	0.187	0.139	0.273	0.198
	avgVelocity	(P)	0.144	0.173	0.091	0.153
	sessTime	(P)	0.606	0.774**	0.595	0.688*

*Correlation is significant at the 0.05 level (2-tailed).
**Correlation is significant at the 0.01 level (2-tailed).

significant between all categories of the CSUQ and the number of direct movements as well as with the number of long direct movements. Hence, all examined attributes of straight movement patterns correlated with all examined usability attributes on a high significantly level. To examine the relevance of direct and indirect movement closer, the percentage proportion of the non-direct movement to the total amount of movements was calculated. This reveals likewise a high statistical significant correlation towards the information quality (INFOQUAL) and the overall satisfaction with the usability and a significant correlation with the system usability (SYSUSE) and the interface quality (INTERQUAL). Further, it revealed that the number of pauses is statistical significant when associated with the perceived system usefulness, information quality and the overall satisfaction with the usability. In addition, it was noted that the time of the session is significantly associated with the information quality and the overall satisfaction with the usability.

6   Discussion

The results of this study showed that several mouse attributes are statistically significant associated with the factors of the satisfaction with the usability, described by the CSUQ. It was shown that mouse movement attributes correlate significantly with factors of the satisfaction with the usability of cloud-based business software solution for managing soft data. In the following, each sub-research questions (see part 3.1) are discussed in more detail.

1. Which direct-movements (straight pattern) attributes can be associated with the satisfaction of the usability?

The results in Table 4 show that both of the direct-moment attributes examined in this study (the number of direct and long-direct movements) are highly statistical correlated with all factors of the CSUQ. The analysation revealed a negative correlation since the highest value in the questionnaire (7-points) was given on a strong disagreement with a statement and reported less satisfaction with the usability. Following [35] all revealed correlations with the attributes of direct movements can be classified as high. It can be summarised that a low number of direct and long direct movement can indicate a low satisfaction with the usability. In researches of [1] a straight pattern including long direct movements is interpreted as familiar with the system.

2. Which non-direct-movements (random pattern) attributes can be associated with the satisfaction of the usability?

Even if the number of direct movements correlated highly significantly to the satisfaction with the usability, no statistical significances were found on the bivariate correlation analysis between the absolute number on non-direct movements and the factors of the CSUQ. Therefore, the percentage quotient of the ratio between the number of non-direct movements and the total quantity of movements during the session was further examined. This showed also a highly statistical association between the calculated quotient and all factors of the CSUQ. It should hence be noted that even if all participant were given the same tasks, the absolute number of direct or non-direct movements seems not to be decisive. Instead, the proportion of direct and non-direct movements should be considered for the consideration of the users' satisfaction with the usability. The number of total movements during the task session does not reveal any statistically significant correlation with the factors of the CSUQ. Since every user has his or her own habits to work with the system and the investigation should observe an everyday working process. Therefore, no concrete click path was prescribed.

3. Which hesitation pattern attributes can be associated with the satisfaction of the usability?

Regarding the examined hesitation pattern attributes, no statistically significant correlation could be found. The absence of a significant correlation with the number of hovers, could possibly be based on the various elements on the interface, which must be constantly crossed while fulfilling a task. Again, there were various possibilities for solving the given task, were some ways might invoke more hovers than others. The absence of a significant correlation with the pause before clicks could be based on the fact, that a high percentage of clicks had pauses in before. During the more detail consideration, it was noticed, that on average over 78% (SD = 0.096389341; SE = 0.03212978) of all clicks had pauses in before for all users. It seemed to be a natural behaviour to make a pause before clicking. This could mean that pause before clicks should be studied more in the field of ECM systems to be a significant factor in the determination of a hesitation pattern. Based on this, hesitation patterns might be determinable by longer pauses before clicks or by other attributes like the task duration time or the covered distance (searching pattern).

4. Which fixed pattern attributes can be associated with the satisfaction of the usability?

In the conducted study, it was revealed that the number of pauses made during the task execution is significantly correlated with the perceived system usefulness, information quality and the overall satisfaction with the usability. It revealed further, that the average of long pauses was significantly associated with the INTERQUAL factor. A more detailed consideration of the data revealed that a low point rating for the INTERQUAL (<3; equal a positive perceived interface), had an average time for long pauses of longer than 8.847 s, while on a higher point ranking (equal a less positive perceives interface) of the INTERQUAL factors the average of long pauses was under 8.847. It can be summarised, that the average of long pauses on a less positive perceived user interface are shorter than on high positive perceived interfaces. During the estimation of the remaining fixed pattern related mouse attributes it was noticed, that no further mouse attributes were statistically correlated with the factors of the CSUQ. It was noticed that the appearance of long pauses differed for each participant. This might be possibly based on various habits within the computer utilisation and not connected to information about the satisfaction with the usability of the ECM system.

5. Which attributes of mouse activity can be associated with the satisfaction of the usability?

During the investigation of the further examined mouse attributes, it revealed that the session time is highly significantly correlated with the INFOQUAL factor and the overall satisfaction of the usability. Therefore, it can be inferred that the design of the interface and therewith its quality have an influence on the length of the session. It is further noted that no other attribute of mouse activity is significantly associated with any of the factors of the CSUQ. The absence of a significant correlation with the average velocity might indicate that the velocity differs for each user and is less connected with the perceived satisfaction of usability.

Based on the above-described found correlations, it can be concluded that the examined pattern-related mouse movements attributes can be useful as implicit feedback of the users towards their satisfaction with the usability. Such an implicit feedback does not interrupt the interaction of the user with the system, but rather interact on an implicit level so that the user can continue his or her usual activity without answering questions. Those systems can be used to infer the users' interests and get more information about the user experience [36]. In contrast to explicit feedback methods, the mouse attribute analysis has the benefit of its validity, since the output of questionnaires is always dependent on the participant accuracy and their willingness to provide feedback.

6.1   Possible Issues and Limitations

The findings of this study correspond with the findings of the study of [2].. Statistical significances correlations were found between the mouse attributes: number of non-direct movements (curved movements), the number of direct movements and the number of long direct movements with the perceived usefulness and perceived ease of use. This corresponds to the finding of the conducted study. However, the study of [2] revealed further statistical significance correlations. For instance, it was discovered that a statistical significant association between the total number of movements and the perceived usefulness, perceived ease of use and the self-efficiency. This could be possibly due to the different, more homogenous and larger group of participants in the study of [2]. For this study, a smaller but representative group of the customers of the tested system were chosen. A major difference however, is the testing within an ECM system. In this study, it was furthermore the focus on effectively finding information within the solution.

Likewise, [2] found a statistically significant association of the number of long pauses and the average time of long pauses with the attribute of self-efficiency. Even if the topic of self-efficiency was covert by the CSUQ within the section SYSUSE, no statistical significance was revealed with this factor. Whereas, it was found a statistically significant correlation between the average time of long pauses and the INTERQUAL factor. This factor encompasses satisfaction-oriented questions (users comfort with the system [15]) about the interface quality and the included functions and capabilities of the system. This might indicate that the average time of long pauses (bigger than 4 s. [2]) could be a potentially important factor in the determination of the users' satisfaction with the interface in ECM systems, while the average time of long pauses in end-user developer tasks seems to be more indicating to self-efficiency.

Every participant was provided with the same hardware (laptop and mouse). These devices differ from the hardware, used in the daily working process. Following [37], different mice are used in different ways. The study [38] researched the impact of different devices while computer usage. Following these two studies and their outcome, it could be hypothesized, that the usage of another mouse could have influences on the task execution. This however, has not been investigated closer, since all users had the same devices at hand.

7   Conclusion and Further Work

The main objective of this study was to investigate the potential correlation between mouse attributes and factors of the users' satisfaction with the usability. Many related studies showed that mouse movement analysis is a variable attempt to access information about the user [1, 8, 10, 21, 23]. In this study, a prototype tool for the analysation and calculation of mouse attributes have been designed and implemented. It requests collected data from the database and visually presents it on an admin panel. It can further determine a characterisation of movements like slow movements, direct or non-direct movements or long direct movements. The results of this study showed multiple statistical significant intersections within the conducted bivariate correlation analysis. It revealed that the number of direct movements, the number of long direct movements, the number of pauses as well as the covered distance and the session time are significant factors in the determination of the users' satisfaction with the usability. The results correspond to related literature, where mouse metrics were correlated to end-user behaviour attributes [2]. The found results were discussed and related to other studies and their outcome.

As mentioned above, a selection of mouse attributes for the examination was made. In future work, further mouse attributes should be examined, and the definition of the characterisation should be studied more closely. In this way, a more narrowed definition of certain mouse movement characterisation should be reached. In addition, measured attributes of this study will be examined in more detail, e.g., their dependence on other variables. For further investigations of mouse attributes, it is important to expand the group of participants and consider more narrowed target groups independently, since it indicates that the mouse usage exhibit huge deviations.

It is further planned to examine the potential validity of mouse attributes on other platforms, like end-customer e-business solutions. A potential study could be the determination of how far specific mouse attributes can be used to individualise the users' content.

Acknowledgements. The research leading to these results has been conducted in collaboration with WorkPoint A/S.

References

1. Mueller, F., Lockerd, A.: Cheese: tracking mouse movement activity on websites, a tool for user modeling. In: CHI 2001, Extended Abstracts on Human Factors in Computing Systems, pp. 279–280 (2001)
2. Tzafilkou, K., Protogeros, N.: Mouse behavioral patterns and keystroke dynamics in end-user development: what can they tell us about users' behavioral attributes? In: Computers in Human Behavior, pp. 288–305, 5 February 2018

3. de Vicente, A., Pain, H.: Informing the detection of the students' motivational state: an empirical study. In: Cerri, S.A., Gouardères, G., Paraguaçu, F. (eds.) ITS 2002. LNCS, vol. 2363, pp. 933–943. Springer, Heidelberg (2002). https://doi.org/10.1007/3-540-47987-2_93
4. McQuiggan, S.W., Lester, J.C.: Diagnosing self-efficacy in intelligent tutoring systems: an empirical study. In: Ikeda, M., Ashley, K.D., Chan, T.-W. (eds.) ITS 2006. LNCS, vol. 4053, pp. 565–574. Springer, Heidelberg (2006). https://doi.org/10.1007/11774303_56
5. Rodden, K.X., Fu, A.A., Spiro, I.: Eye-mouse coordination patterns on web search results pages. In: CHI 2008 Extended Abstracts on Human Factors in Computing Systems, pp. 2997–3002 (2008)
6. Hinbarji, Z., Albatal, R., Gurrin, C.: Dynamic user authentication based on mouse movements curves. In: He, X., Luo, S., Tao, D., Xu, C., Yang, J., Hasan, M.A. (eds.) MMM 2015. LNCS, vol. 8936, pp. 111–122. Springer, Cham (2015). https://doi.org/10.1007/978-3-319-14442-9_10
7. Ferreira, S., Arroyo, E., Tarrago, R., Blat, J.: Applying mouse tracking to investigate patterns of mouse movements in web forms. Universitat Pompeu Fabra, Pompeu (2010)
8. Zimmermann, P., Guttormsen, S., Danuser, B., Gomez, P.: Affective computing–a rationale for measuring mood with mouse and keyboard. Int. J. Occup. Saf. Ergon. 9(4), 539–551 (2003)
9. Tanjim-Al-Akib, M., Ashik, L.K., Al-Walid-Shaiket, H., Chowdhury, K.: User-modeling and recommendation based on mouse-tracking for e-commerce websites. In: 19th International Conference on Computer and Information Technology, Dhaka, Bangladesh (2016)
10. Navalpakkam, V., Churchill, E.: Mouse tracking: measuring and predicting users' experience of web-based content. In: Proceedings of the SIGCHI Conference on Human Factors in Computing Systems (CHI 2012), pp. 2936–2972 (2012)
11. Tzafilkou, K., Protogeros, N., Yakinthos, C.: Mouse tracking for web marketing: enhancing user experience in web application software by measuring self-efficacy and hesitation levels. Int. J. Strateg. Innov. Mark. 1, 233–247 (2014)
12. Mitakos, T., Almaliotis, I., Demerouti, A.: An auditing approach for ERP systems examining human factors that influence ERP user satisfaction. Informatica Economică 14(1), 78–92 (2010)
13. Brooke, J.: SUS - a quick and dirty usability scale. In: Usability Evaluation in Industry, pp. 189–194. Taylor & Francis, London (1996)
14. Nielsen, J.: Usability 101: Introduction to Usability, 4 January 2012. https://www.nngroup.com/articles/usability-101-introduction-to-usability/
15. International Organisation for Standardisation, "ISO9241 Ergonomic, Part 11: Guidance on usability," International Organisation for Standardisation, Geneva, Switzerland (1998)
16. Frøkjær, E., Hertzum, M., Hornbæk, K.: Measuring usability: are effectiveness, efficiency, and satisfaction really correlated? In: CHI 2000 Proceedings of the SIGCHI Conference on Human Factors in Computing Systema, pp. 345–352, 01–06 April 2000
17. Loewenstein, G.: The psychology of curiosity: a review and reinterpretation. Psychol. Bull. 116(1), 75–98 (1994)
18. Bandura, A.: Self-efficacy: toward a unifying theory of behavioural change. Psychol. Rev. 8(2), 191–215 (1977)
19. Blackwell, A.F., Rode, J.A., Toye, E.F.: How do we program the home? Gender, attention investment, and the psychology of programming at home. Int. J. Hum. Comput. Stud. 67, 324–341 (2009)
20. Davis, F.D.: Perceived usefulness, perceived ease of use, and user acceptance of information technology. MIS Q. 13, 319–340 (1989)

21. Atterer, R., Wnuk, M.S.A.: Knowing the user's every move - user activity tracking for website usability evaluation and implicit interaction. In: Proceedings of the 15th International Conference on World Wide Web, Edinburgh, Scotland (2006)
22. Leiva, L.A., Vivó, R.: A gesture inference methodology for user evaluation based on mouse activity tracking. In: Proceedings of the IADIS International Conference on Interfaces and HCI, pp. 18–26 (2008)
23. Chen, M., Anderson, J.R., Sohn, M.: What can a mouse cursor tell us more? Correlation of eye/mouse movements on web browsing. In: Extended Abstracts CHI 2001, pp. 281–282 (2001)
24. Cooke, L.: Is the mouse a "poor man's eye tracker"? Usability and Information Design Magazine, pp. 252–255 (2006)
25. Griffiths, L., Chen, Z.: Investigating the differences in web browsing behaviour of chinese and european users using mouse tracking. In: Aykin, N. (ed.) UI-HCII 2007. LNCS, vol. 4559, pp. 502–512. Springer, Heidelberg (2007). https://doi.org/10.1007/978-3-540-73287-7_59
26. ClickTale Ltd.: ClickTale: Basic System Manual, 1 February 2013
27. Leiva, L.A., Vivó, R.: (SMT) real time mouse tracking registration and visualization tool for usability evaluation on websites. In: Proceedings of IADIS WWW/Internet, pp. 187–192 (2007)
28. Churruca, S.L.: Comparative study of cursor movement patterns between a touchpad and a mouse devices. Master thesis, UPF (2011)
29. Clicktale, "Click maps," 10 June 2018. https://www.internetrix.com.au/services/analytics/clicktale/click-maps/
30. Dijkstra, M.: The diagnosis of self-efficacy using mouse and keyboard input. Faculty of Science theses, Utrecht (2013)
31. Leiva, L., Vivó, R.: Web browsing behavior analysis and interactive hypervideo. ACM Trans. Web (TWEB) 7(4), 20–28 (2013)
32. Fitts, P.M.: The information capacity of the human motor system in controlling the amplitude of movement. J. Exp. Psychol. 47, 381–391 (1954)
33. Naumann, A., et al.: Intuitive use of user interfaces: defining a vague concept. In: Harris, D. (ed.) EPCE 2007. LNCS (LNAI), vol. 4562, pp. 128–136. Springer, Heidelberg (2007). https://doi.org/10.1007/978-3-540-73331-7_14
34. Lewis, J.R.: IBM Computer Usability Satisfaction Questionnaires: Psychometric Evaluation and Instructions for Use. Human Factors Group, Boca Raton (1995)
35. Cohen, J.: Statistical Power Analysis for the Behavioral Sciences. Erlbaum, Hillsdale (1988)
36. Zahoor, S., Rajput, D., Bedekar, M., Kosamkar, P.: Inferring web page relevancy through keyboard and mouse usage. In: International Conference on Computing Communication Control and Automation, pp. 474–478 (2015)
37. Keir, P.J., Bach, J.M., Rempel, D.: Effects of computer mouse design and task on carpal tunnel pressure. Ergonomics 42(10), 1350–1360 (1999)
38. Gerling, K.M., Klauser, M., Niesenhaus, J.: Measuring the impact of game controllers on player experience in FPS games. In: MindTrek 2011 Proceedings of the 15th International Academic MindTrek Conference: Envisioning Future Media Environments, Tampere, Finland (2011)

Next Level Service Performance - Intelligent Order Assistants in Automotive After Market

Joachim Reiter[1(✉)], Andrea Mueller[1], Uwe Hartmann[2],
Michael Daniel Schatz[2], and Larissa Greschuchna[1]

[1] Hochschule Offenburg – University of Applied Sciences, Badstrasse 24,
77652 Offenburg, Germany
joachim.reiter@hs-offenburg.de
[2] Mann+Hummel GmbH, Schwieberdinger Strasse 126,
71636 Ludwigsburg, Germany

Abstract. A car is only useful, when it runs properly – but keeping a car it running is getting more and more complex. Car service providers need a deep knowledge about technical details of the different car models. On the other hand car producers try to keep this information in their ownership. Digital data collection takes place every second on the car's product life cycle and is stored on the car producers' servers. The contribution of this paper is three-fold: we will provide an overview of the current concepts of intelligent order assistant technologies (I). This corpus is used to come to a more precise description of the specific service performance aspects (II). Finally, a representative empirical study with German motor mechanics will help to evaluate the wishes and needs regarding an intelligent order assistant in the garage (III).

Keywords: Automotive after market · Intelligent agents · User acceptance · Car repair service performance · SERVQUAL

1 Introduction: Digital Challenges in Automotive After Market

About 324 million vehicles create a 240 billion Euro aftermarket (parts and labor) in Europe. There are two categories of service providers for vehicle repair: about 84,000 are manufacturer-affiliated ('dependent') and approximately 378,000 are non-manufacturer-affiliated ('independent' or 'IAM' for Independent Aftermarket). Both segments equally occupy about 50% of the entire market volume [1, 2].

In the past years, several trends, including digitalization, have changed and will continue to influence the market metrics and also keep on challenging market players to adapt to disruptions within the industry.

Since March 31st 2018, each new vehicle marketed in the European Union is now equipped with a mandatory emergency call function ("e-call"). From that time on new vehicles are equipped with digital sensors and vehicle manufacturers are now offering connected services through this hardware on a large scale. Each day a car produces up to 20 Gigabyte of data, which is collected primarily by the car manufacturer.

F. F.-H. Nah and K. Siau (Eds.): HCII 2019, LNCS 11589, pp. 114–125, 2019.
https://doi.org/10.1007/978-3-030-22338-0_9

The task for legislation will be to enable independent market players to gain access to this data in order to be able to provide high-quality services to the car owner and therefore maintain fair competition on a level playing field. Only those independent aftermarket players that will adapt to digitalization will be able to adopt a profitable business model adding value as e.g. the German aftermarket revenue will decrease by between 2% and 11% by 2025 [3].

Type approval regulation in Europe demands for an On-Board-Diagnosis (OBD) or OBD II port, which provides open access to car and diagnostics data. Vehicle mechanics then have the possibility to extract relevant information about the service status of the vehicle and the installed parts. The clear identification of the right parts for a car is a key process before beginning the actual repair on the vehicle.

Without correct information, an efficient service and repair of the vehicle is almost not possible and increases costs. This poses a major challenge to IAM players along the entire value chain and it will be vital for suppliers and parts wholesalers to provide additional technical support to the workshops.

An interesting element to help solve this challenging situation could lie in a smart combination of artificial intelligence and technical databases of spare parts identification (e.g. TecDoc) of all brands worldwide. A visual auto part selection combined with a natural voice recognition device would detect the defective parts and could enable the mechanic to order directly the required spare part in the system, thus freeing time that he can now spend working on the vehicle.

Intelligent order assistant technologies could help to solve this problem for the IAM and furthermore generate a service proposition in all the strategic success factors time, quality, and costs for them. By offering a faster, more precise and more cost-effective spare part order process, a better service to the end-customer can be implemented, which directly translates into an improved customer experience [2].

2   AUTO-AL: Intelligent Order Assistants Features

Digital assistants gain more and more acceptance by private users: Applications like Siri by Apple or Alexa by Amazon as well as Cortana by Microsoft are very popular and already included in many software packages. Companies of many branches are very interested to integrate intelligent automated service assistants in their customer interaction. This would allow professional 24/7 support for their customers without extra costs for additional service staff. So digital assistants promise a great chance to enhance marketing and sales activities in the B2C-field.

But, also the B2B area needs a high-level professional service support: the search of complex technical details with standard interaction equipment like laptops and internet browsers is time-consuming and frustrating.

Motor mechanics in a garage for example have to gain information about specific car parts: they need to leave their workplace, clean themselves, go to a computer and find the right products over the internet. A system, which is installed directly at the defective car and interacts via voice could be a very helpful solution for this problem.

The car repair process in independent aftermarket companies is not standardized. Each car is different because each customer can configure it dependent on his or her individual needs and wishes. Thus, motor mechanics need a very broad and detailed knowledge about the car models of different automotive brands worldwide.

The mobile access to a database of all car repair parts of the most common models and brands would be helpful to support the motor mechanics in the repair process. By using a new intelligent order assistant technology, an intuitive and process-integrated system supports all activities in the repair process.

Besides the setup of such a database, there are several user-related requirements on an intelligent order system: Available intelligent dialog systems such as Siri or Cortana are pre-integrated in hardware systems like computers, or smart phones. Alexa is an independent system and extra device with additional functions like a speaker or smart home control. Further hardware options for the installation in a garage could be tablet PCs, telephone headsets, or virtual reality or augmented reality eyeglasses.

Furthermore, it is not obvious, what interfaces the system should offer: Is voice control already accepted by the future users? What about eye blink control? Other interaction modes like text chat, touch screen, or mouse control are already established dialog concepts, which have to be considered (Fig. 1).

Fig. 1. AUTO-AL can support car mechanics in a garage

Based on DIN ISO 9241 110 there are seven significant requirements in user experience: suitability for the task, suitability for learning, suitability for individualization, conformity with user expectations, self-descriptiveness, controllability, and error tolerance [15].

Not all factors are similar important in the AUTO-AL scenario. An intelligent order system as AUTO-AL has to fulfill the individual expectations of the users otherwise they would not be willing to use it. Users might look forward to a system, which allows to accelerate the car repair service process, reduces prices for car repair parts, facilitates as well as speeds up the order process, increases independence of the single mechanic, and creates a better working environment.

There could also be concerns: the system could be error-prone, difficult to integrate, time-consuming, or just not assessed as necessary because the existing process is accepted by all employees. Especially small and medium sized companies might have problems to install this system if it is not intuitive and usable, or it is costly or difficult to install.

Motivations for the usage of the AUTO-AL system could depend on the hardware as well as the functions and service components: E.g. the SERVQUAL-model can help to display the service quality dimensions, like tangibles, assurance, reliability, responsiveness, and empathy.

The users are more motivated to accept new concepts and technologies, if they expect an advantage by the usage: Before developing a system like AUTO-AL these motivations have to be clearly evaluated by empirical research based on a service quality evaluation model.

3   Service Quality Assessment in Car Repair Service Users Minds

In the field of product-related, support services, such as car repair, ensuring high service quality is a key success factor. Changing customer needs, e-mobility, growing connectivity and digital technologies are some of the major challenges for the auto-motive market for the future [4]. Against this background, solutions, and product and service concepts that accompany car repair garages on their way to the future in after-sales service become more and more important.

High service quality can reduce service costs, differentiate from competitors and reduce service times. Cost reduction arises e.g. through a certain standardization of the service or externalization strategy in the sense that the customer performs parts of the service himself [5]. Differentiation advantages compared to competitors can arise in particular from a perceived above-average quality of service. Associated with this, advantages can also arise if, for example, a provider has a high level of responsiveness because he provides a quick service [5].

Customers expect service companies to provide prompt services and they expect the mechanics to inform them about the exact time the services will be performed (high responsiveness). Following Parasuraman/Zeithaml/Berry (1985) they additional expect that service providers keep their promises (reliability), that they themselves are neatly dressed and offer their services in a clean, comfortable business premises (tangibles), that they have knowledge, credibility and will provide the services at the exact time they promise (assurance) and they provide individualized attention (empathy) [6].

SERVQUAL is a recognized and widely used method of measuring service quality, that takes these five dimensions into account. The SERVQUAL approach measures the discrepancies between perceived and expected quality. The dimensions are measured by 22 individual items [7].

The literature review shows some studies focusing on service quality including customers' perceptions on after sales services in the car repair industry. The results of the study of Elistina and Naemah (2011) showed that many customers in the car repair sector had a low and moderate perception of service quality and the repair and maintenance sector of automobiles has received lot of complaints. They conclude that lawmakers in Malaysia are called upon to set standards for car repairs to provide comprehensive consumer protection [8].

Izogo (2015) showed in a study that SERVQUAL can be used as a valid and reliable approach to measure service quality within a non-western context car repair service. In the survey, empathy proved to be the most important dimension of service quality followed by the responsiveness. Overall, customers' perceived level of service quality of car repair services ranks very low. The conclusion is, that car mechanics "should focus on the antecedents that play a crucial role in determining the level of service quality". The study collected data from customers of car repair services in a southeastern Nigerian city. The author pointed out that the results cannot be generalized and a transfer to Western countries is still pending [9].

Also based on the SERVQUAL approach, Lotko (2017) recognizes that the greatest discrepancy between expectations and their fulfilment in car repair services was observed for reliability. The smallest discrepancy was recorded for responsiveness. The respondents manifested the highest expectations with regard to the speed and efficiency of service.

Lotko divided the respondents into different groups concerning the time of being a car user. He found out that the expectation of drivers with many years of driving experience (41–51 years) for responsiveness were lower than the actually perceived value. In comparison driver with less than ten years of driving experience the largest gap was determined. Lotko pointed out that the time of being a car user diversified the assessment results for the dimension responsiveness, assurance and empathy. The study has shown that there are formal car user characteristics, which "significantly diversify the assessment of service quality level" [10].

Kankam-Kwarteng et al. (2016) also comes to conclusion that "customers' perceptions of service quality offered by mechanical service industry did not meet their expectations" and for this they have to improve their service quality. By using SERVQUAL they identified responsiveness, reliability and empathy as the main determinants of service quality in the car repairs and maintenance industry. But all dimensions had a gap meaning expectations were higher than perceptions and customers perception is that mechanics need modern form of technology and equipment. It is eminent that car repair providers match their objectives of being in business with that of the expectations of their customers [11].

Examining the impact of service quality on customer satisfaction and loyalty to Ghanaian car owners is the goal of Famiyeh/Kwarteng/Asante-Darko. The result shows that empathy, assurance, responsiveness and tangibles have a significant positive relationship with customer satisfaction, and that the empathy and reliability of the mechanic have a positive relationship with customer loyalty. The authors conclude that it is important for mechanics to understand that customers want their cars to be maintained by mechanics who have knowledge and empathy and are able to explain customers' services needed as well as likelihood of potentially required repairs. Only then will it be possible to satisfy these customers and thus lay the foundation that they will remain loyal [12].

The aim of the study by Ambekar (2013) was to determine the influence of the five SERVQUAL dimensions on the service of the car repair shops in India. The study thus revealed a significant difference between expected and perceived service quality for private car owners. The reliability was the most expected factor and the tangibility the least expected factor. Perceived scores showed that assurance was best and empathy the worst [13].

The results for commercial car users were similar to that of the private owners (except tangibility, which was statistically insignificant). Ambekar came to the conclusion, that the private car owners have higher expectations of the service providers, since the cars are intended for personal use. The study has shown that despite the availability of modern, digital technology, reliability, responsiveness and empathy has to be desired. In order to improve these points, in particular the responsiveness, the technology and service process has to be improved [13].

The literature review raises the question of which technological developments can help to improve the car repair process to support mechanics and ultimately to be able to increase the quality of service. However, it is questionable which functions a technological support must contain and what barriers and obstacles could appear from the mechanic's perspective.

The filter production company Mann + Hummel, Ludwigsburg, and Hochschule Offenburg conduct an unique research project: The objective is to identify these barriers and obstacles in motor mechanics cognition of intelligent order assistant technologies. Several scenarios of such a system called AUTO-AL are proposed and tested in a representative survey in Germany.

The research focusses on the identification of the needed features of this AUTO-AL-system, like if it should be display-based, an eye-ware, or a speech interaction technology. Motorcar mechanics can use this system to reduce repair time, improve order quality, and facilitate a maintenance. They can do this without discontinuity in the process, e.g. the repairperson does not have to interrupt the repair work to leave the work place.

The motor mechanics do not have to use the computer in the office to search for detailed information about the specific car model and the needed spare parts. They just do the order process on the position, where the car is machined.

To understand the needs and expectations of the future users it is necessary to conduct an empirical study: Therefore Mann + Hummel and Hochschule Offenburg conducted an user inquiry with independent car repair companies in Germany.

4 Study: Evaluating the Acceptance Potential

In a survey among IAM garages with a return of n = 127 completely filled questionnaires, our research was focused on the acceptance potential and the identification of the needed features of such a digital order assistant called AUTO-AL.

The sample covered a wide range of different car repair service providers types, with 57.9% family business, 10.5% contract workshops, 3.0% franchising workshops, and 66.9% single company, whereby multiple answers were possible.

This also applies to the garages' number of employees. Our sample covered 49.2% with less than five employees, 36.4% from five to ten employees, 10.6% from eleven to 20 employees, and 3.8% with more than 20 employees.

In contrast to the SERVQUAL-studies mentioned above, we did not focus on the garages' customers and their evaluation of service quality, but on the car service providers and their employees. That means we evaluated AUTO-AL·as a service component to the garages themselves.

Consequently, the first question was, if AUTO-AL would in general be able to provide a service quality improvement from the workshops' point of view, and in more detail, if there is a basic relevance for such a system.

As there was neither such a system in use yet, nor a hypothetical system configuration – e.g. a prototype – given, we requested in a first row general expectations, importance, and wishes with the main goal to use them as indicators to the acceptance potential of such a system. Concretized to the SERVQUAL approach, there was only a measure of the expected quality, not of the perceived quality and trivially no measure of discrepancies. In general, the items were measured on a metric scale from one (e.g. completely unimportant) to six (e.g. very important).

As a first result, there is a clear potential to place a digital order assistant on the market. We detected room for improvement in the order process' efficiency, as the garages show a certain order frequency, 74% with three and more orders a day, whereby each order takes its time, 79.9% of the orders need more than two minutes. Additionally, 45% of the garages declared a return rate of more than 10%.

Concretizing the evaluation of AUTO-AL's basic relevance, a central item measured the expected importance of such a system's availability. Here, 60.3% classified the potential use of a digital order assistant at least as "rather important", that means with a value of at least four on the scale until six. Consequently, we conclude, that a general acceptance potential for such a system is given.

The further analysis aimed at detecting the essential SERVQUAL-dimensions from the car repair service providers' point of view with respect to the system service, in order to substantiate the acceptance potential deeper. The main goal of the study was to find an importance ranking of the digital order assistant's potential features.

In our questionnaire, specific items evaluated each dimension of SERVQUAL as follows:

As shown in Fig. 2, reliability is represented in the questionnaire by the item 'system stability'. The dimension 'responsiveness' is measured by the correspondent questionnaire item. Empathy is shown in the questionnaire as the items 'confidence generation' and 'reaction like a human being' among other items, which revealed less relevance, however. The questionnaire items 'type of device', 'usage by touchscreen', and 'text chat' cover the dimension tangibles. Finally, assurance is represented by the items 'checking part number' and 'adjustment of faulty insertion'.

Based on the percentages with an evaluation 'rather important or better', that means a value of at least four on the scale until six, the top-rated items determined the following ranking: adjustment of faulty insertion (92%), system stability (91.3%), responsiveness (91.1%), checking part number (87.4%), and confidence generation (86.4%) as you can see in Fig. 3.

Evaluated by the mean values of the corresponding items, the most important SERVQUAL-dimensions are in decreasing order: Reliability (mean 5.43), Assurance (mean 5.35), and Responsiveness (mean 5.21). There was a clear distance to Tangibles (4.16) and Empathy (3.4), see Fig. 4.

SERVQUAL-DIMENSIONS	MEASURED FEATURE(S)
Reliability	System stability
Responsiveness	Responsiveness
Empathy	confidence generation reaction like a human being (among other items, which revealed less relevance, however)
Tangibles	type of device usage by touchscreen text chat
Assurance	checking part number adjustment of faulty insertion

Fig. 2. SERVQUAL-Dimensions and measured features.

TOP-RATED ITEMS	PERCENTAGE IN CATEGORIES ≥ 4
Adjustment of faulty insertion	92.0%
System stability	91.3%
Responsiveness	91.1%
Checking part number	87.4%
Confidence generation	86.4%

Fig. 3. Top-rated AUTO-AL features

SERVQUAL-DIMENSIONS	MEAN VALUES (CORRESPONDING ITEMS)
Reliability	5.43
Assurance	5.35
Responsiveness	5.21
Tangibles	4.16
Empathy	3.40

Fig. 4. Importance of the five SERVQUAL-dimensions for car repair staff

Thus, the potential users prefer a system that supports the operative core process in the first instance. This result is supported by significant ($\alpha \leq 0.01$) correlations (positive values up to 0.74) between the top-rated SERVQUAL-items and corresponding items from a block evaluating the 'expectations on a digital order assistant', as e.g. 'should identify spare parts', 'should generate spare part's supplier list', 'should be able to take and send pictures', 'faster delivery', 'higher delivery quality', and 'simpler ordering'. Additionally, all these items show high mean values of above five.

Analogous results were found for a block evaluating 'obstacle items' such as 'usage needs more time', 'difficult to integrate', 'not desired by colleagues', or 'actual process already optimal' – negative correlations respectively.

Summarized, there is a clear acceptance potential for a digital order assistant indicating high expectations to the service delivery of a system like AUTO-AL. Actually, the focus lies on the process-oriented features. This seems to be a consequence of the fact, that the respondents do not yet use a corresponding system. They had to express their expectations, which were derived from the known operative process and its weak points.

Especially the tangible feature, which is a vital success factor, because it represents the interaction interface, shows an evaluation below average. Related to the digital order assistant's appearance, there is a clear trend towards familiar types of devices. 97% are familiar with devices of low, e.g. headset, or medium, e.g. smart phone or tablet, innovation level – and only 3% are familiar with devices of high innovation level, e.g. VR glasses. Basically, there were the same rates, 90% vs. 10%, for the favored order assistant's appearance.

However, in a more detailed investigation of this aspect, we conducted a cluster analysis with the digital order assistant's appearance items as cluster variables, which result in five clusters. Three of them shall be described in more detail. First, the 'standard cluster', where smartphone and tablet are overrepresented, and all other features are under-represented. This is conform to the mentioned trend towards familiar types of devices. Additionally, it was the largest cluster with 53.85%.

In contrast to this, there is a small group of 'fundamental denier' with 12.5%, where all items are under-represented. But, there is also a small cluster with 11.54%, where items related to a high-innovation level, e.g. VR glasses or smartwatches, are over-represented and items related to a low or medium-innovation level including smartphones and tablets are underrepresented. We conclude that there might be a potential need to differentiate the system.

Future work should focus on the presentation of a prototype system, in order to enable the users to evaluate the system support more fundamental. Complementary, some different configurations should be presented and be ranked by the potential users. Then, essential components can be detected by conjoint analysis measurement.

At last, we tried to get a hint to the potential improvement in customer satisfaction from the cr repair service providers' point of view as expected by AUTO-AL use. For this, we investigated the relationship between acceptance potential as well as the expected system's service delivery and the customer-related garage service quality in general.

We considered as central item 'expectation from AUTO-AL use related to the improvement in customer satisfaction'. As already described above, the most important SERVQUAL-dimensions were evaluated by the mean values of the corresponding items. A correlation analysis between these dimensions and the expected customer satisfaction showed significant ($\alpha \leq 0.01$) positive correlations of medium strength, as follows: Reliability (0.402), Assurance (0.424), and Responsiveness (0.451).

Of course, there are more than these three dimensions and the related items necessary, to determine user satisfaction. Nevertheless, the general tendency shows that the expected service quality of the system also implies service quality on the customers' side.

5 Recommendations

Mann + Hummel is able to develop their intelligent order assistant system corre-spondent to the users' requirements guided by the Hochschule Offenburg survey results. New options of order assistance can also offer new business models, like also supporting the do-it-yourself business with this system. Other companies from different branches can also use the intelligent order assistant system, like domestic appliance, shipping, or power station maintenance.

The system should base on current technologies like a tablet PC or smart phone. In this way, the interaction process between system and user is well known. The content access is familiar. So usage barriers are very low and easy to overcome.

Following four recommendations are the most important for the introduction and the future development of an AUTO-AL-system:

Recommendation 1: Established Devices
Car repair service providers are obviously very wary towards new intelligent tech-nologies: to find acceptance by the users a prototype of the system has to be familiar. The first offered device should be one, which is already well-known and in use by the car mechanics – at least in their private live – like a smart phone or a tablet PC.

Recommendation 2: Best Practice Interaction
Car mechanics have several digital technologies in use – but mostly for private applications. The usage of a touch display, a dialog with Siri or a chat via a messenger system is a daily routine. These are the patterns, AUTO-AL should be based on, especially in the launching phase of the new system.

Recommendation 3: Put Your Best Foot Forward
Future users wish a system, which helps to avoid mistakes. If the supporting intelligent order assistant is introduced in an imperfect stage, users will not accept it in the future. A "stupid" device is disappointing and wastes users' time. A system, which does not support to avoid mistakes, provides no sufficient help for the user.

Recommendation 4: Personal Instruction and Assistance
First introduction should include an individual training on the new service device. Users wish to understand, how this new intelligent order system can be used, and what they need to do to interact with AUTO-AL. Additionally, Youtube videos or chat functions could be helpful.

Our study showed, that in the introduction phase features like the search for suitable spare parts, order support and input check are the most relevant functions the systems should support. In respect of the user requirements based on DIN ISO 9241 110 the factors suitability for the task, conformity with user expectations, self-descriptiveness, controllability, and error tolerance could be identified as the most relevant for the AUTO-AL scenario. This needs to be taken into account in the application design process.

6 Conclusion

The initial assumptions regarding an AI/NVR-system deployment in a vehicle work-shop environment were confirmed through the conducted research. Provided, that a system works properly and is easy to use, the results showed a strong interest in an assisted intelligent ordering process by the car repair service professionals.

In order to become relevant and gain traction throughout the garage space, an industry-wide approach providing the required access to relevant service networks, could therefore add the necessary scale needed for system deployment and is recommended to other users.

Once installed, the AUTO-AL-system could support in other areas relevant for the garage, e.g. point of sales, technical support, administration, etc. For Mann + Hummel, this system could open up new value streams even outside of the traditional automotive parts segment and would support the company's shift towards being more agile and more digital and thus offering to the customer a much more service-oriented package.

7 Limitations and Future Work

Artificial intelligence and predictive maintenance are future technologies, which could enhance AUTO-AL's features: currently the challenge is to assure the car mechanics of the easement of workload using intelligent order assistants.

By the integration of expected and established functions and technologies in the AUTO-AL-system the first step to acceptance by the not-digital-affine target group of car repair service providers is taken. If the system becomes relevant to the user innovative concepts like voice control or augmented reality glasses can follow up.

The need for specific information can fulfill a structured database in the initial phase. The more familiar the user feels with the system, the more intelligence he or she wants the system to perform: for example, the system could identify the age or condition of a car part and predict the moment of repair exactly.

With artificial intelligence, the system could learn from analyzing the order processes of the users of a car repair company, what preferences they have, and automate sections of the order process. An intelligent system could support the car mechanics by searching relevant information about a car model and related problems or even one specific car by analyzing the repair history to solve technical problems faster.

There is a huge acceptance potential in the car repair industry in the future, although the current users cannot yet appreciate the "intelligent" features of AUTO-AL.

Especially, if the car manufacturers give open access to the car tracking databases, an interpretation of the data contents is without the support of intelligent algorithms no longer possible.

So, further research is necessary to identify the full acceptance potential for these types of systems not only for the car repair industry: also maintenance of other machines, like in production companies or household appliances could find a major market.

References

1. Wolk, A., Nikolic, Z., Aboltin, D.: The Car After Market in Europe, Bergisch Gladbach (2017)
2. Mueller, A.: Erfolgsfaktoren für Cross-Media-Publishing-Anbieter, Berlin (2009)
3. Kempf, S., Heid, B.: Ready for inspection – the automotive aftermarket in 2030 (2018)
4. http://www.europarl.europa.eu/news/en/press-room/20180326IPR00510/saving-lives-ecall-mandatory-in-new-car-models-from-this-week. Accessed 21 Dec 2018
5. Parasuraman, A., Zeithaml, V., Berry, L.: Alternative scales for measuring service quality: a comparative assessment based on psychometric and diagnostic criteria. J. Mark. **70**(3), 201–230 (1994)
6. Bruhn: Servicequalität. Konzepte und Instrumente für eine perfekte Dienstleistung (2013)
7. Parasuraman, A., Zeithaml, V., Berry, L.: A conceptual model of service quality and its implications for future research. J. Mark. **1985**(49), 4 (1985)
8. Parasuraman, A., Berry, L., Zeithaml, V.: A multiple-item scale for measuring customer perceptions of service quality. J. Retail. **1998**(64), 1 (1998)
9. Elistina, B., Naemah, A.: Consumers' perceptions on the service quality in the motor vehicle repair and service industry: an exploratory study in Klang Valley, Malaysia. Pertanika J. Soc. Sci. Hum. **19**(2), 409–422 (2011)
10. Izogo, E.: Customers' service quality perception in automotive repair. Afr. J. Econ. Manag. Stud. **6**(3), 272–288 (2015)
11. Lotko, A.: Measuring and assessment of the quality of motorcar maintenance and repair services with using the SERVQUAL model with regard to customer's profile. The Archives of Automotive Engineering – Archiwum Motoryzacji **77**(3), 51–62 (2017)
12. Kankam-Kwarteng, C., Acheampong, S., Amoateng, F.: Service quality and customers' willingness to pay for vehicle repairs and maintenance services. J. Sci. Res. Rep. **10**(5), 1–11 (2016)
13. Famiyeh, S., Kwarteng, A., Asante-Darko, M.: Service quality, customer satisfaction and loyalty in automobile maintenance services: evidence from a developing country. J. Qual. Maintenance Eng. **24**(3), 262–279 (2018)
14. Ambekar, S.: Service quality gap analysis of automobile service centers. Indian J. Res. Manag. Bus. Soc. Sci. **1**(1), 38–41 (2013)
15. DIN EN ISO 9241 110

Foundational UX Research—Process Best Practices

Alwyn Sekhri[✉]

Google LLC, 1600 Amphitheatre Pkwy, Mountain View, CA, USA
alwyn.sekhri@gmail.com

Abstract. The need to create a set of Process Best Practices specifically for Foundational User Experience (UX) Research becomes essential in driving an increase in the success of this type of research, and the continued positioning of UX Research as a strategic partner contributing to ongoing product strategy and business success. These Best Practices have been crafted by author's over 17 years of professional UX Research & Strategy experience across a variety of industries (medical, mobile, printing, IT) and companies (Baxter, Motorola, HP, Google); and they will continue to evolve as emerging technologies and new methodologies continue to impact the UX Research landscape. These foundational projects have varied in scope, depth, and objectives; however, the following of these Best Practices has remained consistent and contributed to many successful and impactful projects over the years. The results of these research projects have directly impacted entire business units, driven the future direction of product portfolios, pivoted product strategy, and created new business opportunities. The Process Best Practices described in this paper are designed to successfully guide a research practitioner step-by-step through a Foundational UX Research project from initiation through insight integration.

Keywords: User experience research · UX research ·
Foundational user experience research · Front end UX research ·
User research best practices · UX research process best practices ·
Design strategy

1 Background and Definitions

User experience (UX) researchers are tasked with investigating users and translating their behaviors, needs, motivations, and responses into appropriate and actionable insights relevant to a multitude of stakeholders. These investigations can take place across different stages of development utilizing different methodologies as deemed appropriate by different researchers. UX researchers start with the objectives or questions that need to be answered and then go through a complex multi-step process aligning the research type and methodologie(s) while incorporating a variety of dimensions from timelines and budgets to product priorities and business objectives.

In an ideal world once the research plan is created, there would be immediate and unilateral buy-in from all stakeholders, budgets would be limitless, time would not exist, research parameters would operate in lab-type settings under full control, and all

© Springer Nature Switzerland AG 2019
F. F.-H. Nah and K. Siau (Eds.): HCII 2019, LNCS 11589, pp. 126–140, 2019.
https://doi.org/10.1007/978-3-030-22338-0_10

insights would be immediately integrated into product strategy. Alas in the real professional world that most of us work in today, this is rarely if ever the case! A majority of our day-to-day activities center not around the actual creation of a solid research plan or even conducting the research itself; but rather in focusing on all of the *other* process steps involved including logistics, communication, coordination, stakeholder buy-in, awareness, education, and insight implementation. The well-known (and commonly associated) *usability studies* that a majority of our stakeholders understand do not typically demand this multitude of steps. It is when a larger ambiguous foundational project is initiated that the importance of implementing those aforementioned process steps really becomes critical in driving a successful foundational project. When using the term 'Foundational' it is important to take a step back and define what this means by distinguishing how it differs from other research phases while referencing the product development process. This differentiation will help to better explain the complexities (scope, timeline, output) involved when tackling a more ambiguous and larger foundational project as compared to other research projects. These research phases are not to be confused with Research *Methods* (Exploratory, Generative, Evaluative) as various methods or combinations of methods can be used during any UX Research Phase. The following three different research phases are author defined and referenced in this paper: Tactical, Strategic, and Foundational. Keep in mind that these definitions are focused on differentiating between the research phases with a goal of helping to identify when a project might fall into the 'Foundational' category. Variations of the names of each of these three phases might exist within different industries, UX teams, etc. The important thing to keep in mind are the distinguishing characteristics of each phase, potential output, and where along the product development process they fall (Fig. 1).

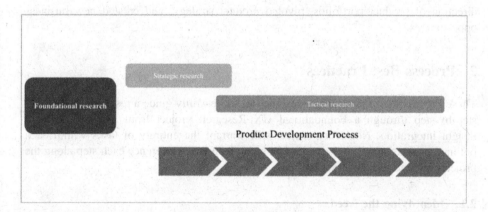

Fig. 1. Visual reference of each UX research phase as aligned with the product development process

Foundational research ideally takes place in the 'fuzzy' front end of development focusing on *attitudinal* and potentially *behavioral* aspect of users. Usually relationships with one or more larger focal areas (i.e. technology, commerce, devices, etc.) drive investigations with a variety of methodologies used. Some output examples of this phase might include personas, strategic frameworks, behavioral mappings, UX road-maps, etc.

Strategic research is usually conducted either prior or during early requirements gathering. Bounded by a portfolio, product, or solution, yet still focusing on deeper understandings of user needs while gathering initial high-level feedback on proposed ideas/concepts. Some output examples of this phase might include mental model development, critical user journeys, concept resonance, etc.

Tactical research tends to be ongoing starting once initial concepts and early designs are created and continues through increased fidelity until designs are 'locked.' Focused on moving from multiple potential experiences to one ideal experience through different types of research methods. Some output examples of this phase might include usability assessments, user preferences, human performance metrics, comparative design analysis, etc.

The need to create a set of proven guidelines, or Best Practices, specifically for the Foundational Research Process becomes essential in driving an increase in successful Foundational UX Research projects, and the continued positioning of UX Research as a strategic partner contributing to ongoing product strategy and business success. These Best Practices have been crafted by author's over 17 years of professional UX Research & Strategy experience across a variety of industries (medical, mobile, printing, IT) and companies (Baxter, Motorola, HP, Google); and they will continue to evolve as emerging technologies and new methodologies continue to impact the UX Research landscape. These foundational projects have varied in scope, depth, and objectives; however, the following of these Best Practices has remained consistent and contributed to many successful and impactful projects over the years. The results of these research projects have directly impacted entire business units, driven the future direction of product portfolios, pivoted product strategy, and created new business opportunities.

2   Process Best Practices

These Process Best Practices are designed to successfully guide a research practitioner step-by-step through a Foundational UX Research project from initiation through insight integration. Not every project will warrant the entirety of tasks within each outlined process step, however it is still recommended to reference each step along the project timeline to help ensure success.

2.1   Identifying the Need

Understand the Space. The first step is to begin to understand the larger space that a foundational project will impact from a design, technology, and business perspective. The time and effort this requires can vary depending on factors like topic familiarity, industry experience, etc. Even if prior work or projects (or even a thesis!) was completed in a space it is still important to take a step back and ensure up to date knowledge is being leveraged prior to the start of a foundational project. The technology industry as an example changes quite quickly as emerging technologies are being discovered and human computer interactions continue to evolve.

Create an Initial List of Questions. An important tangible result of this initial understanding is to create an initial list of ALL of the questions from each different perspective (design, technology, business) within the space. This can initially be from just the researcher's perspective or from other stakeholders/partners as well. At this point there is no maximum or minimum to the amount of questions or the simplicity or complexity of questions, as it is really a divergent phase of thinking. It is critical to capture any and all questions at this stage knowing that not all will be answered with just one foundational project, however it can help provide an initial layout of a multi-year plan of research within that larger space.

Begin Prioritization of the List of Questions. Now it is time to start dividing and conquering that initial list through a variety of tasks.

Performing an Intensive Literature Review is one of the most important tasks in understanding what questions might already be answered and to what extent. This should be done both internally (within your current company) as well as externally (outside of your company). Reading reports, conversing with colleagues, setting up time with people outside of your department, and other ways of gathering information should be used at this stage.

Internal reports and analysis can have more of an analogous business understanding associated with the work, while external references might have to be slightly extrapolated to be properly referenced. Also remember to look at how long ago some of these reports or work might have been completed. For some topics the knowledge may remain pertinent for a long time. For other topics, it may be necessary to re-answer a question or topic in order for it to be relevant (i.e. Market segmentation and Design Personas should be updated on a regular cadence depending on industry). At this stage an understanding of what questions have or haven't been properly answered should be clear.

Highlight Questions with Broader Behavioral or Attitudinal Aspects of a user or their relationship with topics relevant to the space. These questions can range from trying to understand ongoing user motivations, to holistically understanding a full day-in-the-life of a certain user group, to mapping out how/why/when users might interact with technology or product of interest.

2.2   Alignment and Buy-In

Disseminate the List. It is critical at this stage to ensure stakeholders are able to get up to speed on the prioritized list of questions and begin to provide their own perspectives. This can be accomplished in a number of ways depending on the number of stakeholders or company setup. Providing an editable digital copy for the team is always important to allow for time to digest and begin the addition of stakeholder questions. For certain projects it can also be important to hold an alignment meeting with key stakeholders to walk through the list of questions and begin to prioritize them. This will allow not only alignment but also buy-in from those stakeholders whose business needs your project will be addressing. Some will potentially become evangelizers of the work which is instrumental in helping to integrate the final insights as well as continuing to support and drive future Foundational UX Research projects.

Finalize Key Questions and Translate into Objectives. After gathering priorities from the different perspectives and stakeholders an important step is to align those foundational questions with top business objectives/goals for the quarter, year, upcoming year(s), etc. This could have already happened with initial stakeholder alignment, but if not, this really is a critical step for the researcher. Embarking on a foundational project will not be as successful or impactful if it does not relate to a larger business need. Focus at this stage on creating a *sweet spot* at the intersection of user + business needs. This will result in the insights and implications of the project really driving the design strategy.

Another important step at this stage is to translate those questions into UX Research objectives. You want to be very clear with the intent of the project and providing objectives is an effective way to do this. It is recommended (but not necessary) to use action verbs when highlighting these objectives (i.e. identify, discovery, understand, establish, etc.). Keeping in mind that multiple research *questions* might comprise a final research *objective* so be sure to organize and integrate the questions appropriately.

2.3   Kicking It Off

Once alignment has occurred it is time to start building momentum for this Foundational work. Identifying the 'core team' that will be contributing their time and energy is a critical first step. This should ideally be a cross discipline and cross functional group including key stakeholders (when possible) and potentially fellow researchers (depending on the size/scope of the work). This core team will also help to evangelize the work, as they will ideally be contributing to the project in some capacity from start to finish so choose wisely!

Scoping of timeline, budget, and resources is important in understanding the reality of how the project will progress. Not every foundational project will be the same size or require an enormous budget with a huge team. Global foundational projects typically require budget to help procure research vendor facilities (i.e. labs), recruiting, translation (for non-English speaking countries), etc. Non-global projects can also require vendor support; however, the amount of support might be less for a smaller project within just one region. Here are some initial scoping questions that have proved useful over the years:

- What is the total number of desired users for this project?
- When do the results of this research need to be delivered in order to appropriately impact the roadmap, portfolio, business, etc.?
- Does this research need to be run 'blind' (no user awareness of company) to prevent bias? [vendor support is needed]

- Does this research require a global vs. regional vs. local scale? Is the focus on developed versus emerging markets? (The industry, location of current + future users, and objectives should guide this question)
  - Example: Foundational research focused on understanding various aspects of how mobile technology permeates a user's life. Global understanding is important with locations in US, Europe, and Asia chosen although initial focus is only on developed markets.
- Is this research being run in locations where the primary language(s) of that location requires translation + moderation support? [vendor support might be needed]
- Does the timeline require running parallel locations simultaneously which then requires additional moderators, translators, and materials? [vendor support or more UX researchers might be needed]

Every company has a slightly different process for procuring vendors so making sure those processes are in place at this stage is critical if vendor support is needed. Ensure the project budget needs align with actual budget provided and escalate right away if there is a discrepancy. Finally, set an initial timeline thinking through everything from a kick-off through final report delivery and subsequent share-outs.

Kick-Off Meeting. Holding a kick-off meeting is a very successful best practice that is recommended not to be skipped. This meeting could include a larger audience than the identified core team (referred to as extended team), especially if some of the research objectives cross into different businesses. This is a great opportunity to ensure a holistic perspective has been taken in the question prioritization and to gather any relevant internal business information. This meeting will provide an opportunity for the core + extended team to meet each other while allowing the researcher to continue to build rapport and trust.

Background and Introductions are important in ensuring a common starting point is established while everyone gets to know one another. When different disciplines from different business units are gathered together it is a perfect opportunity for sharing of expertise and business goals. Don't assume that everyone in the room knows each other, but rather take the opportunity to help build relationships around your Foundational UX Research project.

Scope, Expectations, and Timeline. There may be stakeholders that have never participated in this type of research (or any UX research for that matter) who are unsure of what is involved with this type of project. This is an opportunity to educate on this type of research (foundational) and your expectations from them as either core or extended team members. Take the time to discuss the research objectives and initial timeline created so that expectations of when involvement is asked for throughout the year – keep in mind that many stakeholders are balancing multiple projects/priorities - so the farther in advance they know of activities the greater chance they can be active participants.

Brainstorming Session. A critical aspect within this meeting is to hold a brainstorming session that frames the research objectives and allows everyone to voice their specific questions most relevant or important to them. One very effective (and one of my favorite) brainstorming techniques is the use Post-its to help capture ideas/questions from each participant. After framing the objectives set aside 10–20 min for silent brainstorming as folks capture their thoughts on post-its. Take the next 20–40 min to have each participant share their post-its one at a time while placing them on a wall, whiteboard, or other common physical space in the room. This tried-and-true technique allows for group sharing of thoughts and the ability to build upon questions, ideas, or even hypotheses. At the end of the session the researcher should spend some time doing a cluster analysis of the post-its to identify any key themes or important topics that have evolved. Taking photos and translating the findings into a share-able format is also recommended for reference and team reflection.

(Remember to take photos during this kick-off meeting to capture data but also capture the collaborative nature of this process step)

Stakeholder Interviews. There are certain stakeholders that are not always able to participate in the official kick-off or it might not be appropriate based on their level of involvement. Sometimes certain stakeholders are acting more as executive sponsors of the research (Sr. Directors, VPs, SVPs, etc.) while others just might not have the bandwidth to full participate but are vested in the results. For these stakeholders, plan on 'interviewing' them by sharing the research objectives and capturing any specific questions, hypotheses, or expectations they have.

2.4 Planning the Logistics

This is an important time to pause and incubate on all of the collaborations, discussions, brainstorming cluster analysis, emerging themes, and stakeholder interviews. Some ongoing questions to ponder might include:

- Are the identified objectives still relevant to answering both user and business needs?
- Does the scope need to be tweaked or are there any missing stakeholder perspectives that have yet to be gathered?
- How is the proposed timeline in relation to core team participation?
- Are any key hypotheses beginning to emerge?

Choose UX Research Method(s). One of the most critical pieces of this entire process is choosing the correct method or combination of methods that will best answer the research objectives with the proper amount of rigor. This paper will not go into great detail on how that can be accomplished, as there are many resources written on that topic that can be referenced. My recommendations at this stage are to make sure enough time is taken to research the research! Reach out to fellow researchers both internally and externally for their input. Look to the past (dust off academic references for research methods) and future (read articles, blogs, attend a conference on emerging UX Research techniques) for inspiration. Think through past experiences and successful methods used. Any and all are encouraged to ensure proper alignment of objectives with research method(s).

Craft UX Research Plan. This will be the source of truth of all of the steps taken thus far and the constant reference of what will and will not be accomplished within this Foundational UX Research project. It should be the organized culmination of all information to date and should include the following:

- Project background (business landscape for the space, high level focus of project, references to past relevant research)
- Core + extended Team with contact information and role
- Research objectives
- Key Questions (this highlights the key questions that will feed into answering the objectives)
- Method(s) including details of location, high level participant criteria and overall rationale
- Timeline with a breakdown of each primary activity (Kick-off, Asset creation, Recruiting, In-field, Debriefs, Analysis, Report delivery, Share-outs)

In-Field—Signup and Best Practices. It is a good rule of thumb to adequately space out travel across different regions with 1 to 2 week breaks in between when possible (i.e. 2 week in-field break between US cities and European cities). It is not always reasonable for team members to be away from their other work responsibilities, family, or other commitments for extended periods of time, so please keep that in mind when scheduling all of the in-field work. Balancing the schedule with the amount of in-field participation is important. On the other extreme, there can be instances when working with a critical timeline can cause all locations to be back-to-back. If this is the case, ensure all team members are aware ahead of time and can plan accordingly.

For those foundational projects taking place across multiple cities or regions, it is recommended to have a sign-up sheet, so it is clear who is planning to attend what sessions and where. I would actually recommend this for every project with more than one location as it is a good way to keep track of the overall participation across different stakeholders. This sheet should list the dates, locations, and approximate times of sessions in each location. Including specific locations of sessions if a UX lab will be used can also help with planning travel logistics for hotel stays. Remember the capacity of each session may vary depending on the method chosen (ex. ethnography sessions should be kept to 2–4 total people versus in-lab study that can hold 20+ in the back room) so be sure to include the total number of allowable spots for each location. Remember that as the sole researcher your presence at every location is a critical part of the success of this foundational work. If you have multiple researchers supporting it can be easier to divide and conquer, although I would still recommend if this is your first Foundational UX Research project that you attend every location. Keep in mind you might not have to be at every *session* within that location but will still be responsible for running debriefs and championing the project along the way (continue reading to Sect. 2.5 In-Field below for more details).

Once there is an understanding of who will be traveling to each location, send out a some in-field best practices (list, packet, presentation, etc.) to ensure everyone knows what to expect. Again, keeping in mind, you might have stakeholders that have never participated in a project like this and will be unsure as to what to expect or how to act.

This is primarily needed for immersive research (in-home ethnographies, intercepts, field observations) as stakeholders will be in direct contact with end users. Some of these best practices might include:

- Refrain from wearing anything that could be deemed offensive, or with company logos (especially if running a blind study)
- Maintain an attentive body language during sessions
- Refrain from asking questions during a session until the researcher (or moderator) opens up the discussion to allow them
- Check with your researcher if bringing laptops vs. pen and paper is more appropriate
- Arrive at each destination a few minutes early with the ideal being to travel together as a team
- Don't take any photos in a user's home without making sure it is allowed first

2.5   In-Field

Roles & Responsibilities. Assigning every team member a role to play during each session provides a continued sense of active contribution as well as helping to maintain focus during longer (2+ hour) sessions. These roles may vary depending on the type of sessions (ethnographic vs. in-lab) and the number of stakeholders. Some roles might include pure notetaker, camera/audio setup and takedown, prototype prep, etc. These roles could be in addition to the ongoing capturing of notes (observations, reactions, questions, quotes, etc.). Please remember that the importance of note taking by each stakeholder is crucial in ensuring different perspectives are captured while in-field.

Debriefs. I have found the use of debrief sessions to be one of the most crucial activities conducted in-field. These sessions can happen at the end of each day in-field or after each individual session, depending on the type of research being conducted. The important thing is that they do happen in a timely fashion! I personally recommend holding debriefs after *each* session for ethnographic (or other more immersive techniques) where an in-lab study could go either way – after each session, or at the end of each day. These sessions allow the sharing of each stakeholder's observations and perspectives and should be viewed as the starting point for future analysis and synthesis. Some of my personal best practices include debriefing over food or caffeine breaks which help to naturally break up longer days in-field. Assume you will need about 30–60 min per debrief session depending on the number of stakeholders and complexity of sessions.

The structure of a debrief might vary but I recommend following something similar to the following (assuming each person has been capturing notes to some extent):

- Allow 5–10 min for each stakeholder (researcher/moderators included) to write down their top observations, notes, quotes, 'a-ha moments' etc.
  - Recommend using Post-its + Markers (i.e. Sharpie)
  - One idea/observation/quote per Post-it
  - Record participant number and location in the upper right or left of the Post-it (example: P3, Chicago)

- Allow each stakeholder time to share each of their Post-its to the group (rotating through the order of who starts after each session or debrief)
- Physically collect all Post-its at the end of each debrief
- Repeat as needed

Over the years I have found that in addition to these sessions I will also reflect at the end of each day and begin to jot down emerging themes, initial opportunities, cultural deltas, potential innovations, etc. I continue to track if future debriefs continue to support or oppose these initial perspectives as I find this greatly assists in upcoming synthesis.

Immersions. One of the benefits of conducting research in different areas of the world is the opportunity to fully immerse yourself in that culture. This can be directly related to your research objectives and specified within the UX Research plan, or it can be more of an ad-hoc series of activities. These immersions enrich the team's knowledge of that location and contribute towards building rapport among the core team. These shared experiences have a way of cementing team relationships and will prove vary valuable in the continued support of your Foundational UX Research project.

Let's say that you are doing Foundational UX Research in Hong Kong focused on understanding various aspects of how mobile technology permeates a user's life.

Specified Research. An example of a specified research immersion could be a shopping trip to the local mobile phone markets. This immersion could tackle the buying process of the mobile technology user journey specific to that market and would be in addition to specific user sessions planned in Hong Kong. For an immersion like this it should be organized in advance with native language speakers, clear goals for the immersion (i.e. successfully purchase 2 mobile phones), and transportation for the entire group of stakeholders.

Ad-hoc Activities. These might vary depending on the interest level and time in market with stakeholders. A trip to Victoria Peak to see the vast views of Hong Kong might be appropriate, or perhaps a visit to the Temple Street Night Market to sample local snacks and grab souvenirs. Try and understand interest in these activities prior to arriving in-field so that any needed reservations can be made ahead of time. Food immersions are one of my personal favorites (everyone has to eat) as it is a great way to indulge in a local culture.

2.6 Following Fieldwork

Now that all of the in-field travel has been completed (thousands of miles traveled, dozens of hotel stays, infinite coffee drinks, and hopefully hundreds of debrief Post-its) it is time analyze and synthesize all of the data into a cohesive story.

Project Debriefs. Once everyone has returned from field it is important to gather all in-field attendees in one room for some larger scale debriefs. These vary from the smaller in-field session debriefs in that the focus could be on the entire project, or for a specific region that just finished in-field work. As aforementioned, try to provide a week or two in between in-field regions, with the assumption of holding debriefs with all the stakeholders who attended that region (i.e. European debrief) *as well as* a final project debrief after ALL fieldwork has been completed.

These debriefs provide an opportunity for all those in-field attendees (present at one or multiple locations) to both share and learn while discussing different observations, findings, and initial insights. For smaller projects the entire core team could have attended all sessions, while for larger projects each team member could only have potentially participated in just one region. Regardless of the specific makeup, the primary goal of these gatherings should be to think holistically about the project and what has been discovered thus far. The structure of these sessions can vary depending upon project size and scope, but I typically recommend referencing the initial UX Research objectives, some key questions, sharing any initial themes/learnings, and then asking each team member to share some of the biggest take-aways from in-field. This step helps further probe on those emerging themes, opportunities, and insights tracked over the course of the project while allowing stakeholders to reiterate what was their biggest take-aways were.

Analysis Immersion. As a researcher and huge fan of immersions, I came up with this phrase to help describe the check-in with stakeholders completed in the midst of analysis. This should take place a few weeks (potentially longer depending on complexity) after project debriefs with a goal of sharing the progress made from an analysis and synthesis perspective. One of the reasons I call this an immersion is that I like to physically immerse stakeholders in my analysis and synthesis process. Some of the ways to accomplish this might include:

- Physically showcase all Post-its in their current state of cluster analysis
- Print out relevant in-field photos of users, homes, environments, etc.
- Print and post user scales (i.e. Likert Scale or Semantic Differentials)
- Showcase initial concept sketches

The physical placement of the different data gathered in-field shown in a mid-synthesis context is found to have a very powerful effect on stakeholders. It also provides a level of education while showcasing some of the very complex analysis processes many researchers go through with larger qualitative studies. I recommend providing all in-field attendees time to walk through the analysis immersion thinking through what they are seeing and how it relates to what they experienced while in-field. This is also an excellent time to take note of any missing focal areas voiced by stakeholders that they aren't seeing from the analysis as of yet. Repeat as necessary.

Initial Report Share-Out. At this stage you should be in process of compiling an initial layout of the report to be shared out and referenced (hopefully) for many years. The exact form this report may take can vary across projects, however an initial structure commonly seen may include sections like research objectives, methods, executive summary, literature review, insights, implications and opportunity spaces. In addition to your own critical assessment of the report, it is advantageous to have an initial report share-out with only those stakeholders (core team or extended) that have been heavily involved throughout the research process. These people have awareness of where the project started, the in-field work, multiple debriefs, and knowledge of the analysis process. They are an excellent audience to test out key insights and implications as well as giving feedback on the overall flow of the report. They should be able to provide a critical eye as well as supportive feedback which will only improve your final report.

Opportunity Brainstorming Session. This final step might be optional depending on the research objectives but still worth noting. If one of the outcomes of the foundational work is opportunity spaces, it can be worthwhile to hold some deep dive brainstorming sessions with specific core or extended team members. These sessions should be geared towards discussing the opportunity spaces with a focus on prioritization, relevance, potential solutions, etc. It is important to keep in mind that as a researcher it is part of our job to properly analyze and synthesize data in order to craft insights, implications, and opportunity spaces, however the further dissection of opportunity spaces can benefit from a collaborative approach with multiple disciplines with varying overall knowledge of the space.

2.7 Sharing the Story

Now the time has finally come to officially share the story. For every Foundational UX Research project completed to date, there has always been a report. This report is the culmination of all of the incredible work accomplished along the Foundational UX Research journey and provides the opportunity to tell that project's story. This paper won't go into best practices for report writing but I will always recommend referencing those initial objectives and critically looking at what you discovered and how you are conveying your insights, implications, and any potential opportunity spaces.

Craft Multiple Versions. One important lesson I've learned over the years is to plan on crafting multiple versions of this research story. One primary reason for this is tied into the different audiences and potential contexts that the story will be shared. Keep a 'master copy' which has ALL of the extensive details of every step along the project journey, which very few people might ever fully read. Create more of an executive summary report intended for those Senior Stakeholders (VPs, SVPs, Directors) as well as multiple other versions specifically tailored towards other specific audiences (engineers vs. product managers vs. marketing vs design). Finally, it is very important to create at least one version of the report that is optimized for presenting (as opposed to reading). This presentation version can sometimes require even more work than initially writing the report, so please remember not to take it lightly.

Include Next Steps. A very impactful ending to every story is including a 'Next Steps' section. This is an opportunity to ensure the learnings from this research project have a forward trajectory and set the proper expectations with stakeholders. There can be a large variety of next steps included in this section ranging from a specific project direction decided, to a next phase of research needed, to a timeline showcasing when different opportunity spaces should be investigated. The important thing to remember here is that just because the research has been completed does not mean the *impact* of this research is complete. Think critically about how the insights from the research align with business goals to showcase that interaction sweet spot of user + business perspectives.

Share with Diverse Audiences. Plan on beginning share-outs with those stakeholders directly involved with the research, or within business units or groups related to the topic. After those have been completed, try to reach out to different teams or business groups in your larger organization to schedule share-outs. Initially this might not feel very relevant, but you would be surprised how many different groups of people will be interested in learning about not only your findings, but the overall Foundational UX Research process. Just as it is important to create those stakeholders who will evangelize the research, it is also important to be your own evangelizer of your current work. Opportunities might arise to work cross functionally or cross-organizationally on a future Foundational Research Project as well as continuing to educate the larger community on the importance of these types of UX Research projects.

2.8 Maintain the Momentum

With the report and associated share-outs complete, it might feel like it is time to move onto the next project. At this stage the process could be complete for a smaller project, or for a project with more narrow objectives. For those projects with more ambiguous objectives and multiple resulting insights or opportunity spaces, there are a few more activities that can help to really drive your Foundational UX Research home.

'Next Steps' Prioritization Sync. After highlighting your proposed next steps in the report and potentially talking to them in a presentation, it is time to solidify the priority by bringing back together all relevant stakeholders. This is an opportunity to discuss what steps are realistic and in what timeframe according to your core and extended teams. Larger scale research can yield multiple implications and so it is important to realign from a business, technical, and design perspective to create a clear priority. Use this opportunity to integrate next steps directly into a quarterly business goals, product roadmaps, new portfolios, vision statements, etc.

Run a Sprint or Workshop. One very enjoyable post-report activity is bringing people together to deep dive on one of the learnings (insight, implication, opportunity space, etc.) from the project. Enough time has passed to incubate on learnings from those heavily involved with the UX Research and including fresh perspective from multiple disciplines is also highly recommended. I would recommend taking a prioritized learning (decided from the previous sync) and creating goals for the session based on what outcome would be most beneficial in moving that learning forward. As an example, if I am focusing on a prioritized opportunity space, I might run a Sprint tailored towards generating possible solutions using 'how might we' statements with a team of designers, engineers, product managers, and marketing teams.

Create Tangible Artifacts. This final momentum builder is not always possible or applicable but still something to ponder. At this stage try and think if there is a way to create any physical artifacts summarizing some key insights or learnings from your Foundational Research. Perhaps you created a framework, or day in the life mapping of an important target group that you could print out on a large poster and place in your workspace? Maybe design personas were a key output, and you create quick 'cheat sheet booklets' to be distributed to all team members (one of my personal favorites). Try to be creative at this stage remembering that there is something to be said about the power of physically taking up space when it comes to reminding those around us of key research learnings.

2.9   Reflection

We have finally reached the end of our Foundational UX Research Process which allows us to take a step back and reflect on the overall journey. This is a special last activity, because it allows the researcher to pause and focus on key highlights and lowlights of the project. There is no right or wrong way to do this as long as some time is spent in reflection. Some of the questions that are beneficial to ask might include:

- What 3 things went really well with this project?
- What 3 things did not go as smoothly with this project?
- What did I enjoy most on this project?
- What did I struggle most with on this project?
- What would I have done differently?
- What would I have done the exact same way?
- What did I learn about myself along this journey?
- Am I excited or leery about tackling another project like this?

As you are answering these, please record them while lightly categorizing where along the process these highs and lows fell, as sometimes patterns can emerge which helps pinpoint where some of your own strengths or weaknesses might lie. The focus of this reflection is to acknowledge the incredible work completed, and then add a lens of constant improvement knowing that it will only help you continue to improve upon your ability to successfully conduct these types of research projects.

3   Conclusion

In conclusion many steps and sub-steps have been outlined with the goal of helping any research practitioner successfully complete a Foundational UX Research project. As aforementioned, not every sub-step is necessary when conducting a project like this, however I strongly recommend following the larger step outline (2.1, 2.2, 2.3 etc.) ensuring some contributions from each are completed along the way.

These Process Best Practices are designed to be used across Foundational UX Research projects of varying size and scope from global to regional and developed to emerging markets. They were not created with just one specific research project in mind, but rather developed over many years taking various successes and lessons learned into account. If I were to summarize the key take-aways from this paper they would be as follows

- Communicate a clear story defining WHY the research is important to the user, the business, the industry, the company, etc. ensuring buy-in

- Drive stakeholder collaboration early and often to help educate and create forever ambassadors of the work
- Ensure all key stakeholders have directly contributed to the primary objectives or secondary questions of focus
- Be meticulous with your UXR Plan and use it as *the* source of truth
- Take advantage of time spent in-field with activities or immersions outside of the research sessions with your core/extended team
- Debrief, debrief, debrief
- Passionately tell the research story to as many people as you can get to listen
- Always continue the conversation utilizing your 'next steps' as a guide

I hope that you find these as useful as I did while compiling them, and that they serve as a guide in empowering you to effectively conduct your first or hundredth Foundational UX Research project.

Soccer Competitiveness Using Shots on Target: Data Mining Approach

Neetu Singh[1]($\boxtimes$), Apoorva Kanthwal[2], and Prashant Bidhuri[3]

[1] University of Illinois at Springfield, Springfield, IL 62703, USA
nsing2@uis.edu
[2] SEI Investments, One Freedom Valley Dr, Oaks 19456, USA
akanthwal@seic.com
[3] Enterprise Cloud Solutions, 600 Third Avenue, 2nd Floor,
New York, NY 10016, USA
prashant.bidhuri@eclouds.co

Abstract. This paper presents the model for the competitiveness of soccer matches played in the top four European soccer leagues. Every soccer match in every league holds some importance and contributes towards the overall performance of the league compared to other leagues. These individual results constitute a single season. A lot of aspects of a team and a season are attributed to their final positions in the league. These positions, however, do not detail the competitiveness of a single match. This research aims to highlight the competitiveness in each match without any relation to how the season may have ended. A match gives out a lot of details towards how it was approached by a team. A win may not constitute competitiveness, but the approach does. The idea is to look at individual statistics of a match and use them to construct a model using SEMMA approach of data mining, that classifies the matches based on how competitive they were. This research constructs various models for classification as each model provides its own variant based on the different methodologies used in the individual models. Our analysis is mainly depended on, but not limited to, the number of attempted shots on goal and on the number of those shots that were on target. An important characteristic of the attempts on goals is that they are subjective to the performance of a team and its ability to try and secure a win in a match. This performance formulates competitiveness which is the basis of our research.

Keywords: Competitiveness · Data mining · Shots on target ·
Performance evaluation · Misclassification rate

1 Introduction

Competitiveness in sports, especially in leagues, is often characterized as a measure of the toughness of the sport. Sports leagues throughout the world have multiple measures of competition and success. In soccer, a team's success in the league is determined by the points scored at the end of a season. These points are a total of the points accumulated based on the result of each match, where a win gives 3 points and a draw gives 1 point. The difference between these points and a team's league position at the end of a

© Springer Nature Switzerland AG 2019
F. F.-H. Nah and K. Siau (Eds.): HCII 2019, LNCS 11589, pp. 141–150, 2019.
https://doi.org/10.1007/978-3-030-22338-0_11

season is considered as the level of competition during that season, which are some measures of competitive balance used in sports [1]. This research is focused more towards the competitiveness of each match played in the top 4 soccer leagues of Europe and not the inter-league competitiveness which is one of the main reasons why the measure of 'competitive balance' was not considered to measure the competitiveness in the study. The different approach to the competitive analysis led to the research question: "How competitive are matches in Top European Leagues?".

Competitiveness of a soccer match can be based on many factors such as possession of the ball, chances created, total goals scored, total shots attempted. Although crucial to a soccer match, the total points accumulated, the final position in the league, or number of goals scored provide a singular approach to measure competitiveness [2]. An important statistic in a team's attacking prowess is the number of shots on target that team attempted in a match. Combining the total shots on target of the two teams in a match gives the information about how much both teams attacked in a match. The difference of these shots on target by both teams gives the actual difference of the level of performance of both the teams in a match. As, this research is not focused on the outcome of a match or a season, but the performance of individual matches.

Another reason for this approach is because, in soccer, and in any team sport, a team that dominates the match in terms of statistics may not always have the result in their favor at the end of the game. Due to which, the number of goals or number of points were not considered as a measure of competitiveness. Significant research has been done in competitiveness in soccer in Europe using competitive balance and many other factors [1]. However, extant literature does not emphasize on competitiveness in soccer matches based on difference between shots on target.

2 Literature Review

Competitiveness in sports often give rise to a term called "Competitive Balance". It assesses the wins of teams within a season and performance within a team [1]. Although it is great for percentages and numbers, it only gives out competitiveness of leagues with respect to the teams playing in it [3]. Lower the balance, bigger the difference between stronger and weaker teams. What is usually missed out in this comparison is the competitiveness of each match played in these soccer leagues. A single strong team can alter the competitive balance of a league if it is far superior to the other teams. But that does not necessarily mean that the rest of the teams are not equally competitive amongst themselves.

Additionally, the competitive balance measures the competitiveness within a season. One single season does not define a league or a team. Consistency matters in sports and that's what defines the strength or weakness in a league. As Brad [3] concludes by providing his alternative solution to competitive balance, "CBR: This computationally simple statistic scales average team-specific variation in won-loss ratio during a number of seasons by the average within-season variation in won-loss percentage during the same period", the gap remains on measuring competitiveness based on the way the matches were played and not the outcome.

Other methods devised to measure competitiveness in soccer follow the age old competitive balance where the competitive balance was either used as the base to formulate a different method of measurement [4, 5] or there are attempts to overcome the shortcomings of the original method [6]. The method used in this research attempts to provide the measurement of competitiveness in European soccer a new approach in this field of study.

While researchers argue the frailties of the older method, few have provided ways to measure competitiveness of each match played over the years in the top European leagues. This research attempts to fill that gap with the method of measuring the difference between shots on target of two teams in each match played over the period of 12 years in the top European leagues.

However, newer methods have started to come up in the measurement of competitiveness. The most notable being the "Situational Score Line" devised by Wibowo [7]. He proposes two new methods to consider the outcome of a match apart from the score line:

- Away Rating: The impact of performances of a team in away matches to negate home field advantage.
- Opponent Rating: Quality of the opponent team in a match.

Another method to measure teams' performances in soccer was used by Julen [8] by comparing the statistics of matches played between teams to identify the success of teams playing in the football world cup. Although, the intended outcome was not competitiveness, it emphasizes the importance of individual match statistics.

This research employs similar methodology in the way that it uses match statistics of over 17000 matches played over the period of 12 years in the top four European leagues, but the intended outcome is not to measure success, but to measure competitiveness.

3   Data Analysis

The data was acquired from the website 'Football Data' which contains details of football matches being played in all European soccer leagues. Finding a data set that is in multiple formats, locations and files is an obstacle that is most common with researchers and analysts [9]. We collected information of matches of top 4 European leagues, English Premier League, German Bundesliga, Italian Serie A and Spanish La Liga. The initial sample consisted of data between 2000 and 2017.

The data set included 64 variables, out of which 42 were the betting odds of each match, hence we excluded those from the data set completely. Keeping in mind the main focus of analysis was to analyze competitiveness, we also excluded the count of penalty yellow cards and red cards given by the referee during the match as these do not factor in when considering competitiveness of a match in terms of game play. The final sample had 22 variables which included some derived variables as well with 17030 records.

3.1 Data Cleaning

The data gathered for the analysis is generally raw form of data that has lots of discrepancies including but not limited to missing and inconsistent values. Data set like this can lead to misdirected analysis, false conclusions and biased results. The data errors are mainly caused by mistakes in data entry, different methods of measurement used, integration errors etc. [10]. There are two types of data quality problems, single source problems and multi-source problems and both types were encountered in the data. In case of single source problem, duplicate rows were deleted, and null values were removed. In case of multi-source problems, the inconsistencies like extra columns were removed. The data was formed by combining multiple files into one and some additional fields had to be removed to keep the dataset consistent. The data obtained from a European website and hence needed date format corrections as well.

3.2 Data Preparation

Once the data is cleaned and the formats are uniform and appropriate, the next stage is preparing the data to get the best result out of the available data. Data preparation is a pre-requisite for successful data mining process and it has been generally seen that data preparation takes up 80% of the total time in analysis [11]. The different steps involved in data preparation were, extracting appropriate data, checking integrity of data, integrate data, create new variables if required [12]. Another important part of data preparation is preparing the score data. In this case 20% of the total data was used as score data. Score data included data from all the four leagues to maintain the homogeneity of the data. 52 different csv files containing one soccer season each from each league were collected and then command prompt was used to successfully combine data set into one csv file.

3.3 Variable Selection

In any kind of data analysis, once the data is cleaned and prepared the next step involves selecting the variable that will be used for the analysis. Identification of the appropriate predictors and the target variable is of utmost importance [13]. The variable selection will determine the results of classification, prediction and data analysis [14]. As explained before, as to why shots on target is an important factor in determining competitiveness, DST (Difference between shots on target) was the first choice of target variable. While exploring the dataset we observed wide range of values for DST ranging from 0 to 21. It would have been difficult to make a list of the values and then determine the result based upon these values. Thus, the values were categorized into '0' and '1'. The value of DST from 0 to 5 was categorized as '0' being the most competitive and the value of DST 6 or greater than 6 was categorized as '1' being least competitive. Categorizing the DST values into 0 and 1 had the advantage as it made the target variable binary. The values '0' and '1' were in the variable 'Class' which is a derived variable. Observing the variables DST and Class, they came out to be highly collinear as Class was derived from DST. To benefit the analysis, the variable DST was rejected, and Class was selected as the target variable. One of the cases in multi-collinearity is when two variables are correlated and could lead to greater standard errors. More indifferent results are possible by avoiding collinearity, thus, it was important to reject and select the appropriate variables [15].

3.4   Data Mining Techniques

The SEMMA (Sample, Explore, Modify, Model, and Assess) data mining approach is used to develop the classification model using SAS® Enterprise Miner. The choice of model/technique depends on many factors such as how big the data is, type of target and predictors, and also on the end result that we are looking forward to i.e. whether we are trying to classify or predict in our analysis [16]. Based on the type of data that is selected there are two types of techniques that can be used to analyze the data, namely supervised learning technique and unsupervised learning technique [17]. When we consider supervised learning techniques, we are already aware of the various groups that exist (target variable is known), and this information is used for the analysis. Whereas, in unsupervised learning technique such as clustering we have no information about the target variable and try to look for patterns [18].

As our target variable is 'Class' which has two categories '0s' and '1s' and our predictors were continuous (interval variables), our analysis fits in the category of supervised learning technique with categorical response and continuous predictors. We decided to use three techniques which are Logistic Regression, Neural Networks, and K-Nearest Neighbors (Memory Based Reasoning) for the analysis of our data set.

Regression because of its flexibility in application is most widely used analysis technique. Further using logistic regression, it is possible to represent the chances of target variable falling in one category or class as compared to the other [19]. As we have a categorical target variable 'class' and we are trying to classify the percentage of matches of European League which fall in the respective classes '0' and '1', thus logistic regression with the help of iterations helps in identifying the predictors that will have the maximum likelihood of identifying the desired outcome. For Logistic regression we developed exhaustive regression, forward regression, backward regression, and stepwise regression.

The second technique that we used was Neural Networks. It is also known as Artificial Neural Networks and is one of the techniques that is used for classification and prediction. As neural network tries to understand and mimic how the human brain works, so it is possible to train a neural network efficiently thereby using it for pattern recognition and problem solving [20]. Neural network consists of input node, output node, hidden layers, and the weights are determined for the networks. Iterations keep improving the knowledge of the neural network thereby helps in giving nearly accurate predictions [21]. Neural networks have some disadvantages, with the main disadvantage being the inability to explain the networks and their relationships [22]. Hence, to avoid this black box problem, we also used a decision tree model to compare with the neural network models. We used Neural Network with hidden units as 3 named 'Neural' and second with hidden units as 5 and named it as 'Neural 2'. The decision tree node was also kept to default as it was added to avoid the black box problem because of the ease of interpretation of the leaf nodes of the decision tree model.

Apart from logistic regression and neural networks, K-Nearest Neighbors also known as Memory Based Reasoning is used for the analysis. By using this technique with the help of mathematical formula like Euclidean distance it is possible to determine the k nearest neighbors, and class having majority is put under the values of k determined [18]. By using this technique, we can find k records in the training data set which are identical to the records that we are trying to do classification for [16]. All the above-mentioned techniques helped us in analyzing our data and gave an insight how the various predictors were affecting the target variable which is 'class'. MBR was developed for two different values of K $(K = 16 \ and \ K = 7)$.

When the target variable is categorical in nature then one of the factors on which the models or techniques are compared is misclassification rate of the validation data set. If misclassification is high in the model it makes the analysis bias and also the statistical efficiency of the model is reduced [23]. To see that whether the model is performing good or bad we compared the misclassification rate of validation data set with the baseline misclassification [24]. This baseline misclassification also referred to as the naïve rule helps to examine how well the model is performing [16]. Thus, it is important to calculate the baseline misclassification rate, which in our case is 17.47%. In addition, Receiver Operator Characteristics (ROC) curve is used to evaluate the performance of our classification models. To further our analysis, final model comparison was conducted where the best models out of all the three techniques were compared to obtain the overall best model.

4   Results and Discussions

After model comparison Memory Based Reasoning with $K = 7$ turned out to be the best model with misclassification rate of 0.069094 or 6.9%, which is also less than the baseline misclassification rate of 17.47%. Thus, this also supported that the model was performing better than the baseline misclassification. Also, misclassification rate of neural network also improved to 0.079272 or 8%, and for logistic regression (stepwise) the misclassification rate was 0.138188 or 13.8%. The accuracy of the best model came out to be 93.09%, and ROC curve (Fig. 1) was further used to see how well the model is performing. As it is the graph plotted between true positive and false positive so more the graph is towards the upper left (towards true positive) better is the model. From the ROC curve shown in Fig. 1 it is evident that the model performs best for Memory Based Reasoning (MBR).

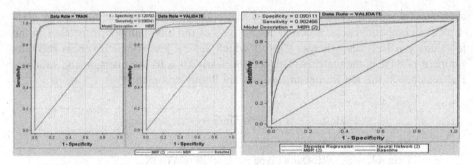

Fig. 1. Receiver Operator Characteristics (ROC) for model performance

Therefore, with final model comparison and taking all parameters into consideration Memory Based Reasoning with k = 7 came out to be the best model for our
analysis.

The classification chart for the best model MBR (k = 7) with target variable 'class'
was also plotted to further see how well the model classified, which in our case is the
percentage of matches which fall in class '0' which is competitive and class '1' un-
competitive. The classification chart for the two classes is shown in Fig. 2.

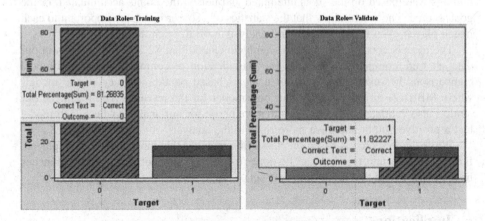

Fig. 2. Classification chart for MBR (k = 7)

The graph depicts that in target class 0, the total percentage is 81.26 which shows
that the competitiveness is more as class 0 depicts more competitiveness. Similarly,
target class 1, shows 11.82% of the matches fall under this category. This class 1, in our
case is less competitive. It can also be summed as; that for class '0', the model classifies
81.26% of matches as competitive, and on the other hand for class '1', 11.82% of
matches are classified as non-competitive by the MBR model.

We wanted to conduct extensive analysis, so we decided to score our data and used
20% our main data as score data. The results obtained after scoring also validated our

analysis. The results (Table 1) depicted that class 0, which in our case is the class depicting competitiveness, accounts for 82.15% of the total number of matches in the top European Leagues, whereas Class 1 which depicts less competitiveness accounts for mere 17.84% of the matches. This results clearly answers our question and validates that matches in the top European Leagues are highly competitive.

Table 1. Class variable summary statistics output

Class variable summary statistics				
Data role = SCORE Output type = CLASSIFICATION				
Variable	Numeric value	Formatted value	Frequency count	Percent
I_Class	.	0	2795	82.1576
I_Class	.	1	607	17.8424

5 Conclusion

This research offers a new dimension to the measurement of competitiveness in soccer. The variables used in the research have been used in previous research, but the target variable used has not been used in classifying competitiveness in soccer before. The findings were based on the shots attempted and not on the points accumulated, or the goals scored. The results show that the statistics of a soccer match are important to each match played even if the research and analysis have different targets.

The models constructed in the research concluded that 82% of the matches in our data set were competitive based on the classification of competitiveness. The model comparisons however, improved our analysis based on the accuracy of the models where MBR (2) turned out to be our best model for the research. The results of our models also validated the techniques that we chose for our analysis where each model had a positive output and gave more rigor to the analysis.

While this research is based on classifying matches that have already been played, further research into the data can be done to forecast competitiveness of the matches between the teams that are in this data set.

6 Implications

Competitiveness in soccer matches is rarely done based on matches. The general discussion of competitiveness has been taking place based on domestic leagues. This comparison, although extensive, is done using "Competitive Balance", which is a common method to compare competitiveness in team sports. We recommend that "Difference Between Shots on Target" should also be considered as an important factor in assessing competitiveness.

This research also adds "Shots on Target" as a new dimension to the debate of determining competitiveness in soccer. Any future research on the topic should keep in mind that there is big difference in a final outcome of a match and how a match actually unfolds. Predefined factors such as points, goals and league standings will predict outcomes but cannot tell the actual story of the match, which we believe our methodology of analyzing a soccer match will. Teams who have played other teams previously can predict the approach of their opponent based on the previous level of competitiveness in matches between them and assert the competitiveness of the upcoming match with that team and strategize for accordingly.

References

1. Pawlowski, T., Christoph, B., Hovemann, A.: Top clubs' performance and the competitive situation in European domestic football competitions. J. Sports Econ. **11**(2), 186–202 (2010)
2. Jessop, A.: A measure of competitiveness in leagues: a network approach. J. Oper. Res. Soc. **57**(12), 1425–1434 (2006)
3. Humphreys, B.R.: Alternative measures of competitive balance in sports leagues. J. Sports Econ. **3**(2), 133–148 (2002)
4. Criado, R., García, E., Pedroche, F., Romance, M.: A new method for comparing rankings through complex networks: model and analysis of competitiveness of major European soccer leagues. Chaos **23**(4), 043114 (2013)
5. Owen, P.D.: Limitations of the relative standard deviation of win percentages for measuring competitive balance in sports leagues. Econ. Lett. **109**(1), 38–41 (2010)
6. Eckard, E.W.: The NCAA cartel and competitive balance in college football. Rev. Ind. Organ. **13**(3), 347–369 (1998)
7. Wibowo, C.P.: Clustering seasonal performances of soccer teams based on situational score line 1, vol. 1, no. 1, May 2016
8. Castellano, J., Casamichana, D., Lago, C.: The use of match statistics that discriminate between successful and unsuccessful soccer teams. J. Hum. Kinet. **31**, 139–147 (2012)
9. Brown, J.G.: Using a multiple imputation technique to merge data sets. Appl. Econ. Lett. **9**(5), 311–314 (2002)
10. Hellerstein, J.M.: Quantitative Data Cleaning for Large Databases. United Nations Economic Commission for Europe, February 2008
11. Zhang, S., Zhang, C., Yang, Q.: Data preparation for data mining. Appl. Artif. Intell. **17**(5/6), 375 (2003)
12. Refaat, M.: Steps of data preparation. In: Data Preparation for Data Mining Using SAS. Morgan Kaufmann, San Francisco (2007)
13. Bagherzadeh-Khiabani, F., Ramezankhani, A., Azizi, F., Hadaegh, F., Steyerberg, E.W., Khalili, D.: A tutorial on variable selection for clinical prediction models: feature selection methods in data mining could improve the results. J. Clin. Epidemiol. **71**(Supplement C), 76–85 (2016)
14. Trappenberg, T., Ouyang, J., Back, A.: Input variable selection: mutual information and linear mixing measures. IEEE Trans. Knowl. Data Eng. **18**(1), 37–46 (2006)
15. Yoo, W., Mayberry, R., Bae, S., Singh, K., (Peter) He, Q., Lillard, J.W.: A study of effects of multicollinearity in the multivariable analysis. Int. J. Appl. Sci. Technol. **4**(5), 9–19 (2014)
16. Schmueli, G., Bruce, P.C., Patel, N.R.: Data Mining for Business Analytics, Third. Wiley, Hoboken (2016)
17. Asheibi, A., Stirling, D., Sutanto, D.: Analyzing harmonic monitoring data using supervised and unsupervised learning. IEEE Trans. Power Delivery **24**(1), 293–301 (2009)
18. Baxter, M.J.: A review of supervised and unsupervised pattern recognition in archaeometry. Archaeometry **48**(4), 671–694 (2006)

19. Stoltzfus, J.C.: Logistic regression: a brief primer. Acad. Emerg. Med. **18**(10), 1099–1104 (2011)
20. Boritz, J.E., Kennedy, D.B., De Miranda e Albuquerque, A.: Predicting corporate failure using a neural network approach. Int. J. Intell. Syst. Account. Finan. Manag. **4**(2), 95–111 (1995)
21. Ince, H., Aktan, B.: A comparison of data mining techniques for credit scoring in banking: a managerial perspective. J. Bus. Econ. Manag. **10**(3), 233–240 (2009)
22. Tsai, C.-F., Chiou, Y.-J.: Earnings management prediction: a pilot study of combining neural networks and decision trees. Expert Syst. Appl. **36**(3), 7183–7191 (2009). Part 2
23. Barron, B.A.: The effects of misclassification on the estimation of relative risk. Biometrics **33**(2), 414–418 (1977)
24. Kayhan, V.O.: SAS Enterprise Miner Exercise and Assignment Handbook for Higher Education, Second. Valor Onur Kayhan (2016)

Recommendation as a Service in Mergers and Acquisitions Transactions

Yu-Chen Yang[1]([✉]), Yi-Syuan Ke[1], Weiwei Wu[2],
Keng-Pei Lin[1], and Yong Jin[2]

[1] National Sun Yat-Sen University, Kaohsiung, Taiwan
ycyang@mis.nsysu.edu.tw
[2] The Hong Kong Polytechnic University, Hung Hom, Hong Kong

Abstract. Mergers and acquisitions (M&A) happens frequently between corporations to combine and/or transfer their ownerships, operating units and assets. The purpose of the study is to develop a service that is able to recommend a feasible M&A deal. We integrate the support vector machine model with the kernel tricks to automatically determine M&A deals. In the end of the study, our proposed technique is empirically validated, and the results show the effectiveness of the recommendation service.

Keywords: Mergers and acquisitions · Machine learning ·
Support vector machine · Financial kernel · Recommendation service

1 Introduction

Mergers and acquisitions (abbreviated M&A) happens frequently between corporations to combine and/or transfer their ownerships, operating units and assets. The major objective of M&A is to improve companies' financial and operating performances with potential synergies, such as market share, profits, economies of scale, influence in the industry etc. Thomson Reuters reports that the value of worldwide M&A deals in the first nine months of 2018 reached $3.3 trillion, increased by 39% from 2017, and almost half of the deals worth more than $5 billion[1]. Thomson Reuters also shows that the largest M&A market is in the United States, following by Europe, Asia Pacific, Japan, and Africa-Middle East[2]. The volume of global M&A is continuing to grow rapidly, and M&A is one crucial trend of business behavior.

The purpose of the study is to develop a service that is able to recommend a feasible M&A deal. We propose the recommendation service integrating with the support vector machine (abbreviated SVM) model. Prior studies attempt to use various techniques of machine learning to evaluate a M&A firm, for example, logistic regressions (Meador et al. 1996; Pasiouras and Gaganis 2007), rule induction (Ragothaman et al. 2003), neural networks (An et al. 2006) and decision tree (Yang et al. 2014) etc. However, few studies implement the support vector machine (abbreviated SVM)

---

[1] https://www.ft.com/content/b7e67ba4-c28f-11e8-95b1-d36dfef1b89a.
[2] https://www.nytimes.com/2018/07/03/business/dealbook/mergers-record-levels.html.

© Springer Nature Switzerland AG 2019
F. F.-H. Nah and K. Siau (Eds.): HCII 2019, LNCS 11589, pp. 151–159, 2019.
https://doi.org/10.1007/978-3-030-22338-0_12

algorithm as M&A recommendation models. Comparing with the above models, the SVM model is very efficient for binary classification, including quickly finding hyperplanes to separate data and shorter training time (Cristianini and Shawe-Taylor 2000). Furthermore, our work incorporate three different kernels, including a Gaussian kernel, a polynomial kernel (Cristianini and Shawe-Taylor 2000) and a financial kernel (Cecchini et al. 2010). Finally, prior studies such as Yang et al. (2014) provide a novel technique to evaluate the M&A deals, but they only work on the Asia Pacific market, which may not be representative of the whole M&A markets. The study focuses on the major market, that is, the United States, and we will validate the proposed recommendation technique in M&A transactions in the U.S.

The remainder of the paper is organized as follows. Section 2 lists the related work to our study. Section 3 formulates the proposed M&A forecasting model based on the integration of SVM and kernels. Section 4 presents the evaluation of the proposed technique. Finally, the conclusions and possible directions for future research are provided in Sect. 5.

2 Related Work

We will present the two major related works in the section. First, we review the related studies of M&A recommendation techniques. Second, the SVM model and the kernel methods are introduced. The proposed service model is based on the combinations of SVM and kernels.

2.1 M&A Recommendation

The popular analysis techniques applied to developing M&A recommendations/predictions include logistic regression (Meador et al. 1996; Pasiouras and Gaganis 2007), rule induction (Ragothaman et al. 2003), and decision tree (Yang et al. 2014). First, logistic regression is the most common model. Meador et al. (1996) use logistic binary regression analysis to examine the accounting, financial, and market variables to predict the M&A target companies as well as horizontal and vertical subsamples of merged companies over the period 1981 to 1985. Their model shows the strongest predictive ability for horizontal acquisitions. Pasiouras and Gaganis (2007) also employ the model of logistic regression to examine the financial characteristics of Asian banks during the period of 1998 to 2004. They further indicate that high asset risky portfolios and high liquidity increase the probability of being involved in an acquisition. Ragothaman et al. (2003) apply the techniques of artificial intelligence (AI)-based rule induction to identify acquisitions targets. Decision tree is a new application in the section of M&A. Yang et al. (2014) propose a M&A prediction technique that incorporates a comprehensive set of technological indicators, the technological profiles of both the bidder firm and a candidate target firm. Different from prior studies, they derive some technological indicators derived via patent data analyses. The work of Yang et al. (2014) is the latest study that explores the M&A predictions so far. We will extend their work and the related indicators in the study.

2.2 Support Vector Machine and Financial Kernels

The support vector machine is a popular classification method created by Vapnik and colleagues (Boser et al. 1992; Cortes and Vapnik 1995; Cristianini and Shawe-Taylor 2000). Sometimes, we may have to deal with high-dimensional feature space. In order to reduce the dimensionality, some techniques can be employed, and one of the popular techniques is "kernel methods" – providing a powerful tool for learning non-linear relations with a linear machine. The basic philosophy is that a certain type of similarity measure, i.e. a kernel, maps the data set into a high-dimension feature space, in which linear methods are used for learning and estimation problems. We use the symbol K to represent a kernel matrix such that $K(\mathbf{u}, \mathbf{v}) = \langle \phi(\mathbf{u}), \phi(\mathbf{v}) \rangle$, where $\phi : X \to F$ means an implicit mapping ϕ from an input attribute space X onto some feature space F, and $\mathbf{u}, \mathbf{v} \in X$. A kernel matrix K is required to satisfy these conditions: symmetric, positive semidefinite, and the Cauchy-Schwarz inequality (Cristianini and Shawe-Taylor 2000).

Several common types of kernel functions are listed in Cristianini et al. (2002) and the number is ever growing. One typical example is the polynomial kernel, which is defined as $K(\mathbf{u}, \mathbf{v}) = (K_1(\mathbf{u}, \mathbf{v}) + R)^d$, where $K_1(\mathbf{u}, \mathbf{v})$ is the normal inner product kernel, d is a positive integer, and R is fixed. Another typical example is the Gaussian kernel (or called the radial basis function kernel): $K(\mathbf{u}, \mathbf{v}) = \exp\left(\frac{\|\mathbf{u} - \mathbf{v}^2\|}{2\sigma^2}\right)$, where σ is a free parameter and determines the width of the kernel.

Cecchini et al. (2010) propose a useful financial kernel to determine management fraud. The financial kernel is denoted as $K_F(\mathbf{u}, \mathbf{v})$ and computes all ratios of input attributes as well as year-over-year ratio. It begins with n attributes and produces $3n(n-1)$ features, which can be broken into six feature types. The mapping ϕ is represented as:

$$\phi(\mathbf{u}) = \left(\frac{u_{i1}}{u_{j1}}, \frac{u_{j1}}{u_{i1}}, \frac{u_{j2}}{u_{i2}}, \frac{u_{i2}}{u_{j2}}, \frac{u_{i1}u_{j2}}{u_{j1}u_{i2}}, \frac{u_{j1}u_{i2}}{u_{i1}u_{j2}} \right)', i, j = 1, \ldots, n, \quad i < j.$$

The financial kernel is also working on other financial analyses even though initially it is proposed for detecting management fraud. We are following the work of Cecchini et al. (2010) and apply the financial kernel into the M&A recommendation.

3 The Proposed Recommendation-as-a-Service Technique in M&A Transactions

In the section, we detail the design of our proposed recommendation-as-a-service technique in M&A transactions. Following the work of Yang et al. (2014), we replace the forecasting technique with the SVM model integrated with a Gaussian kernel, a polynomial kernel, or a financial kernel presented by Cecchini et al. (2010). Figure 1 shows the details of our proposed technique, where a training phase and a forecasting phase are involved.

The training phase involves two major steps: kernel mapping and inductive learning. First, we follow the previous studies and extract the values of the related

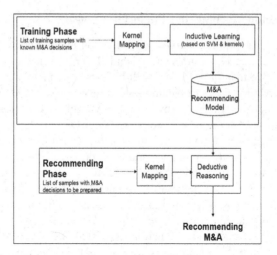

Fig. 1. Overall process of the proposed recommendation-as-a-service technique in M&A transactions

financial variables for each training sample (see Table 1). Then all the values of the financial variables will be mapped via a kernel function such as a polynomial kernel, a radial basis kernel or a financial kernel. Following kernel mapping is the inductive learning step, and we choose the R package "e1071" (Hornik et al. 2006; Dimitriadou et al. 2008), a supervised learning technique that provides computational efficiency and excellent interpretability. The package "e1071" offers a powerful function "svm()" with flexible parameter tuning methods. In the inductive learning step, we employ SVM integrated with a kernel to induce M&A recommending models from the set of training instances. In the recommending phase, we use the recommending model induced by SVM in the training phase to recommend an M&A candidate deal.

4   Empirical Evaluation

In this section, we express how we collect the data and design the evaluation. We then show the preliminary results from the evaluation of the proposed M&A recommendation service model.

4.1   Data Collection

The M&A cases are collected from the SDC Platinum database, which is available at https://financial.thomsonreuters.com/en/products/data-analytics/market-data/sdc-platinum-financial-securities.html. Totally 5,804 cases are collected, and the M&A cases are within 2000 and 2011 in technology-related industries of North America. These industries include hardware (with first-two-digit SIC code 35), software (with first-two-digit SIC code 36), and computer related business service (with first-three-digit SIC code 234). We further check whether these cases are available for our empirical evaluation purpose.

Table 1. Definitions of financial indicators of M&A

Indicator	Definition
3-year average dividend (DVT3)	A company's dividend payments to its shareholders over the last three years
Capital-expenditures-to-total-asset (CETA)	(Current assets – current liabilities)/(total assets)
Cash flow (CF)	Amount of money moving into and out of a business
Common shares traded divided by common shares outstanding (CSTRCSHO)	(Shares traded)/(shares outstanding)
Cost of goods sold (COGS)	Carrying value of goods sold during a particular period
Cost of goods sold divided by average inventory (COGSNI)	(Costs of goods sold)/inventory
Current ratio (CURRENTRATIO)	(Current assets)/(current liabilities)
Debt-to-assets ratio (DEBTTOASSETS)	(Sum of long-term and short-term debt)/(total assets)
Dividend (DVT)	A company's dividend
Debt-to-equity ratio (DEBTTOEQUITY)	(Sum of long-term and short-term debt)/(book value of equity)
Earnings before interest and taxes or operating income after depreciation (EBIT)	Revenue minus expenses, excluding tax and interest
Tobin's Q (Q)	(Sum of short-term and long-term debt)/(total assets)
Price-to-earning ratio (PE)	A company's share price to its per-share earnings
Profit margin (PROFITMAT)	Net income divided by revenue, or net profits divided by sales
Ratio of tangible (fixed) assets to total assets (TANGIBLEAT)	(Tangible assets)/(total assets)
Return on assets (ROA)	(Net income)/(total assets)
Return on equity (ROE)	(Net income)/(book value of equity)
Return on investment (ROI)	(Gain from investment – cost of investment)/(cost of investment)
Sales to total assets or asset turnover (ASSETTURNOVER)	(Net sales)/(total assets)
Tax shield effects (TAXSHIELD)	Taxable income reduces claiming deductions

If the M&A case is not likely technology-oriented, we remove it from the dataset. As a result, we end up with retaining a data set consist of 83 M&A cases and 680 non-M&A cases. The ratio between M&A cases and non M&A cases in the data set is 83/680 = 0: 12205.

For each case, the values of the corresponding financial variables (see Table 1) are collected from the Compustat database in the Wharton Research Data Services

(WRDS, available at https://wrdsweb.wharton.upenn.edu/wrds/). In order to transforming values taken from different sources into a consistent format, we further standardize the range of financial variables by this way:

$$x' = \frac{x - \min(x)}{\max(x) - \min(x)},$$

where x is an original value, and x' is the standardized value. Furthermore, the decision on M&A deal in a constantly changing business environment is usually dynamic and oscillated over time. We use lagged variables to incorporate feedback over time and capture the year-over-year effect. Hence, for each case, the values of 20 pairs financial variables are extracted from WRDS, and each pair of variables include one variable for the current year and one corresponding lagged variable for the previous year. Each M&A case (or each training instance) is expressed as:

$(DVT3, DVT3_{lag}, DVT, DVT_{lag}, CETA, CETA_{lag}, CF, CF_{lag}, CSTRCSHO, CSTRCSHO_{lag},$
$COGS, COGS_{lag}, COGSNI, COGSNI_{lag}, CURRENTRATIO, CURRENTRATIO_{lag},$
$DEBTTOASSETS, DEBTTOASSETS_{lag}, DEBTTOQUITY, DEBTTOEQUITY_{lag}, EBIT,$
$EBIT_{lag}, Q, Q_{lag}, PE, PE_{lag}, PROFITMAT, PROFITMAT_{lag}, TANGIBLEAT,$
$TANGIBLEAT_{lag}, ROA, ROA_{lag}, ROE, ROE_{lag}, ROI, ROI_{lag}, ASSETTURNOVER,$
$ASSETTURNOVER_{lag}, TAXSHIELD, TANGIBLEAT_{lag}).$

4.2 Evaluation and Preliminary Results

In this section, we measure the effectiveness of our proposed M&A forecasting technique on the basis of the complete data set. The criteria used to measure the performance evaluation are "accuracy", "precision", "recall", and "F_1". We compare with different kernels in order to determine the optimal model based on the proposed M&A recommendation technique. Totally three different kernels are considered, including Gaussian, polynomial, and financial.

In order to determine the optimal model, we fine tune the parameters, measure the effectiveness, and compare the proposed technique with different kernels. Tables 2 and 3 show the tuning results of the technique integrated with the Gaussian kernel and the polynomial kernel, respectively. Apparently, the Gaussian kernel performs best as the parameter $\gamma = 0.5$, and the polynomial kernel is best with $\gamma = 0.5$ and 0.7. After detecting the proper parameter values, we further measure the performance of these three models, i.e., the proposed technique with three different kernels: Gaussian ($\gamma = 0.5$), polynomial ($\gamma = 0.5$), and financial. The results are shown as Table 4. First, the Gaussian kernel beats the financial kernel. It shows higher accuracy (84:81% > 83:54%), higher precision (50% > 33:33%), higher recall (16:67% > 8:33%), and higher F1 (25% > 13:33%). Second, although the recall values are low, the Gaussian kernel's precision is 50%, much higher than the polynomial kernel's precision (23.53%). The result further indicates that the Gaussian kernel still has a 50% opportunity to correctly identify the M&A cases, while most predictions made with the polynomial kernel are incorrect (23.53%).

Table 2. Turning results of the proposed model with the Gaussian kernel

Gaussian kernel	Accuracy	Precision	Recall	F_1
$\gamma = 0.3$	83.54%	33.33%	8.33%	13.33%
$\gamma = 0.5$	84.81%	50.00%	16.67%	25.00%
$\gamma = 0.7$	84.81%	50.00%	8.33%	14.29%

Table 3. Turning results of the proposed model with the Polynomial kernel

Polynomial kernel	Accuracy	Precision	Recall	F_1
$\gamma = 0.3$	70.89%	21.05%	33.33%	25.81%
$\gamma = 0.5$	73.41%	23.53%	33.33%	27.59%
$\gamma = 0.7$	73.41%	23.53%	33.33%	27.59%

Table 4. Evaluation of different kernels

Kernel	Accuracy	Precision	Recall	F_1
Gaussian	84.81%	50.00%	16.67%	25.00%
Polynomial	73.41%	25.53%	33.33%	27.59%
Financial	83.54%	33.33%	8.33%	13.33%

5 Conclusion

M&A is a very common business activity and happens frequently in the high-technology industries because these IT companies are motivated for the speedy innovation and required to extend their resources and capabilities through the M&A transaction. In this study, we aim to provide a recommendation service that automatically determine a feasible M&A deal. We extend the work of Yang et al. (2014) and propose the M&A recommending technique on the basis of SVM. We also derive 40 financial variables and develop a training and recommending method for the technique. The M&A cases in the U.S. market are collected to validate the effectiveness of the proposed model.

However, the study is an initial exploration of the application of SVM in M&A recommending and forecasting. Our works still contains some limitations and may need to be improved in the future. First, we plan to show the performance of our proposed technique by incorporating other benchmark models, such as decision tree (C4.5), neural networks, or other machine learning techniques. Second, our proposed technique does not consider the possible negative outcomes, e.g. declining market shares and profits. Third, the study only focus on North America and only collect M&A cases from there. A generalized technique is still required although most M&A deals are made in North America. We plan to collect the M&A cases from other markets, including Europe and Asia Pacific to verify the generalization of our proposed technique.

Acknowledgement. This work is supported by the Ministry of Science and Technology of Taiwan (106-2410-H-110-082), and the Intelligent Electronic Commerce Research Center from the Featured Areas Research Center Program within the framework of the Higher Education Sprout Project by the Ministry of Education (MOE) in Taiwan.

Appendix

See Table 5.

Table 5. Reference of financial indicators

Indicator	Reference
3-year average dividend (DVT3)	Barnes (2000)
Capital-expenditures-to-total-asset (CETA)	Barnes (2000); Ragothaman et al. (2003)
Cash flow (CF)	Ragothaman et al. (2003); Ali-Yrkkö et al. (2005); Song et al. (2009)
Common shares traded divided by common shares outstanding (CSTRCSHO)	Meador et al. (1996)
Cost of goods sold (COGS)	Meador et al. (1996)
Cost of goods sold divided by average inventory (COGSNI)	Meador et al. (1996)
Current ratio (CURRENTRATIO)	Meador et al. (1996); Barnes (2000); Ragothaman et al. (2003); Tsagkanos et al. (2007)
Debt-to-assets ratio (DEBTTOASSETS)	Barnes (2000); Pasiouras and Gaganis (2007)
Dividend (DVT)	Barnes (2000)
Debt-to-equity ratio (DEBTTOEQUITY)	Meador et al. (1996); Ragothaman et al. (2003); Song et al. (2009)
Earnings before interest and taxes or operating income after depreciation (EBIT)	Meador et al. (1996)
Tobin's Q (Q)	Meador et al. (1996); Barnes (2000); Ragothaman et al. (2003); Song et al. (2009)
Price-to-earning ratio (PE)	Meador et al. (1996); Barnes (2000); Ragothaman et al. (2003); Song et al. (2009)
Profit margin (PROFITMAT)	Tsagkanos et al. (2007)
Ratio of tangible (fixed) assets to total assets (TANGIBLEAT)	Ali-Yrkkö et al. (2005)
Return on assets (ROA)	Meador et al. (1996); Pasiouras and Gaganis (2007)
Return on equity (ROE)	Meador et al. (1996); Barnes (2000); Tsagkanos et al. (2007)
Return on investment (ROI)	Ali-Yrkkö et al. (2005)
Sales to total assets or asset turnover (ASSETTURNOVER)	Meador et al. (1996); Barnes (2000); Tsagkanos et al. (2007)
Tax shield effects (TAXSHIELD)	Song et al. (2009)

References

Ali-Yrkkö, J., Hyytinen, A., Pajarinen, M.: Does patenting increase the probability of being acquired? evidence from cross-border and domestic acquisitions. Appl. Financ. Econ. **15**(14), 1007–1017 (2005)

An, S., He, Y., Zhao, Z., Sun, J.: Measurement of merger and acquisition performance based on artificial neural network. In: 2006 5th IEEE International Conference on Cognitive Informatics, pp. 502–506. IEEE, Beijing (2006)

Barnes, P.: The identification of UK takeover targets using published historical cost accounting data Some empirical evidence comparing logit with linear discriminant analysis and raw financial ratios with industry-relative ratios. Int. Rev. Financ. Anal. **9**(2), 147–162 (2000)

Boser, B.E., Guyon, I.M., Vapnik, V.N.: A training algorithm for optimal margin classifiers. In: Proceedings of the Fifth Annual Workshop on Computational Learning Theory, pp. 144–152. ACM, Pittsburgh (1992)

Cecchini, M., Aytug, H., Koehler, G.J., Pathak, P.: Detecting management fraud in public companies. Manag. Sci. **56**(7), 1146–1160 (2010)

Chapelle, O., Haffner, P., Vapnik, V.N.: Support vector machines for histogram-based image classification. IEEE Trans. Neural Netw. **10**(5), 1055–1064 (1999)

Cortes, C., Vapnik, V.: Support-vector networks. Mach. Learn. **20**(3), 273–297 (1995)

Cristianini, N., Shawe-Taylor, J.: An Introduction to Support Vector Machines and Other Kernel-Based Learning Methods. Cambridge University Press, Cambridge (2000)

Cristianini, N., Shawe-Taylor, J., Lodhi, H.: Latent semantic kernels. J. Intell. Inf. Syst. **18**(2–3), 127–152 (2002)

Dimitriadou, E., Hornik, K., Leisch, F., Meyer, D., Weingessel, A.: Misc functions of the Department of Statistics (e1071), TU Wien. R package, 1, 5–24 (2008)

Hagedoorn, J., Duysters, G.: The effect of mergers and acquisitions on the technological performance of companies in a high-tech environment. Technol. Anal. Strat. Manag. **14**(1), 67–85 (2002)

Hornik, K., Meyer, D., Karatzoglou, A.: Support vector machines in R. J. Stat. Softw. **15**(9), 1–28 (2006)

Hu, X., Pan, Y.: Knowledge Discovery in Bioinformatics: Techniques, Methods, and Applications, vol. 5. Wiley, Hoboken (2007)

Hua, S., Sun, Z.: A novel method of protein secondary structure prediction with high segment overlap measure: support vector machine approach. J. Mol. Biol. **308**(2), 397–407 (2001)

King, D.R., Slotegraaf, R.J., Kesner, I.: Performance implications of firm resource interactions in the acquisition of R&D-intensive firms. Organ. Sci. **19**(2), 327–340 (2008)

Meador, A.L., Church, P.H., Rayburn, L.G.: Development of prediction models for horizontal and vertical mergers. J. Financ. Strat. Decis. **9**(1), 11–23 (1996)

Pasiouras, F., Gaganis, C.: Financial characteristics of banks involved in acquisitions: Evidence from Asia. Appl. Financ. Econ. **17**(4), 329–341 (2007)

Ragothaman, S., Naik, B., Ramakrishnan, K.: Predicting corporate acquisitions: an application of uncertain reasoning using rule induction. Inf. Syst. Front. **5**(4), 401–412 (2003)

Song, X.-L., Zhang, Q.-S., Chu, Y.-H., Song, E.-Z.: A study on financial strategy for determining the target enterprise of merger and acquisition. In: 2009 IEEE/INFORMS International Conference on Service Operations, Logistics and Informatics, SOLI 2009, pp. 477–480. IEEE, Chicago (2009)

Tsagkanos, A., Georgopoulos, A., Siriopoulos, C.: Predicting Greek mergers and acquisitions: a new approach. Int. J. Financ. Serv. Manag. **2**(4), 289–303 (2007)

Yang, C.-S., Wei, C.-P., Chiang, Y.-H.: Exploiting technological indicators for effective technology merger and acquisition (M&A) predictions. Decis. Sci. **45**(1), 147–174 (2014)

Social Media and Big Data Analytics in Business

The Privacy Paradox in HCI: Calculus Behavior in Disclosing PII Online

Cheryl Booth[(⊠)] and Shuyuan Mary Ho

Florida State University, Tallahassee, FL, USA
clbl4h@my.fsu.edu, smho@fsu.edu

Abstract. The Privacy Paradox is an information privacy behavioral phenomenon wherein individuals are aware that the personally identifiable information (PII) they disclose in an online transaction may be compromised, yet disclose it nonetheless. One explanation that has been given for this phenomenon is that the decision to disclose information online is informed by a risk/reward analysis, referred to as Privacy Calculus. However, the broad privacy calculus framework does not necessarily provide insight into specifically how an individual assesses either risk or reward. In our study, we evaluate several behavioral factors in an effort to assess whether and to what extent each informs or influences an individual's risk assessment when deciding whether to disclose or withhold their PII in a given online transaction. Specifically, we report findings from a recent survey we administered, examining factors included in three different behavioral models. Results from this survey were analyzed using exploratory factor analysis, which provided insights as to the salience of each variable vis-à-vis online information behavior. Of the factors included in our study, our results surfaced four variables – *perceived trustworthiness*, *perceived vulnerability*, *"cyber" self-efficacy*, and *perceived controllability* – that appear to be particularly salient in an individual's decision to withhold or disclose PII online.

Keywords: Information privacy · Human computer interaction ·
Personally identifiable information (PII) · Information privacy behavior ·
Privacy paradox

1 Introduction

In 1890, legal scholars Brandeis and Warren famously wrote that privacy consists in "the right to be let alone" [1, p. 193]. Moreover, they asserted that a person's right to be let alone is violated not only when an unwanted or uninvited individual accesses that person's physical space, but also when that individual accesses *facts and information about them* without their prior knowledge and permission [1] (emphasis supplied). Core to this construct of information privacy is the idea that, at a minimum, individuals have a legally protected interest (if not a right as such[1]) in controlling the time, place, manner, and audience when they disclosing their personal information. Individuals are

---

[1] The reader should be mindful that there is no specific "right" to privacy in the U.S. Constitution.

© Springer Nature Switzerland AG 2019
F. F.-H. Nah and K. Siau (Eds.): HCII 2019, LNCS 11589, pp. 163–177, 2019.
https://doi.org/10.1007/978-3-030-22338-0_13

particularly vulnerable, and their interest in controlling their personal information is greatest, when the personal information in question can connect them back to the information to the exclusion of any other individual. That is, our interest in information privacy is perhaps highest when our *personally identifiable information* (PII) is involved. PII refers to information about the individual that can be connected back to that individual to the exclusion of any other [2]. However, because online transactions necessarily entail the individual to be using a computer with specific internet protocol (IP) and media access control (MAC) addresses, these online transactions can be easily tagged back to the individual who was logged in at that IP address at that time. In other words, virtually any online transaction involving personal information in fact involves PII, rather than anonymized information. Thus, as the use of computers to collect, store and disseminate information about us has become virtually ubiquitous, protecting our information privacy – controlling who learns what about us, how they learn it and when they learn it - has increasingly become a challenge.

Organizations often assert that their collection and use of customers' PII is necessary to facilitating the computer based interaction between the individual and their organization: it allows the organization to more effectively and efficiently tailor and personalize the goods and services offered to a specific customer. Customer PII is also exchanged between and among organizations. Disclosing PII is a part of the cost incurred by individuals when obtaining goods, services, or even information online. In addition, it is increasingly the case that there are no viable alternatives for obtaining the good or service than to complete the online transaction and disclose their PII. That is, engaging in this particular type of human-computer interaction requires disclosure of some amount of PII. The result is that individuals who are unwilling to disclose their PII may not have access to the goods, services, and even information that individuals who are willing to disclose their PII have access to. This, in turn, results in a significant imbalance in bargaining power as between the individual consumer and the organizations with which they interact online. While this shift in bargaining power has become increasingly noticeable during the 2010s, privacy scholar Gandy [3] observed as long ago as the mid 1990s that:

> [T]he power that the individual is able to exercise over the organization when she withholds personal information is almost always insignificant in comparison with the power brought to bear when the organization chooses to withhold goods or services unless the information is provided [3, p. 19].

Given omnipresent and increasing inter-organizational competition, organizations engaging with customers online should begin to imagine and plan for a universe in which there are online goods and services providers who do not barter in their customers' PII, and who allow consumers to retain meaningful control over their PII. In this regard, organizations engaging with customers online (i.e. through a computer interface) should revisit their respective information privacy policies and practices as if such a universe existed; this, in turn, requires them to more fully acknowledge their customers' actual concerns and, in sum, to understand their information behaviors around information privacy when engaging with their virtual marketplace. According to a 2014 Pew research center study, which investigated the perceptions of the American public with respect to issues of personal privacy, provides some initial insights [4], lack of control over the further dissemination of information is a core concern. 91% of the study participants indicated that they believe consumers have lost control over their personal information online.

Consumers are clearly concerned about online information privacy. However, the continued proliferation of goods and services available online provides evidence that few of these individuals actually modify their online information-sharing behaviors - much less simply decline to disclose information online in the first instance. Privacy scholars Norberg, Horne and Horne [5] referred to this phenomenon - wherein we disclose personal information online even though we know there are risks associated with doing so - as the *privacy paradox*.

To understand the privacy paradox, we need to first understand what drives our basic propensity to disclose PII online. Our research thus aims to explore online information privacy behaviors – that is, those behavioral factors that influence our decisions to disclose PII online. More specifically, we examine the privacy paradox through the lens of the privacy calculus framework. That is, we start by examining the privacy paradox as being explained by a risk/reward analysis. We raise the research question: *which behavioral factors are salient in forming our perception of risk vis-à-vis disclosing our PII online?*

In this paper, we first provide a brief discussion of privacy calculus, and introduce several theoretical frameworks that may inform an individual's online information privacy behavior. Next, we outline and position the specific behavioral factors included in the study, which comprise our theoretical framework. Then, we discuss our research method, and present our data analysis. Finally, we present our conclusion(s), acknowledge the particular limitations of our study, and outline the future direction of our research.

2   Privacy Calculus

There are a number of theoretical behavioral frameworks that have the potential to explain our apparent propensity to share our PII online despite realizing that doing so exposes us to the risk of having that information compromised. In particular, information privacy behavior has frequently been discussed in terms of a behavioral risk/rewards analysis, referred to in the literature as *privacy calculus* [6].

Privacy calculus was initially proposed by Culnan and Bies [6], as an extension of a broader analysis by Laufer and Wolfe [7]. Privacy calculus suggests that, when an individual interacts with an organization or institution, their propensity to disclose personal or private information to that organization or institution is essentially a function of whether the individual believes they are being given a fair exchange for that information – that is, the benefits they receive for doing so outweigh, or, are, in any case, not outweighed by, the potential risks undertaken in disclosing the personal information. In essence, this model suggests that, in order for an organization or institution to entice or encourage individuals to disclose personal information, it ought to both enhance the rewards and benefits offered as part of the transaction, and work to reduce perceived risk. To this latter end, Culnan and Bies [6] position trust as having direct (negative) influence on perceived risk. In particular, Culnan and Bies [6] point out that the unwarranted (i.e. unauthorized) disclosure of personal information undermines trust when an organization discloses information to someone other than the person who the customer initially expected or authorized to receive it, and, in particular, when the customer considers some or all of that information to be sensitive.

Dinev and Hart [8] likewise take the perspective that propensity to disclose personal information online is a function of an individual's cost/benefit analysis with respect to the online transaction. Accordingly, Dinev and Hart [8] proposed a privacy calculus model in which they framed the result of the cost/benefit analysis as a "cumulative antecedent to information disclosure" [8, p. 62]. Smith and Dinev [9] examined the role of privacy concern in influencing propensity to disclose PII, particularly the extent to which an individual's level of privacy concern might inform their risk analysis.

3   Study Framework

Privacy calculus analysis offers a straightforward way in which to think about our online information behaviors (specifically, our decision to either disclose or withhold our PII when interacting online). However, this risk/reward analysis does not address foundational questions concerning how we perceive the potential risk and potential reward of disclosing or withholding PII when interacting online. To attempt to answer these questions, we must look at other behavioral factors. We start by using the foundational factors suggested in Bauer's seminal work on *perceived risk* [10] to analyze the salience of each with respect to an individual's decision to disclose or withhold information when interacting online. We also consider the salience of an individual's fundamental level of *privacy concern* on their disclose/withhold decision [8, 9, 11]. Finally, we consider the potential salience of other, more general behavioral factors. For example, an individual's decision to disclose or withhold PII when interacting online may be informed by the *subjective or social norms* to which they have been exposed, their *attitude* toward either disclosing PII or interacting online, or their sense of *perceived behavioral control* with respect to their ability to retain control over and protect their PII.

Figure 1 below depicts our initial framework. Each of the foregoing factors is incorporated into the theoretical framework we are investigating. In the following subparagraphs, we discuss and define each of these factors, and present our initial theoretical framework.

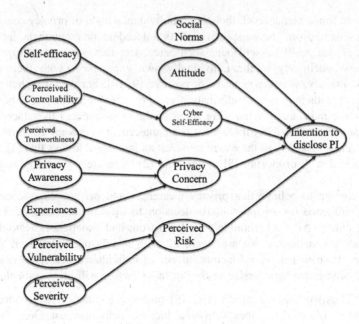

Fig. 1. Initial study framework

3.1 Perceived Risk

Bauer defined *perceived risk* as consisting of two fundamental components: uncertainty of outcome and seriousness of outcome [10]. Bauer further wrote that perceived risk includes multiple types of risks – including social risk, psychological risk, time risk, financial risk, and performance risk. Pavlou and Featherman expanded on Bauer's discussion, framing 'uncertainty' in terms of perceived vulnerability, and 'seriousness' as "perceived severity" [12]. Featherman and Pavlou's discussion of perceived risk also included privacy risk as an additional risk facet [12].

Following Featherman and Pavlou, in the context of our study we consider the extent to which, in deciding whether to disclose PII online, an individual considers both the likelihood of their PII being compromised (*perceived vulnerability*) and the specific consequences of having the information compromised (*perceived severity*). We suggest that the basic perceived risk framework holds up in this context, and hypothesize that both *perceived vulnerability* and *perceived severity* are salient factors in an individual's decision whether or not to disclose PII online.

3.2 Privacy Concern

"Privacy concern" may be broadly thought of as referring to how much concern or anxiety an individual experiences with respect to the treatment of their PII. At a high level, privacy concern speaks to a variety of potential PII handling issues - specific events or occurrences that we can point to as making us generally concerned about the privacy of our PII online.

At a more fundamental level, though, an individual's level of privacy concern may also be examined from the perspective of its antecedent or component factors. As Smith, Dinev and Xu [9] assert, once such antecedent factor is *privacy experiences*, which refers specifically to the individual's own experiences with their personal information privacy, whether negative or positive [9, 13]. For example, has the individual ever had their personal information compromised? Has their PII been compromised more than once? What were some of the consequences they faced? Smith et al. also suggest that *privacy awareness* is an antecedent to privacy concern. Privacy awareness refers generally to the extent to which an individual knows that (1) there are risks associated with disclosing PII online; and (2) there are ways they can mitigate these risks [9].

It is tempting to believe that privacy awareness and privacy experience have a significant influence on an individual's decision to disclose or withhold PII when interacting online. After all, shouldn't we learn from bad experiences? Shouldn't we avoid negative situations if we are aware of them in advance? However, from the perspective of which behavioral factors inform an individual's perceived risk in disclosing PII online, we hypothesize neither of these factors will prove salient.

Perceived Trustworthiness. Smith et al. [9] further posit that privacy concern both informs and is informed by other behavioral factors, including trust. Deutsch defined trust in terms of the personal characteristics of the person being trusted (the trustee), as they are perceived by the person who trusts (the trustor) [14]. The trustor's assessment of the trustee's abilities to perform the particular task in question, as well as their general reliability and overall predictability are the key components in the formation of trust. Deutsch further framed trust with respect to the trustor allowing themselves to be vulnerable to the trustee in a given situation: the trustor effectively gives up control over the situation (including its outcome) to the trustee [15].

One of the defining characteristics of online transactions, however, is that the individual is providing their PII to an anonymous entity, over which they have little or no control or oversight. The trust analysis in this case is a bit different: the inquiry is not so much whether the online organization (or individual) is capable or reliable; rather, the trustor is more likely to be asking themselves how likely it is that their PII will be compromised or mishandled in some way, and how badly it is compromised or mishandled. The trustor relies on not only the ability, but also the integrity and benevolence of the online organization with which they are interacting to protect their PII, and ensure it is not compromised or mishandled. These elements (ability, integrity, and benevolence) are hallmarks not of trust, but of the subjective construct of *perceived trustworthiness* [c.f. 16–20]. Accordingly, we assert that *perceived trustworthiness*, rather than trust, is the more appropriate factor to consider in our framework.

We hypothesize that *perceived trustworthiness* is a significant, salient factor in an individual's decision to disclose or withhold PII online. Moreover, as suggested above, the perceived trustworthiness analysis speaks directly to the perception of risk.

The more we feel that an online organization has not only the ability and integrity to "do the right thing" by us, but also the benevolence to do so, the less likely we are to perceive that interacting with them is risky for us.

3.3   Perceived Behavioral Control: Cyber Self-efficacy

Ajzen [21] asserted that perceived behavioral control is best understood as a hierarchical construct, consisting of two lower-order factors—perceived self-efficacy and perceived controllability—that collectively inform the higher order factor perceived behavioral control. To distinguish between these two constructs, perceived self-efficacy refers to the level of ease or difficulty the individual ascribes to the particular behavior while perceived controllability looks at the degree to which actual performance is up to (within the control of) the individual.

We note that perceived self-efficacy and perceived controllability are aggregative concepts. Virtually all tasks/behaviors consist of multiple steps. The individual performing the behavior may feel that most (if not all) of these steps are easy for him/her to do (perceived self-efficacy) or within their control; but, if the individual feels that one of these steps is very difficult for them, they may well decide not to perform the behavior—even though they know that if they perform the steps of the behavior, they will achieve the desired outcome. Similarly, if the individual feels that most of the steps in the behavioral outcome are within their control, but may nonetheless not perform the behavior (or even attempt it) because they believe they will ultimately lack those resources for which they must rely on others (materials; time; money; personnel) to complete the behavior, they may simply not attempt it. Framed in terms of perceived self-efficacy and perceived controllability, an individual may have high perceived self-efficacy, but due to low perceived controllability (i.e. as to the outcome), they may not attempt to perform the behaviors. Conversely, an individual may know that if she performs certain behaviors, a desired outcome is guaranteed (if you save enough money, you can purchase a new TV). However, if the individual has low perceived efficacy (feels unable to save, has too many financial commitments), they will likely not attempt the behavior despite the fact that it will, in fact, achieve a desired outcome. In this regard, Ajzen [21] suggested that perceived behavioral control should be understood to refer simply to the individual's sense that the ability to attempt the performance of a particular behavior is within their purview, rather than the outcome per se.

In the context of disclosing PII online, what we term "cyber self-efficacy" considers, on the one hand, the extent to which an individual believes they are able to identify situations in which it is/is not safe to disclose PII, what information is/is not safe to disclose in a given situation (control over task), and, on the other hand, the individual's belief that they can control what information is/is not disclosed and who accesses and uses it (control over outcome). Our study framework thus considers the extent to which cyber self-efficacy informs an individual's decision to disclose or withhold PII when interacting online. We predict that *cyber self-efficacy* is an important factor in the disclose/withhold decision.

3.4   Attitude

Allport [22] defines an individual's attitude as "a mental and neural state of readiness, organized through experience, exerting a directive or dynamic influence upon the individual's response to all objects and situations with which it is related" [22, p. 810]. He notes that the effect of attitude on behavior can be viewed on a continuum from driving (motivating) behavior to simply directing it. Allport [22] further notes that attitude had generally been discussed and studied as a binary concept (i.e., favorable/unfavorable; good/bad; positive/negative). Fishbein [23] defines attitude similarly, referring to attitudes as "learned predispositions" which cause us to respond to specific people, places and things in a particular, predetermined way (whether favorable or unfavorable).

In our study framework, we investigate whether an individual's attitude toward interacting online (whether with organizations or individuals) influences their intention or propensity to disclose PII online. In particular, we consider whether or not an individual's perceived risk in disclosing PII online is informed by their fundamental attitude toward interacting online. We posit that attitude is not a salient factor in predicting or explaining an individual's intention or propensity to disclose PII online. Accordingly, we further hypothesize that attitude is also not a salient factor in the individual's perception of the risk associated with disclosing PII online.

3.5   Social Norms

Social norms, resulting from general consensus and/or negotiation in a society, is a collective construct, which essentially provide an informal, custom-based and socially enforced set of rules for acceptable behavior within that society [24]. These rules encompass the customs, traditions, standards, mores, and fashions of that particular culture, as well as similar indicia of membership in or belonging to that society. Social norms reflect standard or characteristic behaviors to be expected of, from and by members of that society or culture. Accordingly, they provide guidance in situations where expectations are ambiguous and the appropriate response behavior is uncertain. Moreover, based on the principles or rules of conduct and behavior established in the society, social norms serve to both foster desirable behavior and to sanction undesirable behaviors.

Cialdini and Trost [24] described two types of social normative behavior: descriptive norms, and injunctive norms. Descriptive norms are those behavioral norms that function to encourage socially desirable behavior. Descriptive norms influence behavior by providing a positive, socially successful model on which to base one's own behavior. Injunctive norms influence behavior by imposing sanctions of varying severity on the society's miscreants. These sanctions are often loosely constructed, informal forms of indictment within one's own social network[2]. As noted in the

---

[2] The most essential and widely shared norms (both descriptive and injunctive) within a society are usually formally codified in the laws of the society, which are then subject to enforcement by the State. Thus, a miscreant may be subject not only to social sanction but also to legal sanction.

preceding paragraph, injunctive and descriptive norms are not mutually exclusive, and may serve to inform each other.

Fishbein and Ajzen [25] discussed social norms with specific reference as to how they influence behavioral intention and outcome – i.e. how they influence us to perform (or not) a particular behavior. Fishbein and Ajzen [25] note that descriptive norms have both direct and indirect effects on behavior. That is, we observe the direct effect of a behavior: is it rewarded or punished? Such observation may also inform our awareness of a related injunctive norm (discussed below). We may also observe that – whether initially rewarded or not – a behavior may have indirect consequences – i.e. subsequent positive or negative consequences. Moreover, we can also observe any resources we may require, or barriers we may need to deal with, in order to perform the behavior. Injunctive norms, on the other hand, are those behavioral norms that operate to sanction socially undesirable behaviors. The Ajzen and Fishbein framework incorporates both injunctive and descriptive social norms into what they refer to as *subjective norms*, which they define as "an individual's perception that most people who are important to [them] think [they] should (or should not) perform a particular behavior" [25, p. 131]. In other words, subjective norms are one's perception of applicable social norms, and reflect the "total social pressure experienced with respect to a given behavior" [25, p. 131].

It is tempting to believe that online information privacy behaviors are influenced by social norms. On a daily basis, we observe others interacting and sharing PII online. If they do it, why shouldn't we? If they have a problem resulting from sharing PII online, shouldn't we think twice before doing it ourselves? However, we predict that the influence of subjective norms is actually not significant in terms of our ultimate decision to disclose or withhold PII online.

4 Method

This study attempts to investigate the extent to which the behavioral factors discussed in the previous section inform and, in turn, are informed by an individual's subjective assessment of the risks and rewards associated with disclosing PII online in a particular transaction. That is, the basic model remains the very straightforward privacy calculus model described above; however, we include the behavioral factors described in the previous section in our framework to determine which, if any, are salient in terms of explaining and predicting how the risk/reward analysis is conducted. The data were analyzed using exploratory factor analysis (EFA) techniques.

4.1 Data Collection and Survey Instrument

The survey was recently administered to students enrolled in an undergraduate-level technical writing course at a large southeastern state university. A total of 69 surveys were returned, of which 67 were complete and used for analysis. The participants were all between the ages of 18 and 40, with the vast majority being between the ages of 18–25 (n = 64). Approximately two-thirds (n = 47) were male. Nearly all (n = 51) indicated having previous information technology (IT) experience.

The survey uses questions covering perceived behavioral control, attitude and social norms, which were adapted from Ajzen's Theory of Planned Behavior (TPB) model questionnaire [26] to be specific to online information privacy behaviors. The adapted TPB items were combined with questions intended to measure the participant's level of privacy concern (as defined in Smith, Milberg [13] and Smith, Dinev [9]), as well as perceived risk. Questions concerning privacy calculus, suggested by Dinev and Hart [8], were also incorporated.

The instrument consisted of 39 items, with each item being scored on a 7-point Likert-type scale (-3 = strongly disagree; 0 = neutral; 3 = strongly agree). Two specific questions concerning the participants' declared intention to disclose personal information online within a specified timeframe were excluded as ultimately irrelevant to the research questions to be addressed. Accordingly, the final analysis consisted of 37 observed variables. In addition, anonymized demographic information (i.e. age range and gender) were also collected, but not analyzed for this study.

4.2   Analysis

Because we have no pre-conceived ideas with respect to how the factors described in the previous sections may interact in this specific context, our first step is to apply EFA techniques to the survey data. EFA allows us to determine whether or not the data surface any (or all) of these factors as being salient in explaining online information privacy behavior. We performed our analysis using IBM's SPSS (v25). We used Principal Axis Factoring as the extraction method, and, to facilitate interpretation of the factors, we applied factor rotation (specifically, Oblimin with Kaiser Normalization).

As a preliminary matter in conducting EFA, we consider both the Bartlett's test of sphericity and the Kaiser-Meyer Olkin (KMO) measure of sampling adequacy. The first iteration of EFA yielded a Bartlett's Test result that was statistically significant ($p < 0.001$)[3]. Thus, although the KMO was marginal (.546), we felt justified in proceeding with the EFA. The extraction values in the communalities table, reflecting the amount of variance each measured variable could be reproduced by the factors as a whole [27], were fairly homogeneous. The majority of the extraction values fell between .5 and .8, with only items 4 and 10 falling below .4. In this first iteration, 12 factors were surfaced with initial Eigenvalues >1 [28, 29]. Cumulatively, these factors explain approximately 66.3% of the variance between and among the 37 variables.

As noted above, items 4 and 10 had the least explanatory value of the initial 37 items (i.e. measured variables). While there is no magic cut-off number for selecting extraction values, the factors as a set did not produce more than 40% of the variance of

---

[3] To avoid unnecessary repetition, we note here that the Bartlett's test remained statistically significant ($p < 0.001$) through each iteration of EFA.

either item 4 or 10. Accordingly, items 4 and 10 were not useful in surfacing salient factors, and we removed them in our second iteration. The results of the Bartlett's test and the KMO test were similar to those obtained in the first iteration, although the KMO results were slightly higher (.569). The extraction values resulting from this iteration were, again, fairly homogeneous, with the exception of item 16 (which was <.4). 11 factors were surfaced having Eigenvalues > 1. Cumulatively, these 11 factors also explain 66.3% of the variance between and among the remaining 35 variables.

When we removed item 16 in the next iteration of EFA, the KMO value again improved, but was still marginal (.578). The extraction values of the variables in the communalities table were all >.4, with the exception of v35. Although there were again 11 factors with Eigenvalues >1, the overall percentage of variance between and among the remaining 34 variables explained by these factors increased to 67.33%.

Continuing to eliminate variables with limited contributions to the factors being surfaced, we next removed item 35. The KMO value increased to .582. The extraction values of the variables remained homogeneous, with the exception of one of the variables (item 14), which was <.4. This fourth EFA iteration also surfaced 10 factors with Eigenvalues >1; the overall percentage of variance between and among the remaining 33 variables explained by these 10 factors decreased (slightly) to 65.89%.

When we next removed item 14, the KMO value decreased slightly – to .578. No additional factors were eliminated, so we still had 10 factors at the end of this fifth iteration of EFA. However, the overall percentage of variance between and among the remaining 32 variables explained by these 10 factors increased to 66.7%.

Finally, in our sixth and last iteration of EFA, we removed item 20 – the only extraction factor <.4 from the previous EFA iteration. This iteration of EFA had no further variables with extraction values <.4. In addition, there was virtually no change in the KMO value from the previous iteration and there are still 10 factors with Eigenvalues >1. These remaining 10 factors explain 67.69% of the variance between and among the remaining 31 variables.

Given the level of homogeneity achieved in the extraction values of the remaining variables, we suggest that further extraction would be of marginal/limited value. Accordingly, we next examined the corresponding pattern matrix to identify which items correspond with which factors (i.e., which variables load most strongly on which factors). The end result of this part of the analysis reveals four factors that have strong loadings of multiple items. Three of these four factors had at least four item structure coefficients of >|.6|, which is generally held to be the minimum factor loading value needed for factors consisting of four or fewer variables [27]. The fourth factor (*perceived controllability*) had four total items loading on it, of which three were >|.6|. The final EFA pattern and structure coefficient matrix is presented in Table 1 (Appendix), and summarizes the factors and loadings in our final model.

Figure 2 below is a representation of the study framework as tested by our study. The lighter arrows and circles reflect factors that did not load well with the survey data, and the darker arrows and circles denote factors having good loadings. As can be seen, while EFA reduced the data collected across the original 37 items to 10 factors, our final framework includes just four factors. Four of the 10 factors had only weak loadings (loadings <.4). In addition, items 11, 15, 19, 22, 28, and 29 loaded across three additional factors, but they did not load cohesively such that the resulting factors were meaningful. Accordingly, these weak-loading and non-loading items were eliminated, leaving us with four factors.

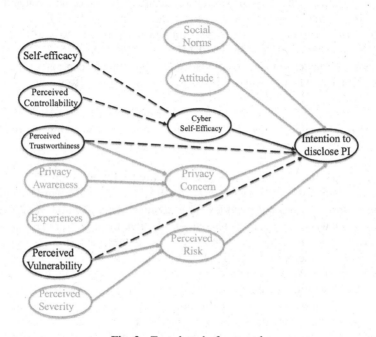

Fig. 2. Tested study framework

4.3 Discussion of Research Question

Based on the results of EFA discussed above, we can answer our research question as follows: *perceived trustworthiness*, *cyber self-efficacy*, and *perceived vulnerability* appear to be the most salient of the factors we studied in terms of predicting or explaining an individual's decision to disclose or withhold PII when interacting online. With respect to an individual's perception of risk in disclosing PII online, we can also assert that these are salient factors. Our findings are illustrated in Fig. 3 below, which depicts our final study framework. Note that, because both of the lower-order factors of which *Cyber Self-Efficacy* is compromised loaded well, our final framework includes the higher-order factor only.

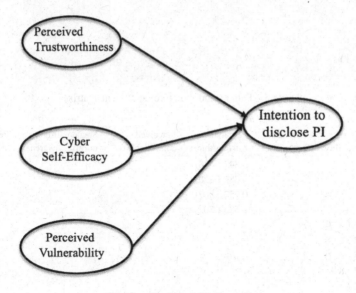

Fig. 3. Final study framework

5 Conclusions, Limitations, and Future Work

Applying this study findings in an organizational context, we note that our findings suggest that organizations that emphasize normative behaviors or attempt to influence attitudes in order to make individuals more likely to transact/disclose PII online are perhaps missing out on more significant behavioral influencers. Likewise, severity of outcome doesn't appear to be a salient behavioral factor in this context, suggesting that the simple fact of having customers' or users' PII compromised matters less to them than the consequences to them of the compromise. Further and as suggested by the privacy paradox, even making individuals aware of the potential for the PII they disclose online to be compromised seems insufficient (including invoking the individual's own experiences with this issue) to deter disclosure.

A main limitation of the study we discuss in this paper is that our sample size was small (n = 67). However, as discussed in Thompson [27], sample size may be less important when the factors have structure coefficients greater than |.6|, as was the case here (see Appendix). In addition, the external validity of the study is problematic because only a single, fairly homogeneous, group from a single location participated in the survey.

Future research will focus on the other factors surfaced from the EFA - specifically, *perceived vulnerability* and *perceived trustworthiness* – along with *cyber self-efficacy* - to assess how effectively these three factors explain (or predict) propensity to disclose personal information. Moreover, as part of our future work, we will not only examine these factors individually vis-à-vis online information privacy behavior, but will also operationalize each of them in an experimental design in order to gage the relative importance of each in an individual's risk/reward analysis when disclosing PII online as well as explore the relationships between and among them to assess whether one or more of these factors influences and/or moderates the interactions between and among the others.

Appendix

(See Table 1)

Table 1. Pattern and structure coefficient matrix

Items	Factors						
	Perceived vulnerability	Cyber self-efficacy	Perceived trustworthiness	Perceived controllability	Social norms	Privacy awareness	Perceived severity
Q7			0.842 (.888)				
Q8			0.789 (.820)				
Q6			0.757 (.807)				
Q9			0.625 (.703)				
Q34	0.376 (.427)						
Q33	0.912 (.889)						
Q32	0.885 (.884)						
Q31	0.782 (.828)						
Q30	0.672 (.689)						
Q2					0.856		
Q1					0.737		
Q3					0.419		
Q13						−0.809	
Q12						−0.788	
Q37							0.917
Q36							0.836
Q27				−0.891 (−.885)			
Q26				−0.765 (−.803)			
Q17				−0.759 (−.789)			
Q18				−0.313 (−.474)			
Q25		0.797 (.765)					
Q24		0.686 (.777)					
Q21		0.618 (.726)					
Q23		0.501 (.677)					
Q5		0.417 (.487)					

· For each of our final 4 factors, the Structure Coefficient corresponding to the Pattern Coefficient is noted in the parentheses.

References

1. Warren, S.D., Brandeis, L.D.: The right to privacy. Harv. Law Rev. **4**(5), 194–220 (1890)
2. Office of E-Government and Information Technology, M-06-19: Reporting Incidents Involving Personally Identifiable Information and Incorporating the Cost for Security in Agency Information Technology Investments, O.o.M.a. Budget, Editor, Washington, D.C (2006)
3. Gandy, O.H.: The Panopic Sort: A Political Economy of Personal Information. Westview Press, Boulder (1993)

4. Pew Research Center, Public Perceptions of Privacy and Security in the Post-Snowden Era. Pew Research Center (2014)
5. Norberg, P.A., Horne, D.R., Horne, D.A.: The privacy paradox: personal information disclosure intentions versus behaviors. J. Consum. Aff. **41**(1), 100–126 (2007)
6. Culnan, M.J., Bies, R.J.: Consumer privacy: balancing economic and justice considerations. J. Soc. Issues **59**(2), 323–342 (2003)
7. Laufer, R.S., Wolfe, M.: Privacy as a concept and a social issue: a multidimensional developmental theory. J. Soc. Issues **33**(3), 22–42 (1977)
8. Dinev, T., Hart, P.: An extended privacy calculus model for e-commerce transactions. Inf. Syst. Res. **17**(1), 61–80 (2006)
9. Smith, H.J., Dinev, T., Xu, H.: Information privacy research: an interdisciplinary review. MIS Q. **35**(4), 989–1015 (2011)
10. Bauer, R.A.: Consumer behavior as risk taking. In: Cox, D.F. (ed.) Risk Taking and Information Handling in Consumer Behavior, pp. 23–33. Harvard University, Boston (1967)
11. Malhotra, N.K., Kim, S.S., Agarwal, J.: Internet users' information privacy concerns (IUIPC): the construct, the scale and a causal model. Inf. Syst. Res. **15**(4), 336–355 (2004)
12. Featherman, M.S., Pavlou, P.A.: Predicting e-services adoption: a perceived risk facets perspective. Hum.-Comput. Stud. **59**, 451–474 (2003)
13. Smith, H.J., Milberg, S.J., Burke, S.J.: Information privacy: measuring individuals' cocnerns about organizational practices. MIS Q. **20**(2), 167–196 (1996)
14. Deutsch, M.: Trust and Suspicion. J. Conflict Resolut. **2**(4), 265–279 (1958)
15. Deutsch, M.: Trust and suspicion: theoretical notes. In: The Resolution of Conflict: Constructive and Destructive Processes, pp. 143–176. Yale University Press, New Haven (1973)
16. Ben-Ner, A., Putterman, L.: Trusting and trustworthiness. Boston Univ. Law Rev. **81**, 523–551 (2001)
17. Colquitt, J.A., Scott, B.A., LePine, J.A.: Trust, trustworthiness, and trust propensity: a meta-analytic test of their unique relationship with risk taking and job performance. J. Appl. Psychol. **92**(4), 909–927 (2007)
18. Hardin, R.: Trustworthiness. Ethics **107**(1), 26–42 (1996)
19. Hosmer, L.T.: Trust: the connecting link between organizational theory and philosophical ethics. Acad. Manag. Rev. **20**(2), 379–403 (1995)
20. Zand, D.E.: Trust and managerial problem solving. Adm. Sci. Q. **17**(2), 229–239 (1972)
21. Ajzen, I.: Perceived behavioral control, self-efficacy, locus of control and the theory of planned behavior. J. Appl. Soc. Psychol. **32**(4), 665–683 (2002)
22. Allport, G.W.: Attitudes. In: Murchison, C. (ed.) A Handbook of Social Psychology, pp. 799–844. Clark University Press, Worcester (1935)
23. Fishbein, M. (ed.): Readings in Attitude Theory and Measurement. Wiley, New York (1967)
24. Cialdini, R.B., Trost, M.R.: Social influence: social norms, conformity, and compliance. In: Gilbert, D.T., Fiske, S.T., Lindzey, G., Aronson, E. (eds.) The Handbook of Social Psychology, pp. 151–192. McGraww-Hill Companies, Inc., New York (1998)
25. Fishbein, M., Ajzen, I.: Predicting and Changing Behavior: The Reasoned Action Approach. Routledge Taylor & Francis Group, New York (2010)
26. Ajzen, I.: Constructing a theory of planned behavior questionnaire: conceptual and methodological considerations (2002)
27. Thompson, B.: Exploratory and Confirmatory Factor Analysis. American Psychological Association, Washington (2004)
28. Guttman, L.: Some necessary conditions for common-factor analysis. Psychometrika **19**(2), 149–161 (1954)
29. Kaiser, H.F.: The varimax criterion for analytic rotation in factor analysis. Psychometrika **23** (3), 187–200 (1958)

A Classification Framework for Online Social Support Using Deep Learning

Langtao Chen[✉]

Department of Business and Information Technology,
Missouri University of Science and Technology, Rolla, MO 65409, USA
chenla@mst.edu

Abstract. Health consumers engage in social interactions in online health communities (OHCs) to seek or provide social support. Automatic classification of social support exchanged online is important for both researchers and practitioners of online health communities, especially when a large number of messages are posted on regular basis. Classification of social support in OHCs provides an efficient way to assess the effectiveness of social interactions in the virtual environment. Most previous studies of online social support classification are based on "bag-of-words" assumption and have not considered the semantic meaning of words/terms embedded in the online messages. This research proposes a classification framework for online social support using the recent development of word space models and deep learning methods. Specifically, doc2vec models, bag-of-words representations, and linguistic analysis methods are used to extract features from the text messages that are posted in OHC for online social interaction or social support exchange. Then a deep learning model is applied to classify two major types of social support (i.e., informational and emotional support) expressed in OHC reply messages.

Keywords: Online health communities · Social support · Machine learning · Deep learning · Word embedding · Doc2vec

1 Introduction

Health consumers are increasingly participating in online health communities (OHCs) to seek social support from others to better deal with their health conditions [1, 2]. With the advancement and wide adoption of the Internet, social support exchange, which traditionally occurs in a physical setting with face-to-face interactions between the giver and the recipient, has been gradually moved to the online setting such as an online health community. An important task for OHC research and practice is to automatically categorize social support embedded in online messages, especially when a large amount of social support is exchanged in the virtual environment. The automatic classification of social support helps practitioners and researchers to better understand social interactions in OHCs and thus provides insights regarding how the OHCs can be managed to better serve the needs of community participants. For example, assessing social support contribution of participants can provide a way for the OHC to detect leaders in the community so that social support seekers can be more

© Springer Nature Switzerland AG 2019
F. F.-H. Nah and K. Siau (Eds.): HCII 2019, LNCS 11589, pp. 178–188, 2019.
https://doi.org/10.1007/978-3-030-22338-0_14

efficiently directed to these leaders. In general, evaluation of social interactions in online communities sets a basis for more advanced motivational mechanisms (or affordances) such as voting and commenting that can incentivize ongoing engagement and contribution of participants [3]. As OHC participants tend to use particular writing styles and elements in expressing social support in their online messages [4], social support classification based on linguistic features extracted from online messages has been shown to be efficient. However, previous studies on online social support classification (e.g., [2, 4, 5]) are based on the approach of bag-of-words (BOW), which represents a document as a vector of terms ignoring their positions and semantic connections between them.

This study applies deep learning methods to the classification of social support exchanged in online health communities. Particularly, this study applies the doc2vec model to represent each OHC message. The doc2vec model [6] is an extension of the word2vec model [7]. Two variants of doc2vec are distributed memory model of paragraph vectors (DM) and distributed bag of words (DBOW). The word space models trained by word2vec and doc2vec have been shown to be able to capture semantic meanings and perform well in a variety of natural language processing tasks such as sentiment analysis [8], Wikipedia article quality assessment [9], and news classification [10]. However, there is no extant study that applies and evaluates the recent development of word space models as well as deep learning methods for online social support classification. The current research aims to fill the knowledge gap by addressing the following research question:

Research Question: How can we use deep learning and word space models to classify social support exchanged in online health communities?

The organization of this paper is as follows. First, research background is introduced in the next section. Then, the framework of online social support classification is proposed, followed by an experiment to evaluate the proposed method. Lastly, preliminary results and conclusions are discussed.

2   Background

2.1   Online Social Support Exchange

Social support refers to the degree to which a person's fundamental social needs such as affection, approval, belonging, identity, and security are met through interactions with others [11, 12]. Online social support is usually exchanged in online health communities (OHCs) where health care consumers can ask questions, share experience/information, or seek/provide support. A typical scenario of social support exchange in OHCs is initiated by a participant posting a message on a specific health condition or topic, followed by other participants' replies to this discussion. Online social support exchange plays an essential role for the self-management of health conditions and the change of health behaviors, as it has been found to benefit participants by improving their health knowledge and attitudes [2].

The two types of social support most frequently exchanged in OHCs are: (1) *informational support* that refers to the offering of detailed information, facts, suggestions, or news about the health situation or ways of better dealing with the situation; and (2) *emotional support* that expresses emotional concerns such as care, love, sympathy, understanding, and encouragement. This study focuses on the classification of these two major types of social support exchanged in online health communities, using deep learning and word-embedding methods as reviewed in the following subsections.

2.2 Deep Learning

Machine learning methods have been applied in various applications such as image recognition, default detection, customer churn prevention, and sentiment classification. Deep learning is a representation learning method that employs multiple processing layers of neural networks to learn a hierarchy of abstract representations of data for regression or classification [13]. A deep learning neural network architecture contains a stack of multiple layers, each layer mapping the input to output. Those multiple layers (usually non-linear) can learn complicated yet minute features from the raw data. Compared with classical machine learning methods in which features need to be refined/extracted by human experts, deep learning methods learn the multi-layer abstract representations of raw data for subsequent regression or classification. Thus, deep learning has a great potential for empowering many business applications such as Fintech [14], manufacturing [15], and enterprise social media management [16].

2.3 Word Embedding

Application of machine learning algorithms to textual data analysis such as social support classification and sentiment analysis requires a way of representing the unstructured textual data as numerical numbers. Previous studies on online social support classification (e.g., [2, 4, 5]) used the bag of words (BOW) approach to quantify textual messages exchanged in OHCs. That is, OHC messages are represented as a form of term-by-document matrix. The BOW representation assumes that a document is a collection of words/terms, thus important information regarding the positions of words and semantic connections between words is not captured. Also, BOW method usually leads to feature vectors with very high dimensionality, which often need a manual or algorithm-driven feature selection procedure to reduce the dimensionality of data for machine learning algorithm training. A general BOW method involves multiple steps including tokenizing textual data, stemming, filtering out stopwords, creating term-by-document matrices, and selecting features.

Word embedding refers to a set of techniques that represent words or phrases of a vocabulary in a continuous low-dimensional vector space. Word embedding methods minimize the distance between a word and its context words in the vector space such that similar words are close to each other in the space model. Compared to methods based on bag of words, word embedding approaches can build a word vector space that captures the syntactic and semantic characteristics of words, thus improving the performance of various regression or classification tasks. Recently word2vec model [7] has become attractive as a word embedding method that is learned from artificial neural networks.

A primary benefit of word2vec model is that it can be trained by a large amount of unlabeled data (i.e., unsupervised learning) using a neural network structure with two layers. Two techniques of word2vec, as depicted in Fig. 1, include: (1) continuous bag of words (CBOW) which predicts a word from its context words, and (2) skip-gram which, on the opposite direction, predicts context words from the current word.

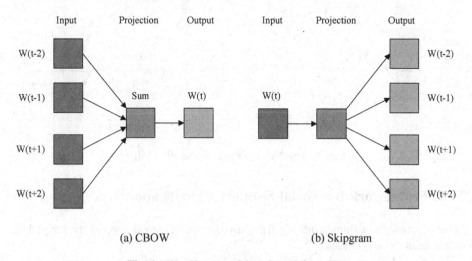

(a) CBOW   (b) Skipgram

Fig. 1. Word2vec models (adapted from [7])

As word2vec models only provide vector representation for individual words, the results cannot be directly used for social support classification or other text classification that is at the document (or message) level. A typical way of representing documents is to aggregate all the vectors of words occurring in a document as the embedding representation of the document [e.g., 17]. However, such aggregation does not guarantee an appropriate representation of similar documents.

The doc2vec model [6] extends the word2vec approach to unsupervised leaning of continuous representations of documents, paragraphs, or sentences. Two variations of doc2vec are: (1) distributed memory (DM) model of paragraph vectors which is similar to the CBOW model in word2vec, and (2) distributed bag of words (DBOW) which is analogous to the skip-gram model in word2vec. As shown in Fig. 2, the DM model uses both the document/paragraph vector and word vectors to predict the center word in the context, while the DBOW model trains the document/paragraph vector to predict words in a small window. This study applies both the DM and DBOW models to represent OHC messages.

182   L. Chen

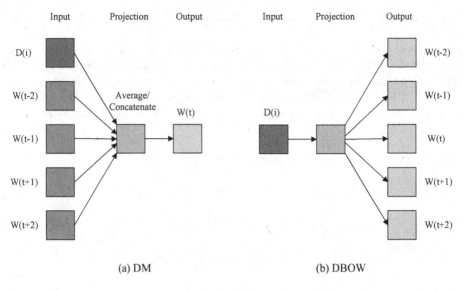

(a) DM   (b) DBOW

Fig. 2. Doc2vec models (adapted from [6])

3 A Framework for Social Support Classification

Figure 3 presents a framework for the classification of social support exchanged in online health communities.

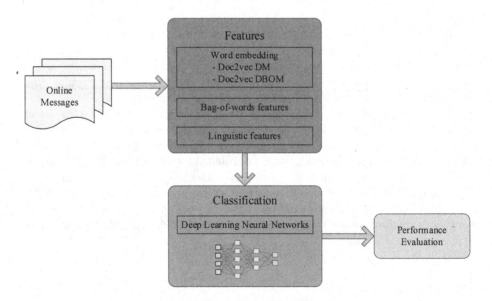

Fig. 3. Framework of online social support classification.

First, textual messages are collected from OHCs. These messages are then cleaned and various features including document embedding features using doc2vec, bag-of-words features, and linguistic features are trained or extracted from the textual data. All these features are treated as the input of a deep learning model which classifies whether an OHC message expresses informational support or emotional support. At the evaluation stage, various performance measures such as accuracy, AUC (area under curve), precision, recall, and F1 score can be used to evaluate the performance of the trained algorithm.

4   Research Method

An experiment was conducted to evaluate the proposed framework of social support classification. The details are explained in the following subsections.

4.1   Dataset

A dataset of 1830 forum reply messages was collected from a US-hosted online health community dedicated to the topics of depression. Each message was manually coded as whether it expresses informational support or emotional support. The manual labels were treated as the ground truth for validation. This is an imbalanced dataset with 249 messages expressing informational support and 417 messages expressing emotional support among all 1830 replies. The whole dataset was split into a training set of 1281 observations (70%) and a test set of 549 observations (30%).

4.2   Textual Data Processing

The raw OHC messages were preprocessed to extract important features for classification modeling. In total, 1055 features were trained or extracted from the textual data. These features include the following four major types that capture significant textual characteristics of social support expression in these messages. The total number of features of each type is shown in parentheses.

- Doc2vec DM features (300)
- Doc2vec DBOW features (300)
- Bag-of-words TF-IDF features (362)
- Linguistic features (93)

The doc2vec features (both DM and DBOW) were trained by using the Python implementation of doc2vec in the Gensim package [18]. Word embeddings were trained on the same research dataset.

To extract bag-of-words features, reply messages collected from the online health communities were first tokenized and changed to lower case. Non-letter terms were filtered out in the data analysis. Stop words such as "the", "is", "of", "an", and "a" were removed from the documents. Then, the Porter stemming method [19] was applied to remove term suffices. Finally, a TF-IDF (term frequency-inverse document frequency) matrix was created to represent the relative importance of frequent terms in OHC reply

184   L. Chen

(a) Informational support messages   (b) Emotional support messages

Fig. 4. Word clouds of social support messages in online health communities.

messages. Figure 4 shows the word clouds of the 150 most frequent stemmed terms occurring in informational support messages and emotional support messages respectively.

The linguistic features were calculated by the software tool LIWC [20]. LIWC is a widely used linguistic analysis tool, with its reliability and validity verified by many studies [20–22].

4.3   Feature Importance

The importance of the four sets of features was assessed by applying a random forests algorithm on informational support classification. Figure 5 shows the importance scores of all features. Table 1 summarizes the top 200 most important features from all the 1055 features. A substantial portion of the top 200 most important features are trained from doc2vec models, with 52% of features trained from the distributed memory (DM) model and 42% trained from the distributed bag of words (DBOW) model. In contrast, only 6% of the top 200 most important features come from the traditional bag of words approach and the LIWC linguistic analysis. This provides clear evidence that the word2vec models can better capture important features for online social support classification than the traditional bag of words and linguistic analysis methods.

4.4   Predictive Modeling

A deep learning neural network was used to classify whether an OHC reply message expresses informational and emotional social support. As an OHC reply may provide both informational and emotional support, two classifiers were trained and evaluated,

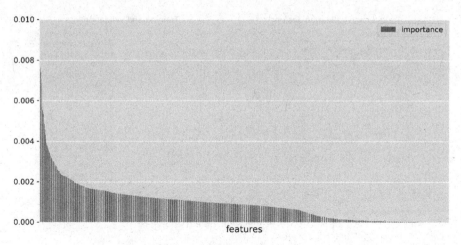

Fig. 5. Feature importance.

Table 1. Summary of top 200 most important features.

Feature level	Number of features	Percent
Doc2vec DM	104	52.0%
Doc2vec DBOW	84	42.0%
LIWC	9	4.5%
BOW	3	1.5%

each classifying one type of social support. As the dataset is imbalanced, classification algorithms tend to introduce bias by predicting the more frequent classes. To deal with the imbalanced dataset, class weights were set to be inversely proportional to their frequency in the training set.

5 Preliminary Result

Figure 6 shows the accuracy and loss of each social support classifier over time. Overall, the informational support classifier reaches an accuracy of 87.4%, while the emotional support classifier has an accuracy of 83.8%.

For the future work, a couple of other classification methods including logistic regression, support vector machine, decision tree, and random forests will be used to compare with the suggested deep learning neural network. Grid search strategy will also be used to tune hyper-parameters in the learning algorithms, in order to further improve the classification performance of the algorithms. Further, other performance metrics such as AUC, precision, recall, and F1 score can be applied to more comprehensively evaluate the performance of deep learning classification method. In addition, using pre-trained word embeddings may also improve the performance of text classification [23]. Lastly, more labelled data can be collected as deep learning needs a lot of training samples.

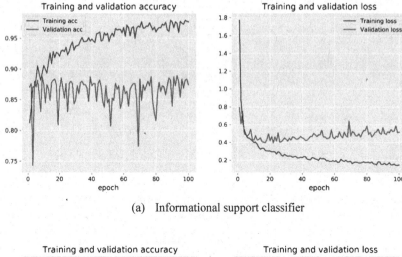

(a)   Informational support classifier

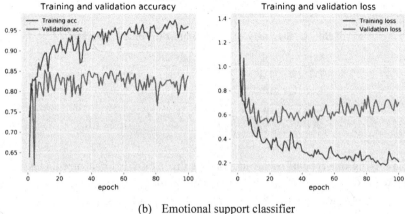

(b)   Emotional support classifier

Fig. 6.   Performance of social support classifiers over time.

6   Conclusion

Online health communities have attracted significant attention from both academic communities and practice [1, 2, 24, 25]. This study proposes a framework that incorporates doc2vec representation models and deep learning methods into the classification of social support exchanged in online health communities. The findings will provide important implications for both research and practice of online health communities. The same approach can also be applied in or extended to a variety of other settings such as online knowledge communities where an important effort is to assess the quality of knowledge contribution expressed in participants' posts [3].

References

1. Chen, L., Straub, D.: The impact of virtually crowdsourced social support on individual health: analyzing big datasets for underlying causalities. In: Proceedings of the 21st Americas Conference on Information Systems, pp. 1–8 (2015)
2. Chen, L., Baird, A., Straub, D.: Fostering participant health knowledge and attitudes: An econometric study of a chronic disease-focused online health community. J. Manag. Inf. Syst. **36**(1), 194–229 (2019)
3. Chen, L., Baird, A., Straub, D.: Why do participants continue to contribute? Evaluation of usefulness voting and commenting motivational affordances within an online knowledge community. Decis. Support Syst. **118**, 21–32 (2019)
4. Wang, Y.-C., Kraut, R., Levine, J.M.: To stay or leave?: the relationship of emotional and informational support to commitment in online health support groups. In: Proceedings of the ACM 2012 Conference on Computer Supported Cooperative Work, pp. 833–842. ACM, 2145329 (2012)
5. Wang, X., Zhao, K., Street, N.: Social support and user engagement in online health communities. In: Zheng, X., Zeng, D., Chen, H., Zhang, Y., Xing, C., Neill, D.B. (eds.) ICSH 2014. LNCS, vol. 8549, pp. 97–110. Springer, Cham (2014). https://doi.org/10.1007/978-3-319-08416-9_10
6. Le, Q., Mikolov, T.: Distributed representations of sentences and documents. In: International Conference on Machine Learning, pp. 1188–1196 (2014)
7. Mikolov, T., Chen, K., Corrado, G., Dean, J.: Efficient estimation of word representations in vector space. In: Proceedings of Workshop at the International Conference on Learning Representations (2013)
8. Liang, H., Fothergill, R., Baldwin, T.: Rosemerry: a baseline message-level sentiment classification system. In: Proceedings of the 9th International Workshop on Semantic Evaluation (SemEval 2015), pp. 551–555 (2015)
9. Dang, Q.V., Ignat, C.-L.: Quality assessment of Wikipedia articles without feature engineering. In: Proceedings of the 16th ACM/IEEE-CS on Joint Conference on Digital Libraries, pp. 27–30. ACM (2016)
10. Trieu, L.Q., Tran, H.Q., Tran, M.-T.: News classification from social media using twitter-based doc2vec model and automatic query expansion. In: Proceedings of the Eighth International Symposium on Information and Communication Technology, pp. 460–467. ACM (2017)
11. Thoits, P.A.: Conceptual, methodological, and theoretical problems in studying social support as a buffer against life stress. J. Health Soc. Behav. **23**, 145–159 (1982)
12. Kaplan, B.H., Cassel, J.C., Gore, S.: Social support and health. Med. Care **15**, 47–58 (1977)
13. LeCun, Y., Bengio, Y., Hinton, G.: Deep learning. Nature **521**, 436–444 (2015)
14. Siau, K., et al.: Fintech empowerment: Data science, AI, and machine learning. Cutter Bus. Technol. J. **31**, 12–18 (2018)
15. Wang, J., Ma, Y., Zhang, L., Gao, R.X., Wu, D.: Deep learning for smart manufacturing: Methods and applications. J. Manuf. Syst. **48**, 144–156 (2018)
16. Moqbel, M., Nah, F.F.-H.: Enterprise social media use and impact on performance: the role of workplace integration and positive emotions. AIS Trans. Hum.-Comput. Interact. **9**, 261–280 (2017)
17. Enríquez, F., Troyano, J.A., López-Solaz, T.: An approach to the use of word embeddings in an opinion classification task. Expert Syst. Appl. **66**, 1–6 (2016)

18. Rehurek, R., Sojka, P.: Software framework for topic modelling with large corpora. In: Proceedings of the LREC 2010 Workshop on New Challenges for NLP Frameworks. Citeseer (2010)
19. Porter, M.F.: An algorithm for suffix stripping. Program **14**, 130–137 (1980)
20. Pennebaker, J.W., Boyd, R.L., Jordan, K., Blackburn, K.: The development and psychometric properties of LIWC2015. University of Texas at Austin, Austin, TX (2015)
21. Tausczik, Y.R., Pennebaker, J.W.: The psychological meaning of words: LIWC and computerized text analysis methods. J. Lang. Soc. Psychol. **29**, 24–54 (2010)
22. Pennebaker, J.W., Francis, M.E.: Cognitive, emotional, and language processes in disclosure. Cogn. Emot. **10**, 601–626 (1996)
23. Lau, J.H., Baldwin, T.: An empirical evaluation of doc2vec with practical insights into document embedding generation. arXiv preprint arXiv:1607.05368 (2016)
24. Chen, L., Baird, A., Straub, D.: An analysis of the evolving intellectual structure of health information systems research within the information systems (IS) discipline. J. Assoc. Inf. Syst. 1–48 (2019, forthcoming)
25. Chen, L., Baird, A., Straub, D.: The evolving intellectual structure of the health informatics discipline: a multi-method investigation of a rapidly-growing scientific field. Working Paper, Georgia State University (2014)

Identifying Essential Factors for Deriving Value from Big Data Analytics in Healthcare

Brenda Eschenbrenner[(⊠)]

University of Nebraska at Kearney, Kearney, NE 68845, USA
eschenbrenbl@unk.edu

Abstract. Big data analytics is emerging in many industries and is a prominent undertaking in healthcare. The healthcare industry has more opportunities now to garner insights and advantages from data than ever before. Big data analytics has the potential to enhance many aspects of the industry from enhancing quality of patient care to revenue cycle improvements. However, successfully leveraging big data analytics poses challenges as well, such as data standardization and integrity. Therefore, it will be important to identify the essential factors that will facilitate the ability to derive the maximum value from big data analytics for such endeavors. This research proposes to identify these pivotal factors of big data analytics in healthcare by utilizing value-focused thinking (VFT). VFT will entail interviews with both healthcare data analysts and management to identify these important factors. The findings can provide guidance to practitioners when considering the essential factors for big data analytics success, as well as provide topics for future research.

Keywords: Big data analytics · Value-focused thinking · Healthcare analytics

1 Introduction

Big data analytics has the potential to provide increased, improved, and more salient insights that were previously unfathomable. With the increased usage of and continuous improvements in technology and its capabilities, utilizing massive amounts of data to improve healthcare services is now possible and being explored [1]. The healthcare industry has been exploring and using big data from a variety of sources such as electronic health records and health information exchanges [2]. Healthcare systems can leverage this data to gain new insights into reducing costs, generating new revenue streams, and, most importantly, improving quality of care and patient outcomes. Hence, utilizing data to assist healthcare and administrative professionals, is a significant focus [1]. Leveraging this data and applying big data analytics to derive value is a current topic of concern in healthcare.

With the escalating use of big data analytics in many industries, many opportunities as well as challenges emerge. Being able to utilize data analytics software applications, develop new insights into the data, having the skills and analytical prowess to extract the relevant data and model it in the most insightful manner, as well as develop and decipher the many different representations of data that are possible can be beneficial and problematic. Being able to garner the full potential of big data analytics will require

© Springer Nature Switzerland AG 2019
F. F.-H. Nah and K. Siau (Eds.): HCII 2019, LNCS 11589, pp. 189–198, 2019.
https://doi.org/10.1007/978-3-030-22338-0_15

more than just data, such as knowledge of and ability to utilize appropriate analytic techniques and tools [3]. Some organizations have not realized the benefits that were intended and are re-addressing their strategies, which makes identifying factors that will lend to deriving value essential.

Although the amount of data continues to grow, some healthcare organizations are not sure what the true potential is of big data analytics [4]. Also, organizations are trying to identify cost-effective and optimal ways to deploy their resources to gain the most benefit from data analytics. For example, leveraging predictive analytics to create definite business value has not been fully realized [5]. Factors that have been challenges in this endeavor include the volume and complexity of data, analysts who are not fluent with data analytic techniques, and being able to demonstrate a salient impact. Deriving value from big data analytics is a major undertaking in healthcare [1]. In order to derive the full value that big data analytics can offer to healthcare, it's essential that we identify the factors that will contribute to this endeavor. Therefore, the research question being pursued for this study is: What are the factors essential to deriving value from big data analytics in healthcare?

Shedding light on the perspectives of various individuals, at varying levels or areas of the organization, impacted by big data analytics will be important for realizing the true value from big data analytics in healthcare [1]. This research proposes to address this research question by interviewing data analysts and management using value-focused thinking to identify the factors essential to deriving value from big data analytics. The outcome from these interviews and subsequent analysis will be a means-ends objective network. This approach will allow the essential factors (i.e., means) needed to derive the value (i.e., ends) from big data analytics in healthcare to be identified.

2 Literature Review

Big data has been defined with various characteristics. Big data has been described with the attributes of volume, velocity, variety, veracity, value, variability, and valence [3, 6]. Volume refers to the amount of data. Velocity is the speed that data is being created and delivered. Variety is a multifarious gamut of structured and unstructured data. Veracity is the quality, uncertainty, and imprecision in the data. Value is the data's worth such as developing competitive advantages. Variability refers to continuous modification. Valence is connectedness or relational aspects of the data.

Healthcare information systems and big data analytics are prominent in the healthcare industry. Healthcare information systems can be classified as clinical information systems (CIS) and administrative information systems (AIS), although some systems combine both [1]. CIS support the service provider and delivery of the service (e.g., electronic health records). AIS support administrative functions (e.g., payroll systems). Types of big data analytics include descriptive, predictive, and prescriptive [6]. Descriptive analytics provide insights into what has occurred in the past and is currently taking place. Examples include dashboards and standardized reporting. Predictive analytics provide projections regarding what could occur. Examples include Monte Carlo simulations and data mining. Prescriptive analytics provide guidance and suggestions regarding recommended courses of actions. Examples include adaptive algorithms.

Big data analytics can be leveraged to provide valuable insights and support decision-making processes in organizations [6]. Specific applications, such as predictive analytics, have been utilized to refine business processes, discover unanticipated opportunities, and proactively identify problems [5]. For instance, predictive analytics are being used to assess the probabilities of patient readmissions and identify patients with higher risks of certain diseases. Insurance companies can create such predictive models based on medical claim data. Some argue that insurers' experience and history with predictive analytics, along with magnitude of the institution, provides an advantage over healthcare systems capabilities.

Also, sources of data used in analysis can be more expansive and diverse [5]. Analysis can include not only data seen by payers but include clinical as well as psycho-socioeconomic data. This can then be leveraged to identify at-risk patents. For example, if a patient is not filling a necessary prescription, their healthcare provider can be given this information who can then intervene by communicating with the patient about his or her treatment plan. Another possibility is to develop a treatment plan based on the patient's current status including levels of activity and health condition (e.g., weight).

The healthcare industry has utilized big data in areas of bioinformatics and exchanging healthcare information to improve patient care, for example disease diagnosis [2]. Opportunities for big data analytics in healthcare include improvements in medical diagnoses, predicting disease epidemics, improving quality of care, identifying discontinuity in the delivery of healthcare services, reducing costs, discovering trends associated with reactions to medicines and hospital readmissions, and deriving treatments or cures and doing so based on an individual's personal circumstances (e.g., previous treatments and reactions, medical history) [1, 6, 7]. Healthcare models are evolving to be more personalized as well as proactive versus reactive, such as identifying categories of individuals with similar biological basis of a disease for better treatment plans [8, 9]. Healthcare systems have leveraged clinical data to gain better insights into populations' concerns and improving accuracy in predictions [5].

In an accounting context, big data analytics has been used for endeavors such as health care charge capture, fraud detection, continuous auditing/monitoring, anomaly identification or gaining other insights during an audit, and vendor payment transactions [5, 7, 10–12]. The value of big data analytics is still emerging and will require users who can apply advanced technical and analytical skills making the factors needed for competent usage potentially unique in comparison to other system usage such as enterprise resource planning systems. Also, identifying new uses of the data that will benefit one's organization will require attributes, skills, and knowledge capabilities that expand many users' existing repertoires. Hence, existing frameworks may need adaptation to properly align with the needs of big data analytics.

Big data analytics in healthcare is replete with challenges. This includes issues such as security as well as privacy [2, 7]. Other potential issues some have posed include the use of big data analytics over healthcare professional services. Greater reliance may be placed on big data analytics with less reliance on healthcare professionals' opinions and diagnoses, creating lesser need for their services [7].

Data governance issues have emerged such as fragmented data sets that could be integrated to decrease costs and improve integrity, accessibility, reliability, standardization, sharing, integration, transmission, processing, storage, and security [5, 6]. Data, such as electronic health record data, can be in both unstructured and structured formats [9]. Unstructured data, such as clinical notes, can be problematic to analyze because formats may vary, unnatural grammar or misspellings may be included, and domain-specific acronyms may be used. The frequency of data collection also varies. Some tests only occur once (e.g., genome), while others can be several times in one day (e.g., labs) or continuous (e.g., respiration). Data can also be generated from sensor devices, self-reporting data, videos, and medical images [6].

Data may be incomplete (e.g., pharmacy data for an entire population), substantial costs may be incurred, and extensive amounts of time to generate a return on investment can all be considered barriers to overcome [5, 6]. Data can have a significant amount of dimensions and highly heterogenous, and the quality of the data can be problematic [6, 9]. For instance, inadequate signal-to-noise ratios, errors in data entry, and gaps in data [9]. Effective utilization of predictive analytical models can be problematic due to data analysts' lack of medical knowledge creating inabilities to provide recommendations [5]. Also, healthcare professionals are deficient on time to participate in predictive model development and need to integrate these predictive models into existing work routines.

Some healthcare professionals may be averse to change [1]. Recommendations to effectively leverage data analytics include understanding the impact desired, consolidating data into a single location, integrating data analytics when deciding upon patient care and treatment, and utilizing qualitative as well as quantitative data [5]. Also, achieving the benefits that big data has to offer is dependent upon the correct assembly of technology, methods, and skill sets [1]. Organizations will need to consider effective approaches to integrate big data analytics in their current IT infrastructures. Also, for those who have historically used analytics, they will need to integrate big data analytics in a complementary fashion.

Previous research has addressed some aspects of leveraging information technology to achieve its full potential and the greatest return on investment. For instance, the abilities of the users. Previous literature has conceptualized information systems user competency or the ability of some users to obtain the greatest benefits possible from IS usage [13]. Also, previous research has explored critical success factors in domains such as ERP implementations (e.g., [14]). However, users of big data analytics can have unique challenges because of the inherent and potentially unstructured nature of the tasks to accomplish. For example, the objective may not be clearly defined and entail more exploratory, innovative, and unplanned discovery. Big data analytics is unique in that it can also entail statistics and machine learning [6]. The importance of proficient big data analytics usage needs to permeate the organization and not be centralized to just a few. In addition, this research focuses on ongoing usage of big data analytics versus its implementation.

Previous research has explored aspects of big data analytics in healthcare such as improving models, enhancing the richness of the data used, and identifying more optimal methods of processing data to improve hospital readmission predictive analytics [15]. Research has explored the use of variegated -omic and electronic health record data to facilitate precision medicine [9]. Research has put forth frameworks for studying big data and business-IT alignment from a social dynamics perspective [1]. However, previous research has not identified the elements needed to realize the desired value of big data analytics in healthcare. In other words, a gap in the literature can be filled by focusing on identifying the essential factors needed to derive the desired value from big data analytics in healthcare.

3   Research Methodology

This study proposes to utilize value-focused thinking (VFT) to identify essential factors associated with deriving value from big data analytics in healthcare. VFT can be more readily understood using Means-Ends Chain (MEC) Theory and a laddering interviewing technique [16]. According to MEC, product or service attributes are linked to the values that individuals are trying to achieve through the consequences associated with consumption [16, 17]. These values are pivotal drivers in decision making [17]. When individuals identify items (such as product or service attributes) that have the potential to fulfill what one values, these items can be categorized as such. Items or attributes used to create these categories are derived from one's values and originate from distinctions which "are dichotomies that represent *the end points of dimensions along which objectives may be compared*" [17, p. 63]. In other words, item or attribute categories are created based on their association with or ability to achieve a desired value or end state.

Consequences are the outcomes derived from an activity, whether they are experienced immediately or in the future, and are evaluated based on situational circumstances [17]. These consequences of engaging in an activity are associated with that activity in one's memory. Consequences can be directly derived from the activity, or indirectly from external sources (e.g., other individuals' reactions) after the activity occurs. The basic tenet is that decision making among various activities is based on achieving consequences that are deemed favorable or desirable and reducing unfavorable or undesirable outcomes. In some circumstances, trade-offs can occur in that achieving certain consequences means having to tolerate unfavorable consequences or sacrificing some other favorable consequences.

Values are arranged in one's value system by their importance [17]. Accordingly, consequences associated with more cardinal values or desired ends are more salient. Whereas, consequences associated with less vital values are less salient. Therefore, its important to understand the correlations between attributes and the consequences that can be derived in order for a decision to be made.

Attributes are considered *means* and the lowest level of the hierarchy of one's memory [16, 17]. The next level is considered *means* as well and consists of the consequences generated from consuming the product or service. The consequences can be physical, psychological, or social. The final level is the *ends* or the value that is derived from the consequences. Hence, in the decision-making process, individuals identify the means (or attributes and consequences) that ultimately provide the desired ends (or values). This chain can then shed light on the means that are important to achieving the ends.

Laddering allows deeper probing into cognitive structures and has been used with techniques such as Repertory Grid [18, 19]. This is accomplished by first prompting the interviewee to identify attributes that differentiate products or services [16]. Then, to reveal the ladder or means-ends chain (i.e., attribute, consequence, and end value), the interviewee is asked questions about the attribute elicited such as "Why is that important to you?" [16, p. 29]. The answers provided represent levels of abstraction and are subsequently used for additional questioning to further understand the chain or ladder until the highest level of abstraction is revealed. In the context of means-ends chains, this technique provides a mechanism to expose the relationship between the means/attributes, consequences, and values. Content analysis can then be utilized to identify pivotal elements of means/attributes, consequences, and values elicited from interviewees. Then, a cognitive map is created by the salient relationships among the elements.

VFT provides a mechanism to illuminate what individuals consider important to them and the manner to successfully attain it [16]. In other words, VFT focuses on the means-ends value chain. Values are identified by stated objectives, or something one aspires to accomplish. These objectives include "a decision context, an object, and a direction of preference" [16, p. 30]. Two types of objectives can be elicited – fundamental and means objectives. Fundamental objectives represent the values or end state one desires [16, 20, 21]. The means objectives are the methods to accomplish or bring to fruition these end states. The goal of VFT is to identify both of these objectives as well as their relationships, with the result being a means-ends objective network that is representative of decision-making in a given context.

Considering that VFT explicitly elicits the methods of obtaining a desired end state, this research method is considered appropriate considering the focus of this research is identifying those factors (i.e., methods of achieving the end state) associated with value from big data analytics in healthcare. VFT also places no restrictions on the objectives (i.e., means and ends) that participants can generate and facilitates a comprehensive approach to obtaining these objectives [22]. VFT is considered most ideal for this study because other methods, such as surveys, may not shed light on the relationships between means and ends.

VFT has been utilized previously in contexts such as strategic management and decision making, mobile technology in education, mobile technology's strategic impact, information system security, terrorism, system architecture assessment, and emerging technologies [16, 20–26]. The VFT approach allows the uncovering of what an individual values, or a desired objective, and the means with which it can be achieved. In the context of big data analytics, this study can utilize VFT to identify the values that data analysts have and the means to achieve these values. This study can also use VFT to identify management's values and the means with which they believe that they can be achieved. These means represent factors necessary to derive value from big data analytics in healthcare, and this study intends to identify these factors both from analysts' and management's perspectives to provide a more complete understanding of the relevant factors.

The VFT procedures are noted in Table 1 [16, 25, 27]:

Interviews with both data analysts and management will be recorded and transcribed. Research participant interviews will continue until the point of saturation is

Table 1. Value-focused thinking procedures

Step	Procedure
1	Research participants will be interviewed and asked to identify what they value in big data analytics or the value they see in big data analytics. This will include identifying issues, goals, and potential benefits. Participants will include both data analysts and management who are most familiar with these aspects of big data analytics (e.g., issues, desired value) so a more inclusive view of essential factors can be identified. Also, these factors will be identified by those who are interacting with, or responsible for the analysis, and are more likely directly impacted by or are familiar with objectives associated with big data analytics. Others, such as medical professionals, may be considered end users which can be addressed in future research studies. Specific questions to identify values will include: 1. What are the goals of using big data analytics in healthcare? 2. What are the potential benefits that can be derived from using big data analytics in healthcare? 3. If there were no limitations with big data analytics, what value could be derived? 4. What are the issues with effectively using big data analytics? After participants have identified all values they can generate, additional questions will be asked to identify additional values. For example, the pros and cons of big data analytics as well as the use of big data analytics in specific contexts. Also, questions will be posed to identify potential issues such as cost versus benefits and expertise. All participants' value lists will then be aggregated. Objectives will be reviewed by two individuals and consistent themes or meanings will be grouped together
2	The identified values are then transformed into objectives which will then be classified as either fundamental or means objectives. As mentioned previously, an objective is considered "something one wants to strive towards" and "has three features: a decision context, an object, and a direction" [27, p. 535]. Discerning these objectives can be accomplished by asking probing questions about the importance of each objective. More specifically, during the interviews, participants will be asked "Why is that important" in order to clearly distinguish means from fundamental objectives. Fundamental objectives are goals that the individual would like to achieve. Means objectives are methods of achieving other objectives. Hence, fundamental objectives will be identified as those that provide end values states and additional objectives cannot be derived
3	A means-ends objective network will then be constructed from the findings in the previous step in which the relationships between the means and fundamental objectives are depicted. The network will include any sub-objectives as components of the overarching fundamental objective

reached, or no new objectives emerge. Two individuals will code the results and identify means and fundamental objectives, and inter-rater reliability will be assessed using Cohen's Kappa coefficient [28]. Yin's [29] Principles of Data Collection will be utilized to enhance the reliability and validity of this study. This will include utilizing various sources of evidence, a database, and chains of evidence.

Utilizing various sources of evidence will be fulfilled by triangulation of the data in which two individuals will independently code the data and inter-rater reliability assessments made using Cohen's Kappa coefficient. Coefficients that are above .65 will be considered acceptable based on previous recommendations [30]. Also, both data analysts and management will be interviewed. To address the principles regarding creating and maintaining a database and chains of evidence, a database of all transcripts and notes taken during the interviews will be created. Also, all coding and the results obtained through each iteration will also be maintained in a database, and done so separately so a chain of evidence is created.

Based on the research participants responses to the probing question "Why is that important" and the objectives identified, the means-ends objective network will be derived. The ladders or relationships between the objectives will be included in the network if at least four participants have generated it, based on previous recommendations [16].

4 Expected Contributions, Implications, and Conclusion

Big data analytics is being heavily adopted in healthcare. However, deriving the full value it has to offer is a challenge for many organizations. The findings from this research study can potentially improve outcomes in the healthcare industry by identifying the pivotal factors needed to successfully leverage big data analytics. This model of means and fundamental objectives can provide insights into the most important factors (i.e., means objectives) needed to realize the greatest benefits from big data analytics in healthcare.

Practitioners can utilize the findings from this study to address the factors needed to realize the greatest return on their investment in big data analytics, as well as achieve successful performance outcomes. This can provide guidance regarding mechanisms that need greater investment or development to derive the desired values. Organizations may have already identified some of these mechanisms and not others. Hence, organizations can receive confirmation that current investments may be justified, and new investments may be needed. Also, current investments in mechanisms that are not identified in the network may need to be re-addressed in regard to the contribution they are making to achieve the end goal, i.e., the desired value from big data analytics.

Leveraging Means-Ends Chain (MEC) Theory and a laddering interviewing technique, value-focused thinking uncovers the methods or means to achieve the desired end or value. In this context, the means to achieve the desired value from big data analytics in healthcare (i.e., ends) will be identified. The research results from this study will provide a means-ends objective network that can provide future research directions. For example, the importance of means or essential factors for deriving value from big data analytics in healthcare can be addressed. Also, the findings can be explored or used in future research studies such as experiments entailing the assessment of identified means or mechanisms for deriving value from big data analytics. The network could be applied in action research studies of big data analytics in a healthcare institution as well, for example. Also, the findings can be assessed for generalizability to other domains, such as the financial services industry. Overall, big data analytics has the potential to make a significant contribution to improvements in healthcare, and identifying essential factors to derive its value is pivotal to this endeavor.

References

1. Weerasinghe, K., Pauleen, D., Scahill, S., Taskin, N.: Development of a theoretical framework to investigate alignment of big data in healthcare through a social representation lens. Australas. J. Inf. Syst. **22**, 1–23 (2018)
2. Guha, S., Kumar, S.: Emergence of big data research in operations management, information systems, and healthcare: past contributions and future roadmap. Prod. Oper. Manag. **27**(9), 1724–1735 (2018)
3. Grover, V., Chiang, R.H.L., Liang, T.-P., Zhang, D.: Creating strategic business value from big data analytics: a research framework. J. Manag. Inf. Syst. **35**(2), 388–423 (2018)
4. Angood, P.B.: Data and information critical for health care's future. Phys. Executive **40**(4), 4–5 (2014)
5. Appold, K.: Turn data into insight: how predictive analytics can capture revenue. Managed Healthc. Executive **27**(7), 16–21 (2017)
6. Saggi, M.K., Jain, S.: A survey towards an integration of big data analytics to big insights for value-creation. Inf. Process. Manag. **54**(5), 758–790 (2018)
7. Alexandru, A.G., Radu, I.M., Bizon, M.-L.: Big data in healthcare – opportunities and challenges. Informatica Economica **22**(2), 43–54 (2018)
8. Whelan, D.: Big data analytics, digital health platforms, and precision medicine tools: moving towards individualized and personalized care practices. Am. J. Med. Res. **5**(2), 28–33 (2018)
9. Wu, P.-Y., Cheng, C.-W., Kaddi, C.D., Venugopalan, J., Hoffman, R., Wang, M.D.: Omic and electronic health record big data analytics for precision medicine. IEEE Trans. Biomed. Eng. **64**(2), 263–273 (2017)
10. Raphael, J.: Rethinking the audit. J. Account. **223**(4), 29–32 (2017)
11. Tschakert, N., Kokina, J., Kozlowski, S., Vasarhelyi, M.: The next frontier in data analytics. J. Account. **222**(2), 58–63 (2016)
12. Tysiac, K.: How financial statement audits deliver key business insights: increased use of data analytics is helping auditors find more information that could be helpful to clients. J. Account. **223**(6), 44–45 (2017)
13. Eschenbrenner, B., Nah, F.F.-H.: Information systems user competency: a conceptual foundation. Commun. Assoc. Inf. Syst. **34**(1), 1363–1378 (2014)
14. Reitsma, E., Hilletofth, P.: Critical success factors for ERP system implementation: a user perspective. Eur. Bus. Rev. **30**(3), 285–310 (2018)
15. Zolbanin, H.M., Delen, D.: Processing electronic medical records to improve predictive analytics outcomes for hospital readmissions. Decis. Support Syst. **112**, 98–110 (2018)
16. Sheng, H., Siau, K., Nah, F.F.-H.: Understanding the values of mobile technology in education: a value-focused thinking approach. DATA BASE Adv. Inf. Syst. **41**(2), 25–44 (2010)
17. Gutman, J.A.: A means-end chain model based on consumer categorization processes. J. Mark. **46**(2), 60–72 (1982)
18. Kelly, G.A.: A Theory of Personality. W.W. Norton, New York (1963)
19. Kelly, G.A.: The Psychology of Personal Constructs. W.W. Norton, New York (1955)
20. Kunz, R.E., Siebert, J., Mütterlein, J.: Combining value-focused thinking and balanced scorecard to improve decision-making in strategic management. J. Multi-Criteria Decis. Anal. **23**(5–6), 225–241 (2016)
21. Kunz, R.E., Siebert, J., Mütterlein, J.: Structuring objectives of media companies: a case study based on value-focused thinking and the balanced scorecard. J. Media Bus. Stud. **13**(4), 257–275 (2016)

22. Dhillon, G., Torkzadeh, G.: Value-focused assessment of information system security in organizations. Inf. Syst. J. **16**(3), 293–314 (2006)
23. Keeney, G.L., von Winterfeldt, D.: Identifying and structuring the objectives of terrorists. Risk Anal. **30**(12), 1803–1816 (2010)
24. Lesinski, G.: Application of value focused thinking and fuzzy systems to assess system architecture. Procedia Comput. Sci. **61**, 168–175 (2015)
25. Sheng, H., Nah, F.F.-H., Siau, K.: Value-focused thinking and its application in MIS research. J. Database Manag. **18**(3), I–V (2007)
26. Sheng, H., Nah, F.F.-H., Siau, K.: Strategic implications of mobile technology: a case study using value-focused thinking. J. Strateg. Inf. Syst. **14**(3), 269–290 (2005)
27. Keeney, R.L.: The value of internet commerce to the customer. Manag. Sci. **45**(4), 533–542 (1999)
28. Cohen, J.: A coefficient of agreement for nominal scales. Educ. Psychol. Measur. **20**(1), 37–46 (1960)
29. Yin, R.K.: Case Study Research: Designs and Methods, 2nd edn. Sage Publications Inc, Thousand Oaks (1994)
30. Sun, H., Zhang, P.: Adaptive IT use: conceptualization and measurement. In: Proceedings of the Fifth Annual Workshop on HCI Research in MIS, Milwaukee, WI, pp. 65–69 (2006)

A Medical Decision Support System Using Text Mining to Compare Electronic Medical Records

Pei-ju Lee[1]([⊠]), Yen-Hsien Lee[2], Yihuang Kang[3],
and Ching-Ping Chao[1]

[1] National Chung Cheng University, No. 168 University Rd., Minhsiung 621,
Chiayi County, Taiwan
pjlee@mis.ccu.edu.tw
[2] National Chiayi University, No. 300 Syuefu Rd., Chiayi City 600, Taiwan
[3] National Sun Yat-sen University, No. 70 Lianhai Rd., Gushan District,
Kaohsiung City 804, Taiwan

Abstract. The electronic medical records (EMRs) contain information about the patient such as their date of birth and blood type as well as other medical information such as prescription history and previous syndromes. Physicians usually have limited time to identify critical information on medical records and to provide a summary before they make a decision. However, the content of EMRs usually be complicated, repeated, and contain many consistency problems; these issues are not only cost a lot of time for physicians to filter information out from the medical records but also increase the probability of wrong medical decisions. Therefore, this study proposed a new EMR interface to identify the new medical information such as new syndromes or the turning point in the medical records. The Metathesaurus database which contains medical information such as medical terms or classification codes in the Unified Medical Language System will be used. This study uses MetaMap tools to compare medical terms within EMRs using MetaMap and also compares the vocabulary using the bigram technique to highlight the similarities in the EMR.

Keywords: Electronic medical records · Decision support system · MetaMap

1 Introduction

The electronic medical record (EMR), or the digital medical record, contains the interactive information between patients and medical staffs (Jardim 2013), as well as patients information such as the blood type and the physical condition. This standardized information helps hospitals collect patients' data for further analysis and allows healthcare professionals to make reference decisions for the patients (Senteioet al. 2018). The EMR is stored electronically in the cloud database of the Ministry of Health and Welfare in Taiwan, so that the Ministry of Health and Welfare can grasp the basis of people's medication and the hospital's declaration of health insurance points, and can fully store patients' information for the follow-up research and analytical uses of the government.

© Springer Nature Switzerland AG 2019
F. F.-H. Nah and K. Siau (Eds.): HCII 2019, LNCS 11589, pp. 199–208, 2019.
https://doi.org/10.1007/978-3-030-22338-0_16

With the implementation of EMRs, it has brought convenience and speed of the whole process of medical records. Most EMR systems enable physicians to use the functions of copy and paste or automatically import previous clinical data. However, the efficiency also brings a part of problems: when physicians use the copy and paste functions, it may cause the repeatability of some contents in EMRs, prolongs the length of whole EMR or the prescriptions prescribed by the physicians do not match the current situation of patients. These situations make it very difficult for medical staff to read medical records and take a longer time to find useful information (Zhang et al. 2017).

When physicians read EMRs, often suffer from the difficulty of data connection due to access a large amount of medical information (Prados-Suárez et al. 2012). Most of the literature is to redefine the data structure, reorganize file information, or provide a new medical system (Jerding and Stasko 1998; McAlearney et al. 2010; Prados-Suárez et al. 2012). Some studies does not directly dealing with amount problems but performing knowledge mobilization (i.e. calling professionals prepared for the action) and ubiquitous computing (i.e. people can process and capture information whenever and wherever they want) (Judd and Steenkiste 2003; Kang et al. 2006; Prados-Suárez et al. 2012), exchange of information using standardized medical information systems (Cayir and Basoglu 2008; Lähteenmäki et al. 2009; Nagy et al. 2010b; Prados-Suárez et al. 2012), or based on the user's background needs to improve data retrieval, so that the data retrieval model can better meet the real needs of customers (Prados-Suárez et al. 2012). Zhang et al. (2017) conducted a medical information semantic similarity study based on the n-gram method to find redundant EMRs.

The above research did not enable physicians to quickly identify new information on medical records and summaries in no time. Instead, they simply identified information and did not perform other function such as medical abstracts, labeling information, etc. Therefore, the medical data retrieval method of this study is to unitize the words in multiple EMRs of a single patient and use the n-gram and MetaMap comparison method to find the parts of the EMRs that are similar to the selected comparison cases. This study also proposes an interface, use it in a teaching hospital in central Taiwan as the research data, compare the medical records in an n-gram manner, and output new condition of the patient and a summary of the patient's medical records. In addition, the color-coding is used to highlight the differences between these EMRs, so that the physicians can pay attention to the information on the new condition in time. Furthermore, the medical related terms in the medical record are labeled and the medical record summary of the physician's EMR is provided using MetaMap. In turn, a decision support system was developed to identify the problem from the original data, documents, and personal knowledge, to find a solution to the problem so that the user can make better decisions (Hwang et al. 2018). The information can be shown on different devices, such as computers, cell phones, etc., in a responsive webpage, so that physicians can obtain new medical record information ubiquitously and make decisions more quickly.

2 Background

The types of decision support system consists of databases, computational model libraries, and knowledge outcome libraries; and the efficiency of the mining process and the information processed by the operations can be improved through visualization (Reyes et al. 2014; Tejeda et al. 2013; Zhang et al. 2017; Demergasso et al. 2018).

In the hospitals, because the medical information is very complicated, it may cause many medical problems, such as misadmission and misdiagnosis if we want to rely on the medical professionals to record the patients' medication, meals, etc. Therefore, the well-designed medical decision support system can then be used to remind physicians of medications and other information, or to provide physicians advice when reading reports of X-ray, CT, etc., and to alert them when the prescribed dosage is abnormal. Alerts and suggestions are provided to enable healthcare professionals to reduce the risk of medical malpractice (El-Sappagh and El-Masri 2014).

There are many different applications in the medical decision support system. For example, El-Sappagh and El-Masri (2014) collects medical information and transformed it into electronic format in various hospitals, and pre-processes electronic medical information with data mining technology. The format is unified, and then the knowledge is generated into a knowledge base by means of association rules, classification, grouping, etc. Finally, the knowledge is encoded by the prediction model, so that the knowledge engine can provide information to the medical professionals through the generated knowledge and speed up the decision of the physician. Parshutin and Kirshners (2013) pre-processed the data query form containing 28 attributes and 840 records using the classification methods C4.5 and CART as the basic classifier to find a better medical decision support system and to provide extra help to the professionals. Khan and Shamsi (2018) proposed a neural network-based clinical decision-making system that helps medical staff diagnose diseases and identify disease categories by performing natural language processing and multi-label classification techniques on patients' EMRs. deWit et al. (2015) used pharmacists' help to optimize clinical rules, to prune rules for less relevant rules in the medical decision support system and reduce false alarms in the medical decision support system. Almasri (2017) proposes an automated clinical decision-making system based on a neural network to assess multi-factor health problems, using a multi-layer perceptron to predict the risk of thromboembolic disease to provide decision-making for healthcare professionals. Nazari et al. (2018) proposed a medical decision support system based on fuzzy analysis, which was studied in four steps: (1) selection of criteria and sub-criteria, (2) weighted sub-criteria, (3) assess the patient's condition, (4) finally assessed the risk of heart disease in patients with heart disease by fuzzy analysis of risk factors. Wulff et al. (2018) proposed that when the medical decision support system generates knowledge-intensive problems, it will cause problems such as high cost and operational difficulty in the medical decision support system. Therefore, in order to solve these problems, they propose to use openEHR, which is a database queried with the Archetype Query Language syntax; when the rules in the database are touched, a warning is sent to alert the health care provider. Shanmathi and Jagannath (2018) proposed a remote health monitoring clinical decision-making system that can use multiple signs of life (such as blood pressure, heart rate, etc.), using multi-label classification, clinical terminology, and context-aware technology, then the information can be passed to the telemedicine monitoring center for the physician to make clinical decisions when the patient is in a critical situation.

Medical information retrieval refers to the use of a retrieval model to find medical information that meets the needs of medical professionals from a large number of medical databases in hospitals. Rui et al. (2015) mentioned that when searching for medical information, he often encounters search difficulties such as searching for fever and rash when the EMR contains "the patient has fever and rash" but because of the symptoms are not very obvious so many other symptoms are found when searching for these keywords and causing ambiguity in the search. Therefore, the authors use Consumer Health Vocabulary to convert words that are not medical words into medical words and use WordNet to find possible similar words to form a search vocabulary to avoid blurring medical information search. Shamna et al. (2018) proposed an unsupervised image retrieval framework based on spatial matching patterns of visual words, which can effectively calculate the spatial similarity of visual words. Ma et al. (2017) proposed to combine semantic and visual similarity and use context-related similarity for medical image retrieval to improve image retrieval. Zhao et al. (2018) proposed a semantic search of graphics based on file relevance and document popularity. Choi et al. (2014) proposed using MetaMap to analyze medical records to find concepts and use concept identifiers to make medical information search concepts more correct. Rui et al. (2017) proposed six steps to find new information in the medical records: (1) data pre-processing, (2) delete stop words and use TF-IDF to find high frequency but not important word deletion, (3) normalize words, (4) apply rules to classify words, (5) establish bigram semantic similarity model, and (6) generate semantic similarities by formulas modified from Pedersen (2010).

The medical record is dynamic information that continuously monitors the health of patients through clinical records and medical plans. Electronic Health Record (EHR) or EMR stores the medical activities received by patients are recorded in time order, recording the patient's treatment time, diagnosis and treatment, and treatment location (Jardim 2013). In various medical information retrieval methods, for file comparison, traditional information retrieval mainly uses two elements for document ranking: text relevance and text content views. The text-related index indicates whether the search results match the user's needs; and the number of text content views can show which words are more important for users (Zhao et al. 2018). However, there is not much research in the medical information comparison.

3   Methodology

The structure of the research is shown in Fig. 1. It is expected to use the admission record and the progress note of a regional teaching hospital in Taiwan. Visual Studio will be used as the development tool and Windows 7 environment. This research also uses the Python3's natural language processing tool - Natural Language Toolkit (NLTK) to perform medical data processing on the medical data set (SpellChecker kit), stemming (PorterStemmer kit), sentence break, punctuation, etc. Then, the binary comparison is performed and the MetaMap medical dictionary is searched to obtain new information and a summary of the medical record.

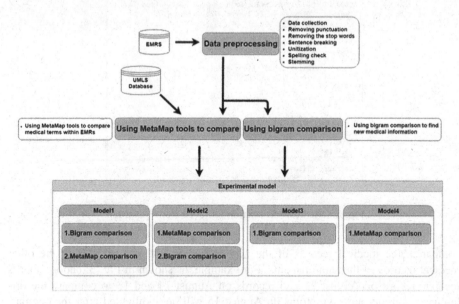

Fig. 1. Research structure.

When the EMR is processed through data integration, sentence segmentation, unitization, spelling check, stemming, removing punctuation, removing the stop word, etc., the data set without noise can be obtained. The purpose of this study is to use the hospital's EMRs to find new medical information such as new syndromes or the turning point in the medical records. The UMLS (Unified Medical Language System) Metathesaurus database will be used and which contains medical information such as medical terms, classification codes, etc. This study uses MetaMap tools to compare medical terms within EMRs, and comparing the vocabulary in the Metathesaurus database with the EMRs using the bigram comparison method to find the same vocabulary and highlight these words.

This study will use medical data from UMLS which is a system developed by the National Library of Medicine (NLM). The medical information in the system is numerous and credible. UMLS utilizes the Metathesaurus database to retrieve medical information such as Concept, Concept Unique Identifier (CUI), Semantic Type, Definition, etc. as shown in Fig. 2. And using MetaMap, the researcher can get the medical terminology of the hospital's EMR, and use the obtained medical terminology to carry out a short medical summary, so that physicians can understand the patient's condition quickly.

This study also adopts bigram to construct experimental models. In this study, the EMR in the database are first segmented, and then each EMR is unitized using a binary language model that using two words as a group. When the medical records are

```
Processing 00000000.tx.1: my leg pain.
                         Patient's condition
Phrase: my leg pain.
Meta Mapping (1000):
   1000   C0023222:LEG PAIN (Pain in lower limb) [sosy]
Processing 00000000.tx.2: I have a cold.

Phrase: I
Meta Mapping (1000) Concept Unique Identifier
   1000   C0021966 I- (Iodides) [inch]
Meta Mapping (1000):
   1000   C0221138:I NOS (Blood group antibody I) [aapp,imft]

Phrase: have

Phrase: a cold.
Meta Mapping (1000):
   1000   C0009264:Cold (Cold Temperature) [npop]
Meta Mapping (1000):
   1000   C0009443:Cold (Common Cold) [dsyn]
Meta Mapping (1000):
   1000   C0041912:Cold (Upper Respiratory Infections) [dsyn]
Meta Mapping (1000):
   1000   C0234192:Cold (Cold Sensation) [phsf]
```

Fig. 2. Medical information retrieved from MetaMap.

compared, the medical records of the new symptoms are compared with the other medical records of the same patients. For example, as shown in Fig. 3: choose John's medical record on August 15 and records on August 14 and 13 to compare the differences, and any new symptoms on August 15 will be highlighted after the comparison. This allows physicians to quickly read the differences in medical records.

Present Illness :

This 47-year-old woman has past history of breast cancer s/p oral chemotherapy treatment Her activity of daily living was independent at home She had acute onset of right throbbing headache and right face numbness at around 2AM this morning She also had vertigo with nausea/vomiting , left limbs numbness and general weakness She denied having sluured speech , double vision , or focal limb weakness She was brought our emergency department At ED , IV tradol 60mg and Valium 0 5amp were administered for headache and vertigo The brain CT scan showed not remarkable Antiplatelet agent was administered IV Novomin 1amp and Primperan 1amp were administered for persistent vertigo with vomiting She could not swallowing smoothly Brain MRI was performed later Then , she was admitted to ward for further and evaluation and management .

Assessment and Plan :

★ 1 . Acute right medullar infarction

■ Assessment

acute onset of right ptosis , right throbbing headache and right face numbness at around 2AM this morning , vertigo with nausea/vomiting , left limbs numbness and general weakness , dysphagia was also noted , no sluured speech , double vision , or focal limb weakness → favor brain stem infarction , brain MRI showed acute right lateral medullar infarction , compatible with clinical symptoms → unstable neurological deficit

Fig. 3. Example of EMRs comparison.

According to the physicians' clinical suggestion, because the medical record system of the hospital is too complicated, it will cause inconvenient and a waste of time when reading and comparing multiple EMRs. Therefore, this study will construct a new interface based on the new information on the EMR and construct a medical decision support system that facilitates reading by healthcare professionals. At present, the web language HTML and PHP will be used for interface presentation. The initial design contains the EMR search page, the EMR comparison page, and the new information page (shown in Figs. 4, 5, and 6 respectively). The webpage will be the respond page that allows medical staff to view new medical records and medical record summaries on different devices.

Fig. 4. Example of EMR search page.

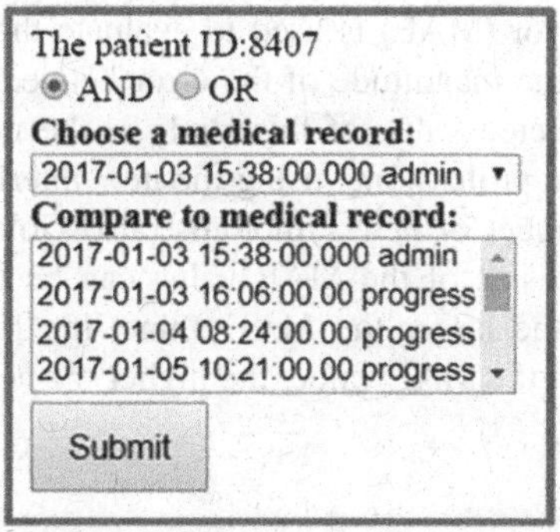

The patient ID:8407
◉ AND ◯ OR
Choose a medical record:
2017-01-03 15:38:00.000 admin ▾
Compare to medical record:
2017-01-03 15:38:00.000 admin
2017-01-03 16:06:00.00 progress
2017-01-04 08:24:00.00 progress
2017-01-05 10:21:00.00 progress ▾

Submit

Fig. 5. Example of EMR comparison page.

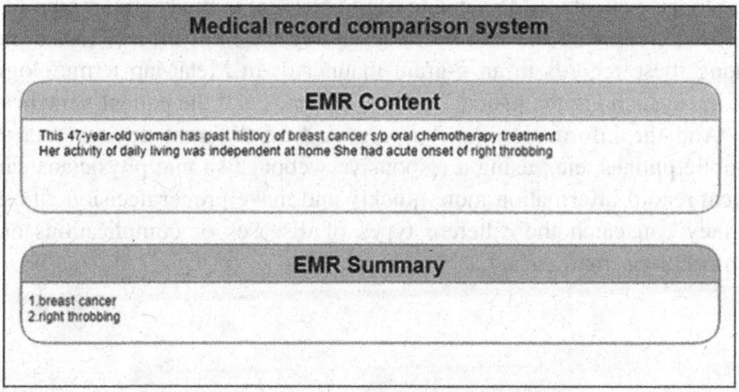

Medical record comparison system

EMR Content

This 47-year-old woman has past history of breast cancer s/p oral chemotherapy treatment Her activity of daily living was independent at home She had acute onset of right throbbing

EMR Summary

1.breast cancer
2.right throbbing

Fig. 6. Example of the new information page.

4 Evaluation

This study is expected to collect neurological EMR, and carry out the MetaMap and bigram model to find out new medical information in different EMRs and compare with the medical information found in traditional EMR interface in our experimental hospital. Before the experiment, the physician expert was asked to mark the medical information on all experiment datasets as the Gold Standard for these medical records. This study will recruit 12 medical professionals and divided them into two groups. The first group will use the new EMR interface to find new symptoms, and then use the old interface to find out new symptoms; the second group first uses the old interface, and then uses the new interface. Each group of participants will receive two different electronic medical records for the new interface and the old interface for the experiment to avoid the given knowledge of previous EMR will affect the speed and correctness of the answer. In addition, two different EMRs will be randomly selected from the experiment EMR database to avoid the difficulty varied between EMRs and will affect the outcome of the answer. Finally, evaluate the medical narrative written by the participants after reading the EMR within five minutes, and evaluate the correct rate of each participant of the experimental model according to the Gold Standard.

The Mean Absolute Error (MAE) is used to evaluate the performance. The MAE value can clearly indicate the magnitude of the error between the predicted value and the actual value. The predicted value of this study is the number of new symptoms found by recruiting medical professional using the new interface and the old interface. The actual value is the number of new symptoms (also Gold Standard) found for the neurological clinician. The size of the MAE value can be used to indicate the error value of the experiment; the larger the MAE value, the lower the accuracy of the experiment, and the smaller the MAE value, the higher the accuracy of the experiment.

5 Conclusion

This research is expected to collect EMRs, and carry out the MetaMap and bigram comparison using Python and presented using the web page as an interface. This study is expected to use patients' EMRs in a teaching hospital in the central region of Taiwan as research data, compare the medical records at a different time to locate the differences among these records in an n-gram manner or in MetaMap terminologies. The outputs of the system are the patient's new syndromes and the patient's medical record summary. And the information can be presented on different devices such as computers, mobile phones, etc., using a responsive webpage so that physicians can obtain new medical record information more quickly and make proper decision efficiently; in addition, they can catch the different types of diseases or complications and other medical information more easily.

References

Almasri, N.: Clinical decision support system for venous thromboembolism risk classification. Appl. Comput. Inform. (2017). https://doi.org/10.1016/j.aci.2017.09.003

Cayir, S., Basoglu, A.N.: Information technology interoperability awareness: a taxonomy model based on information requirements and business needs. In: Proceedings of PICMET: Portland International Center for Management of Engineering and Technology, pp. 846–855 (2008). https://doi.org/10.1109/PICMET.2008.4599692

deWit, H.A.J.M., et al.: Evaluation of clinical rules in a standalone pharmacy based clinical decision support system for hospitalized and nursing home patients. Int. J. Med. Inform. **84** (6), 396–405 (2015). https://doi.org/10.1016/j.ijmedinf.2015.02.004

Demergasso, C., et al.: Decision support system for bioleaching processes. Hydrometallurgy **181** (September), 113–122 (2018). https://doi.org/10.1016/j.hydromet.2018.08.009

El-Sappagh, S.H., El-Masri, S.: A distributed clinical decision support system architecture. J. King Saud Univ. Comput. Inf. Sci. **26**(1), 69–78 (2014). https://doi.org/10.1016/j.jksuci. 2013.03.005

Hwang, B.G., Shan, M., Looi, K.Y.: Knowledge-based decision support system for prefabricated prefinished volumetric construction. Autom. Constr. **94**(June), 168–178 (2018). https://doi. org/10.1016/j.autcon.2018.06.016

Jardim, S.V.B.: The electronic health record and its contribution to healthcare information systems interoperability. Procedia Technol. **9**, 940–948 (2013). https://doi.org/10.1016/j. protcy.2013.12.105

Jerding, D.F., Stasko, J.T.: The information mural: a technique for displaying and navigating large information spaces. IEEE Trans. Visual Comput. Graphics **4**(3), 257–271 (1998). https://doi.org/10.1109/2945.722299

Jiang, J.J.: Semantic Similarity Based on Corpus Statistics and Lexical Taxonomy (Rocling X) (1997)

Judd, G., Steenkiste, P.: Providing contextual information to ubiquitous computing applications. In: 1st IEEE International Conference on Pervasive Computing and Communications (PerCom 2003), pp. 133–142 (2003). https://doi.org/10.1007/s00703-015-0406-0

Kang, D.O., Lee, H.J., Ko, E.J., Kang, K., Lee, J.: A wearable context aware system for ubiquitous healthcare. In: Proceedings of Annual International Conference of the IEEE Engineering in Medicine and Biology, pp. 5192–5195 (2006). https://doi.org/10.1109/ IEMBS.2006.259538

Khan, S., Shamsi, J.A.: Health quest: a generalized clinical decision support system with multi-label classification. J. King Saud Univ. Comput. Inf. Sci. (2018). https://doi.org/10.1016/j. jksuci.2018.11.003

Lähteenmäki, J., Leppänen, J., Kaijanranta, H.: Interoperability of personal health records. In: Proceedings of the 31st Annual International Conference of the IEEE Engineering in Medicine and Biology Society: Engineering the Future of Biomedicine, EMBC 2009, pp. 1726–1729 (2009). https://doi.org/10.1109/IEMBS.2009.5333559

Ma, L., Liu, X., Gao, Y., Zhao, Y., Zhao, X., Zhou, C.: A new method of content based medical image retrieval and its applications to CT imaging sign retrieval. J. Biomed. Inform. **66**, 148–158 (2017). https://doi.org/10.1016/j.jbi.2017.01.002

McAlearney, A.S., Robbins, J., Hirsch, A., Jorina, M., Harrop, J.P.: Perceived efficiency impacts following electronic health record implementation: an exploratory study of an urban community health center network. Int. J. Med. Inform. **79**(12), 807–816 (2010). https://doi. org/10.1016/j.ijmedinf.2010.09.002

Nazari, S., Fallah, M., Kazemipoor, H., Salehipour, A.: A fuzzy inference-fuzzy analytic hierarchy process-based clinical decision support system for diagnosis of heart diseases. Expert Syst. Appl. **95**, 261–271 (2018). https://doi.org/10.1016/j.eswa.2017.11.001

Parshutin, S., Kirshners, A.: Research on clinical decision support systems development for atrophic gastritis screening. Expert Syst. Appl. **40**(15), 6041–6046 (2013). https://doi.org/10.1016/j.eswa.2013.05.011

Pedersen, T.: Information content measures of semantic similarity perform better without sense-tagged text, pp. 329–332, June 2010

Senteio, C., Veinot, T., Adler-Milstein, J., Richardson, C.: Physicians' perceptions of the impact of the EHR on the collection and retrieval of psychosocial information in outpatient diabetes care. Int. J. Med. Inform. **113**(February), 9–16 (2018). https://doi.org/10.1016/j.ijmedinf.2018.02.003

Shamna, P., Govindan, V.K., Abdul Nazeer, K.A.: Content-based medical image retrieval by spatial matching of visual words. J. King Saud Univ. Comput. Inf. Sci. (2018). https://doi.org/10.1016/j.jksuci.2018.10.002

Shanmathi, N., Jagannath, M.: Computerised decision support system for remote health monitoring: a systematic review. IRBM **39**, 359–367 (2018). https://doi.org/10.1016/j.irbm.2018.09.007

Zhang, R., Pakhomov, S.V.S., Arsoniadis, E.G., Lee, J.T., Wang, Y., Melton, G.B.: Detecting clinically relevant new information in clinical notes across specialties and settings. BMC Med. Inform. Decis. Mak. (2017). https://doi.org/10.1186/s12911-017-0464-y

Zhao, Q., Kang, Y., Li, J., Wang, D.: Exploiting the semantic graph for the representation and retrieval of medical documents. Comput. Biol. Med. **101**(May), 39–50 (2018). https://doi.org/10.1016/j.compbiomed.2018.08.009

An Incremental Clustering Approach to Personalized Tag Recommendations

Yen-Hsien Lee[1] and Tsai-Hsin Chu[2(✉)]

[1] Department of Management Information System,
National Chiayi University, Chiayi City, Taiwan
yhlee@mail.ncyu.edu.tw
[2] Department of E-Learning Design and Management,
National Chiayi University, Chiayi City, Taiwan
thchu@etech.ncyu.edu.tw

Abstract. Volumes of user-generated contents have caused the problem of information overload and hindered Internet users from browsing and retrieving information. Social tagging that allows users to annotate resources with free preferred keywords to ease the access to their collecting resources. Though social tagging benefits users managing their resources, it always suffers the problems such as diverse and/or unchecked vocabulary and unwillingness to tag because tags are freely and voluntarily assigned by users. Tag recommender systems, which follow some criteria to select from the tag space the most relevant tags to the user's annotating resource, drastically transfer the tagging process from generation to recognition to reduce user's cognitive effort and time. This study takes personalized tag recommendation as an incremental clustering problem and proposes a Progressive Expansion-based Tag (PET) recommendation technique. The incremental clustering assumes each object appears in sequence and then is incrementally clustered into either an appropriate existing category or a created new category. The PET technique can classify each resource into multiple categories (i.e., tags) or label it as new. While a resource is labelled as new, it will recommend a set of tags that have been used by other users and are relevant to the target user's practices. Finally, our empirical evaluation results suggest that the proposed PET technique outperforms the traditional popularity-based tag recommendation methods, while the performance rates achieved by both techniques are not satisfying.

Keywords: Tag recommender systems · Personalized tag recommendation · Incremental clustering · Progressive tag expansion · Social tagging

1 Introduction

Applications of Web 2.0 enable people to create and share information on the Internet; however, volumes of user-generated contents have in turn caused the problem of information overload and hindered users from browsing and retrieving information [1]. If not properly addressed, the users would be frustrated by the increasing number of online resources. Recently, some Web 2.0 platforms provide tagging mechanism, namely social tagging, that allows users to annotate resources (e.g., websites, articles,

© Springer Nature Switzerland AG 2019
F. F.-H. Nah and K. Siau (Eds.): HCII 2019, LNCS 11589, pp. 209–220, 2019.
https://doi.org/10.1007/978-3-030-22338-0_17

photos, videos, music, and etc.) with free, preferred keywords to ease the access to their collecting resources in the future. For example, Del.icio.us, a social bookmarking website, enables individuals to bookmark any URLs on the World Wide Web. CiteU-Like, a digital library, allows users to upload abstracts or full-texts of research articles with relevant tags (or labels) and afterward they can retrieve documents through their corresponding tags. Social tagging that takes into account users' notion of a specific resource [2] is helpful in organizing, browsing and retrieving their own resources [3]. In other words, social tagging allows resources to be categorized in the way a particular user prefers to, and therefore is considered as a substitute for taxonomy [4, 5].

Social tagging can benefit people managing their online resources; on the other hand, tags from individual users represent their personal preferences and can be used to improve the performance of personalized recommendation if properly utilized [6]. However, social tagging always suffers the problems such as diverse and/or unchecked vocabulary and unwillingness to tag because tags are freely and voluntarily assigned by users [7, 8]. The problem of diverse vocabulary may result from users' forgetfulness and bounded rationality. Ebbinghaus hypothesized that the memory retention declines over time and people may lose about 70% of the information received two days ago without any attempt on retention [9]. Though the loss of information can be mitigated by constant recall, it persists when people fail to review frequently [10]. Furthermore, the bounded rationality also limits users' ability to process information that disabled them from recalling all the tags they have used [11]. As a result, users might tend to reuse the most frequent terms (vocabularies) or use different terms each time they annotate similar resources. Thus, as the number of annotated resources increased, the tag space would become vast and the resources related to a tag would become heterogeneous. Both might frustrate users in accessing resources due to the cognitive dissonance [12, 13].

To address the problems faced by social tagging, some studies have shifted focus on tag recommender systems to assist individual users in tagging resources and converge the tags attached [3, 14–18]. Tag recommendation service has been provided by some websites, such as Delicious, BibSonomy, and Last.fm, that implies the needs in real-world situation. The task of tag recommender systems is to identify a set of tags that might be considered relevant to a resource by the focal user. Specifically, given a user u and a resource r, the task of traditional recommendation is to predict the class of $preference(u, r)$; while that of tag recommendation is to predict the set of $tags(u, r)$ what the user u will assign to the resource r [7].

For making tag recommendations, previous research assumed the number of tags was static; that is, users are limited to annotating resources with existing tags. For example, they followed collaborative filtering methods by identifying users whose used tags or annotating resources are similar to that of the focal user and suggest those tags annotating to the similar resources by these users [19]. On the other hand, some research addresses the tag recommendation problem by content-based approaches. For example, while annotating a resource, some studies tried to identify the resources that share similar content with the focal resource and then recommended the top-ranked tags annotated to them to the user [20]. Chen and Shin proposed several textual features and social features for each tag used by each particular user and use which to construct a classifier to predict the representative tags that the focal user is interested in [21].

Though prior studies have shown the effectiveness of their proposed approaches in making tag recommendations, they still have some limitations needed to be addressed. A resource will be suggested one or more used tags compulsorily no matter whether they are relevant or not. However, the tags that people used to annotate resource might evolve over time. Some tags that receive less notice will be left behind; while some tag shall emerge from as annotating new resources. Reasonably, these tags shall be relevant to the annotating resource and related to the particular user's topics of interest (the tags he or she has used to annotate resources) to better help users retrieve the resources later. That is, the new tags must to some degree conform to or associate with users' practices. In a nutshell, a tag recommender system shall make suggestion on the basis of existing tags and is able to recommend new tags that are appropriate and associated with users' practices.

Nevertheless, prior research focused most on the reuse of existing tags and accordingly attempted to recommend people those tags that are popular among the referred users or frequently used to annotate similar resources. Generally, people annotate resources one by one, and each resource will be assigned one or more tags. The assigned tags can be existing ones that people used to annotate previous resources (including the previous one), or created by the users if there is no proper tag existing, or both. As a result, this study intends to improve the personalized tag recommendations by suggesting appropriate existing tags or new tags to the target user. Instead of multi-label classification, we adopt the content-based approach and model personalized tag recommendation as an incremental clustering problem. The incremental clustering assumes each object (or resource) appears in sequence and then is incrementally clustered into either an appropriate existing category or a created new category [22, 23]. This study extends the incremental clustering approach and propose a progressive expansion-based tag (PET) recommendation technique. The proposed PET recommendation technique assumes the resources to be annotated are fed in sequence and will be assigned one or more existing categories (i.e., existing tags) and/or suggested appropriate new categories (i.e., new tags). In addition, when determining the appropriate existing tags for a resource, the PET technique will consider the focal user's topics of interest. For example, instead of identifying similar resources to make tag recommendations, PET tries to measure the relevance between a new resource and a tag. It measures the content similarity between the resource to be annotated and all resources annotated by the tag. Furthermore, to suggest new tags, the PET will identify the representative term(s) in the resource to be annotated by measuring not only the term frequency but also the relevance to existing tags. The remainder of this study is organized as follows: In Sect. 2, we review the literature relevant to this study. Then we depict our proposed Progressive Expansion-based Tag (PET) recommendation technique in Sect. 3. In Sect. 4, we describe the empirical evaluation including the data collection, evaluation design, followed by the evaluation results in Sect. 5.

2 Literature Review

In this section, we briefly review the research works relevant to our proposed progressive expansion-based tag recommendation technique, including prior research in tag recommender systems and an overview of incremental clustering.

2.1   Tag Recommender Systems

Tag recommender is one kind of recommender systems. Instead of recommending objects such as books, music, or movies, the purpose of tag recommender is to suggest appropriate tags to users who are annotating objects in the social media; especially the social bookmarking and the media sharing websites. Such websites generally provide the social tagging mechanisms that allow users to annotate objects with free keywords. For example, the social bookmarking website, Del.icio.us enables individuals to bookmark any URLs in the World Wide Web; the digital library, CiteULike allows users to upload the abstract or full-text of research articles with some relevant tags (or labels); the famous video sharing website, YouTube allows users to upload their videos with some tags. Though user-generated content is the core to Web 2.0, Internet users have been overloaded with the great volumes of information that hinders them from browsing and retrieving information [1]. Social tagging can benefit users managing and accessing their online resources; on the other hand, the tags annotated by an individual user may represent his or her notions of a resource that can facilitate the personalized recommendation if properly utilized [2, 3, 6].

Use of tags allows users to annotate resources in the way they like, and therefore, tagging is somehow considered as a substitute for the taxonomy of user's resources [4, 5]. Nevertheless, social tagging always suffers the problems such as diverse and/or unchecked vocabulary and unwillingness to tag because tags are freely and voluntarily assigned by users [7, 8]. Besides, users tend to reuse the frequent tags or to create new tags, which will diminish the coherence or distinctness of the resources with a specific tag and adversely affect users' resource searches and access due to the cognitive dissonance [12, 13]. To address the problems faced by social tagging, prior research attempts to develop tag recommender systems to support users in annotating resource to converge the tags attached [3, 14–18]. Tag recommendation may drastically transfer the tagging process from generation to recognition which reduces user's cognitive effort and time [20]. A tag recommender system follows some criteria to select from the tag space the most relevant tags to the user's uploading resource. Specifically, given a user u and a resource r, the task of tag recommendation is to predict a set of tags(u, r) from a finite set of tags T that the user u may prefer to annotate the resource r [7].

Prior research broadly divided the tag recommendations into content-based, collaborative filtering, and graph-based (or ranking-based) approaches according to their adoptive algorithms [3, 7]. The content-based approaches focus on content analysis and are mainly applied textual resources like webpages and textual documents [21, 24–31]. Instead of analyzing contents, the collaborative filtering approaches for tag recommendation resemble traditional collaborative filtering recommendation approaches which make recommendations on the basis of the preferences of a referent group [19, 20, 32]. Finally, the graph-based or ranking-based approaches are inspired from the Web ranking. They make recommendations based on the ranking score that is computed according to spectral attributes extracted from the underlying folksonomy data structure (i.e., the 3-way relationship among users, resources, tags) [7, 17, 33, 34].

Overall, prior research focused most on the reuse of existing tags and attempted to recommend people those tags that are popular among the referred users or frequently used to annotate similar resources. Though users' interests may evolve over time, they seldom take into consideration the user's topics of interest when making tag recommendations. Besides, people annotate resources one by one and always create new tags combining with existing tags to annotate them. Tag recommendations shall be made with consideration of user's interests and that is what we intend to address in this study.

2.2 Incremental Clustering

Clustering analysis methods usually employ the batch mode strategy to discover the structure hidden in the whole unlabeled data at a time. However, the sheer volume of data available for clustering analysis has made the memory-based approach impractical, and thus raise the need of incremental clustering approaches, which process one object at a time and require less memory space for data storage [35]. One of the well-known incremental clustering algorithms is sequential k-means [36], which is an incremental variant of Lloyd's algorithm [37]. The sequential k-means algorithm targets on finding a set of cluster means M that minimizes the cost function $\sum_{\forall o_j \in O} \min_{m \in M} \|o_j - m\|^2$. It randomly initials k data points as cluster means $M = (m_1, m_2, ..., m_k)$ and set to 1 the size of each cluster $N = (n_1, n_2, ..., n_k)$. As an object o_j arrives, Euclidean distance between the object o_j and each of the cluster means will be calculated in sequence. Assume the object o_j is classified into its closest cluster c_i, the size of cluster c_i (i.e., n_i) will be increased by 1 and the mean of cluster c_i (i.e., m_i) will be updated by $m_i + (o_j - m_i)/n_i$.

Yang et al. [23, 38] addressed the news event detection problem by proposing INCR, a single-pass incremental clustering algorithm, produces nonhierarchical clusters incrementally for both retrospective and online detection. For supporting online detection, INCR was designed to sequentially process news documents. It employed an incremental IDF to respond the effect of continuously incoming documents on term weighting and vector normalization during online detection. The incremental IDF is defined as $idf(w, p) = \log_2(\frac{N(p)}{n_{,(w,p)}})$, where w is the focal term, p is the current time point, $N(p)$ is the number of documents accumulated up to the current time point (including the retrospective corpus if used), and $n(w, p)$ is the document frequency of term w at time point p. Furthermore, INCR incorporated a time penalty, which can be a uniformly weighted time window (i.e., a time window of m documents before x is imposed) or a linear decaying-weight function, to adjust the similarity between a document x and any cluster c in the past. The similarity measure can be cosine similarity or any distance measure like Euclidean distance. The $Similarity'(x, c)$ is defined as $\left(\begin{matrix} (1 - \frac{i}{m}) \times Similarity(x, c) & \text{if } c \text{ has any member in the window} \\ 0 & \text{otherwise} \end{matrix} \right)$, where i is the number of documents between x and the most recent member document in c, and m is the time window of documents before x. Finally, a document x is absorbed by the most similar cluster in the past if the similarity between the document and cluster is larger than a pre-selected *clustering threshold* (t_c); otherwise, the document becomes the seed of a new cluster.

3 Progressive Expansion-Based Tag (PET) Recommendation Technique

Our study intends to propose a Progressive Expansion-based Tag (PET) recommendation technique by revising an incremental clustering algorithm. The PET technique considers a focal user's interests to recommend the appropriate categories (tags) to the resources for the focal user. On the other hand, the PET tries to recommend tags by identifying the relevant tags from the tags annotated to the focal resource by other users if the focal user's own tags are less appropriate. As shown in Fig. 1, the overall process of the PET technique comprises four phases, including feature extraction and selection, resource representation, candidate tag generation, and tag recommendation. The PET technique takes as inputs a focal user's resource profile (i.e., resources with their respective annotated tags) and the resources to be annotated and produces a list of tags to be recommended. Because the PET considers user's (resources) interests, we first group the resources in the user's profile by their attached tags. Reasonably, two resources that attached the same tag may discuss similar topic or share similar content. A set of important features will then be selected and used to represent resources in each tag cluster. Subsequently, an incremental clustering algorithm is applied to determine a set of appropriate tag clusters for the resources to be annotated. A resource will be classified into a tag cluster if the content similarity between them is over a pre-specified threshold and these tag clusters then become the candidates for recommendations. If a resource could not be classified into suitable tag cluster, the PET will access appropriate tags used by other users. In the following, we describe the preliminary design of the proposed PET technique.

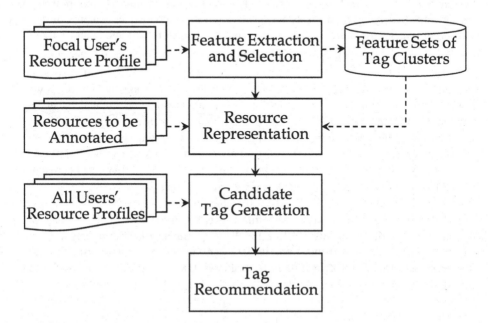

Fig. 1. Overall process of progressive expansion-based tag recommendation technique

Feature Extraction and Selection: In the feature extraction and selection phase, the resources in the user's profile are groups by their respective attached tags to form a set of tag clusters. One resource could belong to multiple groups since it might be attached more than one tags. The PET then extracts from the textual resources a set of representative features (i.e., nouns and noun phrases) for representing the resources themselves. We adopted the rule-based part-of-speech tagger developed by Brill to syntactically tag each word in these resources [39]. Subsequently, we employed a parser for extracting nouns and verbs from each syntactically tagged document. The global dictionary scheme was adopted and the chi-square statistic was used to measure to the weight of each feature for constructing the representative feature set of each cluster [40].

Resource Representation: In the resource representation phase, the resources in each cluster are represented by its set of representative features. In this study, we employed TFxIDF measure as the representation scheme to re-represent the resources in each cluster.

Candidate Tag Generation: The purpose of candidate tag generation phase is to assess and identify the tags relevant to the resource to be annotated. This phase comprises two stages, including tag cluster identification and new tag generation. At the stage of tag cluster identification, this study revised the INCR algorithm [23, 38] to enable supporting multi-label classification. Specifically, INCR algorithm assumes each object belongs to one and only one cluster. However, in our study, a resource can belong to any number of tag cluster; that is, a resource might be different to the resources in the focal user's profile or belong to more than one tag cluster. As a result, we accommodate INCR algorithm to be able to assign a resource into multiple tag clusters or create a new cluster for it if needed. We followed the INCR algorithm by employing a clustering threshold. The tag clusters that share similarities with a resource higher than the clustering threshold will be viewed as candidate tags for recommendations. However, when a resource is labeled as new; that is, all the similarities it achieves are lower than the clustering threshold, we will try to identify suitable tags for recommendation from the annotated resources of other users. Thus, the task of new tag generation is to assess suitability of the tags that was annotated to the focal resource by other users. We rank those tags by considering their respective frequency appearing in the whole resources, their relevance associated to the resources that the focal user has annotated, and their temporal distance to the resource to be annotated. The frequency *TF* is defined as the number of a tag that is used to annotate resources; the relevance *TR* is defined as the content similarity between a specific tag cluster (i.e., the resources received the specific tag) and the resources in the focal user's profile; the temporal distance *TD* is defined as $e^{-\frac{|Now - Date(t_i)|}{Now - Date(T)}}$ where t_i is the tag to be assessed, T is the set of all candidate tags, $Date(t_i)$ is the starting date to use tag t_i and $Date(T)$ is the starting date to use anyone of the candidate tags. We finally defined the ranking score of a specific tag t_i as $Score(t_i) = TF \times TR \times TD$.

Tag Recommendation: The task of the final phase of PET technique is to make tag recommendations. PET will first recommend tags identified at the stage of tag cluster identification, and if needed, the tags identified at the new tag generation stage will be recommended to satisfy the number of recommending tags. The candidate tags from focal user's profile will be ordered by their achieved similarities and those from other users' profile will be ordered by their ranking scores.

4 Empirical Evaluation

4.1 Data Collection

We adopted the MovieLens 20M database (ml-20m) as our evaluation corpus. This database contains 465,564 tag applications across 27,278 movies, created by 138,493 users who have rated at least 20 movies between January 09, 1995 and March 31, 2015. Among the database, the max, min, and average number of tags used by a user is 2,330, 1, and 58.1; the max, min, and average number of tags received by a movie is 197, 1, and 15.14; the max, min, and average number of movies that a specific tag was annotated to is 1,093, 2, and 18.03. Because the tags annotated to the movies in the evaluation corpus is sparse, we adopted the p-core scheme to tri-partite hypergraphs to trim the corpus and keep its dense part for the evaluation purpose [41, 42]. Finally, we set the level k to 3 for the p-core scheme to make sure that each user, tag and resource has/occurs at least 3 times in the evaluation corpus. After the trimming, there exists 7,801 users, 19,545 movies, and 364,804 tagging records in the evaluation corpus. Besides, we also collected the synopsis of each annotated movie for the experiments. We implemented a crawler to gather the overview of each movie from TheMovieDb website (https://www.themoviedb.org/) through the movie ID provided by MovieLens database.

4.2 Experiment Design

For each user in the evaluation corpus, we take his or her last annotating movie and corresponding tags as testing examples, and all users' tagging histories (i.e., all other annotating movies and corresponding tags) as training examples. In this study, we implemented two popularity-based recommendation approaches, namely PAT and PUT as the performance benchmarks. In PAT, the top-n tags that are frequently used to annotate resources by all users will be recommended; on the other hand, in PUT, the top-n tags that are frequently used to annotate resources by the focal user will be recommended. Furthermore, we adopted Precision, Recall, Hamming Loss, Mean Reciprocal Rank (MRR) [43], Average Precision (AP) [44], and Average Utility

(AU) as the evaluation criteria. These criteria are defined as $Precision = \frac{1}{|D|}\sum_{i=1}^{|D|}\frac{|P_i \cap T_i|}{|T_i|}$,

$Recall = \frac{1}{|D|}\sum_{i=1}^{|D|}\frac{|P_i \cap T_i|}{|P_i|}$, $Hamming\ Loss = \frac{1}{|D|}\sum_{i=1}^{|D|}\frac{|P_i \Delta T_i|}{|P_i|}$, $MRR = \frac{1}{|D|}\sum_{i=1}^{|D|}\sum_{j \in P_i \cap T_i}\frac{1/Rank_j}{|P_i \cap T_i|}$,

$AP = \frac{1}{|D|}\sum_{i=1}^{|D|}\sum_{j \in P_i \cap T_i}\frac{Precision_j}{|P_i \cap T_i|}$, and $AU = \frac{1}{|D|}\sum_{i=1}^{|D|}\sum_{j \in P_i \cap T_i}\frac{Precision_j}{|P_i|}$, where $|D|$ is the number of target movies, P_i is the set of recommended tags for the target movie d_i, and T_i is the set of true tags annotated to the target movie d_i, Δ is the XOR operation, $Rank_j$ is the rank of the recommended tag j, and $Precision_j$ is the precision at the time tag j is recommended. Finally, we set the clustering threshold for incremental clustering algorithm to 0.05 and examine the overall effectiveness of our proposed PET and benchmark techniques by averaging the recommendation performance across all users.

5 Evaluation Results

We investigate the effectiveness of both evaluation techniques when the number of recommended tags is three and five. As shown in Table 1, our proposed PET outperforms the benchmarks, i.e., PAT and PUT techniques, across all performance metrics when making recommendation of three and five tags. Though the performance of PET is advantageous over the benchmarks, the rates it achieves across all performance metrics are not satisfying. Furthermore, as the number of recommended tags increased, there is a tradeoff existing in precision and recall rates. However, almost all the rates it achieves are lower than 0.1 except for the recall rate. The evaluation results imply the difficulty of tag recommendation that must identify relevant tags among thousands of candidate tags. Overall, the performance of the proposed PET technique is better than the benchmark technique, which make tag recommendations on the basis of tag's popularity. Besides, the low performance rates may be raised by the sparse data, that is still a problem needed to be addressed in the study of tag recommendation.

Table 1. Comparative evaluation results

	Precision	Recall	HL	MRR	AP	AU
Number of recommending tags = 3						
PAT	0.021	0.015	0.990	0.011	0.042	0.015
PUT	0.034	0.064	0.973	0.038	0.059	0.021
PET	0.060	0.107	0.954	0.062	0.099	0.038
Number of recommending tags = 5						
PAT	0.022	0.027	0.987	0.013	0.050	0.011
PUT	0.037	0.097	0.969	0.046	0.069	0.019
PET	0.062	0.173	0.949	0.078	0.120	0.031

6 Conclusion

This study based on the concept of incremental clustering to propose a progressive expansion-based tag recommendation technique. The PET technique can recommend appropriate tags to the resources to be annotated in consideration of the focal user's preference and tag usage practices. The preliminary evaluation results indicated that the proposed PET technique is more effective than the popularity-based tag recommendation approaches across all evaluation criteria. The progressive expansion approach can identify tags to meet user's needs in annotating online resources. However, this study has some limitations need to be addressed which in turns become the future research directions. First, we only adopted one database (i.e., MovieLens 20M database) to evaluate and compare the investigated techniques. More experimental datasets shall be collected from the other social bookmarking websites, such as BibSonomy, CiteULike, and Last.fm for carrying out more empirical evaluations. Second, this study employed two popularity-based recommendation approaches as the performance benchmarks. Other approaches to tag recommendation shall also be examined in the future. Finally, the experimental evaluations we conducted in this study are preliminary, and thus it requires more analyses on the effects of the proposed PET technique.

Acknowledgement. This work was supported by Ministry of Science and Technology of the Republic of China under the grant MOST 106-2410-H-415-009.

References

1. Lee, B.K., Lee, W.N.: The effect of information overload on consumer choice quality in an on-line environment. Psychol. Mark. **21**, 159–183 (2004)
2. Wu, H., Zubair, M., Maly, K.: Harvesting social knowledge from folksonomies. In: The 17th Conference on Hypertext and Hypermedia, pp. 111–114. ACM Press (2006)
3. Musto, C., Narducci, F., de Gemmis, M., Lops, P., Semeraro, G.: A Tag recommender system exploiting user and community behavior. In: Jannach, D., et al. (eds.) The ACM RecSys 2009 Workshop on Recommender Systems & the Social Web, vol. 532. CEUR-WS. org (2009)
4. Heckner, M., Heilemann, M., Wolff, C.: Personal information management vs. resource sharing: towards a model of information behaviour in social tagging systems. In: The Third International AAAI Conference on Weblogs and Social Media Conference, pp. 42–49 (2009)
5. Marvasti, A.F., Skillicorn, D.B.: Structures in collaborative tagging: an empirical analysis. In: The Thirty-Third Australasian Conference on Computer Science, vol. 102, pp. 109–116 (2010)
6. Yang, C.S., Chen, L.C.: Personalized recommendation in social media: a profile expansion approach. In: The 18th Pacific Asia Conference on Information Systems (2014)
7. Marinho, L.B., et al.: Social tagging recommender systems. In: Ricci, F., Rokach, L., Shapira, B., Kantor, P.B. (eds.) Recommender Systems Handbook, pp. 615–644. Springer, Boston, MA (2011). https://doi.org/10.1007/978-0-387-85820-3_19
8. Bischoff, K., Firan, C.S., Nejdl, W., Paiu, R.: Can all tags be used for search? In: The 17th ACM Conference on Information and Knowledge Management, pp. 193–202 (2008)
9. Ebbinghaus, H.: Memory: A Contribution to Experimental Psychology. Columbia University, New York (1885)
10. García, R.R., Quirós, J.S., Santos, R.G., González, S.M., Fernanz, S.M.: Interactive multimedia animation with macromedia flash in descriptive geometry teaching. Comput. Educ. **49**, 615–639 (2007)
11. Simon, H.A.: Models of Bounded Rationality. MIT Press, Cambridge (1997)
12. Oliver, R.L.: A cognitive model for the antecedents and consequences of satisfaction. J. Mark. Res. **17**, 460–469 (1980)
13. Wei, C.P., Hu, P., Lee, Y.H.: Preserving user preferences in automated document-category management: an evolution-based approach. J. Manag. Inf. Syst. **25**, 109–143 (2009)

14. Cattuto, C., et al.: Network properties of folksonomies. AI Commun. **20**, 245–262 (2007)
15. Jäschke, R., Marinho, L., Hotho, A., Schmidt-Thieme, L., Stumme, G.: Tag recommendations in social bookmarking systems. AI Commun. **21**, 231–247 (2008)
16. Shepitsen, A., Gemmell, J., Mobasher, B., Burke, R.: Personalized recommendation in social tagging systems using hierarchical clustering. In: The 2008 ACM Conference on Recommender Systems, pp. 259–266. ACM (2008)
17. Symeonidis, P., Nanopoulos, A., Manolopoulos, Y.: Tag recommendations based on tensor dimensionality reduction. In: The 2008 ACM Conference on Recommender Systems, pp. 43–50. ACM (2008)
18. Tso-Sutter, K.H.L., Marinho, L.B., Schmidt-Thieme, L.: Tag-aware recommender systems by fusion of collaborative filtering algorithms. In: The 2008 ACM Symposium on Applied Computing, pp. 1995–1999. ACM (2008)
19. Marinho, L.B., Schmidt-Thieme, L.: Collaborative tag recommendations. In: Preisach, C., Burkhardt, H., Schmidt-Thieme, L., Decker, R. (eds.) Data Analysis Machine Learning and Applications, pp. 533–540. Springer, Heidelberg (2008). https://doi.org/10.1007/978-3-540-78246-9_63
20. Sood, S., Owsley, S., Hammond, K., Birnbaum, L.: TagAssist: automatic tag suggestion for blog posts. In: The International Conference on Weblogs and Social Media (2007)
21. Chen, X., Shin, H.: Tag recommendation by machine learning with textual and social features. J. Intell. Inf. Syst. **40**, 261–282 (2013)
22. Hartigan, J.: Clustering Algorithms. Wiley, New York (1975)
23. Yang, Y., Carbonell, J.G., Brown, R.D., Pierce, T., Archibald, B.T., Liu, X.: Learning approaches for detecting and tracking news events. IEEE Intell. Syst. **14**, 32–43 (1999)
24. Brooks, C.H., Montanez, N.: Improved annotation of the blogosphere via autotagging and hierarchical clustering. In: The 15th International Conference on World Wide Web, pp. 625–632. ACM Press (2006)
25. Lee, S., Chun, A.: Automatic tag recommendation for the web 2.0 blogosphere using collaborative tagging and hybrid ann semantic structures. In: The 6th Conference on WSEAS International Conference on Applied Computer Science, Stevens Point, Wisconsin, pp. 88–93 (2007)
26. Heymann, P., Ramage, D., Garcia-Molina, H.: Social tag prediction. In: The 31st Annual International ACM SIGIR Conference on Research and Development in Information Retrieval, pp. 531–538 (2008)
27. Tsoumakas, G., Katakis, I.: Multi-label classification: an overview. Int. J. Data Warehouse. Min. **3**, 1–13 (2007)
28. Gonçalves, T., Quaresma, P.: A preliminary approach to the multilabel classification problem of Portuguese juridical documents. In: Pires, F.M., Abreu, S. (eds.) EPIA 2003. LNCS (LNAI), vol. 2902, pp. 435–444. Springer, Heidelberg (2003). https://doi.org/10.1007/978-3-540-24580-3_50
29. Boutell, M.R., Luo, J., Shen, X., Brown, C.M.: Learning multi-label scene classification. Pattern Recogn. **37**, 1757–1771 (2004)
30. Lauser, B., Hotho, A.: Automatic multi-label subject indexing in a multilingual environment. In: Koch, T., Sølvberg, I.T. (eds.) ECDL 2003. LNCS, vol. 2769, pp. 140–151. Springer, Heidelberg (2003). https://doi.org/10.1007/978-3-540-45175-4_14
31. Zhang, M.L., Zhou, Z.H.: ML-kNN: a lazy learning approach to multi-label learning. Pattern Recogn. **40**, 2038–2048 (2007)
32. Mishne, G.: Autotag: a collaborative approach to automated tag assignment for weblog posts. In: The 15th International Conference on World Wide Web, pp. 953–954. ACM Press, New York (2006)

33. Hotho, A., Jäschke, R., Schmitz, C., Stumme, G.: Information retrieval in folksonomies: search and ranking. In: Sure, Y., Domingue, J. (eds.) ESWC 2006. LNCS, vol. 4011, pp. 411–426. Springer, Heidelberg (2006). https://doi.org/10.1007/11762256_31

34. Rendle, S., Marinho, L.B., Nanopoulos, A., Schmidt-Thieme, L.: Learning optimal ranking with tensor factorization for tag recommendation. In: The 15th ACM SIGKDD International Conference on Knowledge Discovery and Data Mining, Paris, France, pp. 727–736. ACM Press (2009)

35. Ackerman, M., Dasgupta, S.: Incremental clustering: the case for extra clusters. In: 2014 Annual Conference on Neural Information Processing Systems, Montreal, Quebec, Canada, pp. 307–315 (2014)

36. Charikar, M., Chekuri, C., Feder, T., Motwani, R.: Incremental clustering and dynamic information retrieval. In: The Twenty-Ninth Annual ACM Symposium on Theory of Computing, pp. 626–635. ACM Press (1997)

37. Lloyd, S.P.: Least squares quantization in PCM. IEEE Trans. Inf. Theory 28, 129–137 (1982)

38. Yang, Y., Pierce, T., Carbonell, J.G.: A study on retrospective and on-line event detection. In: 21st Annual International ACM SIGIR Conference on Research and Development in Information Retrieval, pp. 28–36, Melbourne, Australia. ACM Press (1998)

39. Brill, E.: Some advances in rule-based part of speech tagging. In: Proceedings of the 12th National Conference on Artificial Intelligence (AAAI-94), pp. 722–727. AAAI Press (1994)

40. Apté, C., Damerau, F., Weiss, S.: Automated learning of decision rules for text categorization. ACM Trans. Inf. Syst. 12, 233–251 (1994)

41. Jäschke, R., Marinho, L., Hotho, A., Schmidt-Thieme, L., Stumme, G.: Tag recommendations in folksonomies. In: Kok, J.N., Koronacki, J., Lopez de Mantaras, R., Matwin, S., Mladenič, D., Skowron, A. (eds.) PKDD 2007. LNCS (LNAI), vol. 4702, pp. 506–514. Springer, Heidelberg (2007). https://doi.org/10.1007/978-3-540-74976-9_52

42. Vladimir, B., Matjaž, Z.: Generalized cores. arXiv preprint (2002)

43. Deshpande, M., Karypis, G.: Item-based top-n recommendation algorithms. ACM Trans. Inf. Syst. 22, 143–177 (2004)

44. Chowdhury, G.: Introduction to Modern Information Retrieval. Facet Publishing, London (2010)

Motivating User-Generated Content Contribution with Voluntary Donation to Content Creators

Lili Liu[✉]

College of Economics and Management, Nanjing University of Aeronautics
and Astronautics, Nanjing, Jiangsu, People's Republic of China
llili85@nuaa.edu.cn

Abstract. Donating money to online content creators is gaining popularity in
the last few years, especially in Mainland China. Different from mandatory
payment mode (e.g., pay subscription fee to access online content), despite some
user-generated content (UGC) is free and openly available, audiences are
allowed to voluntarily donate money to content creators after their consumption.
As a relatively new phenomenon, little is known about audiences' donation
behavior. Drawing on value-based adoption model (VAM), this study unearths
perceived value as a key factor that determines audiences' donation behavior. In
addition, antecedents of perceived value are explored, including the benefits
(hedonic benefit, utilitarian benefit, and social benefit) and sacrifice (perceived
fee) of UGC consumption. A conceptual framework with following hypotheses
is then proposed: (1) benefits of UGC consumption are positively related to
perceived value, (2) sacrifice of UGC consumption is negatively related to
perceived value, (3) perceived value of UGC positively influences audiences'
intention to donate money to content creators. Data will be collected to test the
framework and verify the hypotheses in the future. Donating for UGC is an
emerging topic in new media era, and this study represents the first step toward
explaining voluntary donation behavior in UGC consumption.

Keywords: Voluntary donation to content creators ·
Value-based adoption model · Hedonic benefit · Utilitarian benefit ·
Social benefit · Perceived fee · Perceived value

1 Introduction

User-generated content (UGC) encompass a wide range of content such as text, video,
digital images, and audio files that created by end-users of an online system or service
[3]. Although coming in different types, UGC can be summarized as media content
created by the general public and openly available on the Internet [6]. UGC is crucial to
the success of various websites (e.g., Wikipedia, YouTube), yet prior research indicates
that the majority of UGC is produced by very few content creators [17], because they
incur costs in terms of time, effort, opportunity costs, reputation risks, and money to
contribute content [24]. In order to motivate UGC contribution, websites managers
have attempted to raise the benefits received from creating UGC so that benefits

F. F.-H. Nah and K. Siau (Eds.): HCII 2019, LNCS 11589, pp. 221–230, 2019.
https://doi.org/10.1007/978-3-030-22338-0_18

outweigh the potential costs [4, 14]. In general, there are three methods by which content creators can directly obtain revenue: (1) advertisement revenue (e.g., any YouTuber can market their videos and profit from advertisements), which varies depending on the viewership and types of advertisements run on the UGC [2], (2) subscription revenue (audiences pay a fixed price to content creators to enjoy content updates over a period) [18], and (3) donation revenue (audiences donate money to content creators though the UGC is free and openly available) [26]. Different from mandatory payment mode (e.g., advertisement and subscription), donating money to content creators has been introduced on a voluntary basis.

Facing with the challenge of attracting content creators' attention and contribution, many websites have introduced the donation function that allows audiences to directly give monetary incentives to content creators. In recent years, implementing donation function has gained great popularity [26]. For instance, Sina Weibo, the most famous microblogging platform in Mainland China, has provided the donation function since 2014, and earned approximately 7 million US dollars through donation in 2015. Twitch. tv—a user-generated live video streaming website in U.S.—raised over 75 million dollars via donation in 2017 [20]. Figure 1 displays an example of voluntary donation to content creators on WeChat (the leading social media in Mainland China). After reading an article on WeChat, a donation button and list of previous donors appear below the article. Clicking on the donation button, a payment page that shows optional donation amounts will pop-up. Thereafter, audiences are able to decide whether they would like to donate and the donation amount (either select an optional donation amount provided by the content creator or set up an amount by themselves) freely.

Fig. 1. An example of voluntary donation to content creator on WeChat (source: http://img0. imgtn.bdimg.com/it/u=4277826650,1812296389&fm=214&gp=0.jpg)

One of the best way to motivate content contribution is to have it supported, either financially or non-financially (e.g., the comments and likes to YouTube videos). While in traditional business model, content creators mostly earn from advertisement and subscription, the introduction of voluntary donation function has enabled a more complex interaction that involves the three main parties of a website: audiences, content creators, and website managers. In the long run, adopting donation function is beneficial to these three main parties (see Fig. 2). On one hand, voluntary donation to content creators fulfills a variety of their basic needs (e.g., food, shelter) and higher-level needs (e.g., entertainment, interactivity, and social recognition). Earning an income from content contribution may free the content creators' schedule, and encourage the transition from part-time to full-time content creators. On the other hand, audiences and website managers are also beneficiaries of the donation function. For example, by donating to content creators, audiences are able to experience entertainment and interactivity. Content creators who receive donations might be motivated and put more effort on producing UGC in the future. Consequently, audiences have an opportunity to enjoy UGC with improved quality and increased quantity. Moreover, effects of voluntary donation on content creators are often translated into benefits for website managers. Donation to content creators provides website managers with the means to enhance their shared monetary revenue, as well as the engagement of audiences and content creators [16], thereby ensuring the long-term sustainability of a website.

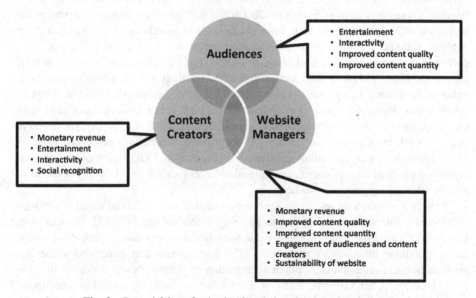

Fig. 2. Potential benefits by implementing the donation function

Although there are many potential advantages by enabling donation to content creators, it is not a simple endeavor to facilitate content creators' contribution of UGC, primarily because most UGC are free of charge and audiences do not necessarily need to donate after consumption of UGC [15]. In this condition, encouraging audiences to voluntarily donate money to free UGC becomes a big challenge. Apparently, incorporating the donation function is not sufficient, unless we understand the motivations behind audiences' voluntary donation [26]. Given that donation function is relatively new and very limited research has investigated this phenomenon so far, this paper intends to develop an analyzable model that summarizes the predictors of donation behavior. In light of value-based adoption model (VAM), this study unearths perceived value as a key factor that determines audiences' donation behavior. In addition, antecedents of perceived value are explored, including the benefits (hedonic benefit, utilitarian benefit, and social benefit) and sacrifice (perceived fee) of UGC consumption. Theoretically, the proposed model can serve as the basis for future empirical study on donation to content providers. Practically, our research provide website managers with important implications on how to understand and motivate audiences' donation behavior to free content, therefore they can successfully operate the donation function to maintain website sustainability.

2 Theoretical Background

2.1 Conceptualization of Perceived Value

Day [8] describes consumer perceived value as the trade-off between the "get" and "give" components of a product. More specifically, the "get" components refer to the benefits a consumer derives from a product while the "give" components represent the sacrifices of acquiring a product. Prior studies are comprehensive in explaining the benefits audiences obtain from product consumption. For instance, Holbrook [9] contends that perceived value consists of eight types of value: convenience, quality, success, reputation, fun, beauty, virtue, and faith. Sheth et al. [21] illustrate perceived value as functional value, social value, emotional value, epistemic value, and conditional value. However, these conceptualizations omit the sacrifices associated with product consumption, which apparently should be captured to fully explain perceive value. Therefore, according to Zeithaml [30], this research defines perceived value of UGC consumption as an audience's overall estimation of UGC based on the consideration of the benefits and sacrifices required to access and/or use it, which is the most widely adopted by previous studies.

A review of previous research suggests that audiences' perceived value is a critical factor that influences user intention to pay for online content [10, 27]. For example, Chu and Lu [5] argue that perceived value of online music positively influence online music purchase intention. Wang et al. [27] demonstrate that perceived value has positive impacts on audiences' purchase intention of online content services. In addition, Hsiao and Chen [10] find that perceived value is positively related to consumers' intention to pay for e-book subscriptions. Following existing research, we identify perceived value as the key factor affecting audiences' intention to donate money to content creators. Based on audiences' overall estimation of UGC, they decide whether donate money to content creators or not.

2.2 Value-Based Adoption Model

Despite perceived value has been frequently used to explain intention to pay for UGC, few studies have explored what factors drive audiences' perceived value from the perspective of perceived benefits and perceived sacrifices. To fill this gap, Kim et al. [12] propose the value-based adoption model (VAM) that explains customers' mobile Internet service adoption from the benefit-sacrifice perspective. In VAM, beneficial factors (i.e., hedonic benefit, utilitarian benefit, and social benefit) and sacrificing factor (i.e., perceived price) have been treated as determinants of perceived value. VAM's benefit-sacrifice framework represents a novel approach to understanding intention to pay for UGC, which has been widely applied in subsequent research [10, 22, 27].

Basically, VAM posits that beneficial factors have positive impacts on perceived value while sacrificing factors are negatively associated with perceived value, which in turn affects purchase intention [12]. In light of VAM, this study develops a comprehensive model for explaining and predicting audiences' intention to donate money to content creators. The following section elaborates the research model and hypotheses in greater detail.

3   Research Model and Hypotheses

This study seeks to better understand why audiences are willing to donate money to content creators, even though the UGC is free of charge. To this end, we rely on the VAM benefit-sacrifice framework mentioned earlier to investigate audiences' donation behavior in the UGC consumption context. A conceptual model is developed and presented in Fig. 3.

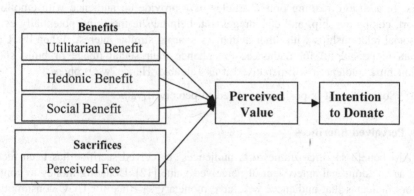

Fig. 3. Research model

3.1   Perceived Benefits

According to previous research, the benefits audiences obtain from UGC consumption consist of utilitarian benefit (e.g., UGC usefulness) [22], hedonic benefit (e.g., perceived enjoyment) [12, 27], and social benefit (e.g., social knowledge-image expression and social relationship support) [13].

In particular, utilitarian benefit refers to the perceived utility of UGC based on its overall usefulness [29]. Utilitarian benefit is goal-related, cognitive, and functional. Similar UGC exists on various websites, audiences seek for distinctive UGC with great utilitarian benefit, which provides them with more useful and detailed information. Empirical findings have supported the observation that utilitarian benefit in terms of

UGC usefulness positively influences perceived value of UGC [10]. When the UGC is complete, accurate, well-formatted, relevant, and up-to-date, audiences are more likely to perceive them as valuable. We thus propose:

H1. Utilitarian benefit is positively related to perceived value.

Hedonic benefit is defined as the perceived utility of UGC based on its capacity to arouse feelings or affective states [23]. Different from utilitarian benefit, hedonic benefit is intrinsically and emotionally evaluated. Taking YouTube as an example, audiences could perceive enjoyment and excitement while watching videos, thus hedonic benefit is derived. Prior studies has demonstrated that perceived enjoyment, as a representative of hedonic benefit, positively affect perceived value [12, 27]. UGC that arouses audiences' feeling of delight will evoke a better value appraisal. Therefore, we propose:

H2. Hedonic benefit is positively related to perceived value.

Social benefit is described as the perceived utility of UGC based on its ability to enhance audiences' social well-being [13]. Social benefit refers to the extrinsic advantages that UGC provide, which fulfill audiences' needs for establishing social image and gaining social support [11]. For example, people read online articles to enhance their social image (one's image in the eyes of others), as the knowledge conveyed by these articles can be helpful to communicate one's symbolic meaning to others. In addition, reading online articles may provide an audience with emotional support, companionship, and encouragement, help he/she meet and potentially establish social relationships with other audiences sharing similar interest. When the UGC appears to be helpful for audiences to enhance their social image or build social relationships, audiences will perceived it as valuable. Hence, we propose:

H3. Social benefit is positively related to perceived value.

3.2 Perceived Sacrifices

In VAM benefit-sacrifice framework, audiences' perceived sacrifice has been recognized as an additional antecedent of perceived value [12]. Donating money to content creators indicates that audiences will have monetary sacrifice for UGC consumption. Instead of using subjective amount of money, we use perceived fee to measure monetary sacrifice. That is because: (1) audiences have the authority to decide the donation amount; (2) given the same amount of donation, different audiences' perception of fee may vary dramatically. We define perceived fee as the extent to which an audience believes that the amount of donation is considerable. It has been suggested that perceived fee is negatively related to perceived value of UGC. For instance, in the context of online content service, Wang et al. [27] suggest a negative relationship between perceived fee and perceived value. When audiences consider the fee they need to pay for online content service as high, the overall evaluation of the service value will decrease. Therefore, we hypothesize:

H4. Perceived fee is negatively related to perceived value.

3.3   Intention to Donate to Content Creators

As noted earlier, our definition of perceived value reflects an audience's overall assessment of the benefits and sacrifices of acquiring and/or using UGC. It is believed that audiences are economically rational and try to achieve maximum utility or satisfaction through UGC consumption, given their resource limitations (e.g., time limitation). Since donating money to content creators is completely voluntary, after consuming UGC, audiences will firstly evaluate the trade-off between benefits they receive and sacrifices they make. Based on the evaluation, audiences then conclude whether the UGC is valuable, which in turn serve as a basis for their following behavioral decision [30]. In VAM, perceived value is identified as the key factor affecting purchase behavior. Researchers have found that, in the contexts of online content services [27] and e-book subscription services [10], perceived value has a significant and positive impact on intention to pay. Following their findings, we propose:

H5. Perceived value is positively related to audiences' intention to donate.

4   Methodology

4.1   Measures

We will test the research model and hypotheses empirically. Based on our literature review, we developed a questionnaire to collect data. The questionnaire consists of six sections: utilitarian benefit, hedonic benefit, social benefit, perceived fee, perceived value, and intention to donate. A 7-point Likert scale ranging from 1 (strongly disagree) to 7 (strongly agree) was used as a measurement scale. All measurement items in this study were adapted from prior studies, in order to ensure the content validity. In particular, measurement items for utilitarian benefit were adapted from Kim et al. [12] and Chu and Lu [5]. The scale for hedonic benefit was modified from Kim et al. [12] and Agarwal and Karahanna [1], while social benefit items were adapted from Kim et al. [13] and Sweeney and Soutar [23]. The items for measuring perceived fee were adapted from Kim et al. [12] and Voss et al. [25]. Finally, the items used to measure intention to donate was adapted from Kim et al. [12] and Davis et al. [7]. In the present study, the wording of the measurement statements was modified to reflect the UGC consumption context.

4.2   Data Collection and Analysis

Data will be collected from websites that allow audiences to donate money to content creators (e.g., Sina Weibo and WeChat in Mainland China). We have develop the questionnaire on a professional survey website (wjx.cn). Invitation emails including the survey link will be distributed to target participants. We aim to collect approximately 200 valid responses. In terms of data analysis, we follow the partial least squares (PLS) approach. SmartPLS software will be used to conduct a two-step analysis [19]: (1) all measurement models will be examined for the psychometric properties, and

(2) the structural model and hypotheses will be tested. PLS is a convenient approach that simultaneously assess the measurement model (including reliability and validity of the measures for theoretical constructs) and structural model (relationships among theoretical constructs), which is widely adopted in information science research [28].

5 Conclusion

This study is one of the first that aims to investigate determinants of audiences' voluntary donation to UGC content creators through IS wisdom. Drawing on value-based adoption model [12], we propose an analytical conceptual model to explain audiences' donation behavior. More specifically, in the research model, (1) perceived value (the overall estimation of the gap between audiences' perceived benefits and sacrifices) has been identified as the key predictor of audiences' intention to donate money, (2) antecedents of perceived value have been further explored, including benefits of UGC consumption (utilitarian benefit, hedonic benefit, and social benefit) and sacrifice of UGC consumption (perceived fee).

The contributions of this study to research on donation to content creators are threefold. First, it will expand the literature on perceived value and audiences' donation behavior. The present work is one of the first that conceptualize the benefits and sacrifices of UGC consumption, and empirically investigate how these antecedents affect audiences' perceived value and donation behavior. Second, while prior research focuses primarily on exploring how the benefits of UGC consumption influence audiences' donation behavior [22, 26], this study will contribute to the knowledge of UGC consumption by distinguishing sacrifices from benefits, and investigating their effects on donation behavior respectively. Third, this study will contribute to the value-based adoption model by adapting and verifying it in the UGC consumption context. Upon completion, this research are expected to provide effective implications for content creators and website managers, that is, audiences are more likely to donate money to content creators when the benefits (utilitarian benefit, hedonic benefit, and social benefit) gaining from UGC are improved, or when the sacrifice (perceived fee) of UGC consumption is reduced.

Acknowledgement. This study was supported by the Fundamental Research Funds for the Central Universities: No. NR2018002 awarded to the author.

References

1. Agarwal, R., Karahanna, E.: Time flies when you're having fun: cognitive absorption and beliefs about information technology usage. MIS Q. 24, 665–694 (2000)
2. Arantes, M., Figueiredo, F., Almeida, J.M.: Understanding video-ad consumption on YouTube: a measurement study on user behavior, popularity, and content properties. Paper presented at the Proceedings of the 8th ACM Conference on Web Science (2016)
3. Beal, V.: What is User-Generated Content? Webopedia (2018). https://www.webopedia.com/TERM/U/UGC.html. Accessed 9 Feb 2018

4. Cabrera, A., Cabrera, E.F.: Knowledge-sharing dilemmas. Organ. Stud. **23**(5), 687–710 (2002)
5. Chu, C.-W., Lu, H.-P.: Factors influencing online music purchase intention in Taiwan: an empirical study based on the value-intention framework. Internet Res. **17**(2), 139–155 (2007)
6. Daugherty, T., Eastin, M.S., Bright, L.: Exploring consumer motivations for creating user-generated content. J. Interact. Advert. **8**(2), 16–25 (2008)
7. Davis, F.D., Bagozzi, R.P., Warshaw, P.R.: User acceptance of computer technology: a comparison of two theoretical models. Manag. Sci. **35**(8), 982–1003 (1989)
8. Day, G.S.: Managing market relationships. J. Acad. Mark. Sci. **28**(1), 24–30 (2000)
9. Holbrook, M.B.: Consumer Value: A Framework for Analysis and Research. Psychology Press, London (1999)
10. Hsiao, K.-L., Chen, C.-C.: Value-based adoption of e-book subscription services: the roles of environmental concerns and reading habits. Telematics Inform. **34**(5), 434–448 (2017)
11. Keller, K.L.: Conceptualizing, measuring, and managing customer-based brand equity. J. Mark. **57**(1), 1–22 (1993)
12. Kim, H.-W., Chan, H.C., Gupta, S.: Value-based adoption of mobile internet: an empirical investigation. Decis. Support Syst. **43**(1), 111–126 (2007)
13. Kim, H.-W., Gupta, S., Koh, J.: Investigating the intention to purchase digital items in social networking communities: a customer value perspective. Inf. Manag. **48**(6), 228–234 (2011)
14. Kollock, P.: The economies of online cooperation: gifts and public goods in cyberspace. In: Smith, M.A., Kollock, P. (eds.) Communities in Cyberspace. Routledge, London (1999)
15. Lee, M.R., Yen, D.C., Hsiao, C.Y.: Understanding the perceived community value of Facebook users. Comput. Hum. Behav. **35**, 350–358 (2014)
16. Lu, Z., Xia, H., Heo, S., Wigdor, D.: You watch, you give, and you engage: a study of live streaming practices in China. Paper presented at the CHI, Montreal, QC, Canada (2018)
17. Nonnecke, B., Preece, J.: Shedding light on lurkers in online communities. In: Buckner, K. (ed.) Ethnographic Studies in Real and Virtual Environments: Inhabited Information Spaces and Connected Communities, Edinburgh, pp. 123–128 (1999)
18. Pulizzi, J.: The Only 10 Ways to Make Money From Content Marketing (2017). http://contentmarketinginstitute.com/2017/05/make-money-content-marketing/. Accessed 9 Feb 2018
19. Ringle, C.M., Wende, S., Becker, J.-M.: SmartPLS 3. Boenningstedt: SmartPLS GmbH (2015). http://www.smartpls.com
20. Schroeder, A.: 2017 Charity Update: Twitch community gives back at record pace! (2017). https://blog.twitch.tv/2017-charity-update-twitch-community-gives-back-at-record-pace-a687f86001bd. Accessed 9 Feb 2018
21. Sheth, J.N., Newman, B.I., Gross, B.L.: Consumption Values and Market Choices: Theory and Applications. Southwestern Publishing, Cincinnati (1991)
22. Su, L., Zhang, R., Li, Y., Li, W.: What drives trust in online paid knowledge? The role of customer value. Paper presented at the Proceedings of the 22nd Pacific Asia Conference on Information Systems, Japan (2018)
23. Sweeney, J.C., Soutar, G.N.: Consumer perceived value: the development of a multiple item scale. J. Retail. **77**(2), 203–220 (2001)
24. Tedjamulia, S.J.J., Dean, D.L., Olsen, D.R., Albrecht, C.C.: Motivating content contributions to online communities: Toward a more comprehensive theory. Paper presented at the Proceedings of the 38th Annual Hawaii International Conference on System Sciences, Hawaii (2005)
25. Voss, G.B., Parasuraman, A., Grewal, D.: The roles of price, performance, and expectations in determining satisfaction in service exchanges. J. Mark. **62**(4), 46–61 (1998)

26. Wan, J., Lu, Y., Wang, B., Zhao, L.: How attachment influences users' willingness to donate to content creators in social media: a socio-technical systems perspective. Inf. Manag. **54**(7), 837–850 (2017)

27. Wang, Y.-S., Yeh, C.-H., Liao, Y.-W.: What drives purchase intention in the context of online content services? The moderating role of ethical self-efficacy for online piracy. Int. J. Inf. Manag. **33**(1), 199–208 (2013)

28. Wei, P.-S., Lu, H.-P.: Why do people play mobile social games? An examination of network externalities and of uses and gratifications. Internet Res. **24**(3), 313–331 (2014)

29. Xu, J., Benbasat, I., Cenfetelli, R.T.: Integrating service quality with system and information quality: an empirical test in the e-service context. MIS Q. **37**, 777–794 (2013)

30. Zeithaml, V.A.: Consumer perceptions of price, quality, and value: a means-end model and synthesis of evidence. J. Mark. **52**(3), 2–22 (1988)

Deal Communication Through Microblogging

Yi Liu[✉]

Rennes School of Business, Rennes, France
yi.liu@esc-rennes.com

Abstract. Social media facilitates information dissemination and narrows the distance between merchants and consumers. However, how to better integrate social media and how to communicate promotional messages to consumers have not been fully understood by merchants. Anchoring on the concept of psychological distance, we argue that the effectiveness of social media communication depends on the degree to which consumers perceive the psychological distance of the deal communication. The social media communication data of the group-buying website were obtained from its national and city accounts. Data on the featured deals in these two cities were collected, and the sales performance of these deals was used as the indicator of the effectiveness of promotional message communication. The results indicate that promotional messages conducted on the national account induce better sales performance.

Keywords: Social media · Microblogging · Group-buying

1 Introduction

The rise of social media has provided a revolutionary form of communication media for narrowing the distance between merchants and consumers. However, the understanding of such issue remains limited. Explicit engagement in social media to communicate product information to consumers potentially increases sales [1–3]. In practice, how to integrate social media into commercial activities is unclear. Mangold and Faulds [4] echo similar concerns as they claim that the degree to which the media is effectively utilized determines its value realization. We aim to address this concern by contextualizing the research in group-buying context where group-buying websites use microblogging for deal communication and sales generation.

Anchoring on Construal Level Theory (CLT), we propose that effective use of social media depends on the degree to which consumers perceive the distance of deal communication based on who communicates it. CLT indicates that psychological distance is linked to the level of mental construal, such that psychologically distant (proximal) objects will be construed at a higher (lower), abstract (detailed) level; and high (low) level construal will bring to mind distant (proximal) objects [5]. Psychological distance is determined by the spatiotemporal distance of the event or object from the self, here and now. Spatiotemporal distance of social media communication

© Springer Nature Switzerland AG 2019
F. F.-H. Nah and K. Siau (Eds.): HCII 2019, LNCS 11589, pp. 231–241, 2019.
https://doi.org/10.1007/978-3-030-22338-0_19

perceived by consumers can affect their construal level, which in turn, guides how they evaluate the communication [6]. Deal communication in social media varies in their spatial distances. For instance, consumers perceive the postings at the city-level social media account of merchants as spatially proximal compared with the postings at the account of the headquarters (i.e., national-level). Psychologically distant and proximal postings could be evaluated differently. The relationship between the construal level and evaluation (purchasing willingness) has been investigated in existing CLT literature. However, the results differ. Trope et al. [6] suggest that consumer willingness to purchase a product is higher for distant objects because abstract thinking focuses more on the desirability of the object (e.g., how interesting the product is) and less on the feasibility of the object (e.g., how expensive or useful the product is). By contrast, Williams et al. [7] argue that the purchasing willingness of a consumer is higher for proximal objects because distance promotes emotional detachment. The present study empirically tests these conflicting arguments.

This study contributes to researchers by addressing the means through which social media can be best integrated into daily commercial activities from the merchant perspective. This study adds to the existing social media literature that mainly focuses on the effects of consumer generated contents, such as consumer reviews and product ratings, on sales performance [8, 9].

2 Literature Review

The popularity of social media motivates researchers to examine how business and economic values can be realized through social media communication, which is an important indicator of communication effectiveness for merchants. Most studies focus on word-of-mouth (WOM) communication through social media. For instance, several studies investigate the effects of WOM on the box office sales of movies. Liu [9] discovers that the volume, instead of valence (percentage of positive/negative messages), of WOM messages offers significant explanatory power for both aggregate and weekly box office revenue. Duan et al. [8] examine the awareness effect of online user reviews on daily box office performances of movies, and reveal that the volume of online posting significantly influences box office sales. Chen and Xie [10] consider online user reviews as endogenous factors that influence movie sales. In addition, the volume of online reviews, which indicate the importance of the awareness effect, significantly influences box office sales. However, the rating of online user reviews has no significant impact on the box office revenues of movies, which indicate little persuasive effect on consumer purchase decisions. Moon et al. [11] find that high advertising spending on movies supported by high ratings maximizes movie revenues. In other contexts, Ye et al. [12] reveal that user ratings positively affect hotel room sales, which imply that ratings as a new form of communication on social media have business values for retailers. Besides the volume of WOM communication, Chevalier and Mayzlin [13] determine a significant relationship between the length of reviews and online book sales. Clemons et al. [14] reveal that the variance of ratings and the strength of the most positive quartile of reviews play a significant role in determining which new products grow fastest in the market. The effectiveness of reviews is also affected by other factors. Forman et al. [15] suggest that consumers use reviewer disclosure of identity-descriptive information to supplement or to replace product information when making purchase decisions and evaluating the helpfulness of online reviews in the online community. Consumers can rate reviews that contain identity-descriptive information more positively, and the prevalence of reviewer disclosure of identity information is associated with increases in subsequent online product sales. User-generated social media content conveys more information compared with conventional online platforms. Luo et al. [16] argue that social media-based metrics, such as consumer ratings and blogs, are significant indicators of firm equity value compared with web traffic and Google searches.

The abovementioned studies focus on investigating social media communication generated by consumers. Social media affords communication among consumers, which generate economic values for merchants. Although the findings are valuable, the fact that merchants have limited or no control over what users post in social media indicates that improvements still need to be introduced in terms of how social media communication can be utilized by merchants to increase sales. Thus, a few studies have started to explore how to communicate promotional messages to consumers on social media sites. For instance, Goh et al. [2] show that the information richness of social media communication generated by merchants on Facebook positively affects sales. Our study aims to enrich the understanding of effective social media communication by merchants.

3   Construal Level Theory (CLT)

We propose that social media communication generated by merchants are processed by consumers, and the manner how consumers construe communication affects its effectiveness. This process can be explained by CLT. CLT is an account of how psychological distances between individuals and their targets influence individual construal levels of those targets. The theory suggests that psychological distance is an important determinant of whether the primary or the secondary peripheral characteristics are used as the basis of individual evaluation [5, 6]. CLT assumes that people mentally construe objects that are psychologically near in terms of low-level, detailed, and contextualized features, while, at a distance, they construe the same objects or events in terms of high-level, abstract, and stable characteristics [6]. Psychological distance is egocentric, and its reference point is the self, here and now. Differences in time, space, social distance, and hypotheticality constitute different distance dimensions [17]. Various empirical studies have investigated the effects of psychological distance on construal level. Liberman et al. [18] examine temporal differences in construal and report that people think about a set of objects in more superordinate abstract terms in the distant future condition as compared with in the near future condition. Fujita et al. [19] show that the events in a film are described by more abstract language for people who believe such events were located in a spatially distant location. Social distance is influenced by the similarity or power difference among individuals [6]. Liviatan et al. [20] report that students prefer subordinate and superordinate action identifications to describe the activities of students of similar (similar targets) and different (dissimilar targets) classes, respectively. Aside from temporal, spatial, and social distances, hypotheticality affects psychological distance. An improbable event would seem more distant than a probable event [21]. Different dimensions of psychological distance affect mental construal, and these construals guide prediction, evaluation, and behavior [6]. Prediction, evaluation, and behavior are based on high-level construal aspects as psychological distance increases. Nussbaum et al. [22] study the manner by which temporal distance influences the confidence of predicting future outcomes. They find that temporal distance enhances confidence when deriving from a high-level construct. Concerning evaluation, Liberman and Trope [23] examine desirability concerns, which high-level construals of an activity should emphasize, and feasibility concerns, which low-level construals of an activity should emphasize. As temporal distance increases, desirability effect increases, while feasibility effect decreases. Applying desirability and feasibility concerns in consumer purchasing behavior, abstract mental construal increases consumer willingness to purchase a product because abstract thinking focuses more on the desirability of the object (e.g., how interesting the product is) and less on the feasibility of the object (e.g., how expensive or useful the product is) [5]. Thus, psychological distance could promote the purchasing willingness of consumers. Similar arguments can be found in several consumer behavior studies. For instance, consumers who have higher construal level place more importance on perceived fit in evaluating brand extensions [24]. Based on the above arguments, effectiveness of social media communication depends on whether consumers perceive communication messages distant (spatially).

However, recent studies question this main proposition of CLT and re-examine the relationship between psychological distance and construal level. Williams et al. [7] argue that psychological distance and construal level are actually two separate concepts. They suggest that distance promotes emotional detachment, whereas abstract thinking promotes a focus on positivity. Other studies have also shown that consumers have weaker emotional responses to distant stimuli, e.g., [25]. van Boven et al. [26] suggest that emotional intensity reduces perceived psychological distance. Given that psychological distance reduces the intensity of emotional reactions during judgment and choice, they find that consumer willingness to purchase highly desirable products decreases [7]. The influence of emotional reactions on consumer behavior and advertising communication has been widely studied in consumer research literature, e.g., [27]. The effect of emotional reactions on purchasing behavior has been studied in the online context. For instance, Hausman and Siekpe [28] find that emotional reactions toward a website positively affect online purchasing intentions. Park and Kim [29] show that consumer emotional reactions to products are key influential factors for consumer commitment, which results in higher purchasing intentions. According to this stream of studies, for social media communication, which is distant to consumers and causes emotional detachment [7], the effectiveness decreases. The present study examines how the distance between consumers and social media communication affects the effectiveness of communication. Hypotheses are developed based on these two opposite views.

4   Hypotheses Development

According to CLT, spatial distant object increases psychological distance and is construed at a high level [5]. By construing the object in a high level, the abstract and stable characteristics of the object would be presented [6]. Liberman and Trope [23] find that desirability effect increases and feasibility effect decreases when psychological distance increases. High-level construals of the objects emphasize desirability concerns, whereas low-level construals of the object emphasize feasibility concerns. Therefore, spatially distant object induces abstract thinking from consumers who will focus more on the desirability of the object and less on the feasibility of the object [5]. Increases in desirability effect would enhance consumer willingness to purchase. Conversely, feasibility concerns should be more prominent in decisions regarding the spatially proximal object. Ironically, although feasibility aspects are often more multifaceted compared with desirability aspects, increasing reliance on low-level construal for spatially proximal objects often reduces consumer confidence and decisiveness [5]. Therefore, the increase of feasibility effect would diminish consumer willingness to purchase.

One company can have multiple accounts in the same social media site based on the level of its business operations. A company can have one account as its national (headquarter and country-level) account and other accounts for each of its branches (city-level), which are mainly used to deliver information from the local branches. From the perspective of local consumers, the national account of a company is spatially distant, whereas its local account is spatially proximal. Accordingly, local consumers will have high mental construals of communication sent through the national account of a company. The prevalence of desirability (high mental construal) over feasibility (low mental construal) should increase consumer confidence and decisiveness, and attract better sales performance of the promoted product. Thus, we hypothesize:

H1a: Compared to promotional messages on local accounts, promotional messages on national accounts result in higher sale performance.

The above counterintuitive view of CLT is still debatable. The gist of CLT is that psychological distance has a linear relationship with abstract thinking. These two variables are often treated as identical and interchangeable. However, a recent study has contested this relationship and has found evidence suggesting that these variables should not be treated as identical because they are not interchangeable. Specifically, distance promotes emotional detachment [7], and reduces emotional concern [25, 26].

Abstract thinking promotes a focus on positivity in which the objects are perceived more pleasant [7]. Therefore, being psychologically distant from an object does not necessarily mean that consumers will construe the object at a high level or in an abstract manner. Given that psychological distance promotes emotional detachment, a psychologically distant object, which results in lower emotional reactions, diminishes consumer willingness to purchase, e.g., [28]. Therefore, compared with promotional messages communicated through the local account of a company, those communicated through its national account should have worse sales performance of the promoted product. Thus, we hypothesize:

> *H1b: Compared to promotional messages on local accounts, promotional messages on national accounts result in lower sales performance.*

5 Research Methodology

Two sources of data were collected, namely, merchant communications on social media site and the sale performance of the merchant, which represents the effectiveness of the communications. We selected a daily-deal group-buying website, Meituan, one of the most popular Groupon-like daily-deal group-buying websites in China. Sina-Weibo, which is a Twitter-like micro-blogging site in China, is the most widely used social media site in major cities in China and hosts a verified company account of almost every business in the country. Thus, we selected SinaWeibo as the social media site in our study and crawled the messages posted by Meituan. In this study, we only collected deals featured in the Beijing and Shanghai websites, the two biggest cities in China where the website first started its business. Data were collected from December 2011 to February 2012. The number of coupons sold for the deals in the Meituan Beijing and Shanghai sites was crawled hourly. At the same time, all deal-related data (i.e., face value of the deal, price, title, start time, end time, tipping point, availability, and expiration time of the coupon) were also captured. After excluding lucky draw deals, for which the price is 0, and the deals without expiration date, 1131 deals were collected (583 deals from Meituan Beijing branch and 548 deals from Meituan Shanghai branch). Among these 1131 deals, 184 deals were sold out before the end of feature time online. Thus, we only considered 947 deals for the analysis on total number of coupons sold. To control the product types, the deals were categorized into grocery/dining, leisure/entertainment, and others. This categorization is widely applied in Chinese daily-deal websites. The feature duration of the deal refers to the number of days the deal is featured on the group-buying website. The expiration time of the coupon refers to the number of days the coupon is valid for redemption after the end time of the deal.

In SinaWeibo, we crawled the number of followers from the headquarter account of Meituan and its two local accounts in Beijing and Shanghai hourly. All tweets, including contents and posting times on these three accounts were also crawled and saved. In total, we obtained 1128 tweets from headquarter account, 2219 tweets from local account in Beijing, and 2490 tweets local account in Shanghai. These tweets were classified into three categories based on their contents, namely, promotional tweets (information on the promoted product), business-related tweets other than promotions (e.g., company news and lucky draws), and non-business-related tweets (e.g. jokes and weather conditions). We used three count variables for each deal to determine how many times they were promoted in the Meituan headquarter/branch accounts. We control the frequency and types of tweets on the national and local accounts of the company. The number of tweets for each type and from each account is calculated for the duration when a particular deal is featured on the group-buying website. We also control the number of followers on each account, which is calculated as the average number of users for the duration when a particular deal was featured on the group-buying website.

6 Data Analysis and Results

According to H1a and H1b, promotional messages on the national account had higher or lower sales performance as compared with promotional messages on the local account. We used the negative binomial regression to test this hypothesis, given that our dependent variable, i.e., the total number of coupons sold for each deal, was counted with over-dispersion ($\mu = 1395$, $\sigma = 3600$). The frequency of promotion of each deal on the national account (both explicit and implicit) and the respective local account (both explicit and implicit) were the independent variables. Control variables were obtained from two sources. First, deal-related variables from group-buying retailers, such as the category of the deals, tipping point, availability, price, and expiration time of the coupon, were included in the analysis. Three deal-related variables, namely, the city where the deal is featured, face value of the deal, and duration of the feature, were dropped because of a multi-collinearity problem in the analysis. Second, social media communication-related variables, such as the number of followers on the national and the respective local accounts as well as the number of tweets for each account level and category were included in the analysis. Due to the multi-collinearity problem of the control variables, we ran four models with different sets of control variables. For each set, we used control variables that did not have a multi-collinearity problem.

Table 1 indicates that the number of sold coupons could increase up to 5.12 ($10^{0.709}$) times by posting a promotional message on the headquarter account, whereas the number of sold coupons could increase up to 1.36 ($10^{0.135}$) times by posting a promotional message on the local account. The national account was a more effective social media communication tool. Thus, H1a is supported, while H1b is not supported. This finding supports the CLT.

Table 1. Field data results

Main variables	#Coupon sold	#Coupon sold	#Coupon sold	#Coupon sold
Promotional message headquarter	0.631*** (0.103)	0.586*** (0.105)	0.604*** (0.104)	0.630*** (0.104)
Promotional message local	0.100* (0.043)	0.115** (0.043)	0.112** (0.043)	0.097* (0.043)
Control variables				
Deal category (grocery/restaurants drinks (food) as the base)				
Entertainment	0.449*** (0.068)	0.435*** (0.069)	0.421*** (0.068)	0.455*** (0.068)
Others	−0.124 (0.084)	−0.159 (0.086)	−0.149 (0.085)	−0.125 (0.085)
Tipping point	0.065*** (0.019)	0.021 (0.018)	0.029 (0.018)	0.073*** (0.020)
Value	5.16e−05 (8.67e−05)	1.068e−04 (8.98e−05)	8.86e−05 (8.82e−05)	4.71e−05 (8.7e−05)
Price	−0.002*** (0.000)	−0.002*** (0.000)	−0.002*** (0.000)	−0.002*** (0.00)
Expiration time	−0.003** (0.001)	−0.003*** (0.001)	−0.003*** (0.001)	−0.003*** (0.001)
Feature duration				0.014 (0.011)
Follower headquarter (Log)	−5.791*** (1.551)	−4.616** (1.533)	−5.828*** (1.559)	−4.532** (1.442)
Follower local (Log)	1.020*** (0.162)	0.864*** (0.174)	1.211*** (0.161)	0.942*** (0.160)
Number of messages promotional messages headquarter			0.011*** (0.003)	
Number of messages biz headquarter	0.014*** (0.004)	0.014* (0.005)	0.013** (0.004)	0.015*** (0.004)
Number of messages nonbiz headquarter		0.010*** (0.002)		
Number of messages promotional messages local	0.005*** (0.001)			0.006*** (0.001)
Number of messages biz local		0.005** (0.002)		
Number of messages nonbiz local	0.004* (0.002)		0.005*** (0.002)	
Constant	67.000*** (19.857)	54.299*** (19.791)	65.703*** (20.016)	51.779** (18.679)
Log likelihood	−6911.154	−6929.375	−6921.138	−6913.355
Akaike information criteria (AIC)	13852.31	13888.75	13872.28	13856.71
Bayesian information criteria (BIC)	13925.11	13961.55	13945.08	13929.51

*** $p < 0.001$, ** $p < 0.01$, * $p < 0.05$; N = 947

7 Discussion

Inspired by the question on how to integrate social media into daily commercial activities, this study investigates how psychological distances, reflected by the spatial distance, between social media communication and consumers affect the effectiveness of the communications. Based on CLT, spatially distant social media communication should increase the effectiveness of communication because of the high mental construal of consumers, which increases the desirability and decreases the feasibility concern. However, there is an opposing view on this stand where psychological distance could promote emotional detachment. According to this view, spatially distant social media communication could decrease the effectiveness of communication because of consumer emotional detachment from the message. One way to increase its effectiveness is by making the message more abstract. To address this opposing view, we analyze the sales performance of online group-buying website and their respective microblogs. We find that promotional messages that are posted on the company national account, which is spatially distant from consumers, generate better sales performance than message posted on the local account. This finding is consistent with CLT.

This study offers several implications. First, we introduce and empirically examine an opposing view to CLT, which argues that psychological distance and construal level are two separate constructs, and that the former is linked to emotional detachment, e.g., [28, 29]. Second, this study enriches social media literature. Although social media is attracting more attention from the industry, empirical studies, especially theoretical frameworks anchored studies, still lack. This study relies on the concept of psychological distance and on the two opposing views of construal level and emotional reactions to explain social media phenomenon. Third, this study contributes to the group-buying literature. The daily-deal group-buying phenomenon has attracted researchers from different fields, such as information systems [30] and marketing [31]. The optimization of the sales performance, which is measured by the number of sold coupons, is a central topic in this area. We confirm in this study that the herding behavior/observational learning effect exist in group-buying websites. We have also extended group-buying studies to social media platforms. Existing studies on group-buying mostly focus on data derived from group-buying websites, such as the number of sold coupons, to determine consumer purchasing behavior on such websites [30], and characteristics of deals, websites, and merchants [31]. By integrating social media and group-buying data, studies on group-buying can attract a broader audience and offer more valuable implications.

References

1. Culnan, M., McHugh, P., Zubillage, J.: How large U.S. companies can use Twitter and other social media to gain business value. Manag. Inf. Syst. Q. Executive 9(4), 243–259 (2010)
2. Goh, K., Heng, C., Lin, Z.: Social media brand community and consumer behavior: quantifying the relative impact of user- and marketer-generated content. Inf. Syst. Res. 24(1), 88–107 (2013)

3. Xia, L.: Effects of companies' responses to consumer criticism in social media. Int. J. Electron. Commer. **17**(4), 73–100 (2013)
4. Mangold, G., Faulds, D.: Social media: The new hybrid element of the promotion mix. Bus. Horiz. **52**(4), 357–365 (2009)
5. Trope, Y., Liberman, N.: Construal-level theory of psychological distance. Psychol. Rev. **117**(2), 440–463 (2010)
6. Trope, Y., Liberman, N., Wakslak, C.: Construal levels and psychological distance: effects on representation, prediction, evaluation, and behavior. J. Consum. Psychol. **17**(2), 83–95 (2007)
7. Williams, L., Stein, R., Galguera, L.: Beyond construal: specifying the distinct emotional consequences of psychological distance and abstract construal (2012)
8. Duan, W., Gu, B., Whinston, A.: Do online reviews matter? - an empirical investigation of panel data. Decis. Support Syst. **45**(4), 1007–1016 (2008)
9. Liu, Y.: Word of mouth for movies: its dynamics and impact on box office revenue. J. Mark. **70**(3), 74–89 (2006)
10. Chen, Y., Xie, J.: Online consumer review: word-of-mouth as a new element of marketing communication mix. Manag. Sci. **54**(3), 447–491 (2008)
11. Moon, S., Bergey, P., Iacobucci, D.: Dynamic effect among movie ratings, movie revenue, and viewer satisfaction. J. Mark. **74**(1), 108–121 (2010)
12. Ye, Q., Law, R., Gu, B.: The impact of online user reviews on hotel room sales. Int. J. Hospitality Manag. **28**(1), 180–182 (2009)
13. Chevalier, J., Mayzlin, D.: The effect of word of mouth on sales: online book reviews. J. Mark. Res. **43**(3), 345–354 (2006)
14. Clemons, E., Gao, G., Hitt, L.: When online reviews meet hyperdifferentiation: a study of the craft beer industry. J. Manag. Inf. Syst. **23**(2), 149–171 (2006)
15. Forman, C., Ghose, A., Wiesenfeld, B.: Examining the relationship between reviews and sales: the role of reviewer identity disclosure in electronic markets. Inf. Syst. Res. **19**(3), 291–313 (2008)
16. Luo, X., Zhang, J., Duan, W.: Social media and firm equity value. Inf. Syst. Res. **24**(1), 146–163 (2013)
17. Liberman, N., Forster, J.: Distancing from experienced self: how global-versus-local perception affects estimation of psychological distance. J. Pers. Soc. Pyschol. **97**(2), 203–216 (2009)
18. Liberman, N., Sagristano, M., Trope, Y.: The effect of temporal distance on level of construal. J. Exp. Soc. Psychol. **38**, 523–535 (2002)
19. Fujita, K., Henderson, M., Eng, J., Trope, Y., Liberman, N.: Spatial distance and mental construal of social events. Psychol. Sci. **17**, 278–282 (2006)
20. Liviatan, I., Trope, Y., Liberman, N.: The effect of similarity on mental construal. J. Exp. Soc. Psychol. **44**, 1256–1269 (2008)
21. Wakslak, C., Trope, Y., Liberman, N., Alony, R.: Seeing the forest when entry is unlikely: probability and the mental representation of events. J. Exp. Psychol. Gen. **135**(4), 641–653 (2006)
22. Nussbaum, S., Liberman, N., Trope, Y.: Predicting the near and distant future. J. Exp. Psychol. Gen. **135**, 152–161 (2006)
23. Liberman, L., Trope, Y.: The role of feasibility and desirability considerations in near and distant future decisions: a test of temporal construal theory. J. Pers. Soc. Psychol. **75**, 5–18 (1998)
24. Kim, H., John, D.: Consumer response to brand extensions: construal level as a moderator of the importance of perceived fit. J. Consum. Psychol. **18**(2), 116–126 (2008)

25. Williams, L., Huang, J., Bargh, H.: The scaffolded mind: higher mental processes are grounded in early experience of the physical world. Eur. J. Soc. Psychol. **39**(4), 1257–1267 (2009)
26. van Boven, L., Kane, J., McGraw, P., Dale, J.: Feeling close: emotional intensity reduces perceived psychological distance. J. Pers. Soc. Psychol. **98**(6), 872–885 (2010)
27. Westbrook, R.: Product/consumption-based affective responses and postpurchase processes. J. Mark. Res. **24**, 258–270 (1987)
28. Hausman, A., Siekpe, J.: The effect of web interface features on consumer online purchase intentions. J. Bus. Res. **62**(1), 5–13 (2009)
29. Park, C., Kim, Y.: Indentifying key factors affecting consumer purchase behavior in an online shopping context. Int. J. Retail Distrib. Manag. **31**(1), 16–29 (2003)
30. Liu, Y., Sutanto, J.: Buyers' purchasing time and herd behavior on deal-of-the-day group-buying websites. Electron. Mark. **22**(2), 83–93 (2012)
31. Kumar, V., Ranjan, B.: Social coupons as a marketing strategy: a multifaceted perspective. J. Acad. Mark. Sci. **40**(1), 120–136 (2012)

The Effects of Privacy Awareness and Content Sensitivity on User Engagement

Martin Stabauer[✉] [iD]

Johannes Kepler University, Linz, Austria
martin.stabauer@jku.at

Abstract. To increase user engagement is an important goal and major business model for many web applications and online publishers. An established tool for this purpose is online polling, where user opinions, preferences, attitudes and possibly personal information are collected to help publishers to a better understanding of their target audiences. These polls are often provided as supplements to online newspaper articles, the topics of which are typically also reflected in the content of the polls. We analyzed and categorized this content, and related it with the user engagement rate given as the proportion of people who voluntarily disclose personal information. Recently, public privacy awareness has increased, especially since the introduction of the European Union's General Data Protection Regulation (GDPR). Extensive media coverage has led to public discussions about data protection and privacy. This study additionally investigated the effect of increased public privacy awareness on individual privacy awareness and subsequently user engagement. The results are based on live data of more than 60,000 polls and more than 22 million user votes, mainly collected in German-speaking countries, and give insights into user behavior when confronted with requests for personal information in various settings and over time.

Keywords: Online polls · Online profiling · Privacy awareness · Informed consent · User engagement

1 Introduction

Although there is broad consensus that internet users' privacy awareness should be increased and encouraged and that informed consents can strongly support highly sustainable means of income, the effects of privacy regulations and privacy awareness on the profits of IT businesses remain unclear. Numerous studies have sought to quantify the value internet users allocate to their personal data, but the topic continues controversial [1]. User consent to the processing of personal data is typically requested at the beginning of an interaction; however, the literature suggests that the consent may change over time and should therefore be considered an ongoing activity [2] (cf. Sect. 3.2).

Generally speaking, user engagement has become essential for many websites and publishers [3], and in most cases it involves collecting and processing

© Springer Nature Switzerland AG 2019
F. F.-H. Nah and K. Siau (Eds.): HCII 2019, LNCS 11589, pp. 242–255, 2019.
https://doi.org/10.1007/978-3-030-22338-0_20

users' personal data at some level of aggregation. One of the major sources of income for these businesses is behavioral targeting, which has become widely used throughout many web applications. However, the decision to employ behavioral targeting should be based on nuanced consideration: For small publishers whose advertising space is in low demand traditional advertising may be preferable under certain circumstances [4].

Responsible treatment of the personal data collected is essential for businesses, as the legal requirements and corresponding fines are becoming increasingly restrictive and severe. However, sometimes this need for privacy is mixed up with the need for data security, and there is evidence that 38% of organizations address the latter but not the former [5]. Furthermore, in recent years users have become better informed and aware of their privacy rights.

The contribution of this work is twofold: It (a) follows earlier evidence that privacy concerns are greater in the context of sensitive goods and investigates the effect of the sensitivity of a website's content on its user engagement rate, and (b) examines the engagement rate over time before and after introduction of the General Data Protection Regulation (GDPR).

2   Privacy

Protection of personal data and the concept of privacy in general is currently one of the most widely discussed topics in the IT sector. At a very abstract level, two fundamental perspectives on privacy can be distinguished:

- Privacy of the personal sphere as *"the right to be let alone"*, which was already introduced in 1890 by Warren and Brandeis [6]. Their influential work defined privacy as (a) the secrecy of everyone's own thoughts, properties and actions and (b) the flow towards the individual of these data about others and that might affect him or her.
- Privacy of one's own personal data as *"the right to select what personal information about me is known to what people"* [7]. This is the traditional viewpoint of many computer scientists, where the focus is on control over information about oneself, one's conversations and actions. Unlike the concept of solitude, privacy of personal data is actively determined by the individual.

Both perspectives play an important role in the process of designing and implementing new applications that make use of personal data, and should be considered accordingly. Equally important is the extent to which users are aware of what happens to their personal data (and similar privacy-related issues) and whether they act accordingly. Several studies have shown that people's intentions and their self-reported privacy preferences are not always reflected in their behavior, as many tend to disclose significantly larger amounts of personal data than they their initial assertions would indicate *("Privacy Paradox")* [8,9].

2.1 Privacy Awareness

As previously mentioned, not only are data protection and privacy by themselves important in the context, but it is also of interest whether users are aware of the usage of their personal data. As a generic term, awareness can be defined as an individual's attention to, perception of or cognition about both physical and non-physical objects. It plays a crucial role in the field of privacy, where privacy awareness comprises attention to, perception of and cognition about [10]:

- *whether* others receive or have received personal information about oneself,
- *which* personal information is affected,
- *how* this information can or could be processed and used, and
- *what amount* of information about others flows towards, and might affect, one.

When users are aware of privacy-related information, they are able to come to an informed decision on whether they agree to a specific request. In essence, this can be expressed by a very basic utility function [11]:

$$U(X) = Benefit - Cost,$$

where *Benefit* is the individual value of a personalized service and *Cost* a combination of previous privacy invasion, consumer privacy concern, and the perceived importance of privacy policies and information transparency. Other scholars conceived of a similar function by substituting *Cost* with (privacy) *Risks*, for which they identified seven dimensions [12]:

- *Physical Risk:* Fearing the loss of physical safety, arising from access to personal data
- *Social Risk:* Fearing a change in one's social status
- *Resource-Related Risk:* Fearing the loss of resources
- *Psychological Risk:* Fearing a negative impact on one's peace of mind
- *Prosecution-related Risk:* Fearing that legal actions will be taken against one
- *Career-related Risk:* Fearing negative impacts on one's career
- *Freedom-related Risk:* Fearing a loss of freedom of opinion and behavior.

Recent literature also shows that the willingness to disclose personal information differs across cultures [13] and that a big data fair collection and use policy could assist in building awareness of data collection and usage [14]. These policies are also encouraged by the legal regulations presented in the next section.

2.2 GDPR and ePrivacy Regulation

The European Union's General Data Protection Regulation came into effect in 2016, and since May 25, 2018, organizations have been required to comply to it. In contrast to its predecessor – the Data Protection Directive, which required local regulations for implementation – the GDPR is self-executing and legally binding in all EU member states. This promises to eliminate inconsistencies and different perceptions. The GDPR defines rights for individuals in the EU regarding protection of their personal data and requirements for organizations regarding collection, storage and processing of these data. One of the most important aspects of the GDPR is *Privacy by Design*, for which the European Union Agency for Network and Information Security defined 8 strategies for organizations [15]:

- *Minimize:* Restricting the amount of personal data to be processed to a minimum
- *Hide:* Hiding personal data and their interrelations from plain view
- *Separate:* Processing of personal data in a distributed way whenever possible
- *Aggregate:* Processing of personal data at the highest level of aggregation and the lowest level of detail possible
- *Inform:* Informing data subjects whenever they are being processed, and thus increasing transparency
- *Control:* Providing data subjects with agency over the processing of their personal data
- *Enforce:* Compliance with a privacy policy compatible with legal requirements
- *Demonstrate:* Ability to demonstrate this compliance with privacy policies.

Aspects of the technical implementation of Privacy by Design are well researched, while other steps of the Design Science Research Methodology Process Model, such as *Design and Development* or *Demonstration*, have hardly been covered in recent literature [16].

The ePrivacy Regulation is meant to replace the current ePrivacy Directive and to particularize and complement the GDPR. At the time of writing, it is still a draft and under discussion, but it aims to protect *"fundamental rights and freedoms of natural and legal persons in the provision and use of electronic communications services"* (Art. 1(1) ePR-Draft) while ensuring *"free movement of electronic communications data and electronic communications services"* in the EU (Art. 1(2) ePR-Draft).

The consequences of both regulations remain partly unclear; in particular, the draft of the ePrivacy Regulation leaves many questions open, for instance, in the area of consent for setting cookies [17]. Some studies have identified uncertainties for both businesses and consumers and have therefore suggested standardized privacy labels [18], while others have even claimed negative effects of the GDPR on investment in the European IT sector [19] – clear reasons to research this topic further.

3   User Engagement

This section gives an introduction to the subject of online polls and to user engagement in this field.

3.1 Online Polls

One of the main attributes many modern internet applications have in common is that they rely heavily on engaging their users to provide content, to spread this content, or simply to make their personal data available. These business models are working well [3], as internet users increasingly desire to share their opinions and contribute to website content. The literature shows that this phenomenon can be observed in various forms, for instance, in the comments sections of online newspapers [20] and in social media [21].

However, as investments in online personalization can be very expensive, their justification can be severely undermined if consumers do not value them because of privacy concerns [22]. Including online polls in websites' content is an way of increasing user engagement at relatively low cost. A typical poll is structured as a single question with typically between two and five answer options. Figure 1 shows such an online poll after the voting process.

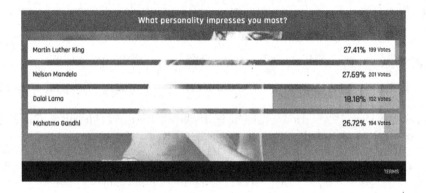

Fig. 1. Example online poll

Publishers either have their polls programmed in house or employ commercial systems. In many cases, these systems – like other analytics tools – make use only of polling metadata. However, previous studies have shown that user opinions in the form of poll responses are an untapped source of knowledge that can help publishers to monetize their content [23]. Combining poll responses with polling metadata allows even better profiling. One way of combining these two sources of information is a request for providing more personal information after the poll, as shown in Fig. 4. Requests of this kind are frequently integrated into another form of *Benefit* (see Sect. 2.1), for example, prize games.

3.2 Engagement Process

O'Brien and Toms [24] defined a process model of engagement consisting of the phases of initiating and sustaining engagement, disengaging, and potentially reengaging during a single interaction. The *Point of Engagement* with an online poll is typically a news article in which it is included. Reading the article, users see the poll and want to share their opinions or see what others think about the topic. This is the start of the *Period of Engagement*, which typically ends after seeing the results of the poll (*Disengagement*). Means of *Reengagement* are for example, showing subsequent polls with related content or showing additional offers, such as prize games or other forms that request personal data.

These phases all have attributes that emerge during and affect further inter-action, such as aesthetics, novelty, interest, motivation, awareness, interactivity, and challenge. Most of these attributes are also relevant to the polling system under investigation. The definition of engagement used here is therefore *"a quality of user experiences with technology that is characterized by challenge, aesthetic and sensory appeal, feedback, novelty, interactivity, perceived control and time, awareness, motivation, interest, and affect"* [24].

4   Empirical Study

4.1   Theoretical Model

Our research is based on the model by Awad and Krishnan [11], which examines the effects of consumers' demographic attributes (gender, education and income) and other factors on the perceived importance of information transparency. These factors are specifically:

- Previous Online Privacy Invasions: Many users have already experienced various forms of privacy invasion, such as e-mail spam and identity theft. These individuals may place less value on personalization and therefore tend not to accept corresponding requests.
- Privacy Concerns: A higher level of privacy concern will likely lead to a lower willingness to be profiled online.
- Importance of Privacy Policies: Consumers who value the privacy policy as an aggregate view are also likely to value specific information transparency features.

In the first step, these factors are aggregated in the perceived importance of information transparency, which in the second step has an effect on both the willingness to be profiled online for personalized services and the willingness to be profiled online for personalized advertising. Figure 2 shows the described basis for our model.

These findings are in line with other research in the field, suggesting that the effect of user concerns for information privacy on their willingness to transact in an e-commerce setting is mediated by risk perceptions and trust, and that information privacy is more important in the context of well-known than of lesser known merchants [25].

In an earlier study, we extended this model by introducing the variables of *Actual Information Transparency* and *Real-World Setting*, and examined their influence on the willingness to be profiled online [26]. Additionally, the question

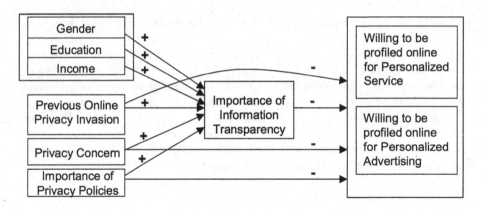

Fig. 2. Basic theoretical model [11]

arose of whether the constructs of *Privacy Awareness* and consequently *Information Transparency* also have a direct effect on the user engagement rate. This work extends the basic model to include the independent variables of *Content Category and Sensitivity* and *Public Privacy Awareness*; the relevant parts of this extension can be seen in Fig. 3. We expected both variables to be inversely correlated with the users' willingness to be profiled, which is expressed by the dependent variable *User Engagement Rate*. The reasoning behind this extension is discussed in the next section.

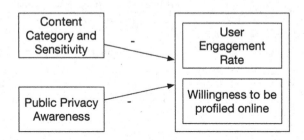

Fig. 3. Research model

4.2   Motivation and Methodology

This empirical study was carried out as part of an ongoing research project in collaboration with an industry partner providing a tool for creating online polls to publishers and other website owners as described in Sect. 3.1. In work published earlier, we sought to make the formerly discrete online polls more intelligent by applying semantic technologies [27] and examined variations of visualization [28]. One of the main findings was that the profiling capabilities of an online polling system can be improved by adding more general knowledge about the pollees and classifying the knowledge coming from the polling responses.

The following analyses are based on a real-world data pool of more than 22M votes in more than 60k polls with more than 65k individual user data sets collected mainly in German-speaking countries. These polls, many of which were supplements to online newspaper articles, were published on a variety of websites. As the polling system investigated is a commercial system utilized by publishers, it is considered a third-party data processor as defined by the GDPR. Users have to accept the terms and conditions of the polling system before they use it for the first time, thereby performing a revocable opt-in.

Fig. 4. Request for personal information

Fig. 5. Consent notification

While the literature shows that opt-outs should remove personal user data from use rather than simply result in termination of sending out marketing messages [2], users in our case study showed little interest in this option. Only 191 people (i.e., 0.002%) out of 7,366,014 unique visitors in the period under consideration clicked on the corresponding link shown in Fig. 5. Further, interest in the terms and conditions of the polling system was also somewhat limited: only 12,513 people (0.15%) clicked on the link leading to the terms (see Figs. 1 and 4).

The first question investigated was, how a poll's content sensitivity affects the user engagement rate. Online polls are often provided as supplements to online newspaper articles, the topics of which are typically also reflected in the polls. In our setting, we defined the user engagement rate as the proportion of users who voluntarily disclose personal data, and expected it to differ between categories of poll content. Since earlier studies had shown that privacy concerns can be greater when dealing with sensitive goods [29], we assumed that this also applies to polls with sensitive content, which is reflected in the first hypothesis:

Hypothesis 1 (H1). *The pollees' willingness to participate in online profiling is lower after answering polls with more sensitive content.*

Hypothesis 1 was tested by categorizing polls that included some kind of request for personal data and were published within the period from October 1, 2018, to November, 30, 2018. We established a categorization system based on the top level (Tier 1) of the IAB Tech Lab Content Taxonomy[1] with minor adaptions to better reflect the polling system investigated. We then allocated each poll to one of the resulting 23 categories (see Table 1). Publishers chose a variety of requests, for instance, for e-mail addresses (see Fig. 4), or more complex forms for postal addresses or for demographic data. These requests were shown to the user after voting in a poll. We calculated the engagement rate (ER) by relating the number of unique visitors seeing the requests for personal data after voting to the actual number of data sets collected.

The next step built on an online questionnaire (October 2018, N = 41) in which we asked internet users to express their views on the sensitivity of the established categories. The median results of this survey were then consolidated to assign to each category a content sensitivity score between 1 (=low) and 5 (=high). We then again calculated a mean engagement rate for each group of categories with the same score. By employing an ordinal regression, we investigated the correlation between content sensitivity and engagement rate.

As a second research focus, we investigated the effect of public privacy awareness on users' personal privacy awareness and consequently on the user engagement rate. We expected the user engagement rate to change over time, especially during the phase of GDPR introduction. Media coverage of privacy topics was exceptionally high during that time and public discussion around data protection very intense. We assumed that a correlation between these factors would emerge. This led to the second hypothesis:

Hypothesis 2 (H2). *The pollees' willingness to participate in online profiling decreases with high public privacy awareness.*

---

[1] available at https://iabtechlab.com/standards/content-taxonomy/.

4.3 Results

The results presented in Table 1 show each category's number of unique visitors, number of collected data sets and engagement rate. Furthermore, the statistical evaluation of the online survey regarding perceived sensitivity of content categories is given; the median scores were used to distinguish between content sensitivities. There are clear differences between the categories of polls identified: While in categories such as *Education* and *Family & Parenting* the acceptance rate of submitting personal information was more than 0.6%, it did not even reach 0.1% in *Health*.

Table 1. Engagement Rate (ER) by Poll Category and sensitivity

Category	Visitors	Data sets	ER	M	SD	Mdn
Arts & Entertainment	734, 106	515	0.070%	1.90	0.625	2
Automotive	679,645	910	0.134%	1.27	0.501	1
Business	239,105	346	0.145%	2.83	0.704	3
Careers	122,064	181	0.148%	2.95	0.805	3
Education	35,335	232	0.657%	3.17	0.704	3
Family & Parenting	25,810	168	0.651%	4.29	0.901	5
Finance	11,267	29	0.257%	3.76	0.767	4
Food & Drink	475,838	500	0.105%	1.88	0.678	2
Health & Fitness	5,250,520	233	0.004%	4.56	0.743	5
Hobbies & Interest	189,787	346	0.192%	2.90	1.020	3
Home & Garden	53,410	206	0.386%	3.66	0.762	4
Law, Governm. & Politics	618,200	484	0.078%	4.44	0.709	5
News	2,245,371	247	0.011%	1.88	0.678	2
Pets	57,583	196	0.340%	3.27	1.001	4
Real Estate	53,180	59	0.111%	2.66	0.825	3
Religion & Spirituality	19,452	189	0.972%	4.68	0.471	5
Science	24,373	16	0.066%	3.49	1.003	4
Shopping	233,310	832	0.357%	1.39	0.628	1
Society	241,792	539	0.223%	2.56	0.896	3
Sports	6,481,887	785	0.012%	1.44	0.634	1
Style & Fashion	302,111	100	0.033%	2.10	0.800	2
Technology & Computing	1, 063, 370	204	0.019%	1.71	0.901	2
Travel	108,739	202	0.186%	1.56	0.808	1
Total	19,266,255	7,537	0.039%			

Table 2 presents the results of aggregating the poll categories according to sensitivity. A significant effect of content sensitivity on the engagement rate cannot be postulated ($\mathcal{X}^2 = 93.572$, $p = 0.223$, Nagelkerke Pseudo $R^2 = 0.286$). The highest ER was found for the – generally perceived as sensitive – category of *Religion & Spirituality*, while the third lowest rate was observed for the minimally sensitive category of *Sports*. Thus, we can neither accept *Hypothesis* 1 nor reject the null hypothesis, as there are more influential factors than content sensitivity. For example, the relatively high ER of *Careers* can presumably be explained by pollees wishing to be contacted by potential employers.

Table 2. Engagement Rate (ER) by content sensitivity (1 = low, 5 = high)

Sensitivity	Visitors	Data Sets	ER
1	7,503,581	2,729	0.036%
2	4,820,796	1,566	0.032%
3	881,263	1,721	0.195%
4	146,633	447	0.305%
5	5,913,982	1,074	0.018%

To test *Hypothesis* 2, we redefined the engagement rate as the proportion of people voting in a poll, regardless of their willingness to disclose any further personal data, thereby taking into account all polls during the time from January 2017 until November 2018. We compared the phases before and after May 25, 2018, the date on which the GDPR came into force. At the same time, the polling system investigated introduced a cookie consent notification (see Fig. 5) and an option to opt out. Whenever visitors used the polling system for the first time, they had to accept the terms and conditions for their vote to be counted. In contrast to the previous analysis, the ER in this case was calculated by dividing the unique views of all polls by the number of actual votes during the same period; in other words, we calculated the proportion of all users who saw a poll and decided to vote in it. Table 3 summarizes the results.

Table 3. Impact of GDPR introduction on Engagement Rate (ER)

Time frame	Visitors	Votes	ER
2017/01/01 – 2017/05/24	29,583,496	2,465,083	8.33%
2017/05/25 – 2017/12/31	38,581,186	3,530,410	9.15%
2018/01/01 – 2018/05/24	102,051,356	9,246,200	9.06%
2018/05/25 – 2018/11/30	68,411,600	7,504,811	10.97%

Contrary to our expectations, introduction of the consent notification and applicability of the GDPR did not have a negative effect on the engagement rate. Holt's exponential smoothing shows an almost continuous growth with an

R^2 of 0.752 and RMSE of 0.685. The engagement rate climbed from around 9% to nearly 11% in the months after GDPR, thereby disproving *Hypothesis* 2. Generally speaking, these are remarkably high numbers in the context of online marketing applications.

5   Conclusion and Future Research Directions

The research presented in this paper forms part of a research project that is currently being carried out together with an industry partner focused on providing online polls to website owners and publishers. It concentrates mainly on investigating two questions: (i) How likely are users to disclose personal information after voting in polls from various content categories, and does the sensitivity of the content correlate with their willingness to be profiled? (ii) How does the public discussion around data protection and privacy that was triggered by introduction of the GDPR and the related media coverage affect the users' individual privacy awareness and thus their engagement rate?

To answer these questions, live data from online polls published by various websites was analyzed. The polls were categorized using an industry standard taxonomy, and the user engagement rate was calculated by dividing the number of collected data sets by the number of unique participants in these polls. An online survey was then conducted to determine each category's sensitivity and the engagement rates for the established sensitivity groups were calculated. We found that the engagement rate differed considerably between categories, but a significant effect of sensitivity on engagement rate could not be identified. Additionally, the engagement rate given by the number of unique visitors and their votes in polls published over time before and after GDPR introduction in May 2018 was investigated. The result showed that – contrary to our expectations – the engagement rate did not decrease post-GDPR.

User behavior in the context of online polling offers several further interesting avenues for research. For example, we expect users' privacy awareness and engagement rate to differ across categories of websites, for instance, professional journals, tabloid press or companies from various lines of business. Furthermore, since the period after GDPR introduction considered in this work was relatively short, it would be interesting to see how the engagement rate continues to develop.

Acknowledgement. This research was funded in part by the Austrian Research Promotion Agency (FFG) within the scope of a joint project on *Poll Analytics*.

References

1. Wagner, A., Wessels, N., Buxmann, P., Krasnova, H.: Putting a price tag on personal information - a literature review. In: Proceedings of the 51st Hawaii International Conference on System Sciences, pp. 3760–3769 (2018)
2. Whitley, E.A., Kanellopoulou, N.: Privacy and informed consent in online interactions: evidence from expert focus groups. In: Proceedings of the 31st International Conference on Information Systems (2010)

3. Steinfeld, N.: Trading with privacy: the price of personal information. Online Inf. Rev. **39**(7), 923–938 (2015)
4. Chen, J., Stallaert, J.: An economic analysis of online advertising using behavioral targeting. MIS Quart. **38**(2), 429–449 (2014)
5. Ernst & Young: Can privacy really be protected anymore? (2016). https://www.ey.com/Publication/vwLUAssets/ey-can-privacy-really-be-protected-anymore/$FILE/ey-can-privacy-really-be-protected-anymore.pdf
6. Warren, S., Brandeis, L.: The right to privacy. Harv. Law Rev. **4**, 193–220 (1890)
7. Westin, A.: Privacy and Freedom. Atheneum, New York (1967)
8. Norberg, P.A., Horne, D.R., Horne, D.A.: The privacy paradox: personal information disclosure intentions versus behaviors. J. Consumer Aff. **41**(1), 100–126 (2007)
9. Spiekermann, S., Grossklags, J., Berendt, B.: E-privacy in 2nd generation e-commerce: privacy preferences versus actual behavior. In: Proceedings of the 3rd ACM Conference on Electronic Commerce, EC 2001, pp. 38–47. ACM, New York (2001). https://doi.org/10.1145/501158.501163
10. Pötzsch, S.: Privacy awareness: a means to solve the privacy paradox? In: Matyáš, V., Fischer-Hübner, S., Cvrček, D., Švenda, P. (eds.) Privacy and Identity 2008. IAICT, vol. 298, pp. 226–236. Springer, Heidelberg (2009). https://doi.org/10.1007/978-3-642-03315-5_17
11. Awad, N., Krishnan, M.: The personalization privacy paradox: an empirical evaluation of information transparency and the willingness to be profiled online for personalization. MIS Quart. **30**(1), 13–28 (2006)
12. Karwatzki, S., Trenz, M., Veit, D.: Yes, firms have my data but what does it matter? measuring privacy risks. In: Proceedings of the 26th European Conference on Information Systems (2018)
13. Bauer, C., Schmid, K.S., Strauss, C.: An open model for researching the role of culture in online self-disclosure. In: Proceedings of the 51st Hawaii International Conference on System Sciences, pp. 3637–3646 (2018)
14. Perreault, L.: Big data and privacy: control and awareness aspects. In: Proceedings of the International Conference on Information Resources Management. AIS (2015)
15. ENISA: Privacy and data protection by design, January 2015. https://www.enisa.europa.eu/publications/privacy-and-data-protection-by-design
16. Kurtz, C., Semmann, M., Böhmann, T.: Privacy by design to comply with GDPR: a review on third-party data processors. In: Proceedings of the 24th Americas Conference on Information Systems (2018)
17. Härting, N., Gössling, P.: Study on the impact of the proposed draft of the ePrivacy-regulation. Comput. Law Rev. Int. **19**(1), 6–11 (2018). https://doi.org/10.9785/cri-2018-190103
18. Fox, G., Tonge, C., Lynn, T., Mooney, J.: Communicating compliance: developing a GDPR privacy label. In: Proceedings of the 24th Americas Conference on Information Systems (2018)
19. Jia, J., Wagman, L.: Data as a driver of economic efficiency. Report, Illinois Institute of Technology (2018). https://datacatalyst.org/wp-content/uploads/2018/11/Data-as-a-Driver-of-Economic-Efficiency-Final-1.pdf
20. Weber, P.: Discussions in the comments section: factors influencing participation and interactivity in online newspapers' reader comments. New Media Soc. **16**(6), 941–957 (2014). https://doi.org/10.1177/1461444813495165. http://nms.sagepub.com/content/16/6/941.abstract

21. Hanna, R., Rohm, A., Crittenden, V.L.: We're all connected: the power of the social media ecosystem. Bus. Horiz. **54**(3), 265–273 (2011). https://doi.org/10.1016/j.bushor.2011.01.007

22. Chellappa, R.K., Sin, R.G.: Personalization versus privacy: an empirical examination of the online consumer's dilemma. Inf. Technol. Manag. **6**(2), 181–202 (2005). https://doi.org/10.1007/s10799-005-5879-y

23. Stabauer, M., Grossmann, G., Stumptner, M.: State of the art in knowledge extraction from online polls: a survey of current technologies. In: Proceedings of the Australasian Computer Science Week Multiconference, pp. 1–8. ACM (2016). Article no. 58

24. O'Brien, H.L., Toms, E.G.: What is user engagement? A conceptual framework for defining user engagement with technology. J. Am. Soc. Inform. Sci. Technol. **59**(6), 938–955 (2008)

25. Van Slyke, C., Shim, J., Johnson, R., Jiang, J.: Concern for information privacy and online consumer purchasing. J. Assoc. Inf. Syst. **7**(6), 415–444 (2006)

26. Stabauer, M.: The impact of UI on privacy awareness. In: Nah, F.F.-H., Xiao, B.S. (eds.) HCIBGO 2018. LNCS, vol. 10923, pp. 513–525. Springer, Cham (2018). https://doi.org/10.1007/978-3-319-91716-0_41

27. Stabauer, M., Mayrhauser, C., Karlinger, M.: Converting opinion into knowledge. In: Nah, F.H., Tan, C.-H. (eds.) HCIBGO 2016. LNCS, vol. 9751, pp. 330–340. Springer, Cham (2016). https://doi.org/10.1007/978-3-319-39396-4_30

28. Burgstaller, F., Stabauer, M., Morgan, R., Grossmann, G.: Towards customised visualisation of ontologies: state of the art and future applications for online polls analysis. In: Proceedings of the Australasian Computer Science Week Multiconference, ACSW 2017, pp. 26:1–26:10. ACM, New York (2017). https://doi.org/10.1145/3014812.3014839

29. Jentzsch, N.: Auctioning privacy-sensitive goods: In: Preneel, B., Ikonomou, D. (eds.) APF 2014. LNCS, vol. 8450, pp. 133–142. Springer, Cham (2014). https://doi.org/10.1007/978-3-319-06749-0_9

Effect of Firms' Responsive Strategies in Crisis: Based on Big Data Analysis in Social Media

Xiaolun Wang[(✉)] and Lin Liu

Nanjing University of Science and Technology, Nanjing, China
wxl@njust.edu.cn

Abstract. In the age of social media, after a crisis event, firms will immediately take responsive actions and publicly announce what they do in news media, in order to attenuate the potential negative impact of crisis. Afterwards, the public in social media will freely discuss and deliver their opinions in the form of word-of-mouths (WOMs), which directly reflect their feeling of firms' responsive strategy. Therefore, based on big data analysis in social media, we attempt to establish the link between crisis firms' responsive actions and public perceptions reflected in online WOMs. Large quantities of secondary panel data are crawled from both search engine and social media. To obtain a robust result, we adopt Panel Vector Auto Regression model to conduct our data analysis. The results show that increased responsive strategies of crisis firms will lead to a significant increasement in the strength of online WOMs, while a more positive responsive strategy can significantly decrease the strength of online WOMs in contrary. Our research provides profound theoretical and practical contributions.

Keywords: Responsive strategy · Firm crisis · Social media · Big data ·
Online WOM

1 Introduction

Crisis is an emergent event which can bring serious threat to an organization, damaging its survival, development, and reputation. To eliminate the potential negative consequences, firms in crisis always take immediate responsive strategies as soon as a crisis event breaks out. These strategies are composed of various responsive types ranging from positive to negative ones, such as denying, justification, apology, and so on.

In the age of social media, firms are able release their responsive strategies to the public with the highest speed through social media platforms. Meanwhile, they lose full control of the public voice. Everyone can express his opinion arbitrarily in social media (i.e., Sina Microblog), no matter how extreme and reckless the sentence seems. Therefore, development of social media brings both opportunities and challenges to today's enterprises.

In previous literatures, there are two major research directions concerning firms' responsive strategies in crisis. The first one is based on experiment, questionnaire, and case study methodology, which aim to compare the effect of different responsive

© Springer Nature Switzerland AG 2019
F. F.-H. Nah and K. Siau (Eds.): HCII 2019, LNCS 11589, pp. 256–265, 2019.
https://doi.org/10.1007/978-3-030-22338-0_21

strategies, but lacks objectivity with limited subjective behavioral data. The other approach is based on stimulation, which only select a few crisis events as examples to investigate the effect of responsive strategy on the public. The generality cannot be guaranteed with such a small sample. Fortunately, the open environment of social media provides new research opportunity for scholars, where we can crawl everyday real data about firms' responsive strategy and public word-of-mouth, so as to conduct empirical analysis through big data methodology.

In a word, we attempt to solve one research question in this paper: Based on objective big data analysis from social media (news media and social networking sites), what is the real effect of crisis responsive strategy on public perception? Specifically, will the strength and attitude of crisis firms' responsive strategy affect the strength of online WOMs in social media?

To answer the problems, we crawl large quantities of secondary panel data from both search engine and social media to conduct the empirical research. We do not generally analyze the total effect of crisis responsive strategy as usual, but consider the change of everyday responsive strategy of crisis firms and corresponding everyday public opinions. In total, 59 crisis events were selected, and related news reports as well as public WOMs in social media were collected within 30 days after each crisis event. We also quantify the everyday responsive strategies and public perceptions manually through certain standards. Finally, we adopt Panel Vector Auto Regression model to conduct our data analysis. The results show that increased responsive strategies of crisis firms will lead to a significant increasement in the strength of online WOMs, while a more positive responsive strategy can significantly decrease the strength of online WOMs in contrary. Our research provides profound theoretical and practical contributions.

The article is organized as follows. First, we review the relevant literatures from the following three parts: research on crisis firms' responsive strategies and effects; research on the role of social media in responsive to firm crisis; research on the relationship between firm crisis and public perception. Second, we propose our research model and hypotheses. Then, we introduced the methodology of data collection and analysis. Finally, we discuss our results, and conclude this article's contributions and limitations.

2   Literature Review

2.1   Research on Crisis Firms' Responsive Strategies and Effects

Crisis event is a sudden accident with serious threats to organizations, whose existence may cause huge losses to firms' survival, development, and reputation. Different crisis responsive theories proposed different responsive strategies from different views. Representative theories include Situational Crisis Communication Theory (SCCT) [1], Corporate Apologia Theory [2], Theory of Image Restoration [3] and so on. These theories all focus on the responsive strategies after a crisis event.

Although classified by many different standards in past literatures, crisis responsive strategies are generally distinguished into positive and negative ones. Marcus and

Goodman [4] identified two kinds of responsive strategies by a typical standard: Accommodative-Defensive. Accommodative strategy means recognizing accountability and taking remedy actions, while defensive strategy means denying their own problems and fault. The most well-recognized theory was proposed by Coombs [5], in which he divided the responsive strategies into seven kinds from the most negative to the most positive: Attack Accusers, Denial, Excuse, Justification, Ingratiation, Correction, and Apology. Later, Griffin [6] increased the two-dimensional strategy to three dimensions, and proposed Reticence strategy. In other words, some firms do nothing and have no response to a crisis. In this article, we combine both standards of Coombs [5] and Griffin [6], and divide responsive strategies of firms in crisis into eight kinds.

In fact, past scholars have already conducted a few researches on crisis responsive strategies and corresponding effects. However, the research methodology is relatively subjective, because they are mainly based on questionnaire, experiment, case analysis and stimulation methods. Furthermore, most research are only based a single crisis event, which is insufficient in explaining the impact of crisis responsive strategy from a generally macro view. In this article, we attempt to fill in the research gaps based on big data analysis in social media.

2.2 Research on the Role of Social Media in Responsive to Firm Crisis

Generally speaking, social media are regarded as a tool and platform based on interpersonal information communication, sharing and dissemination, with feathers like participation, openness, connection, sense of community, and so on. On a broad view, social media include not only social networking sites (i.e., Sina Microblog), but also professional forums (i.e., News Media), both of which have a prominent influence on the dissemination and response of a crisis event.

In recent years, some scholars began to compare the different impacts when firms choose different channels in responsive to firm crisis. Sweetser and Metzgar [7] found that when an organization uses blogs to manage crisis, it will convey as much information as possible to the public in a short time, which helps to leave a good impression of the firms on the public. Through an experiment, Schultz [8] found that in contrast to traditional media, microblog plays a more prominent role in crisis management, which can gain more recognition by investors. These studies demonstrate that social media has substantial increasement in dissemination speed and scope, thus offer a new opportunity for firms in crisis.

In fact, as an important kind of intermediary, social media plays a double-edged role in the process of crisis response. On one hand, companies can convey their responsive strategies to the public directly and immediately through social media such as news media. On the other hand, because companies lose control of public opinions, people can freely express their opinions and discuss with other users in social media such as Sina Microblog.

Overall, social media influence public perception on firm crisis and responsive strategies through two main channels: news media and social networking websites. So, we attempt to crawl information from both social networking websites and news media to analyze the effect of crisis responsive strategy on the public perception, thus probe the role of social media in crisis response.

2.3 Research on the Relationship Between Firm Crisis and Public Perception

Unsurprisingly, firm crisis will necessarily influence public perceptions, thus a few scholars have made a number of researches on their relationships. For instance, a crisis event will decrease consumer's purchase intention and perceived loyalty to a specific brand [9, 10]. These studies are mainly based on experiment and questionnaire methods, so as to explore the change of public perception (i.e., trust, loyalty) after a crisis event.

In fact, with the popularity of social media, the real public perception will be reflected directly in online users' posts in social networking websites. A few literatures have already crawled user reviews after a crisis event, so as to analyze the public's changes after companies take responsive strategies. For example, Xu [11] found that using microblog in responsive to firm crisis can prominently improve public emotions and even raise company's stock price. However, these researches are too general to distinguish the different effects of different crisis response strategies, especially under the social media context.

Therefore, previous studies on the relationship between crisis response strategies and public perception are mainly based on a single event and have less universality. Besides, they hardly focus on the everyday changes of firms' crisis response strategies, thus cannot reflect the time-sequence of both crisis response strategies and public perceptions. Therefore, In this study, we attempt to solve the above problems.

3 Research Model and Hypotheses

3.1 Research Model

In this paper, we want to explore the effect of crisis responsive strategy on public perception. Specifically, we propose that the strength and attitude of crisis firms' responsive strategy will affect the strength of online WOMs in social media. More details are displayed in Fig. 1.

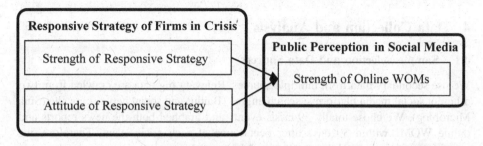

Fig. 1. Research model

3.2   The Relationship Between Responsive Strategy of Firms in Crisis and Public Perception in Social Media

After the occurrence of a crisis event, the information dissemination speed and influence scope will increase exponentially, thus the popularity of the firm will increase in both news media and social media. Then, this crisis event will gradually involve more and more participants to share and express their opinions. In the era of social media, a hot event can lead to hot discussions in online platforms. Based on Negativity Bias Theory [12], negative events will be more easily to catch people's eyes. The same thing will happen when the firms in crisis announce their response strategies. The public likes to follow the trends of crisis events, and keep an eye on company's responsive strategy, so as to deliver their opinions in social media at first time. Therefore, when more responsive strategies are released in news media, more WOMs will be generated in social media correspondingly. We propose Hypothesis 1:

> *Hypothesis 1: There is a positive linear correlation between the strength of crisis firms' responsive strategy and the strength of online WOMs about crisis event in social media.*

The crisis firms' responsive strategies can reflect the firms' positive or negative attitudes to the crisis events. When a company takes a positive response strategy to solve a crisis, such as apology, product recalls, and compensate the customer loss, public trust and satisfaction on the firm will be recovered. In other words, only by positively taking the responsibility and admitting own faults, can organizations radically prevent the deterioration and expansion of a crisis event, thus relevant discussions will be fewer and fewer. Otherwise, the firms will definitely see a serious negative effect. Therefore, when a company takes a more positive responsive strategy to cope with crisis event, the discussions in social media will be less as the public begins to forgive the firm. We propose Hypothesis 2:

> *Hypothesis 2: There is a negative linear correlation between the attitude of crisis firms' responsive strategy and the strength of online WOMs about crisis event in social media.*

4   Data Collection and Analysis

4.1   Sample Selection and Data Sources

We use secondary data from multiple sources. Relevant big data are crawled from two different social media platforms: search engine (Baidu) and social networking site (Sina Microblog). We chose totally 59 crisis events and grabbed both the news reports and online WOMs within 30 days after occurrence of each crisis event. Therefore, we constructed an integrated panel data set. Main variables and definitions are shown in Table 1.

News Data. Based on the biggest search engine in China (Baidu), we used the tool "Webripper" and chose the name of each crisis event as keywords, so as to search and grab all the links and contents of relevant news reports posted on professional public news media within 30 days after the occurrence of each crisis event. After deleting repetitive news articles, we acquired a final data set containing 6892 items of news, including news links, news titles, post time, detailed content, and so on.

Responsive Strategy Data. Because not all the news reports are related to crisis responsive strategies, we first filtered the news by titles and keywords in the content. Then, according to the standards of Coombs [5] and Griffin [6], we manually classified these responsive strategies into eight kinds from the most negative to the most positive: attack accusers, denial, excuse, justification, reticence, ingratiation, correction, and apology, and numbered them from 1 to 8.

Finally, on the basis of the manually-operated data, we computed two key indicators on responsive strategies. First, to reflect the proactivity of firms under a crisis event, we counted the volume of everyday responsive strategies within 30 days after occurrence of each crisis (Action Volume, AC_VO). Second, we computed the mean value of everyday responsive strategies' types to demonstrate the firms' attitudes on the crisis (Action Attitude, AC_AT), with a value ranging from 1 to 8. The higher the value, the more positive the firms are in responsive to the crisis event.

Online WOMs Data. By the tool C#, we crawled the online WOM data from the most famous social networking sites, Sina Microblog, which has the largest user base in China. Again, we used the name of each crisis event as keywords, and collected crisis-relevant WOMs within 30 days after occurrence of each crisis. Finally, our sample included a panel data set with 225,491 pieces of online WOMs in Sina Microblog. We counted the volume of everyday posts, forwards and comments related to each crisis event in Sina Microblog, and defined this variable as WOM_VO (WOM Volume) (Table 1).

Table 1. Main variables and definitions

Variable name (Abbreviation)		Definition	Data source
Independent variable	Strength of Responsive Strategy (AC_VO)	Log of the volume of everyday responsive strategies within 30 days after occurrence of each crisis	Baidu Search Engine
	Attitude of Responsive Strategy (AC_AT)	Mean value of everyday responsive strategies' types/attitudes	Baidu Search Engine
Dependent variable	Strength of Online WOM (WOM_VO)	Log of the volume of everyday posts, forwards and comments in social media related to each crisis event	Sina Microblog

Table 2. Descriptive statistics and correlation matrix

	1	2	3
1. AC_VO	1.000		
2. AC_AT	−0.043	1.000	
3. WOM_VO	0.429**	0.048	1.000
Mean	1.900	4.740	4.133
Standard variance	1.160	0.913	1.835
Observations	437	437	265

Notes. *p < 0.1; **p < 0.05.

4.2 Research Model

We use PVAR model (Panel Vector Auto Regression) to conduct our data analysis [13]. Due to the following three reasons, PVAR is very suitable for this research. First of all, PVAR can capture both the direct and indirect impact among endogenous factors, so this method can help us to explore the mutual influence between firm' crisis responsive strategy and public perception, which is similar to Simultaneous Equation Models. Second, result of PVAR is robust even if problems such as heteroscedasticity and serial correlation exist [14]. Third, we can incorporate the fixed panel effect vector u and time trend vector T in PVAR models, which are difficult to observe in simple models.

Our analysis of PVAR model follows the standard steps. First, based on Granger Causality Test, we prove the appropriateness of PVAR model in this research. Then, based on results of Unit Root Test, we try to judge our model validity. The Panel Unit Root Test rejected the null hypothesis, and verified that all the results of endogenous variables are smaller than critical value (see Table 3). Therefore, we can use the three endogenous variables to estimate our model. In the end, based on Information Criterion, we determine the time lag of the PVAR model. Specifically, the result of SBIC (Schwarz-Bayesian Information Criterion) showed that lagging one day is the most fitted to our PVAR model.

Table 3. Result of Unit Root Test

Variable	Test statistics	P value
AC_VO	277.2208	<.0001
AC_AT	297.6315	<.0001
WOM_VO	111.0674	<.0001

4.3 Data Analysis Results

We analyze how responsive strategies of crisis firms influence public perceptions in social networking sites, data regression results are shown in Table 4. It is worth to note that in PVAR model, the coefficients reported in Table 4 are not the general coefficients as we know. Differently, they represent the iterative cumulative effect of one-unit shock of each endogenous variables [15].

Table 4. Results of Panel Vector Auto Regression

One-unit Shock Endogenous variables	DV: WOM_VO$_{i, t}$
AC_VO$_{i, t-1}$	0.964*** (0.186)
AC_AT$_{i, t-1}$	−3.864*** (1.095)
WOM_VO$_{i, t-1}$	0.582*** (0.112)

Note. This model is a balanced PVAR model with fixed effect; Numbers in parentheses are standard variance; *p < 0.1; **p < 0.05; ***p < 0.01.

According to the data analysis results, increased responsive strategies of crisis firms will lead to significant increasement in the strength of online WOMs in social media the next day, which supports Hypothesis 1. Meanwhile, when the firms adopt more positive responsive strategies to cope with a crisis event, the strength of online WOMs significantly decreased, in accordance with Hypothesis 2. In other words, the public will talk more when firms take more responsive actions, but talk less if they take effective positive actions since they forgive the firms.

5 Discussion and Implications

5.1 Discussion of Findings

Based on the empirical research from big data crawled from Baidu and Sina Microblog, we answer our research questions about how the responsive strategies of crisis firms impact the public perceptions in social media. We find an opposite effect between the strength and attitude of responsive strategies on the strength of online WOMs. In specific, respond more after a crisis may induce more discussions in social media, whether it is good or bad still needs more investigation. In contrast, positive response is a relatively safe way because these actions can make the public quiet, which implies that the public might forgive the firms in crisis and don't want to condemn them anymore.

5.2 Implications, Limitations and Future Research

This research has profound theoretical and practical contributions. From the theoretical perspective, past researches on crisis responsive strategy usually adopted methods like questionnaire, experiment, stimulation, and so on. Our empirical research method based on big data in social media is more objective and can be generalized. Besides, most relevant studies do not take the time effect in consideration. We look at the everyday changes of firms' crisis response strategies, thus can reflect the time-sequence of both crisis response strategies and public perceptions. In practice, firms should not only respond more when a crisis event happens, because what matters is their attitudes. A positive responsive strategy can help firms to recover from the negative crisis more quickly.

There are also a few limitations in our research, and need to be improved in the future. First, although we used panel data in this article, the data set is a little too small. We need to collect more crisis events and corresponding responsive strategies, thus explore their relationships more systematically. Second, the measurements of responsive strategies only include strength and attitude. In future research, we will try to include more indexes to analyze the effect of crisis firms' responsive strategies, such as strategy consistency, continuity, and so on. Third, there are many other factors influencing the effect of crisis responsive strategy such as crisis types. We did not control them in our study. These are all gaps for us to investigate in further researches.

Acknowledgement. This work was supported by National Science Foundation of China (#71802108), Research Funds for Young Scholars in School of Economics & Management of NJUST (#JGQN1802), Fundamental Research Funds for the Central Universities (30918013104), Ministry of Education Humanities and Social Sciences Fund Project (#18YJC630099).

References

1. Coombs, W.T.: Parameters for Crisis Communication. Blackwell Publishing Ltd., Hoboken (2010)
2. Hearit, K.M.: Corporate Apologia: When an Organization Speaks in Defense of Itself. Sage, Thousand Oaks (2001)
3. Benoit, W.L.: Accounts, Excuses and Apologies: A Theory of Image Restoration. State University of Press, Albany (1995)
4. Marcus, A.A., Goodman, R.S.: Victims and shareholders: the dilemmas of presenting corporate policy during a crisis. Acad. Manag. J. **34**(2), 281–305 (1991)
5. Coombs, W.T.: An analytic framework for crisis situations: better responses from a better understanding of the situation. J. Public Relat. Res. **10**(3), 177–191 (1998)
6. Griffin, M., Babin, B.J., Attaway, J.S.: An empirical investigation of the impact of negative public publicity on consumer attitudes and intentions. Adv. Consum. Res. **18**(1), 334–341 (1991)
7. Sweetser, K.D., Metzgar, E.: Communicating during crisis: use of blogs as a relationship management tool. Public Relat. Rev. **33**(3), 340–342 (2007)
8. Schultz, F., Utz, S., Goritz, A.: Is the medium the message perceptions of and reactions to crisis communication via Twitter, blogs and traditional media. Public Relat. Rev. **37**(1), 20–27 (2011)
9. Cleeren, K., Dekimpe, G., Helsen, K.: Weathering product-harm crises. J. Acad. Mark. Sci. **36**(2), 262–270 (2008)
10. Siomkos, G.J., Kurzbard, G.: The hidden crisis in product-harm crisis management. Eur. J. Mark. **28**(2), 30–41 (1994)
11. Xu, S.: The public crisis sentiment management of listed company: an empirical analysis of Microblog's effect. Master thesis, Central South University (2013)
12. Rozin, P., Royzman, E.B.: Negativity bias, negativity dominance, and contagion. Pers. Soc. Psychol. Rev. **5**(4), 296–320 (2001)

13. Pesaran, M.H., Binder, M., Hsiao, C.: Estimation and inference in short panel vector autoregressions with unit roots and cointegration. Econom. Theory **21**(4), 5–69 (2005)
14. Enders, W.: Applied Econometric Time Series, 3rd edn. Wiley, Hoboken (2010)
15. Hendricks, K.B., Hora, M., Singhal, V.R.: An empirical investigation on the appointments of supply chain and operations management executives. Manag. Sci. **61**(7), 1562–1583 (2015)

Understanding User Engagement Mechanisms on a Live Streaming Platform

Xinwei Wang[1] and Dezhi Wu[2(✉)]

[1] University of Auckland, Auckland, New Zealand
xinwei.wang@auckland.ac.nz
[2] University of South Carolina, Columbia, SC 29208, USA
dezhiwu@cec.sc.edu

Abstract. As part of new emerging eCommerce innovations, live streaming has started to gain lots of attention in business world because of its potential capability to boost sales online. Enabling interactions among a real-time seller, users (i.e., viewers) and peer users in e-Commerce platforms, live streaming is promising to facilitate real-time interactions among seller, users and peers online, which are likely to alleviate the physical separation between sellers, users and products in cyber space. Although some businesses are proactive to invest on this new living stream platform with a goal to more effectively engage their users, it is still largely unknown whether this effort can ultimately increase their consumer conversion rates. Accordingly, this research aims to gain more in-depth insights into users' acceptance of live streaming shopping. Based on multimedia learning and information foraging theories, this research conceptualizes user engagement mechanisms (i.e., *product interactivity*, *communication immediacy*, and *peer cues*) associated with a live streaming platform and furthermore explores how these mechanisms are likely to improve users' *product evaluation* and their *serendipity* to explore more unexpected products, and in turn how they impact users' attitude and intention to buy products on a live streaming platform. Through an online survey study with 200 users on a live streaming platform, this study finds that the identified three user engagement mechanisms significantly improve users' capability to evaluate products and their serendipity behavior online, which also have a positive impact on users' attitude and intention to shop on a live steaming platform.

Keywords: Live streaming · User engagement · Interactivity · Serendipity · Product evaluation

1 Introduction

Live streaming is defined as "the broadcasting of real-time, live video to an audience over the internet" [1]. Its increasing popularity makes the live streaming an important evolving innovation, which has started to change the landscape of the traditional e-Commerce due to its potentials to significantly increase consumer conversion rates. Hence, a new notion of live commerce is being formed. As an example, the Chinese

---

The original version of this chapter was revised: The word "conversation" has been corrected to "conversion" in two occurrences. The correction to this chapter is available at https://doi.org/10.1007/978-3-030-22338-0_40

© Springer Nature Switzerland AG 2019
F. F.-H. Nah and K. Siau (Eds.): HCII 2019, LNCS 11589, pp. 266–275, 2019.
https://doi.org/10.1007/978-3-030-22338-0_22

live-steaming market was forecast to grow US$4.4 billion in 2018 with viewer numbers topping 456 million [2]. Lately, in mainland China, Taobao Live, one of the most popular live streaming platforms, has achieved a consumer conversion rate of 32%, "meaning 320,000 products are added to customers' carts per million views" [2]. In the United States, businesses such as Facebook, YouTube, Instagram, Periscope etc. also started to adopt this new live streaming platform. For instance, Kohl's, as one of the primary retail chains, has made its first live streaming held through Periscope during the New York Fashion Week, so they were able to effectively guide their remote consumers to find relevant products and looks online [3]. Despite many companies' efforts in using live streaming to increase their user awareness and engagement of their products, it remains a challenge to gain their investment returns off these efforts [2, 3]. Therefore, it is important to understand underlying user engagement mechanisms and how effective user engagement enabled by live streaming technologies is to convert live streaming viewers to real consumers who can make immediate decisions to purchase their products online. As an initial step, this research aims to explore the user engagement mechanisms that can be uniquely identified on the live streaming platform and their impact on users' perceived capability of product evaluation and serendipity, which in turn influence the users' attitude and intention to use the live streaming for shopping.

2 Related Theoretical Background

Live streaming is unique in terms of its channels for sellers to engage and interact with its online users (i.e., viewers) through live product demonstrations by sellers and synchronous user interactions enabled by live streaming platform's functionalities, such as live videos, real-time online chat, conversation and other additional capabilities to leverage two-way instantaneous communications (1) between viewers and the seller and (2) between peer online viewers on the platform. As a result, live streaming is likely to create a sense of spatial and communication immediacy, which makes viewers immerse themselves *in-the-moment* and not *behind-the-screen* [3]. Its real-time functionality on rich media communication entices users to actively interact with the seller to acquire authentic sensory information about a product through touching, seeing, hearing and following online peers' cues on the live streaming platform, and therefore, influences users' purchase decision making process.

In this research, we theorize the user engagement mechanism in a living steaming context through multimedia learning and information foraging theories, in that they are associated with users' learning process to gain a product knowledge and their serendipity behavior, which we believe to further influence users' attitude and intention to make purchase decisions on a live streaming platform.

2.1 Multimedia Learning

How users learn a product's features demonstrated on a live streaming platform is somewhat similar to how students learn a new subject in a multimedia environment through multiple sensorimotor channels including auditory, visual, and other external cues from peers and teacher. Prior studies [4, 5] have documented that appropriate use of multiple sensory cues in multimedia can enhance learners' spatial perceptions of objects. In a live streaming context, consumers are likely to more effectively build their respective mental representations through both auditory and visual cues delivered through static and live videos of a product, and thereafter facilitate them to learn about a product and gain heightened product knowledge. Hence, compared with traditional e-Commerce shopping platforms where consumers typically gain product information through browsing static product presentations, live streaming shopping platforms afford consumers better capability to evaluate a product through simultaneous online interactions with sellers, other consumers and products.

2.2 Information Foraging Theory

Information foraging theory is often applied to understand users' strategies and technologies to seek, gather, appraise and acquire information based on their environmental cues [6]. In our study context, live streaming platform allows users to directly interact with the seller, view other viewers' activities, such as what inquiries they asked, buyers' feedback, and other users' posting, adding products to shopping carts, or processing order and making payment in a real time. They are exposed to a very rich environment that is full of seller and peer user-generated contents in real-time live video, text message formats and beyond.

Serendipity has been widely studied in information science, marketing and various other domains. It is defined as "the faculty or phenomenon of finding valuable or agreeable things not sought for" in Marriam-Webster online dictionary, so it represents the unexpected or unplanned valuable occurrence of events through an accidental discovery. Users' serendipity behavior by interacting with certain technologies refers to as the extent to which a user believes that a platform triggers her/him to discover useful but unexpected products in a search process [7, 8].

Based on the multimedia learning and information foraging theories, we theorize three mechanisms of user engagement: (1) *Product interactivity*: Live streaming videos, which the seller uses to demonstrate product features, enable multiple channels of sensory product information disclosure, and three-way real-time interactions between seller and viewers and between peer viewers online, open up new opportunities for users to clarify the product uncertainty, so users are likely to be more effectively engaged to acquire the product features before they make purchase decisions; (2) *Communication immediacy*: Flexible non-verbal and verbal communication channels in real time together immerse and reinforce the user engagement; (3) *Peer cues*: Live streaming shopping provides users the opportunity to observe other peer users' online shopping activities. Such observational learning can generate unexpected triggers, driving users to seek and gather more relevant information to understand their own product preferences or needs or even to be further persuaded to consider some unplanned products. Therefore, exposing a user to peers' online shopping activities can potentially be an effective way to engage consumers due to their social influence. In this study, focusing on these three user engagement mechanisms, we proposed a research model, which is presented in Fig. 1.

**User Engagement
Mechanisms**

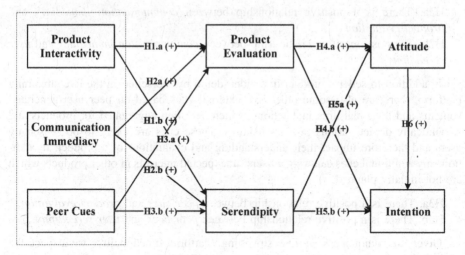

Fig. 1. Proposed research model

3   Brief Hypothesis Development

Based upon online interactions at e-Commerce websites, users can gain actual product knowledge, which refers to "the extent to which consumers understand product information" [9, p. 478]. According to multimedia learning theory, rich product interactivity through triggering multiple sensory channels and real-time interactions among the seller and peer viewers afforded by the live streaming platform is likely to significantly reduce users' uncertainty of a product and improve users' capability to evaluate a product. In addition, it is also possible to entice users' new interests to explore unplanned products that are initiated and acquired by other peer viewers, so we hypothesize:

H1a. There is a positive relationship between *product interactivity* and *product evaluation*.

H1b. There is a positive relationship between *product interactivity* and *user serendipity*.

Users are empowered to communicate product information along with the seller synchronously on a live streaming platform, and thus the live streaming platform can cause communication immediacy among the sellers and users, especially when users are immersed in an entertaining environment, associated with how the sellers strategize to promote products and attract online viewers. Communication immediacy enabled by the live streaming platform can make users feel like thrilling and you are there yourself, similar to the spatial immediacy effects by arts [10], so the live streaming can significantly mimic a real shopping environment where users can communicate easily without being constrained by the online channel. This communication immediacy is likely to positively affect users' product evaluation and to arouse their serendipity behavior:

H2a. There is a positive relationship between *communication immediacy* and *product evaluation*.

H2b. There is a positive relationship between *communication immediacy* and *user serendipity*.

In addition to seller's product live video demo by the seller on the live streaming platform, there are also some other live external cues based on peer user-generated contents and their real-time interactions, which are often aggregated for products and semantically depict various product features. These cues are likely to be sensed by users and therefore impact their understanding and evaluations of a product. In addition, any additional cues can trigger users' unexpected interests in other products which are not initially planned.

H3a. There is a positive relationship between *peer cues* and *product evaluation*.

H3b. There is a positive relationship between *peer cues* and *user serendipity*.

Given the uniqueness of live streaming platform functionality, we expect the identified three user engagement mechanisms are likely to be more persuasive than the traditional e-Commerce platforms, where real-time interactions and rich sensory product information are lacking. The amount of information shared and gathered through live streaming is likely to boost sales through converting viewers to consumers who buy products online. It adds some fun entertainment features for viewers and to have real-time options to clarify complex procedures/features of a product while enabling the ways to take control of the current fan base for certain product brands. According to [11], product evaluation is likely to have a positive influence on people's purchase intention. While users acquire more information about a product, they become more capable of evaluating their product needs and preferences to meet their psychological standards before making the order. Because of reduced product uncertainty and more confidence to evaluate certain products, the users are expected to make a sounder decision in a real-time manner, and their intentions of using the live streaming for shopping are likely to be strengthened. User serendipity behavior can also be triggered through real-time observations, interactions and synchronous user-generated contents posted by their peer viewers. For example, while the users are acquiring intended product information, they can often be enticed to some unexpected product search paths introduced by other peer users' inquiries about other unintended products to the seller. This peer social influence is likely to foster more unexpected product discovery. We thus expect users' product evaluation and their serenity behavior will have a positive impact to users' attitude and intention to purchase on the live streaming platform.

H4a. There is a positive relationship between *product evaluation* and *user attitude*.

H4b. There is a positive relationship between *product evaluation* and *user intention*.

H5a. There is a positive relationship between *user serendipity* and *user attitude*.

H5b. There is a positive relationship between *user serendipity* and *user intention*.

The attitude measures how people think about their product experiences by ways of watching real-time product demonstration on the live streaming platform. The intention in our study context refers to as how likely users will use the live streaming platform for shopping in the future. Based on the theory of reasoned action, an individual's behavioral intention is impacted by one's attitude toward the action and one's subjective judgement on performing the action [12]. So, we echo the following hypothesis, that has been widely proved:

H6. There is a positive relationship between *user attitude* and *intention*.

4   Study Design

An online survey study was conducted in mainland China. To attract user participation, every participant was led to the lucky draw after submitting their answers. The online survey consisted of two sections: First section was an introduction to live streaming e-Commerce platform and second section was the user questionnaire, which we adopted instruments that have been validated in previous research studies shown in Table 1. In total, we received 247 responses. Forty-seven were excluded because of their ages younger than 18 or missing questions, so we eventually had 200 valid user responses.

Table 1.   Measurement instruments

Construct	Item	Questions	Source
Attitude	ATT1	Bad—Good	[13]
	ATT2	Unappealing—Appealing	
	ATT3	Unpleasant—Pleasant	
	ATT4	Boring—Interesting	
	ATT5	Dislike—Like	
Intention	INT1	It is likely that I will buy products via the live streaming e-commerce platform	[14]
	INT2	I will use the live streaming e-commerce platform the next time I want to shop online	
	INT3	I will definitely try the live streaming e-commerce platform	
Product evaluation	PEV1	If I had to purchase the product on the live streaming e-commerce platform today, I would need to gather very little information elsewhere in order to make a wise decision	[13]
	PEV2	I feel very confident about my ability to judge the quality of the product displaying on the live streaming e-commerce platform	
	PEV3	I could accurately evaluate the capability of the products from the interaction between sellers and other buyers	
	PEV4	I could accurately evaluate the quality of the products from the interaction between sellers and other buyers	

(continued)

Table 1. (*continued*)

Construct	Item	Questions	Source
Serendipity	SER1	From the communication between sellers and other buyers, I could find some clothes which I like but I had not planned for	[15]
	SER2	Watching clothes displaying on the live streaming e-commerce platform could provide some unexpected but useful findings	
Communication immediacy	COM1	Live streaming e-commerce platform allows me to give and receive timely feedback regarding the products	[16]
	COM2	Live streaming e-commerce platform allows me to use rich and varied language (varied words expressions or emoji) in my messages	
	COM3	The live streaming e-commerce platform allows me to communicate about the product as I would in the store	
Product interactivity	PIN1	Live streaming e-commerce platform allows me to acquire a wide variety of product features (such as texture, appearance of clothes on different models, different possible clothes combination and so on)	[14]
	PIN2	The live streaming e-commerce platform provides accurate sensory information about the products	
	PIN3	The experience on live streaming e-commerce platform gives me as much as sensory information about the product as I would experience in a store	
Peer Cues	PEC1	Live streaming e-commerce platform allows me to view other buyers' actions (e.g. adding product to shopping cart; processing orders or making payment) in real time	Self-developed
	PEC2	Live streaming e-commerce platform allows me to view inquiries asked by other buyers and receive timely feedback	

5 Data Analysis and Results

We used SEM modeling approach to examine our proposed research model for this study. The following Table 2 presents the measurement model analysis results, which are satisfying. Data analysis results demonstrate most of our hypotheses are significantly supported except H 2.b, meaning that communication immediacy does not impact users' serendipity behavior (See Fig. 2).

Table 2. Measurement model analysis results

Construct	Item	1	2	3	4	5	6	Composite reliability	Average variance extracted
Attitude	ATT1	.728						0.936	0.745
	ATT2	.864							
	ATT3	.750							
	ATT4	.813							
	ATT5	.848							
Intention	INT1	.769						0.905	0.760
	INT2	.782							
	INT3	.646							
Product evaluation	PEV1		.567		.532			0.858	0.668
	PEV2		.649						
	PEV3		.626						
	PEV4		.723						
Serendipity	SER1			.820				0.858	0.751
	SER2			.680					
Communication immediacy	COM1			.658				0.838	0.722
	COM2				.814				
	COM3				.656				
Product interactivity	PIN1					.828		0.826	0.704
	PIN2					.593			
	PIN3		.466			.412			
Peer cues	PEC1						.722	0.805	0.674
	PEC2						.720		

Note: PEV1 and PIN3 were deleted for loading on multiple constructs. COM1 was deleted for loading on unintended construct.

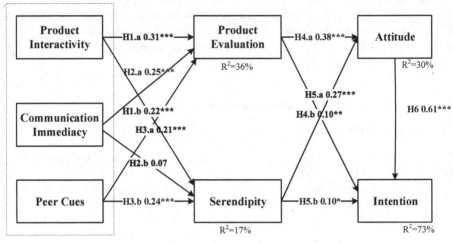

Notes: * p<0.10, ** p<0.05, *** p<0.01

Fig. 2. Proposed research model and SEM results

6 Study Findings and Implications

In sum, this study successfully identified three user engagement mechanisms on the live streaming platform, which are useful for online businesses to develop their own strategies to effectively engage their potential consumers (i.e., viewers). We reported that the live streaming platform can effectively empower users to be more capable of evaluating whether a product meets their needs and preferences due to rich sensory product cues enabled by live streaming's user engagement mechanisms.

We expect this study will contribute to the understanding of the current popular live streaming commerce phenomenon and raise the interests in our community to further explore more in-depth the user engagement mechanisms, and to effectively design more enjoyable user experiences, so businesses can achieve their goals to convert more online viewers to consumers, who are likely be persuaded to make immediate purchase decisions on such a platform. Future research can be expanded in multiple ways through integrating more marketing strategies and fostering more persuasive user experiences to boost online business sales and transactions in field studies with authentic online consumers and live streaming businesses.

References

1. What is live streaming? https://www.thinkuknow.co.uk/parents/articles/what-is-live-streaming/. Access 30 Jan 2019
2. Soo, Z.: Attention all shopaholics: now you can shop online and watch live streaming at the same time (2018). https://www.scmp.com. Accessed 30 Nov 2018
3. Amoah, K.: How to use live streaming to promote your E-Commerce brand (2018). https://kudobuzz.com. Accessed 26 Nov 2018
4. Mayer, R.E.: The promise of multimedia learning: using the same instructional design methods across different media. Learn. Instruct. **13**, 125–139 (2003)
5. Mayer, R.E., Moreno, R.: Aids to computer-based multimedia learning. Learn. Instruct. **12**, 107–119 (2002)
6. Pirolli, P.: Information foraging. In: Encyclopedia of Database Systems (2009). https://doi.org/10.1007/978-0-387-39940-9_205
7. McCay-Peet, L., Toms, E.G.: Exploring the precipitating conditions of serendipity. In: Proceedings of 2nd Annual Graphics, Animation New Media NCE Conference, Vancouver, BC, Canada (2011)
8. Sun, T., Zhang, M., Mei, Q.: Unexpected relevance: an empirical study of serendipity in retweets. In: Proceedings of 7th International Conference Weblogs and Social Media, Boston (2013)
9. Jiang, J., Benbasat, I.: The effects of presentation formats and task complexity on online consumers' product understanding. MIS Q. **31**(3), 475–500 (2007)
10. Tortum, H.Z.: Embodies montage: reconsidering immediacy in virtual reality. Master's thesis, MIT (2016)
11. Li, H., Daugherty, T., Biocca, F.: Characteristics of virtual experience in electronic commerce: a protocol analysis. J. Interact. Mark. **15**(3), 13–30 (2001)
12. Fishbein, M., Ajzen, I.: Belief, attitude, intention and behavior: an introduction to theory and research (1975)
13. Suh, K.S., Chang, S.: User interfaces and consumer perceptions of online stores: the role of telepresence. Behav. Inf. Technol. **25**(2), 99–113 (2006)
14. Fiore, A.M., Kim, J., Lee, H.H.: Effect of image interactivity technology on consumer responses toward the online retailer. J. Interact. Mark. **19**(3), 38–53 (2005)
15. Yi, C., Jiang, Z., Benbasat, I.: Designing for diagnosticity and serendipity: an investigation of social product-search mechanisms. Inf. Syst. Res. **28**(2), 413–429 (2017)
16. Carlson, J.R., Zmud, R.W.: Channel expansion theory and the experiential nature of media richness perceptions. J. Acad. Manag. **42**(2), 153–170 (1999)

Identifying Opinion Leaders in Virtual Travel Community Based on Social Network Analysis

Jinbi Yang[1]([⊠]), Yukang Zhang[2], and Libo Liu[3]

[1] Jiangnan University, Wuxi, China
yangjinbi@jiangnan.edu.cn
[2] Shanghai Jiao Tong University, Shanghai, China
[3] Swinburne University of Technology, Melbourne, Australia

Abstract. With the thriving development of internet industry and continuous increase of consumer demand in outbound tourism in China, opinion leaders in virtual community have significant effects on consumers' decision making process. Hence, identifying the opinion leader in virtual travel community (VTC) is significantly important for virtual community of outbound tourism. This study proposes the opinion leader recognition model based on social network analysis (SNA), and identifies leader value presented by construal influence, content influence, and activity to measure and evaluate the effect of opinion leader on consumers' cognition. Based on the empirical data, this study examines the soundness of SNA in VTC dimensionally and comprehensively, and establishes the opinion leader recognition, which can be used in future research to explore the assessment mechanism of opinion leader' effect on consumers.

Keywords: Opinion leaders · Virtual travel community ·
Social network analysis · Leader value

1 Introduction

The outbound tourism market is experiencing a thriving development globally. In 2016, the number of Chinese outbound tourists reached 122 million, increased by 4.3% compared with the number of 2015 [1]. The new movement of Chinese outbound tourism is deemed as a second wave of tourism by Arlt [2], therein more and more resorts outside of Asia become priorities for independent travelers. Travel is an informative-intensive activity. Since outbound tourism often happens in an environment of entirely different cultural and language background, which increases the difficulty for planning and traveling. However, since the mid-1990s, ever-emerging virtual travel communities (VTCs) provide travelers and tourism providers with an accessibility for exchanging information and maintaining relationships [3]. The development of supporting travel network products began from the original BBS to the user generating content (UGC) platform, from the professional generated contents (PGC) content to the vertical growth of the Raiders, accompanied by refined content. In China, tourists are more inclined to VTCs, because the cultural norms encourage people to live in a community-minded way [4].

© Springer Nature Switzerland AG 2019
F. F.-H. Nah and K. Siau (Eds.): HCII 2019, LNCS 11589, pp. 276–294, 2019.
https://doi.org/10.1007/978-3-030-22338-0_23

VTCs allow people to share their suggestions or stories based on their knowledge and tourism experience [5]. Other tourists are able to refer to other's experience or word-of-mouth to design their own journey or communicate for fun [6]. In this process, opinion leader in tourism exert a great impact on VTCs' users community involvement [7]. Opinion leader has also been proved the best marketing object in terms of diffusion speed and maximum cumulative number of adopters [8]. In consideration of the demand for outbound tourism, a number of opinion leaders are active in the outbound tourism virtual community, in addition to many potential opinion leaders. In e-commerce, opinion leaders are excellent channels for information dissemination. They have special marketing advantages as word-of-mouth communicators in the outbound tourism market. With their unique structural position and social assets, they can achieve excellent marketing results. For virtual communities, opinion leaders also play an important role - opinion leaders are the foundation of the community and the most important members of the virtual community, which can activate the community atmosphere and enhance the popularity of the virtual community.

Given the popularity of outbound tourism and growing importance of VTCs utilization in outbound tourism, it is vital for us to identify opinion leaders rather than merely understand their characteristics. This study empirically to use social network analysis (SNA) combined with some feathers (Title Certificate, User Level) of outbound UGC virtual travel community (VTC) to identify opinion leaders in Qyer.com, an outbound VTC in China. The experiment study on real dataset reveal that our identification method is effective to identify opinion leader in outbound tourism virtual community. This study seeks to establish an outbound VTC opinion leader identification model and test this model with social networking analysis combined with outbound TVC's features using the data extracted from a Chinese outbound VTC called Qyer.com.

2   Literature Review

2.1   Opinion Leader in Virtual Travel Community

Virtual Travel Community relies mainly on information sharing by its users. Such information is a kind of online word-of-month (WOM), which is informal, person-to-person communication between a perceived noncommercial communicator and a receiver about a product, service or organization [9]. The research indicated that although the number of "travel opinion leaders" or "central travelers" is relatively lower, they play a key role in supplying information to others [10], they are those influential, respected, WOM-spreading individuals [11].

The connotation of opinion leaders was gradually discovered, and its influence mechanism was also concerned by researchers. Zhu [12] defines the concept of "network opinion leader" and discusses its influence on online speech and its social influence; defines the concept of "network opinion leader post" and considers its progressive significance. On the basis of distinguishing the two, think about the ambiguity, fusion and transformation between the two concepts.

In tourism virtual community behavior, Liu [13] studies the influence and mechanism of opinion leaders in the process of college students' participation, based on social capital theory, social influence theory and herd behavior theory and tests the influence of opinion leaders on college students' participation in tourism virtual community behavior. In addition, Zhu [14] believes that with the "snowball"-style communication structure, the Internet circle confirms the role of the opinion leader of the information initiator in the virtual community, that is, the power center of the communication network; at the same time, because the Internet circle is infiltrated by the blood of different social relationships, its authorization is formed. The opinion leader is unbalanced in practical role.

Opinion leader could affect people's knowledge and attitude [15]. Much research has been conducted to explore opinion leader in context of VTC. Vasiliki and Kostas [16] pointed that travel opinion leaders are more willing to provide information, and they were more accessible by others through abundant incoming links. Further, Yoo et al. [17] concluded that travel opinion leaders relied on their rich travel experience and official statues to be trusted by others. According to the study of Jeong and Jang [18], opinion leaders were more active in exploratory behavior and dispersed more eWOM that non-leaders. Gabriela et al. [19] found that group leaders in VTC seemed to be active participants, and they had more experience with products related to group's interests or have more refined tastes.

2.2   Opinion Leader Value Measurement Model

Opinion leaders are important in improving communication and encourage team members to achieve a higher level of information exchange [20]. Many studies have proposed innovative opinion leader recognition and value measurement models to identify and evaluate them across different platforms or groups. With regard to how to identify opinion leaders, Li and Du [21] proposed an ontology-based BARR framework to analyze Weibo content, user characteristics and user relationships in popular Weibo to identify opinion leaders in Weibo.

Besides, in terms of structural influence, the Analytic Hierarchy Process (AHP) was used to implement the opinion leadership impact assessment, and an evaluation system consisting of four first-level indicators and 13 second-level indicators was constructed [22]. Moreover, Zhang [23] constructed a directed right network that characterizes the interpersonal influence of the community from the perspective of social network, and constructed a user influence model, exploring the rules of interpersonal communication, communication and influence within the community, and provided a theoretical basis for community word-of-mouth marketing practical guidance. Further, Aghdam et al. [24] proposed a framework using trust relationship between the users and evaluates the total trust value (TTV) of primary opinion leaders between other users to select the highest of them. Top in-degree method, top out-degree method, top centrality method and hybrid IO-degree method were proved have better results in social network marketing campaigning.

From the perspective of content impact and activity, Cao and Zhang [25] explained the characteristics and trends of social network structure changes, and pointed out that opinion leaders will still play a central role in social media. Ding and Wang [26] took

"Douban Net" as the research object, and established four levels of indicators including neutral, active, cohesive and infectious, and whether it is administrator, number of friends, number of followers, number of followers SNS virtual community opinion leader identification index system with 12 secondary indicators such as posting number, posting frequency, posting type, and number of posts. Considering the activity indicator, Yu et al. [27] improved HITS algorithm based on micro-blog user's influence and liveness analysis. Micro-blog user's hierarchy ad their comments were used to build an interactive network based on their weight.

3 Data Source

Founded in 2004, "Qyer.com" has developed into a leading outbound service platform in China. The Travel Quiz section of the "Qyer.com" is a typical outbound travel virtual community with a registered number of 80 million. The members of the section can be divided into three categories: questioners, respondents and bystanders. All the research samples in the article were collected by the web crawler from the poor quiz section. The selected samples only included the questioner and the respondent, excluding the bystanders (users who did not communicate with other users). Because only the number of times the question has been viewed and the number of likes, and the fact that the bystander does not speak cannot be the opinion leader, the opinion leader can be identified by using only the sample of the questioner and the respondent. The daily posting volume of the Travel Quiz section of the "Qyer.com" is less volatile. This article randomly selects posts posted from March 12th to March 14th, using web crawlers to crawl posts, questions, responses, likes, page views, questioners, and respondents. A total of 298 posts were grabbed, 52 unreported posts were removed, a total of 246 posts were collected, and a total of 288 users were sorted out.

4 Study 1

4.1 Method

Participants. This study randomly selects posts posted from March 12 to March 14, 3 days, using web crawlers to crawl the posts, questions, responses, likes, page views, questioners, and respondents. A total of 298 posts were grabbed, removing 52 unreported posts, and then a total of 246 posts were collected. A total of 288 users were sorted out among 246 posts.

Procedure. This paper uses data mining technology to obtain research data, and uses social network analysis to measure the centrality, structural holes and core/edge of outbound tourism virtual community represented by "poor travel network" to analyze the structural influence of leaders. Firstly, the article uses integrated network data analysis to establish an interactive contact between questioners and responders. The interaction between the questioner and the respondent is marked as number 1, and if there is no interaction, it is marked as number "0". Since some answers may be questioned multiple times, this case is also marked as "1". The above data are explained in detail by density analysis, correlation analysis and factional analysis. Next, social network analysis mainly measures the position of members in the network by degree centrality, intermediate centrality and proximity centrality. By intercepting the first 20 users and using Ucinet software, the calculation results of degree centrality, intermediate centrality and proximity centrality are obtained. Then the measurement of structural holes often focuses on four indicators: effective scale, efficiency, limitation and extreme. Run the Ucinet software and click on network → ego network → Structural Holes to calculate the structural holes in the network. Finally, through core/edge analysis, all members are divided into two parts according to the degree of affinity with other members and the density of the network: core members and edge members. Core members are more closely linked with other members and have greater advantages in the process of information exchange. The core and edge members of the network can be directly output through the Ucinet software.

4.2 Results

Based on the analysis of the overall network data, a 288 * 288 matrix is obtained. Numbering 288 users from 1 to 288, a new 288 * 288 matrix is created, which is input into the social network analysis software Ucinet, and the network diagram as shown in Fig. 1 can be obtained.

The social network diagram shown in Fig. 1 shows the network relationships among 288 users, with a blue block representing each user and a number next to it representing each user's number. Because the relationship between all users in the matrix is bidirectional, the arrows between each two users in the graph are bidirectional. The network diagram above intuitively shows the relative position of each user in this virtual community. The most peripheral hanging point represents the user's relationship with other users alienated, only one user contact, and the center user contact is closer. This directly shows the position of each user in this group. Central users are also relatively central in the group, while marginal users are relatively marginal in the group.

By Inputting the finished matrix into Ucinet software, we can get the network density shown in Table 1. According to the results of Table 3, it can be found that the density of the outbound tourism virtual community network is 0.0176, and the standard deviation $\delta = 0.1316$. From the sociological point of view, the density of this network group is small, which is mainly due to the objective reasons of community structure. But in the long run, the density of the group will remain stable. Because most of the questions in the Travel Questions and Answers section are time-sensitive, the answer peak is concentrated on the question within three days. As time goes on, most of the questions will be brushed to the back pages and no one will answer them. Only onlookers will rely on tags to search for relevant questions and answers for browsing. The correlation degree of outbound tourism virtual community network studied in this paper is 0.0176. This is a relatively low degree of association, a low degree of

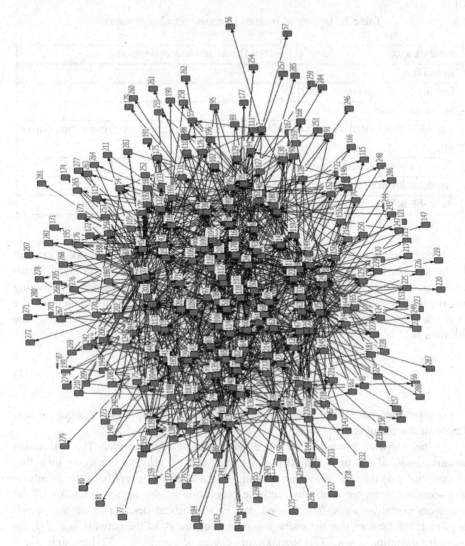

Fig. 1. Social network map of outbound tourism virtual community members

association network with the following characteristics: a. network information and power is more centralized; b. the status of network members is unequal; c. the network is vulnerable to individual users; d. network is a distribution structure. Because the network is a distribution structure, there are many small groups in the network. Ucinet software can be used to calculate the network in this study, including 108 factions, so there are a large number of small groups in the network.

Table 1. Density of outbound tourism virtual communities

Input dataset: matrix (C:\Users\ThinkPad\Desktop\matrix)
Relation: 1
Density (matrix average) = 0.0176
Standard deviation = 0.1316
Use MATRIX>TRANSFORM>DICHOTOMIZE procedure to get binary image matrix.
Density table(s) saved as dataset Density
Standard deviations saved as dataset Density SD
Actor-by-actor pre-image matrix saved as dataset Density Model

When a social network member is in the central position of the network, there will be more social connections with other network members, but also has a higher status and importance, so these users are often the core users of the social network. Measuring the degree centrality of a network, we also pay attention to the central potential of a network. The central potential of a network is the central trend of a network. The formula is:

$$Q = \frac{\sum_{i=1}^{n}(C_{max} - C)}{Max[\sum_{i=1}^{n}(C_{max} - C)]} \tag{1}$$

Q represents the central potential of the whole, and C represents the degree centrality of the member.

Ucinet software is used to calculate the results of degree center. The calculation results consist of two parts. The first part is the result of individual analysis, including the original data number, the specified number, the absolute centrality of the members, the normalized degree centrality, and the proportion of the degree centrality of the members in the network. The second part is a statistical description of the overall results. It can be seen that the average degree of centrality of the network is 8.299, the standard deviation $\delta = 8.837$, the maximum degree of centrality is 37, the minimum is 1, and the centrality of the whole network is 10.07%. The centrality of the network is small because the links between members are mainly mediated by questions. Most of the respondents do not have direct links, but point directly to the questioner, so the network is less centrality.

Contrary to degree centrality, users with high degree of centrality are those who occupy a central position between two users in a social network and act as valves and intermediaries in the flow of information in the social network. The calculation formula of center centrality is:

$$C_j = \sum_{h}^{n}\sum_{i}^{n} b_{hi}, h \neq i \neq j, h < i \tag{2}$$

Where b_{hi} is the number of shortcuts between point h and point i of point j more than the number of shortcuts between point h and point i, and the centrality C_j of point j is obtained by summing up the centrality of all points of point j in the graph.

By using the middle centrality of Ucinet, the results of intermediate center could be obtained. Similar to the degree centrality, the analysis results of the center centrality are also divided into two parts. The first is the original data number, the second is the user ID, the third is the user center, and the fourth is the standardized center. Like point-centricity, the most centralized user in the network is still No. 51, which is nearly 2.5 times more centralized than the second-place user. This shows that No. 51 plays a mediating role in many user interactions and a large amount of information flows can be transmitted through it. Therefore, number 51 user has great power and resources in the network. In this network, there are also a large number of users with zero inter-mediate centrality. They are only associated with a certain member. They appear in the form of hanging points in the network diagram, so their intermediate centrality is 0. The second part is about the statistical description of the whole network. It can be seen that the average intermediate center degree of the network is 716.222, the standard deviation $\delta = 1443.040$, the minimum intermediate center degree is 0, and the maximum is 15594.157. The central degree of the network is 18.19%, which is also a relatively small value. It is also caused by the objective reality of the data.

The proximity centrality is used to determine the location of a point in the network by measuring the sum of the distances between the point and other points. The approximate centrality C_i formula of point i is:

$$C_i = \sum_{j=1}^{n} b_{ij} \tag{3}$$

b_{ij} is the shortcut distance from point i to point j.

Using the Ucinet software, we can get the results of the near-center calculation. The proximity center includes two indicators: the internal proximity to the center (in-closeness) and the external Proximity Center (outcloseness). The greater the internal proximity and the smoother the node passes information to the other nodes, yet the greater the external proximity to the center, the smoother the node gets the information from the other nodes. The results generated by the ucinet contain six columns, of which the first two columns are the same as the center of the midpoint and the middle center, the third column is indegrees away from the degree, the fourth column is a outdegree away from the degree, the five is the indegree of proximity, and the six is the outdegree of proximity. The second part is the statistical description of the network and can be seen in the proximity of the measurement, the number 51st ID is not awake users regardless of the indegree of proximity or outdegree of proximity are ranked first. It is visible that the user interacts frequently with other users in the network, not only answering questions from the questioner, but also making comments and supplementary answers to other answers.

The measurement of structural holes often focuses on four indicators: effective scale, efficiency, limitation and extreme. Run the Ucinet software and click on network → ego network → Structural Holes to calculate the structure hole of the network (intercepting the top 20 members):

Table 2. Outbound tourism virtual community network structure hole analysis

Input dataset:	matrix (C:\Users\ThinkPad\Desktop\matrix)			
Method:	Whole Network			
Output datset	StructuralHoles (E:\ucinet\Ucinet 6\DataFiles\StructuralHoles)			
Display of dyadic redundancy matrix automatically suppressed due to large size.				
Display of dyadic constraint matrix automatically suppressed due to large size.				
Structural Hole Measures				
EffSize	Efficie	Constra	Hierarc	Indirec
-------	-------	-------	-------	-------
1 6.000	1.000	0.167	0.000	0.000
2 7.000	1.000	0.143	0.000	0.000
3 10.800	0.982	0.100	0.034	0.023
4 8.000	1.000	0.139	0.093	0.000
5 16.000	1.000	0.064	0.018	0.000
6 23.638	0.985	0.053	0.058	0.075
7 22.895	0.995	0.049	0.048	0.019
8 21.809	0.991	0.052	0.059	0.021
9 23.000	1.000	0.048	0.064	0.000
10 23.662	0.986	0.052	0.076	0.044
11 29.000	1.000	0.039	0.069	0.000
12 31.813	0.994	0.036	0.069	0.013
13 26.735	0.990	0.044	0.077	0.026
14 29.885	0.996	0.038	0.069	0.008
15 23.968	0.999	0.047	0.072	0.005
16 26.809	0.993	0.043	0.075	0.016
17 24.886	0.995	0.047	0.066	0.022
18 28.776	0.992	0.042	0.065	0.044
19 26.953	0.998	0.041	0.065	0.004
20 27.955	0.998	0.040	0.063	0.008
Structural hole measures saved as dataset StructuralHoles (E:\ucinet\Ucinet 6\Data-Files\StructuralHoles)				

Table 2 shows the results of the operation, the first column is the user ID, the second is valid scale, the third is limited to the system, the fourth list is Level. This is most important, as the extreme higher represents the higher limit on the user's concentration. Combined with the data can be found, such as Level maximum of 1, the lowest is 0, in 288 users, users with numbers 56, 57, 77, 80, 81, 147, 156, 157, 160, 161, 162, 179, 184, 207, and so on, are Level 1, it can be seen that they have a greater degree of restriction in the network.

Through the Ucinet software, the core and edge members of the network can be directly output. As shown in Table 3, all members are grouped into two categories, distinguished by 1 and 2, of which 1 is the core member with 54 members and 2 is the edge member with 234 members. 288 members can be sorted by core/edge values (intercepting the top 20 members). The sorting results are shown in Table 4.

Table 3. Core/edge analysis of outbound tourism virtual community network

Input dataset:	matrix (C:\Users\ThinkPad\Desktop\matrix)
Type of data:	Positive
Fitness measure:	CORR
Density of core-to-periphery ties:	
Number of iterations:	50
Population size:	288Core/Periphery Class Memberships:
1: 1 3 5 6 7 8 9 10 11 12 13 14 15 16 17 18 19 20 21 22 23 24 25 26 27 28 29 30 31 32 33 34 35 36 37 38 39 40 41 42 44 45 46 47 49 50 51 60 61 62 64 65 68 69 72 73 82 83 92 93 97 98 99 100 101 103 104 106 107 108 116 117 118 135 178	
2: 2 4 43 48 52 53 54 55 56 57 58 59 63 66 67 70 71 74 75 76 77 78 79 80 81 84 85 86 87 88 89 90 91 94 95 96 102 105 109 110 111 112 113 114 115 119 120 121 122 123 124 125 126 127 128 129 130 131 132 133 134 136 137 138 139 140 141 142 143 144 145 146 147 148 149 150 151 152 153 154 155 156 157 158 159 160 161 162 163 164 165 166 167 168 169 170 171 172 173 174 175 176 177 179 180 181 182 183 184 185 186 187 188 189 190 191 192 193 194 195 196 197 198 199 200 201 202 203 204 205 206 207 208 209 210 211 212 213 214 215 216 217 218 219 220 221 222 223 224 225 226 227 228 229 230 231 232 233 234 235 236 237 238 239 240 241 242 243 244 245 246 247 248 249 250 251 252 253 254 255 256 257 258 259 260 261 262 263 264 265 266 267 268 269 270 271 272 273 274 275 276 277 278 279 280 281 282 283 284 285 286 287 288	
Output partition:	CorePartition (E:\ucinet\Ucinet 6\DataFiles\CorePartition)
Output clusters:	CoreClasses (E:\ucinet\Ucinet 6\DataFiles\CoreClasses)
Starting fitness: 0.280	
Final fitness: 0.280	

Table 4. Core/marginal analysis ranking

Number	ID	Corene
51	醒不来啊	0.366
60	Cotatu	0.21
6	Minituski	0.188
68	志留纪	0.185
116	唐古拉01	0.172
9	HickeyHsui	0.142
82	Alegria_1122	0.142
14	美好心情521	0.139
64	宇宙人001	0.136
100	自在兰卡	0.132
21	111da	0.131
29	我中迫	0.13
8	盼panda盼	0.126
12	西枣Qin	0.123
18	月123567	0.123
38	13906222081	0.12
98	bestow07	0.12
11	nicy	0.119
49	白隼翱翔	0.119
7	擦心而过	0.118

On the whole, the core value of users who can not wake up is the highest, and is located in the most central position of the network. IDs for Cotaku, Silurian and Tanggula 01 are also relatively high core members, they constitute several cores of the network.

Social network analysis is to study the network relationship among members, and to judge whether opinion leaders exist in a group from the perspective of structure. But this method only focuses on the relationship among members and ignores the content of communication among members. The following research combines social network analysis with index analysis, in consideration of the relationship structure, content influence and activity of network members. Therefore, Study 2 research is carried out.

5   Study 2

As all sample data are taken from the travel question and answer section of "Qyer.com", the members who can be collected in this section are the questioner and the respondents. According to the definition and characteristics of the opinion leader, the questioner is not able to become an opinion leader by merely asking questions in the network and not having a wider exchange with other members. On the contrary, respondents, whether in the form of high-quality answers or broad-based socializing, may have a unique social capital advantage, so they may become opinion leaders in the virtual community, so this article excludes 47 questioners from the remaining 241 respondents to identify the network's opinion leaders.

Social network analysis includes three research interests: dynamic grading, role evaluation, professional and Community discovery [28]. SNA can study the relationship between nodes and reveal the structure of group relationship, which will affect the function of the group [29]. But this approach only focuses on the relationships among members and ignores the content of communication among members. Therefore, this research combines the social network analysis with the index analysis, taking into account the relationship structure, content influence and activity of the network members, and using the analytic hierarchy process to calculate the weight of each index, thus calculating the value of each member leader, and then identifying the virtual community opinion leader under the theme of outbound tourism.

5.1   Development of Opinion Leader Recognition Model

Opinion leaders in different virtual communities show different behavioral characteristics, so the identification indicators of opinion leaders in different virtual communities are different, but can be used for reference in this study. Based on the existing research and social network analysis results, this paper establishes a virtual community member leader value measurement model including three first-level indicators and eight second-level indicators as shown in Fig. 2.

Structural Influence. Structural influence refers to the influence of members in a special position in the network, such as the administrator of the virtual community, member communication intermediary, etc. As they naturally have the position of information valve, they can control the flow of information and become the opinion leaders in the virtual community. The structural influence of virtual community members can be measured by the intermediate center degree, the near center degree, the core/edge degree value, and the structural hole efficiency index in the social network analysis. Here the value of the center degree is inBetweenness; the close to the center degree takes inCloseness. The metric of the structural hole selects the degree, but the smaller the limit, the easier the point i is in obtaining information and transmitting information, so it is inverted and recorded as $i_{s'}, i_{s'} = 1/i_s$; core/Edge analysis selects the Corene value, indicating where the user is in the network.

Content Influence. Opinion leaders in BBS often spread their images to other users by virtue of their large number and excellent quality of posts, so as to maintain high community influence. However, they are often not moderators and administrators. Therefore, it is necessary to calculate these users and measure the influence of their replies. In the "Qyer.com" travel question and answer board, users can be judged by the number of "like" answers and their own authentication.

The number of "like" directly affects the number of page views of users' answers, and the number of likes will be placed on top. In addition, the number of "like" reflects the degree of recognition of users' answers. The more likes, the higher the degree of recognition, the greater the influenee. There are four titles in "Qyer.com": destination players, question and answer pathfinders, elite authors, and experienced users of regions and interests. The four titles were ranked by how easy it was to get, and they were all tied directly to the quality and quantity of responses. For example, the criteria for selecting a pathfinder is: more than 100 high-quality answers in Qyer 2 months before applying for the title, without over-heated comments, and more than one third of the useful answers are clicked; Published a journey of essence 2 months before applying for the title. According to observations, users who answered questions in the Travel Q&A section mainly had the first three titles, of which the number of respondents was the most, and the number of users who received titles was significantly higher than that of users without titles. Quantify the four titles: 1 point, 2 points, 3 points and 4 points for the four titles, and 0 points for users without titles.

Activity. The activity degree is to measure the active degree of users in the virtual network in China. The more active the users who answer the questions, the more connections they have with other members, and the higher the degree of degree center, so the degree center is chosen to measure the active degree of users. In addition, the more active members answered questions and established connections with other members, the higher their community contribution and the corresponding community level would be. Therefore, this study also used the level of members to measure their activity.

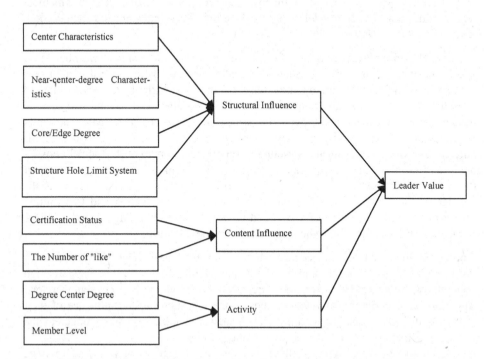

Fig. 2. Measurement model of member leader value of outbound tourism virtual community

5.2   Index Weight Calculation

According to the established virtual community opinion leader value calculation model, the analytic hierarchy process (AHP method) is used to calculate the weight value of each indicator. Yaahp software can be used to obtain each measurement index and its corresponding weight (Table 5):

Table 5.   Weight of opinion leader value of outbound tourism virtual community

Indicators	The weight
Intermediate centrality	0.017
Near centrality	0.052
Core/margin	0.069
Structure hole limit system	0.062
Certification	0.080
The great number	0.320
Degree of center	0.333
Members of the class	0.067

5.3   Identification of Opinion Leaders in Outbound Tourism

The leader value of each member can be calculated by using the above weight and the 8 indicators of each member's leader value. However, the 8 indicators of each member are different in form and size. Therefore, the above 8 indicators data are first processed in a consistent manner, and all data are converted into Numbers between 0 and 100. Taking $i_{c'}$ close to centrality as an example, the consistent formula is as follows:

$$i_{c'} = \frac{i_c}{i_{cmax}} \times 100 \tag{4}$$

$i_{c'}$ represents the nearly centroid value of consistent, i_c represents the close centroid value of point I, and i_{cmax} represents the maximum value of the nearly centroid value of point I. After conversion, the consistent result of the 8 index values of each member can be obtained. Then the leader value of each user can be calculated.

5.4   Results

After comparison and verification, all the opinion leaders identified by the social network analysis indicators were included in the above results, that is, both the pure social network analysis and the index system method that introduced content and activity were considered to have high leader values in the virtual communities under the theme of outbound tourism. Therefore, the opinion leaders in the "Qyer" travel quiz section include the following users: Cotaku, can't wake up, sean3076, silurian, tangula 01, meow on the journey, rockylee, white falcon soaring, wcm360, bestow07, shanghai1973, free lanca, kate9660, bennypsr, cosmic 001, Shadowk, oldbay, fswindy, hui1952, Charlemagn, forty flowers, alegria_1122, Nicolesyo, vasily hussain, mahler, wu Teacher, lin86109, masterio, I travel, SHCHM.

6 Discussion and Contributions

6.1 Discussion

This article uses the social network analysis and the AHP method to identify the opinion leader, and adopts the statistical method to carry on the characteristic analysis to the opinion leader and the non-opinion leader, obtains the following conclusion:

1. From the sociological point of view, the density of the network group is relatively small, which is mainly caused by the objective reasons of the community structure. Through correlation analysis and factional analysis, it can be found that because the network is an allocation structure, there are many small groups in the network. Through the structure hole and core/edge analysis to identify the structure of the 288 outbound tourism virtual community members, while using the AHP method to the center, structure hole and core/edge degree and certification, points like number and membership level together, in 288 members identified 30 opinion leaders. A group that demonstrates the presence of opinion leaders in the virtual community of outbound travel affects the outbound travel decisions and experiences of other users.
2. According to the results of the study, the virtual community of administrators and members of the exchange intermediary can control the flow of information as the opinion leader, because they have the status of natural information valve. It can be used to measure the structure influence of the virtual community members by using the middle Center degree, the Close Center degree, the core/edge degree value and the structure hole efficiency index in the social network analysis.
3. Based on the "social impact model" and "technology acceptance model" and the actual situation of the outbound tourism virtual community, the article puts forward the model of the participation of the virtual community of outbound tourism, and designs the questionnaire to investigate the characteristics of opinion leaders and non-opinion leaders respectively. Through comparison and verification, the opinion leaders identified by the social network analysis are all included in the results of the study, that is, whether it is purely social network analysis, or the introduction of content and activity of the index system method is considered that these members in the outbound tourism theme of the virtual community has a higher leader value. The study found that opinion leaders were significantly higher than non-opinion leaders in their involvement, functional, recreational, social, community identity, interaction, emotional connection, perceived usability, and perceived ease of use. However, there is no significant difference between opinion leaders and non-opinion leaders in the behavior of Internet use.

6.2   Contributions

Theoretical Contributions

1. At present, the research on virtual community Opinion leaders focuses on two levels: first, the opinion leader recognition level, this level discusses the establishment and optimization of the recognition algorithm more. Second, the public opinion control, this level is mainly concerned about emergencies and government micro-blog, discussion is how to define and use the relevant opinion leaders to guide the opinion. However, there are few research on outbound tourism opinion leaders in virtual community at present. On the one hand, outbound travel is often used as a section of virtual community of tourism, overlapping with other sections, difficult to collect data, on the other hand, this kind of post has a long time span of large data and inconvenient handling. However, with the improvement and development of virtual community of tourism and the upgrading of data mining and processing technology, objective obstruction has been solved. The paper analyzes the social network of the outbound tourism opinion leaders in the virtual community, which is a further subdivision of the opinion leaders of the tourism virtual community, which can fill the gap in this area, and facilitate the management of the tourism virtual community, broaden the tourist information sources and help the tourism enterprises to find the marketing objects.
2. This paper mainly has two ideas: the first, the social network analysis of the members of the virtual community of outbound tourism and the combination of analytic hierarchy process to find out which members belong to the opinion leaders, which members are not the opinion leaders, and the second is the characteristics of community participation in the identified opinion leaders through the questionnaire survey, Attempts to clarify the differences between opinion leaders and non-opinion leaders in outbound travel topics, and to supplement existing research.
3. This study combines social network analysis with index analysis, taking into account the relationship structure, content influence and activity of network members, using analytic hierarchy process to calculate the weights of each index, thus calculating the value of each member leader, and then identifying the virtual community opinion leaders under the outbound tourism theme.

Practical Contributions

1. For tourism enterprises, we should pay attention to the special status of opinion leaders and make reasonable use of their social assets value.

   In e-commerce, word-of-mouth marketing has become a very efficient marketing means, opinion leaders in the outbound tourism market as a word-of-mouth communication has a special marketing advantage, with its unique structure and social assets can achieve excellent marketing results. Similar to Weibo's online red economy, more and more tourism companies are now opting to collaborate with opinion leaders in the tourism community, such as full-time and "poor" Japanese version of the Essence of Shenyangoxygen co-author, Gore-Tex outdoor equipment to the user's sponsorship and so on. Therefore, tourism enterprises should use the opinion leader to accumulate the popularity, reputation and other social assets advantages, with opinion leaders as intermediaries to open up the market, in-depth market, and then the company's products or services marketing to vigorously promote.

2. For the relevant departments, the opinion leader is a very good channel of information dissemination.

   For the tourism Bureau, especially the Overseas Tourism Bureau, the information Communication intermediary role of opinion leaders can help the tourist bureau to promote tourism, and can achieve good results. However, in the process of information dissemination, the amplification of opinion leaders will also cause negative information or the expansion of false information, therefore, the relevant departments for opinion leaders should focus on monitoring, maintain good cooperation, so as to use their influence to spread practical information, issued security alerts, to protect the interests of outbound travelers.

3. For virtual communities, use opinion leaders to enhance social linkages in virtual communities.

   Opinion leaders can enliven the community atmosphere and increase the heat of virtual communities, especially in question-and-answer communities, where opinion leaders are the foundation of Community existence, and therefore they are the most important members of a virtual community. To this end, the virtual community can take a combination of online and offline activities to promote the interaction between opinion leaders and other members, the use of virtual community social, mutual influence and other characteristics to create a sense of community for members. So as to enhance the participation of members and promote the generation of opinion leaders.

6.3   Limitations

This paper uses the social network analysis and analytic hierarchy process to identify the opinion leaders of the outbound tourism theme virtual community. There are some limitations as belows.

1. Due to the website structure limitation of "Qyer.com", only 288 members of the information is crawled. The sample size is relatively small. We can improve the network crawler technology, Grab more samples and increase the depth and breadth in future study.

2. The article does not further subdivide the opinion leaders. In outbound tourism, there are different opinion leaders under different issues. For example, trip questions of "Qyer.com" include visas, transportation, accommodation and other issues. In the future study, we could increase the sample size and classify the opinion leaders in each field according to the different fields of outbound tourism.

3. Due to the objective condition of collecting data, the current study just chooses the travel question and answer section of "Qyer.com" to excavate the user relationship. But the "Qyer.com" also has a more popular plate for the travel forum allowing

users to publish their travels, where the number of posts is large, and the relationship between users is more active and complex. Therefore, the data mining and cleaning technology should be optimized in the future research, and the big data in the plate can be analyzed to obtain more accurate results.

References

1. Yang, Y.W., Sun, G.H., Tao, X.B.: Country, destination image and outbound travel intention. Bus. Manag. J. (2017)
2. Arlt, W.G., Burns, P.: The second wave of Chinese outbound tourism. Tour. Plan. Dev. **10**(2), 126–133 (2013)
3. Kim, W.G., Lee, C., Hiemstra, S.J.: Effects of an online virtual community on customer loyalty and travel product purchases. Tour. Manag. **25**(3), 343–355 (2004)
4. Reisinger, Y., Turner, L.W., Long, P.: Cross-Cultural Behaviour in Tourism: Concepts and Analysis, p. 337. Butterworth Heinemann, Oxford (2003). ISBN 0-7506-56689. Int. J. Tour. Res. **6**(1), 54 (2004)
5. Gao, L., Bai, X., Park, A.: Understanding sustained participation in virtual travel communities from the perspectives of is success model and flow theory. J. Hosp. Tour. Res. **41**(4), 1–35 (2017)
6. Kim, D.G., Kang, W.L., Oh, S.T., et al.: Preparation of W-Cu nanocomposite powder by hydrogen-reduction of ball-milled W and CuO powder mixture. Mater. Lett. **58**(7), 1199–1203 (2004)
7. Gretzel, U., Yoo, K.H.: Use and impact of online travel reviews. Inf. Commun. Technol. Tourism **26**(1), 35–46 (2008)
8. Cho, Y., Hwang, J., Lee, D.: Identification of effective opinion leaders in the diffusion of technological innovation: a social network approach. Technol. Forecast. Soc. Chang. **79**(1), 97–106 (2012)
9. Lewis, R.C., Chambers, R.E.: Marketing leadership in hospitality. Found. Pract. (1989
10. Vrana, V., Zafiropoulos, K.: Locating central travelers' groups in travel blogs' social networks. J. Enterp. Inf. Manag. **23**(5), 595–609 (2013)
11. Toledano, M.: Professional competition and cooperation in the digital age: a pilot study of New Zealand practitioners. Public Relat. Rev. **36**(3), 230–237 (2010)
12. Zhu, Y., Yao, C., Bai, X.: Scene text detection and recognition: recent advances and future trends. Front. Comput. Sci. **10**(1), 19–36 (2016)
13. Liu, L., Li, J., Bie, F., et al.: Power list system and construction of modern hospital management system. Contemp. Med. (2018)
14. Yang, J., Zhu, T., Zhao, Y., et al.: Acute intermittent porphyria in the north of china: the acute attack effect on quality of life and psychological condition. Biomed. Res. Int. **2018**(110), 1–6 (2018)
15. Valente, T.W., Davis, R.L.: Accelerating the diffusion of innovations using opinion leaders. In: The Annals of the American Academy of Political and Social Science, pp. 55–67 (1999)
16. Karavasilis, I., Zafiropoulos, K., Vrana, V.: Extending TAM to understand e-governance adoption by teachers in Greece. Commun. Comput. Inf. Sci. **112**, 57–68 (2010)
17. Hahn, W., et al.: Enhanced cardioprotective effects by coexpression of two isoforms of hepatocyte growth factor from naked plasmid DNA in a rat ischemic heart disease model. J. Gene Med. **13**(10), 549–555 (2011)

18. Jeong, J.C., Jang, S.W., Kim, T.H., et al.: Mulberry fruit (Moris fructus) extracts induce human glioma cell death in vitro through ROS-dependent mitochondrial pathway and inhibits glioma tumor growth in vivo. Nutr. Cancer **62**(3), 402–412 (2010)

19. Maier, D.A., Brennan, A.L., Jiang, S., et al.: Efficient clinical scale gene modification via zinc finger nuclease-targeted disruption of the HIV co-receptor CCR19. Hum. Gene Ther. **24** (3), 245 (2013)

20. Weingart, J., Grossman, S.A., Carson, K.A., et al.: Phase I trial of polifeprosan 20 with carmustine implant plus continuous infusion of intravenous O6-benzylguanine in adults with recurrent malignant glioma: new approaches to brain tumor therapy CNS consortium trial. J. Clin. Oncol. **25**(4), 399–404 (2007)

21. Qu, L.L., Zhu, Y.L., Li, Y.Z., et al.: Solvent-induced synthesis of zinc(II) and manganese(II) coordination polymers with a semirigid tetracarboxylic acid. Cryst. Growth Des. **11**(6), 2444–2452 (2011)

22. Ariga, K., Li, J., Fei, J., et al.: Nanoarchitectonics for dynamic functional materials from atomic-/molecular-level manipulation to macroscopic action. Adv. Mater. **28**(6), 1251–1286 (2016)

23. Zhang, Y.J., Tang, L.L., Wang, Z., et al.: Insights into characteristics, sources and evolution of submicron aerosols during harvest seasons in Yangtze River Delta (YRD) region, China. Atmos. Chem. Phys. **15**(3), 1331–1349 (2015)

24. Sepantafar, M., Maheronnaghsh, R., Mohammadi, H., et al.: Stem cells and injectable hydrogels: synergistic therapeutics in myocardial repair. Biotechnol. Adv. **34**(4), 362–379 (2016)

25. Zhang, Y.J., Tang, L.L., Wang, Z., et al.: Insights into characteristics, sources and evolution of submicron aerosols during harvest seasons in Yangtze River Delta (YRD) region, China. Atmos. Chem. Phys. **14**(7), 9109–9154 (2014)

26. Qian, W., Zhou, X.D., Zheng, Q.H., et al.: Distribution of Porphyromonas gingivalis fimA genotypes in chronic apical periodontitis associated with symptoms. J. Endod. **36**(11), 1790 (2010)

27. Yu, H., Huang, T.: Correction: Yu, H.; et al. Molecular mechanisms of floral boundary formation in Arabidopsis. Int. J. Mol. Sci. **19**(7), 1845 (2018)

28. Chen, Q., Yan, M., Cao, Z., et al.: Sperm tsRNAs contribute to intergenerational inheritance of an acquired metabolic disorder. Science **351**(6271), 397–400 (2016)

29. Jeon, J.W., Wang, Y., Yeo, G.T.: SNA approach for analyzing the research trend of international port competition. Asian J. Shipping Logist. **32**(3), 165–172 (2016)

Who Borrows Money from Microloan Platform? - Evidence from Campus E-card

Chenghong Zhang, Shuaiyong Xiao[⊠], Tian Lu, and Xianghua Lu

School of Management, Fudan University, Shanghai 200433, China
{chzhang, syxiao, lutian, lxhua}@fudan.edu.cn

Abstract. As the microloan becomes popular with the advance of information technology, the assessment of credit risk and understanding borrowers become crucial. However, without antithetical individuals, the prediction of loan probability and risk control cannot be so accurate. As an important consumption group in current commercial society, college students usually don't have enough disposable income thus very likely become active lenders in microloan platforms. For microloan platforms, a vital question is how to distinguish the individuals who use the loans for the right purposes. In this study, we combine the student loan data from a microloan platform with student daily consumption data recorded by a campus e-card system to examine the change of consumption behavior for those students who borrowed money from the microloan platform. Our study finds that students with loan do have distinct consumption patterns for both long and short terms. Furthermore, by applying a difference-in-difference regression method, we find significant increases in both consumption frequency and money after students borrow money from the microloan platform for both long and short terms. Our research enriches the literature on microloan in the context of college students as consumers.

Keywords: Microloan · Consumption flow data · Risk control ·
College students

1 Introduction

Information technology provides a convenient channel for people who have microloan demand to seek loans. Microloan platforms (Lending club, Prosper et al.) are thus becoming more and more popular [12]. For microlenders, the borrowers' credit risk assessment and understanding borrowers' behavior are crucial in lending procedure [16]. Prior research often uses the borrowers' demographic characteristics, social capital and credit history to assess the risk (e.g. [10, 16]). However, lacking of antithetical individuals, who have the similar characteristics (e.g. sex, age, enroll year et al.) as the borrower but don't borrow money from the microloan platform, microlenders cannot obtain the unique characteristics of borrowers compared with non-borrowers and can hardly recognize who on earth need to borrow money.

© Springer Nature Switzerland AG 2019
F. F.-H. Nah and K. Siau (Eds.): HCII 2019, LNCS 11589, pp. 295–304, 2019.
https://doi.org/10.1007/978-3-030-22338-0_24

Among the huge borrower group, young people who completed high school are "special" potential consumption group. They usually become to decide what to purchase by themselves without intervention from parents after they enter colleges. In recent years, college students' consumption view has also upgraded. According to a report from iResearch, Chinese college students spend approximately 452.4 billion RMB in 2016[1]. On the one hand, they begin to form their own consumption view out from the childhood. On the other hand, they don't have enough disposable income to satisfy their demand and don't have the qualification to apply credit card. Under such situation, most students are hesitated to seek help from family members or borrow money from friends due to fear of getting blame and feeling of embarrassment. However, because of lacking stable source of income and poor consumption plan, the limited money may not afford the purchasing need of some college students. Thus young people are very likely to seek money from microloan platforms. Meanwhile, the development of microloan business provides a loan channel for college students who are in short of money. Thus they are very likely become a type of active lenders in microloan platform. For microloan platform, how to distinguish the students who use the loan for the right (low-risk) purpose is a vital question. In many instances, college students are not familiar with the loan procedure, and have less responsibility and weak awareness of risk and information security, which leads to negative events such as high default rate, unduly debt collection and information theft. Therefore, how to trace students' subsequent consumption behavior after borrowing money is an important question for college administrators and microloan lenders. For college administrators, how to distinguish the students who have need for financial support and give them some financial support to help them make through the financial difficulties and finish college education is a main concern.

Nevertheless, there is little literature on risk evaluation with daily consumption data and we need find valuable evaluation indicators. Since the digital campus has already been well-developed, almost all aspect of college life can be paid by campus e-card. Thus, our research idea is based on the student daily consumption behavior data acquired from the e-card records, mining features of high-risk borrowers. Furthermore, by investigating on comparing the behaviors before and after obtaining money from microlenders, we can help academia and industry better understand borrowers' behaviors and trace their risk after loan. Moreover, the microlenders can recognize the low-risk financial demand borrowers and provide personalized service. The relevant regulators such as financial governors and college administrators can also recognize the group with real financial demand, thus provide financial support to them and improve the social well-being.

The paper is organized as follows: First, the relevant literature on microloan and e-card is reviewed. Next, we introduce our data set and variables. The research method and results are presented in Sect. 4. Finally, we summarize the conclusion and implications of our research.

---

[1] http://report.iresearch.cn/report/201701/2906.shtml.

2 Literature Review

The literature related to our research includes two streams: microloan and campus e-card.

At individual level, the literature on microloan is very rich. The literature can be approximately categorized into three types. One is about user credit and risk evaluation and prediction [1, 2, 8, 10, 13, 14, 16]. These studies contribute to testing the influential factors related to borrowers' repayment risk, such as loan characteristics, borrower characteristics, credit history, and social capitals. The second strand of literatures analyzed microloan user behavior (e.g. [3, 5, 8, 11, 15]). These studies focus on users' behavioral patterns such as herding, and reveal the existence of home bias. The third group of literature explored the factors related to successful loans, interest rates, as well as the investment patterns of lenders, etc. [4, 6, 7, 15, 21]. These studies face a common dilemma that their research factors are static and from the borrowers' self-reported information, thus can lead to potential endogeneity problem.

To the best of our knowledge, the literature on application of campus e-card data is scarce. In the limited literature, a few papers employ e-card data to investigate the factors that may influence students' study performance [17, 19], and they find that students' breakfast frequency, consumption habit are strongly correlated with their study performance. Another stream of studies investigates student behavioral patterns such as dinning frequency, dinning money, shopping money and frequent canteen windows with data mining method such as clustering [9, 18]. Fu et al. [20] use the MapReduce method to visualize the student consumption behavior among different season and grade in the Hadoop framework. However, the extant research does not: (1) make full use of the e-card consumption data, (2) have a deep investigation in the data, (3) associate the data to the student financial status, and (4) allocate students with economic difficulties.

In summary, the prior literature has not empirically investigated the factors revealing why individuals borrow money from microloan with second-hand consumption flow data; and there is a gap in literature on tracing and comparing borrowers' purchasing behaviors before and after loan attainment. Campus e-card data of college students can trace the daily consumption activities and thus provide good opportunities to fill in the above research gaps.

3 Data Description

Our dataset contains two parts: loan data from the online lending platform and campus e-card consumption data. The loan data is from a Chinese microloan platform whose business mainly targets college students. We obtained 520 student borrowers from a unique school in China. The school has both college and university students according to their scores in higher-education entrance examination. All loans were applied from June 2014 to February 2015, and are the first time for these students to experience in the platform. The dataset includes students' basic information such as whether he/she is an undergraduate student, gender, age, study major, etc. We also have borrowers' self-reported loan purpose, and we categorize them into two types: daily consumption and emergency consumption. Loan information includes interest rate, loan term and loan size. Detailed repayment records are also included in the loan data. The descriptive statistic of loan data is shown as Table 1.

Table 1. Description of student loan data.

Variables	Definition	Borrowers (Obs. = 520)			
		Mean	S.D.	Min	Max
Overduedays	The number of overdue days	34.788	42.365	0	92
Overdueflag	Dummy (=1 if overdue, else = 0)	0.554	0.498	0	1
Baddebtflag	Dummy (=1 if bad debt, else = 0)	0.275	0.447	0	1
Loan purpose	Dummy (=1 if loan reason is daily consumption, else = 0)	0.513	0.5	0	1
Loan size	The amount of loan	2805.915	523.45	300	3000
Loan term	The loan time that borrow	6.179	1.336	3	10
Interest rate	The annual interest rate of loan	15.892	2.305	13	21
Income_m	The monthly income of borrower	1.198	0.57	1	5

We obtained campus e-card consumption data from the same school of the 520 students who borrowed money from the microloan platform. With the agreement of students and help of school managers, we totally got 12,282 students' over 40 million consumption data records from 2009 to 2017. The dataset contains student basic information such as gender, age, year of attendance, hometown, and very detailed consumption flow data such as amount, time and consumption purpose (i.e., consumption in canteen, shopping in stores, and recharge the e-card). Notably, the platform doesn't have the information on students' daily consumption and do not use them in risk assessment, so there is no sample selection bias from the platform employers. We match the 520 sample students' loan information with their campus e-card records by phone numbers with the help of a third-party e-campus service providers. We do not have any information that could identify the authentic identity of every student in our dataset.

Without the students who don't borrow money from the platform, we can't control the unobservable heterogeneity in student characteristics. Furthermore, randomly picking unborrowed student can't make sure that the borrowed group and unborrowed group are comparable. Thus, we use propensity score matching (PSM) method to find the antithetical individuals. First, we use the logit regression method to find the significant variables that may influence the two group, the logit regression result is shown in Table 2. Then we use these variables to match the two group in the full sample and compare the mean difference of these variables between the two groups. We get a perfect match for each student who borrow money from microlenders.

Table 2. Logit regression for PSM.

Variables	Description	Coefficient	Std. Error
Custtype	Dummy(=1 if the student is undergraduate, else 0	1.936***	0.191
Inyear	The enroll year of the student	0.204***	0.087
Sex	The gender of the student (=1 if female, else 0)	−0.915***	0.101
Age	The age of the student	−0.139***	0.040
CityGDP_10k	The per capital GDP of the city that the student born in (a unit is 10,000 RMB)	−0.044	0.044
Specialty_Dummy	The specialty of the student	Included	–
Log Lik.			−1914.07
Chi Square			368.86***
Observations			12282

Note: * $p < 0.10$, ** $p < 0.05$, *** $p < 0.01$. The same below.

After PSM, we had 1,040 students (520 borrowers and 520 non borrowers) with 1,572,803 e-card consumption records. Then we code the student dinning behavior, shopping behavior and recharge behavior for both long and short terms. The long terms include a year before borrowing and borrowing date to repayment date. The short terms include a month before borrowing money and a month after borrowing. For the long-term variables, we also code the regularity using the corresponding standard deviation of each student. By comparing the mean value of each variable, we preliminarily find that students without loan have more consumption frequency and money than students with loan on average.

4 Method and Results

For the first research question: what kind of student will borrow money from the microloan platform, we use logit regression to find the answer. However, since there are endogeneity problems because the students who borrow money may have special consumption behavior pattern, which will lead the causality relationship unreliable. In order to avoid this issue, we use the average amount of all the students who are in the same period as the student who borrows money expect his/her own consumption amount as an instrumental variable. We set a year before borrowing money from the platform as a long-term period and a month before borrowing money from the platform as a short-term period. The long-term and short-term regression results are shown in Table 3.

Table 3. Regression of "who will borrow money from platform".

Variables	DV: Loan	
	(long term)	(short term)
Breakfast frequency	−0.484***	−0.133***
	(0.0653)	(0.0207)
Dinner frequency	0.0111	−0.0201***
	(0.0177)	(0.0063)
Shopping frequency	−0.174	−0.136***
	(0.124)	(0.0357)
Recharge frequency	0.514***	−0.176***
	(0.133)	(0.033)
Dinning money	−0.00875	−0.186***
	(0.195)	(0.078)
Shopping money	−0.287	−0.086
	(1.51)	(0.502)
Recharge money	−0.673***	−0.277***
	(0.234)	(0.073)
Intercept	343.0*	−36.76
	(191.5)	(174.3)
Control variables	YES	YES
Pseudo R^2.	0.339	0.193
Log Lik.	−476.7	−581.8
Observations	1040	1040

Note: * $p < 0.10$, ** $p < 0.05$, *** $p < 0.01$.

In long term, we can find that the recharge frequency has a significant positive effect on whether borrowing money, whose coefficient is approximately 0.514. Both the breakfast frequency and the recharge money have significant negative effect on whether borrowing money from the platform and their parameters are −0.484 and −0.673 separately. This indicates that students with a healthy breakfast eating habit are less likely to borrow money since they maybe more organized. Furthermore, the students with less recharge money and more recharge frequency are more likely to spend all their money quickly and seek for extra financial support.

Similarly, we can know that almost all the consumption behaviors have significant negative effect on the probability of borrowing money in the short term. The significance and value of each variable indicates that if a student decrease the consumption in campus suddenly in recent month and there exists a large chance that the student will need an additional financial support and loan money from online microlenders if the demand is not satisfied.

For the second research question: whether the students with loan behave differently after borrowing money from the microloan platform, we use the Difference-in-Difference (DID) method to test this question. We generated a dummy variable "time" and set time equal to 1 if the period of the variables is after borrowing else set time equal to 0. Our dependent variables can be divided into three categories. One category is dinning variable, including dinning frequency, dinning money and dinning regularity. The second category is shopping variable, including shopping frequency, shopping money and shopping regularity. The third category is recharge variable, including recharge frequency, recharge money and recharge regularity. We analysis the long-term effect and short-term effect. We controlled the demographic characteristics such as gender, age, enroll year. We also controlled the number of days of holiday, vacation and weekend. The long-term behavior change is shown in Table 4.

Table 4. The difference of consumption behavior after borrowing in long term.

Variables	Bre_freq	Din_freq	Shop_freq	Rech_freq	Din_mny	Shop_mny	Rech_mny
Loan	−3.130***	−11.36***	−5.246***	−1.099***	−120.8***	−32.72***	−98.42***
Time	0.0996	1.281*	0.265	0.953***	16.46**	0.108	31.12***
LoanxTime	**0.16**	**2.655***	**0.00396**	**0.315***	**19.00****	**2.083**	**22.40****
Age	−0.140**	−0.435	−0.374***	−0.225***	−7.690**	−2.694***	−8.172***
Custtype	1.247***	13.57***	4.234***	2.004***	110.1***	25.41***	115.8***
Inyear	0.0145	−0.392	−0.733***	−0.13	−3.436	−3.524***	−3.611
Gender	0.487**	1.785*	−1.380***	0.154	−48.14***	−13.18***	−10.46
CityGDP_10 k	−0.0145	0.307**	0.121**	0.0904***	5.361***	1.088***	5.540***
Weekend	0.0365	−0.0866	−0.481	−0.344*	1.164	−2.735	−15.86
Vacation	−0.316	−2.159	0.61	0.0854	−10.87	5.635	−5.725
Holiday	1.035	8.464	−0.22	1.135	34.77	−9.569	88.3
Intercept	−23.66	806	1489.0***	268.6	7264.9	7196.9***	7599
R^2	0.217	0.127	0.193	0.107	0.18	0.188	0.124
Observations	2080	2080	2080	2080	2080	2080	2080

Note: * $p < 0.10$, ** $p < 0.05$, *** $p < 0.01$.

In long term, the students with loan do have an increase in consumption frequency and consumption money. Significant increase exists in dinner frequency, recharge frequency, dinning money and recharge money. The increase in consumption means that students borrow money from the microloan platform in order to improve their living quality other than because of some irrational consumption psychology and impulse buying.

The short-term behavior change is shown in Table 5. In short term, the increase of the consumption behavior of the student borrowers in campus are more significant. All the consumption variables are significant and positive. This further indicates the student are merely lack of money to improve their life quality.

The DID regression results with the student campus e-card data shows that the students didn't borrow money for irrational consumption reasons or impulse buying, which is different from the common knowledge and intuitive feeling. It's an important finding for the college administrator to recognize the student with real financial difficulties, offer financial support to them and help them get through.

Table 5. The difference of consumption behavior after borrowing in short term.

Variables	Bre_freq	Din_freq	Shop_freq	Rech_freq	Din_mny	Shop_mny	Rech_mny
P2P	−3.438***	−11.21***	−6.265***	−1.116***	−125.5***	−38.42***	−104.9***
Time	−0.540**	−5.752***	−1.283***	−0.850***	−30.87**	−8.687***	−55.97***
P2PxTime	0.444*	2.887*	1.119**	0.604*	23.45*	9.060***	38.39**
Age	−0.257**	−0.969*	−0.593***	−0.356***	−14.66***	−4.340***	−15.36***
Custtype	2.354***	23.28***	4.425***	2.897***	173.7***	26.53***	178.7***
Inyear	0.304*	1.608**	−0.711***	−0.0514	15.56**	−3.178**	4.556
Gender	0.487	2.449*	−2.337***	−0.0229	−47.40***	−19.40***	−26.81*
CityGDP_10 k	0.0281	0.634***	0.158**	0.153***	7.020***	1.133**	10.90***
Weekend	−0.344	3.124	1.484**	1.426***	26.5	7.554*	51.58***
Vacation	−0.0472***	−0.357***	−0.0655***	−0.0528***	−2.834***	−0.380***	−3.381***
Holiday	0.109*	0.146	−0.132	−0.0869	0.218	−0.868	0.431
Intercept	−598.4*	−3258.6**	1427.1***	89.05	−31255.6**	6418.7**	−9573.2
R^2	0.171	0.138	0.156	0.06	0.142	0.147	0.112
Observations	2080	2080	2080	2080	2080	2080	2080

Note: * $p < 0.10$, ** $p < 0.05$, *** $p < 0.01$.

5   Conclusion and Implications

College students are at a special period. Their financial demand is an important issue that need concern. How to find the target students that need financial support and trace their consumption behavior is a meaningful question both for academia and practice. Many universities have constructed campus e-card system in the proceeding of digital campus, which provide abundant student consumption data to investigate students' consumption behavior. By combining student consumption data from a university in China and student borrowing data from a microloan platform, our study finds that students with less breakfast frequency, more recharge frequency but less recharge money are more likely to borrow money from the platform in long term. We infer that this is because this kind of students do not have a reasonable plan for using money. In short term, almost all the consumption behavior will decrease for the student borrowers. This indicates that the students will decrease their temporary consumption if they are short of money. This can be an important indicator for college managers to recognize the students with financial difficulties. Furthermore, we find that the students with loan have a significant improvement in their campus consumption for both long term and short term. This means the students borrow money from the platform for improving life quality other than for impulse consumption needs.

Our findings have some theoretical contributions. Firstly, we investigated the consumption characteristic of the students who borrow money from online lending platform with a unique empirical data and find out some valuable indicators. Secondly, we analyzed the consumption behavior difference of the students before borrowing and after borrowing, which is not investigated by prior literature. Thirdly, we researched the microloan platform risk management with campus e-card data. Last, we enriched the literature on campus e-card and microloan. Our findings also have practical implications for university, government and corporation. For universities, the conclusion can help them distinguish the students who need financial support, provide financial aids for these students, trace their consumption behaviors after borrowing, and provide a better solution for the problems of campus loan. For managers of microloan companies, they may better supervise the risk with students' daily consumption data.

Acknowledgments. This work was supported by the National Natural Science Foundation of China (grant # 91546104) and the Scientific Research Project of Shanghai Science and Technology Committee (grant #17DZ1101002).

References

1. Agarwal, S., Liu, C.: Determinants of credit card delinquency and bankruptcy: macroeconomic factors. J. Econ. Finance **27**(1), 75–84 (2003)
2. Allen, T.: Optimal (partial) group liability in microfinance lending. J. Dev. Econ. **121**, 201–216 (2016)
3. Cai, S., Lin, X., Xu, D., et al.: Judging online peer-to-peer lending behavior: a comparison of first-time and repeated borrowing requests. Inf. Manag. **53**(7), 857–867 (2016)
4. Canales, R., Greenberg, J.: A matter of (relational) style: loan officer consistency and exchange continuity in microfinance. Manag. Sci. **62**(4), 1202–1224 (2016)
5. Gonzalez, L.: Online Social Lending: The Effect of Cultural, Economic and Legal Frameworks. Economic and Legal Frameworks (2014)
6. Guo B.: Research on the factors affecting the successful borrowing rate of P2P network lending in China—taking the case of Renrendai online lending as an example. In: International Conference on Industrial Economics System and Industrial Security Engineering, pp. 1–5. IEEE (2016)
7. Herzenstein, M., Andrews, R.L.: The democratization of personal consumer loans? Determinants of success in online peer-to-peer lending communities. Boston Univ. Sch. Manag. Res. Pap. **14**(6), 1–36 (2008)
8. Herzenstein, M., Dholakia, U.M., Andrews, R.L.: Strategic herding behavior in peer-to-peer loan auctions. J. Interact. Mark. **25**(1), 27–36 (2011)
9. Nan, J., Weisheng, X.: Student consumption and study behavior analysis based on the data of the campus card system. Microcomput. Appl. **31**(2), 35–38 (2015)
10. Lin, M., Prabhala, N.R., Viswanathan, S.: Judging borrowers by the company they keep: friendship networks and information asymmetry in online peer-to-peer lending. Manag. Sci. **59**(1), 17–35 (2013)
11. Lin, M., Viswanathan, S.: Home bias in online investments: an empirical study of an online crowdfunding market. Manag. Sci. **62**(5), 1393–1414 (2015)
12. Liu, D., Brass, D.J., Lu, Y., et al.: Friendships in online peer-to-peer lending: pipes, prisms, and relational herding. MIS Q. **39**(3), 729–742 (2013)
13. Lu, Y., Gu, B., Ye, Q., et al.: Social influence and defaults in peer-to-peer lending networks (2012)
14. Pötzsch, S., Böhme, R.: The role of soft information in trust building: evidence from online social lending. In: Acquisti, A., Smith, S.W., Sadeghi, A.-R. (eds.) Trust 2010. LNCS, vol. 6101, pp. 381–395. Springer, Heidelberg (2010). https://doi.org/10.1007/978-3-642-13869-0_28
15. Puro, L., Teich, J.E., Wallenius, H., et al.: Bidding strategies for real-life small loan auctions. Decis. Support Syst. **51**(1), 31–41 (2011)
16. Serrano-cinca, C., Gutiérreznieto, B., Lópezpalacios, L., et al.: Determinants of default in P2P lending. PLoS ONE **10**(10), e0139427 (2015)

17. Rui, T.: The Study on Academic Record Prediction and Students' Friendship Network Detection Based on Consumption Data of Campus Card. Central China Normal University, Hubei (2016)
18. Fang, W., Zhuosheng, J.: Constructing student conduct analyzing system based on campus smart card system. Comput. Sci. **35**(10), 212–215 (2008)
19. Jian, X.: The research and analysis of consume behavior and grades relativity on the basis of campus cards' data. Nanchang University, Nanchang (2010)
20. Fu, Y., Jing, M., Cheng, D.: Analysis on data of the Campus IC Card based on Hadoop. Wirel. Internet Technol. **15**, 77–79 (2016)
21. Zvilichovsky, D., Inbar, Y., Barzilay, O.: Playing Both Sides of the Market: Success and Reciprocity on Crowdfunding Platforms. Social Science Electronic Publishing (2015)

Collaboration, Decision Making and Open Innovation

Skill and the Art of Tax Filing Excellence: Comparison of Two Cultures

Craig C. Claybaugh[1(✉)], Peter Haried[2], and Linjia Tang[3]

[1] Missouri University of Science and Technology, Rolla, USA
claybaughc@mst.edu
[2] University of Wisconsin - La Crosse, La Crosse, USA
pharied@uwlax.edu
[3] Zhejiang University of Technology, Hangzhou, China
tlj@zjut.edu.cn

Abstract. Tax filing is a mandatory part a company's tax compliance every year. This research looks at how the competence of the tax preparing professional and the tax forms are perceived by two different Small and Medium sized firm (SME) groups: one from a developed country (US) and one from a developing country (China). The competence of the tax preparing professional and the tax forms perception by the firms impacts a firm's future intention to use the tax service provider again. Drawing upon skill assessment literature and expectation-confirmation theory, this study presents an attitude change model of a firm's tax preparation organization in two countries: SMEs in the US and SMEs in China. In particular, this study focuses on how perceptions of competence in the tax professional influences satisfaction and attitude change related to the tax services received by a firm.

Keywords: Tax filing · Attitude change · Satisfaction

1 Introduction

The tax filing process has come a long ways from the paper based systems used for decades [1]. Now tax filing is a global endeavor and involves a major commitment by the firm to meet compliance regulations [2]. Yet all might not be ideal under the surface as different cultures approach the mandatory filing process differently [3]. Intuit, for example provides a comprehensive tax service for business users that completely utilizes the cloud for its data exchange [4]. The way companies in different countries approach tax filing is not consistent and has been shown to be influenced by national culture and perceptions of institutional effectiveness [5].

As corporations operate they seek to adhere to accounting principles in the jurisdictions in which they operate. Since these can change from year to year it is important to have a trusted tax advisor and tax service you can rely on to provide advise on how the filing process works [6]. As the firm relies on this service they decide when they should continue to use the service or not. Moreover, certain cultures with different perceptions of perfect service should respond to the service encounter differently [7]. The tax form is also at the root of the assessment as it should be designed to be

F. F.-H. Nah and K. Siau (Eds.): HCII 2019, LNCS 11589, pp. 307–315, 2019.
https://doi.org/10.1007/978-3-030-22338-0_25

appealing to the user and not get them to turn off the tax paying processes, even when cultural differences are present [8]. As a result, this study seeks to understand how loyalty and commitment to the tax filing firm is formed. In order to explore the behavioral perspective of attitude and continuance, the variables of filing competence, tax form assessment, and satisfaction are proposed as antecedents of the tax filing behavior.

2 Tax Filing and Expectation-Confirmation Theory (ECT)

Today many tax preparation companies provide tax services for firms to submit their forms and be paid in short order [9]. Given the mandatory nature of tax filing the use of these third parties being given sensitive information should not be overlooked. By requiring this annual activity, the government is in effect encouraging a significant risk taking behavior by firms [10]. However, this is a better alternative than not using a service as the firm can then focus on their own core competencies and competitive advantages. This mandatory task might also not be something that is done poorly or perceived poorly, this might be due to the tax professional's knowledge taking precedent over their ability to provide service [11].

One of the ways to reduce the risk is to ensure that the accountants providing the service are competent and exhibit the right skills to their service recipients [12]. This perception of the service being provided impacts the continuance intention of using the service in the future [13, 14]. This proposed study employs this concept through the lens of the expectation-confirmation theory.

The Expectation-Confirmation Theory (ECT) describes how preconditions to a stimulus are used to measure a pre and post social perception or attitude [15]. The ECT comprises four primary constructs or ideals: expectations, perceived performance, confirmation, and satisfaction [16]. The ECT posits that an individual's expectations and perceived performance affect positive or negative disconfirmation after an event takes place (like tax filing). If a service beats expectations (positive disconfirmation) post-procurement satisfaction will be increased. If a service fails to meet initial expectations (negative disconfirmation), the firm filing the tax forms through the service is likely to be dissatisfied. Individuals who had a positive experience will be likely to repurchase a product or service, while, at the same time, an individual who is dissatisfied would be less likely to buy the service again [17, 18]. IS researchers have applied the theory to explain information technology usage [19, 20] and web consumer satisfaction [21]. In the context of this study the theory will be applied to a mandatory process required by a firm: annual tax filing.

3 Proposed Model of Continuance Intention

Figure 1 below examines tax filing in two different contexts, one in the US and one in China for SMEs. In this study the difference between the two samples is expected to moderate the perceptions of each relationship between the constructs. The factors driving continuance intention are explored in this unique setting.

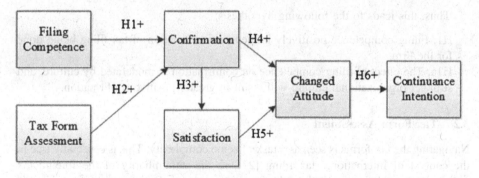

Fig. 1. Proposed model of continuance intention of tax filling

3.1 Service Provider Filing Competence

Service provider tax filing competence is seen as a sense of the firm's perception of the overall service being provided by the tax preparation professionals [22]. The needs of those firms searching for the tax filing service stem from the lacking of professional knowledge on the task filing task. With this sense of competence being formed a firm is then in a position to rely on the service provider to fulfill these needs by properly filling out the required tax forms. When a firm has a high sense of competence then they can feel confident the tax filing process is going to be done correctly and efficiently. Higher filing competence will increase the client firm's confidence on the problem solving and enhance the overall satisfaction about the service [23]. This also reduces their risk assessment of the relationship and increases the chance of the firm continuing to use the service.

Culture plays an important part in this assessment process when the tax filing work is done and needs to be double checked. Culture factors assert their different effects on the professional financial service in several aspects, including the institutional-level cultural difference, organization-level cultural difference and individual-level cultural difference [24]. All of these cultural differences will result in the gap from high satisfactory to merely decent work, or even complaints on the tax filing service. Cultural gap will be particularly prominent between the western developed countries and those eastern developing countries as the economic disparities will further widen cultural differences [25]. In some western developed countries, such as the United States, tax filing services have been provided in a more mature way and the organizational culture has been formed that the customers will appreciate those services provided by the professional service. On the other hand, the situations in some eastern developing countries, such as China, are more likely to get worse assessments over the tax filing service they receive as the organizational culture has not yet yielded a comprehensive evaluation process [26]. In this sense the assessment of the service being provided by a firm in a developed country is seen as being less of an influence relative to a developing country.

Thus, this leads to the following hypothesis:

H1: Filing competence positively influences confirmation of tax filing being done for the firm.
H1a. The effect of filing competence on confirmation is moderated by culture, and stronger organizational culture will result in greater positive confirmation.

3.2 Tax Form Assessment

Navigating the tax forms is seen as a task of some complexity. This is especially true in the context of international tax filing [27], as the unfamiliarity of the foreign tax policies and regulations raise the risk of making mistakes. One major difference in this task is the mandatory nature of annual tax filing and the need to be in compliance. To conclude, tax filing work may differ in various aspects from nation to nation, and the tax form assessments provide ways to investigate if the tax filing work was completed correctly as well as efficiently [28]. It is expected that professional service providers are more likely to get better feedbacks from their customers.

It is also suggested that culture may influence the outcome of the tax form assessment. Enterprise customers in the context of stronger organizational cultures will have a much lower burden of tax filing considering the expected difference by location and purpose [29]. On the other hand, companies in stronger institutional culture contexts who receive competent tax professionals working on the forms will get a better experience from the assessment and assurance that the forms have been completed correctly. Thus, this leads to the following hypothesis:

H2: A positive assessment of the tax forms positively influences confirmation of tax filing being done for the firm.
H2a. The effect of tax form assessment on confirmation is moderated by culture, and stronger organizational culture will result in greater positive tax form assessment.

3.3 Confirmation of Service Provided

Confirmation is defined as the firm's awareness of the comparison between the expectations of the tax service used and the perceived tax filing outcomes [30]. The difference between the firm's preliminary expectations of the tax filing service and the outcome of the tax filing service is captured in the confirmation construct. It can also be viewed as a deviation from the initial anticipations of the event being done [15]. It is expected that this deviation will get larger when the customer's anticipation is low while the service satisfactory is high, and get smaller when the anticipation is high while the satisfactory is low. The outcome will be getting more complicated when these two variables change in the similar direction.

Differences in organizational and national culture are expected to result a higher confirmation on the tax filing being done correctly. In this sense a firm in a developed country should recognize the tax service being completed in compliance with local standards and receive a better experience on the service confirmation [31]. However, it might be possible for a corporation in a developing country finds the event to be done perfectly whereas they might not have high confirmation on the service being provided. Thus, this leads to the following hypothesis:

H3: Confirmation of service provided positively influences satisfaction of the tax filing service.

H3a: The effect of confirmation of service on satisfaction is moderated by culture, and stronger Organizational culture will result in greater positive service confirmation.

Confirming the expectations of the tax service provided proposes that firms are able to understand the potential benefits of filing taxes successfully. This might include getting a bigger refund or finding out about deductions that the firm was not aware of in the past. This validation of the confirming belief would increase attitude change towards the service performed. Firms who strongly confirmed the tax filing outcome assessment would have a more positive post-attitude than a pre-attitude assessment of the tax filing service [32]. Alternatively, those firms who did not experience what they expected would be likely to have a negative attitude towards the tax filing service, and this performance evaluation will have a more negative impact on the company's attitude towards tax filing in the future and further affect the change of its financial management decision-making behavior.

This sense of the service being provided is expected to differ under different cultural contexts. In China where the culture is more collectivist [33] the assessment of confirmation is seen as smaller due to the culture when high expectations on the tax filing service already received. While firms in the United States, where the culture values the strength of the individual, this gap is seen to be much wider. Thus, this leads to the following hypothesis:

H4: Confirmation of service provided positively influences changed attitude of the tax filing service.

H4a: The effect of confirmation of service on changed attitude is moderated by culture, and stronger individual culture will result in greater positive service confirmation.

3.4 Satisfaction with Service Provided

Satisfaction is defined as an individual's affective feelings about the tax service achieved through the tax filing process [19]. In the context of IT usage and service encounters multiple studies have found a significant link between the association of satisfaction and attitude towards service provisioning [34]. Thus, a firm's high satisfaction of a tax filing service would result in increased feelings toward that service. Some research has also argued that the evaluation against the service expectation will increase the positive attitude towards the service provider via the satisfaction of the service. In other words, completing tax filing in a high quality will not directly increase the management attitude unless this fulfillment comes to the satisfaction on the firms performance in the past. Nonetheless, satisfaction with the tax filing service plays a core role in the management attitude towards the service and also its provider.

Again, these perceptions of service satisfaction are expected to differ by culture [35]. First, organizational culture affects the evaluation on the job of tax filing being done correctly by a tax service provider. Stronger organizational culture as is the more common in developed countries will make the evaluation process under a more formal way and yield a more positive attitude towards the service provider. Besides, we should take the manager's own decision process into consideration as well because in many cases the manager's individual cultural difference will impact their attitude on similar tax service providers jobs. Thus, this leads to the following hypothesis:

H5: Satisfaction of the service provided positively influences changed attitude toward the tax filing service.

H5a: The effect of satisfaction of service on changed attitude is moderated by culture, and stronger organizational and individual culture will result in greater positive changed attitude.

3.5　Attitude Change and Continuance Intention

Changed attitude refers to individual firm's altered (increased or decreased) assessment from the experience of the tax filing service being completed [36]. The purpose of the tax filing process is to ensure the company is in compliance with current tax practices and does not violate any requirements in the jurisdictions they operate. These individual firms engaging the tax filing service with the third party would have a positive attitude on use when this is done flawlessly. On the other hand, continuance intention refers to the willingness to continue to use the previous tax filing service provider. Attitude change will determine the continuance intention in two different ways, including the positive performance of past tax service received, as well as the professional and stability of future tax service offerings [37]. This positive appraisal of the tax service provider will induce the firm to continue to use the service in the future.

Attitude change by a firm is not automatically formed [38], nor is the attitude change guaranteed to lead to a behavior modification by a firm [39]. Different cultures are expected to have significant influence on their attitude towards the continuance of the tax service provider. Considering in the stronger organizational cultural context, attitude change will be linked with the future selection of the tax service provider as the management decision is based on an objective assessment of the company's past tax management performance. Lower organizational culture will involve more complex factors into the decision process and the former tax provider would be substituted by a new tax provider even if its previous work turned out to be satisfying. In addition, the individual culture will also influence the final decision on whether to continue to use the previous tax service or not, and managers who hold stronger individual cultures tend to increase the probability of the continuance intention. Thus, this leads to the following hypothesis:

H6: Changed attitude toward the tax filing service positively influences intention to continue to use the tax service.

H6a: The effect of changed attitude on continuance intention is moderated by culture, and stronger organizational and individual culture will result in greater positive continuance intention.

4 Method (Proposed)

A survey will be used to evaluate tax filing perceptions of firms located in two countries; China and the United States. The proposed methodology is similar to other studies looking at national culture and mandatory tasks [8, 40]. The test of the proposed relationships would be done through a transversal, cross cultural quantitative study. An equal number of questionnaires would be distributed to both a US and a Chinese audience, where the focus would be on SME institutions. Qualified subjects would be the primary tax filer for both the US and Chinese SMEs. The questions will be focused on the last year of tax collection and filing for revenue earned in the last year.

Established scales for the constructs would be found in existing literature and translated into the native language where the survey will be administered. The model would be tested using SEM as the data analysis choice. To test the impact of national culture a multi-group analysis will be conducted to identify the moderating effect of national culture in this setting. Data will be analyzed using PLS-SEM as this method allows for group nesting of comparisons and for formative and reflective indicators.

5 Expected Contribution and Discussion

This study has the potential to validate how two different cultures view tax filing and the forms that make up the process in two countries. It is possible that no discernable differences will be detected in the study. In this sense the samples might find the mandatory process to both be counter intuitive. Understanding how businesses approach the problem of tax filing and antecedents of their attitude reinforcement will assist government agencies with making changes in the future [41].

A future study might look at how to design a tax form to make it more appealing. Moreover, a form might be designed to be the same for both counties and look at a common set of accounting principles. Another study might also look at how willing either country might be to share data with outside third parties. Popular press has a number of stories of data breaches and how they affect a company's operation [14].

References

1. Chen, J.V., Jubilado, R.J.M., Capistrano, E.P.S., Yen, D.C.: Factors affecting online tax filing–an application of the IS Success Model and trust theory. Comput. Hum. Behav. **43**, 251–262 (2015)
2. Nisha, N., Iqbal, M., Rifat, A.: Innovativeness, privacy, and trust as determinants of electronic tax filing: an empirical investigation and new research agenda. In: Optimizing Current Practices in E-Services and Mobile Applications, pp. 181–202. IGI Global (2018)
3. Cummings, R.G., Martinez-Vazquez, J., McKee, M.: Cross cultural comparisons of tax compliance behavior (No. paper0103). International Center for Public Policy, Andrew Young School of Policy Studies, Georgia State University (2001)
4. Anders, S.B., Fischer, C.M.: Top choices in tax software: 2015 annual survey of New York State practitioners. CPA J. **85**(11), 22 (2015)

5. Strielkowski, W., Čábelková, I.: Religion, culture, and tax evasion: evidence from the Czech Republic. Religions **6**(2), 657–669 (2015)
6. Wang, Y., Butterfield, S., Campbell, M.: Effects of earnings management, compensation, insider equity holding on tax structure. Int. Manag. Rev. **13**(2), 5–15 (2017)
7. Van Rooij, B.: Weak enforcement, strong deterrence: dialogues with Chinese lawyers about tax evasion and compliance. Law Soc. Inq. **41**(2), 288–310 (2016)
8. Van Rooij, B., Fine, A., Zhang, Y., Wu, Y.: Comparative compliance: digital piracy, deterrence, social norms, and duty in China and the United States. Law Policy **39**(1), 73–93 (2017)
9. Albring, S., Robinson, D., Robinson, M.: Audit committee financial expertise, corporate governance, and the voluntary switch from auditor-provided to non-auditor-provided tax services. Adv. Acc. **30**(1), 81–94 (2014)
10. Guo, J.T., Harrison, S.G.: Tax policy and stability in a model with sector-specific externalities. Rev. Econ. Dyn. **4**(1), 75–89 (2001)
11. Claybaugh, C.C., Haseman, W.D.: Understanding professional connections in LINKEDIN—a question of trust. J. Comput. Inf. Syst. **54**(1), 94–105 (2013)
12. Jimenez, P., Iyer, G.S.: Tax compliance in a social setting: the influence of social norms, trust in government, and perceived fairness on taxpayer compliance. Adv. Acc. **34**, 17–26 (2016)
13. Hung, S.Y., Chang, C.M., Yu, T.J.: Determinants of user acceptance of the e-Government services: the case of online tax filing and payment system. Gov. Inf. Q. **23**(1), 97–122 (2006)
14. Claybaugh, C.C., Chen, L., Haried, P., Zhou, D.: Risk and information disclosure in Google Drive sharing of tax data. In: Nah, F.F.-H., Xiao, B.S. (eds.) HCIBGO 2018. LNCS, vol. 10923, pp. 42–50. Springer, Cham (2018). https://doi.org/10.1007/978-3-319-91716-0_4
15. Bhattacherjee, A., Premkumar, G.: Understanding changes in belief and attitude toward information technology usage: a theoretical model and longitudinal test. MIS Q. 229–254 (2004)
16. Kwak, D.H., Srite, M., Hightower, R., Haseman, W.D.: How team cohesion leads to attitude change in the context of ERP learning. In: International Conference on Information Systems, Milan (2013)
17. Oliver, R.L.: A cognitive model for the antecedents and consequences of satisfaction. J. Mark. Res. **17**(4), 460–469 (1980)
18. Spreng, R.A., MacKenzie, S.B., Olshavsky, R.W.: A reexamination of the determinants of consumer satisfaction. J. Mark. **60**, 15–32 (1996)
19. Bhattacherjee, A.: Understanding information systems continuance: an expectation-confirmation model. MIS Q. **25**(3), 351–370 (2001)
20. Venkatesh, V., Goyal, S.: Expectation disconfirmation and technology adoption: polynomial modeling and response surface analysis. MIS Q. **34**(2), 281–303 (2010)
21. McKinney, V., Yoon, K., Zahedi, F.M.: The measurement of web-customer satisfaction: an expectation and disconfirmation approach. Inf. Syst. Res. **13**(3), 296–315 (2002)
22. Carter, L., Christian Shaupp, L., Hobbs, J., Campbell, R.: The role of security and trust in the adoption of online tax filing. Transform. Gov.: People Process Policy **5**(4), 303–318 (2011)
23. Carter, L., McFadden-Wade, G., Wells, J.T.: Exploring the impact of organizational citizenship behavior on perceptions of e-filing success. Int. J. Public Adm. Digit. Age (IJPADA) **3**(1), 43–52 (2016)
24. Haried, P.J., Claybaugh, C.C.: Evaluating information systems offshore project success: can success and failure coexist? J. Global Inf. Technol. Manag. **20**(1), 8–27 (2017)
25. Morgeson III, F.V., Sharma, P.N., Hult, G.T.M.: Cross-national differences in consumer satisfaction: mobile services in emerging and developed markets. J. Int. Mark. **23**(2), 1–24 (2015)

26. Gupta, G., Zaidi, S., Udo, G., Bagchi, K.: The effect of espoused culture on acceptance of online tax filing services in an emerging economy. Adv. Bus. Res. **6**(1), 14–31 (2015)
27. Kerzner, D.S., Chodikoff, D.W.: International Tax Evasion in the Global Information Age. Springer, Cham (2016). https://doi.org/10.1007/978-3-319-40421-9
28. Claybaugh, C.: To believe or not to believe a call to action: an empirical investigation of source credibility. In: Nah, F.F.-H., Tan, C.-H. (eds.) HCIB 2015. LNCS, vol. 9191, pp. 53–63. Springer, Cham (2015). https://doi.org/10.1007/978-3-319-20895-4_6
29. Claybaugh, C.C., Haried, P., Chen, Y., Chen, L.: ERP vendor satisfaction: from communication and IT capability perspectives. J. Comput. Inf. Syst. 1–12 (2019)
30. Claybaugh, C.C.: Flow and the art of ERP education. In: Nah, F.F.-H.F.-H., Tan, C.-H. (eds.) HCIBGO 2016. LNCS, vol. 9752, pp. 39–46. Springer, Cham (2016). https://doi.org/10.1007/978-3-319-39399-5_4
31. Lee, K.C., Kirlidog, M., Lee, S., Lim, G.G.: User evaluations of tax filing web sites: a comparative study of South Korea and Turkey. Online Inf. Rev. **32**(6), 842–859 (2008)
32. Nambisan, S., Agarwal, R., Tanniru, M.: Organizational mechanisms for enhancing user innovation in information technology. MIS Q. 365–395 (1999)
33. Newell, S.J., Wu, B., Leingpibul, D., Jiang, Y.: The importance of corporate and salesperson expertise and trust in building loyal business-to-business relationships in China. J. Pers. Selling Sales Manag. **36**(2), 160–173 (2016)
34. Savitri, E.: The effect of taxpayer awareness, tax socialization, tax penalties, compliance cost at taxpayer compliance with service quality as mediating variable. Proc.-Soc. Behav. Sci. **219**, 682–687 (2016)
35. Laroche, M., Ueltschy, L.C., Abe, S., Cleveland, M., Yannopoulos, P.P.: Service quality perceptions and customer satisfaction: evaluating the role of culture. J. Int. Mark. **12**(3), 58–85 (2004)
36. Pothukuchi, V., Damanpour, F., Choi, J., Chen, C.C., Park, S.H.: National and organizational culture differences and international joint venture performance. J. Int. Bus. Stud. **33**(2), 243–265 (2002)
37. Claybaugh, C.C., Srite, M.: Factors contributing to the information technology vendor-client relationship. J. Inf. Technol. Theory Appl. (JITTA) **10**(2), 3 (2009)
38. Abdul Rashid, Z., Sambasivan, M., Abdul Rahman, A.: The influence of organizational culture on attitudes toward organizational change. Leadersh. Organ. Dev. J. **25**(2), 161–179 (2004)
39. Jung, L.: A study on the relationship with attitude and satisfaction of the continuance intention in Fintech. Int. Inf. Inst. (Tokyo) Inf. **20**(8), 5817–5824 (2017)
40. Kassim, N., Asiah Abdullah, N.: The effect of perceived service quality dimensions on customer satisfaction, trust, and loyalty in e-commerce settings: a cross cultural analysis. Asia Pac. J. Mark. Logist. **22**(3), 351–371 (2010)
41. Peña-García, N., Gil-Saura, I., Rodríguez-Orejuela, A.: E-loyalty formation: a cross-cultural comparison of Spain and Colombia. J. Electron. Commer. Res. **19**(4), 336–356 (2018)

Humanoid Robots as Interviewers
for Automated Credibility Assessment

Aaron C. Elkins[(⊠)], Amit Gupte[(⊠)], and Lance Cameron[(⊠)]

San Diego State University Artificial Intelligence Lab,
San Diego State University, 5500 Campanile Dr, San Diego, CA 92182, USA
{aelkins,agupte,lcameron}@sdsu.edu

Abstract. Humans are poor at detecting deception under the best conditions. The need for having a decision support system that can be a baseline for data-driven decision making is obvious. Such a system is not biased like humans are, and these often subconscious human biases can impair people's judgment. A system for helping people at border security (CBP) is the AVATAR. The AVATAR, an Embodied Conversational agent (ECA), is implemented as a self-service kiosk. Our research uses this AVATAR as the baseline and we plan to augment the automated credibility assessment task that the AVATAR performs using a Humanoid robot. We will be taking advantage of humanoid robots' capability of realistic dialogue and nonverbal gesturing. We are also capturing data from various sensors like microphones, cameras and an eye tracker that will help in model building and testing for the task of deception detection. We plan to carry out an experiment where we compare the results of an interview with the AVATAR and an interview with a humanoid robot. Such a comparative analysis has never been done before, hence we are very eager to conduct such a social experiment.

This research paper deals with the design and implementation plan for such an experiment. We also want to highlight what the considerations are while designing such a social experiment. It will help us understand how people perceive robot agent interactions in contrast to the more traditional ECA agents on screen. For example, does the physical presence of a robot encourage greater perceptions of likability, expertise, or dominance? Moreover, this research will address the question on which interaction model (ECA or robot) elicits the most diagnostic cues to detecting deception. This study may also prove very useful to researchers and organizations that want to use robots in increasing social roles and need to understand its societal and personal implications.

Keywords: Human-Robot interaction · Credibility assessment ·
Social experiment with robots · AI

1 Introduction

Borders and airports are becoming increasingly congested as more people are traveling. In this environment, border guards must make rapid decisions with myriad distractions, pressures, and limited vigilance. Credibility assessment which is a vital task to secure borders and other points of entry of the country is generally carried out manually by a

© Springer Nature Switzerland AG 2019
F. F.-H. Nah and K. Siau (Eds.): HCII 2019, LNCS 11589, pp. 316–325, 2019.
https://doi.org/10.1007/978-3-030-22338-0_26

border security/law enforcement officer. But this task is hindered by obvious human bias. A technology-based solution to support credibility assessment has been investigated leading to the AVATAR [7], an embodied conversational agent (ECA) with integrated sensors that conducts automated credibility assessments on travelers. The AVATAR is implemented as a self-service kiosk with an integrated screen where the ECA is represented as a law enforcement officer, interviews passengers while integrated sensors measure nonverbal/verbal and physiological behaviors of the interviewees. An important aspect of the AVATAR is its ECA's human/intelligent appearance and demeanor to interviewees. Great attention to detail has been placed on the ECA's demeanor, voice/inflection, clothes, language, and appearance and their effect on the perceptions and behaviors of interviewees.

With the improvements to Artificial Intelligence (AI) for predictive modeling and the accessibility of programmable robots, this next logical step for this research in credibility assessment is to make the interaction more human and intimate.

The transition for humans seeing robots in science fiction films and having robots working and assisting them in the day to day tasks has been swift. George Devol, an American inventor from Kentucky designed the first industrial robot: Unimate in the 1950s. But we have come a long way since then. Mindful of the ethics [17] involved with AI and governed by Asimov's Laws of robotics, companies are now developing cutting edge robots that can do various tasks not just faster but better than humans. Robots are being made that look like humans. Softbank Robotics is one such company whose robots we are using in our research whose programmable robots are pictured below in Fig. 1.

Fig. 1. Programmable humanoid robots (Source: SoftBank Robotics)

These humanoid robots are capable of realistic dialogue and nonverbal gesturing. Most of the initial applications for these robots are confined to tasks in customer service, greeting visitors and providing product and service descriptions. Various industrial sectors like automobile, aerospace, construction, and defense have adopted robots to make life easier for humans around them. In contrast, this research aims to investigate richer interactions that rely on interpersonal communication and credibility assessment theories to study the emerging area of human-robotic interaction.

The study will have participants come and interview with both AVATAR and a programmable humanoid robot. We plan to use the robot augmented with additional behavioral and physiological sensors that are essential to detect deception cues on it. These sensors include microphone, video and eye tracker. The robot will iterate through around 14 questions few of which are to establish a baseline for the deception model. The robot exhibits various interactive cues like blinking of eyes, hand gestures to intuitively convey the question.

2 Literature Survey

As automation becomes increasingly prevalent in the service and manufacturing industries additional applications such as automated law enforcement and border control technologies are being explored. Within the many possible applications of automation to law enforcement, automated interviewing and credibility assessment using a humanoid robot interviewer are the focus of this study and related literature.

2.1 The Need for Better Credibility Assessment in Law Enforcement

In the law enforcement realm, determining if someone is telling the truth is a critical step in any investigative effort. Whether they are trying to cross a border or give a witness statement, what a person says and the way their words are interpreted are crucial to the next investigative steps. Despite our belief in our ability to detect deception, novice human interviewers are only able to correctly determine if an interviewee is deceiving 54% of the time, correctly detecting deception 47% of the time and detecting truths as nondeceptive 61% of the time [2]. The higher than chance accuracy for truth detection reflects an intrinsic truth bias where novice interviewers classify most statements as true. Conversely, experts and law enforcement often reverse their accuracies and demonstrate a lie bias, assuming most statements are deceptive. Although some law enforcement personnel receive training in deception detection, a study in 2004 by Garrido, Masip, and Herrero [13] found law enforcement officers assessment of credibility to result in the same near-chance levels.

The polygraph is the most well-known method for determining veracity in the law enforcement setting. To administer a basic polygraph test requires the participant to physically attach sensors in several parts of their body to measure cardiovascular activity, respiratory activity, and electrodermal activity [16]. Attaching these sensors to a participant is an invasive and time-consuming process that can itself make a non-deceiver uncomfortable and elicit responses that can influence polygraph measurements [19]. Aside from being an invasive and time-consuming process, modern scientific opinion on the polygraph is highly polarized. None of the dominant methodologies for analyzing polygraph sensor data have achieved an acceptable degree of empirical support when investigating crimes in progress [16].

2.2   AVATAR for Credibility Assessment

In addition to only detecting deception at chance levels, human interviewers introduce individual variability to each interview they give. A human interviewer has their own personal interview style in addition to fluctuations in their disposition, both of which can influence how an interviewee answers questions and behaves [4]. To eliminate interviewer variance [7], Nunamaker et al. proposed the creation of an Embodied Conversational Agent (ECA) to run on a kiosk that would conduct interviews while collecting sensor data about the interviewees. Figure 2 illustrates the current prototype of the AVATAR system used. This original ECA kiosk design was later field tested by Elkins, Derrick, and Gariup in 2012 [10]. The AVATAR can administer interviews consistently removing the behavioral variance caused by a human interviewer by asking interview questions in a systematic and controlled way while measuring behavioral and physiological reactions.

Fig. 2. AVATAR kiosk for automated creditability assessment

In the 2012 experiment, human participants passed through a mock visa checkpoint by conducting an interview with the AVATAR. Some participants holding fake visas were instructed to lie during the interview. Using a microphone and eye-tracking sensor the AVATAR obtained a 94% overall detection accuracy rate for identifying imposters. 100% of imposters were correctly categorized, with only two false positives [10].

According to Interpersonal Deception Theory, first proposed by Buller and Burgoon in 1996, deception is a strategic interaction between sender and receiver. During a deception, a deceiver must manage additional cognitive demands which result in leakage of deception cues [3]. As summarized by Elkins et al., deceivers speak with a greater and more varied vocal pitch, shorter durations, less fluency, and with greater response latencies [4]. Deceivers also have ocular cues that can indicate arousal from deception and plausibility management. Different blink duration, blink frequency, pupil dilation, and eye-gaze fixation all can be indicative of an attempt at deceit [4]. The camera, eye tracker, and microphone sensor data from the AVATAR are fused and reviewed by a classification engine which benefits from not relying on a single indicator of deception [9].

The AVATAR kiosk can administer consistent interviews and make quick, accurate decisions on the veracity of responses to a set of predefined questions. The use of non-invasive sensors like the microphone and eye tracker camera offers a way to collect physiological data from the interview participants without introducing variation due to discomfort from physical sensors.

3   Study Objectives

This research will help us understand how people perceive robot agent interactions in contrast to the more traditional ECA agents confined to a screen. Also, certain perception-based changes that a person might have during this interaction with the robot are metrics we would like to consider.

3.1   The Following List Outlines the Objectives

- Find out which interaction (ECA or humanoid robot) elicits the most diagnostic behavioral cues for detecting deception
- Study if does the physical presence of a robot affect perceptions of interaction and speaking partner such as likability, expertise, or dominance
- Comparison of deception detection accuracy results of AVATAR vs Robot Interview
- Understand the societal and personal implications of human-robotic interactions
- Determine how to surreptitiously incorporate and calibrate multiple behavioral sensors (e.g., eye tracker) into a humanoid robot form factor and interview environment.

4   Conceptual Background of Research

An important aspect of the AVATAR is the use of an ECA represented by a face on the kiosk screen that asks interview questions. Having a face that interviewees speak to creates a more interactive social context for the deception to take place with access to visual, auditory, verbal, and environmental channels. According to Buller and Burgoon, a less interactive social context for the interaction limits the cues that would be produced [3]. This paper proposes a comparison between the current animated face ECA and a physically present humanoid robot as the interviewer to see how a humanoid robot changes the presence and robustness of deception cues elicited by the interviewee.

There is evidence people view humanoid robots in positions of authority as less authoritative and credible. A study by Edwards, Edwards, and Omilion-Hodges conducted simulated medical interviews with a human physician and a robot physician using a Softbank supplied Nao robot. Survey results after the interviews reported the human physician scored higher on positive affect, perceived credibility, and social presence [8].

Wood et al. found that children interviewed by humanoid robots interacted very similarly with a robot interviewer as with a human interviewer. There were however differences in the duration of robot interviews, the eye gaze patterns towards robot interviewers, and the response time of robot interviewers [5]. There is concern that if the alternative eye gaze behavior applies broadly to how people look at humanoid robots, our humanoid robot may induce eye behavior that confounds the AVATAR classification engine.

Alternatively, the robots humanoid appearance could produce stronger responses from interview participants due to its humanoid appearance. Latikka, Turja, and Oksanen found that when testing different robot types in an elderly care facility to assist human workers, humanoid robots found faster acceptance by human staff and higher reported self-efficacy [15]. Self-efficacy in this scenario is the beliefs a worker has about their ability to use robots effectively. The fact the humanoid robot performed better than non-humanoid robots in this measure suggests a familiarity with humanoid robots that could translate into a more interactive social context for our deception experiment. In this richer context, more open communication channels could lead to more visible deception cues [3].

5   Experimental Design

The most challenging aspect of conducting research into nonverbal deception detection regardless of the interviewer is establishing internal validity. Obtaining ground truth which is clear and unambiguous behavioral examples of deception is challenging. Generally, credibility assessment research focuses on three experiment profiles in increasing ecological validity at the expense of experimental control and production of clear unambiguous lie examples: Deceptive Interviews, Mock Crime, and Field Experiments.

5.1   Deceptive Interviews

In this paradigm (example studies: [11, 12]), participants are recruited to participate in a study ostensibly on job interviewing strategies or student intelligence for example. When the participants arrive in the lab they are instructed to complete an interview with their primary task being to be perceived as credible as possible by the interviewer (human, AVATAR, or humanoid robot). Participants are incentivized monetarily to be successful and often induced with an experimental prime, such as tying their performance to their identity or self-efficacy.

During the interview, participants are asked a wide variety of question types such as: biographical, ethical dilemmas, and short or long form answers. During the interview, participants are randomly instructed to lie or tell the truth to the questions via a teleprompter that is obscured from the interviewer. After sets of questions, the interviewee reports how credible they were in their answers to the questions, and their overall confidence level in their performance. After completing the interview, participants complete a post-survey where they report their perceptions, beliefs, and feelings during the interview.

The strength of this experimental design is that there is a high level of control and many clear truthful and deceptive behavior examples are generated. Additionally, with interviewees reporting how credible they were, deception is treated as a continuous variable of truth rather than binary true or lie. There is a difference between a white lite and a complete fabrication. Also, the ability to create a diverse pool of question responses also improves the models built to classify deceptive behavior.

The primary weakness of this design is that participants feel no jeopardy or concern making the measured behaviors partially incongruent to a high-stakes security environment. How detrimental this weakness is to the research is often overstated as a concern only specifically activates arousal and physiological cues, while there are many other categories of cues expected by liars such as cognitive load, memory, emotion, behavioral control, and communication strategies.

5.2   Mock Crime

In contrast to the previous experiment design, the mock crime experiment increases ecological validity and perceived participant jeopardy by instructing participants to commit a crime and subsequently completing an investigative interview (example studies: [6, 7, 18]). There are many scenarios that have been evaluated including: impostership where participants take on a fake identity, smuggling drugs or a bomb, self-selecting to cheat on an exam, or stealing a valuable object.

After committing the crime, participants then complete a security interview. For example, in a bomb smuggling study, participants would attempt to conceal a bomb hidden in their bag and complete a border security interview credibly, which would inquire about their travel plans, destination, identity, contents of their bag, and other customs-related questions.

The primary strength of this design is its relevance to how automated credibility systems would be used. Moreover, there is no universal cue to all lies. To develop a reliable system for deception detection, the context, questions, and situation must be modeled from data uniquely. A deception detection model based on border security interviews would not necessarily function if applied to a criminal investigation or a fraud interview.

The major downside to this approach is the reduced experimental control and collection of much fewer examples of deceptive behavior. Often, 80% of the questions asked are irrelevant questions and only 20% of the asked questions require the participant to lie (e.g., Are you carrying a prohibited object?). Despite its limitations, this experimental design is the most common in the field.

5.3 Field Experiment

After establishing the validity of the technology in the lab, the next step is to take it to the field such as airports, border crossings, and law enforcement facilities. In these locations, the ecological validity is highest, and participants can be recruited from the local population (e.g., passengers disembarking from international flights). In this scenario, participants can be given instructions (experimental manipulation) or simply asked to complete an interview naturally.

This type of study is typical in the later stages of the research and offers valuable insight into how technology is perceived by actual future users of the technology. The major downside of this type of study is the reduced experimental control, reliable lie examples or ground truth can be impossible to collect without experimental manipulation.

6 Discussion

For this research, we will be starting with a more controlled scenario such as a deceptive interview. This will allow for a more direct comparison between deceptive interviews conducted by AVATAR and its humanoid robot counterpart.

The implications of this research depend on if the humanoid robot interviewer is found to be more effective, less effective, or not significantly different at eliciting deception cues than the AVATAR. The various implications of each scenario are separated and discussed below.

6.1 Scenario: Humanoid Robot Outperforms AVATAR

In the case that the humanoid robot performs better at eliciting deception cues from interviewees, than very serious consideration to transitioning to humanoid robot interviews must be considered. This will introduce a new set of research questions necessary to deploying a humanoid robot into the field, such as sensor placement, power requirements, interview positioning (e.g., seated or standing), just to name a few.

In the job market there is a need to determine the veracity of applicants for certain high-stakes positions, but in recent years controversy has surrounded and limited the use of the most popular credibility assessment for job screening – the polygraph [14]. If a robot equipped with the AVATAR sensor suite could perform quick, noninvasive, and reliable job screening then employers could hire with more confidence in their candidates.

The use of the polygraph for credibility assessment in general law enforcement has come under similar scrutiny to job screening. According to Ben-Shakhar, Bar-Hillel, and Lieblich, many of the studies supporting the effectiveness of the polygraph were found to have several types of methodological contamination [1]. A robot equipped with AVATAR sensors could administer interviews for determining veracity and possibly have those determinations submitted as evidence in the courtroom someday.

Future research on the successful pairing of the AVATAR with humanoid robots could incorporate different voice and appearances. Interpersonal Deception Theory specifies that the sender's (deceiver) communications are affected by the communications of the receiver robot). Changes to the robot's demeanor or costuming the robot in a uniform could communicate perceived authority and possibly elicit stronger deception cues from the deceiver.

6.2   Scenario: Robot Under Performs Against AVATAR

If the robot performs worse than the AVATAR then analysis of the participant's perceptions toward the robot and AVATAR interviewers will be critical. Survey questions given to study participants after their interview should indicate what potential moderators or mediators affected the elicitation of cues to deception. Further studies on different robot heights, voices, dispositions, and other variations in the interview should still be conducted.

Regardless of how well a humanoid robot interviewer performs in the task of credibility assessment this research is only the beginning of the investigation into human-robotics interaction and socialization as humanoid robots continue to become more commonplace in society as social actors and increase in their AI and emotional intelligence.

References

1. Ben-Shakhar, G., et al.: Trial by polygraph: scientific and juridical issues in lie detection. Behav. Sci. Law 4(4), 459–479 (1986)
2. Bond Jr., C.F., DePaulo, B.M.: Accuracy of deception judgments. Pers. Soc. Psychol. Rev. 10(3), 214–234 (2006)
3. Buller, D.B., Burgoon, J.K.: Interpersonal deception theory. Commun. Theory 6, 203–242 (1996)
4. Burgoon, J., et al.: Unobtrusive Deception Detection. In: Oxford Handbook of Affective Computing, pp. 503–515 (2014)
5. Dautenhahn, K., et al.: Robot-mediated interviews - how effective is a humanoid robot as a tool for interviewing young children? PLoS One 8(3), e59448 (2013)
6. Derrick, D.C., et al.: Border security credibility assessments via heterogeneous sensor fusion. IEEE Intell. Syst. 25, 41–49 (2010)
7. Derrick, D.C., et al.: Embodied conversational agent-based kiosk for automated interviewing. J. Manag. Inf. Syst. 28(1), 17–48 (2011)

8. Edwards, A., et al.: How do patients in a medical interview perceive a robot versus human physician? In: Presented at the Proceedings of the Companion of the 2017 ACM/IEEE International Conference on Human-Robot Interaction (2017)
9. Elkins, A.C., et al.: Predicting users' perceived trust in Embodied Conversational Agents using vocal dynamics. In: Proceedings of the Annual Hawaii International Conference on System Sciences, pp. 579–588 (2012)
10. Elkins, A.C., et al.: The voice and eye gaze behavior of an imposter: automated interviewing and detection for rapid screening at the border, pp. 49–54 (2012)
11. Elkins, A.C.: Vocalic markers of deception and cognitive dissonance for automated emotion detection systems. University of Arizona (2011)
12. Elkins, A.C., Stone, J.: The effect of cognitive dissonance on argument language and vocalics. In: Forty-Fourth Annual Hawaii International Conference on System Sciences, Koloa, Kauai, Hawaii (2011)
13. Garrido, E., et al.: Police officers' credibility judgments: Accuracy and estimated ability. Int. J. Psychol. **39**(4), 254–275 (2004)
14. Horvath, F.: Job screening. Society **22**(6), 43–46 (1985)
15. Latikka, R., et al.: Self-efficacy and acceptance of robots. Comput. Hum. Behav. **93**, 157–163 (2019)
16. Synnott, J., et al.: A review of the polygraph: history, methodology and current status. Crime Psychol. Rev. **1**(1), 59–83 (2015)
17. Taddeo, M., Floridi, L.: How AI can be a force for good. Science **361**(6404), 751LP–752LP (2018)
18. Twyman, N.W., et al.: A rigidity detection system for automated credibility assessment. J. Manag. Inf. Syst. **31**(1), 173–202 (2014)
19. Yankee, W.: An investigation of sphygmomanometer discomfort thresholds in polygraph examinations. Police **9**(6), 12 (1965)

ICT Use as Mediator Between Job Demands and Work-Life Balance Satisfaction

Catherine Hellemans[(✉)], Pierre Flandrin, and Cécile van de Leemput

Université Libre de Bruxelles (ULB), 1050 Brussels, Belgium
{catherine.hellemans,pierre.flandrin,
cecile.van.de.leemput}@ulb.ac.be

Abstract. The use of mobile technologies potentially alters the boundaries between professional and private spheres. Some studies report the negative overflow of work on private life, but also the possibility of a better work-life balance (WLB). As the results of previous studies are not homogenous, aiming some authors to speak about "double-edge sword" for ICT use for professional purpose after hours, workers' attitudes were considered as mediator variables. The main hypothesis was that ICT use after hours and segmentation preference are sequential mediators in the relation between job demands and WLB satisfaction. The on-line survey has been completed by 142 workers from various sectors. The results showed that job demands, ICT use and segmentation preference explained WLB satisfaction for 30% of the variance. In more details, high job demands contributed to more ICT use for professional purposes after hours, which contributed to weak segmentation preference, this weak segmentation preference increasing WLB satisfaction. In other words, integration preference, explained itself by ICT use after hours, contributed to WLB satisfaction. The results, highlighting the determinant role of boundary management attitudes, are an innovative contribution in the HCI and WLB research: it allows to better understand the "double-edged sword" phenomena by supplying some first conditions under which ICT use turns negative issues into positive ones.

Keywords: Mobile technology · Boundary management · Quality of life

1 Introduction

We knew that job demands played a major role on work-life conflict [1], but the use of mobile technologies potentially alters the boundaries between professional and private spheres that were previously better delineated [2]. Some studies on ICTs use report the negative overflow of work on private life, but also the possibility of a better work-life balance (WLB), beyond the situation of teleworking during the working hours [3, 4].

In this way, one might think that the use of ICT for professional reasons outside of conventional working hours [5–7] plays a mediating role between job demands and WLB. However, as the results of previous studies are not homogenous, aiming some authors to speak about "double-edge sword" for ICT use for professional purpose after hours [8–10], the process can be more complex. Workers' attitude may have to be considered as the preference for segmentation or for integration [11].

© Springer Nature Switzerland AG 2019
F. F.-H. Nah and K. Siau (Eds.): HCII 2019, LNCS 11589, pp. 326–337, 2019.
https://doi.org/10.1007/978-3-030-22338-0_27

Hence, we propose to analyze, starting from job demands, in which way the use of ICTs can lead to more flexible attitude or, at the opposite, a more rigid one relating to the boundaries between work and life spheres. This chain of variables could mediate the dynamic of the relationship between job demands and WLB, in the current context where ICTs are integrated in all levels of activities.

1.1   Job Demands and Work-Life Balance Satisfaction

Work-Life Balance (WLB) can be defined as the "individual's relative perception of the relation between work and private life" [12]. The use of "balance" rather than "work-family conflict" induces a neutral, even a positive situation. Clark [3] defined balance as satisfaction and good functioning at work and at home, with a minimum of role conflict; Syrek and colleagues [13] defined it as an absence of conflict between different areas of life or different roles.

This said, for lots of researchers a satisfying balance between work and life is not easy to obtain, seeing the strong demands and duties in each domain [1, 13–16]. The specific role of job demands on work-life conflict is confirmed by lots of researchers for a long time [17, 18]. Furthermore, the workers are more and more flexible: from the temporal perspective ("flextime" [19]): working hours are getting longer, overtime is legion, and home-work journeys are complicated by congestion in the big cities [20, 21]. From the physical perspective ("flexplace" [19]): remote work and teleworking are flourishing, including sometimes contacts with colleagues on the other side of the planet, expanding workplace, bringing it at home, with rules that remain external to that of the private domain [22]. This leads the worker to have to "make do" with these external rules in his·her private life space, to let them invade him·her, to impose them on the members belonging to his·her private life, or to create new internal rules, and so building his.her new own psychological boundaries [23]. As Kossek and colleagues [24] pointed, it seems necessary to investigate these psychological boundaries or "boundary management characteristics" to affine the comprehension of the relation between job demands and WLB satisfaction.

1.2   ICT Use and Preference for Segmentation as Psychological Boundaries Management Mediators

ICT use for professional reason after hours is an essential variable to consider for discussing the WLB satisfaction, because this use is considered as potentially pertaining to the blurredness between life domains [10]. Researchers noted the great ambiguity relating to ICT use during nonwork time, even the "double edged sword" [5, 8–10, 25]: the negative aspects of the constant connection concern the further burden of work, an invasion of the work domain on the private one, accepted willy-nilly. The positive ones are in relation to autonomy and flexibility, as the opportunity to finish the tasks in a more comfortable environment, the opportunity to anticipate problems at work for the next day, and, generally, the opportunity for a better work-life balance, for example thanks to the possibility to leave earlier the workplace, before all the work done, to manage the responsibilities and duties of private life, and then to finish his work tasks thanks to ICT in the evening. So, the ambiguity seems at least for a part to be linked with worker's constrains and duties in his different areas of life. Boswell and Olson-Buchanan [5] showed how worker' ICT use varies among as well his personal characteristics as his organizational affective commitment, his job involvement and his ambition.

In this way, it seems necessary to investigate the workers' preference model of work-life balance [24]. The model has been described, at extremes, as segmentation of life spheres, characterized by high contrast in role identities, inflexible and impermeable role boundaries *vs* integration of life spheres characterized by low contrast in role identities, flexible and permeable role boundaries [11, 23, 26, 27].

For researchers such as Young and Kleiner [2], there was some ultimately desirable compartmentalization or segmentation between the professional and the private spheres. Nevertheless, since the massive arrival of ICTs in particular, research questions concern the still current adequacy of the preference for segmentation. It may be thought that the use of ICTs may alter preferences in terms of segmentation towards a preference for integration, if ICTs use contributes to the definition of a socially sustainable work for workers [28] or, better, a WLB satisfaction.

Hence, we propose to test the following hypotheses (see also Fig. 1 for visual view):

H1: High job demands contribute to decrease WLB satisfaction.
H2: ICT use for professional purpose after hours and segmentation preference are sequential mediators in the relation between job demands and WLB satisfaction:
H2a: there is no explanatory discontinuity in the process: job demands explain ICT use, ICT use explains segmentation preference, and segmentation preference explains WLB satisfaction.
H2b: Taking together, ICT use and segmentation preference explain indirectly the relation between job demands and WLB satisfaction.
H2c: Each of both the mediators (ICT use and segmentation preference) mediatize the relation between job demands and WLB satisfaction.
H3: Boundary management attitudes aiming for domains integration increase the WLB satisfaction.

2   Method

2.1   Procedure and Participants

We contacted the potential respondents by social and professional networks. They were requested to fill an online questionnaire, which has been hosted on our University website.

The survey has been completed by 142 workers from various sectors such as public service, medical sector, or teaching. The sample included 29% of women and 71% of men. Their age was well distributed: 24.5% of respondents were less than 35 years, 29.7% between 35 and 45 years, 32.4% between 45 and 55 years, and 13.7% more than 55 years old. They had different hierarchical positions in their organisation: 45.7% were a team member, 22.1% a team supervisor, 11.4% a supervisor of supervisors, and

20.7% were outside the hierarchical line (advisor...). Their family situation was also varied even if a great part of the sample was in couple with children at home for at least half-time: 12% lived alone, 7.7% were single with at least one child at home for at least half-time, 26.8% were in couple without children, 45.1% were in couple with children at home for at least half-time, 5.6% were in another situation (with parents, apartment-sharing...), 2.8% did not answer to the question.

2.2 Measures

The questionnaire integrated four variables to evaluate, and some demographic data: sex, age, professional responsibility, and family situation.

Work-life balance satisfaction (Dependent Variable) was measured with the 5-items Work-Life Balance Scale developed by Syrek and colleagues [13]. Examples of items are: "It's hard for me to combine work and private life" (to reverse), "I achieve a good balance between stressful and restful activities in my life".

Job demands (Independent Variable) were measured with the "External effort" dimension of Effort-Rewards Imbalance model [29]. An example of item is: "I have constant time pressure due to a heavy work load". The items were to evaluate on a 5-point Likert scale, from "not agree at all" to "totally agree".

ICT use (Mediator Variable 1) was measured with three questions, each concerning the use, for professional reasons outside the workplace and outside normal working hours, (1) of smartphone, (2) of laptop. The three questions were: "during the morning or in the evening (before or after the normal working hours)", "during the weekend or the days of rest", "during the days off". The response possibilities were binary ("no" or "yes"), leading to a total score between 0 (no use) and 6 (use of smartphone and laptop at the three proposed periods).

Workplace segmentation preferences (Mediator Variable 2) were measured with the four-item measures for workplace segmentation preferences and supplies created by [11]. This scale is defined as the degree to which the individual prefers a workplace that helps to segment work and home domains. We used a Likert-type scale from 1 to 5, with 1 = "strongly disagree", and 5 = "strongly agree" to evaluate the preference for segmentation. An example of item is: "I don't like to have to think about work while I'm at home".

3 Results

To analyze the results and test the hypotheses, we used SPSS 25.0 for the descriptive analyses and SmartPLS for the path analyses. SmartPLS aims to study causal relations between latent variables as an alternative to structural equation models: it does not use maximum likelihood estimations of the parameters but least squares, allowing to test models with smaller samples, and with fewer distributional assumptions than structural equation models as LISREL or AMOS.

3.1 Descriptive Analyses

Table 1 presents the descriptive analyses: mean and standard deviation, and correlations between the variables. The composite scores are the means of items retained following SmartPLS model (see Fig. 1). The participants show an average WLB satisfaction, some quite high job demands, a preference for work life segmentation (vs integration), and an average ICT use for professional purposes after hours that implies that respondents use their smartphone or laptop at two occasions on the three proposed ones outside working hours, in average.

Table 1. Descriptive analyses: scale, mean, standard deviation (SD), and correlation. Note: WLB SAT = work-life balance satisfaction, JOB DEM = job demands, SEG PREF = preference for segmentation; $*p < .05$; $** \ p < .01$

		Scale	M	SD	2.	3.	4.
1.	WLB SAT	1–5	3.30	.92	−.48**	−.18*	−.32**
2.	JOB DEM	1–5	3.64	.93		.20*	.28**
3.	ICT USE	0–6	3.12	2.20			−.17*
4.	SEG PREF	1–5	3.73	1.10			

We tested the mean differences among sex (man, woman), age (25–35, 35–45, 45–55, 55+) and professional responsibility (team member or tm, team supervisor or ts, supervisor of supervisors or ss, outside hierarchical line or out) on the composite scores: there were a significant mean difference in segmentation preference among sex (M_{men} = 3.43, M_{women} = 3.88), a significant difference in ICT use after hours among age (M_{25-35} = 2.70, M_{35-45} = 3.52, M_{45-55} =3.47, M_{55+} = 2.05), and among professional responsibility (M_{tm} = 2.65, M_{ts} = 3.35, M_{ss} = 4.31, M_{out} = 3.24) – see Table 2. These results show that women had a higher preference for segmentation than men, and that ICT is more used among the 35–55 years old respondents, especially among the supervisors of supervisors.

Table 2. Differences (ANOVA) on composites scores among sex, age, professional responsibility, and family situation. Notes: WLB SAT = work-life balance satisfaction, ICT USE = ICT use after working hours, SEG PREF = preference for segmentation.

	WLB SAT	JOB DEMANDS	ICT USE	SEG PREF
Sex	$F(1, 137) =$ .54, p = .46	$F(1, 137) =$ 3.77, p = .05	$F(1, 137) = 4.07$, p = .05	$F(1, 137) =$ 4.77, p = .03*
Age	$F(3, 138) =$ .08, p = .97	$F(3, 138) =$ 1.27, p = .29	$F(3, 138) = 2.86$, p = .04*	$F(3, 138) =$ .49, p = .69
Professional responsibility	$F(3, 139) =$ .89, p = .45	$F(3, 139) =$ 2.21, p = .09	$F(3, 139) = 2.81$, p = .04*	$F(3, 139) =$ .58, p = .63
Family situation	$F(1, 100) =$ 3.54, p = .06	$F(1, 100) =$ 5.12, p = .03*	$F(1, 100) =$ 11.74, p = .00**	$F(1, 100) =$ .02, p = .90

Note: * significant

We tested also the differences among family situation, comparing people living in couple without children with those living in couple with children seen the weak proportion in the other sub-categories. The results indicated that people living in couple with children reported higher job demands (M = 3.87) than those living in couple without children (M = 3.44); a mean difference was greatly present on ICT use: people living in couple with children reported higher ICT use (M = 3.75) than those without child (M = 2.32).

3.2 Reliability of the Latent Variables

SmartPLS provided different indicators, aiming to improve the fit of the used measures. Information about outer loads allowed to decide if retaining or not each considered item for the latent variables. In the final model, WLB satisfaction was loaded by 2 items, job demands by 3 items, and segmentation preference by 3 items; ICT use was loaded by the two sums of use (for smartphone and for laptop) – see Fig. 1. The reliability indicators for the latent variables (Cronbach alpha, rho A, composite reliability and AVE - Average Variance Extracted) were calculated on the basis of the retained items following outer loads analysis. Cronbach's alpha and composite reliability are greater than .70 - excepted for the ICT use (alpha = .67), and rho A and AVE are greater than .50, as expected. In this way, we can consider that the reliability indicators for the latent variables are good (see Table 3).

Table 3. Reliability indicators for the latent variables.

	Cronbach alpha	rho_A	Composite reliability	Average Variance Extracted (AVE)
Job demands	0.755	0.765	0.860	0.673
ICT use	0.670	0.844	0.848	0.738
Segmentation preference	0.905	0.908	0.941	0.841
WLB satisfaction	0.855	0.901	0.931	0.872

3.3 Model Fit

SmartPLS provides some indices to evaluate the fit of the proposed model. It is considered that a value for SRMR less than .10 or of .08 in a more conservative version [30] indicates a good fit. For NFI, it is generally considered that the fit is good if greater or equal to .90, but, it is also considered that this fit is sub-estimated when the sample is little.

We obtained a SRMR of .077 and a NFI of .756. Another indicator is the ratio between Chi-square and the degrees of freedom (df). There were 89 df and the Chi-square was 162.28, so the ratio Chi-square/df = 1.823, a good fit. We can consider that our model fits well our data.

332   C. Hellemans et al.

3.4 Testing Path Model

Overall, job demands, ICT use and segmentation preference explained WLB satisfaction for 30% - see Fig. 1. Outer load of items, path coefficients (or direct effects:
beta), and R^2 (in the circles of the mediators and the dependent latent variables) are
presented in Fig. 1. Path coefficients (or direct effects or beta), total indirect and
specific indirect effects, and also total effects are presented in Table 4, with their
interval confidences following the bootstrap analysis. All the direct effects (d.e.) were
significant. High job demands decrease WLB satisfaction (d.e. = −.389).

In more details, high job demands contribute to more ICT use for professional
purposes after hours (d.e. = .204), which contributes to weak segmentation preference
(d.e. = −.237), this lack of segmentation preference increasing WLB satisfaction (d.e. =
−.232). In other words, integration preference, explained itself by ICT use after hours,
contributes to WLB satisfaction.

Concerning the indirect effects, we obtained a significant total indirect effect
between job demands and WLB satisfaction (ind. e. = −.104). More specifically, ICT
use was a partial mediator of the relation between job demands and segmentation
preference (specific indirect effect = −.048), but was not a significant mediator between
job demands and WLB satisfaction; segmentation preference was a complete mediator
between ICT use and WLB satisfaction (as direct effect = −.167*, specific indirect
effect = −.055*, but total effect = −.112[NS]), and a partial mediator between job
demands and WLB satisfaction (specific indirect effect = −.081). These results highlight the role of ICT use and, in a more importantly part, of segmentation (or integration) preference on the dynamic between job demands and WLB satisfaction: the
negative link between job demands and WLB satisfaction.

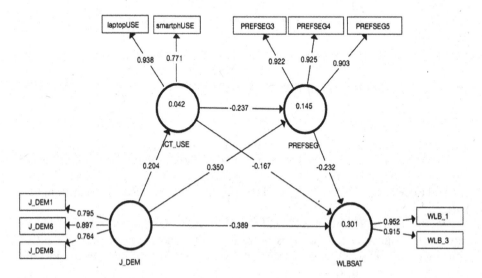

Fig. 1. Results of path analysis. J_DEM = Job demands, PREF_SEG = Preference for
segmentation, WLBSAT = Work-life balance satisfaction.

Table 4. Direct, indirect and total effects, and their interval confidence

	Initial sample	2.5% IC	97.5% IC
Path coefficients/direct effects (beta)			
JDEM -> ICT USE	0.204*	0.001	0.377
JDEM -> PREFSEG	0.350*	0.189	0.509
JDEM -> WLBSAT	−0.389*	−0.507	−0.264
ICT USE -> PREFSEG	−0.237*	−0.398	−0.070
ICT USE -> WLBSAT	−0.167*	−0.315	−0.012
PREFSEG -> WLBSAT	−0.232*	−0.361	−0.099
Total indirect effects			
ICT USE -> WLBSAT	−0.055*	0.012	0.117
JDEM -> WLBSAT	−0.104*	−0.184	−0.043
Specific indirect effects			
JDEM -> ICT USE -> PREFSEG	−0.048*	−0.108	−0.000
JDEM -> ICT USE -> WLBSAT	−0.034	−0.080	0.001
JDEM -> PREFSEG -> WLBSAT	−0.081*	−0.152	−0.026
JDEM -> ICT USE -> PREFSEG -> WLBSAT	0.011	−0.000	0.030
Total effects			
EXI -> ICT USE	0.204*	0.001	0.377
EXI -> PREFSEG	0.302*	0.121	0.464
EXI -> WLBSAT	−0.493*	−0.589	−0.384
ICT USE -> PREFSEG	−0.237*	−0.398	−0.070
ICT USE -> WLBSAT	−0.112	−0.250	0.044
PREFSEG -> WLBSAT	−0.232*	−0.361	−0.099

Note: *significant

4 Discussion

The aim of this paper was to evaluate the role of two boundary management charac-teristics: ICT use for professional purpose after hours and segmentation preference, as mediators of the relation between job demands and WLB satisfaction. The results indicated that 30% of variance of WLB satisfaction was explained by the three studied variables.

More specifically, the first hypothesis was that high job demands contribute to decrease WLB satisfaction. With a direct effect of −.389 from job demands on WLB satisfaction, we can confirm the first hypothesis: high job demands contribute heavily to decrease WLB satisfaction. This result is classic and coherent with a lot of contri-butions as those of [1, 17], or yet [18].

The second hypothesis concerned the sequential explanatory process between job demands and WLB satisfaction, *i.e.* the mediator roles of ICT use for professional reasons after hours and segmentation preference. To discuss this hypothesis, different criteria (cf. sub-hypotheses) had to be filled: first of all (H2a), no explanatory dis-continuity in the process. The results showed that job demands explained ICT use, that ICT use explained segmentation preference and that segmentation preference explained

WLB satisfaction, confirming H2a and so, giving a first global credit to this second hypothesis. Second criterium (H2b), the total indirect effect of both mediators (taken together) between job demands and WLB satisfaction had to be significant, what was, giving a second credit to the global hypothesis 2. To be completed, the third criterion (the more challenging one, H2c) was that each of both the mediators had to mediatize the relation between job demands and WLB satisfaction. The analysis of specific indirect effects showed that segmentation preference completely mediatized the relation between ICT use and WLB satisfaction, that ICT use partially mediatized the relation between job demands and segmentation preference, but no specific indirect effect of ICT use between job demands and WLB satisfaction was observed. In other words, ICT use explained WLB satisfaction only through segmentation preference. So, the H2c is only partially confirmed. Nevertheless, giving all the results for the global hypothesis 2 and the fact that third criterion was the most challenging and was partially received, we can consider that hypothesis 2 is confirmed: ICT use and segmentation preference are sequential mediators in the relations between job demands and WLB satisfaction.

The latest hypothesis (H3) concerned the direction of the relations between variables. We supposed that boundary management attitudes aiming to domains integration (ICT use for professional purpose after hours and integration preference) would increasing WLB satisfaction, ICT use (itself linked to high job demands) increased integration preference and that this integration preference increased WLB satisfaction. So, the mediator processes allowed to turn the issue of high job demands upside down. This result, highlighting the determinant role of boundary management attitudes on WLB satisfaction, as pointed by Kossek and colleagues [24], is an innovative contribution in the WLB research: it allows to better understand the "double-edged sword" phenomena [8–10] by supplying some first conditions under which ICT use turns negative issues into positive ones.

One can guess that the boundary management process highlighted can have been a voluntary strategy developed willy-nilly by the workers to reach to a good WLB satisfaction. This strategy has perhaps (or probably) implied a complete revision of worker's organization in his different spheres of life. The mean differences analyses had, by the way, revealed a higher ICT use among 35–45 and 45–55 people, among supervisor of supervisors, and among people in couple with children than among the others, situations typically including a lot of duties. It can therefore be understood that people with heavy work and family responsibilities, probably out of necessity, have resorted to ICTs to help them juggle their different duties, and leading them to prefer an integration of spheres, which at final allows them to achieve a WLB satisfaction. These results are consistent with the comments of [28], describing how ICTs are used in the definition of a socially sustainable work for workers.

Nevertheless, our research is not flawless: it was cross-sectional, the sample was quite small, and did not come from the same organizational culture. Consequently, the previous comments have to be proven: there are indeed others research programs to implement.

Our results could delight many organizations, since they highlight that working out of working hours can under certain conditions increase the WLB satisfaction. Obviously, it must be understood that these results do not mean that the organizations can escape their social responsibility: firstly, we can anticipate that there are limits to not be exceeded to job demands, ICT use, even if preference for integration. This aspect needs to be further explored in future research. Secondly, workers have the right to expect reciprocity from their organization: if there is ICT use after hours for professional reasons, is the ICT use for private reasons during working hours also permitted? Is it just tolerated or accepted? Is it totally considered as normal in the organization?

Another question concerns the point of view of the other members of the private sphere: how do they feel the preference of integration of the concerned individual? Do they consider his integration preference as normal, do they just tolerate it, or do they think that it causes conflicts never resolved? Does the ICT use for professional reasons outside normal working hours tend to modify the balance and distribution of roles and tasks within the family sphere? Is the other member of the couple also satisfied of his WLB? Or is he in fact the regulator (at his expense) of his partner's integration preference? Is it the same process among gender? Among age? Among level of professional responsibility of one of the partners inside the couple?

Anyway, following our results, it is not, per se, the organization's disconnection policies that have the greatest need to be questioned, but well the opportunities of flexibility allocated by organizations, outside their walls, but also inside them, during the working time.

Traditionally, this flexibility is relatively present among senior managers and accepted by the organization, because these people have reached these hierarchical levels, and this is an evidence of a respected psychological contract and of a mutual trust, but the question is no doubt much more delicate for employees with lower grades. It will then be up to companies themselves to be flexible and trusting in accepting the introduction of new forms of organization at all hierarchical levels, as long as the tasks allow it, promoting remote workers autonomy, without forced schedule, despite all the possibilities offered by new technologies for control.

References

1. Voydanoff, P.: The effects of work demands and resources on work-to-family conflict and facilitation. J. Marriage Fam. **66**, 398–412 (2004)
2. Young, L., Kleiner, B.H.: Work and family: issues for the 1990s. Women Manag. Rev. **7** (1992). https://doi.org/10.1108/09649429210016151
3. Clark, S.C.: Work/family border theory: a new theory of work/family balance. https://journals-sagepub-com.ezproxy.ulb.ac.be/doi/abs/10.1177/0018726700536001
4. El Wafi, W., Brangier, E., Zaddem, F.: Usage des technologies numériques et modèles de la perméabilité des frontières entre la vie personnelle et la vie professionnelle. Psychol. Trav. Organ. **22**, 74–87 (2016). https://doi.org/10.1016/j.pto.2015.12.002
5. Boswell, W.R., Olson-Buchanan, J.B.: The use of communication technologies after hours: the role of work attitudes and work-life conflict. J. Manag. **33**, 592–610 (2007). https://doi.org/10.1177/0149206307302552
6. Derks, D., van Duin, D., Tims, M., Bakker, A.B.: Smartphone use and work-home interference: the moderating role of social norms and employee work engagement. J. Occup. Organ. Psychol. **88**, 155–177 (2015). https://doi.org/10.1111/joop.12083

7. Richardson, K.M., Thompson, C.A.: High tech tethers and work-family conflict: a conservation of resources approach. Eng. Manag. Res. **1** (2012). https://doi.org/10.5539/emr.v1n1p29

8. Dén-Nagy, I.: A double-edged sword?: a critical evaluation of the mobile phone in creating work-life balance: impact of mobile phone use on WLB. New Technol. Work Employ. **29**, 193–211 (2014). https://doi.org/10.1111/ntwe.12031

9. Diaz, I., Chiaburu, D.S., Zimmerman, R.D., Boswell, W.R.: Communication technology: pros and cons of constant connection to work. J. Vocat. Behav. **80**, 500–508 (2012). https://doi.org/10.1016/j.jvb.2011.08.007

10. Ďuranová, L., Ohly, S.: Persistent Work-Related Technology Use, Recovery and Well-Being Processes: Focus on Supplemental Work After Hours. Springer, Heidelberg (2016). https://doi.org/10.1007/978-3-319-24759-5

11. Kreiner, G.E.: Consequences of work-home segmentation or integration: a person-environment fit perspective. J. Organ. Behav. **27**, 485–507 (2006). https://doi.org/10.1002/job.386

12. Nam, T.: Technology use and work-life balance. Appl. Res. Qual. Life **9**, 1017–1040 (2014). https://doi.org/10.1007/s11482-013-9283-1

13. Syrek, C., Bauer-Emmel, C., Antoni, C., Klusemann, J.: Entwicklung und Validierung der Trierer Kurzskala zur Messung von Work-Life Balance (TKS-WLB). Diagnostica **57**, 134–145 (2011). https://doi.org/10.1026/0012-1924/a000044

14. Dumas, M.: Conflit Et Enrichissement Travail-Famille Et Implication. Rev. Gest. Ressour. Hum. **23–37**, 51 (2008)

15. Duxbury, L.E., Higgins, C.A., Thomas, D.R.: Work and family environments and the adoption of computer-supported supplemental work-at-home. J. Vocat. Behav. **49**, 1–23 (1996). https://doi.org/10.1006/jvbe.1996.0030

16. St-Onge, S., Renaud, S., Guérin, G., Caussignac, É.: Vérification d'un modèle structurel à l'égard du conflit travail-famille. Relat. Ind. Ind. Relat. **57**, 491–516 (2002). https://doi.org/10.7202/006887ar

17. Jacobs, J.A., Winslow, S.E.: Overworked faculty: job stresses and family demands. Ann. Am. Acad. Polit. Soc. Sci. **596**, 254–255 (2004). https://doi.org/10.1177/000271620459600105

18. Wallace, J.E.: It's about time: a study of hours worked and work spillover among law firm lawyers. J. Vocat. Behav. **50**, 227–248 (1997). https://doi.org/10.1006/jvbe.1996.1573

19. Allen, T.D., Johnson, R.C., Kiburz, K.M., Shockley, K.M.: Work-family conflict and flexible work arrangements: deconstructing flexibility. Pers. Psychol. **66**, 345–376 (2013). https://doi.org/10.1111/peps.12012

20. Batt, R., Valcour, P.M.: Human resources practices as predictors of work-family outcomes and employee turnover. Ind. Relat. J. Econ. Soc. **42**, 189–220 (2003). https://doi.org/10.1111/1468-232X.00287

21. Frone, M.R., Russell, M., Cooper, M.L.: Antecedents and outcomes of work-family conflict: testing a model of the work-family interface. J. Appl. Psychol. **77**, 65–78 (1992)

22. Kossek, E.E., Lautsch, B.A., Eaton, S.C.: Telecommuting, control, and boundary management: correlates of policy use and practice, job control, and work–family effectiveness. J. Vocat. Behav. **68**, 347–367 (2006). https://doi.org/10.1016/j.jvb.2005.07.002

23. Rothbard, N.P., Phillips, K.W., Dumas, T.L.: Managing multiple roles: work-family policies and individuals' desires for segmentation. Organ. Sci. **16**, 243–258 (2005)

24. Kossek, E.E., Ruderman, M.N., Braddy, P.W., Hannum, K.M.: Work–nonwork boundary management profiles: a person-centered approach. J. Vocat. Behav. **81**, 112–128 (2012). https://doi.org/10.1016/j.jvb.2012.04.003

25. Jauréguiberry, F.: Déconnexion volontaire aux technologies de l'information et de la communication (2013)
26. Ashforth, B.E., Kreiner, G.E., Fugate, M.: All in a day's work: boundaries and micro role transitions. Acad. Manag. Rev. **25**, 472–491 (2000)
27. Barber, L.K., Jenkins, J.S.: Creating technological boundaries to protect bedtime: examining work-home boundary management, psychological detachment and sleep: creating boundaries to protect bedtime. Stress Health **30**, 259–264 (2014). https://doi.org/10.1002/smi.2536
28. Grady, G., McCarthy, A.M.: Work-life integration: experiences of mid-career professional working mothers. J. Manag. Psychol. **23**, 599–622 (2008). https://doi.org/10.1108/02683940810884559
29. Siegrist, J., et al.: The measurement of effort–reward imbalance at work: European comparisons. Soc. Sci. Med. **58**, 1483–1499 (2004). https://doi.org/10.1016/S0277-9536(03)00351-4
30. Hu, L., Bentler, P.M.: Cutoff criteria for fit indexes in covariance structure analysis: Conventional criteria versus new alternatives. Struct. Equ. Model. Multidiscip. J. **6**, 1–55 (1999). https://doi.org/10.1080/10705519909540118

Consciousness of Cyber Defense: Boundary Objects for Expansive Learning Through Creation of Contradictions

Shuyuan Mary Ho$^{(\boxtimes)}$, Diogo Oliveira, and Raghav Rathi

College of Communication and Information, School of Information,
Florida State University, Tallahassee, FL 32306-2100, USA
smho@fsu.edu, diogo.oliveira@cci.fsu.edu,
rrl7d@my.fsu.edu

Abstract. Cyber attackers gain access into systems, networks and cyberin-frastructure by escalating privileges to confidential information regardless of the efforts systems engineers put into security. The chess game between cyber offense and defense destabilizes the ability of organizations to protect their information assets. This research employs the lens of Activity Theory to study the interaction through the contradictions embedded between the cyber attackers and cyber defenders. These types of contradictions were forcefully created and simulated in the cyber security virtual lab at Florida State University for the purpose of facilitating real-world scenario-based learning experiences. Both network traffic data and interviews were collected in order to identify the boundary objects that intersect the two activity systems. Natural language processing (NLP) was adopted to explore and extract topics frequently used by both activity systems. Consciousness of cyber defense was expanded by creating contradictions, and boundary objects were identified by comparing the interactions between these two activity systems.

Keywords: Activity theory · Activity system · Human-computer interaction ·
Sociotechnical systems · Boundary objects · Natural language processing (NLP) ·
Cybersecurity · System penetration · Cloud security

1 Introduction

The pervasiveness of technology enables modern organizations to use computer-mediated and cloud-based technologies to share data, information and services through cyberspace. However, putting any information online faces a significant threat from malicious hackers. The global 2018 Verizon Data breach Investigation Report suggests that compared to the last ten years, the number of breaches remains high, while hacking techniques are getting more sophisticated and elaborate. In general, 68% of breaches take a month or longer to discover, and 94% of the security incidents—and 90% of confirmed data breaches—fall into the categories of web hacking, privilege misuse, cyber espionage, compromised assets, crimeware and payment card skimmers [1, pp. 6–7]. Cyber espionage does not occur as frequently as other forms of cyber-crime, but the fundamental goal of such attacks is to capture trade secrets and proprietary

© Springer Nature Switzerland AG 2019
F. F.-H. Nah and K. Siau (Eds.): HCII 2019, LNCS 11589, pp. 338–353, 2019.
https://doi.org/10.1007/978-3-030-22338-0_28

information. Attackers are now developing enhanced mechanisms to bolster penetration speed.

Though systems engineers and IT professionals work diligently to secure the network and block attackers, hackers seem to find better angles for system penetration, understanding system vulnerabilities and backdoors. Hence, they can more quickly perform loophole analysis. This finding suggests either one of two things: (1) systems engineers do not have a holistic view of the computing service environment when configuring the systems, or (2) hackers have a more creative, outside the box understanding of relevant security loopholes and system vulnerabilities, to adopt advanced tools for exploiting systems and networks. Willison and Warkentin [2] suggested that many violations can also be the result of simple mistakes, or non-malicious noncompliance, poor employee awareness training, low motivation and commitment or weak oversight from management. However, security breaches can also be malicious and deceptive in nature. Ho and Hancock [3–6] suggested that disgruntled insiders with malicious intent can threaten an organization's ability to protect their own intellectual property. Our ability to make sense of group communication and group interaction can provide insights into these complex problems. Vance and Lowry [7] offered approaches to reduce insider abuse and policy violation, along with different mechanisms to increase awareness and accountability. Although other studies have offered ways to train, secure and monitor our computing environment (such as awareness training, auditing of electronic presence), there has not been an effective approach proposed to enhance cyber defense activities.

Cyber defense itself is an activity, and the activity itself provides the context [8]. As such, we propose to study the consciousness of cyber defense, and examine the interactions between attackers and defenders as an activity system, as well as to gain insight that might have practical implications for organizational information security. With this goal in mind, our research [9] aims to address the following questions: *How do we uncover the consciousness of cyber defense in a way that can transform organizational information systems security?* More specifically, *what are the boundary objects created through the contradictions embedding between cyber attack teams and cyber defense teams that impact their knowledge and their cyber defense tactics?*

We adopt the lens of Activity Theory [10] to examine the interactions and activities to capture the differences in motivation and behavior between cyber attackers and defenders. To do so, we (1) compare objects, goals, actions, tools, and operations of both groups and (2) examine how the social environment has shaped the values and skillsets demonstrated by each respective team. This will help identify the boundary objects created through contradicting values. In this paper we will first discuss the theoretical lens of activity theory from existing literature. Then, we will describe our own study framework, the research design, method, data collection, data analysis, and research limitations. Finally, this paper concludes with the research contribution to this field, and future works.

2 Activity Theory: Context and Conflict

Activity Theory first originated in the late 70s and early 80s through the work of Soviet developmental psychologist Leont'ev [11] as a response to the work of Vygotsky [12]. This theory embodies a concept in which activity is represented as the interaction between subject and object, and is further defined by the subject's motive. Activity in this context is also a system of processes that reflect the subject's motive. The original generation of this Activity Theory as developed by Vygotsky [12] focused on the interaction between human agents (subject) and the world (object) as mediated by tools and signs [13, 14]. Leont'ev [11] advanced Vygotsky's [12] work by proposing a three-level model of activity. That is, activity does not occur without a motive. The subject would take certain actions directed towards a specific goal. An action is a conscious choice and a representation of progress toward a desired outcome. In this scenario, operations can be subconsciously performed or mediated by tools (e.g., technology). Leont'ev [11] advocated for the notion of collective activity rather than individual focus. However, Leont'ev [11] did not illustrate a model of collective activity until after Engeström [10, 15] proposed the expanded triangle representation and introduced the community, rules and norms, as well as division of labor which became the collective aspects and elements of an activity system, providing a root model of human activity [10, 16].

Since the conception of Activity Theory, it has been adopted in a wide range of domains and studies such as genre systems [17], writing instructions [17, 18], designing learning environments [19], innovation [20], organizational learning [21], strategic practices [22, 23], mobile health systems [24], incident control systems [24], ICT4D [25], CHAT [26, 27], and software development [28]. Kuutti [29–32] suggested this 3×6 (levels × elements) Activity Theory concept to be further adopted in information systems research (ISR) [29, 31], computer-supported cooperative work (CSCW) [32], and human computer interaction (HCI) [30] when studying organizational learning. The three (3) levels refer to top-tier executives, middle management and front-line workers in an organization. The six (6) elements refer to subject, object, tool, rule, community and division of labor of an activity system. Kuutti and Arvonen [32] criticized that limited view of CSCW design, and suggested re-conceptualizing the structure of (work) activity by defining an activity as a *collective* phenomenon, which is "*work by multiple subjects sharing a common object, supported by information technology*" (p. 234). Moreover, an activity not only exists in a material environment, but is historically developed and culturally mediated by a tool (instrument, i.e., information technology). Kuutti and Arvonen [32] illustrated the role and importance of "tools" being able to mediate organizational learning. That is, the creation of new information technology can assist in organizational learning, transfer shared knowledge, meaning, or materials, to construct, maintain and sustain a community (i.e., a community with shared interests). Interestingly, Kuutti and Arvonen [32] emphasized that "contradictions are the force behind the development of an activity" (p. 235). That is, the driving force for an organization to learn, to advance, and to grow is the existence of conflicts, contradictions, and tensions [10].

Since an activity is a collective phenomenon [32] that focuses on the interaction of human activity and consciousness [19, 30, 33] within its relevant context. Jonassen and Ronrer-Murphy [19] emphasized that "an activity cannot be understood or analyzed outside the context" (p. 62). Nardi [8] compared the differences between activity theory, situated action models, and distributed cognition, and emphasized that in activity theory, the unit of analysis is an activity itself whereas the situated actions views the "person-acting in settings" as a unit of analysis. An activity takes place in a particular situation [34]. Distributed cognition, on the other hand, requires a cognitive system composed of individuals and artifacts. The distributed cognition emphasizes the system as the unit of analysis. Distributed cognition is concerned with the structures of the system, and the transformations of these structures, the coordination among the individuals and artifacts, and the process of how individuals align or share information [8, p. 39]. Nardi [8] suggested that activity theory offers a richer framework that can help capture consciousness, intentionality, and history of human-computer interaction when studied in context. That is, context is not a random composite of people and artifacts, but rather a "specific transformative relationship between people and artifacts" (p. 38). People consciously and deliberately generate context through interacting with objects mediated by artifacts. In short, the subject is engaged in an activity, and the object held by the subject can motivate the activity, and can be transformed in the course of an activity (p. 37). An activity can be mediated by artifacts [29] such as signs, symbols, language, machines, information systems, and instruments, etc. That is, "the activity itself is the context" (p. 38).

To help explain this view of the context, Kaptelinin and Nardi [35] provided a checklist to define the "space" of context. Basically, the transformation of activity involves both internalization and externalization activities. Internalization refers to a cognitive process in the transformation of external activities to internal cognition. Externalization transforms the internal cognitive states or activities into external ones (such as for visualization or coordination purposes). This activity checklist includes the following: (1) identifying the hierarchies of goals, (2) actively transforming the objects in the social and physical aspects of the environment, (3) being able to internalize and externalize objects so transformation can take place, and (4) analyzing both history and potential changes in the environment for further development.

In order to understand organizational learning, Virkkunen and Kuutti [21] suggested that we revisit the units of analysis; the "activity system." Organizational learning is a collective learning process. It involves complex interaction between six (6) elements of an activity system. Organizational learning is not only multifaceted and multi-phased, but is always local and situational (p. 293). After examining many frameworks, Virkkunen and Kuutti [21] suggested the unit of analysis for organizational learning as being an activity system. One of the key elements of an activity system is the "object," which refers to the motive of the activity. The subject is motivated to take action to achieve the object. The outcome of an activity may likely become a component of another activity system, and thus the object is further transformed. Because of this transformation phenomenon, the activity system is always "internally heterogeneous" and contains "many competing and partly conflicting views" (p. 301). The contradictions of this process create opportunities for transformation; transitional objects becoming different elements (e.g., a tool, a community, a rule, or a division of labor) of another activity system, and this process represents the cycle of collective or "expansive" learning in an organization.

Contradictions generally refer to incompatible or opposite things [36, p. 369]. *Contradictions* create tension or opposition within an activity system, and this fosters change within organizations [24, p. 840]. However, Engeström and Sannino [36] emphasized that *contradictions* cannot be mixed with paradox, tension, inconsistency, conflict, dilemma or double bind (p. 370), and suggested that based on linguistic cues, *contradictions* can be identified and categorized into four types of discursive manifestations: dilemma (e.g., 'but'), conflicts (e.g., 'no'), critical conflict (e.g., descriptive metaphors), and double bind (e.g., using rhetorical questions) (p. 375). On the other hand, Allen and Brown [24] proposed the concept of *congruencies*, which foster reproduction (p. 841). Allen and Brown [24] studied technology-mediated organizational change through the lens of critical realism by analyzing the contradictions and congruencies within two scenarios: (case one) the paramedic treatment of heart attacks through the mobile health system, and (case two) the ambulance dispatch of an incident control system. In case one, the introduction of a new tool provides congruencies between the internal and the external motivation of the objects, which become a strong stabilizing influence on the activity system. In case two, when the subject accepts the conflicting use of the tools as part of the norm of the activity system, this acceptance leads to the transformation from contradictions into congruencies.

Karanasios [14] proposed a unified view of technology and activity, and worked to re-conceptualize the activity system in order to reposition the technology in terms of its role in resolving contradictions, but further argued for a new form of harmonized congruencies within the organization. Nardi [33] and Kaptelinin [37] pointed out that objects can represent the motivation of the activity system. To distinguish the motivation from the objects, and to control those objects without clearly defined boundaries —called "runaway objects"—the activity system would require and involve multiple and complex links between activities. Karanasios [14] identified this problem as a potential opportunity for the IS field to develop and advance the notion of runaway objects (p. 144), and to transform these runaway objects into something smaller and manageable.

In sum, consciousness of cyber defense can be found embedded in the social arrangements (e.g., motives and intents) and the mediated technologies (e.g., tools). The current study aims to find out how the consciousness of cyber defense manifests itself through creation of contradictions—or contradicting values—in two activity systems. Rather than identifying the differences in the discursive manifestations of contradictions [36], our study aims to identify the "boundary objects" spinning between the two activity systems that represent certain degrees of consciousness of cyber defense. Star and Griesemer [38] suggested that boundary objects are "objects" that are "enough to adapt to local needs, and "yet, robust enough to maintain a common identity across sites" (p. 393). That is, in two different activity systems, the consciousness of cyber defense can be recognized through the boundary objects "as a key process in developing and maintaining coherence across intersecting social worlds" (p. 393).

3 Study Framework

Cyber defense can be represented as an activity system (Fig. 1) where the outcome of the two activity systems is determined by whether the systems or networks have been protected or penetrated. Within a framework of cyber defense, we can assume that the subject is making sense of the object of activity [37]. The subject—as an individual or as a team—requires a long-term motive to defend their information assets, and take actions to achieve short-term goals in protecting these assets. The conscious choice of the subject in taking actions that will achieve certain outcomes is mediated by technologies such as firewalls, intrusion detection systems, networks, and various information systems. This activity system involves routine operations as well as activities occurring in confined conditions and situations [11].

This study aims to investigate the consciousness of the cyber defender as an activity system. In particular, we are interested in examining the interactive activities that explain the differences in behavior demonstrated by the attackers and defenders. Our study framework creates the contradicting values between cyber defense and offense by assigning four teams of cyber professionals (i.e., students with proficient system and network technical knowledge) with short-term goals to understand systems' loopholes and vulnerabilities, and to protect their information assets—as well as long-term goals to acquire pragmatic know-how and skillsets in cyber defense. Each cyber defense team or cyber offense team is considered an activity system. When two competing activity systems are placed together, conflicts are created due to the overlapping outcomes. In this overlapping outcome, security incidents occur and system vulnerabilities are discovered. It is significant to study the relationships and interaction between cyber defenders and attackers in cyberspace where the two activity systems interact. Both theoretically and operationally, we can observe the contradictions of motives, goals, and conditions of cyber operations—for defenders as well as attackers—as they examine and assess system vulnerabilities. Consequently, individuals involved in both roles are likely to have very different motives.

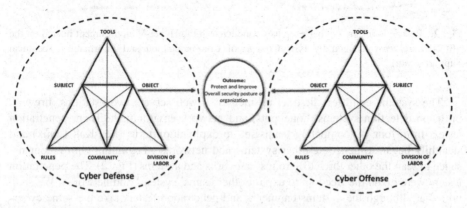

Fig. 1. Cyber defense activity systems

4   Research Design

The research design of this study involved cybersecurity experiments using servers, workstations and network environments that were replicated in four distinct segments, which were enabled by virtual switches in the virtual lab, and managed by Hyper-V software. Four groups with four to five members were formed, each comprising a combination of systems engineers and penetration testers. Systems engineers protected their own systems while penetration testers attempted to exploit other teams' systems.

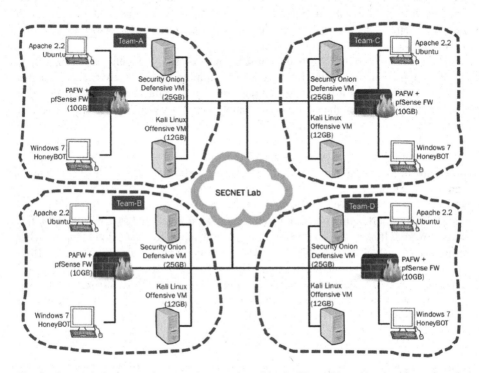

Fig. 2.   Research design—cyber exercises conducted in the Hyper-V environment hosted on the SECNET server (managed by FSU College of Communication and Information Technical Support Team)

The systems engineers first set up their own web servers, workstations, firewall, intrusion detection systems, honeypots, and network environment. Then, penetration testers from four (4) competing teams set up exploitation tools (i.e., Kali Linux) and stealthily began to penetrate other systems and networks—beginning with reconnaissance to scan the other three (3) groups' networks and systems (Fig. 2). The penetration testers were given the freedom to exploit other teams' systems and networks. We shall note that although the systems engineers and penetration testers take the same cybersecurity class, each team's systems configuration settings and credentials differ and are determined within the team. Since these students have extensive systems' knowledge, they are given the freedom to choose and implement their own tools and techniques in order to either (1) protect their own systems, information assets, possessions and territory, or to (2) penetrate and exploit other teams' systems, information assets, possessions and territory.

5 Method

We collected both network traffic data as well as interviews from participants. To understand the consciousness of team interaction, this study employs a triangular mixed method approach by simultaneously collecting both quantitative data in the form of network traffic, and qualitative data in the form of semi-structured interviews. Furthermore, to capture the complexities of the participants' interactive behavior, we observed their behavior as well as extrapolating the meaning of their interactions.

5.1 Data Collection

The experiments and the computing environments were set up on a server powered by Hyper-V management system and maintained by Florida State University College of Communication and Information Technical Support Team. Data was collected from an Advanced Information Security undergraduate class offered at the Florida State University during Spring 2017. There were 18 participants recruited for this study[1]. We first interviewed the systems administrators in the cyber defense team at the beginning phase of the experiments (January through March 2017). After the systems and networks were set up, we interviewed the penetration testers on the cyber offense team during the second phase of the experiment (April and May 2017). These participants had appropriate technical skills in areas like troubleshooting, intrusion detection, etc. because they all took prerequisite classes on Linux, web programming, networking, and database management. The tasks performed by the participants included protecting their systems, fixing vulnerabilities, and engaging in activities to prevent future attacks. A total of 28 interviews were conducted, recorded, and transcribed.

Two types of data were collected. The first type of data was the network traffic logged by the E-Detective traffic monitoring system. The second type of data was the interview transcript. Each participant participated in an hour-long face-to-face semi-structured interview, first as a systems administrator and then as a penetration tester. A member of the research team conducted the interviews with a prepared script of questions and recorded the open-ended responses for audio transcription. The interview included questions about the division of labor, context of work, tools used, activities involved in setting up the environment, in addition to the rules each team applied.

---

[1] The study has been approved by the Florida State University Human Subject Committee, and obtained the Institution Review Board (IRB) protocols #2016.19676, #2017.22357, and #2018.25742.

5.2   Network Traffic Data Analysis

We attempt to treat the number of DNS requests collected from network traffic as representations of routine activities. The number of requests collected from the network traffic is further processed by Python interface; a library used to create a data frame of the entire dataset, which is illustrated in Table 1.

Table 1. Network traffic data (1/1/2017–05/31/2017)

	DNS	FTP	HTTP files	HTTP pages	HTTP videos
Network activities as represented by the number of requests	409980	23199	11385	28071	46

Frequency counts were performed on the collected data frames to get the number of occurrences for each source IP. In our data collection and observation, four (4) IP addresses had the most DNS requests.

Appendix A illustrates the frequency of DNS requests. In retrospect, these high frequency counts reflect the design of the experiments because these four IP addresses were allocated as pfSense firewall used by four (4) teams.

However, this approach can at most help us identify the systems that were up and running, and interacting as the gateways (i.e., pfSense firewalls). We could objectively state that based on the requests made during the experiments, the boundary object that spans the four teams is the firewall (i.e., as represented by the most frequent DNS requests for pfSense); however, there was not much insight provided as to the consciousness of cyber defense.

5.3   Interview Data Analysis

We further analyzed the interview transcripts to explore the consciousness of the cyber defense teams during these exercises. The transcript data contained approximately 77,104 words from the 15 systems administrators, and approximately 68,295 words from the 13 penetration testers. Natural language processing (NLP) was adopted to process and analyze the transcripts. We developed Python codes to truncate the transcripts, and extract phrases and topics most frequently mentioned by the participants during the interview.

More specifically, we parsed the data on the basis of the context of the questions asked by the interviewer in the respective categories of the interacting activity systems (i.e., subject, object, tools, interacting outcomes, rules, community, and division of labor). The subject denotes the actors of the activity system; whether a systems administrator, or a penetration tester. The object denotes the intent, and motive of the actors—a cyber defender (i.e., systems administrator) or a cyber offender (i.e., penetration tester). Tools refer to the systems, software, applications, concepts, or techniques utilized by the actors to achieve their goals and outcome. Rules refer to how and what actors choose to communicate and base their decisions on. Community refers to where these actors mostly interact and obtain their knowledge. Division of labor refers to how actors divide and spread leadership and management tasks.

After dividing the data into the above categories, topic analysis was applied to extract the hidden topics from large volumes of text. Several Python modules such as NLTK (a natural language toolkit) and Gensim (a topic modeling toolkit) were leveraged to generate lists of topics from the respective categories. Below are the four steps programmed in the Python script:

Step 1. Tokenize the transcript file, and eliminate all the stop words (e.g., of, the, an, on, etc.) using the NLTK module. A list of variables for the stop words was created to filter out the stop words from the tokenized list.

```
>>>word_tokens = word_tokenize(file)
>>>stop_words = set(stopwords.words('english'))
>>>filtered_sentence = [w for w in word_tokens if
not w in stop_words]
```

Step 2. After removing the stop words, we attempt to automate the process of extracting the topics from the large corpus of text obtained from the interview. A list of the words as a representation of the context was obtained for further analysis. We adopted an automated algorithm—LDA (Latent Dirichlet Allocation) from Gensim package to segregate topics. This module helps to determine the volume and percentage contribution of each topic so we get a sense of how important each topic is. We employed corpora, a method in the Gensim, to create the terms dictionary.

```
>>>dictionary = corpora.Dictionary(texts)
```

Step 3. A terms matrix was created based on the terms dictionary.

```
>>>corpus = [dictionary.doc2bow(text) for text in
texts]
```

Step 4. An LDA model was created using the above variables.

```
>>>ldamodel = gensim.models.ldamodel.LdaModel(cor-
pus, num_topics=2, id2word = dictionary,
passes=20)
```

6   Discussion

Several Venn diagrams represent the most frequently mentioned topics between two activity systems. From Figs. 3, 4, 5, 6 and 7, the number in brackets next to each word denotes frequency counts.

6.1 Addressing Research Questions

Consciousness of the two activity systems was identified through topic extraction from the transcripts. The subjects obviously have conflicting roles in the study. The responsibilities assigned to the systems administrators were aimed at cyber defense—which included setting up, configuring and protecting their own systems and cyber-infrastructure. They also have another conflicting role, which is to act as the penetration testers—cyber offense—poking at other teams' systems for vulnerabilities, and attempting to break through competing teams' cyber-infrastructure. Students were conscious of the cyber defense when they are facing potential hackers (i.e., classmates of other teams who aim to hack into their own information assets and systems). Through strategizing to exploit other teams' systems' vulnerabilities, students were aware of their own systems' vulnerabilities and made attempts to bolster their own systems by fixing loopholes and solving problems.

Contradictions were manifested not only in the objects and outcome (Fig. 3), but also in the tools (Fig. 4), communities (Fig. 6), and division of labor (Fig. 7). We can identify the differences and conflicts of the intents and motives of the actors from the objects as derived from transcripts. In the cyber defense system (Fig. 3), subjects value the teamwork, and their aims were found in words such as 'install,' 'scan,' 'protect,' 'monitor,' and 'block.' The subjects of the cyber defense systems face 'threats' and 'phishing' attacks from the 'attackers,' and their strategies were to enhance security of the email systems, password, and firewalls. On the other hand, the penetration testers frequently used words such as 'knowing,' 'learning,' and their attempts were manifested in the words of 'change,' 'create,' 'happen,' and 'correlate.' Penetration testers in the cyber offense systems appeared to be more creative and innovative, collaborating about command line scripts, exploits, elevating administrative privileges, random-ware, flooding- and taking down the competing teams' networks. The word 'team' was mentioned 11 times in the cyber defense system, whereas the word 'group' was mentioned 29 times in the cyber offense system. The differences of the word choice ('team' vs. 'group') may imply that the cyber defense system appears to be more organized, whereas the cyber offense system tends to be more ad hoc. One common word; 'tools' seems to be a boundary object across the two activity systems [38–40]. Tools were frequently used in both activity systems, which imply that the professionals' ability to know and use the right tools may have a significant impact on the success of each activity system to achieve their goals. We can confidently state that the boundary objects between both activity systems are the tools used.

There were about 10 tools utilized, such as Wireshark, zenmap, and Metasploit, etc. These were generally identified as being commonly adopted by both activity systems (Fig. 4). This implies that both activity systems may share similar knowledge and technological skillsets. It also implies that the same tools adopted by hackers to exploit other teams' vulnerabilities can also be adopted by systems administrators to identify their vulnerabilities, and vice versa. From Figs. 3 and 4 we learn that knowledge of tools may be important to cyber defense. We further identified that the vulnerability scanners (e.g., Nikto, Nessus, etc.), antivirus (e.g., Kaspersky) and setting up honey-pots (e.g., HoneyBot) were mentioned frequently in the cyber offense activity system. The cyber offense activity system also tended to explore the networks (e.g., NS

Lookup, IP-spoof understanding the DNS) and to crack the passwords (e.g., OPH-Crack, hash).

Moreover, regarding the communities, we found no interacting concepts—frequently-used words—between both activity systems (Fig. 6). However, we identified that the community referred to by the cyber defense system was the 'company,' whereas the community for the cyber offense system was the 'industry.' This difference can be easily explained by the fact that the cyber defense is the goal of IT systems administrators for the company. System administrators defend the company's information assets, adhere to organizational goals, and interact frequently with their colleagues to ensure organizational policy is complied with and to safeguard organizational interests. However, in the cyber offense system, 'industry' is frequently mentioned in terms of community. They identified targets as 'flags' to capture. Cyber offense systems appear to be more open. Subjects in the cyber offense system constantly deal with problems, and figure out new ways to reach their goals. They tend to face 'problems' more 'openly,' and always are ready to 'learn' and find out 'answers.'

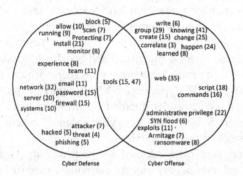

Fig. 3. Objects and outcome of the interaction between two activity systems

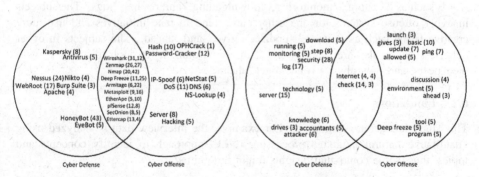

Fig. 4. Tools adopted during the interaction of two activity systems   **Fig. 5.** Rules adopted by two activity systems

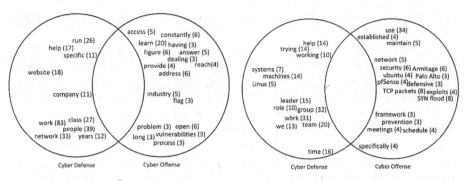

Fig. 6. Communities differentiated between two activity systems

Fig. 7. Division of labor represented by two activity systems

Furthermore, there were no commonly used words—as boundary objects—found between the two activity systems regarding their division of labor (Fig. 7). But, we found that the cyber defense systems tend to be a little more organized as reflected in frequently used words such as 'leader,' 'group,' 'team,' 'roles,' and 'we.' The focus of cyber defense systems was mostly centered on the systems such as Linux, and the subjects in the cyber defense system spend 'time' on 'working' and 'trying.' By contrast, the cyber offense systems 'maintain' and 'establish' hidden connections with their targets. They do not shy away from using tools (e.g., Armitage), penetrating using techniques (e.g., analyzing TCP packets, SYN flooding, exploits) against targets' systems (e.g., Ubuntu) and networks guarded by firewalls (e.g., Palo Alto Network firewalls, and pfSense). Subjects in the cyber offense system also have ad hoc 'frameworks' for 'meetings' and 'schedules.'

Finally, when analyzing rules adopted by both activity systems, we identified 'Internet' and 'checking' as boundary objects, commonly used by both activity systems as they frequently check references and gained knowledge from the Internet (Fig. 5). Subjects in cyber defense systems use more applied technologies, frequently using words such as 'running,' 'monitoring,' 'downloading,' and reading 'logs.' The subjects in cyber offense systems, on the other hand, tend to take initiatives and use more creative terms such as 'launch,' 'update,' 'give,' and 'ahead.' The subjects in cyber defense systems also are more aware of the 'environment' through 'discussion' with their peers, and they always want to get 'ahead.'

6.2   Limitations

This study has certain limitations. For example, the interview data is analyzed using quantitative natural language processing (NLP) approach to identify concepts and topics; thus, some contextual insights might be omitted.

7   Conclusions and Future Work

This study adopts Activity Theory to examine the interaction between cyber defense and offense activity systems. The simulation of interactions between two activity systems helps the participants to gain knowledge and insights from the expansive learning process and outcome. *Contradictions* to the objectives were created through the interaction between these two activity systems. The study identifies the creation of contradicting values, which assist in expanding participants' learning in the domain of cybersecurity. The boundary objects found between two activity systems include the tools, the Internet and the inquiry/searching 'skills' involved in the process of checking for references. The future work will include a qualitative analysis of the interview data to derive context-specific insights, and the participants' subjective consciousness in order to understand the contrast with the current objective approach—natural language processing (NLP).

The practical implications of the study inform the organizations, the practitioners, and the educational institutions to suggest that the best approach to learn, to teach and to enhance the consciousness of cyber defense is through the creation of contradictions; that is, looking through the lens of opposition in the activity systems in cyberspace.

Acknowledgement. The authors wish to thank Alison von Eberstein for the contribution on the interview questionnaire, consent form, and the Institutional Review Board (IRB) protocol approved by Florida State University Human Subjects Committee. The authors also wish to thank Christy Chatmon for the effort on interviewing participants and data collection during Spring 2017, Vanessa Myron for the effort on transcribing interviews, and Sushmita Khan for the effort on interview data analysis during Fall 2018.

Appendix A

(See Table 2).

Table 2. Frequency of DNS requests

Team	System	IP address	Activities as represented by frequency of DNS requests	Team	System	IP address	Activities as represented by frequency of DNS requests
A	A-Apache-03	192.168.72.13	8	B	B-Apache-01	192.168.72.34	3
	A-Apache-04	192.168.72.14	2		B-Apache-02	192.168.72.35	119
	A-Comodo	192.168.72.16	165		B-Apache-04	192.168.72.37	1162
	A-pfSense	192.168.72.22	101412		B-Comodo	192.168.72.39	410
	A-SecOnion	192.168.72.23	15407		B-pfSense	192.168.72.45	48639
	A-Win-02	192.168.72.30	24		B-Win-01	192.168.72.52	6
	A-Win-03	192.168.72.31	3858		B-Win-02	192.168.72.53	1426
	A-Win-04	192.168.72.32	2278		B-Win-03	192.168.72.54	1898
					B-Win-04	192.168.72.55	507
C	C-Apache-04	192.168.72.60	1	D	D-Apache-03	192.168.72.82	2313
	C-Comodo	192.168.72.62	389		D-Apache-04	192.168.72.83	2092
	C-Kali-01	192.168.72.63	1271		D-Comodo	192.168.72.85	259
	C-Kali-03	192.168.72.65	149		D-pfSense	192.168.72.91	138457
	C-pfSense	192.168.72.68	51918		D-Ubuntu-04	192.168.72.96	22
	C-SecOnion	192.168.72.69	424		D-Ubuntu-05	192.168.72.97	2
	C-Ubuntu-03	192.168.72.72	8		D-Win-02	192.168.72.99	3
	C-Win-01	192.168.72.75	3		D-Win-04	192.168.72.101	1916
	C-Win-03	192.168.72.77	6		D-Win-05	192.168.72.102	1

References

1. Verizon 2018 Data breach investigations report. Verizon (2018). http://www. documentwereld.nl/files/2018/Verizon-DBIR_2018-Main_report.pdf. Accessed 5 Nov 2018
2. Willison, R., Warkentin, M.: Beyond deterrence: an expanded view of employee computer abuse. MIS Q. **37**(1), 1–20 (2013)
3. Ho, S.M., Hancock, J.T., Booth, C.: Ethical dilemma: deception dynamics in computer-medicated group communication. J. Am. Soc. Inf. Sci. Technol. **68**(12), 2729–2742 (2017)
4. Ho, S.M., et al.: Demystifying insider threat: language-action cues in group dynamics. In: Hawaii International Conference on System Sciences (HICSS-49). IEEE, Kauai (2016)
5. Ho, S.M., Kaarst-Brown, M., Benbasat, I.: Trustworthiness attribution: inquiry into insider threat detection. J. Assoc. Inf. Sci. Technol. **69**(2), 271–280 (2018)
6. Ho, S.M.: Leader member exchange: an interactive framework to uncover a deceptive insider as revealed by human sensors. In: Proceedings of the 2019 52nd Hawaii International Conference on System Sciences (HICSS-52). Shidler College of Business, Maui (2019)
7. Vance, A., Lowry, P.B., Eggett, D.: Using accountability to reduce access policy violations in information systems. J. Manag. Inf. Syst. **29**(4), 263–290 (2014)
8. Nardi, B.: Studying context: a comparison of activity theory, situated action models, and distributed cognition. In: Nardi, B. (ed.) Context and Consciousness: Activity Theory and Human-Computer Interaction, pp. 69–102. The MIT Press, Cambridge (1996)
9. Ho, S.M., von Eberstein, A., Chatmon, C.: Expansive learning in cyber defense: transformation of organizational information security culture. In: Proceedings of the 12th Annual Symposium on Information Assurance (ASIA 2017), pp. 23–28. Academic Track of the 20th Annual NYS Cyber Security Conference, Albany (2017)
10. Engeström, Y.: Expansive learning at work: toward an activity theoretical reconceptualization. J. Educ. Work **14**(1), 133–156 (2001)
11. Leont'ev, A.N.: The problem of activity in psychology. Soviet Psychol. **13**(2), 4–33 (1974)
12. Vygotsky, L.: Interaction between learning and development. In: Gauvain, M., Cole, M. (eds.) Readings on the Development of Children, pp. 34–40. Scientific American Books, New York (1978)
13. Miettinen, R., Paavola, S.: Reconceptualizing object construction: the dynamics of Building Information Modelling in construction design. Inf. Syst. J. **28**(3), 516–531 (2018). Special Issue: Combined Special issues on Activity Theory and Global Sourcing and Development: New Drivers, Models and Impacts
14. Karanasios, S.: Toward a unified view of technology and activity: the contribution of activity theory to information systems research. Inf. Technol. People **31**(1), 134–155 (2018)
15. Engeström, Y.: Learning by Expanding: An Activity-Theoretical Approach to Developmental Research, 2nd edn, p. 338. Cambridge University Press, New York (1987)
16. Karanasios, S., Allen, D.: Activity theory in information systems research. Inf. Syst. J. **28**(3), 439–441 (2018). Special Issue: Combined Special issues on Activity Theory and Global Sourcing and Development: New Drivers, Models and Impacts
17. Russell, D.: Rethinking genre in school and society: an activity theory analysis. Writ. Commun. **14**(4), 504–554 (1997)
18. Russell, D.: Activity theory and its implications for writing instruction. In: Petraglia, J. (ed.) Reconceiving Writing, Rethinking Writing Instruction, pp. 51–78. Lawrence Erlbaum Associates, Inc., Hillsdale (2002)
19. Jonassen, D.H., Ronrer-Murphy, L.: Activity theory as a framework for designing constructivist learning environments. Educ. Technol. Res. Dev. (ETR&D) **47**(1), 61–79 (1999)
20. Miettinen, R.: The riddle of things: activity theory and actor-network theory as approaches to studying innovations. Mind Cult. Act. **6**(3), 170–195 (1999)

21. Virkkunen, J., Kuutti, K.: Understanding organizational learning by focusing on "activity systems". Acc. Manag. Inf. Technol. **10**(4), 291–319 (2000)
22. Jarzabkowski, P.: Strategic practices: an activity theory perspective on continuity and change. J. Manag. Stud. **40**(1), 23–55 (2003)
23. Jarzabkowski, P., Wolf, C.: An activity theory approach to strategy as practice. In: Golsorkhi, D., et al. (eds.) Cambridge Handbook of Strategy as Practice, pp. 165–183. Cambridge University Press, Cambridge (2015)
24. Allen, D., et al.: How should technology-mediated organizational change be explained? A comparison of the contributions of critical realism and activity theory. MIS Q. **37**(3), 835–854 (2013)
25. Karanasios, S.: Framing ICT4D research using activity theory: a match between the ICT4D field and theory? Inf. Technol. Int. Dev. **10**(2), 1–17 (2014)
26. Foot, K.A.: Cultural-historical activity theory: exploring a theory to inform practice and research. J. Hum. Behav. Soc. Environ. **24**(3), 329–347 (2014)
27. Roth, W.-M.: Emotion at work: a contribution to third-generation cultural-historical activity theory. Mind Cult. Act. **14**(1–2), 40–63 (2007)
28. Dennehy, D., Conboy, K.: Going with the flow: an activity theory analysis of flow techniques in software development. J. Syst. Softw. **133**, 160–173 (2017)
29. Kuutti, K.: Activity theory and its applications to information systems research and development. In: Nissen, H.E., Klein, H.K., Hirschheim, R. (eds.) Information Systems Research: Contemporary Approaches and Emergent Traditions, pp. 529–549. Elsevier North-Holland, Inc., Amsterdam (1991)
30. Kuutti, K.: Activity theory as a potential framework for human-computer interaction research. In: Nardi, B.A. (ed.) Context and Consciousness: Activity Theory and Human-Computer Interaction, MIT Press, Cambridge (1996)
31. Kuutti, K.: Activity theory, transformation of work, and information systems design. In: Engeström, Y., Miettinen, R., Punamäki-Gitai, R.-L. (eds.) Perspectives on Activity Theory, pp. 1–360. Cambridge University Press, Cambridge (1999)
32. Kuutti, K., Arvonen, T.: Identifying potential CSCW applications by means of activity theory concepts: a case example. In: Proceedings of the 1992 ACM Conference on Computer-Supported Cooperative Work (CSCW 1992). ACM, Toronto (1992)
33. Nardi, B.: Activity theory and human-computer interaction. In: Nardi, B. (ed.) Context and Consciousness, pp. 7–16. The MIT Press, Cambridge (1996)
34. Suchman, L.A.: Plans and Situated Actions: The Problem of Human Machine Communication, p. 203. Cambridge University Press, Cambridge (1987)
35. Kaptelinin, V., Nardi, B.A., Macaulay, C.: Methods & tools: the activity checklist: a tool for representing the "space" of context. In: Interactions 1999, pp. 27–39. ACM, New York (1999)
36. Engeström, Y., Sannino, A.: Discursive manifestations of contradictions in organizational change efforts. J. Organ. Change Manag. **24**(3), 368–387 (2011)
37. Kaptelinin, V.: The object of activity: making sense of the sense-maker. Mind Cult. Act. **12**(1), 4–18 (2005)
38. Star, S.L., Griesemer, J.R.: Institutional ecology, 'translations' and boundary objects: amateurs and professionals in Berkeley's Museum of Vertebrate Zoology, 1907-39. Soc. Stud. Sci. **19**(3), 387–420 (1989)
39. Star, S.L.: This is not a boundary object: reflections on the origin of a concept, Sci. Technol. Hum. Values **35**(5), 601–617 (2010)
40. Star, S.L.: The structure of ill-structured solutions: boundary objects and heterogeneous distributed problem solving. In: Distributed Artificial Intelligence, pp. 37–54. Elsevier (1989)

An Improved Grey Multivariable Verhulst Model for Predicting CO_2 Emissions in China

Yi-Chung Hu[1], Hang Jiang[2(✉)], Peng Jiang[3], and Peiyi Kong[4]

[1] Department of Business Administration, Chung Yuan Christian University,
Taoyuan, Taiwan
[2] School of Business Administration, Jimei University, Xiamen, China
hangjiang@jmu.edu.cn
[3] School of Business, Shandong University, Weihai, China
[4] School of Economics and Management, Nanyang University, Xiamen, China

Abstract. A new method for discussing the relationship between CO_2 emissions and bilateral FDI is proposed using grey systems theory. CO_2 emissions and bilateral FDI, GDP are separately regarded as the input to, and output of, a grey system to establish a grey multivariable Verhulst model, GVM(1,N). To improve the prediction accuracy, the residual modification model are combined to the original GVM(1,N) model. Based on data relating to CO_2 emissions and bilateral FDI, GDP in China from 2001 to 2014, empirical research shows that the bilateral FDI help reduce CO_2 emissions, whereas the GDP results in CO_2 emissions.

Keywords: CO_2 emissions · Bilateral FDI ·
Grey multivariable verhulst model · Residual modification

1 Introduction

Since the introduction of China's "Reform and Opening Up" policy, the Chinese government has make great effort to market-oriented reform and the "go out and bring in" strategy [1]. The amount of inward foreign direct investment (IFDI) grew explosively, and now China has become the second largest IFDI host country (behind America) all over the world. Meanwhile, with the rapid economic development, China is gradually transit from FDI recipient to FDI investor. The total amount of outward foreign direct investment (OFDI) is increasing continuously, especially since the proposal of the Belt and Road initiative. There is no doubt that bilateral FDI are the engine and a kind of catalyst for China in economic development. However, for those emerging economies like China, low standards of environmental regulations, cheap labor and energy costs are always used as incentives to attract IFDI. Along with the urgent need of economic development, IFDI brings a series of environmental problems to host country, such as CO_2 emissions. On the other hand, China's OFDI will also have an impact on home country's CO_2 emissions, whereas the results of the relationship between OFDI and CO_2 are still confused. Since the CO_2 emissions must be taken into account for sustainable development in China, this leads to an important issue related to how to accurately predict CO_2 emissions considering bilateral FDI.

F. F.-H. Nah and K. Siau (Eds.): HCII 2019, LNCS 11589, pp. 354–366, 2019.
https://doi.org/10.1007/978-3-030-22338-0_29

Many forecasting methods have been used to CO_2 emissions forecasting, including time series analysis, spatial econometric, artificial intelligence [2–5]. Usually, the above-mentioned methods required a large number of samples to reduce the random interference caused by uncertain factors. Beyond this, econometric methods required the data conform to statistical assumptions, such as normal distribution, as well [6]. However, the data of CO_2 emissions do not often satisfy the assumption, limiting the forecasting capabilities. Therefore, constructing a prediction model that works well with small samples, without making any statistical assumption is the main purpose of this paper. One of the grey prediction models, grey multivariable model GM(1,N), has drawn out attention to CO_2 emissions forecasting. Compared to another widely used grey prediction GM(1,1) model, GM(1,N) model takes account the influence of N-1 relevant factors on the system to improve the prediction accuracy.

The GM(1,N) model is a first order grey multivariable prediction model, contained a system behavior variable and N-1 relevant variables. This model can analyze the effect of multiple relevant variables on the system behavior variable. To improve the simulation and prediction performance of the traditional GM(1,N) model, several improved versions have been proposed, such as a grey prediction model with convolution integral (GMC(1,N)) and an improved GM(1,N) models with optimal background values [7–9]. These existing grey GM(1,N) models and their improved models have linear features with regards structure [10]. However, most of the structure of a real system is non-linear. Therefore, using a linear structure of GM(1,N) model to describe or predict the behavior of a non-linear system can cause unacceptable modeling error [10].

A traditional Verhulst model is mainly used to describe the process with saturation, which is commonly used in population prediction, biological growth forecast, product economic life prediction and so on [11]. It grows slowly in the initial stage, then the growth rate increase quickly, finally, the growth changes from the high-speed to the low-speed until to the cessation of growth, so the data are being the form of S-type [12]. Grey prediction model is established on the randomicity of accumulated generating weakened sequence and the rules of system changes. The model is constructed on the basis of a qualitative analysis, so it generally has higher simulation accuracy and prediction precision, gets preferable results in application. The grey Verhulst model, GVM(1,1), is modeling on base of the raw data from accumulating generation, which expands the available range of the traditional Verhulst model to the approximate single-peak type of data. Therefore, GVM(1,1) model has been widely applied in different fields recently [13–15].

Referring to GVM(1,1) model, this paper proposes a grey multivariable Verhulst model, GVM(1,N), with a view to providing an effective quantitative method to forecast Chinese CO_2 emissions considering the non-linear effect of bilateral FDI. In addition, the residual modification model built on residual obtained from the GVM(1, N) model could improve the prediction accuracy. The proposed improved prediction model is a two-stage procedure; the first stage uses the GVM(1,N) model to generate the predicted value, and the second stage use the traditional GM(1,1) model and Fourier series to modify the residual error, respectively. To verify the validity of the proposed prediction model, the hybrid prediction model is compared with original

GVM(1,N) model in terms of prediction performance using mean absolute percentage error (MAPE).

The rest of this paper is organized as follows: the Sect. 2 is a review of the literature related to this research. Section 3 introduce the GVM(1,N) model and the proposed grey residual modification model combining GVM(1,N) with residual modification model using GM(1,1) and a Fourier series. The empirical analysis of CO_2 emissions in China is presented in Sect. 4. Finally, Sect. 5 discusses the results and presents conclusion.

2 Literature Review

2.1 Forecasting China's CO_2 Emissions

As a developing country, Chinese energy consumption, especially fossil energy consumption is constantly growing with the acceleration industrialization and urbanization, hence, the future changing trend in CO_2emissions is a concern: to that end, many scholars have forecast Chinese CO_2 emissions from different perspectives.

For the prediction of Chinese future CO_2 emissions, the most widely used model is the IPTA, which is also known as the Kaya model. Du, Wang [16] improved the IPTA model and used it to predict and analyze China's per capita carbon emissions in three assumed scenarios up to 2050.

In addition, many scholars have used other methods to forecast Chinese carbon emissions. Zhou, Fridley [17] evaluated the efficiency of Chinese energy consumption and thought that Chinese carbon emissions would reach a peak in 2030. Gambhir, Schulz [18] used the hybrid modeling method to forecast Chinese carbon emissions in 2050. Liu, Mao [19] forecast the gross carbon dioxide emissions and their intensity in China from 2013 to 2020 using a system dynamics simulation.

From the above forecasting results, we know that the traditional EKC method and other forecasting methods have been widely used. As economic growth has a prominent non-linear impact on carbon emissions, if the prediction of carbon emissions were based on the non-linear relationship between carbon emissions and economic growth, it would not only have theoretical support but also could result in more direct policy suggestions for economic growth and environmental quality. In fact, few scholars make such an attempt at present.

2.2 Grey Forecasting Method

To solve the problem of analysis, modeling, prediction and control of uncertain system, Deng [20] proposed the use of a grey system. As this theory had obtained ideal effects of application in practice, the grey theory has been recognized by many scholars at home and abroad in recent years, and its application fields have been extended from control science to many fields such as industry, agriculture, energy, economy, management, and so on [21, 22].

Deng [20] first proposed a multivariable grey model GM(1,N), and it was used in the coordination and development of the planning of the economy, technology, and society of a city in Hubei Province. The GM(1,N) is a first-order multivariable grey model, the model contains a system behavior variable and N-1 influencing factor variables: this model can analyze the effect of multiple influencing factor variables on the behavior of the system. When the changing trends of influencing factor variables were known, we can also predict the behavior variables of the system. Liu and Lin (2006) give approximate whitening time response functions of the GM(1,N). Tien [23] showed that the approximate whitening time response function of the GM(1,N) could lead to unacceptable experimental error at times. The time response function of the GM (1,N) is not always precise and the accuracy of the model is not high. Tien [24] added a control parameter into the grey differential equation of the traditional GM(1,N), meanwhile, used the convolution integral technique to solve the whitening differential equation: the improved model was named GMC(1,N). Hsu [25] used a genetic algorithm to optimize the interpolation coefficient of the background value of the GM(1,N), and the optimization model was applied to predict the output value of the integrated circuit industry in Taiwan, to better forecasting effect. Pei, Chen [8] applied the GA-based GM(1,N) model to forecast the input-output system of Chinese high-tech industry.

3 Methodologies

In this subsection, the algorithm of the grey multivariable Verhulst model is introduced and the inherent definitions of the main parameters are briefly analyzed to gain a better understanding of the relationship between the system behavior variable and the relevant variables. Then, the improved prediction model is proposed based on combining grey multivariable Verhulst model with residual modification model, and its modeling procedure is demonstrated stepwise.

3.1 Grey Multivariable Verhulst Model

Taking into account the fact that the existing grey multivariable model cannot be used to describe the non-linear relationship between CO_2 emission and bilateral FDI, this paper will introduce a Verhulst model into the most widely used grey multivariable model GM(1,N) to describe the non-linear effect that the relevant variables exert on the system behavior variable, and then we will construct the grey multivariable Verhulst model (GVM(1,N)).

Assume that $X_1^{(0)} = (x_1^{(0)}(1), x_1^{(0)}(2), \ldots, x_1^{(0)}(n))$ is original data of a system characteristic sequence (or dependent variable sequence), and $X_i^{(0)} = (x_i^{(0)}(1), x_i^{(0)}(2), \ldots, x_i^{(0)}(n))$, where $i = 2, 3, \ldots, N$ are the relevant variable sequences (or independent variable sequences), which have a certain relationship with sequence $X_1^{(0)}$.

Then the new sequence $x_i^{(1)} = (x_i^{(1)}(1), x_i^{(1)}(2), \ldots, x_i^{(1)}(n))$ can be generated from $X_i^{(0)}$ by the first order accumulated generating operation (1-AGO) as follows:

$$x_i^{(1)}(k) = \sum_{j=1}^{k} x_i^{(0)}(j), \; k = 1, \, 2, \ldots, \, n \tag{1}$$

The background value, $z_1^{(1)}(k)$, is the adjacent neighbor mean generated sequence of $X_1^{(1)}$.

$$z_1^{(1)}(k) = 0.5 \times \left(x_1^{(1)}(k) + x_1^{(1)}(k-1) \right) \tag{2}$$

Then,

$$x_1^{(0)}(k) + az_1^{(1)}(k) = \sum_{i=2}^{n} b_i \left(x_i^{(1)}(k) \right)^2 \tag{3}$$

is called a grey multivariable Verhulst model, abbreviated as GVM(1,N), where a is called the development coefficient of the system, $b_i \left(x_i^{(1)}(k) \right)^2$ the driving term, and b_i the driving coefficient. The corresponding whitening differential equation is written as follows:

$$\frac{dx_1^{(1)}}{dt} + ax_1^{(1)} = \sum_{i=2}^{n} b_i \left(x_i^{(1)}(k) \right)^2 \tag{4}$$

In turn, a and b_i can be obtained by using the original least squares (OLS) method:

$$[a, \, b_i]^T = (B^T B)^{-1} B^T y \tag{5}$$

$$B = \begin{bmatrix} -z_1^{(1)}(2) & \left(x_2^{(1)}(2) \right)^2 & \cdots & \left(x_N^{(1)}(2) \right)^2 \\ -z_1^{(1)}(3) & \left(x_2^{(1)}(3) \right)^2 & \cdots & \left(x_N^{(1)}(3) \right)^2 \\ \vdots & \vdots & \ddots & \vdots \\ -z_1^{(1)}(n) & \left(x_2^{(1)}(n) \right)^2 & \cdots & \left(x_N^{(1)}(n) \right)^2 \end{bmatrix} \tag{6}$$

and

$$y = \left[x_1^{(0)}(2), \, x_1^{(0)}(3), \, \ldots, \, x_1^{(0)}(n) \right]^T \tag{7}$$

The approximate time response sequence of the GVM(1,N) model is given by

$$\hat{x}_1^{(1)}(k) = \left[x_1^{(0)}(1) - \frac{1}{a} \sum_{i=2}^{n} b_i \left(x_i^{(1)}(k) \right)^2 \right] e^{-a(k-1)} + \frac{1}{a} \sum_{i=2}^{n} b_i \left(x_i^{(1)}(k) \right)^2 \tag{8}$$

Finally, using the inverse accumulated generating operation (IAGO), the predicted value $x_k^{(0)}$ is

$$\hat{x}_1^{(0)}(k) = \hat{x}_1^{(1)}(k) - \hat{x}_1^{(1)}(k-1), \ k = 2, \ 3, \ldots, \ n \tag{9}$$

Note that $\hat{x}_1^{(1)}(1) = x_1^{(0)}(1)$ holds.

3.2   The Improved Grey Multivariable Verhulst Model

The improved grey multivariable Verhulst model uses GVM(1,N) model to generate the predicted value, after which the GM(1,1) model and the Fourier series are used to correct the residuals generated by GM(1,N), respectively, abbreviated as RGVM(1,N) and FGVM(1,N). The construction of the GMGMF can be described as follows:

Step 1: Establish a GVM(1,N) model for $x_i^{(0)}$ and generate the predicted value of GVM(1,N), $\hat{x}_i^{(0)}$.

Step 2: Generate the sequence of residual values $\varepsilon_k^{(0)} = (\varepsilon_2^{(0)}, \ \varepsilon_3^{(0)}, \ldots, \ \varepsilon_n^{(0)})$ based on the following equation.

$$\varepsilon_k^{(0)} = x_1^{(0)}(k) - \hat{x}_1^{(0)}(k), \ k = 2, \ 3, \ldots, \ n \tag{10}$$

Step 3: Generating the predicted residual of $\hat{\varepsilon}_k^{(0)}$ by the residual model established as GM(1,1) model (see Appendix A) and Fourier series (see Appendix B) for $\varepsilon_k^{(0)}$, respectively.

Step 4: The predicted value of RGVM(1,N), and FGVM(1,N), $x_1^{'(0)}(k)$, can be calculated as.

$$x_1^{'(0)}(k) = \hat{x}_1^{(0)} + \hat{\varepsilon}_k^{(0)}, \ k = 2, \ 3, \ldots, \ n \tag{11}$$

Figure 1 shows a procedure of the proposed residual modification model.

3.3   Evaluating Prediction Accuracy

In order to compare the forecasting ability of the proposed models against different models, mean absolute percentage error (MAPE) was employed to measure prediction performance. MAPE with respect to $x_k^{(0)}$ is

$$MAPE = \frac{1}{n} \sum_{k=1}^{n} \frac{\left| x_1^{(0)}(k) - x^{'(0)}(k) \right|}{x_1^{(0)}(k)} \tag{17}$$

Lewis [26] proposed MAPE criteria for evaluating a forecasting model, where MAPE $\leq$ 10, 10 < MAPE $\leq$ 20, 20 < MAPE $\leq$ 50, and MAPE > 50 correspond to high, good, reasonable, and weak forecasting models, respectively.

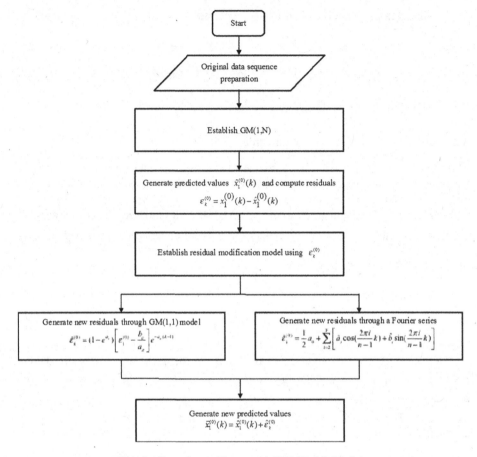

Fig. 1. Procedure of Improved GVM(1, N) Model

4   Empirical Study

4.1   Variables and Data Collection

In order to predict CO_2 emission in China considering the bilateral FDI using proposed RGVM(1,N) model, China's IFDI and OFDI are taken as the relevant variables. Additionally, in accordance with previous studies, GDP is selected as the other relevant variables as well [1]. Table 1 shows the proxies used for the relevant variables and the unit.

All data collected from World Bank Development Indicators between 2001 and 2014 are shown in Table 2. The real data from 2001 to 2012 were reserved for model-fitting, and data 2013–2014 were reserved for the ex post test.

Table 1. Relevant variables of CO_2 emissions in China

Variables	Explanation	Unit
CO_2	CO_2 emissions	Metric tons per capita
GDP	GDP per capita	Current US dollar
IFDI	IFDI per capita	Current US dollar
OFDI	OFDI per capita	Current US dollar

Table 2. Data of CO_2 and relevant variables from 2001 to 2014

Year	CO_2	IFDI	OFDI	GPD
2001	2.74	37.00	7.62	1053.11
2002	3.01	41.45	4.91	1148.51
2003	3.52	44.94	6.56	1288.64
2004	4.04	52.56	6.15	1508.67
2005	4.52	79.86	10.53	1753.42
2006	4.98	94.65	18.25	2099.23
2007	5.33	118.56	13.02	2695.37
2008	5.70	129.49	42.84	3471.25
2009	6.01	98.45	32.97	3838.43
2010	6.56	182.18	43.32	4560.51
2011	7.24	208.37	36.02	5633.80
2012	7.42	178.59	48.10	6337.88
2013	7.56	214.33	53.76	7077.77
2014	7.54	196.51	90.25	7683.50

Source: World Bank Development Indicators

4.2 Empirical Results

Following the calculation procedures, the estimated values of the development and driving coefficients, which can be expressed as $a = -0.28$, $b_2 = 2.47 \times 10^{-8}$, $b_3 = -1.76 \times 10^{-5}$, and $b_4 = -1.51 \times 10^{-4}$. As explained in Ding, Dang [27], the driving coefficient bi has its own actual meaning. Because $b_2 > 0 > b_4 > b_3$, it can be inferred that the GDP contributed significantly to the increase CO_2 in China. Parameter b_3 and b_4 indicate that increasing the bilateral FDI is helpful to reduce the CO_2 emissions. To demonstrate the efficacy and practicability of the proposed model, original GVM(1,N), RGVM(1,N), and FGVM(1,N) are used to comparison, and the predicted results and MAPE for CO_2 emissions in China are summarized in Table 3.

From Table 3, it can be found that the MAPE of the GVM(1,N), RGVM(1,N), and FGVM(1,N) models for model-fitting were 18.07%, 21.82%, and 4.09%, respectively. For ex post testing, the MAPE were 10.03%, 3.21%, and 23.05%, respectively. Obviously, both proposed RGVM(1,N) and FGVM(1,N) model are superior to the original GVM(1,N) model for model-fitting, then RGVM(1,N) model is superior to the GVM(1,N) and FGFM(1,N) models for ex post testing.

Table 3. Prediction precision obtained by different forecasting models for CO_2 emissions

Year	Actual	GVM(1,N)		RGVM(1,N)		FGVM(1,N)	
		Predicted	APE	Predicted	APE	Predicted	APE
2001	2.74	2.74	0.00	2.74	0.00	2.74	0.00
2002	3.01	0.86	71.26	3.01	0.00	2.72	9.63
2003	3.52	1.82	48.46	2.98	15.50	3.84	8.90
2004	4.04	2.94	27.10	3.81	5.77	3.73	7.73
2005	4.52	4.01	11.32	4.61	1.84	4.81	6.31
2006	4.98	4.94	0.80	5.30	6.40	4.74	4.73
2007	5.33	5.85	9.71	6.00	12.47	5.50	3.12
2008	5.70	6.05	6.19	6.02	5.50	5.62	1.47
2009	6.01	7.54	25.53	7.34	22.11	6.00	0.09
2010	6.56	6.64	1.16	6.28	4.23	6.65	1.43
2011	7.24	6.27	13.45	5.78	20.15	7.07	2.42
2012	7.42	7.56	1.84	6.96	6.26	7.67	3.26
MAPE			18.07		8.35		4.09
2013	7.56	8.12	7.42	7.29	3.56	9.97	31.94
2014	7.54	6.59	12.64	7.33	2.87	8.61	14.15
MAPE			10.03		3.21		23.05

5 Discussions and Conclusion

This paper explores the relationship between CO_2 emissions in China and GDP, IFDI, and OFDI based on the proposed grey multivariable Verhulst model incorporating with residual modification model using GM(1,1) and Fourier series.

The comparison of prediction results by different models reveals that the proposed RGVM(1,N) and FGVM(1,N) models perform well on China's CO_2 emissions prediction. The applicability of improved GVM(1,N) model has been proved. For the relationship between CO_2 emissions and GDP, IFDI, and OFDI, the control and driving coefficients indicate that the rapid economic growth would result in larger CO_2 emissions, whereas enhancing environmental protection technology via the spillover effect of IFDI, and transferring the highly polluting industries via OFDI could reduce CO_2 emissions.

In summary, the improved grey multivariable Verhulst model is an effective and practical model for analyzing and predicting CO_2 emissions in Mainland China. The limitation of the new proposed model deserves further attention and research in the future, such as the big error could appear in the data fluctuation. What is more, in regard to the residual modification model, our future research will concentrate on some other approaches, such as the Markov-chain, and neural network.

Appendix A. Residual Modification Model Using GM(1,1) Model

The computational steps for constructing the residual modification using the GM(1,1) model are as follows:

Step 1: Establish a GM(1,N) model for $X_1^{(0)}$. Then, generating the sequence of residual values, $\varepsilon_k^{(0)} = (\varepsilon_2^{(0)}, \varepsilon_3^{(0)}, \ldots, \varepsilon_n^{(0)})$.

Step 2: Perform the accumulated generating operation (AGO). Identify the potential regularity hidden in $\varepsilon_k^{(0)}$ using AGO to generate a new sequence, $\varepsilon_k^{(1)} = (\varepsilon_2^{(1)}, \varepsilon_3^{(1)}, \ldots, \varepsilon_n^{(1)})$.

$$\varepsilon_k^{(1)} = \sum_{j=1}^{k} \varepsilon_k^{(0)}, \ k = 2, 3, \ldots, n \tag{A.1}$$

and $\varepsilon_2^{(1)}, \varepsilon_3^{(1)}, \ldots, x_n^{(1)}$ can be then approximated by a first-order differential equation.

$$\frac{d\varepsilon^{(1)}}{dt} + a_\varepsilon \varepsilon^{(1)} = b_\varepsilon \tag{A.2}$$

where a_ε and b_ε are the developing coefficient and control variable, respectively. The predicted value, $\hat{\varepsilon}_k^{(1)}$, for $\varepsilon_k^{(1)}$ can be obtained by solving the differential equation with initial condition $\varepsilon_2^{(1)} = \varepsilon_2^{(0)}$:

$$\hat{\varepsilon}_k^{(1)} = (\varepsilon_2^{(0)} - \frac{b_\varepsilon}{a_\varepsilon})e^{-a_\varepsilon(k-1)} + \frac{b_\varepsilon}{a_\varepsilon}, \ k = 3, 4, \ldots, n \tag{A.3}$$

Step 3: Determine the developing coefficient and control variable. a_ε and b_ε can be obtained using the ordinary least squares methods (OLS):

$$[a_\varepsilon, \ b_\varepsilon]^T = (B^T B)^{-1} B^T y \tag{A.4}$$

where

$$B = \begin{bmatrix} -z_2^{(1)} & 1 \\ -z_3^{(1)} & 1 \\ \vdots & \vdots \\ -z_n^{(1)} & 1 \end{bmatrix} \tag{A.5}$$

$$z_k^{(1)} = \alpha \varepsilon_k^{(1)} + (1 - \alpha)\varepsilon_{k-1}^{(1)} \tag{A.6}$$

$$y = \left[\varepsilon_3^{(0)}, \varepsilon_4^{(0)}, \ldots, x_n^{(0)} \right]^T \tag{A.7}$$

where $z_k^{(1)}$ is the background value. α is usually specified as 0.5.

Step 4: Perform the inverse accumulated generating operating (IAGO). Using the IAGO, the predicted value or $\hat{\varepsilon}_k^{(0)}$ is

$$\hat{\varepsilon}_k^{(0)} = \hat{\varepsilon}_k^{(1)} - \hat{\varepsilon}_{k-1}^{(1)}, \ k = 2, \ 3, \ldots, \ n \tag{A.8}$$

Therefore,

$$\hat{\varepsilon}_k^{(0)} = (1 - e^{a_\varepsilon}) \left[\varepsilon_1^{(0)} - \frac{b_\varepsilon}{a_\varepsilon} \right] e^{-a_\varepsilon(k-1)}, \ k = 2, \ 3, \ldots, \ n \tag{A.9}$$

and note that $\hat{\varepsilon}_2^{(1)} = \varepsilon_2^{(0)}$ holds.

Appendix B. Residual Modification Model Using Fourier Series

The computational steps for constructing the residual modification using a Fourier series are as follows:

Step 1: Generate the sequence of residual values, $\varepsilon_k^{(0)} = (\varepsilon_2^{(0)}, \ \varepsilon_3^{(0)}, \ldots, \ \varepsilon_n^{(0)})$.

Expressed as a Fourier series, $\varepsilon_k^{(0)}$ is rewritten as:

$$\varepsilon_k^{(0)} = \frac{1}{2}a_0 + \sum_{i=1}^{F} \left[a_i \cos(\frac{2\pi i}{n-1}k) + b_i \sin(\frac{2\pi i}{n-1}k) \right], \ k = 2, \ 3, \ldots, \ n \tag{B.1}$$

where $F = (n-1)/2 - 1$ is called the minimum deployment frequency of the Fourier series and takes on only integer values. Therefore, the residual series can be rewritten as:

$$\varepsilon^{(0)} = PC \tag{B.2}$$

where

$$P = \begin{bmatrix} \frac{1}{2} & \cos\left(\frac{2\pi \times 1}{n-1} \times 3\right) & \sin\left(\frac{2\pi \times 1}{n-1} \times 2\right) & \cdots & \cos\left(\frac{2\pi \times F}{n-1} \times 2\right) & \sin\left(\frac{2\pi \times F}{n-1} \times 2\right) \\ \frac{1}{2} & \cos\left(\frac{2\pi \times 1}{n-1} \times 2\right) & \sin\left(\frac{2\pi \times 1}{n-1} \times 3\right) & \cdots & \cos\left(\frac{2\pi \times F}{n-1} \times 3\right) & \sin\left(\frac{2\pi \times F}{n-1} \times 3\right) \\ \vdots & \vdots & \vdots & \ddots & \vdots & \vdots \\ \frac{1}{2} & \cos\left(\frac{2\pi \times 1}{n-1} \times n\right) & \sin\left(\frac{2\pi \times 1}{n-1} \times n\right) & \cdots & \cos\left(\frac{2\pi \times F}{n-1} \times n\right) & \sin\left(\frac{2\pi \times F}{n-1} \times n\right) \end{bmatrix} \tag{B.3}$$

and

$$C = [a_0, \ a_1, \ b_1, \ a_2, \ b_2, \ldots, \ a_F, \ b_F]^T \tag{B.4}$$

The parameters $a_0, \ a_1, \ b_1, \ a_2, \ b_2, \ldots, \ a_F, \ b_F$ are obtained using the ordinary least-squares method, resulting in the following equation:

$$C = (P^T P)^{-1} P^T \left[\varepsilon^{(0)} \right]^T \tag{B.5}$$

Once the parameters have been calculated, the predicted residual $\hat{\varepsilon}_k^{(0)}$ is then easily obtained based on the following expression:

$$\hat{\varepsilon}_k^{(0)} = \frac{1}{2} a_0 + \sum_{i=1}^{F} \left[\hat{a}_i \cos(\frac{2\pi i}{n-1} k) + \hat{b}_i \sin(\frac{2\pi i}{n-1} k) \right] \tag{B.6}$$

References

1. Zheng, J.J., Sheng, P.F.: The impact of foreign direct investment (FDI) on the environment: market perspectives and evidence from China. Economies, **5**(8) (2017). https://doi.org/10.3390/economies5010008
2. Sun, W., Wang, C.F., Zhang, C.C.: Factor analysis and forecasting of CO_2 emission in Hebei, using extreme learning machine based on particle swarm optimization. J. Clean. Prod. **16**, 1095–1101 (2017)
3. Garcia-Martos, C., Rodiguez, J., Sanchez, M.J.: Modeling and forecasting fossil fuels, CO_2 and electricity prices and their volatities. Appl. Energy **101**, 363–375 (2013)
4. Chen, T.: Analyzing and forecasting the global CO_2 concentration: a collaborative fuzzy-neural angent network approach. J. Appl. Res. Technol. **13**(3), 364–373 (2015)
5. Xu, H.F., Li, Y., Huang, H.: Spatial research on the effect of financial structure on CO_2 emission. Energy Procedia **118**, 179–183 (2017)
6. Feng, S.J., et al.: Forecasting the energy consumption of China by the grey prediction model. Energy Source Part B: Econ. Plan. Policy **7**, 376–389 (2012)
7. Tien, T.L.: The indirect measurement of tensile strength of material by the grey prediction model GMC (1, n). Meas. Sci. Technol. **16**(6), 1322–1328 (2005)
8. Pei, L.L., et al.: The improved GM (1, N) models with optimal background values a case study of Chinese high-tech industry. J. Grey Syst. **27**(3), 223–233 (2015)
9. Wang, Z.X., Pei, L.L.: An optimized grey dynamic model for forecasting the output of high-tech industry in China. Math. Probl. Eng. **2014**, 1–7 (2014). https://doi.org/10.1155/2014/586284
10. Wang, Z.X., Ye, D.J.: Forecasting Chinese carbon emissions from fossil energy consumption using non-linear grey multivariable models. J. Clean. Prod. **142**, 600–612 (2017)
11. Liu, S.F., Lin, Y.: Grey Systems: Theory and Applications. Springer, Heidelberg (2010). https://doi.org/10.1007/978-3-642-16158-2
12. Wang, Z.X., Dang, Y.G., Liu, S.F.: Unbiased grey verhulst model and its application. Syst. Eng.-Theory Pract. **29**(10), 138–144 (2009)
13. Shaikh, F., et al.: Forecasting China's natural gas demand based on optimized nonlinear grey models. Energy **140**, 941–951 (2017)
14. Wang, X.Q., et al.: Grey system theory based prediction for topic trend on Internet. Eng. Appl. Artif. Intell. **29**, 191–200 (2014)
15. Evans, M.: An alternative approach to estimating the parameters of a generalized Grey Verhulst model: an application to steel intensity of use in the UK. Expert Syst. Appl. **41**(4), 1236–1244 (2014)

16. Du, Q., Wang, N., Che, L.: Forecasting China's per capita carbon emissions under a new three-step economic development strategy. J. Resour. Ecol. **6**(5), 318–323 (2015)
17. Zhou, N., Fridley, D., Khanna, N.Z.: China's energy and emissions outlook to 2050: perspectives from bottom-up energy end-use model. Energy Policy **53**, 51–62 (2013)
18. Gambhir, A., et al.: A hybrid modeling approach to develop scenarios for China's carbon dioxide emissions to 2050. Energy Policy **59**, 614–632 (2013)
19. Liu, X., et al.: How might China achieve its 2020 emissions target? A scenario analysis of energy consumption and CO_2 emissions using the system dynamics model. J. Clean. Prod. **103**, 401–410 (2015)
20. Deng, J.L.: Grey Theory. Huazhong University of Science & Technology Press, Wuhan (2002)
21. Liu, S.F., Lin, Y.: Grey Information: Theory and Practical Applications. Springer, London, UK (2006)
22. Wang, J., et al.: A historic review of management science research in China. Omega **36**, 919–932 (2008)
23. Tien, T.L.: A research on the grey prediction model GM (1, n). Appl. Math. Comput. **218**(9), 4903–4916 (2012)
24. Tien, T.L.: The indirect measurement of tensile strength for a higher temperature by the new model IGDMC (1, n). Measurement **41**(6), 662–675 (2008)
25. Hsu, L.C.: Forecasting the output of integrated circuit industry using genetic algorithm based multivariable grey optimization models. Expert Syst. Appl. **36**, 7898–7903 (2009)
26. Lewis, C.: Industrial and Business Forecasting Methods. Butterworth Scientific, London (1982)
27. Ding, S., et al.: Forecasting Chinese CO_2 emissions from fuel combustion using a novel grey multivariable model. Expert Syst. Appl. **162**, 1527–1538 (2017)

User Experiences of Incident Reporting Software in Fire Services: An Integrative Review and Meta-Analysis

Aimee Kendall Roundtree[✉] 🆔

Texas State University, San Marcos, TX 78666, USA
akr@txstate.edu

Abstract. This integrative review gathers data from published articles and user feedback for a meta-analysis of the common problems, use contexts, and recommendations. The project supplements primary interviews with secondary data from prior studies and reports, as well as online feedback and reviews. This approach helps validate user experience findings for rarely-tested products, and it helps to confirm and identify user affordances and system pain points. Findings suggest that poor visibility of system status, lack of match between system and real-world use, and opaque help and documentation are common barriers. NFIRS software programs also do not anticipate the cultural idiosyncrasies endemic to fire services (such as apprenticeship learning) that, if addressed, could help software users better recognize, diagnose and recover from decision-making errors. Firefighters request more functionality, more help to find pertinent codes, and differentiating between nondescript codes. Recommendations for improving the quality of software programs for incident reporting in fire services include improving customization features, providing templates and content guides, and improving the glossaries of common acronyms. Help systems should address the diverse backgrounds and levels of education that comprise fire services.

Keywords: Human factors · Fire services · Integrative review

1 Introduction

This integrative usability review gathers data from published articles and from user feedback to perform a meta-analysis of the common problems, use contexts, and recommendations. The project supplements contextual and individual interviews with data from prior studies and reports, as well as online feedback and reviews. This approach contributes to usability research by enlisting integrative review strategies to find and synthesize data on incident report systems in fire services. Integrative reviews are a type of review more rigorous than standard, narrative reviews insofar as they analyze experimental and non-experimental findings by combining evidence of multiple primary studies in order to derive generalizable findings from consensus [1–4]. Integrative reviews also enable merging qualitative and quantitative findings by reflecting on the interaction between ratings or numbers and unstructured feedback [5, 6]. By using this mixed methods approach, this project aggregates feedback from

© Springer Nature Switzerland AG 2019
F. F.-H. Nah and K. Siau (Eds.): HCII 2019, LNCS 11589, pp. 367–378, 2019.
https://doi.org/10.1007/978-3-030-22338-0_30

usability tests and user public comments for the purpose of formulating general heuristics to help fire services administrators make more informed decisions about the software they choose, rather than singling out a particular problem or issue with any particular vendor's product.

This study also makes a contribution by sharing a comprehensive analysis of feedback regarding incident report writing for firefighters and first responders. While the software in the fire services sector most likely undergoes user testing prior to product launch, the proprietary nature of these test results precludes their wide distribution. Considering preexisting and public user feedback about the software might encourage and inspire innovative developers to help solve the issues that persist in incident report writing software.

The objective of this integrative review is to aggregate and synthesize publicly-accessible user feedback pertaining to incident report software in order to determine the common pain points and problems for designers and developers to resolve. The research question that this article will answer is as follows: What problems with design and help documentation persist across incident reporting software products for firefighters and first responders? Findings reveal that interface design may impact decision making and report quality. In the case of fire services, interface design that facilitates decision making is essential.

Background. Software programs for incident reporting in fire services abound. According to the U.S. Fire Administration, there are 110 active National Fire Incident Reporting System (NFIRS) vendors and 86 registered vendors [7, 8]. The usability of these software programs is integral to accurate reporting which, in turn, ensures that fire services have the best data necessary for making decisions about fire risk, resource allocation, education, and outreach in a community. One fact anchors the most important issues for improving the user experience of incident reporting in fire services: The software must simplify the decision-making process because the complexity of incident reporting often antagonizes and confounds data accuracy.

A recent report on NFIRS found that the Federal system of incident reporting codes has grown too complex and unwieldy [9]. NFIRS incident types include over 175 codes to choose from and interpret; the number of codes has more than tripled from the prior to the current versions of NFIRS. Firefighters use the codes inconsistently due to personal preference, educational background differences, idiosyncrasies of training, and information overload. Fire services have difficulty deciding which are the best software programs to buy, but they have a high standard of accountability not to waste taxpayer dollars. Unfortunately, findings from vendors' usability research and testing of their own software programs often remain proprietary, which disadvantages fire departments around the country insofar as they must gather anecdotal information rather than more robust findings to make decisions about which programs to buy.

Prior studies suggest that several factors play a role in incident report writing difficulties, such as unclear reporting standards, insufficient training and quality control processes, complexity of the NFIRS coding schema, time and stress constraints that characterize the nature of incident response, and uncertainty about the importance and uses of incident report data [10–13]. Three articles also reported problems with software databases and user-friendliness [10, 12, 13]. However, two of these articles did not provide sufficient information about user feedback to integrate into this study; only one of these articles divulged all of the primary data and direct quotes from users, which was integrated into this study. Heuristics derived from this integrative usability review will not only facilitate fire services software selection processes, they will also help designers conceptualize, revise, and authenticate use cases in the fire services as these designers create and improve incident reporting software.

2 Methods

The integrative review was comprised of three sources of content: usability focus group interviews, a review of prior literature, and online review ratings.

2.1 User Focus Group Interviews

Forty-one firefighters from San Marcos and College Station Fire Departments in Texas were interviewed over the course of four weeks about their experiences using two different NFIRS software packages on the NFIRS active vendors list. The focus groups were authorized by the Institutional Review Board at Texas State University. Participants were contacted and recruited through fire chiefs and marshals at San Marcos and College Station Fire Departments. Chiefs and Marshalls sent emails to schedule interviews per shift availability. Participants were asked to fill out a brief background questionnaire. Focus group questions asked participants to share strengths, weaknesses, and suggestions for improvements regarding their current software. Of the 41 participants, 36 were male and 5 were female. Most (n = 28) were between ages 25 and 54. They had served an average of 13.7 years in fire services (Table 1).

Table 1. Focus group demographics

	Category	Number
Age	18–24	2
	25–34	15
	35–44	13
	45–54	8
	55–64	3
Gender	Male	36
	Female	5
Education	High School	2
	Some College	19
	Associate Degree	8
	Bachelor's Degree	9
	Some Grad School	1
	Graduate Degree	2
Years of Service	Average	13.7

2.2   Literature Review

The review of prior literature included English-language reports and peer-reviewed articles published between 2008 and 2018 and cataloged in Google Scholar, Ebsco, IEEE Xplore, and Web of Science. Search terms included the names of active vendors and their respective NFIRS software, as well as the terms user, usability, NFIRS, firefighting, and fire services to delineate studies and research pertaining to user experiences. The abstract and full text of each item from search results were screened for results from usability testing, surveys or other user feedback. Items were eliminated if they contained no user feedback results or if they solely contained hypothetical user models or heuristic evaluations. An Excel spreadsheet was used for data extraction, including the following categories of information from each item: citation, study methods, and results. Findings were combined using content analysis, whereby emerging themes across reports and studies were compiled. Of the 162 articles identified using the keyword searches, seven (7) met inclusion criteria insofar as they reported user feedback rather than overall heuristic evaluations.

2.3   Software Review Ratings

Customer ratings were gathered using Capterra.com. Search terms included the names of active vendors and their respective NFIRS software. Of the 108 active vendors of NFIRS software currently registered with the U.S. Fire Administration, only 24 NFIRS and emergency response programs were included on Capterra.com and received comments for review. Data were analyzed using content analysis, whereby emerging themes across reports and studies were compiled. Text mining tools—Orange.si and RapidMiner—were used to confirm word and phrase frequencies, as well as text clustering. Orange is an open source machine learning and data visualization program for interactive data analysis workflows. RapidMiner is a software platform for data science that includes data prep, machine learning, and predictive model deployment.

2.4   Results Synthesis

In order to synthesize results, all user feedback including negative comments, complaints, and suggestions for improvements were categorized according to the ten usability heuristics for user interface design offered by the Nielsen Norman Group [14]. These heuristics are broad rules of thumb for building user-friendly software products. Definitions of each heuristic are listed below, per the Nielsen Norman Group:

- *System visibility* calls for software to inform users with timely feedback.
- *Match between the system and the real world* calls for the system to follow real-world conventions and use real-world words, phrases, and concepts.
- *User control and freedom* requires that users be permitted to leave an unwanted state without an extended dialogue.
- *Consistency and standards* mean that concepts and actions should carry the same meaning throughout the software.
- *Error prevention* requires that software design prevents problems from occurring.
- *Recognition rather than recall* requires that developers make objects visible and make all instructions retrievable.

- *Flexibility and efficiency of use* allow users to tailor actions.
- *Aesthetics and minimalist design* mean clear relevant info in helpful interface design help.
- *Diagnosing and recovering from errors* dictates that software clearly indicates the problem and solution.
- *Help and documentation* must be concise, easy to search, task-focused, and it must provide steps.

These heuristics served as categories of problems that emerged from the user feedback. They also served as an intuitive schema for combining study results. Only the online ratings from Capterra provided numerical ratings offered by users assessing the overall quality of the software. Therefore, the online review rating section also integrates qualitative and quantitative feedback.

3 Results

3.1 User Focus Group Findings

In 10 transcripts comprised of 7947 lines of exchanges between moderators and participants covering general questions about incident reporting habits, processes, quality control, training, and software, there were 203 suggestions for changes or improvements to the software.

Participants reported several problems with software functioning (n = 25), including insufficient help for quality control, extra keystrokes, too many steps for some functions, and missing features that participants wanted: "You got to put an asterisk or something in it." There were several general statements of discontent about the overall performance of the incident report software (n = 27). Issues included frustration at glitches, general difficulty using the software, and the time-consuming way that the interface was designed: "It is not user friendly in the least little bit." Many of these general problems emerged from comparing the incident report writing software to other software with which they were familiar (n = 37), such as better-designed EMS software: "And the analytics with the [other program] is much better than in [the incident report program], much better." These suggestions point to an error-prone design that failed to prevent problems from happening.

There were problems with interactions between the incident reporting software and the computer-aided dispatch software (n = 16), especially auto-population errors and case sensitivity that complicated the reporting process: "It auto populates a lot of stuff from dispatch." Discrepancies emerged between observations on-site and dispatch information. They also described general limitations with the software's capacity to meet their needs regarding data collection and analytics (n = 8): "[I]t doesn't bring him the other categories for the data collection." Participants also wanted more word processing features included in the software (n = 3) to help them write narratives: "Even the spell check…is very, very, very poor. Terribly poor." Participants did not have the freedom to use the software as their responsibilities required.

There were several requests for better help documentation and software training (n = 20): "The importance of documentation." And "[the help] is too broad."

Participants wished that there were better quality templates to help them write narratives and decide which codes to use (n = 13): "You can have a system…that auto populates a narrative, but they usually aren't very good." System search tools caused problems for participants (n = 6); searches took too long or were not effective finding what participants needed: "You can search it, but it just takes too long." Help and documentation for incident report software are important for participants.

Long lists and drop-down menus (n = 11) made deciding between codes difficult for participants: "There is a long list of options, and when you give somebody like gives us a lot of options, it's difficult to use the right one." There were interface problems (n = 8), including desire for more tabs to make some features more easily accessible and for a more simple login process, as well as a more easy way to work as a team synchronously: "You can put those type of things in there, but not anything that would specify me as the person [who input the info]." Interface design and aesthetics were sometimes unclear to participants and did not aid in usability.

Participants reported dissatisfaction with how the incident reporting software handled errors (n = 5). They wanted better notification and troubleshooting of errors. "Sometimes they'll lose what they typed, and when they have to repeat it because of some error." Participants also felt that incident reporting software used jargon that was sometimes counterintuitive, which, in turn, made it difficult to find what they needed and use the software to capacity: "I wish there was a way that in [the software], I could put plain language in that describes something that happened, and then [the software] give me a whole list of codes that might apply." They wanted plain language options for correcting errors and finding solutions for software problems.

There were requests for more mobile-friendly versions of the software (n = 8), which would help them record incident observations in the field: "You have to be at the fire station to do it." They also wanted more immediate access to newer versions of the software (n = 16). Unfortunately, in the service sector, limited budgets made it difficult to purchase updates: "We had it for 20 years and we're on version seven." Participants wanted the flexibility to use the software in the field and as the job required.

Overall, firefighters reported that technical support for NFIRS software was not easily accessible. They requested more details to help them make decisions about which codes to use. They wanted more detail, such as more code definitions and expert systems to help them make decisions between codes with titles that are very similar or unclear. They wanted easier access to the software, preferring access by tablet or phone over software designed solely for desktops, because their computers were older and limited in number due to constraints on fire services budgets. Firefighters requests more group work features for NFIRS software, such as the ability for two people to work on a report at the same time. They described how some functionality made reporting difficult. In particular, long scrolling menus for reporting personnel, street addresses, and other details made completing reports cumbersome. Search features were limited, which restricted their ability to search for and across incident types, days, and shifts. Firefighters requested more training resources from software developers on NFIRS software. They also wanted more word processing features such as spell check and sentence construction, as well as glossaries for helping decipher and select medical-related acronyms. However, they disliked some of the autofill features of the software because it disincentivized firefighters from writing accurate, event-specific details, and it made it difficult for them to memorize the incident report codes.

3.2   Literature Review Findings

Methodologies varied among the seven studies, including two surveys, two usability tests (with task scenarios, walkthroughs, and think-aloud protocols), a simulation, an interview, and a Delphi group of experts. The findings suggested that mobility of incident report writing software—portability via laptop—helps them record details on-site during an incidence, but mobile phone internet access proved unreliable and difficult to read, given the small screens [15–17] (Table 2).

Table 2.   Prior literature findings.

	Sample methods	Findings	Heuristics
Coleman 2010	Survey of 35 departments	Poor GPS accuracy & mobile usability Inaccessibly small screen	Error prevention Minimal design
Peacock and Forney 2008	Surveys of 400 departments	Language clarifications Programming errors with text strings Automated error checking required Better formatting of input options	Match Error prevention Error recovery Minimal design
Romano et al. 2016	10 usability tests	Interfaces difficult to use Colors confusing or not useful Complex forms with too much & useless info Textual message slow tasks	Flexibility Minimal design Error prevention User control
del Olmon Pueblas 2015	6 cognitive walkthroughs	Awkward interface Hard-to-understand conventions	Minimal design Match
Chronaki et al. 2008	Simulation with 20 organizations, 300 volunteers	Problems over hybrid satellite-WiFi. Problems using PDAs Uncertain security and privacy	Match Flexibility Error prevention
Krueger 2010	Interviews with 20 departments	Text input problems Insufficient help & glossaries Sign-in problems Antiquated design	Error prevention Help documentation Minimal design
Averill et al. 2011	Delphi group of 37 fire department reps	Problems with data & format standards Problems merging, manage data sets Interfaces difficult to use, maintain Problems with customization No automatic entry or quality control No peer review or data transfer Make software available on multiple platforms	Consistency and standards Error prevention Flexibility Error diagnosis Match

Even when flexibility of platform choice is provided, incident report writing software is still error-prone. Forms must tolerate appropriate sentence and text string lengths, error checking logic must predict common problems, and layout of input options must promote ease of data entry [18]. For example, according to Peacock and Forney, "[f]ormatting of input options was improved to ease the data entry process. In particular, the structure for entering the fire service apparatus and personnel deployed to the scene was improved" [18, p. 66]. The design must anticipate users' needs and expectations in order to stave errors.

Even when actual time on task values are close to anticipated values, and when users self-reported satisfaction with the interface, first responders may not use the interface widely because they might be more accustomed to using affordances or other traditional methods, such as sharing info face-to-face or over the phone [19, 20]. Matching design to accommodate real-world use is important. Users also found color schemes used by interfaces confusing or unclear [19, 20]. The user interface for software must be intuitive and easy-to-use; able to auto-fill objective information from devices and instruments; designed to calculate time estimates needed to complete data entry on the front end; capable of peer review, ease of configuration, customization and maintenance, available for multiple platforms; accommodating of multiple data standards, types, systems and locations; ready to handle different types of data query and archiving; and able to check for report completeness, standards and quality [21]. As Averill et al. describe, overall, "[t]he user interface for software needs to be intuitive and easy-to-use, including business logic." [21, p. 26]. Design that attends to these issues might better predict and avoid errors, enable more flexibility to accommodate users with different skills levels, better enable consistent design and software standards, and better accommodate real-world needs and workflows.

3.3   Software Review Findings

The web findings were analyzed by using Nielsen's heuristics for usability. The ten heuristics are a means by which to assess the accessibility and usability of products. They include the following: system visibility, match between the system and the real world, user control and freedom, consistency and standards, error prevention, recognition rather than recall, flexibility and efficiency of use, aesthetics and minimalist design, help diagnosing and recovering from errors, and help and documentation. Ratings were compared with narrative descriptions of the users' experiences of the products, then they were divided into categories based on the ten heuristics (Table 3).

Table 3. Rating scores per heuristic.

	Overall	Ease of use	Customer service
Visibility of system status	4.5	4.25	4.75
Match between system and the real world	3.8	3.5	3.8
User control and freedom	3.6	3.4	3.7
Consistency and standards	2	1.7	1.7
Error prevention	3.6	3.4	3.6
Recognition rather than recall	3.5	3.3	4
Flexibility and efficiency of use	4.0	3.9	4.1
Aesthetic and minimalist design	2.9	2.5	2.6
Help users recognize, diagnose, and recover from errors	–	–	–
Help and documentation	3.3	3	3.1
Overall Review Scores	4.5	4.3	4.6
Negative Review Scores	4.1	3.9	4.2

Of 150 reviews collected, there were 65 negative reviews with several suggestions for improvements or complaints about limitations. Even though 43.3% of the reviews contained suggestions and complaints, the overall rating average was 4.5 out of 5. Surprisingly, the sub-average of rating for suggestions and complaints was only slightly lower: 4.1 out of 5. Comments about poor help support and documentation, difficulty escaping and avoiding error messages, software inconsistencies, difficulty finding instructions and definitions, repetitive errors or pain points, and poor interface design earned the lowest overall scores, as well as lowest scores for ease of use and customer service. On the other hand, despite the fact that there were more comments about problems with software flexibility and customization than any other feedback, these overall scores, as well as scores for ease of use and customer service, were high.

Most of the suggestions and complaints were about the inability for tailoring software to facilitate frequent actions and meet needs (n = 39). For example, one comment mentioned software limitations when it comes to accommodating their policies: "Limited options for complex...policies & only has bi-weekly accruals." On the other hand, comments also indicated some disadvantages to customization, such as favoring some users over others: "There are times when suggested changes cannot be implemented without affecting all users." Several suggestions and complaints also pertained to poor design leading to errors (n = 20). For example, one comment reported great difficulty with simply setting up the software: "The setup that is done for my application does not work for me."

The language used within incident reporting software was often counterintuitive, and the cost was often exorbitant. These suggestions and complaints spotlighted the mismatch between the system and practical use (n = 19). For example, software often did not populate the correct real-world address of events: "Sometimes the addresses that the residents give us will not come up on the prepopulated drop-down menu. Most of the time the problem is the address may be a store within a building that has a lot and block that are for the entire building and not just that store." There were many suggestions and complaints about the limitations and poor quality of help and tech support (n = 17). For example, several comments criticized poor tech support, customer service, and help documentation: "I contacted Customer Service and it took them 2 weeks to get back to me for a simple database question." There were fewer comments about problems with visibility (n = 4), consistency (n = 3), recognition (n = 3) and aesthetics (n = 5). For example, the software often was said to have "a bit of an older look and feel." Overall, a few comments suggested that the interface design was old and unfriendly and that more—and more intuitive—dialogue boxes would make the software more usable (Table 4).

Table 4. Integrating the findings.

	Focus group	Prior literature	Reviews	Total
Visibility of system status	–	–	4	4
Match between system and the real world	–	4	19	23
User control and freedom	27	1	11	39
Consistency and standards	–	1	3	4
Error prevention	37	6	20	63
Recognition rather than recall	–	–	3	3
Flexibility and efficiency of use	24	3	39	66
Aesthetic and minimalist design	19	5	5	28
Help users recognize, diagnose, and recover from errors	6	2	–	9
Help and documentation	33	1	17	51

4 Conclusion

Incident reporting software for fire services and first responders needs improvement overall. Three different sources—user feedback from interviews, prior literature, and ratings online—revealed several problems with the responsiveness, expensiveness, and accessibility of the software. The most common problems mentioned across all three sources were problems with error-prone conditions built into the design that trigger problems (n = 63), a lack of or too much of flexibility and efficiency of use (n = 66), and poor-quality help and documentation (n = 51). Problems with users being unable to control and escape program functions (n = 39), interface design that was either unhelpful or outdated (n = 28), and mismatches between the system and the real world needs and limitations (n = 23) were also dominant.

These findings suggest that contemporary best practices in user-centered design might very easily resolve the problems with incident reporting software. Several times (n = 37) in the user focus groups, participants compared their incident reporting software to other, better software that they use on the job. This fact only goes to show that there are, indeed, contemporary solutions to database programming, data transfer, and cross-platform usability that would benefit and update the software in this sector. However, the limitations of service sector budgets might be a barrier to applying these solutions to incident report writing software products.

Findings from this review also suggest that poor visibility of system status, lack of match between system and real-world use, and opaque help and documentation are common barriers. Interface design complicated cross-platform use from computer to mobile devices, and systems often did not provide adequate user feedback. NFIRS software programs also do not anticipate the cultural idiosyncrasies endemic to fire services (such as apprenticeship learning, log lag, house rules, and level of education) that, if addressed, could help software users better recognize, diagnose, and recover from decision-making errors. Firefighters request more functionality for reporting medical calls, finding pertinent codes, differentiating between nondescript codes, data management, and interface responsiveness. Artificial intelligence and responsive design could be used to develop solutions that help mitigate these issues.

These findings also shed some light on potential confounders in incident report writing. The software could do a better job providing automation or help documentation to help clarify unclear reporting standards. Software help documentation and services could help fill in the gap in report training and quality control processes. Improving help documentation could also help users better navigate the complexity of the NFIRS coding schema. An error-sensitive design could help minimize time on task, as could better mobile options that would allow reporting to happen on site.

Recommendations for improving the quality of software programs for incident reporting in fire services include, among others, improving customization features, providing templates and content guides, and improving the glossaries of common acronyms. Help systems should also enlist multimodal content to accommodate the diverse backgrounds and levels of education that comprise fire services.

Acknowledgments. The project was funded by State Farm Companies Foundation.

References

1. Hopia, H., Latvala, E., Liimatainen, L.: Reviewing the methodology of an integrative review. Scand. J. Caring Sci. **30**(4), 662–669 (2016)
2. Whittemore, R., Knafl, K.: The integrative review: updated methodology. J. Adv. Nurs. **52**(5), 546–553 (2005)
3. Cooper, H.M.: Scientific guidelines for conducting integrative research reviews. Rev. Educ. Res. **52**(2), 291–302 (1982)
4. Torraco, R.J.: Writing integrative literature reviews: using the past and present to explore the future. Hum. Resour. Dev. Rev. **15**(4), 404–428 (2016)
5. Doolen, J.: Meta-analysis, systematic, and integrative reviews: an overview. Clin. Simul. Nurs. **13**(1), 28–30 (2017)
6. Smith, M.C., Stullenbarger, E.: A prototype for integrative review and meta-analysis of nursing research. J. Adv. Nurs. **16**(11), 1272–1283 (1991)
7. U.S. Fire Administration. National Fire Incident Reporting System active vendors. https://www.usfa.fema.gov/data/nfirs/vendors/active_vendors.html. Accessed 1 Feb 2019
8. U.S. Fire Administration. National Fire Incident Reporting System registered vendors. https://www.usfa.fema.gov/data/nfirs/vendors/registered_vendors.html. Accessed 1 Feb 2019
9. Kinsey, K., Aherns, M.: NFIRS incident types: Why aren't they telling a clearer story? National Fire Protection Association, Quincy (2016)
10. Stefancic, J.: NFIRS Data Entry Analysis, Homeland Security Digital Library (2011). https://www.hsdl.org/?view&did=698931. Accessed 1 Feb 2019
11. Federal Emergency Management Agency (FEMA): Conquering the unknowns: research and recommendations on the chronic problem of undetermined and missing data in the causal factors sections of the National Fire Incident Reporting System, The Foundation, Washington, DC (2013)
12. Smith, M.: Determining NFIRS reporting accuracy by Alachua County Fire Rescue company officers. National Fire Academy, Emmitsburg (2007)
13. Stefancic, J.: Fire Inspection Program Analysis. National Fire Academy, Emmitsburg (2010)

14. Nielsen Norman Group: 10 Usability Heuristics for User Interface Design (1994). https://www.nngroup.com/articles/ten-usability-heuristics/. Accessed 1 Feb 2019
15. Krueger, J.: Garbage in? Evaluating the consistency of the data input into the MTFPD NFIRS compliant database. National Fire Academy, Emmitsburg (2010)
16. Coleman, K.J.: Are low cost accountability, communications, and management systems for emergency first responders using 3G and 4G cellular technologies feasible? Rochester Institute of Technology, Rochester (2010)
17. Peacock, R., Forney, G.: Multi-phase study on firefighter safety and the deployment of Resources (2008)
18. Romano, M., Onorati, T., Aedo, I., Diaz, P.: Designing mobile applications for emergency response: citizens acting as human sensors. Sensors 16(3), 406 (2016)
19. del Olmo Pueblas, S.: Real-time visualization of multi-source, heterogeneous data in emergency. Association for Computer Linguistics, Stroudsburg (2015)
20. Chronaki, C.E., Kontoyiannis, V., Charalambous, E., Vrouchos, G., Mamantopoulos, A., Vourvahakis, D.: Satellite-enabled eHealth applications in disaster management-experience from a readiness exercise. In: Computers in Cardiology, pp. 1005–1008 (2008)
21. Averill, J.D., Moore-Merrell, L., Notarianni, K., Santos, R., Wissoker, D.: Proceedings of the National Fire Services Data Summit (No. Technical Note (NIST TN)-1698) (2011)

A Storm in a Teacup:
On the Necessity/Difficulty of Establishing
a National Taiwanese Opera Troupe in Taiwan

Shin-yi Lee[✉]

China Medical University, Taichung 40402, Taiwan
sylee@mail.cmu.edu.tw

Abstract. In 1999–2000 and 2007, the Ministry of Education, Taiwan, respectively proposed to establish a national Taiwanese opera troupe in the hope of preserving this local art. A national troupe means that the government shows its will to preserve the art, and officially recognizes Taiwanese opera as a "national art." Yet, to our greater surprise, many professionals and artists disagreed on this proposal, for they believed once a national opera troupe was established, the domestic troupes may face the crisis of survival. Competing with a national troupe with more financial and technical support from the government, local and non-governmental troupes by all means would find it hard to survive. In other words, a national Taiwanese opera troupe could be a threat to the existence of the art itself. How would a cultural policy with good intentions turn out to be a controversy and causing conflicts among all? This situation will be explored in this paper: firstly, the government's role will be discussed when it comes to the development of Taiwanese opera. Then, the current condition of the local Taiwanese opera performing industry will be introduced and the relevant cultural policies will also be discussed. The last part will focus on the controversy over the necessity of establishing a national traditional troupe, and the significance of having a national troupe in Taiwan. The aim is to examine the role of the government and discuss the necessity of the political actions when it comes to preserving the local arts.

Keywords: Taiwanese opera · Government · Cultural policies ·
Theatrical company management

1 Introduction

The controversy over whether Taiwan should have a national Taiwanese opera troupe has lasted for more than two decades. In Taiwan, there are already two national opera troupes to date: GuoGuang Opera Company (國光劇團) which performs Peking opera (or Beijing opera) and Taiwan BangZi Opera Company (台灣豫劇團) which performs Bangzi opera, yet none of them performs local Taiwanese opera. GuoGuang Opera Company and Taiwan BangZi Opera Company are funded and subsidized by the government and produce fine and skillful works annually. Yet, as the only art that originated from this island, Taiwan, Taiwanese opera is not treated in the same way as Peking opera and Bangzi opera are when it comes to establishing a national troupe and

F. F.-H. Nah and K. Siau (Eds.): HCII 2019, LNCS 11589, pp. 379–392, 2019.
https://doi.org/10.1007/978-3-030-22338-0_31

receiving the annual fund and subsidy. The pros of this proposal would say this step is a must for the government to recognize Taiwanese opera as a "national opera" for it has long been underestimated officially since the Japanese Occupation Era (1895–1945) and the rule of the Nationalist Party of China (國民黨; *Kuomintang*). However, the cons would say a national Taiwanese opera is nothing but a way to deprive the art of its grassroots energy and life, and then a model would be set, which does not help preserve and promote the art. What's more, many professionals and artists also worry they may not be able to compete with the national troupe, and their market share would decline.

Starting as a daily recess activity and local folk art, Taiwanese opera now is still quite active in the domestic market and could be seen in various local ceremonies and religious celebrations. There are also annual "Golden Melody Awards for Traditional Arts and Music (傳藝金曲獎)," held by National Center for Traditional Arts (國立傳統藝術中心), and National Culture and Arts Foundation (國家文化藝術基金會) that encourages and subsidizes artists and professionals. Apart from these, the Ministries of Culture and Education both organize plans, projects, and events to boost the promotion of the local arts. Except for establishing a national Taiwanese opera troupe, the government, the professionals, artists, opera performers and even the audience may have done a lot to support this local art. Then, why is the necessity of having a national opera troupe so urgent that we need to pay so much social recourses and attention to discuss it, since the art itself is not even on the verge of extinction? Concerning the above-mentioned situation, this paper will discuss the issue and divide the argument into three major parts: firstly, the government's role will be discussed when it comes to the development of Taiwanese opera, especially since 1895, the start of the Japanese Occupation Era, to the 1950s–70s, when the Nationalist Party of China *(Kuomintang)* came in power. Then, the current condition of the local Taiwanese opera performing industry will be introduced and the relevant culture policies will also be discussed to show how the idea of nationalism and local color movement in Taiwan have inspired and influenced Taiwanese people's expectation toward a "national Taiwanese opera troupe," especially after the martial law was lifted. The last part will focus on the controversy over the necessity and significance of establishing a national Taiwanese opera troupe. The aim is to examine the role of the government and discuss the necessity of the political actions when it comes to preserving the local arts.

2 The Development of Taiwanese Opera

Taiwanese opera or *Gezaixi* (歌仔戲) has been one of the most popular operatic arts in Taiwan. *Ge* (歌) or songs are the base of this operatic art. Performers sing songs derived from local folk songs from southern China, such as tea-picking songs, boatman's songs, beggars' songs, lullabies and so on, to tell a story, and then later combine these songs to present a play. Taiwanese opera is a synthetic art composed of song-singing, chanting, stylized character types and dancing. Early immigrants around the 18th century brought local folk songs and chants from China to Taiwan, and sang them as a daily recess activity when they finished their day jobs. Later on, people added dance movements and role-playing to the simple song-singing and presented a simple skit, which paved the foundation for the essence of today's Taiwanese opera.

This simple skit could be seen in local religious festivals and public gatherings, and much appreciated and loved by the locals. During the 19th century, a more comprehensive repertoire was established, and the form of this art was much more professionalized than before and became sophisticated in style.

Starting as a common people's daily entertainment and pastime, "changing with time" seems to be something unchanged for Taiwanese opera. If we look back to the development of Taiwanese opera, we would find the art itself keeps accommodating and adjusting itself to various market demands and political powers. Despite the fact that Taiwanese opera's root is quite plebeian, the art itself has been well-received by all walks of life, and the influence was so strong that even the government sought to control and monitor the performances of Taiwanese opera. During the late 19th and early 20th centuries, people already noticed that the style of Taiwanese opera performances were very interactive and entertaining in order to attract more audiences, and many scholars and the government even advocated to ban the "vulgar" opera, for they believed that these performances might cause negative influence.[1] In order to survive, opera performers absorbed the performing style of Peking opera and later the elements of Japanese drama, and was even accompanied with modern music instruments, which added modern and exotic touches to this traditional local art.

There are two periods of time when the political forces strongly intervened the development of Taiwanese opera: one is during the Japanese Occupation Era (1895–1945), and the controlling reached its peak during the *Kominka* Movement (皇民化運動; 1937–1945); the other is during the time when the Nationalist Party of China *(Kuomintang)* came in power from the 1950s to 1970s. During these two periods of time when the political power got the upper hand, Taiwanese opera once again demonstrated its ability to adjust to the changing time and political reality.

The attitude of the colonial Japanese government towards art shifted along with the outbreak of the war. Before the Second Sino-Japanese War in 1937, generally speaking, the colonial government in Taiwan treated the local arts and customs as the access to understand Taiwanese culture and people's ways of life. At this time, the aim of the government was to pacify the mistrust and anger of Taiwanese people towards the colonial power. Yet, along with the outbreak of the war, the colonial government decided to turn Taiwan into the military base, and then issued a series of political brainwashing orders and Japanizing movements in order to convert everything about Taiwanese people into the Japanese ways, and to turn Taiwanese people into *Komin*, the royal subjects of Japan, which is the *Kominka* Movement. At this time, the institute, *Komin Hokokai* (皇民奉公會, 1941–1945) was established to put these *Kominka*

---

[1] There are some records and reports in the printed papers during the Japanese Occupation Era to prove this situation. For example, two reports of *Taiwan Jih Jih Hsin Pao* (*Taiwan Daily News*) pointed out that tea-picking opera (1898.07.19) and Taiwanese opera (1905.08.18) were so interactive with audience and presented sentimental stories, and the authorities were worried that these performances might make audiences imitate the plot and cause "negative" influence among the viewers. Therefore, the authorities and the scholars proposed to ban the performances that were too sentimental or immoral. Please see Ya-xian Xu, *History and Interpretation: Reports and Materials on Taiwanese Opera During the Japanese Occupation Era* (the title is my translation), Yilan (2006): National Center for Traditional Arts, p. 34, p. 67, p. 88.

orders into effect, such as abandoning Taiwanese religions, speaking Japanese and wearing kimonos.

As the most influential operatic art, Taiwanese opera was forced to adopt the Japanese music, costumes, and story plots. The scripts and performers needed to apply for the permission from the police before presenting the plays. Under this strict censorship, many troupes were disbanded or forced to cooperated with other businesses, such as pharmacists or street vendors. According to Yong-yih Tseng, Taiwanese opera had to be performed in Japanese and the Taiwanese language was completely banned from stage, and the performances should be Japanized in music and style, which caused Taiwanese opera to be severely devastated due to the political control [63–64]. Some scholars also share similar opinions to Tseng. For example, Guang-hua Mo also claims that the Japanese Occupation Era has been a calamity to Taiwanese opera, for the art was distorted to serve as a political propaganda [100–101]. By all means, the political force was the main cause to steer the development of Taiwanese opera, but this is also the turning point for this local art to embrace more possibilities and grow out to be a breed totally different from its Chinese soil and root, and becomes an iconic Taiwanese art. Ho-yi Lin sees this political control as main cause to force Taiwanese opera to change, but this also proves that Taiwanese opera could always survive in all kinds of political conditions [178]. Striving under the political suppression, Taiwanese opera was forced to change and incorporate more elements from different cultures in order to survive. The colonial government may have treated this art as a way to brainwash and monitor Taiwanese people, yet at the same time, Taiwanese opera showed its life and resilience when encountering severe suppression.

As the Nationalist Party of China retreated from China and took over Taiwan, art became one of the weapons for political warfare [Su 98–99].[2] The nationalist government at this time treated theatrical arts as the political propaganda, promoting the ideas of "uniting China with Three Principles of the People (三民主義統一中國)," "national anti-Russia and anti-communism movement (反共抗俄運動)" and so on. Otherwise, the acting troupes might not have the chance to perform in public if their shows did not conform with the above-mentioned ideas. Moreover, it was the Ministry of Education, not Ministry of Culture[3], which took charge of theatrical and artistic activities, which reflects that the government saw the theatrical arts as with educational and political purposes. Only those with nationalist aesthetics and moral teaching could be esteemed as the works worth preserving and promoting.

[2] In 1954, the former president, Chiang Kai-shek, published "Two Amendments of the Principle of *Minsheng* or the People's Welfare" (〈民生主義育樂兩篇補述〉 ; my translation). He pointed out that the goal of artistic and literary works would be promoting the national culture and Three Principles of the People. See "Two Amendments of the Principle of *Minsheng* or the People's Welfare," http://www.ccfd.org.tw/ccef001/index.php?option=com_content&view=category&id=110&Itemid=256 中正文教基金會(Chung Cheng Foundation), 3 Feb. 2019. Web. 3 Feb. 2019. Chiang's words were soon treated as the guideline for making cultural policies and advocated by the political elites at that time, not only for treating Taiwan as the legitimate heir to orthodox Chinese culture, but also for securing the political power of the Nationalist Party in Taiwan.

[3] The Ministry of Culture in Taiwan was established in 2012, and before that, the right to all the cultural affairs belonged to the Council of Cultural Affairs (1981–2012) and the Ministry of Education (before 1981).

In 1946, the Nationalist government issued "the Taiwan Provincial Regulations to Manage Acting Troupes" (台灣省劇團管理規則)[4] to monitor all the troupes. The purpose of these regulations was to abort all the Japanized conventions and practices in theatre, and Sinicized Taiwanese local practices. Thus, all the troupes had to register and applied for a license, and before acting, the troupes had to apply for a permit and submitted the script, the title of the play, the playwright and the list of performers to the authorities. By doing so, the government could control the content of the performances to see if the performances were in concord with the goal that the government set for them, which only reflects the government's denial of freedom of speech. Meanwhile, since they were mostly from China who barely spoke and understood Taiwanese, the officials hardly recognized Taiwanese culture and decided to wipe out the colonial influence of Japan. Taiwanese opera was by all means regarded as the venue to spread the ideas of Japanese colonization, so this "colonized" art needed to be reformed to demonstrate the orthodox Chinese aesthetics. Therefore, many Taiwanese opera performers would blend Peking opera performing techniques and music to show how "Chinese" they were, which once again steered Taiwanese opera to change and adjust itself to the political conditions.

Apart from controlling the content of the performances, dramatic academies were also established in the name of preserving Chinese artistic heritages. However, local Taiwanese opera hardly received equal chance as Peking opera or other operas from China. During the 1950s to 1970s, many Taiwanese opera troupe leaders were aware of the necessity of preserving and refining this local art, and appealed to the authorities for establish the professional school for Taiwanese opera. However, only relevant workshops or lectures were allowed to be held, which could not help much when it comes to preserving and cultivating new blood for this art [Su 117–120]. On the contrary, after 1949, many famous Peking opera performers retreated to Taiwan along with the military and governmental officials, and these performers were highly respected by the authorities and started to teach pupils in public. Peking opera started to be taught in school since 1955, and then National Fu Hsing Dramatic Arts Academy (國立復興劇校), the first public school teaching Peking opera, was founded in 1968 [Lin 233–234]. It was until 1994 when Taiwanese opera was taught as a special field in the public education system in National Fu Hsing Dramatic Arts Academy, which is 26 years apart since the academy was founded. In other words, before 1994, Taiwanese opera remained in the field of civilian and private institute and could be learned through apprenticeship.

Looking back to the history of the development of Taiwanese opera, we could find that the politics actually played a key role in directing the style and contents of Taiwanese opera. When in Japanese Occupation Era, foreign elements, such as Japanese folktales and folk songs or western music, were added to the show in order to evade strict censorship, so the opera might not be recognized as "Taiwanese." Then when the Nationalist Party of China came to power, the contents of Taiwanese opera

---

[4] The title here is my translation. "The Taiwan Provincial Regulations to Manage Acting Troupes" was soon aborted in 1948, and then the government issued "the Taiwan Provincial Regulations to Manage Film and Theatre Industries" (1948).

should be politically correct and see China as the cultural root for this local art. It is until the late 20th century that the government started to realize and preserve the essence of this operatic art and see it as an iconic culture of Taiwan. The political ideology wields such a strong influence on the development of arts in Taiwan. First the colonial government turned the grassroots opera into a hybrid and mixed form; then the Nationalist government upheld Peking opera as the model of authentic Chinese theatrical art and underestimated the value of Taiwanese opera, which forced Taiwanese opera to survive on its own before the martial law was lifted.

One situation caused by the forceful political ideology is that the government used to pay too much attention on the operatic form and politically correct content, and deliberately neglected the social and historical background of Taiwanese opera, which is also a denial of Taiwanese local culture. Taiwanese opera has long been closely connected to Taiwanese religious festivals and ceremonies. Presenting an opera to the deities is one way for people to show their respect and thanks. Apart from that, many classic operas end up with moral teaching and happy endings, which has been considered not only entertaining but educational. We can say that distorting the form and content Taiwanese opera is also devastating what makes a Taiwanese: the belief, system of values and ways of life. However, in the past, no long-term plans were made to promote and preserve Taiwanese opera but the political measures, the government's deliberate neglect of the local culture only made this art decline [Su 144–145]. Thus, the necessity of having a national Taiwanese opera troupe is not just the matter of preserving a local culture, but a gesture to show the political justice of the authorities telling people that they care, and distribute the resources to the long-forgotten Taiwanese opera.

3   The Current Condition of Taiwanese Opera in Taiwan

From the previous discussion, we know that since the beginning of the 20th century, the politics played the key role to direct and steer the development of Taiwanese opera, and the Taiwanese theatre had carried the mission to propagandize the politically correct ideas during the colonial and the Nationalist administrations. Cultural affairs were subordinate to the Ministry of Education and national Peking troupes were even under the Ministry of Defense, which only demonstrates that culture had to serve for the politics. To sum up, the basic principle for cultural affairs during the Japanese Occupation Era and the early rule of the Nationalist Party of China was the "nationalist" approach: the cultural affairs were all "politicized." Different political powers had different say in the definition of politically correct culture; what's acceptable in the Japanese Occupation Era might be aborted under the rule the Nationalist Party of China. Cultural affairs were all controlled by the ruling class. The fluctuating cultural policies and aesthetic standard might make the professionals and staff not know what to follow and feel confused and lost.

For long, culture has been second to the development of the politics and economy. The government did not have a comprehensive plan for protecting and preserving the local arts, not to mention taking care of the life of the professionals and performers. The standard approach that the government would take was to monitor the forms and contents of arts, and to give fund and subsidy, so the troupes were controlled financially and ideologically. In the spectrum of the politics, the private troupes had to take either the nationalist standpoint or the populist approach in order to survive or benefit. Taiwanese opera either reflected the taste of the authorities or entertained the general audience. Thus, we may boldly assume that since the principle of making cultural policies in Taiwan had long been "politicized," the politics has taken the core of the art.

However, during the 80s, the government started to build cultural centers in every city in the name of promoting cultural affairs,[5] which is a sign to show the shift of power control was moving from the central government to the local and the regional. It would be easier for people to get in touch with art and cultural activities, and every city government has been encouraged to demonstrate its local colors via the exploitation of its own cultural center. This is the transitional period for the Nationalist government to move to the civic government when culture has become a civic right no longer in the hand of the central and Nationalist government. Citizens could participate actively in various kinds of art and cultural events, and be encouraged to display the distinctive traits and opinions.

After the 90s when the martial law was lifted, Taiwan was released from the authoritarian rule and embraced full democracy, including the freedom of speech. Now arts no longer serve for the politics and could finally reflect the diversity of Taiwanese culture. One thing worth noting is the lifting of the language ban. In 1976, the passing of Radio and Television Act strictly limited the usage of Taiwanese language in radio and TV shows, which severely suppressed the language and caused the young generation to lose touch of the local language and culture. Students might even be punished for speaking Taiwanese in school or public. Presumably, many performances in Taiwanese found it hard to reach for more young audience, and gradually faded away from the stage of history. Eventually in 1993, the Ministry of Education listed Taiwanese and Hakka languages in the selective curriculum of the elementary school to fix the situation, reviving the language through education. As the language ban was finally lifted, Taiwanese opera by all means has found more ground to grow without the political control. Taiwanese opera clubs in schools or private tutoring classes begin to bloom, which is a counter-reacting movement to the authoritarian suppression on local Taiwanese culture. In 1991, the Taiwanese opera, Lu Bu and Diao Chan (呂布與貂蟬)[6], finally made its way to and premiered in National Theatre Hall, a significant milestone for the Taiwanese opera to move away from the street art to the high art.

---

[5] The late president, Chiang Ching-kuo (the premier then), launched "the Ten Major Construction Projects" focusing on the industrial development (1974–1979) and "the Twelve Major Cultural Construction Projects" promoting the cultural and agricultural development (1980–1985). From 1981 to 1986, cultural centers in every city were built, and 22 cultural centers were finished. See Encyclopedia of Taiwan, http://nrch.culture.tw/twpedia.aspx?id=15406 9 Sep. 2009. Web. 9 Feb. 2019.

[6] Lu Bu and Diao Chan (1991) was produced by a well-known Taiwanese opera performer, Lu-hua Yang (楊麗花, 1944-) who was also a pioneer in producing TV Taiwanese opera shows from the 70s to the 90s.

Despite the government finally recognizes and restores the iconic position of Taiwanese opera, the opera itself still faces the crisis of continuation. Today, although the Ministry of Culture is taking charge of cultural affairs, trying to uphold the importance of culture to the equal position of the politics and economy, yet the government still encourages Taiwanese opera by giving funds and subsidies, and it is more like a political gesture and election concern to distribute resources to the potential electorate. In addition, the language ban has caused the loss of young audience who barely understand the language performed onstage, and the emergence of new media, such as the Internet, also makes the performing industry even more competitive. Today's audience probably would like to stay in front of the screen or monitor, instead of going to the theatre. The taste and viewing habits of the audience have changed so greatly that the government seems to fail to notice today's art industry as well as the market demand. Giving financial support is one thing; the authorities also need to take what Taiwanese opera troupes really need into concerns.

Compared to other operas, Taiwanese opera so far is still the most dynamic and representative local operatic form in Taiwan. After the War, there were about 300 professional Taiwanese opera troupes in Taiwan [Lin 214].[7] Now there are about 107 troupes still active in 2017, and among them, there are about 20 troupes which constantly receive grants, subsidy, fund or support from the local government or the Ministry of Culture.[8] As for the profiting and nonprofit public productions (which is also called "*wen-hua-chang*"/文化場), there are about 430 other than countless productions in the religious festivals or ceremonies (which is called "*min-xi*"/民戲) in 2016.[9] In other words, we could see Taiwanese opera being performed everyday throughout the year. The Ministry of Culture awarded and granted more than 30 million NT dollars (about 1 million US dollars) annually (2013–2017) to excellent troupes, and the local government, about 3 million NT dollars (2013–2016).[10] There are also conferences, journal papers, critiques, research papers and books relating to Taiwanese opera being published every year as well social media, social networks and clubs. Yet despite the fact that Taiwanese opera is active and still popular, and the government

---

[7] The exact number of the troupes might vary based on different investigations done by different researchers. According to Lin, Su-shang Lu (呂訴上), a scholar, estimated that there were more than 200 troupes after the War [214].

[8] See *The 2017 Observation and Analysis Project on Traditional Performing Art Industries in Taiwan* (106年臺灣傳統表演藝術生態觀察與分析計畫), National Center for Traditional Arts (2017) https://www.grb.gov.tw/search/planDetail?id=12079431 Dec. 2017. Web. 5 Feb. 2019, p. 129.

[9] See *The 2017 Observation and Analysis Project on Traditional Performing Art Industries in Taiwan* (106年臺灣傳統表演藝術生態觀察與分析計畫), National Center for Traditional Arts (2017) https://www.grb.gov.tw/search/planDetail?id=12079431 Dec. 2017. Web. 5 Feb. 2019, pp. 144–145.

[10] See *The 2017 Observation and Analysis Project on Traditional Performing Art Industries in Taiwan* (106年臺灣傳統表演藝術生態觀察與分析計畫), National Center for Traditional Arts (2017) https://www.grb.gov.tw/search/planDetail?id=12079431 Dec. 2017. Web. 5 Feb. 2019, pp. 130–133.

keeps funding numerous troupes, there are two major problems endangering the continuation of Taiwanese opera. One is that the vicious price war and competition among the troupes; the other is many troupes are short of professional and long-term human resources.

According to the report of *The 2017 Observation and Analysis Project on Traditional Performing Art Industries in Taiwan,* in 2015, of all the productions of Taiwanese opera, 82.42% were "*min-xi*," and the number went even higher in 2016 to 89.87% [142], which means most of the opera troupes greatly rely on participating religious activities, instead of the funding from the government. Therefore, in order to compete for more chances to perform and to win publicity, many troupes might cut down their budget, and then a vicious price war starts. The cost-down strategy may result in the poor quality and loss of the audience. What's more, since the troupes could not earn much through producing a *min-xi*, human capital is also cut down, and the average monthly wage of the staff and performers of private troupes in 2017 is below 25,000 NT dollars (38.2% earn NT$ 20,009 to NT$ 25,000; 30.77% earn less than NT$ 20,008).[11] Many professional performers are part-timers working for different troupes in order to earn enough for keeping the basic quality of life. Thus, this kind of career environment and conditions might not interest new blood to join in, and even if new members would like to work in this field, many of them may not stay long.

Apart from the price war competition and low monthly wage of the staff, many troupes also face the difficulty of finding long-term and professional human resources. The reasons behind this difficulty might be the unstable and poor quality of life resulted from the low wage. Thus, it is understandable that except the public troupes, 85.78% of members in the private troupes are part-timers, according to the report of *The 2017 Observation and Analysis Project on Traditional Performing Art Industries in Taiwan* [64]. Even though every year, there are about 18 students or more who are well-trained graduating from the Department of Taiwanese Folk Opera, National Taiwanese College of Performing Arts, ready to participate in the profession, yet not all of them would devote themselves into the profession and keep working for Taiwanese opera. In addition to school education, there are also some projects supported by the government or personal clubs to train new blood. However, after those projects are over or the training classes are finished, still not all of the trainees or apprentices would take Taiwanese opera performing as their choice of profession.

---

[11] See *The 2017 Observation and Analysis Project on Traditional Performing Art Industries in Taiwan* (106年臺灣傳統表演藝術生態觀察與分析計畫), National Center for Traditional Arts (2017) https://www.grb.gov.tw/search/planDetail?id=12079431 Dec. 2017. Web. 5 Feb. 2019, p. 66. In fact, the average wage for the staff and performers of the traditional opera troupes has been much lower than the average wage for the labors in general in Taiwan. The minimum wage in Taiwan is NT$ 23,100 in 2019 (See "Ministry of Labor," https://www.mol.gov.tw/topic/3067/5990/13171/19154/ 8 Feb. 2019), and the average wage for labors in general in 2018 is NT$ 46,542 (See "National Statistics, R.O.C," https://www.stat.gov.tw/ct.asp?xItem=43714&ctNode=527&mp=4 8 Feb. 2019). The average wage for the opera staff and performers could hardly reach the standard of the minimum wage.

Apart from the low wage, the challenge that young performers also need to face is the impromptu style of acting. Taiwanese opera began as a street art and many early performers just learned the tunes and lyrics by heart through apprenticeship. For these performers, experience is everything. They had to observe and follow what their masters had taught them, and acted out their own style. One's capability of improvisation demonstrates one's ability of performing. Yet today's school education trains students through pedagogical approaches: musicians perform by reading scores, actors and actresses play by memorizing the scripts, the stage is modern and well-equipped, and no audience shouting and chanting with street vendors, which is completely different from the upbringing of the opera performers in the past. This generation gap also causes the difficulty for the young trainees to fit in the demand of the profession in the eye of the senior performers.

To sum up, we find that statism determined the principle of cultural policies, which means the benefits of the country is above citizens' welfare. After the martial law was lifted, Taiwanese opera comes back to people's life as an iconic cultural sign, showing the government finally recognizes the significance of this local art. However, without a sound and comprehensive plan to promote and preserve the art, the staff and performers of Taiwanese opera could only strive on their own. Living on the limited wage, the troupe members also face the challenge of recruiting new blood. Many young trainees and graduates are reluctant to take Taiwanese opera as their profession choice due to the low wage; the troupes might also find these young students are not well-equipped with the impromptu acting techniques and are also reluctant to hire them. The crisis of the shortage of long-term professionals endangers strongly the continuation of Taiwanese opera.

4 Why a National Taiwanese Opera Troupe?

From the previous discussion, we know since the martial law was lifted, Taiwanese nationalism ideology rose to overtake the Greater China perspective—Taiwan and China are an inseparable entity, which sees Taiwan as an ethnically, politically and legally independent country, as a counter-reaction to the authoritarian suppression on the Taiwanese local culture. Under these circumstances, reviving Taiwanese opera would be one of the options for the authorities to respond to the popular demand of Taiwanese nationalism ideology, and then the issue of having a national Taiwanese opera troupe has been brought up. For the politicians, having a national opera troupe is a political measure to show the government's will to preserve the art, set the artistic standard and basic wage line for the domestic troupes, and also even find more job vacancies for students graduating from schools, public projects or private tutoring classes. However, a doubt simultaneously emerges: is the purpose of the national opera troupe for preserving the art or receiving unemployed graduates? Should a national Taiwanese opera troupe be commercialized or educational?

In 1999–2000 and 2007, the Ministry of Education respectively proposed to establish a national Taiwanese opera troupe and held public hearings for professionals, scholars, artists, and opera lovers. Yet, to many people's surprise, this proposal failed twice. Then in 2018, the budget and subsidy for the only public Taiwanese opera troupe, Lan-Yang Taiwanese Opera Company, affiliated to Cultural Affairs Bureau, Yilan County, were deleted and the company might be forced to be disbanded.[12] Once again, the crisis of Lan-Yang triggered the issue for establishing a national Taiwanese opera troupe, and the debate still goes on.

The first debate about having a national Taiwanese opera troupe was during 1999 to 2001. At that time, both National Fu Hsing Dramatic Arts Academy and National Kuo Kuang Academy of Arts had their own opera troupes. These two school were merged into National Taiwan Junior College of Performing Arts in 1999, so the opera troupes also were merged. Then, in 2000, the government proposed to establish "National Dramatic Arts Center" (國立戲劇藝術中心) to manage the existing Peking opera troupe and further to build up a national Taiwanese opera troupe.[13] The proposal was soon rejected by many professionals, claiming that a national opera troupe may prevail in many ways than the private ones, such as having more resources, attracting more professionals, and having more funds. There will be no way for the private troupes to compete with the national one, which may result in the loss of private troupes, and eventually, the loss of dynamics and life of Taiwanese opera. Take Peking opera troupe as an example. Once the only national Peking opera troupe was established, the private troupes failed to compete with it, and they were either disbanded or merged with other troupes. Gradually, only GuoGuang Opera Company survives and gives Peking opera performances regularly. Without the government's protection, Peking opera may not survive in Taiwan's theatre market, for it has lost the competitiveness and ability to live on its own.

In 2007, the issue was brought up again that the Ministry of Education would like to establish a national Taiwanese opera troupe affiliated to National Taiwan Junior College of Performing Arts. The Legislative Yuan held the public hearing with a subtitle: "is the national Taiwanese opera troupe a remedy? Or a sugarcoated drug?"[14] This subtitle has already suggested the conflicting nature of this issue: the government would like to prescribe "a national opera troupe" as a cure to ease politically the dispute over the distribution of public resources to Taiwanese opera and "non-Taiwanese operas." Once a national opera troupe was established, Taiwanese opera and its

---

[12] Lan-Yang Taiwanese Opera Company was officially established in 1992, and is the only public Taiwanese opera troupe in Taiwan supported by Yilan County. Yet the annual budget and subsidy have been gradually reduced year after year and finally deleted in 2019 due to fluctuating cultural policies, which may force the company to be disbanded. See "The Budget for Lan-Yang Taiwanese Opera Company being Deleted. The Mayor Lin: We Defend Our Culture, but We Can't Raise a Cow just for a Cup of Milk" (蘭陽戲劇團預算遭砍光。林姿妙: 捍衛文化,但不能為一杯牛奶養一頭牛), *The Storm Media*, 29 Jan. 2019, Web. 29 Jan. 2019. <https://www.storm.mg/article/886591>. (The heading of this news report is my translation.)

[13] See Xin-yi Liang, "National Taiwanese Opera Troupe Will be Modeled" (國立歌仔戲團 將進入塑造期, the title is my translation), https://www.ptt.cc/man/NTUTradOpera/D60/D88C/M.984591120.A.html 26 Oct. 2000. Web. 9 Feb. 2019. The original news report was from *Min Sheng Bao* (民生報; 1999/12/14).

[14] The title is my translation. See "Establishing a National Taiwanese Opera Troupe: A Remedy or a Sugarcoated Drug?" (成立「國家歌」仔戲團—是「對症下藥」?還是「糖衣毒藥」?), *Public Hearing Information of Legislative Yuan*, https://www.ly.gov.tw/Pages/Detail.aspx?nodeid=5599&pid=47828 Web. 10 Feb. 2019.

performers could be more revered and have even fairer treatment both financially and socially. The artistic quality of the opera might also be enhanced. However, the doubt still lingers: would a national opera troupe, with the example of the national Peking opera troupe in view, truly protect the grassroots art? Or the life and energy of the art would be smothered, for all the troupes might find it hard to survive except the national one? What's more, if the troupe would be affiliated to the college, what would be the goal of the troupe? To benefit? Or to educate and preserve the art? Why does a school need to support a Taiwanese opera troupe? If so, should the school also establish different troupes for different operatic forms respectively? Then who would be qualified enough to join the troupe? The graduates? The teachers? Or even the professionals? All participants in that hearing were opera lovers and supporters, but had such a huge disagreement on this issue. The reason behind this controversy is still, I think, the standpoint of the government. If the government still sees Taiwanese opera as a political capital to flatter certain ethnic and political groups without having a thorough plan and knowledge of the performing industry, Taiwanese opera would always be second to the politics and economy.

Then, why does this issue still keep going on, since the proposal has failed twice? We can't deny the cultural affairs are still politicized in Taiwan. In the 2010 national population and housing census, there were 81.9 persons out of 100 understanding and speaking Taiwanese, and 83.9 persons out of 100 understanding and speaking Mandarin Chinese. Yet, there are only 6.6 persons out of 100 using Hakka language and 1.4 using indigenous languages.[15] Taiwanese and Mandarin Chinese are two dominating languages in Taiwan, so the supporters of the national Taiwanese opera troupe would consider it as a way to balance resources to the dominating ethnic groups. In 2016, some law-makers of the Legislative Yuan proposed that the Ministry of Culture should establish a national Taiwanese opera in order to fairly balance the distribution of public resources to Peking opera, Bangzi opera, Chinese music and Taiwanese opera. The rationale of this proposal was Taiwanese opera did not receive as much support from the government as Peking opera does, despite Taiwanese opera has been the only art originating from Taiwan.[16] This proposal once again demonstrates the political concern of the government. However, compared to Taiwanese opera, Hakka opera, indigenous cultural dances, and other minor operatic forms are quite underprivileged and need the government's support more desperately. Taiwanese opera could not even be considered as "endangered," since it is still lively and active in the domestic market. When it comes to preserving and protecting the dying arts, wouldn't Hakka opera, indigenous cultural dances and other operatic forms be more worthy our attention and efforts?

The role of the government should not be limited to be the fund-giver or financial supporter, but should transcend the political ideology. Culture belongs to the public sphere and citizens should have equal access to cultural affairs, so the government should guarantee adequate resources would be provided for all cultural and artistic

---

[15] See "Population and Housing Census," National Statistics, http://www.stat.gov.tw/lp.asp?CtNode=5993&CtUnit=2043&BaseDSD=7&nowPage=1&pagesize=25 15 May 2013. Web. 10 Feb. 2019.

[16] See *The Legislative Yuan Gazette*, Vol. 105, Iss. 76, No. 4373, Taipei (2006): Legislative Yuan, 157–219.

activities. Therefore, giving money to the art that is active instead of dying ones is nothing but a political measure. There are still many ways to protect Taiwanese arts other than having a national troupe. What the government should consider first is how Taiwanese opera has been passed down, and how the current social condition affects the teaching and learning system. What is the core value and essence of this art? And what is the current condition of the performing industry in Taiwan? We cannot just uphold the flag of ethnic and transformation justice and start a Taiwanese opera troupe in the name of preserving the dying art, but simultaneously devastate it by retaining it in the museum or cultural centers just for display.

5 Conclusion

In 2017, Kun-liang Ciou referred the controversy over establishing a national Taiwanese opera troupe in the news commentary as a storm in the teacup.[17] He does not explain further why this metaphor is used but only mentions this "small" issue "boils" again now. Yet this metaphor is quite adequate for referring to this issue: it probably would only arouse some people's interest within a limited circle. Althoughthe root of Taiwanese opera is plebeian and the opera itself is strongly connected to the religious activities today, not many people, especially the young generation, would like to watch the show in the outdoor stage. Based on my limited teaching experiences, the majority of my students do not know much about the opera until they take my course. They are far more interested to modern media and fancy foreign plays. Therefore, within this small teacup of the opera market, not many people would be affected. To the public, including those who are not interested in opera, they might see having a national Taiwanese opera troupe as a part of the transformation justice that the government mends the past mistakes through political and judicial measures when Taiwanese language and culture were greatly put down by the authoritarian rule. Yet, apart from the politically correct rationale, the government still needs to pay more attention to the art industry and market conditions. Having a national Taiwanese opera troupe should not be a simple yes/no question, but worth our further understanding. Knowing the historical background and the cultural policies in the past helps us recognize the environment where Taiwanese opera lives in, so that a more comprehensive supporting plan could be designed and constructed to truly continue the art.

---

[17] See Kun-liang Ciou, "Just Can't be Able to Establish a National Taiwanese Opera Troupe," (〈國家級歌仔戲劇團千呼萬喚出不來〉 , my translation), *The Storm Media,* https://www.storm.mg/article/267419 18 May 2017. Web. 10 Feb. 2019.

References

1. Ciou, K.L.: Just Can't be Able to Establish a National Taiwanese Opera Troupe, (〈國家級歌仔戲劇團千呼萬喚出不來〉). The Storm Media. https://www.storm.mg/article/267419. Accessed 11 Feb 2019
2. Ciou, K.L.: The Beautiful Sorrow: Lan-Yang Taiwanese Opera Company (〈美麗的哀愁—生懸命蘭陽戲劇團〉). The Storm Media. https://www.storm.mg/article/263794. Accessed 10 Feb 2019
3. Directorate-General of Budget, Accounting and Statistics, Executive Yuan, R. O. C. (Taiwan). https://www.dgbas.gov.tw/mp.asp?mp=1. Accessed 12 Feb 2019
4. Jie, Y.: Guozuzhuyi dao wenhuagongmin: Taiwan wenhua zhengce chutan, 2004–2005 (From Nationalism to Cultural Citizenship: A Study on Cultural Policies in Taiwan, 2004–2005; 《國族主義到文化公民: 台灣文化政策初探2004–2005》). Council of Cultural Affairs, Executive Yuan, Taipei (2006)
5. Lin, H.Y.: A History of the Taiwanese Theatre (《臺灣戲劇史》), 2nd edn. National Taiwan University Press, Taipei (2015)
6. Ministry of Culture. https://www.moc.gov.tw/. Accessed 12 Feb 2019
7. Mo, G.H.: Taiwan geleixing difang xiqu (All Types of Local Operatic Forms in Taiwan; 《臺灣各類型地方戲曲》), pp. 87–113. SMC Publishing, New Taipei City (1999)
8. National Awards of Art. http://www.ncafroc.org.tw/en/default.aspx. Accessed 12 Feb 2019
9. National Center for Traditional Arts. https://www.ncfta.gov.tw/. Accessed 12 Feb 2019
10. National Center for Traditional Arts. The 2017 Observation and Analysis Project on Traditional Performing Art Industries in Taiwan (106年臺灣傳統表演藝術生態觀察與分析計畫). https://www.grb.gov.tw/search/planDetail?id=12079431. Accessed 12 Feb 2019
11. National Center for Traditional Arts. The 2016 Observation and Analysis Project on Traditional Performing Art Industries in Taiwan (105年臺灣傳統表演藝術生態觀察與分析計畫). https://www.grb.gov.tw/search/planDetail?id=11804141. Accessed 12 Feb 2019
12. National Repository of Cultural Heritage. http://newnrch.digital.ntu.edu.tw/nrch/. Accessed 12 Feb 2019
13. Su, G.Z.: Guojia zhengce xia jingju gezixi zhi fazhan (The Development of Peking Opera and Taiwanese Opera under National Cultural Policies; 《國家政策下京劇歌仔戲之發展》). The Liberal Arts Press, Taipei (2003)
14. Tseng, Y.Y.: Taiwan gezixi de fazhan yu bianqian (The Development and Change of Taiwanese Opera; 《台灣歌仔戲的發展與變遷》). Linking Publishing, Taipei (2007)
15. Workshop for Taiwanese Folk Culture (台灣民俗文化工作室). http://www.folktw.com.tw/. Accessed 11 Dec 2019
16. Xu, Y.X.: Shishi yu quanshi: rizhi shiqi Taiwan baokan xiqu ziliao xuandu (History and Interpretation: Reports and Materials on Taiwanese Opera During the Japanese Occupation Era; 《史實與詮釋:日治時期台灣報刊戲曲資料選讀》), pp. 34, 67, 88. National Center for Traditional Arts, Yilan (2006)

Hidden Champions: A Study on Recruiting Top-Level Staff in Rural Areas

Andrea Mueller[1], Alexander Feldberger[2], Christina Miclau[1],
Philipp Koch[1], Lena Walter[1], Sarah Feige[1(✉)], Nicolas Schmidt[1],
Moritz Neth[1], and Oliver Korn[3]

[1] Offenburg University, Badstr. 24, 77652 Offenburg, Germany
sfeige@stud.hs-offenburg.de
[2] FAMIGO GmbH, Krumme Lache 2, 79341 Kenzingen, Germany
[3] Affective and Cognitive Institute, Offenburg University,
Badstr. 24, 77652 Offenburg, Germany

Abstract. Top-level staff prefers to live in urban areas with perfect social infrastructure. This is a common problem for excellent companies ("hidden champions") in rural areas: even if they can provide the services qualified applicants appreciate for daily living, they fail to attract them because important facts are not presented sufficiently in social media or on the corporate website. This is especially true for applicants with families. The contribution of this paper is four-fold: we provide an overview of the current state of online recruiting activities of hidden champions (1). Based on this corpus, we describe the applicant service gap for company information in rural communes (2). A study on user experience (UX) identifies the applicants' wishes and needs, focusing on a family-oriented information system on living conditions in rural areas (3). Finally, we present the results of an online survey on the value of such information systems with more than 200 participants (4).

Keywords: Hidden champions · Recruiting · Onboarding · Generation Y ·
Employer branding · User experience · UX · Rural areas ·
Family-oriented job information system

1 Introduction

Finding highly qualified employees is a squeezing bottleneck for companies all around the world. In western industrial countries, the market for well-qualified employees is almost empty. Especially companies in rural areas have serious problems to win young professionals.

There are many social media applications, describing personal experiences with the employer – however, they mostly do not show the everyday challenges of a new environment for a family. Thus, the decision-making process needs to be supported by employers in all phases via appropriate communication channels. For generation Y applicants, online-channels as well as mobile applications are the most relevant sources for gaining information about employers.

© Springer Nature Switzerland AG 2019
F. F.-H. Nah and K. Siau (Eds.): HCII 2019, LNCS 11589, pp. 393–407, 2019.
https://doi.org/10.1007/978-3-030-22338-0_32

The application process is digital – even first personal contact, job assessment and contract negotiation processes can be performed online. Several new concepts like edutainment – a trend to enrich recruiting websites with playful elements – help employers to get more attention from the potential applicants [1].

However, there still is an information gap: employees prefer to live in a decent distance (up to about 80 km) to their workplace. However, especially smaller companies do not provide relevant information for potential applicants about the facilities in the area around them.

To enhance the performance of such hidden champions' recruiting activities in rural communes, a case study of the rural region Black Forest in Germany is performed by Offenburg University and the start-up company FAMIGO. Our research aims to identify the needs and wishes of applicants, especially those with families. This objective is achieved by three empiric investigations: a series of expert interviews to gain insights into the companies recruiting practices, a user experience study to identify the needs of families while testing a prototype, and finally an online-survey to learn more about the current process of applying [2].

Quantitative and qualitative studies allow assessing, how attractive new information sources are for the target group and for companies. Furthermore, we identify and evaluate the important needs of applicants with families when relocating for a job. Hidden champions in the Black Forest region, like the Hansgrohe, Duravit, Herrenknecht or Sick can use the outcomes to enhance their job platforms with information the applicants need and thus boost their chances to succeed in the "war for talents" [3]. Moreover, hidden champions in rural areas all over the world can use the strategies described and evaluated in our work.

2 Related Work

An important goal for human resource departments in many companies is to highlight open positions to potential applicants and convince them to apply. There are several characteristics, which influence the effectiveness and success of recruitment. Part of those are payment, the company's benefits, or working hours (job characteristics), but also the company's image, work environment, and the location (organizational characteristics) are important [4]. In this chapter, we discuss relevant work for assessing the effects and the acceptance of a platform, which gathers and presents information for applicants from generation Y.

2.1 Target Group: Generation Y

Considering an enormous number of employees in Germany, who will leave their workplace due to retirement in the next few years, companies will have to replace them with younger staff from generation Y [5]. There are different definitions of the time range for that generation. For our study, we define generation Y as follows: it includes every person, who is born between the years 1980 and 2000 [6]. Thus, nowadays the age range of persons of generation Y is between 19 and 39. By 2020, already 46% of the global workforce are from generation Y [7].

Existing literature evaluates differences between the generations in work values, job satisfaction, attitudes towards work and career as well as the work-family conflict [8]. It is an important to note that generation Y's dedication to family [8] and private life increased compared to previous generations.

Many of young graduates choose their employers based on the companies dedicated to social responsibility also for their staff – preferring organizations, which match their own values and ideas [9]. To be able to recruit the needed young talents in the future, companies should adapt their human resource management to improve the attractiveness for generation Y [5]. If companies do not manage to adjust to the shifting expectations, they may encounter the problem of acquiring less qualified talents from the younger generation and therefore fail to gain a competitive advantage [9].

2.2   Challenge Job Relocation

Moving to a new location still is a big challenge for most potential employees. Recent studies show that apart from the financial aspects, moving has an immense impact on partners, children's education, and care for relatives [10]. When making a work-related decision, employees consider their family situation very carefully.

This can influence their choice in accepting a new job or starting their own business [11]. According to Martin "[…] the more the relocator prepares for his or her move, the better should be their psychological well-being following the move" [12]. The employee's well-being is also important for the company, since content workers are more willing to actively improve their workspace and are more likely to stay with the company for a longer period of time [7].

2.3   SME Employer Branding

According to Sonntag [13], small and medium-sized companies often struggle to communicate their advantages to possible applicants and market their company brand effectively. To counteract this problem, a good public image is necessary. Rampl [14] shows that work content and work culture have the greatest impact on the creation of a strong employer brand.

In order to communicate with generation Y effectively, a company should not only focus on recruiting activities to improve its instrumental attractiveness but also towards symbolic characteristics of an ideal employer. Therefore, companies need to use new applications for inbound marketing on recruitment websites and social media [15].

2.4   Job Decisions with a Family

Typically, the decision to change the job is not an easy one, because it can bring many challenges: adjusting to a new company culture, relocation cost, and changes in family or social life are just a few examples. The most common issues are not doing enough research, overestimating oneself, and only thinking about short-term solutions. Also, the difference between expectations and reality on the job can result in dissatisfaction and poor work performance [16].

Since the assessment of risk is a very important influence factor in the decision-making process, gaining secure knowledge and background information about the future situation and the surrounding environment, e.g. by gathering information a family-orientated platform, reduces the uncertainty of job changes.

2.5 Companies' Problems of Recruiting in Rural Areas

In order to gain more information about companies' recruiting challenges in rural areas, we conducted a semi-structured interview with 18 recruiting professionals. In total, we asked 18 questions regarding the current employee situation and ideas, how a family-oriented information platform should be designed. 15 out of the 18 participants stated that they have problems in recruiting professionals due to their company's rural location. As reasons they mentioned the high competition for employees and the almost full employment in this area. Six out of 16 stated that more than 10% of their applicants do not originate from the area – especially for jobs in leadership positions, IT or marketing. To take these jobs, the applicants might have to relocate. When we asked the companies, what they do to attract persons to their location, we collected several actions: helping employees with social matters like finding a kinder garden place or day nursery, highlighting the beauty of the area, or offering recreation activities.

Nine companies stated that they see no need in integrating additional information on their website to increase the attractiveness of their location. Four affirmed they already do, or are planning to include family-oriented details on their websites. However, after presenting the concept of the family information platform FAMIGO, 15 of 18 companies showed specific interest in this concept. They saw potential in standing out against their competitors, attracting applicants from more distant regions and offering additional information also for the current employees.

3 Information Platform to Increase Companies' Attractiveness

We showed that hidden champions in rural areas often have problems to recruit employees due to their remote location. Furthermore, many do not sufficiently present their specific benefits to potential applicants. To solve this problem, the start-up company FAMIGO offers an online platform that aims to bundle relevant information for applicants and their families in one place. To do so, it connects the municipalities, the associations, the economy, and the citizens with each other to create a regional communication network. All involved parties contribute their existing information. The collected data is enriched with important details, and arranged in a central content hub.

Especially for the companies, FAMIGO offers a service in the form of a white label website. The website works as a mobile and desktop version. Every company can adjust the template to their corporate identity and design. They can combine information about their corporate benefits with relevant data from the network. This allows users to seamlessly transition between the corporate website and the communication platform.

To implement the service easily, it uses standardized Application Programming Interfaces (API) like REST, SOAP, XML and JSON. The access to the platform can be integrated everywhere on the corporate website – for example in the career portal or the page "About Us". The modular system allows companies to freely prioritize and sort the different categories according to the relevance. Thus, applicants with families can easier access the information they need during the application process. Besides, the current employees have the opportunity to learn more about their living environment and attractive activities as well. Thus, FAMIGO potentially helps companies to underline their location factor, strengthen the location marketing and present themselves as family-friendly [17].

Since this application is a prototype, we conducted a user experience study to determine the requirements of the target group. For the study, we created a prototype version of the family-orientated information platform with Adobe XD CC.

4   User Experience Study

The aim of this study was to find out how the target group responds to the concept of a family-oriented information platform, if there is a demand in this kind of service, what information the participants consider as relevant, and the impact on the employer. The prototype was designed for use on an iPhone 6s Plus and adapted to the corporate identity of the company Hansgrohe (see Fig. 1).

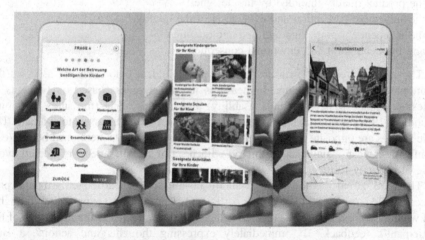

Fig. 1. Prototype of the information platform FAMIGO used for CXT testing.

4.1   Participants and Task

The study was conducted with seven participants who all have a family with children. It was set up in the user experience laboratory of Offenburg University. With the participants' consent, the process was monitored, and recorded. To minimize external influences on the participants' behavior, the procedure contained following steps each time:

- After a short introduction into the topic, the use case was explained.
- Then we asked the participant to answer the first part of the AttrakDiff2 online-questionnaire.
- In the next step, the participants had the following task: "Put yourself in the position of an applicant, interested in the presented job vacancy of Hansgrohe for a position as a business consultant. Imagine having two children between four and eight years who are interested in sports. Your preferred place of residence should be within a 50 km radius of the company's location Schiltach. You are looking for information on available kinder gardens and Waldorf schools."
- While working on the task, the participant should express actions, feelings and thoughts aloud.
- After task completion, the participant answered the second part of the AttrakDiff2 online-questionnaire.
- Following this, we conducted a semi-structured interview.

4.2 Methods

To gain information from the participants three methods were applied: AttrakDiff2 online- questionnaire, think-aloud, and a subsequent interview. AttrakDiff2 is a product evaluation online-questionnaire developed by Hassenzahl, Burmester and Koller [18] to focus both the usability and the pleasurable aspects of an experience. It is based on a model that divides the product experience into four elements:

- the product quality intended by the designer,
- the subjective perception and evaluation of the quality,
- the independent pragmatic and hedonic qualities
- and the behavioral and emotional consequences.

The method does not measure specific physiological emotions, but assesses the emotional impact of a product. It measures its attractiveness based on two sets of scales: pragmatic scale (measures usability) and hedonic scale (measures emotional reactions) [19]. The questionnaire consists of 28 sets of scales for users to evaluate. The scale's poles are opposite adjectives related to the four elements mentioned before (e.g. "confusing—clear", "unusual—ordinary"). Each set of adjective items is ordered into a scale of intensity [20].

The think-aloud method allows gaining insights into a participant's mental processes. While working on the task, the participants were asked to express their thoughts and what they are doing. The great advantage of this technique is the directness of the participant's feedback. By immediately expressing thoughts and actions, a later rationalization of their choice is avoided [21].

The third method, the interview, allows gaining deeper knowledge on the application's overall impression, the didactic design, the operation and navigation, the comprehensibility and the motivation. To guide the interviewer and address all relevant topics, a semi-structured interview with 28 polar and open questions was used. As the interviewer could discuss the participant's answers directly, a deeper qualitative understanding of the participant's insights could be achieved.

4.3 Results

For the question "What do you think about this platform?" the responses regarding the concept are mainly positive. One participant states, "I like it – I really like it" while another says "great idea". On a Likert-scale from 1 (very bad) to 5 (very good) the seven participants rate the overall impression of the prototype in average with 4.5.

When we asked, if they were aware of similar platforms, five out of seven answered negatively. The other two participants stated that one could find similar information on municipal websites and different travel platforms like TripAdvisor with the advantage of having ratings. In total, six out of seven participants stated that they would use this kind of platform and that an employer offers an additional benefit with this service.

To find out which information the users need most, we asked the participants which factors they consider most important for work-related relocation. Since all participants have children, we differentiated between the most relevant information for them and for their children. The most requested data revolved around childcare and schools, since the participants considered this most important both for them and their children. Additionally, they were interested in the environment, trips, and attractions in the area. For their children, the parents consider information on regional sports club as very important. An interest in information about certain residential districts, like pictures and rental prices, was also mentioned.

The opinions on the relevance of information about commuting to work differ. While some perceive this as important or very important, the participants using a car find it less relevant. To show the participant personalized information, six partly personal questions were asked. Since privacy on the internet is a hot topic, the benefits of asking private questions on this platform needed to be investigated. Regarding the particular questions, six persons had no concerns about data privacy at all. Only one person stated that he had a "slightly bad feeling".

One of the most relevant aims was to find out, if providing a family-oriented information platform has an impact on how potential applicants perceive a company. Apart from the fact that persons do not need to search the information on different websites, which makes the relocation easier for them, they also draw conclusions about the company. Indeed, the participants associated a good work climate and increased interest from the company for an employee's personal and family life. They stated that the platform makes the employer more attractive and could increase the chance to apply. Only one participant expressed concerns of a negative influence on the employer. He stated, that for higher positions (e.g. business consultant) the platform might create the impression that the employer underestimates the competency of the applicant.

The evaluation of the AttrakDiff2 online-questionnaire was conducted in form of a portfolio matrix with a diagram of the mean values of the assessment elements. The expectations before the UX-study are represented in blue and the experiences after in orange (see Fig. 2). In the portfolio matrix, the expression of the hedonic quality (HQ) is shown vertically (below = low expression) and the expression of the pragmatic quality (PQ) horizontally (left = low expression). Depending on the expression of the confidence rectangle, the product falls into one or more of the character areas. Both confidence rectangles are small. Therefore, it can be assumed that the test results are more reliable and less coincidental. In both terms of expectations and experiences, the prototype is classified as "desired".

The assignment in terms of pragmatic quality is clear. The prototype is judged to be very pragmatic. For the hedonic quality, the character assignment is not unique, because the confidence interval goes beyond the character range. The user is only encouraged to use the prototype. In general, the expression of the two elements after the experience with the prototype is marginally lower.

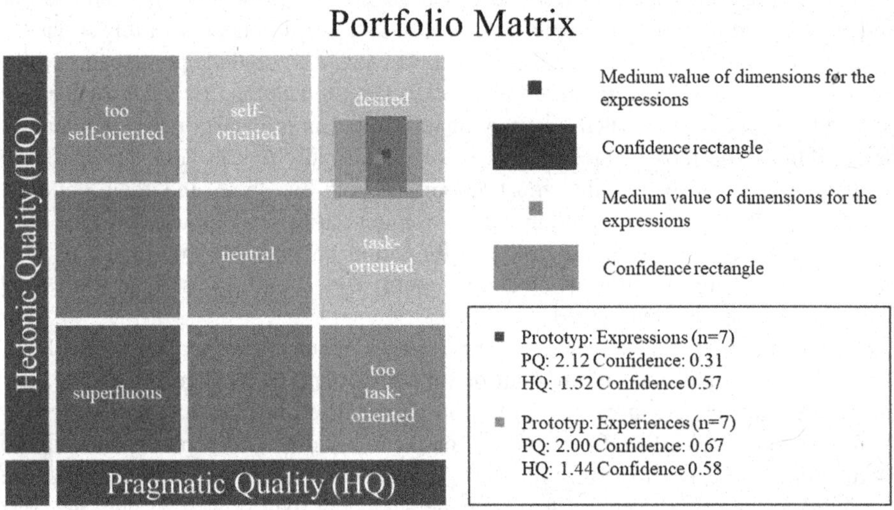

Portfolio Matrix

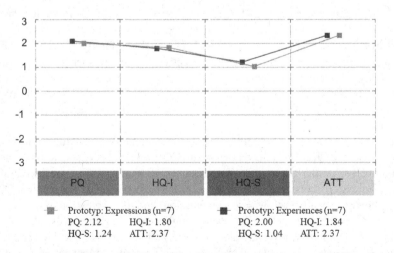

Fig. 2. Portfolio with the average expression of the elements PQ and HQ and the confidence rectangles for the experiences and expectations of the prototype (Color figure online)

Fig. 3. Mean expression of the four elements of the AttraktDiff2

The mean value diagram in Fig. 3 shows the average expressions of the four elements. Regarding the hedonic quality-identity (HQ-I), the prototype is above the average range in terms of expectations (1.80) and experience (1.84). Thus, the prototype offers users a good possibility of identification. Concerning the hedonic quality stimulation (HQ-S), the prototype is within the average range for the expectations (1.24) and the experience (1.04). It corresponds to the usual standards of the users. The attractiveness value (ATT) of the prototype is above average for both, the expectations (2.37) and the experience (2.37).

5 Survey

To gain more information on the process of applying for a job, we conducted an online survey in December 2018. In total, 208 persons completed the survey (61.5% female; 38.5% male). The age ranges between 20 and 69. Only nine were older than 39, which is the maximum age for generation Y. 152 of the participants do not have children yet, while 56 do have children (27%).

We used a five-point Likert scale (1 = strongly disagree to 5 = strongly agree). For some questions, the range was adjusted (1 = very unimportant to 5 = very important). The survey was structured into three parts:

- The first part focused on personal experiences regarding the job search.
- The second part concentrated on how users search for their new place of residence during the application process.
- The last part explained and evaluated the information platform FAMIGO.

5.1 Hypotheses

Based on the related work and the user experience study, we developed and evaluated the following hypotheses (H):

- *H1: For persons with children, the location during the job application phase is more important than for persons without children.*
  We assumed that persons with children start to investigate a company's location during the application process, as for those factors such as school and daycare for children are important.
- *H2: Persons with children prefer to live in rural areas.*
  As one might think, persons with children prefer rural areas as there is less traffic in smaller cities and often a calmer environment for children to grow up. In contrast, persons without children are often expected to live in a city:
- *H3: Persons with children are more likely to inform themselves about the company's location right after viewing the job advertisement.*
  For the human resource department of a company it is important to know when a potential employee starts to investigate the company's location because they must know where to communicate the location's benefits on the website.

402 A. Mueller et al.

- *H4: The platform makes it easier for persons with children to find a job compared to persons without children.*

  It is interesting to see if the platform is preferred by persons with children rather than by those without children. The outcome of this evaluation also gives an indication of the information such a platform should include. If there is no significant difference between persons with children and those without, information for both groups is equally important on such a platform.

- *H5: The higher the level of education, the lower the willingness to share private data.*

  Mostly specialists and management positions are needed in rural areas. Thus, the level of education of potential employees is high. As the platform aims to provide the best information for each user, it needs to ask questions on the family situation and the location preferences. Therefore, it is important to know, if specialists with higher education are concerned about such private data.

5.2 Results

The survey shows that only 28% of the participants look for a job on their mobile phone. The majority of 63% use a desktop PC for the online search and 9% use a tablet. Therefore, other than one might think, for the process of a job search a desktop PC is still very important.

The location becomes important early in the process of applying. The majority of 62% states that they examine the location when they first read the job advertisement. 32% analyze the company's location before sending an application. Thus, the location is important even before application.

When taking a closer look at the process of gaining information on the company's location, the survey shows that the majority uses Google Maps as a source (84%). Thus, Google Maps is the most used website while looking for the location and its surrounding. Furthermore, Wikipedia with 49% and the search engine Google with 45% are used, as well as websites of the city or commune with 37%.

To find out which aspects are important for the career website of a company, participants were asked to rate the statement "I expect data and facts about the company on the career site." The result show that participants do expect such information ($M = 4.46$, $SD = 0.68$). On the contrary, information about the company's location area is less used on the career website ($M = 2.81$, $SD = 1.16$). In general, a company in a city area is preferred ($M = 3.48$, $SD = 1.06$) to a rural area ($M = 2.50$, $SD = 0.97$). When it comes to transport, the connection to public transport is slightly more important ($M = 3.91$, $SD = 1.08$) than a good connection to the highway ($M = 3.37$, $SD = 1.04$). Also, the participants appreciate enough available parking spots ($M = 3.58$, $SD = 1.08$) (Table 1).

Table 1. Participants' preferences: mean values and standard deviations (SD):

Construct	Mean	SD
Company Information on career website	4.46	0.68
Searching information on the region via career website	2.81	1.16
Company's location should be in city area	3.48	1.06
Company's location should be in rural area	2.50	0.97
Great public transportation connection	3.91	1.08
Good connection to the highway	3.37	1.04
Enough available parking spots	3.58	1.08

With $t(103) = 2.14$, $p < .05$ the result supports hypothesis (H1): For persons with children, the location during the application phase is significantly more important ($M = 4.36$, $SD = 0.84$) than for persons without children ($M = 4.07$, $SD = 0.88$).

Regarding hypothesis H2, the preference to live in rural areas, with $t(94) = -0.63$, $p > .27$ there is no significant difference between persons with children ($M = 2.94$, $SD = 1.15$) and persons without children ($M = 3.05$, $SD = 1.21$).

Regarding hypothesis H3 (Persons with children are more likely to inform themselves about the company's location right after viewing the job advertisement), with $t(110) = 2.41$, $p < .01$ there is a highly significant difference between persons with children ($M = 0.75$, $SD = 0.44$) opposed to persons without children ($M = 0.58$, $SD = 0.50$). So indeed the parent will focus on location earlier. For this hypothesis, we used a scale from 0 to 1, as we just looked at the early process in the application ("right after viewing the application").

Regarding hypothesis H4 "The platform makes it easier for persons with children to find a job compared to persons without children", with $t(99) = 2.91$, $p < .01$ there again is a highly significant difference between persons with children ($M = 2.16$, $SD = 0.89$) opposed to persons without children ($M = 2.57$, $SD = 0.90$): persons with children are somewhat more doubtful regarding the platform.

Finally, regarding hypothesis H5 "The higher the level of education, the lower the willingness to share private data", with $t(104) = 0.16$, $p > .43$ we found that the level of education does not significantly impact the willingness to share private data: the mean result for persons with a university degree is $M = 3.96$ ($SD = 0.65$) as opposed to $M = 3.98$ ($SD = 0.73$) for persons without a university degree.

6   Conclusion

As pointed out in the introduction, this work aims to identify the needs and wishes of applicants during their decision process as well as the impact of an information platform for companies, which provides specific information for families aiming to relocate into rural areas (FAMIGO). In this conclusion, we summarize and discuss the results of the UX-study and the three significant hypotheses from the survey.

Finding 1: UX-study Confirms Prototype as "Desired"
For applicants with children looking for a new job, the most relevant information are childcare, schools, attractions, trips and information about the area. Overall, an overview of relevant regional information is considered necessary to make a decision. The FAMIGO-prototype was classified as "desired" in the UX-Testing, which means it supports user during the application process. With regard to the hedonic elements, there is room for improvement. Adding new features and exciting content or interaction styles could further increase the users' motivation, engagement, stimulation and attention. Finally, the information platform is considered "very attractive" by the users.

Finding 2: For Persons with Children, Location Is Especially Important During the Application Phase
Job selection dependents on many factors – but a very important one is the location and region of the company. Especially persons with children must consider several additional factors like availability of childcare institutions, variety of kinder gardens, and quality of schools. It is important to balance children and work. Also, when it comes to location, activities need to be offered for children as well as for parents. In particular, rural areas have to better show their benefits to compensate for the disadvantages in comparison to cities.

Finding 3: Company's Location Is Already Important at the First Sight of a Job Advertisement
The survey showed that persons with children are significantly more likely to inform themselves about the company's location at the first view of the job advertisement. This indicates that the platforms branch point needs to be located directly at the job advertisement, in order to offer support at the right time and place. Furthermore, a branch point to the family information platform needs to be included on the career site and the company's presentation site.

Finding 4: An Information Platform Is Appreciated But Also Looked at More Skeptical by Parents
The platform is rated a helpful tool to find the right place when deciding to relocate for a job. Thus, the overall concept of FAMIGO is supported by the. However, persons with children look significantly more critical at the platform. Thus, the platform should clearly address users with and without children.

Finding 5: A Family-Oriented Information Platform Contributes to the Employer Brand
The platform unites benefits for users as well as for companies. The UX-study showed that a family-oriented information platform, created in the look and feel of a specific company, increased this company's reputation as an employer: it is perceived as family friendly. Furthermore, the platform is seen as an advantage over competitors.

6.1 Recommendations

The results of this study can have an impact on companies in rural areas. Six recommendations have been derived to address location issues and make rural companies more attractive for families:

Recommendation 1: Bring Needs and Information Together
Applicants from Generation Y, and especially those with children, have distinguished needs for their relocation. The most relevant areas of information are childcare and schools. With a family information platform like FAMIGO, it is possible to bring these needs and information together. Although parents have proved to be more skeptical than persons without children, a working family-friendly information platform is considered a helpful tool for finding a job by persons with and without children.

Recommendation 2: Make the Region Easily Likeable
Identify, what is special about the area, select some of the highlights from different cities and villages, as well as from various categories like child care, schools, sportive activity and events. Communicate this information with up-to-date data, appealing pictures or videos and the contact information particularly for childcare and schools.

Recommendation 3: Communicate About the Region Both at the Carrier Site and on the Job Advertisement
Early during the process of applying for a job, location is a key factor to decide whether to apply or not. The majority of users examine the location when they first read the job advertisement and clearly before sending an application. That is why it is important to present information about the region at the career site and even in the job advertisement to convince more persons to apply for the job.

Recommendation 4: Data and Privacy Matter
Data and privacy play an essential role in the recruiting process. If a family-oriented information platform requests personal data to personalize the results, it is crucial to indicate that the data will not be stored or used for purposes. That said, users of Generation Y are willing to provide such information if the benefits are clearly recognizable.

Recommendation 5: Do Not Concentrate on Mobile Devices Only
Be aware that the majority of applicants, even from Generation Y, still uses desktop PCs when searching for a new job. Thus, when developing a family-oriented information platform, the desktop version is at least as important as the mobile one.

Recommendation 6: Strengthen the Employer Brand
Providing a family-oriented information platform has a positive effect on the employer brand. Potential applicants consider employers providing such a service more innovative, expect a better working atmosphere and most of all they look forward to a more family friendly company. This can be a tremendous advantage for a company in a rural area that has to compete with others located in seemingly more attractive urban locations.

6.2 Limitations and Future Work

Some limitations of the study should be noted. First, the study concentrated on the needs of the generation Y as well as companies in rural areas. Further research may consider extending the study to generation Z or companies within another market. An additional limitation is that the study focused on German users, so the cultural characteristics of other countries could not be considered. Future research could explore the impact of these cultural values on the requirements and acceptance of a family information platform.

References

1. Korn, O., Brenner, F., Börsig, J., Lalli, F., Mattmüller, M., Müller, A.: Defining recrutainment: a model and a survey on the gamification of recruiting and human resources. In: Freund, Louis E., Cellary, W. (eds.) AHFE 2017. AISC, vol. 601, pp. 37–49. Springer, Cham (2018). https://doi.org/10.1007/978-3-319-60486-2_4
2. Mueller, A., Gast, O.: Customer Experience Tracking – Online-Kunden conversionwirksame Erlebnisse bieten durch gezieltes Emotionsmanagement. In: Keuper, F. et al. (eds.): Daten-Management und Daten-Services – Next Level, Berlin (2014)
3. Mueller, A., Stopfkuchen, M.: E-Joy - Markenerlebnisse messbar machen. In: Keuper, F., Schomann, M. (eds.) Entrepreneurship heute – Unternehmerisches Denken angesichts der Herausforderungen einer vernetzten Wirtschaft, Berlin (2015)
4. Acikgoz, Y.: Employee recruitment and job search: towards a multi-level integration. Hum. Resour. Manag. Rev. 29(1), 1–13 (2019)
5. Kultalahti, S., Viitala, R.: Generation Y – challenging clients for HRM? J. Manag. Psychol. 30(1), 101–114 (2015). https://doi.org/10.1108/JMP-08-2014-0230
6. Barford, I.N., Hester, P.T.: Analysis of Generation Y Workforce Motivation Using Multiattribute Utility Theory, p. 19 (2011)
7. Soujanen, I.: Young Professionals and the Pursuit of Happiness at Work. The University of Edinburgh, Scotland (2017)
8. Kultalahti, S.: It's so nice to be at work! Adopting different perspectives in understanding Generation Y at work (2015)
9. Fischerová, M., Půbalová, K.: Different approaches in recruiting young professionals. Emerg. Markets J. 8(1), 31–38 (2018). https://doi.org/10.5195/emaj.2018.149
10. Green, A.E., Canny, A.: Geographical Mobility: Family Impacts. Policy Press, Bristol (2003)
11. Greenhaus, J.H., Powell, G.N.: The family-relatedness of work decisions: a framework and agenda for theory and research. J. Vocat. Behav. 80(2), 246–255 (2012). https://doi.org/10.1016/j.jvb.2011.12.007
12. Martin, R.: Adjusting to job relocation: relocation preparation can reduce relocation stress. J. Occup. Organ. Psychol. 72(2), 231–235 (1999). https://doi.org/10.1348/096317999166626
13. Sonntag, J.: Employer Branding - Mit Social Media zur erfolgreichen Personalrekrutierung im Mittelstand. Diplomica Verlag GmbH, Hamburg (2014)
14. Rampl, L.V.: How to become an employer of choice: transforming employer brand associations into employer first-choice brands. J. Market. Manag. 30(13–14), 1486–1504 (2014)
15. Eger, L., Mičík, M., Řehoř, P.: Employer branding on social media and recruitment websites: symbolic traits of an ideal employer. Ekonomie Manag. = Econ. Manag. 1, 224–237 (2018)
16. Alpagut Yavuz, V.: An analysis of job change decision using a hybrid Mcdm method: a comparative analysis. Int. J. Bus. Soc. Res. 6(3), 60–75 (2016)
17. Feldberger, A.: FAMIGO - alle Informationen auf einen Blick (2018)
18. Hassenzahl, M., Burmester, M., Koller, F.: AttrakDiff: Ein Fragebogen zur Messung wahrgenommener hedonischer und pragmatischer Qualität. In: Szwillus, G., Ziegler, J. (eds.) Mensch and Computer 2003, vol. 57, pp. 187–196. Vieweg+Teubner Verlag, Wiesbaden (2003)

19. Hassenzahl, M.: The effect of perceived hedonic quality on product appealingness. Int. J. Hum. Comput. Interact. **13**, 481–499 (2001)
20. Hassenzahl, M., Burmester, M., Koller, F.: Der User Experience (UX) auf der Spur: Zum Einsatz von. In: Brau, H., Diefenbach, S., Hassenzahl, M., Koller, F., Peissner, M., Röse, K. (eds.) Usability Professionals 2008, pp. 78–82. German Chapter der Usability Professionals Association, Stuttgart (2008)
21. Frommann, U.: Die Methode 'Lautes Denken' (2005). https://www.e-teaching.org/didaktik/qualitaet/usability/Lautes%20Denken_e-teaching_org.pdf

Scaling Productivity and Innovation on the Path to Exascale with a "Team of Teams" Approach

Elaine M. Raybourn[1]([⊠]), J. David Moulton[2], and Aimee Hungerford[2]

[1] Sandia National Laboratories, Albuquerque, NM 87185, USA
emraybo@sandia.gov
[2] Los Alamos National Laboratories, Los Alamos, NM 87545, USA
{moulton, aimee}@lanl.gov

Abstract. One of the core missions of the Department of Energy (DOE) is to move beyond current high performance computing (HPC) capabilities toward a capable exascale computing ecosystem that accelerates scientific discovery and addresses critical challenges in energy and national security. The very nature of this mission has drawn a wide range of talented and successful scientists to work together in new ways to push beyond the status-quo toward this goal. For many scientists, their past success was achieved through efficient and agile collaboration within small trusted teams that rapidly innovate, prototype, and deliver. Thus, a key challenge for the ECP (Exascale Computing Project) is to scale this efficiency and innovation from small teams to aggregate teams of teams. While scaling agile collaboration from small teams to teams of teams may seem like a trivial transition, the path to exascale introduces significant uncertainty in HPC scientific software development for future modeling and simulation, and can cause unforeseen disruptions or inefficiencies that impede organizational productivity and innovation critical to achieving an integrated exascale vision. This paper identifies key challenges in scaling to a team of teams approach and recommends strategies for addressing them. The scientific community will take away lessons learned and recommended best practices from examples for enhancing productivity and innovation at scale for immediate use in modeling and simulation software engineering projects and programs.

Keywords: High performance computing (HPC) · Exascale · Team of teams · Computational science & engineering (CSE) · VUCA · Organizational productivity

1 Introduction

Since the collapse of the Soviet Union in the early 90s, the term VUCA (volatile, uncertain, complex and ambiguous) has been used to describe current and future contexts for militaries, industry, and education. However, it is rarely acknowledged that modern *science* driving innovation in each of these domains is *also* VUCA. It is the *scientific discovery*, often executed in rapidly changing and shifting VUCA contexts, that drives advancements in technology and processes that in turn create the

---

The original version of this chapter was revised: The copyright holder name has been corrected. The correction to this chapter is available at https://doi.org/10.1007/978-3-030-22338-0_39

F. F.-H. Nah and K. Siau (Eds.): HCII 2019, LNCS 11589, pp. 408–421, 2019.
https://doi.org/10.1007/978-3-030-22338-0_33

opportunities for breakthrough solutions in computational science & engineering (CSE), modeling, and simulation. Science *is* VUCA, and the teams whose scientific discoveries must anticipate 21st Century challenges are also operating in environments that relentlessly shift in tempo, complexity, and scale.

However, while living in an increasingly VUCA environment is certain, it is also evident that *not everything is unpredictable* [1]. When it comes to drivers for change, innovation, and subsequent modernization the U.S. whole of government must be poised to prepare for, and address stressors to national security. The U.S. Department of Energy (DOE) and the DoD—are, of all the U.S. Federal Executive Departments, in synergistic positions to apply advancements in science and exascale computing to modeling and simulation for national security impact on global trends such as urban concentration, demographic shift, climate change, and technological surprise. Together, federal agencies can prepare for these known global trends that will, and have already begun, to shape our near and distant futures.

1.1 What Is Exascale, and Why Is It a National Security Grand Challenge?

If high performance computing (HPC) today functions above a petaflop (computing speed equal to one million million (10^{15}) floating-point operations per second) then exactly what is exascale computing? Exascale computing is a new class of high-performance computing systems capable of 10^{18} floating point operations per second [2] and whose power is measured in *exaflops*, or computing speed equal to one billion billion calculations per second, and one thousand times more powerful than today's petaflop machines. By 2023, exascale computing will enable us to solve incredibly complex research problems, such as simulating the human brain, hypersonic aircraft, and nuclear tests; predicting space weather, cracking encryption codes, advancing medical research, analyzing 22 million Veteran health records, and modeling the Earth's climate and the global economy [3–5]. Put in layman's terms by the Secretary of Energy, "the jump to exascale would be like going from a flip phone to the latest smartphone or from dial-up to 4G internet speed" [3]. Nevertheless, in the midst of much enthusiasm, there are several pressing trends contributing to the recent sense of urgency. First, impacts on society, energy security, and our everyday lives contribute to the collective pressure to succeed. Second, data is growing exponentially, and while increasingly accessible, is overwhelming. Third, computational power is growing (and largely compounding the challenge). And fourth, flexible, extensible and agile inter-disciplinary approaches and solutions seem most promising when they move toward a capable exascale computing ecosystem.

2 The Path to Exascale

The High Performance Computing Modernization Program (HPCMP) is not a well-known program although it was established in 1992 to modernize the HPC capability of DoD laboratories [6]. The HPCMP was *"assembled out of a collection of small high performance computing departments,* each with a rich history of supercomputing experience that had independently evolved within the Army, Air Force, and Navy laboratories and test centers" (U.S. Army Corps of Engineers HPCMP fact sheet, italics ours). The program's capabilities have been used to accelerate acquisition decision-making, simulate wind tunnels, decrease development timelines [6] for the design of helicopters, and for analyzing weather patterns [7].

As the lead federal agency for fundamental research in energy, and the "single largest supporter of basic research in the physical sciences in the United States" (https://science.energy.gov/about/), the DOE Office of Science has a core mission is to move beyond current HPC capabilities, such as those employed by the HPCMP, toward a capable *exascale computing ecosystem* that accelerates scientific discovery and addresses critical challenges in energy and national security. An *ecosystem* is defined as a group of independent but interrelated elements comprising a unified whole, and the same definition is applied to an *exascale computing ecosystem* in the present paper. The capable exascale computing ecosystem being developed by the DOE Exascale Computing Project (ECP) is an exascale ecosystem which includes applications, system software, hardware technologies and architectures, and critical workforce development —independent, but interrelated elements that comprise a whole. Finally, the DOE Office of Science maintains a research portfolio that includes advanced scientific computing, basic energy science, biological and environmental research, fusion energy science, high energy physics, and nuclear physics. Through scientific discovery and execution of the mission with its semi-autonomous National Nuclear Security Administration (NNSA), the DOE enables application of nuclear science to modeling, simulation, and testing at exascale.

The DOE and modeling, simulation, and test communities can employ lessons learned from organizations leveraging interdisciplinary teams to address VUCA experiences. Recognizing that the path to exascale will draw upon the talents of a workforce enabled primarily by small teams, we take pages from General Stanley McChrystal's playbook [8] and apply them to scaling from small teams to a *team of teams*.

2.1   VUCA Requires Organizational Agility that Scales

High performance computing as an international community of agencies, national laboratories, academia, and industry has largely been defined by the ad hoc assembly of small, agile computational science & engineering (CSE) teams [9]. For many CSE teams, past success may have been achieved by working shoulder-to-shoulder on small, trusted teams (e.g. professor, collaborating students and postdocs, or a modest sized research group) that rapidly innovated, prototyped, and delivered. These aggregate teams are often distributed across organizations, physical locations, time zones, language communities, and cultures. As such, it can be a challenge to foster successful collaboration in larger, distributed teams. The VUCA nature of this socio-technical path to exascale introduces significant uncertainty in HPC scientific software development for future modeling and simulation, and can cause unforeseen disruptions or inefficiencies that impede organizational productivity and innovation critical to achieving an integrated exascale vision.

VUCA contexts require networked configurations—those able to shift in execution and optempo, thereby enabling organizational agility and resiliency at scale (see Fig. 1). A networked configuration should facilitate interdependency, cooperation, and coordination at the level of individuals, teams, and organizations. Therefore, we must reconsider hierarchical "command structures" that are no longer effective when faced with asymmetric threats. Hierarchical "command structures" are designed to be efficient, but efficiency is no longer enough to address a new generation of VUCA threats. Many industrial organizational models in place today were designed to allow organizations to better plan, standardize, and predict output, however, VUCA requires a new approach.

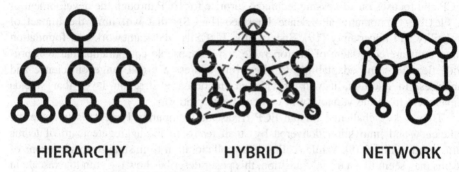

HIERARCHY   HYBRID   NETWORK

Fig. 1. From few to few, toward many to many.

Figure 1 illustrates three types of organizational structures discussed by McChrystal and others [8]: hierarchy, hybrid structure, and network. The hierarchy illustrates the typical "command structure" found in many military organizations. These organizations are characterized by an emphasis on efficiency which leverages silos in predictable ways. On the other hand, the network structure at the right in Fig. 1 focuses on increased interconnectedness and flat, flexible communication. These organizations are more agile, resilient, and well-suited to uncertain environments. Finally, the hybrid structure in the center of Fig. 1 can be employed by hierarchical "command structure" organizations as they adjust their practices toward a more networked system. The hybrid organization encourages more communication across silos. Like many organizations, ECP may be characterized as sets of small teams functioning within a hierarchical structure. Therefore, ECP requires a systems approach that will stimulate interconnectedness for productive and innovative, computational software engineering. On the path to exascale, ECP members will likely need to understand the entire interconnected system, not just their individual areas of expertise or those of siloed teams. Harnessing the entire capability of the distributed organization requires information sharing to achieve levels of transparency that may be entirely new to the organization. According to McChrystal and others [8], the command of teams may be more flexible in some organizations than others, but to be truly adaptable in a VUCA environment, much more than a hierarchical structure is required.

3 Scaling from Small Teams to a Team of Teams: ASC Ristra

The DOE Advanced Simulation and Computing (ASC) program supports the tools to underpin the use of simulations in assessing the current and future stockpile. Within the ASC program the Advanced Development, Technology and Mitigation sub-program (ADTM) focuses on the development of new, production simulation tools for the Nuclear Security Enterprise. The VUCA context faced by the team is created by disruptive trends in hardware, programming models and tools, and in the increasing complexity and diversity of research questions these tools must address. The Los Alamos National Laboratory (LANL) ASC Ristra project (named for the threaded chile strings found in New Mexico) is supported by the ASC-ADTM sub-program as part of ECP and focuses on addressing technical surprise for HCP through the development of a Flexible Computational Science Interface (FleCSI) that will limit the impact of volatility and uncertainty [10]. Specifically, FleCSI is the framework and foundation for a software ecosystem of interoperable and composable components that will provide flexibility and adaptability to effectively address a broad range of science and analyses. In addition, it will provide an important abstraction layer that shields developers from the variability in computational platforms.

Thus, a key challenge for the ECP (Exascale Computing Project) is to scale the efficiency and innovation delivered by small teams to the aggregate team of teams illustrated in Fig. 2 [8]. While scaling agile collaboration from small teams to teams of teams may seem like a trivial transition, this paper describes how the path to exascale in HPC scientific software development for future modeling and simulation would be enhanced by a team of teams approach. We use ASC Ristra, an existing DOE ECP team, as an exemplar in the present paper that illustrates key elements necessary to scale a large organization to a hybrid structure (see Fig. 1) and eventually toward McChrystal and his co-authors' approach of a team of teams (Fig. 2). Subsequent sections discuss shared consciousness, empowered execution, and leading like a gardener. We conclude by recapping key take-aways for the scientific community.

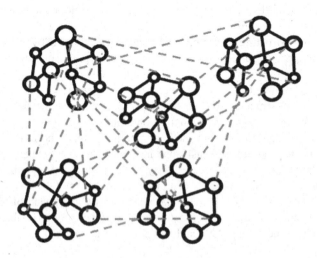

Fig. 2. Team of Teams.

3.1 Shared Consciousness

This section introduces the idea of developing shared consciousness among and within teams as an important step on the path toward scaling the productivity of small teams to a large networked aggregate team, or a team of teams [8]. In our own projects such as ASC Ristra, we have been exploring ways to apply lessons learned from the book, "Team of Teams: New Rules for Engagement in a Complex World" by retired US Army General Stanley McChrystal and others [8]. The authors describe a team of teams as a network of coordinated teams who are interdependent and share trust as well as an awareness of a common purpose, and goal. This connectivity of common purpose, trust, awareness of each other, and transparent communication is referred to as shared consciousness [8]. We don't have to be in project management or a formal leadership role to help our teams reach across rigid organizational structures to achieve shared consciousness.

It has been noted that shared consciousness among teams can enhance organizational productivity and facilitate innovation critical to achieving an integrated vision [8]. Whether we are co-located or distributed, post docs, team members, or group leaders, we can all participate in reaching an integrated vision together. Below we summarize three strategies advanced by McChrystal and others [8] toward developing shared consciousness for and among teams that are distributed and/or co-located.

Identify a Single, Aligning Narrative. Before we can have shared consciousness among our distributed teams, we must first foster a shared mental model of why we are doing what we are doing. That is, before focusing on the technical capabilities to connect, we can take time to engender the willingness to connect [11]. One way to accomplish this is to have a single unifying message that speaks to everyone—consider, each individual, on every team, can see themselves as participants in the story as it unfolds [12, 13]. Repeating this aligning narrative as often as needed, perhaps by opening each meeting with the common purpose, will enable team members to feel comfortable articulating it themselves.

A shared mental model will require, at a minimum, a shared vocabulary. Since the subject matter experts that have come together on the ASC Ristra team represent many different fields of physics, computer science, and HPC, and in many cases, sub-sets of contributors who had worked together on previous teams, the ASC Ristra team was built through the inheritance of smaller software development teams. The inherited teams ranged from academic computational research scientists in astrophysics to LANL production software development teams for multi-scale, multi-physics applications. The software development environments of each group were widely varying on several fronts. Technical fields of expertise were spread across applied mathematics, computer science, and physics with each group bringing its own unique vernacular to the mix. Coding languages and styles from the diverse backgrounds were extremely varied, e.g. Fortran, C, C++, Python and Haskell, and came with code styles that reflected a spectrum of software discipline, from single user research codes to production released community codes. With this diverse background, the ASC Ristra team was faced with engendering a shared vocabulary as a critical step in establishing effective communication and an aligning narrative.

The technical vision of ASC Ristra is to support diversity in science applications and compute architecture through the design and implementation of FleCSI and the ecosystem of supported components (Fig. 3). ASC Ristra uses visualizations such as Fig. 3 to help focus shared consciousness by communicating several key aspects of software design goals and project structure. It makes it easier for team members to understand their roles within and across capabilities, and highlights key mechanisms for mitigating the volatility and uncertainty from external drivers. In addition, visualizing the impact of VUCA on the software design goals as well as project structure gives team members awareness of the breadth of components critical to the software ecosystem, and consequently, the diverse and interdisciplinary nature of the team that is needed to develop and support it. This is an important point in that visualizing VUCA on a regular basis creates shared consciousness of why the vision is urgent, the pressures to succeed, and who can help.

A clear technical vision such as the one illustrated in Fig. 3, and recruitment of strong technical teams are necessary but not sufficient. To develop a successful aligning narrative, ASC Ristra added to their technical vision: embracing their team's diversity and valuing *interpersonal relationships*. These important additions were also key elements in the aligning narrative developed by McChrystal and others [8] and clarified by Fussell and Goodyear [11, pg. 58]. However, it's important to note that fostering interpersonal relationships is the ingredient that is *most often overlooked or dismissed as a low priority* that will simply take care of itself. This is simply not true. By strengthening interpersonal relationships upfront, and with high priority, ASC Ristra is much more likely to succeed. In the following section we expand on how ASC Ristra develops and supports relationships by building trust.

Build Trust. Use a common conceptual model (as shown in Fig. 3) and aligning narrative of the entire, interconnected project to build trust among individuals within a team, and across distributed teams. The terms "within" and "across," may also refer to vertical and horizontal alignment in hierarchical organizations. Many of us who are part of hierarchical organizations may often perceive building trust within vertical alignment to be easiest, although that may not always be the case. Trust may also be built across horizontal organizational alignment with individuals with whom we share common purpose, language, and conceptual models. In the book, "Great at Work," Hansen [14] describes trust as confidence in individuals to consistently and reliably deliver high quality work that is expected from them. If our teams have not reached this level of trust, Hansen recommends applying "trust boosters" to specific trust problems as needed. For example, if distributed team members across a project do not know each other well (they may be strangers), the teams may want to try some bonding exercises or techniques to share personal information.

Many of the initial challenges encountered by ASC Ristra required a willingness for both cultural change and adoption of new technical approaches as well as "trust boosters" Hansen [14]. The team acknowledged and openly welcomed lessons learned from the past efforts, because they saw these as keys to helping plot a different course, rather than harbingers of inevitable doom. This attitude shift was accomplished by paying close attention to the make-up of the team. Diversity of experience, personality and technical expertise were actively considered, even at the team leadership level.

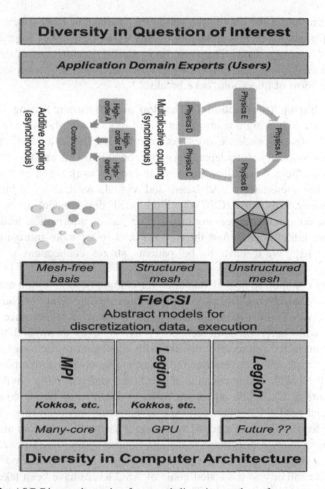

Fig. 3. ASC Ristra schematic of external diversity on the software ecosystem.

A mix of senior and junior staff across a breadth of relevant technical fields was fairly easily achieved. More challenging was finding the right mix of personalities, so that the psychological diversity could accompany that technical diversity.

A "trust booster" the ASC Ristra leadership relies on is *regularly scheduled, informal collaboration time* (in the form of afternoon "Tea" twice a week) to help gauge this balance of diversity, as well as provide a place for creating a shared consciousness within the team. Office co-location had long been a strategy for achieving team cohesiveness at LANL but was not an easy option for ASC Ristra. This was in part due to space limitations, but also because this team required part time engagement from a very large set of subject matter experts. Shared consciousness may be hindered or helped by physical and virtual spaces, and established processes. Creating shared consciousness at scale requires rethinking every process in the organization, including how we approach physical and virtual spaces. The Tea-time concept has been an effective way to overcome lack of co-location, and the Tea-time room has become a natural gathering place for impromptu sub-team meetings at other times. As a result, the general availability of this collaboration space has been a key ingredient for the team's shared consciousness. The trust booster of *"regularly scheduled, informal collaboration time"* has been adopted by at least one other ECP team known by the authors in the form of afternoon "cake breaks."

Commit to Sharing Information to Develop and Maintain Strong Connections Among Teams. Achieving a team of teams will rely on our ability to foster interdependent teams. Interdependence does not merely rely on co-located, "shoulder-to-shoulder" communication. Interdependence must be built on information sharing that is transparent and efficient, and allowing teams to execute work based on their initiative. Since teams are increasingly distributed and virtual, we can try using computer-supported cooperative work (CSCW) cloud-based development tools and video/whiteboard meeting software environments. The use of information technology will help propagate information across the network and foster more transparent communication [12, 13]. We'll have to be patient—strong connections won't happen overnight.

Developing common tools and standards for communication within and across the interdisciplinary teams comprising ASC Ristra presented a variety of challenges. The staff can be divided into two major categories: those with office space in an open environment with fairly modern technology available to them, and those whose workspace is protected for security reasons with significant restrictions on use of cell phones, tablets and other convenience electronics. This created a significant divide in the comfort level with communication tools. Some staff are more comfortable with face-to-face interaction, while others are insistent about using online communication tools and social media. Common software development environments were also not shared by the teams that came together within ASC Ristra. Several team members were not familiar with using a distributed repository control system like Git and were more accustomed to developing from a tar file exchange with collaborators. In addition, activities with similarity to the stated goals of ASC Ristra have been taken on in the past at LANL with limited success. The team started off surrounded by those who had walked their path before and found only disappointment.

Thus, an important topic in the early informal Tea-time gatherings was the exploration of new CSCW tools and approaches that could effectively support a collaborative environment for this diverse team. Specifically, the ASC Ristra team spent its early months seeking a software development tool stack that could fit its needs and be accessible to all the staff involved. The Atlassian tool chain was ultimately adopted and a series of tutorials targeting its use case within ASC Ristra were offered to the whole team. This type of activity is important for creating a shared consciousness, it requires a significant time investment from each member of the team, and often does not generate "results" in any traditional sense of the term. As such, learning-curve activities like this require significant management support so that staff can be shielded in these early phases from product delivery just for delivery's sake. A by-product of this necessary shielding is the headroom to explore higher risk technical ideas as well. ASC Ristra has found significant benefit from having allowed time to chase several higher risk innovative ideas.

In summary, when scaling from small teams to a team of teams, consider how to bootstrap your efforts with the goal of shared consciousness. While this may sound daunting at first, scaling collaboration found in small teams to an aggregate can be made much smoother within our programs by considering the connectivity of an aligning narrative, trust among interdependent teams, and the use of modern CSCW technology to foster transparent communication, and efficient information sharing. Taking time to build trust and a unified sense of purpose within and across teams are important steps in scaling from a small team to a distributed aggregate, or team of teams.

3.2 Empowered Execution

As we discussed in the previous section, the characteristics of effective, small team are trust, common purpose, shared consciousness, decentralized decisions, and autonomy. *But how can we scale up?*

To scale as a team of teams, organizational configurations should foster the delegation of authority to sub-teams and individuals who can act without explicit senior leadership consultation [8]. Providing opportunities for team members to understand each of the interdependent parts of the system will help create a general awareness that will support each team member's specific area of expertise. Introduce transparency in communication and processes to establish a culture of shared consciousness. The synchronization of team cadence in the hybrid model can also reaffirm the aligning narrative.

The importance of preserving both the autonomy and identity of individuals within the context of a team of teams environment cannot be overstated. For example, the ability to respond quickly to new challenges, the confidence to share information openly in integrated, technologically-mediated forums such as videoconferences, the efficient execution of team or individual-specific activities, and the branding associated with both individuals and team capabilities or components can all be enhanced when approvals from a chain of command are not required. Conversely the unnecessary use of vertical approval chains can severely inhibit or even silence these valuable activities.

As discussed earlier, the challenge is to bring the foundational support implicit in a small team, such as trust, common purpose, shared consciousness to the team of teams. This is critical to an effective team of teams environment as it enables periods of empowered execution between broader synchronization points. In the context of large interdisciplinary software development projects this empowered execution can be thought of as disciplined and focused autonomous development within small team environments that is guided by the aligning narrative and technical vision. Although, it is effectively a small team setting, it may be an ad hoc team that includes liaisons or interdisciplinary sub-teams. In addition, it follows the accepted best practices of the broader team, including, styles, tools, communication protocols, and testing protocols.

ECP projects are actively exploring a range of methodologies that can support this hands-off element of empowered execution, while also supporting the accepted best practices. These approaches include the use of bull pens (open-office arrangements for small teams, possibly over specific timeframes), and virtual scrums. In addition, workflows are evolving that allow teams to tune the balance of supervision and autonomy, such as the use of pull requests and code reviews in cloud-based source code management systems like GitHub. In this case, significant freedom and creativity can be leveraged early in the process, but the result put forward in the pull request can be reviewed to ensure it meets development goals, accounts for upstream and downstream dependencies, and follows the software standards of a project. In addition, these methodologies and tools still support an "eyes-on" overall situational awareness, as activities are naturally captured by the interaction and logging that development leveraging these tools and workflows creates. Finally, as discussed in the subsequent section, scaling work flows and project processes through empowered execution requires a paradigm shift in the execution of leadership.

3.3   Leading like a Gardener

A successful shift to a team of teams structure that maintains shared consciousness and enables empowered execution must also be accompanied by a fundamental shift in the leadership style. The most useful and intuitive metaphors describing this shift are from chess master to humble gardener [8]. Specifically, as we strive to accelerate scientific discoveries in this VUCA environment, the critical observation is that centralized control is too slow. It hinders cross-fertilization, and stifles innovation. Even with the amazing wealth of real-time digital information available to leaders today, it is unreasonable to expect them to perform as chess masters and effectively use this information to micro manage a reductionist view of teams and resources.

Instead, to create and nurture an environment that enables "smart autonomy" and shared consciousness, leaders must adopt the role of the humble gardener [8]. Specifically, this environment uses the hybrid and network structures to extend and enhance the qualities implicit in the cultures and processes of successful small teams. To be effective this environment must foster trust, transparency, and free-flowing conversations, both within and across teams. When high-quality liaisons are identified and used as critical nodes in cross-team networks, they can play a significant role in supporting this transparent and effective communication. Furthermore, the leader, as the gardener, plays a critical role in sustaining this environment by consistently reaffirming the aligning narrative, continuously demonstrating respect and appreciation for everyone's contributions, and reinforcing empowered execution with an eyes-on, hands-off, approach [15]. Thus, gardening in reality and in this metaphor, is not passive. The gardener, drives the rhythm and transparency of the team of teams, and builds and maintains the trust needed for cross-functional cooperation.

ASC Ristra started before McChrystal and others wrote "Team of Teams," and at a time when the uncertainty and volatility of computational science had reached a tipping point and the community was searching for approaches to restore or enhance overall productivity. Lessons learned from previous work on multi-physics applications and frameworks, advances in tools and languages, and the growth of agile methodologies began to fuel the vision of a software ecosystem that would provide the flexibility and adaptability required to meet 21st Century VUCA contexts. During this time, it became apparent that the leadership style needed to change as well. ASC Ristra were among those keenly aware of these changes and adopted many aspects of the humble gardener to support their aligning narrative and effectively develop this new software ecosystem.

4 Conclusion

Take-aways have been provided in each section of the present paper and now we recap key concepts by presenting the following questions and advice for consideration as your own organizations scale with a team of teams approach:

1. What is your aligning narrative? Fussell and Goodyear [11, pg. 61] offer the following question to consider as you create your narrative: *In your organization's current state, how would an aligning narrative be best emphasized and contextualized for your teams?*
2. Do your partnerships need a "trust booster?" Fussell and Goodyear [11, pg. 61] offer the following question as you consider how well your aligning narrative is supported by trust: *Your teams might claim to trust and have open lines of dialogue with one another—but can they demonstrate examples of how this trust is helping accomplish your organization's strategy?*
3. Do you leverage a geographically distributed organization to your advantage? Fussell and Goodyear [11, pg. 108] offer the following question as you consider how well your aligning narrative is supported by trust: *Could your organization leverage both physical and virtual spaces to drive cross-silo coordination and improve communication on strategy?*
4. Do you practice disciplined, empowered execution to scale and adapt your organization's response to emerging threats? McChrystal et al. [8, pg. 291] offer the following advice: *"Individuals and teams closest to the problem, armed with unprecedented levels of insights from across the network, offer the best ability to decide and act decisively."*
5. Does your organization reflect a model that is out of date? McChrystal et al. [8, pg. 232] offer the following advice: *"Although we intuitively know the world has changed, most leaders reflect a model and leader development process that are sorely out of date. We often demand unrealistic levels of knowledge in leaders and force them into ineffective attempts to micromanage...Persuading teams to network with other teams will always be difficult, but this is a culture that can be planted, and if maintained, can flourish."*

The present paper described how HPC CSE software development for future modeling and simulation projects would be enhanced by fostering a team of teams environment. Our discussion of the team of teams approach conceived by General Stanley McChrystal and his co-authors highlighted shared consciousness, empowered execution, and leading like a gardener through the use of an exemplar from DOE ECP. The path to exascale introduces significant uncertainty in HPC scientific software development and can cause unforeseen disruptions or inefficiencies that impede organizational productivity and innovation critical to achieving an integrated vision. We hope our discussion has illuminated a key element that while *often underreported,* is integral to the scientific discovery process—workforce development toward enhanced organizational productivity. According to the ECP vision statement, an exascale ecosystem will incorporate applications, system software, hardware technologies and architectures, along with critical workforce development. The success of the program depends on its people. Essentially, it is necessary to scale a shared consciousness intrinsic to smaller teams, which enables autonomous periods of heightened productivity, to a productive and sustainable ecosystem of teams of teams.

Acknowledgements. *Sandia National Laboratories is a multimission laboratory managed and operated by National Technology and Engineering Solutions of Sandia, LLC, a wholly owned subsidiary of Honeywell International, Inc., for the U.S. Department of Energy's National Nuclear Security Administration under contract DE-NA-0003525. Images in Figs. 1 and 2 copyright by NTESS LLC and reproduced with permission. **This work was supported by the U.S. Department of Energy Office of Science, Office of Advanced Scientific Computing Research (ASCR), Office of Biological and Environmental Research (BER), and by the Exascale Computing Project (17-SC-20-SC), a collaborative effort of the U.S. Department of Energy Office of Science and the National Nuclear Security Administration. Figure 3 reproduced with permission. Special thanks to the ADTM-ASC Ristra project for their willingness to be highlighted as an exemplar for the approach, challenges, and successes discussed in the present paper.

References

1. McNulty, E.J.: Leading in an increasingly VUCA world. Strategy-business.com, 27 October 2015. http://www.strategy-business.com/blog/Leading-in-an-Increasingly-VUCA-World?gko=5b7fc. Accessed 4 Feb 2019
2. Reed, D.A., Dongarra, J.: exascale computing and big data. Commun. ACM **58**(7), 56–68 (2015). https://cacm.acm.org/magazines/2015/7/188732-exascale-computing-and-big-data/abstract. Accessed 4 Feb 2019
3. Perry, J.R.: The future is in supercomputers. Whitehouse Art.: Infrastruct. Technol. 3 May 2018. https://www.whitehouse.gov/articles/the-future-is-in-supercomputers/. Accessed 4 Feb 2019
4. Simonite, T.: The US again has the world's most powerful supercomputer. Wired 8 June 2018. https://www.wired.com/story/the-us-again-has-worlds-most-powerful-supercomputer/. Accessed 4 Feb 2019
5. Lohr, S.: Move over, China: U.S. is again home to world's speediest supercomputer. The New York Times, 8 June 2018. https://www.nytimes.com/2018/06/08/technology/supercomputer-china-us.html. Accessed 4 Feb 2019
6. Walker, J.: The DoD office you've never heard of—and why that's about to change. Defense News, 1 January 2018. https://www.defensenews.com/opinion/commentary/2018/01/11/the-dod-office-youve-never-heard-of-and-why-thats-about-to-change/. Accessed 31 Jan 2019
7. Vanian, J.: Hewlett Packard enterprise signs big supercomputer deal with Department of Defense. Fortune.com, 15 February 2018. http://fortune.com/2018/02/15/hewlett-packard-enterprise-supercomputer-department-defense/. Accessed 31 Jan 2019
8. McCrystal, S., Collins, T., Silverman, D., Fussell, C.: Team of Teams: New Rules of Engagement for a Complex World. Penguin Random House LLC, New York (2015)
9. McInnes, L.: What Are Strategies for More Effective Teams? December 2017. https://bssw.io/resources/what-are-strategies-for-more-effective-teams. Accessed 4 Feb 2019
10. Moulton, D.J., Raybourn, E.M., McInnes, L., Heroux, M.: Enhancing Productivity and Innovation in ECP with a Team of Teams Approach. SAND2018-3987 C. figshare. https://doi.org/10.6084/m9.figshare.6151097.v1 (2018)
11. Fussell, C., Goodyear, C.W.: One Mission: How Leaders Build a Team of Teams. Penguin Random House LLC, New York (2017)

12. Raybourn, E.M.: A new paradigm for serious games: transmedia learning for more effective training and education. J. Comput. Sci. **5**(3), 471–481 (2014). Elsevier
13. Raybourn, E.M.: Addressing changing mindsets: transforming next generation leader development with transmedia learning. In: Hailes, T.C., Wells, L. (eds.) Changing Mindsets to Transform Security: Leader Development for an Unpredictable and Complex World. National Defense University, Washington (2013)
14. Hansen, M.T.: Great at Work: How Top Performers Do Less, Work Better, and Achieve More. Simon & Schuster, New York (2018)
15. Mui, C.: Lead like a gardener. Forbes (2016). https://www.forbes.com/sites/chunkamui/2016/07/14/to-nurture-innovation-lead-like-a-gardener-not-napoleon-or-kasparov/#5ef2ce7a3d83. Accessed 4 Feb 2019

Time to Track Cross-Sector Collaboration: Digital Prescriptions for Governing Fragmented Governments

Khadijeh Roya Rouzbehani[✉]

University of Victoria, 3800 Finnetry Road, Victoria, Canada
royarouzbehani@uvic.ca

Abstract. Cross-sector collaborations are a noteworthy addition to the tools of public administration and authorities seek to collaborate in order to deal with cross-sector wicked problems. However, the rate of success is not noticeable due to the barriers to reach collaboration. This study identifies the barriers of different phases of cross-sector collaboration. A synergy map is used to classify the barriers in three clusters to address them via conceptual frameworks, visual thinking and online collaboration platforms to facilitate collaboration.

Keywords: Collaborative governance · Digital tools · Barriers

1 Introduction

While collaborative governance is a fashionable cache in the public administration literature, its literature remains idiosyncratic its use inconsistent [1]. It also does not bring the positive spine because of the challenges and barriers which must be met. Little research has been conducted on identifying the barriers to boundary less collaboration. In this research, inspired by design thinking, the article draws on the case study analysis to produce a synergy map, which provides a comprehensive view for scholars and practitioners to overcome several barriers. Then, I discuss the utilities illustrated in the synergy map to describe the potential role of digital tools, and the cognitive perspective in addressing the barriers of cross-sector collaboration.

2 Collaborative Governance: The State of Theorizing

Several important holistic frameworks for understanding cross-sector collaboration have been published since early 2000. The earlier ones include [2–5], which were based on prior works [6–9]; the latter ones include [1, 10]. The literature has delineated different uses and concepts of collaboration, which will be reviewed briefly in Table 1.

Most of these frameworks do not pay attention to critical steps to facilitate collaboration, but some do contribute important insights. This study focuses on the barriers by focusing on these questions: What are the barriers and how they can be addressed? What is the potential for digital tools to address barriers?

© Springer Nature Switzerland AG 2019
F. F.-H. Nah and K. Siau (Eds.): HCII 2019, LNCS 11589, pp. 422–431, 2019.
https://doi.org/10.1007/978-3-030-22338-0_34

Table 1. Major cross-sectoral theoretical frameworks

Publication	Theory Base	Major Component	Particular Emphasis
Thomson and Perry (2006)	Diverse, including organization theory, public admin theory, and strategic management theory	Antecedents, Processes, and outcomes	Organizational autonomy, and leadership
Ansell and Gash [2]	Diverse, including organization theory, public admin theory, and environmental management studies	Starting conditions, Processes, and outcomes	Face-to-face dialogue, incentives, and remedying power imbalance
Agranoff [3]	Diverse, including organization theory, public admin theory, and strategic management theory	Decision networks, and processes	Leadership, Capacity building, and learning
Provan and Kenis [5]	Network Theory	Ideal types of network governance, tensions, and contingencies	Governance structures
Emerson et al. [1]	Diverse, including organization theory, public admin theory, and environmental management studies	System context, collaborative governance regime, and collaboration dynamics	Collaborative regimes, and capacity building
Koschmann et al. [10]	Communication Theory	Communication, and Trajectory of authoritative texts	Authoritative texts

3 Research Methodology

A Systematic Literature Review (SLR) was conducted using the Thomé et al.'s [11] step-by-step approach. The search relied on these key words: collaboration, cross-sector collaboration, collaborative governance, public-private partnership. Armed with a working definition of collaborative governance to identify a wide range of case studies from the peer-reviewed journals, the search generated articles across a wide range of disciplines, including specialist journals in public health, public administration, social welfare, environmental studies, etc. I also followed up on the literature cited in the cases and finally after excluding the additional studies, it led to 162 case studies. Although international in scope, my search was restricted to case studies in English, following this distribution: North America (78), Europe (59), Asia (22), Australia (3).

The universe of the cases reviewed were studies of an attempt to implement collaborative governance in different sectors and they differed in quality and methodology. The level of collaboration in the cases differed; in most cases a few partners collaborated, while the rest were either at regional level or they were cases in which the government collaborated with non-profits and for profits. As the language used to describe in the cases was far from standardized, it was virtually impossible to find a common language to code studies, and along with the problem of missing data, a quasi-experimental approach could not work. To move from abstract vague concepts to the more concrete ones in a step-by-step fashion, I applied a meta-analytic strategy called successive approximation [12]. A subset of the cases was selected based on their clarity and diversity to identify the barriers of each phase of collaboration. A second subset of cases was randomly selected to test the items developed in the first round. A third sample of cases was used to test the findings, and the list of barriers was finalized after being compared with the fourth sample of cases. As I proceeded, variables and causal relationships proliferated beyond what I felt would ultimately be useful for scholars and practitioners. Therefore, judgement was exerted to develop a nuanced but parsimonious representation of key variables.

4   Cross-Sector Collaboration Barriers

Table 2 provides a visual representation of my most central findings. The process of successive approximation yielded nine broad variables, which were the challenges. Nine barriers were identified which are clustered in three main groups "*communication*": siloed institutions, insufficient representation of world views, inadequate communication methods; "*cognitive*": disintegrated solutions to wicked problems, misunderstanding of core concepts, ineffective thinking paradigms; and "*power*": limited power and resource, inability to participate effectively in talks, lack of inclusive engagement.

Table 2. Barriers of collaborative governance

Barriers	Components
Communication	Siloed institutions, Insufficient representation of world views, Inadequate communication methods
Cognition	Disintegrated solutions, Misunderstanding of core concepts, Ineffective thinking paradigms
Power	Limited power and resource, Inability to participate effectively in talks, Lack of inclusive engagement

These barriers emerge over three main phases of collaboration that is pre-condition, the main iterative phase of collaboration to effectively address the public problem, and finally outcomes and accountability.

5   Barriers and the Potential of Digital Tools

The systematic review of the cases led to the identification of nine barriers crucial to facilitating collaboration. These problems gradually emerge as collaboration unfolds over time.

Asymmetry of power and also lack of incentive of siloed institutions exist in the first phase of most cross sector collaborations [13–16]. Power imbalance is the source of challenge [6, 17, 18] and when some stakeholders do not participate on an equal footing with other stakeholders, the collaborative governance process will be prone to manipulation by stronger actors. Power imbalance is inter-related to two other barriers: some stake holders do not have the organizational infrastructure to participate in collaborative governance processes [19], and some others may not engage in discussions about highly technical problems since they are overpowered by other stakeholders [20, 21].

In the second cycle of phase one, frequent, informal social networking plays an important role in promoting formal collaborative partnerships [22, 23]. However, there are two barriers in this part: some stakeholders may not have the organizational infrastructure to participate, and some other ones, mainly weak ties [24], are under-represented due to lack of access to appropriate communication platforms. Since the phases are inter-related, the barriers of phase one create the challenges of the second phase of collaborative process. When some actors and stakeholders are absent, the thinking paradigm of participants might be reductionist and insufficient to structure the problem effectively. Moreover, if there is no ambidextrous leader to nullify asymmetry of power and encourage inclusivity, core concepts might be misunderstood, hence the solutions either partial or disintegrated [25, 26]. The synergy map (Fig. 1) describes the relationships among barriers and tools.

5.1 Conceptual Frameworks

Conceptual frameworks, which are described with schematic images, are tools to help us think but they are also built on particular world views, depending on the background and experiences of their developers. By revealing some concepts and excluding others, they act as a lens through which we perceive the world [27]. Considering the wicked problems in a collaborative process from a single perspective can only provide a limited understanding and some ideas and methods will be easily overlooked [28], which makes collaboration more time and resource consuming.

Two prominent examples of conceptual frameworks which have not fully integrated with public policy are "design thinking" and "integral theory". Design thinking, which emerged in 1950s and recently migrated to public sector as an emerging field of practice [29, 30], introduces many methods for creating harmonious and organizational context-sensitive solutions to complex problems which are multi-faceted, vaguely defined and socially contested [31], which makes this tool an ideal choice to address these two barriers: disintegrated solutions and misunderstanding of core concepts. Integral theory, on the other hand, unites objective, subjective, individual and collective perspectives into a more complete, complementary approach [32] which is pertinent to behavioral and psychological dimensions of collaboration, and provides the breadth of scope and the agility required for collaboration. Integral theory, by definition, is capable of dealing with siloed institutions and insufficient representation of world views, the first two barriers in Fig. 1.

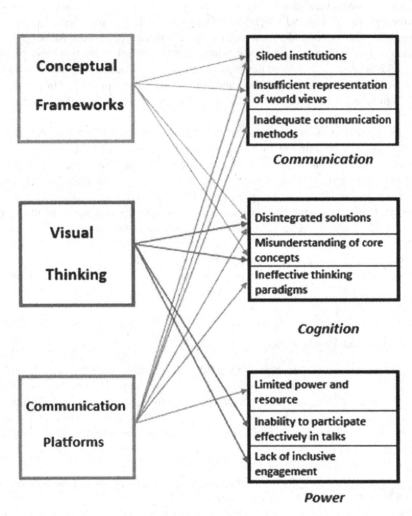

Fig. 1. Synergy map

5.2   The Potential of Visual Tools

By employing visual communication, stakeholders and actors can expand their ability
to clarify, inspire, collaborate and think [33] since the symbolic systems affect how we
perceive, and communicate about the world. Written words encode meaning into
sequence of statements, which is only a fraction of what an image can illustrate. Over
reliance on words, in the second phase of collaboration, fails to reflect the complexities,
and further nuance and complexity must then be communicated by articulating color,
size, shape, pattern and composition [34, 35]. Digital platforms expand this palette to
include user interaction and movement [36]. When it comes to visual thinking and

collaboration, two theories must be discussed: situation awareness theory [37] and theory of grounding in communication [38, 39].

Situation awareness theory suggests that visual information improves coordination by giving actors an accurate view of the task state and one another's activities [37]. It is important to note that the visual information does not need to be identical for all group members for it to support situation awareness, as long as it allows them to form an accurate view of the current situation and appropriately plan future actions [40]. For example, two fighter pilots can converge on a target aircraft, even if one of them uses the visual line of sight and the other uses radar to see the target. However, if the differing displays lead them to form different situational representations, then their performance is likely to suffer. In other words, if visual sighting allows one pilot to distinguish between friendly and enemy aircraft but the radar fails to support this discrimination for the other pilot, then the two fighters are unlikely to coordinate their attack purely on the basis of the situation awareness provided by the visual information. Situation awareness, therefore, has the potential to address disintegrated solutions in collaborative process.

Theory of grounding indicates that in communication, visual information improves coordination by supporting the verbal communication surrounding a collaborative activity [41–43]. This theory suggests that successful communication relies on a foundation of mutual knowledge or common ground. Conversational grounding is the process of establishing common ground, an essential entity over the second phase of collaboration while discussing the core concepts to structure the problem. In conversational grounding, speakers form utterances based on an expectation of what a listener is likely to know and then monitor that the utterance was understood, whereas listeners have a responsibility to demonstrate their level of understanding [44, 45]. Throughout a conversation, participants are continually assessing what other participants know to formulate the steps [38, 39, 44], and unite various views of stakeholders to structure the problem, which makes it a promising choice to deal with the following barriers: misunderstanding of core concepts, inability to participate effectively in talks and lack of inclusive engagement.

5.3 Online Collaboration Platforms

By providing a platform for knowledge sharing and collaboration, online networks can help to address several barriers to collaboration. Free from geographic constraints, online networks can ideally connect people from different organizations, disciplines and communities. If the interface allows, these communication channels can promote sharing of knowledge across silos. Real-time feedback loops can foster a more rapid evolution of ideas than annual conferences or quarterly publications. Dialogues between different cultural groups can help to critique and develop societal values. Inclusive, multi-way dialogues across disciplinary boundaries can go a long way towards integrating diverse knowledge and perspectives for more inclusive conceptual frameworks of sustainability.

When people and computers interact via networks, new intellectual pursuits become possible [46]. By facilitating and structuring collaboration between people with different expertise, online networks can aid creative problem solving [47]. For example, existing online networks assist in collective design (e.g., Linux), decision-making (e.g., Threadless), data analysis (e.g., citizen science) and idea generation (e.g., Flood of Ideas). Being ambitious in their goals, these online platforms can address an array of barriers: siloed institutions, limited power and resource, inadequate communication methods, insufficient representation of world views, ineffective thinking paradigms, and disintegrated solutions.

5.4 Synergy Among Tools

Conceptual frameworks, visual tools, and collaborative platforms are powerful tools on their own, but when combined successfully, each tool enhances the effectiveness of the others. The synergy among them is as follows: "Conceptual frameworks" provide a clear structure of ideas making "visual communication" effective. *Visual tools* in turn allows for a high density of information and expression of complex relationships and emergent properties. Moreover, "Visual tools" provide the right input for conceptual frameworks. "Conceptual frameworks" support online collaboration platforms by providing a meaningful structure for knowledge sharing and discussions across the disciplines, helping researchers and practitioners to avoid a reductionist approach and develop more integrated frameworks. This leverage, in fact, make them prime candidates for further research and investment to facilitate cross-boundary collaboration.

As discussed above, human and computers thinking together, that is cognitive collaboration [46], is ideally a promising way to work with diverse stakeholders to address the barriers of collaborative governance regimes, facilitate collaboration, and reach an understanding of the elephant [48].

6 Conclusion

In this research, I reviewed the cross-sector collaboration case studies from various sectors in order to identify the barriers and developed a synergy map to show the potential of digital tools in addressing them. This research argues that these digitally driven tools are capable of enhancing cross sector collaboration and further the aspiration of democratic governance [49]. In calls for future research, a number of themes are apparent, including, most obviously, the need to view collaborations as complicated dynamic systems. Within these systems, a better understanding is needed of, for example, how to analyze all moving parts of collaboration simultaneously; how digital tools and conceptual frameworks facilitate collaboration and bring cognitive collaboration on the stage.

References

1. Emerson, K., Nabatchi, T., Balogh, S.: An integrative framework for collaborative governance. J. Public Adm. Res. Theor. **22**(1), 1–29 (2011)
2. Ansell, Ch., Gash, A.: Collaborative governance in theory and practice. J. Public Adm. Res. Theor. **18**(4), 543–571 (2008)

3. Agranoff, R.: Managing within Networks: Adding Value to Public Organizations. Georgetown University Press, Washington, DC (2007)
4. Agranoff, R.: Collaborating to Manage: A Primer for the Public Sector. Georgetown University Press, Washington, DC (2012)
5. Provan, K.G., Kenis, P.: Modes of network governance: structure, management, and effectiveness. J. Public Adm. Res. Theor. **18**(2), 229–252 (2008)
6. Gray, B.: Collaborating: Finding Common Ground for Multi-party Problems. Jossey-Bass, San Francisco (1989)
7. Huxham, C., Vangen, S.: Managing to Collaborate: The Theory and Practice of Collaborative Advantage. Routledge, New York (2005)
8. Ostrom, E.: Governing the Commons. Cambridge University Press, Cambridge (1990)
9. Ring, P., Van de Ven, A.: Developmental processes of cooperative interorganizational relationships. Acad. Manag. Rev. **19**(1), 90–118 (1994)
10. Koschmann, M.A., Kuhn, T.R., Pfarrer, M.D.: A communicative framework of value in cross-sector partnerships. Acad. Manag. Rev. **37**(2), 332–354 (2012)
11. Thomé, A.M.T., Scavarda, L.F., Scavarda, A.: Conducting systematic literature review in operations management. Prod. Plann. Control **27**(5), 408–420 (2016)
12. Homans, G., Curtis Jr., Ch.: An Introduction to Pareto. Knopf Publishers, New York (1934)
13. Fawcett, S.B., et al.: Using empowerment theory in collaborative partnerships for community health and development. Am. J. Commun. Psychol. **23**, 677–697 (1995)
14. Lasker, R.D., Weiss, E.S.: Broadening participation in community problem solving: a multidisciplinary model to support collaborative practice and research. J. Urban Health: Bull. N.Y. Acad. Med. **80**, 14–60 (2003)
15. Bruce, M.: Participatory partnerships: engaging and empowering to enhance environmental management and quality of life? Soc. Indic. Res. **71**, 123–144 (2005)
16. Schuckman, M.: Making hard choices: a collaborative governance model for the biodiversity context. Wash. Univ. Law Q. **79**, 343 (2001)
17. Susskind, L., Cruikshank, J.: Breaking the Impasse: Consensual Approaches to Resolving Public Disputes. Basic Books, New York (1987)
18. Warner, J.F.: More sustainable participation? Multi-stakeholder platforms for integrated catchment management. Water Resour. Dev. **22**(1), 15–35 (2006)
19. English, M.: Who are the stakeholders in environmental risk decisions? Risk Health Saf. Environ. **11**, 243–254 (2000)
20. Gunton, T.I., Day, J.C.: The theory and practice of collaborative planning in resource and environmental management. Environments **31**(2), 5–19 (2003)
21. Bryson, J.M., Crosby, B., Bloomberg, L.: Public value governance: moving beyond traditional public administration and the new public management. Public Adm. Rev. **74**(4), 445–456 (2014)
22. Andrew, S.A., Carr, J.B.: Mitigating uncertainty and risk in planning for regional preparedness: the role of bonding and bridging relationships. Urban Stud. **50**(4), 709–724 (2013)
23. Hawkins, C.V., Hu, Q., Feiock, R.C.: Self-organizing governance of local economic development: Informal policy networks and regional institutions. J. Urban Aff. **38**(5), 643–660 (2016)
24. Granovetter, M.: The strength of weak ties: a network theory revisited. Sociol. Theor. **1**, 201–233 (1983)
25. Van der Voet, J., Kuipers, B.S., Groeneveld, S.: Implementing change in public organizations: the relationship between leadership and affective commitment to change in a public sector context. Public Manag. Rev. **18**(6), 842–865 (2016)

26. Rouzbehani, kh.: A new paradigm: collaborative governance. In: Canadian Association for Programs in Public Administration (CAPPA) Conference, Regina-Saskatchewan, 31 May and 1 June (2018)
27. Mann, S.: Sustainable Lens: A Visual Guide. Createspace Independent Pub., New Zealand (2011)
28. Sousanis, N.: Unflattening. Harvard University Press, Massachusetts (2015)
29. Bellafontaine, T.: Innovation Labs: Bridging Think Tanks and Do Tanks. Policy Horizons Canada, Ottawa (2013)
30. Tonurist, P., Kattel, R., Lember, V.: Innovation labs in the public sector: what they are and what they do. Public Manag. Rev. 1–25 (2017)
31. Glanville, R.: Designing complexity. Perform Improv. Quart 20(2), 75–96 (2007)
32. Brown, B.: The four worlds of sustainability: drawing upon four universal perspectives to support sustainability initiatives. Integral Institute, Boulder, Colorado (2007)
33. Lindquist, E.A.: Visualization practice and government: strategic investments for more democratic governance. In: Gil-Garcia, J.R., Pardo, T.A., Luna-Reyes, L.F. (eds.) Policy Analytics, Modelling, and Informatics. PAIT, vol. 24, pp. 225–246. Springer, Cham (2018). https://doi.org/10.1007/978-3-319-61762-6_10
34. Elleström, L.: Modelling human communication: mediality and semiotics. In: Olteanu, A., Stables, A., Borţun, D. (eds.) Meanings & Co. Numanities - Arts and Humanities in Progress, vol. 6, pp. 7–32. Springer, Cham (2019). https://doi.org/10.1007/978-3-319-91986-7_2
35. Langer, S.K.: Philosophy in a New Key: A study in the symbolism of Reason, Rite, and Art, 3rd edn. Harvard University Press, Cambridge (1973)
36. Agrawala, M., Li, W., Berthouzoz, F.: Design principles for visual communication. Commun. ACM 54(4), 60–69 (2011)
37. Endsley, M.R.: Toward a theory of situation awareness in dynamic systems. Hum. Factors 37, 32–64 (1995)
38. Clark, H.H., Marshall, C.R.: Definite reference and mutual knowledge. In: Joshi, A.K., Webber, B.L., Sag, I.A. (eds.) Elements of Discourse Understanding, pp. 10–63. Cambridge University Press, Cambridge (1981)
39. Clark, H.H., Wilkes-Gibbs, D.: Referring as a collaborative process. Cognition 22, 1–39 (1986)
40. Bolstad, C.A., Endsley, M.R.: Shared mental models and shared displays: an empirical evaluation of team performance. In: Proceedings of the 43rd Meeting of the Human Factors & Ergonomics Society. Human Factors and Ergonomics Society, Houston (1999)
41. Gergle, D., Kraut, R.E., Fussell, S.R.: Using visual information for grounding and awareness in collaborative tasks. Hum.-Comput. Interact. 28(1), 1–39 (2013)
42. Monk, A., Watts, L.: Peripheral participation in video-mediated communication. Int. J. Hum.-Comput. Stud. 52, 933–958 (2000)
43. Whittaker, S., Geelhoed, E., Robinson, E.: Shared workspaces: how do they work and when are they useful? Int. J. Man-Mach. Stud. 39, 813–842 (1993)
44. Brennan, S.E.: How conversation is shaped by visual and spoken evidence. In: Trueswell, J.C., Tanenhaus, M.K. (eds.) Approaches to Studying World-Situated Language Use: Bridging the Language-as-Product and Language-as-Action Traditions, pp. 95–129. MIT Press, Cambridge (2005)
45. Brennan, S.E., Kuhlen, A.K., Charoy, J.: Discourse and Dialogue. The Stevens' Handbook of Experimental Psychology and Neuroscience. Volume 3 Language and Thought, vol. 3, pp. 149–205, 23 March 2018
46. Malone, T.W., Laubacher, R., Dellarocas, C.: The collective intelligence genome. IEEE Eng. Manag. Rev. 38(3), 38 (2010)

47. Yu, L.L., Nickerson, J.V., Sakamoto, Y.: Collective creativity: where we are and where we might go. In: Proceedings of Collective Intelligence (2012)
48. Attwood, M., Pedler, M., Pritchard, S., Wilkinson, D.: Leading Change: A Guide to Whole System Working. The Policy Press, England (2003)
49. Rouzbehani, K.: Problem-structuring methods: collaborative action with an application to the healthcare sector in Iran. Asia Pac. J. Public Adm. **38**(4), 281–288 (2016)

Human-Centered Framework for Managing IT Project Portfolio

Hamed Sarbazhosseini[(✉)], Saeed Banihashemi, and Sisira Adikari

University of Canberra, Bruce, ACT 2601, Australia
Hamed.Sarbazhosseini@canberra.edu.au

Abstract. Human-Centered interaction (HCI) has played a significant role in different areas of, software engineering, robotics, programming, facial recognition, and IT systems. To date, Project Portfolio Management is a field that HCI has not yet received much attention. However, the project management field and more specifically, software of Portfolio Management has been encouraged in the practise of HCI and design thinking concepts to improve outcomes of projects. This study aims to develop a framework in portfolio management that improves the understanding of HCI in portfolio management and assist's software developers to better engage design thinking in their approach. Furthermore, it develops a framework that can rectify issues identified from within the Organisational State Transition Approach of Portfolio Management, such as, unclear actions and strategic goals, uncertainty of success measures and key people being unsure of their purpose and what they were trying to achieve. We have applied a PACT framework as well as incorporating project management process groups to assist organizations to achieve their strategic goals. The outcome of this study assists portfolio managers to explore the requirements of their organization and enhance the success rate of their IT projects.

Keywords: Human-centered framework · Project Portfolio Management · Organizational State Transition Approach

1 Introduction

This work was motivated by the need to develop a framework within which to conduct research in a domain that has received a lot of attention in academic circles as well as industry. The Project Portfolio Management (PPM) literature has been studied from different perspectives and different framework, methods and models have been developed to assist practitioners to achieve optimum benefits. However, there seems to be a missing Human-Centered design element in PPM, which would help add design thinking to their processes and add agility within achieving strategic goals for organizations.

In the search for Organizational State Transition Approach (OSTA) of Portfolio Management, there seemed to offer some possibilities how to better manage IT portfolios; However, the OSTA by itself cannot help organizations to achieve their goals as it doesn't match the current and desired state of the organization. Th issues were identified from a study of OSTA that included, uncertainty of actions being undertaken

F. F.-H. Nah and K. Siau (Eds.): HCII 2019, LNCS 11589, pp. 432–442, 2019.
https://doi.org/10.1007/978-3-030-22338-0_35

to achieve strategic goals, uncertainty of success measures, key people being unsure of their purpose and what they were trying to achieve. This further motivated us to research how the OSTA framework can be improved in this domain.

This paper proceeds as follows. It first discusses some of the findings of the use of OSTA in PPM. It then outlines the principles of Human-Centered framework namely; PACT and Project Management process groups. It concludes how the developed framework can be used in this field of research.

2   The OSTA in Project Portfolio Management

The idea behind the State-Transition Approach was simple. McDonald and Sabrazhosseini [1] explained that "for example, the lighting in a room with a push button light switch. When the lights are off (state 1) and someone presses the button (event 1) the system turns on the lights (action) and changes the state to on (state 2). When the same event occurs again, the lights are turned off and the system returns to state1. Figure 1 shows this simple case can be modelled in an STA table". The OSTA was applied in PPM with a purpose to better structure the domain as Watson [2] says that "calls continue for a good theory in Information Systems and development of our own theory". While the idea of OSTA is simple, PPM is imperfect and complex in content [Sarbazhosseini 3].

The two characteristics of the OSTA that made it useful for description and specification are its clarity and completeness [1, 2]. According to Sarbazhosseini [3] and McDonald and Sarbazhosseini [1], the clarity of OSTA comes from "the specification within the table cells - the action the system takes and the new state it moves into are unambiguously described" and the completeness comes from "the table capturing all known states and events. The more controlled a system is, like the one used in the example, the higher the level of completeness".

While the State-Transition Model (STM) was used in clinical, ecological, computer science, and software engineering since late 1990s, there were incomplete research of this approach in project management. PMI [4] developed a standard called P3M3 (Project, Program, Portfolio Management Maturity Model) [5] where organizations can apply this to assess their maturity of their projects. Similar to STM, the central idea of P3M3 assessment is to find what the current status of organizations is and where do they want to be and how to get there. This evaluation takes place at different times because the management environment is dynamic [3].

Therefore, PPM could benefit from OSTA's ongoing, continuous nature of systems that makes the STM useful in looking at organizational state, change and responsiveness. The general OSTA has been represented in Fig. 1.

This figure includes state indicators which shows the current state, desired state and transition actions that require to get from current to desired state and finally learning from this process that updates the state indicators can be concluded in organisational system.

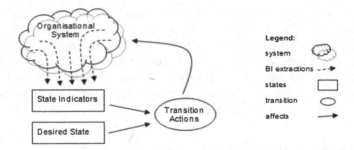

Fig. 1. The general form of OSTA (adapted from McDonald & Sarbazhosseini [1] & Sarbazhosseini.et al. [13])

2.1 The OSTA in PPM Domain

There are number of reasons why OSTA was applied in PPM domain. Based on Killen, et al. [6] findings, empirical studies reported on mixed findings regarding the link between particular PPM methods and goals. Research reveals that most organizations feel that their project portfolio contains too many projects for the available resources; however, no research has demonstrated a significant empirical link between a PPM method and better performance of projects [3].

Filippov et al.'s [7] study in Netherlands indicated that despite the recognized importance of the PPM topic and numerous academic and practice-oriented publications on PPM, the research is lacking a critical mass of empirical evidence. Their finding, based on five case-studies, indicates that organizations should know exactly what they want to achieve before embarking on a transition towards PPM.

Jamieson and Morris [8] reported on the results of four exploratory case studies and seventy-five responses from a Project Management Institute (PMI) European survey on moving from corporate strategy to project strategy. The survey results show that 50 percent of respondents' organisations have a PPM process; however, most respondents do not understand the goals of PPM and perceive it to be for managing projects around a theme rather than for balancing and selecting the best projects.

In the study of Sarbazhosseini [3], the OSTA was applied to the literature of PPM from different perspectives including academic, industry and software literature to ensure that it covers both academic and practitioner's perspective as presented in Fig. 2. Over 100 articles were studied in different data sources along with over 90 software developer's perspective to understand what or how PPM has been conducted [9].

In this analysis, several reasons were identified for why organizations apply PPM in the first place such as too many projects in the pipeline, shortage of resources, projects not liked to their strategic goals, wrong projects and slowing project progress. The desired state/goals for organizations stated as strategically aligned or linking portfolio to the strategy, maximizing the value of portfolio, reducing risks, increase agility, reduce project failures etc. The study of transition actions discovered that organizations are tempted to take different actions such as top down or bottom up approaches, portfolio maps, bar charts, scoring models etc.

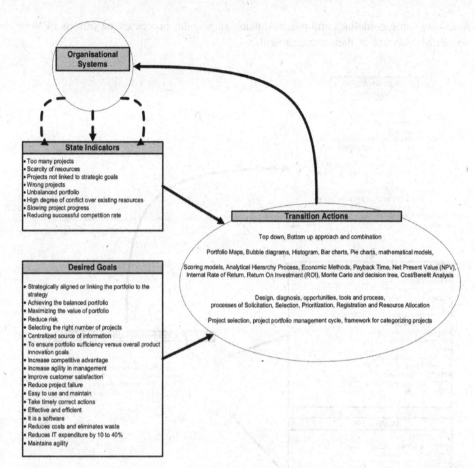

Fig. 2. The OSTA from literature perspective (adapted from Sarbazhosseini [3])

While the analysis of PPM literature indicates that these transition actions do not necessarily assist organizations to achieve their desired state, the proposed framework was further explored in seven government and non-government case-studies and were investigated through several interviews with portfolio managers and document reviews such as strategic plan and P3M3 assessments.

In this paper, it is not intended to discuss how the results were conducted; however, the research followed case-study research procedures following Yin' [10] guide in which appropriate pilot study was conducted and data were collected and analyzed in terms of thematic coding and pattern marching models [3].

The analyzed data helped to develop the following OSTA from empirical study findings (see Fig. 3). The empirical data analysis shows somehow different reasons for applying PPM and what they desire to achieve. It can be highlighted that organizations are applying PPM because they have lower visibility, transparency, accountability and consistency in their portfolio and hoping that they can achieve a higher level of that by following some guidelines and policies, using stage gates processes, or various PPM or non-PPM software in their management.

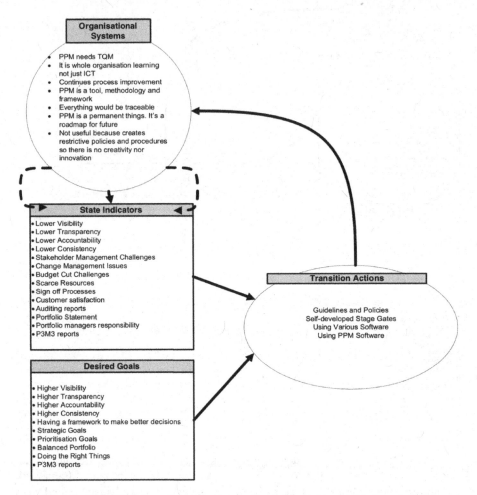

Fig. 3. The OSTA from literature perspective (adapted from Sarbazhosseini [3])

2.2   Findings of the Developed OSTA Within an Empirical Perspective

The analysis of OSTA from an empirical perspective shows a number of interesting findings that leads us to understand why it is necessary to apply a Human-Centered framework in PPM.

The results showed a remarkable gap between transition actions and desired goals where there is no clear evidence that these actions can lead to a desired state. In addition, looking at action that organizations take to achieve a goal does not provide the evidence to assist them in meeting future goals. It was clear that the participating organizations of the study did not have a clear understanding of strategic goals and the actions required to deliver them. The actions taken by the cases/organizations could be categorized mainly into guidelines and policies, self-developed stage-gates and software, but they could not ensure achievement of their set goals.

Another issue explored from this study was the lack of appropriate means for measuring PPM progress or success. It was discovered from PPM literature that there is no success measure for goals (e.g., strategic goals) or for determining a measurement for doing the right things or right projects. This study discovered that organizations were experiencing the same dilemma. It showed that even when organizations knew their desired goals, they were unsure of how to measure achievement of these goals.

From organizational system learning, it was discovered that PPM is a continuous battle with big changes in projects, resources, scope, and quality. In such a battle, there is a need for clear visibility throughout organizations to manage changes effectively. Therefore, better visibility and having an effective framework assists in the management of portfolios. The clarity that a better framework provides, would assists projects to be efficiently traced, and decisions to be consistently made according to strategic goals.

Looking at above analysis led us to develop a framework in which organizations receive a better result in applying PPM. The following will discuss a Human-centred framework in PPM domain.

3 Developing a Human-Centered Framework for Managing IT Project Portfolios

Being human-centered is about "putting people first to support people and for people to enjoy" [11]. In human-centered interactions, we think about what people want to do rather than what the technology/applications can do [11]. It's about designing new ways to connect people and involve them in the design process [11].

To design a human-centered framework, organizations require to understand PACT (People, Activities, Contexts and Technologies) see Fig. 4. PACT is a framework which would assist organizations to understand what the requirements are to design an interactive system where puts the people first. The main emphasis of the framework is that people use technologies to undertake activities in specified contexts.

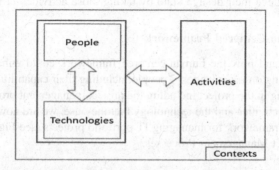

Fig. 4. The general form of PACT (adapted from Benyon [11])

Understanding people assists managers to understand their people's skill, knowledge, experience, role, their capabilities and the purpose of applying portfolio management concepts.

Understanding activities allows organizations to better understand their management activities such as time, cost, quality, risk, communication. The activities include all decision making, strategic alignment and program or portfolio level decisions such as initiating projects, planning, monitoring & controlling, executing and completing projects. These activities are mainly taking place in project management process groups defined by PMI [12] see Fig. 5. In this process groups, initiating process helps to set a vision what is to be achieved. In the planning process, the total scope of the project including timing, costing, communication, procurement, design and development planning happens. In the executing process, all the planned work is to be executed. In the monitoring and controlling process, all the staged of planning, executing are monitored and controlled to understand if the project is still worth doing it or should be stopped. Also, a decision for the next steps can be set up. In the closing process, the project formally closes and all the contracts get sign-off [12].

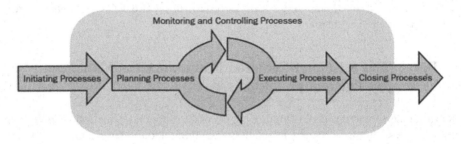

Fig. 5. The general form of PMBOK Process Groups (adapted from PMI [12])

Understanding context of activities are important as it allows organization to realize whether the activities are appropriate to people and the context of the projects such as IT, consultation, research & development, new product development, innovation projects, etc.

It is also important to understand what technologies organizations are using or should use to achieve their desired state by taking those activities in the context.

3.1   The Human-Centered Framework

To better understand how the human-centered framework could enhance the project success by focusing on organizations' people including their capabilities, the activities that they are taking in the project including the project management process groups, the context of these activities and the technology that they use, we are now developing the human-centered framework for managing IT portfolio projects (see Fig. 6) considering PACT and Project Management Processes.

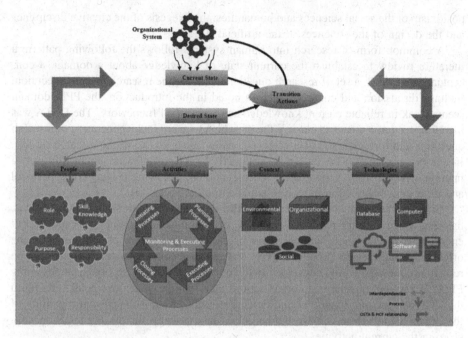

Fig. 6. The Human-Centered Framework for Managing Project Portfolios

The above Human-Centered Framework (HCF) (highlighted in Green area) combines the knowledge from interactive systems design with project management process groups. As the orange arrow connects the HCF to OSTA, it represents that it is a two-way connection. This connection relates four major states of the OSTA to PACT. Meaning that organizations to understand their current state require to analyze PACT. More specifically, they should understand the capability of their people and the purpose of having people in their organization to understand what they want to achieve. Then understand the activities that people are taking within the context and technology to better formulate their desired state.

Organizations with unclear understanding of their people and activities involved in their portfolios are less likely to achieve their strategic goals. Because the organization does not have the clarity of their current state. The HCF can complete the OSTA by allowing organizations to understand their current state and formulating their desired goals and respectively planning their activities.

The HCF also assist with understanding organizational learning. As it helps the organization to assess their current situation and better relate it to their goals and analyze if the goals are achievable. This also allows them to evaluate the current state according to their capabilities and understand what they can achieve or plan to achieve.

3.2   The Use of HCF

There are many different forms of research ranging from the experimentation of the physical sciences; the argument and logic of mathematics and philosophy; the antipositivism of the social sciences and humanities; the exegesis of the creative disciplines and the design of the 'sciences of the artificial' [1].

A common form of research into human systems follows the following pattern: a literature review to establish the current state of knowledge about a domain, a conceptual framework, a set of research questions or aims, the research design, execution, findings discussion and contributions. As noted in the introduction, the PPM domain seems weak in reliable current knowledge and conceptual framework. The OSTA was therefore used as a means to classify the literature, to assist in the generation of research questions and formulate the data gathering and analysis phases of the research project. In that process, the OSTA itself was critiqued. As a result of data sought from set of interviews which were supported by documentation, following the interview protocol and procedures resulted in exploring some empirical issues [3].

Given the conceptual structure of the PPM domain as seen through the OSTA lens, the next issue for the research was how to formulate the framework and collect empirical data that might address them. Because of the nature of the literature, the original thematic review produced a very varied set of constructs. An ends-means type research framework would suggest research questions like Why do organisations apply PPM? What kind of actions do organisations take in order to achieve goals? etc. From the HCF perspective, suggested questions are around: what is the current capability of the organization? How can we define achievable strategy for the organization considering the current activities?

Data is being sought from a set of interviews and observations of decision-making processes from portfolio managers and portfolio office team supported by documentation they make available. The interview protocol involves a set of procedures and instruments used to specify interactions between researchers and study participants including designs for participant contact, an interview data collection instrument, observation of decision-making processes, the interview script and analysis techniques. The protocol should desk-checked by the researchers before use.

To conclude this section of the paper, the HCF for managing IT project portfolios, is being used to frame the phases of a research project. It has offered a structure within which to evaluate this literature, frame research questions and collect and assess empirical data. The use of OSTA is being conducted in parallel with the HCF to understand organizations and better manage their portfolios to achieve their maximum benefits.

4   Conclusion

In this paper we have argued that the Project Portfolio Management domain has aspects that make research difficult and we considered and discussed the use of the developed OSTA to overcome some of these issues. We adapted the approach to human interaction design, calling it HCF for managing IT portfolios.

Our tentative conclusion is that OSTA is an effective framework for the analysis of literature, research question formulation, research design and data collection and analysis. However, this approach requires a better understanding of organizations through analysing PACT. This means that organizations are better learning their current portfolio through analysing, their people, activities they are undertaking and in which context and the technology used to communicate. We also incorporated project management process groups which is an efficient method to explain how or what organizations are doing within this framework. And furthermore, to help organisations better define and set an achievable desired state and accordingly develop an action plan.

The contribution of this paper is that it presents a means for managing IT portfolio domains. It is too early to claim practical contributions however, OSTA is an effective management analysis framework in parallel use with HCF in managing IT portfolios, particularly when well supported by new data, information and knowledge management systems.

This research suggests a number of areas for further development. First, we speculate that PPM is an example of a class of problematic, complex phenomena of interest to the IS discipline. The use of OSTA in parallel with HCF seems to offer a useful conceptual framework for research in PPM so it may offer the same to other problem areas in the class. Second, the definition of the relationship between concepts in OSTA and HCF has not yet begun. Lastly, there is a need for research to build the evidence-based for general HCF and management action across the domain.

References

1. McDonald, C., Sarbazhosseini, H.: A state transition approach to conceptualising research: the project portfolio management domain. In: Proceedings of the 24th Australasian Conference on Information Systems, Melbourne, Australia, pp. 1–10 (2013)
2. Watson, R.: Research in information systems: what we haven't learned. MIS Q. 25(4), v–xv (2001)
3. Sarbazhosseini, H.: Conceptualising project portfolio management in terms of oranisational state-transition approach, Ph.D. thesis, University of Canberra, August 2015
4. PMI: Project Portfolio Management (PPM): The Natural Evolution of Project Management. PMI Virtual Library, pp. 1–4 (2011)
5. OGC.: Portfolio, Programme, and Project Management Maturity Model (P 3M3), Introduction and Guide to P3M3. UK's Office of Government Commerce (2012). http://www.p3m3-officialsite.com/P3M3Model/Model_mhtry.aspx/. Accessed 30 July 2013
6. Killen, C., Hunt, R., Kleinschmidt, E.: Managing the new product development project portfolio: a review of the literature and empirical evidence. In: PICMET Proceedings, Porland, Oregon (2007)
7. Filippov, S., Mooi, H., Van der Weg, R.: Strategic project portfolio management: an empirical investigation. RISUS 3(1), 9–23 (2012)
8. Jamieson, A., Morris, P.W.G.: Moving from corporate strategy to project strategy. In: Jeffery, M., Leliveld, I. (eds.) The Wiley Guide to Managing Projects, pp. 177–205. Wiley (2004a). Best Practices in IT Portfolio Management. MIT Sloan Manag. Rev. 45. no.3 (2007)
9. Sarbazhosseini, H., Young, M.: Mind the gap: exploring the divergence between PPM software and PPM theory. In: Australian Institute of Project Management (AIPM), Melbourne, Australia (2012)
10. Yin, R.K.: Case Study Research: Design and Methods, 4th edn. Sage Publications, USA (2009)

11. Benyon, D.: Designing Interactive Systems: A comprehensive Guide to HCI, UX and Interaction Design, 3rd edn. (2014)
12. PMI: A Guide to the Project Management Body of Knowledge: PMBOK® Guide, 4th edn. (2008)
13. Sarbazhosseini, H., Adikari, S., Keighran, H.: Design thinking framework for project portfolio management, HCI 2016, Toronto, Canada (2016)

Human Collaboration on Crowdsourcing Platforms – a Content Analysis

Navid Tavanapour[(⊠)] and Eva A. C. Bittner

University of Hamburg, Hamburg, Germany
{tavanapour,bittner}@informatik.uni-hamburg.de

Abstract. The crowdsourcing phenomenon offers the opportunity to address an open call to the crowd. Crowd workers may work together to find a solution that satisfies the open call. One of the major benefits for a crowdsourcer is the pool of crowd workers that can be accessed over crowdsourcing platforms. However, the produced outcomes of crowd workers are often on a low level with weak elaboration and quality. The key to high quality work is the collaboration of crowd workers. This has already been addressed in the collaboration process design framework for crowdsourcing (CPDF). At this point we position this work and widen our view by conducting a content analysis on crowdsourcing platforms in order to understand the collaboration of crowd workers on real world crowdsourcing platforms better as well as investigate the weaknesses of the collaboration process design framework for crowdsourcing to improve work practices. By doing so, we redesign the CPDF based on the results of the content analysis and present an improved collaboration process of crowd workers within the CPDF.

Keywords: Human collaboration · Crowdsourcing · Content analysis ·
Design science research · Crowd work · CPDF

1 Introduction

Crowdsourcing has spread through many fields in recent years and shown potential for problem solving and innovation creation for different kind of tasks [1]. It has an increasing role in the area of work and knowledge generation for organizations. While only a few years ago students were predominantly crowd workers, the picture is changing and becoming more heterogeneous. In addition, the diversity of crowd-sourcing platforms is enormous. This allows the practice of crowdsourcing in many industry sectors and areas. Howe [2] describes the crowdsourcing phenomenon with the outsourcing of tasks "to an undefined generally large group of people in an open call" [2]. Consequently, crowdsourcing delivers opportunities for organizations to widen the range of their organizational boarder and consider other sources to solve problems, accomplish tasks and generate innovation [3]. One of the major benefits for the crowdsourcer is the pool of crowd workers (individual members of the crowd [4]) that can be accessed over crowdsourcing platforms. Furthermore, crowdsourcing platforms enable crowdsourcers to address different types of tasks to crowd workers in open calls. Some tasks can be divided into different parts and distributed to different

© Springer Nature Switzerland AG 2019
F. F.-H. Nah and K. Siau (Eds.): HCII 2019, LNCS 11589, pp. 443–458, 2019.
https://doi.org/10.1007/978-3-030-22338-0_36

crowd workers for accomplishment. Other tasks need, due to their complexity, the collaboration of some crowd workers for accomplishment. Collaboration research has shown that the collaboration between different heterogeneous individuals can lead to better outcomes. Especially, if tasks are involved with high complexity level and if they go beyond individuals' skills to be accomplished [5–8]. The collaboration between crowd workers is one key to value creation [9]. However, less is known about the collaboration process among crowd workers [9–13] and most research in this field has an explorative focus for a special domain of crowdsourcing. For example, the elaboration on ideas on web platforms to improve the quality of ideas is in the scope of Kipp [14]. Hutter et al. [15] investigate the tension between collaborative and competitive behavior, the balance and the impact of them on the quality of the outcome in design contests. The management of the crowd through the platforms' process is in the scope of Malhotra and Majchrzak [16] by utilizing the knowledge integration process [17] to guide the crowd workers. However, the collaborative interaction among crowd workers constitutes a gap in prior research [9]. Moreover, the collaboration of crowd workers could lead to better outcomes and help towards preventing or weakening some identified problems on this field. For example, handling enormous user generated input in form of unstructured and/or low quality work with lack of details as well as input that already exists on the platform by recognizing same or similar content and linking them up to each other, finding any weakness in contributions of others and making suggestions for improvement [11]. Therefore, Tavanapour and Bittner [10, 11] introduced the collaboration process design framework for crowdsourcing (CPDF), that considers three different phases to structure the collaboration of crowd workers. In their work they also point out that the CPDF lacks of more detailed process steps to structure the collaboration more accurately. For example according to the CPDF the crowd worker enters the collaboration with other crowd workers in a "prototyping" process step by working on a/n prototype/artefact [11]. Even though the "prototyping" step is evidenced through the research of Tavanapour and Bittner [11], they also point out that more research is needed to explore this deeper. This leaves room for the question of how the participation of crowd workers leads to the process of prototyping an artefact [10, 11]. At this point, more explorative research could shed light to unanswered aspects as shown with the example above. Since the investigation of how far the CPDF is covered on crowdsourcing platforms and covers the collaboration between crowd workers on crowdsourcing platforms was done in recent work (see [11]), we widen our scope to understand the collaboration of crowd workers more in detail and to explore and investigate which process steps the CPDF is still missing. We ask the following research questions for this purpose. **Q1**: How do crowd workers proceed to submit a solution on crowdsourcing platforms? **Q2**: Which process steps, functionalities and problems does the CPDF miss with respect to the collaboration among crowd workers on crowdsourcing platforms?

Initially, the CPDF was derived from and is limited to the literature, this is why we use a different source in this research to identify the missing pieces of the CPDF closer to real world crowdsourcing projects with less limitations to answer Q2. Therefore, we need to understand the patterns that lead to a submission on real world crowdsourcing platforms by answering Q1. To answer Q1 and Q2 we conduct a content analysis (according to Mayring [18, 19]) on existing crowdsourcing platforms. For this purpose, we derive a category system [18] and use the categories for the coding process [20] on crowdsourcing platfoms.

This paper is structured as follows: first, we explain the background of the research by mainly zooming to the CPDF more in detail. Second, we present the methodology before third, presenting the findings of the conducted content analysis. Based on the findings, we redesign the collaboration process of crowd workers. Forth we discuss the collaboration process and close with a conclusion.

2   Research Background

The CPDF according to Fig. 1 considers the phases before (Pre Collaboration Phase) and after (Post Collaboration Phase) the actual collaboration process among crowd workers to consider relevant factors that can influence the collaboration [10]. The Pre Collaboration Phase suggests to consider incentive systems to motivate the crowd workers (in S1), deliver guidance in form of instructions to help the crowd workers through the process of contribution (in S2), give opportunities to get access to per-quisite knowledge for participation as well as understanding of others' contribution (S3) and create content for one specific type of participation (S4) [10].

The Collaboration Process Phase (CPP) provides a design of an interaction process among crowd workers with the goal to create a solution collaboratively that satisfies the open call. Starting with S5 – Prototyping – crowd workers elaborate towards creating a first artefact/prototype of a solution, which serves as a basis to get feedback in S6 for improvement, before submitting a final solution. The revise step (S7) either considers the given feedback to improve, finalize and submit the solution (S8) or can be used to go back to S5 and start over with constructing a prototype [10]. At this point, the Post Collaboration Process starts with documenting the process (S9), sharing the special insights that lead to the solution (S10) and learning from the shared experience of others, towards gaining more expertise (S11) [10].

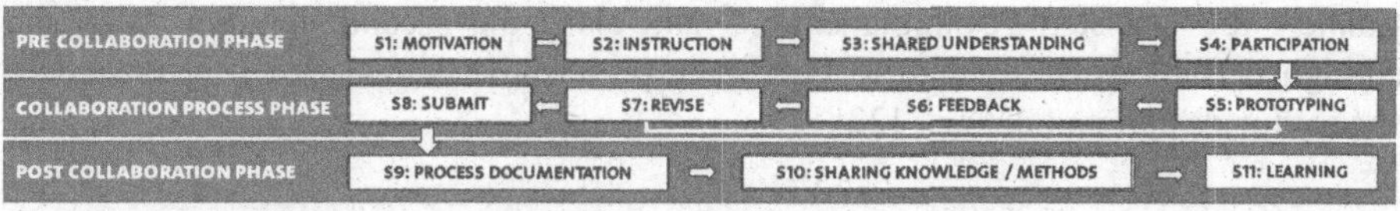

PRE COLLABORATION PHASE	S1: MOTIVATION	—	S2: INSTRUCTION	—	S3: SHARED UNDERSTANDING	—	S4: PARTICIPATION
COLLABORATION PROCESS PHASE	S8: SUBMIT	—	S7: REVISE	—	S6: FEEDBACK	—	S5: PROTOTYPING
POST COLLABORATION PHASE	S9: PROCESS DOCUMENTATION	—	S10: SHARING KNOWLEDGE / METHODS	—	S11: LEARNING

Fig. 1. Collaboration process design framework for crowdsourcing (according to [10, 11])

If we zoom into the Collaboration Process Phase, we can see a jump from S4 to S5 (Fig. 1) and with it the entry to another phase and to the collaborative setting. However, this jump leaves room for the question of how the participation of crowd worker leads to the process of prototyping an artefact [10, 11]. Thus, specially the Collaboration Process Phase (Fig. 1) needs more investigation for more accurate matching to real world crowdsourcing needs [11].

3 Design Science Research Approach

This research starts the second iteration of a larger Design Science Research project (DSR) [21–24] according to the six-steps approach (see Fig. 2) of Peffers et al. [25].

Problem Identification	Objectives of a Solution	Design & Development	Demonstration	Evaluation	Communication
High complexity in understanding how crowd worker produce high quality solutions. Lack of knowledge in the collaboration process among crowd worker on crowdsourcing platforms.	Using recent explorative studies out of the literature to ground a first suggestion for a collaboration process among crowd worker.	Define and derive criteria for the collaboration process for crowdsourcing to analyze the collaboration processes among crowd worker on crowdsourcing platforms.	Use the criteria and the collaboration process design framework for crowdsourcing on different projects on different crowdsourcing platforms to analyze the collaboration process among crowd worker.	Evaluation of the criteria and the framework using the results out of the previous step (Demonstration)	Dissemination of a theory of design and action that guides researchers and practitioners to analyze the collaboration among crowd worker on crowdsourcing platforms

Fig. 2. The six-step DSR approach [11] according to Peffers et al. [25]

The "Problem Identification" and "Objectives of a Solution" remain from the first iteration (see [10, 11]). Therefore, the entry point of this research is taking the loopback after the first iteration to the third step "Design and Development" by using the results of previous research to redefine the categories and criteria of a conducted content analysis on running crowdsourcing platforms (see [11]) and continues with the fourth step "Demonstration" by conducting a content analysis on existing crowdsourcing platforms to gain insights on the collaboration among crowd workers. We analyze the results in the "Evaluation" step and propose a redesigned Collaboration Process Phase for the CPDF to answer the research questions (Q1 and Q2). With this paper, we aim to complete the last step "Communication" and close the second iteration. With the redesigned framework, we aim to contribute prescriptive knowledge [23] towards a "theory for design and action" [22].

4 Analysis and Findings

We conduct the content analysis according to Mayring [18] by deriving a category system to code the relevant content on current ongoing crowdsourcing platforms to gather insights on the collaboration among crowd worker towards solutions.

4.1 Content Analysis

Since we posses a category system from a previous study (see [11]), we utilize it in this paper for more accurate process steps based on the previous results. The previous category system considered each step S1-S11 (Fig. 1) of the CPDF as a category to find evidence for each step in ten real world crowdsourcing projects [11]. As the scope of this paper is on the Collaboration Process Phase (CPP) and the identification of missing steps for the collaboration among crowd workers we exclude the Pre Collaboration Phase and the Post Collaboration Phase from this content analysis. This also results from previous research and the observed insights such as lack and potential for missing process steps in the CPP on real world crowdsourcing platforms [11]. Therefore, we still consider the steps of the CPP S5-S8 as categories for the content analysis. We go one step further and consider, based on the data of prior research (in [11]), four new categories (category 1, 3, 5 and 7) additionally to the previous four (category 2, 4, 6 and 8) resulting from S5-S8. The four new categories are mainly constructed to represent the interaction around the steps S5 "Prototyping", S6 "Feedback" and S7 "Revise" to close the gap in the CPP. The categories are as follows:

- **Category 1 - Before the Prototyping:** This category considers the interaction before the creation or elaboration of or on a first artefact/prototype: The criteria for the coding process is to capture all the activities among crowd worker related to an open call before the actual "Prototyping" step S5 in form of posts (all kind of files) and text segments.
- **Category 2 - Prototyping:** Activities among crowd workers that lead towards the creation of any kind of first artefacts or prototypes. The criteria is to capture (related) crowd workers contributions of first prototypes and artefacts such as ideas, solutions, designs, source code etc. [11].
- **Category 3 - After the Prototyping before the Feedback:** This category considers the interaction after the creation or elaboration of or on a first artefact/prototype and before any feedback by others than the owners is given: The criteria for the coding process is to capture all the activities among crowd workers related to an open call after the actual "Prototyping" step S5 and before the Feedback step S6 in form of posts (all kind of files) and text segments.
- **Category 4 - Feedback:** The first created prototype/artefact is in the scope of this category and any provided feedback in any form related to the produced prototype/artefact. The criteria are to cover any kind of positive or negative feedback in form of rating e.g. like or dislike button, voting ranges or scales, in form of text segments or files highlighted improvement suggestions or pointing out weaknesses to any aspects of the prototype/artefact [11].
- **Category 5 - After the Feedback before the Revision:** This category captures all the activities before revising the prototype/artefact by considering the feedback. The criteria for coding is to capture all the activities among crowd worker related to an open call after the "Feedback" step S6 and before the actual "Revise" step S7 in form of posts (all kind of files) and text segments.

- **Category 6 - Revise:** Activities among crowd workers that lead towards any kind of revised artefacts or prototypes based on the given feedback. The criteria are to capture (related) crowd workers' contribution of revised (improved) prototypes and artefacts such as ideas, solutions, designs, source code etc. [11].
- **Category 7 - After the Revision before submitting:** This category captures all the activities before submitting the constructed solution this far and after considering the feedback to construct a revised solution. The criteria for coding is to capture all the activities among crowd workers related to an open call after the "Revise" step S6 and before the actual "Submit" step S7 in form of posts (all kind of files) and text segments.
- **Category 8 - Submit:** "This category captures necessary formalities for submitting a solution. But before that the crowd workers have to meet the needs for submitting" [11]. Relevant are finalized submitted solution to recognize the end of the collaboration among crowd worker with the reached goal to shape a solution that satisfies the open call.

We coded the content of the considered platforms to the categories [20] and considered produced content of crowd workers in form of texts and files [11] and references to them (e.g. comment from crowdsourcer to crowd workers contribution). In the coding process, on each platform, we went through the first ten open calls and gathered the crowd workers' contributions of any kind and references to them. Additionally, for each of the gathered data, we examined one by one whether they meet the criteria of one category or not.

4.2   The Considered Crowdsourcing Platforms for the Content Analysis

Table 1 shows the platforms we considered for the content analysis. Most of the platforms were selected, because they displayed a certain number of parallel ongoing projects on which the interaction of crowd workers is possible. For our research, the crowding mechanisms as well as the interaction among crowd workers and crowd workers with crowdsourcer are of importance. Some open calls on the considered platforms revealed a high amount of interaction among a multiple number of actors such as crowd workers and crowdsourcer. On most of the platforms, the interaction among actors was restricted to two to five individuals. One reason for this could be the high amount of contributions and the complexity to get an overview of all contributions. We collected the data on each platform from different open calls between February 2017 and March 2018. We conducted the content analyses with data from 13 different platforms. According to Table 1, the diversity of domains is considered with different submitted artefacts.

Table 1. Platforms (P) considered for the content analyses

P. Nr.	Name of platforms (P)	Domain	Link	Artefact(s) considered
P1	Agentur für Arbeit	Government (Germany)	https://ideenwerkstatt. arbeitsagentur.de	Ideas/designs
P2	Postbank	Bank	https://ideenlabor. postbank.de/project	Designs for application/source code
P3	Crowdguru	Human as resource	https://www.crowdguru. de	Task accomplishment
P4	OpenIdeo	Healthcare/education	https://www.openideo. com/challenges	Ideas
P5	Zooniverse	Science	https://www.zooniverse. org/projects	Task accomplishment
P6	Cccinnovation-center	IT-Healthcare	https://www. cccinnovationcenter. com/challenges/	Concepts and designs/source code
P7	NASA	Spacecraft	https://www.nasa.gov/ directorates/spacetech/ centennial_challenges	Designs
P8	Movingideas	Transportation	https://moving-ideas.net	Ideas
P9	Textbroker	Literature and journalism	https://www.textbroker. de	Texts
P10	Testbirds	Software testing	https://www.testbirds.de	Reports about software bugs/improvement suggestions
P11	99designs	Visualization	https://99designs.de/ contests	Designs
P12	Designenlassen	Visualization	https://www. designenlassen.de	Designs
P13	Startnext	Entrepreneurship	https://www.startnext. com/Projekte	Products

4.3 Findings

Table 2 lists the platforms on which we found content according to the criteria of the categories.

We identified the most insightful contents for categories 1 and 4. For category 7 ("after the revision before submitting"), we hardly found content on platforms except for the ones listed in Table 2. One reason for this might be that on most platforms feedback was available (category 4) but ignored by crowd workers. Therefore, no revision took place and this leads to less content for categories 5, 6 and 7.

Category 3 reveals little room among prototyping and receiving feedback. If a prototype/artefact is constructed, crowd workers tend to wait for feedback.

Table 2. Overview corresponding platforms with relevant content for the categories

Category	Content form platforms
1	P1, P2, P3, P4, P5, P6, P8, P9, P10, P11, P12, P13
2	P1, P2, P3, P5, P6 P7, P9, P10, P13
3	P2, P5, P6, P7, P10
4	P1, P2, P4, P5, P7, P8, P9, P10, P11, P12, P13
5	P1, P2, P7, P10, P11, P12
6	P1, P2, P5, P7, P10, P11, P12
7	P2, P5, P7
8	P1 P2, P3, P4, P5, P6, P7, P8, P9, P10, P11, P12, P13

Category 8 contains all platforms as displayed in Table 2. However, we could not identify any other content than submitted solutions.

At this point, we examine each category in more detail and describe the insights and interaction patterns we found in the conducted content analysis.

Starting with **Category 1**, the coding of the content belonging to this category reveals different patterns of the first entry point and interaction among crowd workers. In contrast to the "Prototyping" step in the CPDF, crowd workers do not always start with creating an artefact. The results show that either one idea is shared which leads to collaboration (P1, P3, P4, P5, P6, P8, P9, P10, P11, P12, P13) or an ideation process is started in from of a discussion towards an approach (P1, P2, P6, P10, P13). In both cases, the crowd has the opportunity to discuss the ideas and/or rates the ideas by preference. After the discussion and/or rating a small amount of crowd workers, who are interested in further elaboration find a constellation to elaborate on different parts towards a prototype/artefact of a solution (P1, P2, P6, P10, P13).

Fig. 3. Process pattern in category 1

In some cases (P3, P4, P5, P7, P8, P9, P11, P12), the described process above is not available because the idea is presented directly with a/n prototype/artefact. Before that, we found no interaction or any kind of pattern.

In sum, the entry point for the collaboration process varies from platform to platform and from open call to open call. Different forms of how crowd workers participate lead to a diversity of the entry points at different states of the process (ideation, discussion, ratings, suggestions etc.).

Category 2 considers patterns for the actual "Prototyping". If no prototype/artefact is presented with the idea, the crowd workers discuss parts of the solution and organize themselves by splitting tasks (P1, P2, P6, P10, P13) and elaborate by contributing the divided tasks towards the prototype/artefact (P1, P2, P3, P5, P6 P7, P9). If all subtasks are accomplished, they merge them to complete the first prototype/artefact (P1, P2, P3, P5, P6, P7, P9).

| CONSTRUCTION OF PROTOTYPE/ARTEFACT | ← | ELABORATION | ← | TASK(S) DEFINITION & ASSIGNMENT |

Fig. 4. Process pattern in category 2 "Prototyping"

In **Category 3** after the "Prototyping & before the Feedback", we could identify one specific pattern. Depending on the type of the artefact/prototype, they checked (proof of concept (P2, P5, P6, P7), (re)producing results (P5, P7, P10)), if the prototype/artefact fulfills its purpose (P2, P6) as in an "evaluation". Based on the result of the evaluation some of the prototypes were adjusted or improved (P2, P5, P7, P10).

Category 4 contains any kind of "Feedback". The analysis of the coding revealed the existence of three main kinds of feedback givers. First, the crowd itself in form of ratings (e.g. scales, like/dislike), by providing suggestions for improvement, hints of errors or weaknesses in comments on prototypes/artefacts or in discussions about the prototype/artefact (P2, P4, P5, P7, P8, P11, P12). Second, the platform itself (one platform worker) or experienced crowd workers, who provide detailed feedback on the prototype in an early stage of the process (P1, P2, P7, P9, P10, P11, P12). Third, the crowdsourcer, who also mostly delivered feedback, but at a late state of the process (P1, P4, P5, P8, P9, P10, P11, P12, P13).

In **Category 5** after the "Feedback & before the Revise", we could identify patterns regarding the available feedback. The feedback was discussed with the feedback giver and among the crowd workers, who constructed the prototype/artefact (P1, P2, P7, P10, P11, P12). In some cases, the responsible crowd workers for the prototype filtered the feedback for revising (P2, P7).

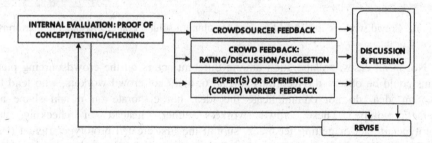

Fig. 5. Process iteration and pattern from category 3, 4, 5, 6 and 7: evaluation, feedback and revise

Category 6 contains any kind of revised prototype/artefact. In this category, the prototypes/artefacts show minor changes. It appears that most of the crowd workers do not invest much effort to shape the prototype with major changes (P1, P2, P5, P7, P10, P11, P12). Even though, valuable feedback is available, it appears that it is not considered for the final submitted solution (P1, P2, P5, P7, P10, P11, P12). Moreover, the feedback from crowdsourcers are more often considered than the feedback from the crowd (P11, P12).

In **Category 7** after the "Revision & before the Submission", the crowd workers evaluated the changes as in category 3, to check whether the prototype still fulfills its purpose (P2, P5, P7). Figure 5 displays the loop back to the "internal evaluation" at this point.

Category 8 contains the submission of a solution. The crowd workers were mostly following the instructions to fulfill the conditions for submission. Finalizing the prototypes/artefacts were mainly in the scope in this category (all platforms P1-P13). No other patterns or content for other patterns were identified.

Figure 6 summarizes the collaboration of crowd workers on the crowdsourcing platforms which we analyzed in real world by merging the patterns we found in the categories as presented in Figs. 3, 4 and 5. The process is initialized by an idea or an ideation process mostly in the form of brainstorming and ends with a submission of a solution to fulfil the open calls' needs.

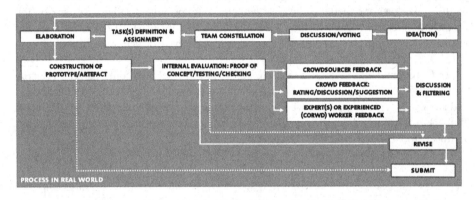

Fig. 6. Crowd workers' real world process to submit a solution on crowdsourcing platforms

Not in all cases, collaboration among different actors on the crowdsourcing platforms could be observed. According to Fig. 6, there are crowd workers, who tend to have an idea, do not communicate the idea, but elaborate on it and shape an artefact/prototype. These crowd workers either, instead of checking the prototype/artefact or getting feedback, submit the first created prototype/artefact (P2, P3, P6, P9, P10, P13) or they "evaluate" the prototype by themselves, make some changes and then submit it. Thus, no collaboration or interaction is recognized here. In some cases, we detected that feedback is provided, but ignored (P2, P5, P8). Therefore, there might be potential to motivate crowd workers to revise their own work.

If we exclude the above mentioned cases, due to the fact that these cases do not show collaboration on crowdsourcing platforms, we can derive a new collaboration process for the CPDF as displayed in Fig. 7. According to Fig. 7 the steps ST1-4 and ST18-20 remain the same as before in the Pre- and Post Collaboration Phase as well as ST16 and ST17 remain the same as before in the CPP (compare to Fig. 1). The new process steps ST5-15, which we derived, are considered for the new CPP. Additionally, we considered the different process entry points of the crowd workers in ST4. Not only

ST5 is a possible entry point but also ST6, ST7, ST8 and ST13 as described before. ST13 is the latest entry point to just give feedback to others' prototype/artefact and work out suggestions for improvements.

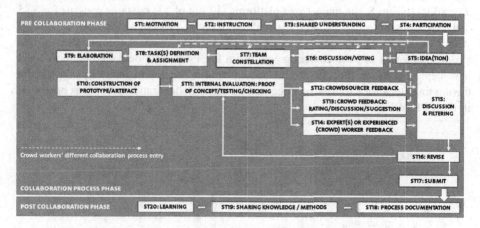

Fig. 7. CPDF with new CPP (with renamed (new) steps (ST))

Table 3 displays the platforms, that were utilized to derive the content for each of the CPPs' new process step. Furthermore, it shows which steps are missing on which platforms to improve the collaboration of crowd workers. In sum, content from all 13 platforms could be utilized for the new process steps. According to Table 3 P4 and P6 contributed content to the same steps as well as P11 and P12. In both cases the type of the constructed prototype/artefact is similar. According to Table 1 for P4 and P6 those

Table 3. Overview of the new derived process steps ST5-ST15 of the CPP and the corresponding analyzed platforms (P)

	ST5	ST6	ST7	ST8	ST9	ST10	ST11	ST12	ST13	ST14	ST15
P1	•	•	•	•	•	•		•		•	•
P2	•	•	•	•	•	•	•		•	•	
P3	•	•			•	•					
P4	•	•						•	•		
P5	•	•			•	•	•	•	•		
P6	•	•	•	•	•	•	•				
P7					•	•	•		•	•	•
P8	•	•						•	•		
P9	•	•			•	•		•		•	
P10	•	•	•	•			•	•		•	•
P11	•	•						•	•	•	•
P12	•	•						•	•	•	•
P13	•	•	•	•				•			

are ideas and for P11 and P12 designs. At this point, the produced outcome could have an influence on the interaction pattern of crowd workers. This needs more investigation in future research.

Figure 8 presents the number of steps the content from each platform contributed to and for each steps from how many various platforms the content was gained. According to Fig. 8, the majority of platforms (12 out of 13) contains patterns for ST5 and ST6. Content from P2 was considered for 10 out of 11 steps followed by P1 and P9 with 9 out of 11. On the other end, ST7, ST8 and ST11 benefit from content of five various platforms and the content gained from P3, P4 and P8 delivered patterns for 4 new steps. Therefore, those platforms show potential for improvement by considering the missing steps for a more structured and managed collaboration process as presented in the CPP of Fig. 7.

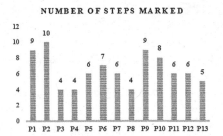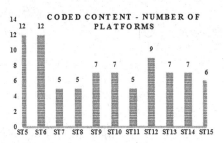

Fig. 8. Comparison of the coded content of platforms with the derived new steps

5   Discussion and Conclusion

Based on the content analysis which relies on current crowdsourcing platforms, we could gain insights about real world process of crowd workers from the beginning of an idea generation to submitting a solution regarding an open call. The scope of our research refers to the CPDF and mainly focusses on the collaboration process of crowd workers on crowdcourcing platforms. Therefore, the CPP of the CPDF was considered for the analysis of this research. The process steps of the CPP, at the beginning of this paper, grounded the choice of categories for the qualitative content analysis. With the approach to investigate, if gaps exist between the process steps of the previous CPP, we could explore and understand the collaboration of crowd workers in more detail. Moreover, we could model the real world process of crowd workers creating and submitting a solution (see Fig. 6) to address an open call and in sum answer Q1.

The real world process of crowd workers creating and submitting a solution on crowdsourcing platforms (according to Fig. 6) does not necessarily need collaboration as described before. The crowd workers could skip ST5-ST9 construct a prototype/artefact (in ST10) and submit it (in ST17) or check the solution (in ST11) and than submit (in ST17). If crowdsourcing platforms aim to prevent such process lifecycle to reduce the probability of receiving a high number of early stage or low quality submitted solutions the management of the crowd [26–31] and guidance of the crowd [27, 32–38] towards supporting the process of the new CPP of the CPDF (Fig. 7) is purposeful.

With the gained insights form the categories 1, 2, 3 and 4 as we could identify missing patterns before a first prototype/artefact is presented, how the previous "Prototyping" step of the CPP could be extended to cover the collaboration better and to capture the variety of feedback and feedback givers. The content analysis also revealed that the revision and submission steps of the further CPP remained mostly unchanged. After the elaboration of a prototype/artefact the majority of crowd workers considered the revision of the prototype/artefact with minimum effort, although helpful feedback was provided. At least that is what we can report form this study. More investigation regarding this is needed in future research to get clarity of the reasons why helpful feedback might not be considered by crowd workers with higher effort. Even though, we excluded the Pre Collaboration Phase of the CPDF, considering incentive systems [32, 33, 39–50] for crowd workers to revise the prototype/artefact by considering the majority of helpful feedback (e.g. with remuneration for revise) could be one option to address this issue. Incentive systems should not be limited to motivate the crowd workers to just participate in an open call and may trigger their motivation [32, 33, 39–50] even at later process state. For example, provoking crowd workers' motivation with incentive systems for ST15 and ST16 could lead the crowd worker to invest more effort to improve the prototype/artefact.

More investigation is also needed in future research to gain insight on why crowdsourcers' provided feedback even at a later stage is considered more often than that of the crowds. One reason could be that valuable feedback might be overseen or might not be detected due to an overload of contributions on crowdsourcing platforms. Another reason could be that responsible crowd workers for the prototype/artefact do not have the experience to detect the valuable feedback of the crowd or share a different vision. If crowd workers are willing to provide more effort to improve their prototype/artefact it seems that they are more motivated by crowdsourcers' feedback, because at the end the crowdsourcer needs to be satisfied with the submitted solution and not the crowd.

With this paper we close the second iteration of the design science research project as described in Sect. 3 (Fig. 2). Our research aims to contribute towards a "theory of design and action" according to Gregor [22] and provides prescriptive knowledge [23] with the real world process of crowd workers creating and submitting a solution (Fig. 6) and a redesigned framework for crowd workers' collaboration on crowdsourcing platforms (Fig. 7 (which also answers Q2)). The framework can serve to design and deploy collaborative environments and structured collaboration processes for crowd workers on crowdsourcing platforms towards more elaborated and improved submitted solutions.

References

1. Leimeister, J.M., Durward, D., Zogaj, S.: Crowd worker in deutschland. Hans-Böckler-Stiftung, Düsseldorf (2016). (in German)
2. Howe, J.: The rise of crowdsourcing. Wired Mag. **14**(6), 1–4 (2006)

3. Howe, J.: Crowdsourcing: Why the Power of the Crowd is Driving the Future of Business. Crown Business, New York (2008)
4. Durward, D., Blohm, I., Leimeister, J.M.: Crowd work. Bus. Inf. Syst. Eng. **58**, 281–286 (2016)
5. Bowers, C.A., Pharmer, J.A., Salas, E.: When member homogeneity is needed in work teams a meta-analysis. Small Group Res. **31**, 305–327 (2000)
6. Bittner, E.A.C., Leimeister, J.M.: Creating shared understanding in heterogeneous work groups: why it matters and how to achieve it. J. Manag. Inf. Syst. **31**, 111–144 (2014)
7. Langan-Fox, J., Anglim, J., Wilson, J.R.: Mental models, team mental models, and performance: Process, development, and future directions. Hum. Factors Ergon. Manuf. **14**, 331–352 (2004)
8. Wegge, J., Roth, C., Neubach, B., Schmidt, K.H., Kanfer, R.: Age and gender diversity as determinants of performance and health in a public organization: the role of task complexity and group size. J. Appl. Psychol. **93**, 1301–1313 (2008)
9. Agafonovas, A., Alonderiene, R.: value creation in innovations crowdsourcing: example of creative agencies. Organ. Markets Emerg. Econ. **2**, 32 (2013)
10. Tavanapour, N., Bittner, E.A.C.: Collaboration among crowdsourcees: towards a design theory for collaboration process design. In: Proceedings of the 50th Hawaii International Conference on System Sciences, Hawaii (2017)
11. Tavanapour, N., Bittner, E.A.C.: The Collaboration of crowd workers. In: Proceedings of the 26th European Conference on Information Systems, Portsmouth, UK (2018)
12. Kittur, A., et al.: The future of crowd work. In: Proceedings of the 2013 Conference on Computer Supported Cooperative Work, pp. 1301–1318. ACM, New York (2013)
13. Pedersen, J., et al.: Conceptual foundations of crowdsourcing: a review of IS research. In: 46th Hawaii International Conference on System Sciences (HICSS), Hawaii (2013)
14. Kipp, P.: Engineering Tool Supported Collaboration Processes for Web-based Platforms. Research on IT / Service / Innovation / Collaboration. 9 (2015)
15. Hutter, K., Hautz, J., Füller, J., Mueller, J., Matzler, K.: Communitition: the tension between competition and collaboration in community-based design contests. Creativity Innov. Manag. **20**, 3–21 (2011)
16. Malhotra, A., Majchrzak, A.: Managing Crowds in Innovation Challenges. Calif. Manag. Rev. **56**, 103–123 (2014)
17. Grant, R.M.: Prospering in dynamically-competitive environments: organizational capability as knowledge integration. Organ. Sci. **7**, 375–387 (1996)
18. Mayring, P.: Qualitative content analysis: theoretical foundation, basic procedures and software solution, Klagenfurt (2014)
19. Mayring, P., Brunner, E.: Qualitative inhaltsanalyse. In: Buber, R., Holzmüller, H.H. (eds.) Qualitative Marktforschung. Gabler, pp. 669–680. Springer, Heidelberg (2009). https://doi.org/10.1007/978-3-8349-9441-7_42
20. Coffey, A., Atkinson, P.: Making Sense of Qualitative Data: Complementary Research Strategies. Sage Publications, Thousand Oaks (1996)
21. Simon, H.A.: The Sciences of the Artificial. MIT Press, Cambridge (1996)
22. Gregor, S.: The nature of theory in information systems. MIS Q. **30**, 611–642 (2006)
23. Gregor, S., Hevner, A.R.: Positioning and presenting design science research for maximum impact. MIS Q. **37**, 337–355 (2013)
24. Gregor, S., Jones, D.: The anatomy of a design theory. J. AIS **8**, 19 (2007)
25. Peffers, K., Tuunanen, T., Rothenberger, M.A., Chatterjee, S.: A design science research methodology for information systems research. J. Manag. Inf. Syst. **24**, 45–77 (2007)

26. Andersen, R., Mørch, A.I.: Mutual development in mass collaboration: identifying interaction patterns in customer-initiated software product development. Comput. Hum. Behav. **65**, 77–91 (2016)
27. Dow, S., Kulkarni, A., Bunge, B., Nguyen, T., Klemmer, S., Hartmann, B.: Shepherding the crowd. In: Tan, D. (ed.) Proceedings of the 2011 Annual Conference Extended Abstracts on Human Factors in Computing Systems, p. 1669. ACM, New York (2011)
28. Mok, R.K.P., Li, W., Chang, R.K.C.: Detecting low-quality crowdtesting workers. In: IEEE 23rd International Symposium on Quality of Service (IWQoS), pp. 201–206. IEEE, Piscataway (2015)
29. Peng, X., Ali Babar, M., Ebert, C.: Collaborative software development platforms for crowdsourcing. IEEE Softw. **31**, 30–36 (2014)
30. Skopik, F., Schall, D., Dustdar, S.: Discovering and managing social compositions in collaborative enterprise crowdsourcing systems. Int. J. Coop. Inf. Syst. **21**, 297–341 (2012)
31. Yang, P., Zhang, N., Zhang, S., Yang, K., Yu, L., Shen, X.: Identifying the most valuable workers in fog-assisted spatial crowdsourcing. IEEE Internet Things J. **4**, 1193–1203 (2017)
32. Ankolekar, A., Balestrieri, F.E., Asur, S.: MET: an enterprise market for tasks. In: Gergle, D., Morris, M.R., Bjørn, P., Konstan, J. (eds.) ACM Conference on Computer-Supported Cooperative Work and Social Computing and Association for Computing Machinery and CSCW. CSCW 2016, pp. 225–228, New York (2016)
33. Tian, F., Liu, B., Sun, X., Zhang, X., Cao, G., Lin, G.: Movement-based incentive for crowdsourcing. IEEE Trans. Veh. Technol. **66**(8), 7223–7233 (2017)
34. Hassan, U., Curry, E.: A capability requirements approach for predicting worker performance in crowdsourcing. In: Bertino, E., Georgakopoulos, D., Srivatsa, M., Nepal, S., Vinciarelli, A. (eds.) 2013 9th International Conference on Collaborative Computing: Networking, Applications and Worksharing (Collaboratecom). IEEE, Piscataway (2013)
35. Hirth, M., Scheuring, S., Hossfeld, T., Schwartz, C., Tran-Gia, P.: Predicting result quality in crowdsourcing using application layer monitoring. In: 2014 IEEE Fifth International Conference on Communications and Electronics (ICCE), pp. 510–515 (2014)
36. Li, G., Wang, J., Zheng, Y., Franklin, M.J.: Crowdsourced data management: a survey. IEEE Trans. Knowl. Data Eng. **28**, 2296–2319 (2016)
37. Naderi, B., Wechsung, I., Moller, S.: Effect of being observed on the reliability of responses in crowdsourcing micro-task platforms. In: Seventh International Workshop on Quality of Multimedia Experience (QoMEX), pp. 1–2. IEEE, Piscataway (2015)
38. Abhinav, K., Dubey, A., Jain, S., Bhatia, G.K., McCartin, B., Bhardwaj, N.: Crowdassistant: a virtual buddy for crowd worker. In: IEEE/ACM 5th International Workshop on Crowd Sourcing in Software Engineering (CSI-SE), pp. 17–20 (2018)
39. Jiang, L., Wagner, C., Nardi, B.: Not just in it for the money: a qualitative investigation of workers' perceived benefits of micro-task crowdsourcing. In: Bui, T.X., Sprague, R.H. (eds.) 48th Hawaii International Conference on System Sciences (HICSS), pp. 773–782. IEEE, Piscataway (2015)
40. Chittilappilly, A.I., Chen, L., Amer-Yahia, S.: A survey of general-purpose crowdsourcing techniques. IEEE Trans. Knowl. Data Eng. **28**, 2246–2266 (2016)
41. Frey, K., Lüthje, C., Haag, S.: Whom should firms attract to open innovation platforms? The role of knowledge diversity and motivation. Long Range Plan. **44**, 397–420 (2011)
42. Schultheiss, D., Blieske, A., Solf, A., Staeudtner, S.: How to encourage the crowd? A study about user typologies and motivations on crowdsourcing platforms. In: IEEE/ACM 6th International Conference on Utility and Cloud Computing (UCC), pp. 506–509. IEEE, Piscataway (2013)

43. Hossain, M.: Users' motivation to participate in online crowdsourcing platforms. In: Proceedings of the 2012 International Conference on Innovation Management and Technology Research, Malacca, Malaysia (2012)
44. Soliman, W., Tuunainen, V.K.: Understanding continued use of crowdsourcing systems: an interpretive study. J. Theor. Appl. Electron. Commer. Res. **10**, 1–18 (2015)
45. Dai, W., Wang, Y., Jin, Q., Ma, J.: An integrated incentive framework for mobile crowdsourced sensing. Tsinghua Sci. Technol. **21**, 146–156 (2016)
46. Faradani, S., Hartmann, B., Ipeirotis, P.G.: What's the right price? Pricing tasks for finishing on time. Hum. Comput. **11**, 11 (2011)
47. Mason, W., Watts, D.J.: Financial incentives and the performance of crowds. ACM SIGKDD Explor. Newsl. **11**, 100–108 (2010)
48. Wu, H., Corney, J., Grant, M.: Relationship between quality and payment in crowdsourced design. In: Hou, J.L. (ed.) Proceedings of the 2014 IEEE 18th International Conference on Computer Supported Cooperative Work in Design (CSCWD), pp. 499–504. IEEE, Piscataway (2014)
49. Xie, H., Lui, J.C.S., Jiang, J.W., Chen, W.: Incentive mechanism and protocol design for crowdsourcing systems. In: 52nd Annual Allerton Conference on Communication, Control, and Computing (Allerton), 2014, pp. 140–147. IEEE, Piscataway (2014)
50. Zhang, Y., van der Schaar, M.: Reputation-based incentive protocols in crowdsourcing applications. In: Proceedings of the 2012 IEEE INFOCOM, pp. 2140–2148. IEEE, Piscataway (2012)

Using Big Data Analytics and Visualization to Create IoT-enabled Science Park Smart Governance Platform

Hsiao-Fang Yang, Chia-Hou Kay Chen,
and Kuei-Ling Belinda Chen[✉]

Digital Service Innovation Institute,
Institute for Information Industry, Taipei, Taiwan
klchen@iii.org.tw

Abstract. Science parks are important industrial clusters in the development of Taiwan's technology industry. Nearly 280,000 employees commute to the science parks on a daily basis. Thus, traffic congestion not only wastes the time of and creates extra fuel costs for the road users, but also leads the vehicles to release more pollutants in the environment. With the rise of Internet of Things technology, the science park administration has established multiple IoT-enabled systems since 2017, in order to collect data and monitor traffic flow and air quality in a more accurate manner.

However, it is still a question that how emerging technology should be applied to provide accurate and timely information to assist administration to observe the historical trends and current status of traffic congestion and air quality, so as to formulate traffic control and air pollution prevention strategies. To that end, there are two purposes in this paper: (1) to establish a Science Park Smart Governance Platform to collect data collected from the IoT devices, and (2) to design and develop data visualization functions for the smart management of traffic and air quality.

The research garners three results from the smart traffic monitoring service: (1) helping administration check the traffic status in real time, in order to facilitate traffic control; (2) presenting the historical trends of traffic flow on a typical day, month, and year, and allowing administration to understand in what intersections and at what periods traffic congestion is more prone to take place; (3) creating a predictive model of how traffic flow and weather can influence the traffic volume interactively to predict traffic flow for every intersection in the following 10 min, so that administration can operate the traffic lights in order to reduce traffic congestion.

Besides the aforementioned results, three other results from the smart air quality monitoring service are presented in the study: (1) allowing administration to monitor real-time air quality status in various areas of the science parks; (2) presenting a historical trend of air quality, and allowing administration to understand in what month/time air pollution is occurring; (3) when the concentration of certain air pollutant exceeds a particular threshold, the smart environmental monitoring Chabot service will push warning messages to the managers.

© Springer Nature Switzerland AG 2019
F. F.-H. Nah and K. Siau (Eds.): HCII 2019, LNCS 11589, pp. 459–472, 2019.
https://doi.org/10.1007/978-3-030-22338-0_37

Keywords: Taiwan Science Park · IoT · Traffic congestion · Air quality · Science Park Smart Governance Platform · Map-based dashboard

1 Introduction

Currently, with the rapid economic development in all parts of the world, most of the population resides in urban areas. According to UN statistics, by 2050 more than 2/3 of the global population will reside in cities. In addition to the sharp increase in demand for services, in the future it can be expected that issues regarding energy, water resources, transportation, disaster prevention, public security, health, education, and medical care will come into existence. Hence, the planning of smart cities [1] and smart services has become social issues that local governments and companies in relevant industries must pay attention to. According to the IDC's statistics [2], the Asia/Pacific region represents over 40% of total spending on smart cities initiatives, while the Americas represent around one third, and Europe, Middle East and Africa around one quarter of the global opportunity. With various countries promoting the development of smart cities around the world, the Ministry of Science and Technology in Taiwan initiated the four-year Smart Science Park Project in 2016 [3], using ICT, Internet of Things (IoT), and other state-of-the-art technologies to transform the science parks into living labs for new smart services, focusing on transportation, sustainability, and governance.

Hsinchu Science Park [4] was established in 1980 as the first science park in Taiwan. The top three industrial focuses are integrated circuits, optoelectronics, and computers and peripheral merchandise. Southern Taiwan Science Park [5] was established in 1997. The top three industrial focuses are biotechnology, precision machinery, and optoelectronics. Central Taiwan Science Park [6] was established in 2003. The top three industrial focuses are precision machinery, biotechnology, and optoelectronics. Currently, more than 850 companies have been stationed in the three science parks, and the number of employees has reached 276,000, and the overall turnover in 2018 has reached 80 billion dollars. According to statistics, 95% of the 153,000 commuters in Hsinchu Science Park use private vehicles (cars or motorcycles) as their means of transportation. Traffic congestion during peak hours of commuting is hence very serious. The traffic congestion not only puts drivers in a gridlock, but also gives rise to economic loss of time and fuel cost, as well as excessive emissions of pollutants while the cars are functioning at low speeds, rendering an even worse impact on the environment [7]. In the long run, losses accumulated can be extremely considerable. In the early days, limited by technology, the administration could only collect traffic and air quality data manually in the science parks. Now in conjunction with the Smart Park Project, the administration built a variety of IoT-enabled systems in 2017, with the eTag [8] system and continuous emission monitoring systems (CEMS) to collect traffic and air quality data and it was expected that such data would be conducive to helping perform traffic management and monitor air quality more accurately.

Many organizations have begun to use big data analytics technology to develop smart applications to achieve smart sustainability, smart governance, smart management and other goals [9]. IoT Innovation [10] indicates that there are three differences between big data and IoT: concept, time sequencing, and analytical goals. The big data, which is analyzing large amounts of mostly human-generated data to support longer-duration use cases such as predictive maintenance. The IoT, which is aggregating and compressing massive amounts of low latency, low duration, and high volume machine-generated data coming from a wide variety of sensors to support real-time use cases such as operational optimization. Although big data and IoT are different, they are intricately linked. Therefore, it is important to find out how to use the emerging technology to support IoT-enabled big data management in order to provide accurate information in real time to help administration observe the historical trends and current conditions of traffic congestion and air pollution, and to formulate research questions on traffic controls and air pollution prevention strategies.

Many previous studies [11–17] point out that data visualization technology and dashboard can bridge the gap between user and data, and improve decision-making quality and efficiency. Based on the statement above, this paper has two research purposes: (1) to build a Science Park Smart Governance Platform [18] to collect, process, and demonstrate data from the Science Park IoT device systems; (2) via big data and visualization technology, to design and develop two smart application services for traffic dynamics and air quality monitoring respectively, and, in the shortest time possible, to convert complicated raw data into dynamic charts and provide them to the administration in the form of dashboards. To that end, this paper plans to gather the traffic flow data of eTag and air quality monitoring data via the standardized data exchange technology tool (e.g. application programming interface, API). Then, the data are parsed and stored in the database of the platform. Finally, the traffic flow data and air quality data are visualized by describing and building modules via statistical analysis and data visualization technology.

2   Related Works

In recent years, with the advances in software and hardware technologies, research on big data is increasing day by day. This paper summarizes the findings of Nuaimi et al. [10] and Mehmood et al. [19] to list out the main applications of big data in smart cities. As shown in Table 1, IoT combined with big data analysis can improve service quality and improve decision-making efficiency. However, real-time IoT big data has high technical requirements for big data management, big data processing platform, algorithm, open standard technology, etc. Therefore, in the absence of relevant technologies, it is difficult for the administration to further explore the value of IoT-enabled big data.

Table 1. Services of big data applications in smart city

Services	Applications
Smart healthcare E-healthcare	Using smart devices to obtain personal health data for monitoring health and sending warnings/notifications in case of abnormalities
Smart energy Smart energy metering	Instantly monitoring energy usage with smart devices; using big data analysis technology to achieve prediction and energy saving
Smart transportation Smart parking	Using smart devices to grasp road traffic and the number of remaining parking spaces in parking lots, through parking guidance the reduction of energy waste and carbon emission can be achieved
Smart safety Safety and security	Collecting spatial and temporal geographic area data to predict future environmental changes or natural disasters (such as earthquakes); using smart devices to identify the location of young children or the elderly to prevent them from going missing
Smart environment	Using smart devices to collect climate data and use big data to predict climate information to promote agriculture, reduce disaster loss, and better manage energy use
Smart waste management	Using smart devices to detect how full the trash cans are in urban areas to achieve smart cleaning and reduce carbon emissions
Smart education	Using big data technology to analyze students' digital learning data, allowing educational institutions to grasp the allocation and utilization of resources
Smart governance	Stakeholders using big data technology to analyze government open data to provide suggestions for improvement

Data visualization [20] is a new research area in recent years. The objective of data visualization is to support the collection and interpretation of heterogeneous data in more clear and effective ways. Previous researches [10–16] have pointed out that data visualization technologies can bridge the gap between user and data, and thus improve decision-making quality and efficiency. Some studies such as [11–13, 16] even present the core information which is most relevant to decision-makers in the form of dashboard. Practically, studies [11, 13] present multiple sources of data on one interface with multiple dashboards, while study [12] presents multiple sources of data on a single dashboard in various colors and graphs. Besides the above-mentioned studies, study [16] utilizes cross-theme dashboards to allow users to execute data exploration, extraction, visualization, transformation, etc. in an interactive manner. Since dashboard offers a comprehensive viewpoint for decision-makers to access all key information in an intuitive way, it has been adopted in the area of city governance [21–23] in recent years. Examples such as the London City Dashboard [24] and the Boston Smart City dashboard [25] present information of multiple categories (e.g. traffic, weather, finance, news, etc.) on a single dashboard, whereas examples such as Bandung City Dashboard [26] and Smart CEI Moncloa Dashboard [27] have a list of categories (e.g. education, population, environment, etc.) on the left of the dashboard for users to click on, and on the right, there is another page or a drop-down menu to present relevant information. Last but not least, in the example of Dublin Dashboard [28], there are different dashboard interfaces which present different information. (See Figs. 1 and 2)

| London City Dashboard | Boston Smart City Dashboard | Bandung City Dashboard |

Fig. 1. The three examples of city dashboard (Source: [24–26])

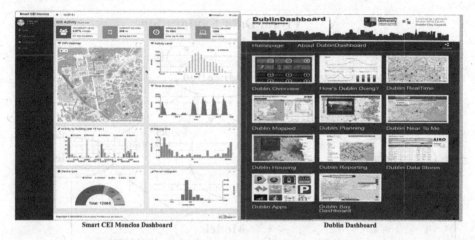

| Smart CEI Moncloa Dashboard | Dublin Dashboard |

Fig. 2. The two examples of city dashboard (Source: [27, 28])

As discussed in the above studies, after being analyzed and visualized, and then presented with all the key information via dashboard, big data generated by smart cities services can help decision makers achieve better efficiency. Therefore, this paper will use the standardized data exchange format technology tool application programming interface (API) to obtain traffic flow data and air quality monitoring data in the science parks. Then, data analysis and storage are performed to the platform back-end database. Finally, via statistical analysis and data visualization technologies, the traffic and air quality data are visually interpreted by the dashboard via the building of the model. The details will be explained in the next section.

3 Methods

Previous studies [20, 29, 30] have established the framework of "visual analytics pipeline" (see Fig. 3), which has four core concepts: (1) Data, which refers to the collection and pre-processing of heterogeneous raw data. Common pre-processing includes data parsing, data integration, data cleaning (e.g. getting rid of redundancy, errors, and invalid), data transformation (e.g. normalization), and data reduction; (2) Models, which refers to the conversion from data to information. Common conversion methods include feature selection and generation, model building, selection and validation, etc.; (3) Visualization, which refers to the visualization and abstract transformation of data, such as visual mapping (e.g. parallel coordinates, force-directed graph, chord graph, scatter matrix), view generation and coordination (e.g. overview + detail, small-multiples), human-computer interaction, etc.; (4) Knowledge (or called intelligence-gaining, sense-making, decision-making, or concept-building), which refers to the process in which humans interact with machines so as to spark knowledge.

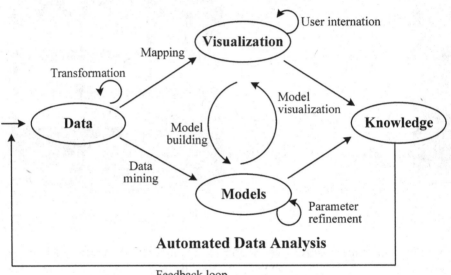

Fig. 3. Visual analytics pipeline (Source: [20, 29, 30])

This paper applies the theoretical framework of the visual analytics pipeline to illustrate the establishment of the smart traffic monitoring service and the smart air quality monitoring service. The objective of Data and Model is to collect, process, and discover the value of data, whereas the purpose of Visualization and Knowledge is to present the results of data and model visualization. Therefore, this paper will first explain the two phases of Data and Model in this section. The two phases of Visualization and Knowledge will be further explored later in Sect. 4.

3.1   Smart Traffic Monitoring Service

In the Data phase, this paper collects the raw traffic data in the science parks and converts it into a format accessible by the database. There are three steps in the establishment process (see Fig. 4): (1) Using APIs to interface with the eTag device system and collect the traffic data at intersections; (2) Writing a program to parse the data structure in the JSON file format; (3) Cleaning and converting the data.

Fig. 4. Data flow of smart traffic monitoring service

In the Model phase, this paper builds a traffic prediction model to predict the traffic volume in the next 10 min. There are three steps in the establishment process (see Fig. 5): (1) manually collecting the map and traffic data from 10 intersections from Google Maps. (2) comparing the color of the Google traffic map image and the traffic volume at the intersections. If the color of the road segment is red (indicating traffic congestion), it is marked as 1, otherwise it is marked as 0 (indicating smooth traffic); (3) integrating climate information [31] (e.g. rainfall probability, highest temperature, lowest temperature) and a traffic flow prediction model for each intersection with Multiple Logistic Regression Analysis [32]. The equation is specified as Eq. 1.

$$y = \beta_0 + \beta_1 x_1 + \beta_2 x_2 + \beta_3 x_3 + \beta_4 x_4 \tag{1}$$

where the variable y indicates the traffic congestion at the intersection (0 means smooth traffic, 1 means congestion), the variables $\beta_0 - \beta_3$ are regression coefficients, the variable x_1 is traffic flow, the variable x_2 is rainfall probability, the variable x_3 is the highest temperature of the day, and the variable x_4 is the lowest temperature of the day.

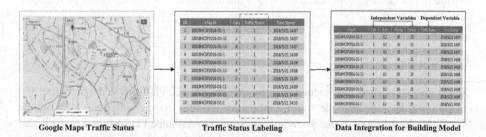

Fig. 5. Model building of smart traffic monitoring service (Color figure online)

3.2   Smart Air Quality Monitoring Service

In the Data phase, this paper collects the air quality data in the science parks and converts it into a database-accessible format. The establishment process has three steps (see Fig. 6): (1) using APIs to interface with CEMS and collecting air quality data from the monitoring station(s) in the area; (2) writing a program to parse the data structure in the XML file format; (3) cleaning and converting the data.

Fig. 6. Data flow of smart air quality monitoring service

In the Model phase, this paper converts air quality data into Air Quality Index (AQI). For the calculation, see Eqs. 2, 3, 4 and 5.

$$AQI_{s1} = \max\left(\max\left(O_{3,8hr},\ O_3\right),\ PM_{2.5},\ PM_{10},\ CO,\ SO_2,\ NO_2\right) \qquad (2)$$

$$AQI_{s2} = \max\left(\max\left(O_{3,8hr},\ O_3\right),\ PM_{2.5},\ PM_{10},\ CO,\ SO_{2,24hr},\ NO_2\right) \qquad (3)$$

$$AQI_{s3} = \max\left(O_3,\ PM_{2.5},\ PM_{10},\ CO,\ SO_{2,24hr},\ NO_2\right) \qquad (4)$$

$$AQI = \max\left(AQI_{s1},\ AQI_{s2},\ AQI_{s3}\right) \qquad (5)$$

where the variable $O_{3,8\,hr}$ is the average concentration of ozone (trioxygen) in the last eight hours; the variable O_3 is the instantaneous concentration of ozone (trioxygen); the calculation of $PM_{2.5}$ and PM_{10} is ($0.5 \times$ the average in the first 12 h + $0.5 \times$ the average in the first 4 h); the variable CO is the average concentration of carbon monoxide (CO) in the last eight hours; the variable SO_2 is the instantaneous concentration of sulfur dioxide; the variable $SO_{2,24\,hr}$ is the average concentration of sulfur dioxide in the last 24 h; the variable NO_2 is the instantaneous concentration of nitrogen dioxide.

4   Results

This study established the Science Park Smart Governance Platform to manage the IoT-enabled big data and provide smart application services. Its user interface is shown in Fig. 7. All the features of the Science Park Smart Governance Platform are listed in the menu on the left. From top to bottom, they are front end, back end, front end settings,

IoT data management center, statistics of water/electricity consumption, back end settings, map-based smart application services, and IoT data stream monitoring. The IoT data management center allows the administration to manage all IoT-enabled big data in the science parks. The two functions of IoT data management center are (1) converting unstructured data into structured data, and (2) converting data into three file formats (i.e. CSV, JSON, and XML). Map-based smart application services allow the administration to visually examine data processing and analysis results. Similar to researches [11, 13], this paper also integrates multiple data into a single dashboard, with the purpose of reducing the time and cognitive effort that users need to spend in order to understand the information presented.

Fig. 7. User interface of science park smart governance platform (Source: [18])

4.1   Smart Traffic Monitoring Service

In the Visualization phase, this paper visualizes traffic-related data or information, and the user interface established is shown in Fig. 8. The user interface has five main blocks; from top to bottom they are (1) the big data exploration block, (2) the intersections block, (3) the traffic predication block, (4) the traffic flow block, and (5) the weather condition block. The intersections block presents the traffic flow of 10 intersections simultaneously via data visualization. The traffic prediction block predicts the traffic flow change of each intersection in the next 10 min. The traffic flow block provides the instantaneous traffic flow data of each intersection. The weather condition block provides the local rainfall probability, temperature, as well as other weather conditions described in text.

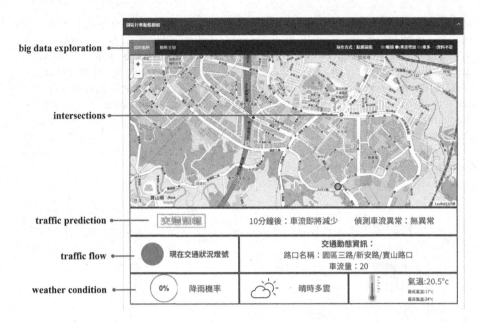

Fig. 8. User interface of smart traffic monitoring service

In the Knowledge phase, this paper accumulates the traffic data from 10 intersections since July 2018 (approximately 500,000 pieces of data per week) and presents it in a line chart (as shown in Fig. 9). Users can click on the buttons at the top right to view the trend of traffic flow history data define in different timeframes (i.e. the current day, the current month, and the current year). For example, the traffic volume on the 14th is abnormally high, and the traffic volume in the first half of the month is higher than that in the second half.

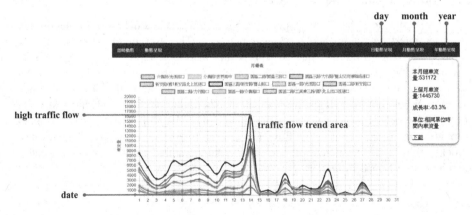

Fig. 9. User interface of data exploration area

In short, the smart traffic monitoring service provides three services: (1) providing accurate traffic flow data, allowing the administration to instantly (updated per minute) grasp the traffic status; (2) providing three kinds of traffic flow history data trends, allowing the administration to know at what time traffic congestion occurs; (3) predicting traffic flow for the next 10 min, and the administration can use this information to further adjust the traffic lights at intersections.

4.2 Smart Air Quality Monitoring Service

In the Visualization phase, this paper presents information such as air quality index (AQI), wind direction, wind speed, etc., and the results are shown in the upper part of the dashboard (see Fig. 10). Therefore, users can directly know in which directions pollutants are diffused the air quality status of each monitoring station from the colors shown on the dashboard. Green (0–50) indicates good air quality. Yellow (51–100) indicates normal air quality. Orange (101–150) indicates the air quality is unhealthy for sensitive groups. Red (151–200) means that air quality is unhealthy for all people. Purple (201–300) means that air quality is very unhealthy, and maroon (301–500) means air quality is harmful.

In the Knowledge phase, this paper collects the data of air quality per hour since mid-May 2018 (approximately 3,600 pieces of data per month) and sets an air pollution warning threshold for the platform. When the AQI exceeds the threshold, the time, location, and AQI value of air pollution will be listed at the lower left of the dashboard. Therefore, the administration can further explore whether there exist regional or seasonal trends in air quality anomalies.

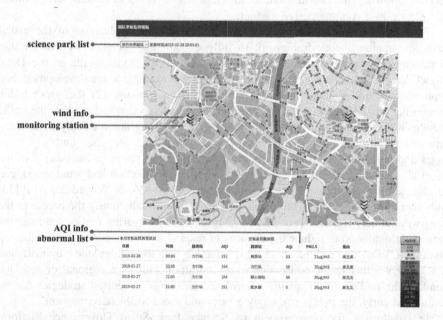

Fig. 10. User interface of smart air quality monitoring service (Color figure online)

In short, smart air quality monitoring service provides three services: (1) the hourly concentrations data of air pollutant from three monitoring stations are collected, allowing the administration to monitor the air quality status in various areas of the science parks immediately; (2) the hourly concentration data of air pollutant, wind direction and wind speed data from the three stations has been collected from mid-May 2018, presenting a historical trend of air quality, and allowing the administration to understand in what month/time air pollution is occurring; and (3) when the concentration of certain air pollutant exceeds a particular threshold, the smart environmental monitoring Chabot service will push warning messages to the administration in the science park.

5   Conclusion and Future Work

Big data and visual analysis technology have been widely used to tackle real-world problems such as network traffic analysis, engaging education, sport analysis, database analysis, and biological data analysis. In recent years, relevant industries and the academia have begun to pay attention to data visualization applications such as time-oriented data, spatio-temporal data, network data, etc. Different from previous researches, this paper discusses the IoT-enabled big data and its visualization in smart application services. First, the researchers developed the IoT-enabled Science Park Smart Governance Platform, which allows the administration to manage all on-site IoT-enabled data using IoT data management. Next, the researchers introduced the dashboard concept to the smart traffic monitoring service and smart air quality monitoring service, allowing the administration to view traffic congestion and air pollution information in a comprehensive manner.

The contribution of this paper is as follows: (1) the application of the visual analytics pipeline theory framework to fully explain the operation of smart traffic monitoring service and smart air quality monitoring service at various phases (i.e. Data, Model, Visualization, and Knowledge), adding a new example to the development and application of IoT-enabled big data presented via dashboard; (2) the smart traffic monitoring service presents the traffic volume at the intersection and predicts the traffic change in the next 10 min, and the traffic sign technology automatically adjusts the time of red lights to improve the issue of congestion and reduce the number of stoppages and the amount of fuel consumption; (3) instant air pollution monitoring of the smart air quality monitoring service, with data of wind direction and wind speed, can be accessed through digital signage or the Science Park Mobile Wizard 2.0 APP [33] and other terminal devices. The system will also automatically notify the people in the downwind to carry out self-protection strategies (such as wearing masks, reducing the time spent outdoors) to reduce the chances of respiratory dysfunctions, cardiovascular diseases (CVDs), and asthma attacks; (4) using big data technology, the administration can know whether traffic congestion or air pollution follows a regional or seasonal trend. If the traffic and air quality control and pollution prevention strategies can be formulated early, the public can enjoy a safer and more livable environment.

In conclusion, the development of Science Park Smart Governance Platform enables administration to accurately observe and grasp the trends, be it historical or current, of traffic congestion and air pollution. There are three directions worthy of further exploration in the future: (1) warning service should be developed in the future to detect data reception abnormality from the IoT devices in real time, in order to enable administration to check and repair the devices/systems in the shortest time to improve preventive maintenance; (2) the research can present the integrated multi-data analysis results via map-based dashboard visualization, in order to provide administration with more comprehensive information to optimize the quality and efficiency of decision-making process; and (3) traffic congestion and air quality issues need to be more thoroughly investigated in future studies, in order to increase the accuracy of the information dashboard provided by the Science Park Smart Governance Platform.

Acknowledgments. This paper is supported by the Ministry of Science and Technology, the Hsinchu Science Park, the Central Taiwan Science Park, and the Southern Taiwan Science Park.

References

1. Smart City. http://www-07.ibm.com/tw/dp-cs/smartercity/overview.html. Accessed 22 Feb 2019
2. IDC's Smart Cities Spending Guide Expands Its Coverage to More Than 100 Cities. https://www.idc.com/getdoc.jsp?containerId=prUS44817419. Accessed 14 Mar 2019
3. Chen, K.L.B.: Smart park ICT re-engineering initiative. In: 2017 Energy Smart Communities Initiative (ESCI). http://esci-ksp.org/project/smart-park-ict-re-engineering-initiative/. Accessed 22 Feb 2019
4. Hsinchu Science Park. https://www.sipa.gov.tw/. Accessed 12 Feb 2019
5. Southern Taiwan Science Park. https://www.stsp.gov.tw/. Accessed 12 Feb 2019
6. Central Taiwan Science Park. https://www.ctsp.gov.tw/. Accessed 12 Feb 2019
7. Zhang, K., Batterman, S.: Air pollution and health risks due to vehicle traffic. Sci. Total Environ. **450–451**, 307–316 (2013)
8. Electronic Toll Collection (Taiwan). https://en.wikipedia.org/wiki/Electronic_Toll_Collection_(Taiwan). Accessed 16 Feb 2019
9. Nuaimi, E.A., Neyadi, H.A., Mohamed, N., Al-Jaroodi, J.: Applications of big data to smart cities. J. Internet Serv. Appl. **6**(1), 1–15 (2015)
10. IoT Innovation. https://internet-of-things-innovation.com/insights/the-blog/differences-between-big-data-iot/#.XIn8YiIzbIV. Accessed 14 Mar 2019
11. Graves, A., Hendler, J.: Visualization tools for open government data. In: Proceedings of the 14th Annual International Conference on Digital Government Research, pp. 136–145 (2013)
12. Burkhardt, D., Nazemi, K., Parisay, M., Kohlhammer, J.: Visual correlation analysis to explain open government data based on linked-open data for decision making. Int. J. Digit. Soc. **5**(3), 947–955 (2014)
13. Bera, P., Sirois, L.P.: Displaying background maps in business intelligence dashboards. IT Prof. **18**(5), 58–65 (2016)
14. Krishna, C.N., Suneetha, M.: Business intelligence solutions for processing hugedata to the business user's using dashboards. In: 2016 International Conference on Signal Processing, Communication, Power and Embedded System (SCOPES), Paralakhemundi, India, pp. 1672–1677 (2016)

15. Pokorný, P., Stokláska, K.: Graphics visualization of specific dashboards in transport technologies. In: 2016 Third International Conference on Mathematics, and Computers in Sciences and in Industry (MCSI), Chania, Greece, pp. 203–206 (2016)
16. More, R., Goudar, R.H.: DataViz model: a novel approach towards big data analytics and visualization. Int. J. Eng. Manuf. 6(7), 43–49 (2017)
17. Gledson, A., Dhafari, T.B., Paton, N., Keane, J.: A smart city dashboard for combining and analysing multi-source data streams. In: IEEE 16th International Conference on Smart City, Exeter, United Kingdom, pp. 1366–1373 (2018)
18. Science Park Smart Governance Platform. https://www.twsp.org.tw/MOST/. Accessed 13 Feb 2019
19. Mehmood, Y., Ahmad, F., Yaqoob, I., Adnane, A., Imran, M., Guizani, S.: Internet-of-things-based smart cities: recent advances and challenges. IEEE Commun. Mag. 55(9), 16–24 (2017)
20. Sun, G.D., Wu, Y.C., Liang, R.H., Liu, S.X.: A survey of visual analytics techniques and applications: State-of-the-art research and future challenges. J. Comput. Sci. Technol. 28(5), 852–867 (2013)
21. Suakanto, S., Supangkat, S.H., Suhardi, Saragih, R.: Smart city dashboard for integrating various data of sensor networks. In: International Conference on ICT for Smart Society, Jakarta, Indonesia, pp. 1–5. (2013)
22. Kitchin, R., Lauriault, T.P., McArdle, G.: Knowing and governing cities through urban indicators, city benchmarking and real-time dashboards. Reg. Stud. Reg. Sci. 2(1), 6–28 (2015)
23. McArdle, G., Kitchin, R.: The dublin dashboard: design and development of a real-time analytical urban dashboard. In: International Society for Photogrammetry and Remote Sensing IV-4/W1, pp. 19–25 (2016)
24. City Dashboard: London. http://citydashboard.org/london/. Accessed 8 Mar 2019
25. Boston Smart City dashboard. https://boston.opendatasoft.com/page/smart-city-2/. Accessed 8 Mar 2019
26. Bandung City Dashboard. http://data.bandung.go.id/dashboard/. Accessed 8 Mar 2019
27. Smart CEI Moncola Dashboard. https://ceiboard.dit.upm.es/dashboard/. Accessed 8 Mar 2019
28. DublinDashboard. https://www.dublindashboard.ie/pages/index. Accessed 8 Mar 2019
29. Keim, D., Kohlhammer, J., Ellis, G., Mansmann, F.: Mastering the Information Age - Solving Problems with Visual Analytics. Eurographics Association (2010)
30. Wang, X.M., Zhang, T.Y., Ma, Y.X., Xia, J., Chen, W.: A survey of visual analytic pipelines. J. Comput. Sci. Technol. 31(4), 787–804 (2016)
31. Open Weather Data. https://opendata.cwb.gov.tw/index. Accessed 12 Feb 2019
32. McDonald, J.H.: Handbook of Biological Statistics, 3rd edn. Sparky House Publishing, Baltimore (2014)
33. Science Park Mobile Wizard 2.0 APP, Android. https://play.google.com/store/apps/details?id=tw.gov.nsc.mobileApp.NSCApp_ns&hl=zh_TW. Accessed 14 Feb 2019

Research on Visual Management of State Key Laboratory Environment

Chongwen Yuan[✉] and Huang Zhang

School of Art and Design, Wuhan University of Technology,
No. 123 Luoshi Road, Hongshan District, Wuhan 430070, China
348791916@qq.com, 664782154@qq.com

Abstract. National laboratories can promote the construction of academic teams, improve the level of scientific and technological innovation, improve the quality of personnel training, improve academic material conditions, and create a strong academic atmosphere. It is an important support for creating world-class disciplines. Visual elements are one of the main components of the laboratory environment, and strengthening the construction of visual management is of great significance. However, visual management laboratories are not perfect in most countries, and even some laboratories have not yet been established, lacking in structural layout, laboratory equipment display, lighting, walls, ground color, signs, slogans, guiding laboratory settings, etc. The visual programming of the system also brings up some new problems, mainly reflected in the efficiency and safety of the human, equipment, environmental, psychological and emotional experience of the experimenter. Therefore, how to strengthen the visual management of national laboratories has become a new topic in the construction of national laboratories.

Keywords: Laboratory · Visualization · Visual recognition · Management

1 Introduction

According to the current research status, visual management has been researched and applied in the fields of nuclear power, electric power, railway, coal, petrochemical, etc., but there are still many gaps in the application of visual management. Most of the research on laboratory construction is centered on management and sociology to complete the standardization of the management process. From the design point of view, combined with management, psychology, semiotics and other multidisciplinary, this paper uses the concept of visual management to study how to enhance the information visualization of the laboratory to ensure the safety of the experiment. Improve the laboratory's space environment and make students feel comfortable in the face of a complex and indifferent laboratory environment. The corresponding design methods are proposed to improve students' visual recognition ability in the experimental environment.

© Springer Nature Switzerland AG 2019
F. F.-H. Nah and K. Siau (Eds.): HCII 2019, LNCS 11589, pp. 473–481, 2019.
https://doi.org/10.1007/978-3-030-22338-0_38

2   Visual Management of National Laboratories

2.1   Information Visualization

Information visualization refers to the visualization of non-spatial data. With the advancement of experiments and the use of student lab machines and laboratories, the source of information is growing. In addition to the need to store, transfer, retrieve and classify these data, it is more urgent to understand the interrelationships and trends of data. In order to understand the relationship and development trends between data, we can turn to visualization technology. Modern data visualization technology refers to the theory, method and technology of using computer graphics and image processing technology to convert data into graphics or images on the screen and interactive processing. It involves computer graphics, image processing, computer-aided design, computer vision and human-computer interaction technology. Data can be displayed with images, curves, 2D graphics, 3D volume and animation, and its mode And visual analysis of the relationship. Information visualization can be seen as an adjustable mapping from data information to visualizations to human perception systems. Information visualization not only uses images to display multi-dimensional non-spatial data, but also allows users to deepen their understanding of the meaning of the data, and uses visually intuitive images to guide the retrieval process and speed up retrieval. Thomas, a scholar at the University of Illinois in the United States, said that information visualization solves the problem of how to talk to information resources. The main problem to be solved in information visualization is how to achieve mapping, transformation and interaction control between information resources. Information visualization technology is not the same as geographic information technology. It visualizes and maps information with geographic attributes, and then analyzes and maps according to relevant conditions, so that various information and analysis results can be seen at a glance. Therefore, information visualization can accurately transfer the cumbersome text information of the laboratory's experimental arrangement, experimental identification, and experimental results to each classmate in an image manner.

2.2   Visual Management System

Visualization is a theory in the field of graphic imaging that weakens the obscurity of traditional digital signals. The construction of visual management information system is based on this theory, which uses computer technology to convert several complex and diverse media signals into graphics or images to make it more simplified. The current virtual reality technology is a typical application based on visualization technology. The visualized management information system for big data, according to the business function, regularizes and analyzes the massive target data in the computer to form simple and easy-to-understand graphic and text information, and then uses the screen projection and other media to display.

As a small environment complex, the university laboratory includes teaching, scientific research and other aspects. Through the visual media presentation form of the visual management system platform, the laboratory management behavior can be simplified and the management level can be improved. The visual management information system is transformed into an integrated integrated media display platform.

2.3   Problems in Visualization of University Laboratory Environment

Visual recognition is confusing and information transmission is not comprehensive. The laboratory usually has the following characteristics: 1. The number of laboratories is large, involving many disciplines, many professions, different scales and relatively independent, and difficult to manage; 2. Full laboratory functions, excellent equipment, and a large number of valuable precision instruments; There are many categories and projects, and the experimental conditions are complex. Some of the experiments are dangerous. 4. The experimental equipment is used frequently, and the personnel are concentrated and the mobility is large. For these reasons, the laboratory's visual identity has been documented for use by students of all majors. The information is repetitive and confusing, and the information transmission is not comprehensive. There are certain security risks.

Visual recognition ignores beauty. On the one hand, the lack of aesthetics of visual recognition is reflected in the basic design of the logo. When designing the logo, there is a relatively high requirement in the meaning of the logo. The logo must have a very rich cultural connotation, but the simplification of the logo is often neglected. And beauty. On the other hand, the lack of aesthetics is reflected in the overemphasis on the practicality of the application system, while ignoring the aesthetics of the application system. This type of design causes students to experience visual fatigue during the long-term operation of the laboratory, and there are certain safety hazards.

The system was introduced and scattered, and the recognition effect of the system was not formed. The system import is not comprehensive, too fragmented, and can not form the recognition effect of the system. After importing visual recognition systems, many college laboratories often only import the basic design part, basically staying in the standard use of the logo and standard words, the application system part is basically not imported, or only a part of the import when importing, resulting in The use of the visual identity system of the entire laboratory is not standardized, and the visual image cannot be uniformly transmitted to the outside world, failing to meet the original intention of the visual recognition system.

Lack of visual management system. In the university laboratory, it is very rare to use the visual management system to present the results of experiments and experimental processes. In the course of the experiment, most people only rely on hand-written records to allocate experimental machines. The experimental period and the time required for experiments cannot be displayed to others. This has led to an imbalance in the use of laboratory machines.

3   Visual Management Information System

3.1   Data Presentation Forms Are Diverse

In the laboratory visual management construction, the business data exchange of the application system is based on the data center and standardized standard data. The construction concept of the only basic data center and unified data specification enables the system data to be highly shared and shared. With the advancement of the concept of clustered information platform, the capacity of the basic data center and distributed sub-database has increased dramatically, and the data density has become larger and larger. High-density big data analysis and high-speed convergence of cloud computing make the visual application management system's functional application module display style richer. Dynamic text, graphics, animation, audio and video technologies are widely used in visual management information systems. The complex and industry data is humanized by the visual management system platform. The data analysis based on big data is no longer a boring data, but is transformed into a variety of dynamic, simple and easy to read forms. This visualization technology has become the main technical means in the visualized management information system, which greatly reduces the difficulty of traditional laboratory management, reduces secondary analysis behavior, and improves management efficiency.

3.2 Visualization Data

All kinds of sensors based on the Internet of Things in the laboratory are generating various types of business data at all times, and structured and unstructured data such as text, numbers, images, audio, and video become the basic data storage format. Based on the preliminary analysis and calculation of big data, the management information system platform based on visualization technology develops secondary analysis and calculation, and displays the analysis results with more intuitive and visual visualization media, supplemented by interactive dynamic display. The application of visual management information system enables managers to quickly make scientific management decisions by relying on more intuitive and simple multi-dimensional visual media data.

3.3 Omnidirectional Visibility

With the support of the network and big data technology, a comprehensive 24-hour data record is conducted on all aspects of the laboratory's teaching activities. Relying on the visualized management information system, it can get rid of the boring data statistics process, and can quickly process the target object to achieve real-time tracking and post-complete activity tracking. The visual management system retrieves the most valuable key media data, and presents the historical activity information of the target object from multiple angles and multiple directions, thereby giving decision makers a reliable decision basis based on reliable facts and scientific analysis.

3.4 Realize Laboratory Visual Management

In the visual management of the laboratory, the intelligent terminal objects based on the Internet of Things can realize interoperability, comprehensively acquire and perceive the latest data information of laboratory activities, use the visual management information system to find actual problems and analyze the causes, and visually and remotely control the targets. Feedback related information. The visual laboratory management system can provide a full range of visualization services for laboratory management, and promote the humanization, scientific and intelligent management of laboratory management. It can comprehensively apply a variety of services such as teacher and student attendance management, identification, traffic statistics, and experimental information management. Through sensors installed in key areas of the laboratory, sensors and sound image acquisition devices that can sense light, sound, and temperature. Visually monitor the laboratory environment and teacher and student behavior, intelligent management, and fully realize the intelligent management of the laboratory environment and teaching activities.

3.5 Promote the Construction of a Visual Teaching Environment

With the development of network technology and audio and video digital media technology, various online teaching classrooms with short video as the core have become a new type of education and teaching. The Internet combines this virtual learning environment with real-life teaching to achieve the interconnection of physical space and digital space. In the online classroom, students can not only perceive the real teaching scene, but also break through the traditional learning space, and can learn from leading experts and scholars at home and abroad. The visualized management information system integrates such online educational resources, changes the form of one-way network communication, improves learning efficiency, strengthens communication and learning between teachers and students, and promotes the harmonious development of interpersonal relationships.

3.6 Visualization Technology in Laboratory Resource Management System

Using information visualization technology, the experimental resources can be displayed on different graphs at any time, so that the laboratory manager can keep abreast of the situation. Usually, the laboratory administrator fills in the test registration form according to the experimental course, and transmits the use of the test equipment to the control center in time, and uses the information visualization technology to display in real time. In this way, the use of each test equipment can be known at any time, and the overall utilization of the test resources of the entire school can be displayed, providing an accurate basis for the rational use and deployment of laboratory equipment.

4   Visual Management Process

Most project management themes are to achieve "better, faster, more economical." [1] Visual management can effectively control the elements of management through process models, reduce errors, reduce detours, and succeed in the fastest way, ending failures with minimal cost. For projects that need to apply cross-disciplinary knowledge to apply, visual management is the best way to achieve effective information understanding by communicating with each interdisciplinary.

4.1   Secure Visual Identification

The design of environmental visualization can be seen as the study of the relationship between people and the environment, so the analysis of laboratory information visualization design from "people" and "environment". University laboratories usually have the following characteristics: 1. The number of laboratories is large, involving many disciplines, many professions, different scales and relatively independent, and difficult to manage; 2. Full laboratory functions, excellent equipment, and a large number of valuable precision instruments; There are many experimental categories and projects, and the experimental conditions are complex. Some of the experiments are dangerous. 4. The experimental equipment is used frequently, and the personnel are concentrated and the mobility is large.

According to the characteristics of university laboratory safety work, learn from other industry experience, establish a university laboratory safety visual identification system, visualize the safety concept and safety culture of university laboratories, and use visual colors and symbols that are perceptible, understandable and transmissible. Interpretation can enable the audience (mainly teachers and students) to understand the information to be conveyed by the safety culture at a glance, consciously restrain the behavior in the laboratory, avoid safety accidents, and establish a safe culture atmosphere of the university laboratory.

The main content of the university laboratory security visual identification system The university laboratory security visual identification system consists of three components, namely the basic concept, the basic part and the application part. 1. The basic concepts include the laboratory safety work concept, guiding ideology and work policy. 2. The basic part consists of basic design elements and safety signs. The basic design elements include safety contrast color design specifications, standard colors, auxiliary colors and special Chinese and English printed fonts; safety signs are mainly various safety signs stipulated by national standards. 3. The application part includes the environment series, office series and publicity series. The environmental series mainly includes laboratory safety information cards, safety evacuation instructions, pipeline signs, warning lines, laboratory waste collection labels, glass ribbons, laboratory labels, system cards, biohazard warning signs, operating procedures signs, etc. Warnings, prohibitions, instructions and indications; office series mainly include business cards, letterheads, envelopes, fax papers, folders (boxes), badges, notebooks, safety training certificates, safety training handouts, and safety monitoring rectification submissions and receipts Etc. The propaganda series mainly includes safety warning bells, overalls, helmets and so on.

5   Steps to Create a University Laboratory Security Visual Identity System

The establishment of a university laboratory security identification system should generally follow the following steps: 1. Research and analysis of the environment, audience, and information. Environmental analysis is the laboratory safety management personnel and laboratory teachers for the specific work environment, jointly analyze, find security risks, assess the dangerous situation, analyze and determine the environmental information identification and local information identification. Audience analysis, that is, through surveys to obtain the audience's needs (mainly teachers and students) for security knowledge, acceptance habits and receiving channels.

Information analysis, which classifies the information to be communicated to the audience, such as regulations, skills, common sense, advocacy and prohibition. 2. Elemental exploration. Including: the discovery of laboratory safety concepts, to make the concept of safety more clear. 3. Design and development. Including: university laboratory safety standard color, safety contrast color, safety mark design, laboratory safety standard introduction, language expression of university laboratory safety concept and media confirmation; design should pay attention to easy identification, system and timeliness, And maintain identity with the school identity system. 4. Write an application manual. After revision and feedback, all design and development elements are determined, and all design, description, copywriting, field application examples, and production requirements are compiled into a "safe visual identification system specification manual" to distribute the audience. 5. Application. According to the safety status of different laboratories, the content, material, size and placement of various safety information identifications are separately evaluated and determined, which are identified by the information of the environment series.

5.1 Using Color Design

The feeling conveyed by color and its physical properties have certain universality. "All visual performance is produced by color and brightness," Rudolf Arnheim wrote in his book Art and Visual Perception. That is, the three characteristics of color: hue, brightness and purity, of which hue is the most intuitive factor affecting visual perception. In 1801, the British scientist Thomas Young proposed the theory of three primary colors. Hermann Helmholtz further perfected the theory of three primary colors and formed the theory of color. It is pointed out that human color perception is the result of stimulating human visual cells by red, green and blue colors. National Security Color (GB2893-2008) stipulates that red indicates ban, stop, dangerous or rapid fire preparedness, facility information; blue indicates compliance with command information; yellow indicates attention and warning information; green indicates safety alert. Therefore, the laboratory's main logo color can use the most intuitive red, yellow, green, and blue colors for clear identification.

5.2 Using Metaphor Design

There are two types of metaphors in the metaphor of information visualization: the most important and the most common metaphors: temporal metaphors and spatial metaphors. In the laboratory visual design, traditional spatial metaphors include windows, panels, desktops, rooms, and so on. Metaphors in the laboratory environment include the design of tables, chairs, machines, and rooms, which affect students' psychological perception and visual perception of the laboratory. The color of these items as a means of visual perception can motivate students to have positive emotional effects on the current environment. Students' psychological emotions can be improved by applying the psychological effects of color, thereby improving the efficiency of experiments and reducing fatigue. At present, there are many mechanical equipments and instruments in university laboratories, mainly neutral colors of gray tone (see Fig. 1). Indifferent machines combined with excessive colorless color matching can easily lead to visual fatigue and psychological depression. In the laboratory, you can create a relaxed or warm emotional experience by changing the surface color of the tables, chairs, rooms, and bulletin boards (see Fig. 2).

Fig. 1. The gray tone environment in the university lab (www.baidu.com).

Fig. 2. The color of the robot lab (www.baidu.com). (Color figure online)

6 Research Results

In the actual establishment and application of the laboratory visual management system, attention should be paid to the consistency of the basic concepts and basic performance elements. In practical applications, we should also pay attention to the diversity that is inevitable due to differences in time and space, audience differences, and differences in appeals, and strive to achieve clear goals and targeted. The construction of information visualization system should be greatly strengthened, and the safety visual identification design of the laboratory should be improved. In the specific application process of the safety visual identification system, the laboratory safety management personnel should fully consider various potential safety hazards, jointly find safety hazards, and properly use the safety visual identification mark at a reasonable location and location. If the laboratory's safety hazard or source of danger changes, the laboratory safety status must be re-evaluated and a corresponding safety information logo should be produced. The safety information logo set on site should be eye-catching, have good lighting conditions, and give the audience enough time to pay attention to what it expresses, generally not on movable objects. The safety mark shall be inspected at least once every six months. If it is found that there is damage, deformation, fading, etc. that do not meet the requirements, it shall be repaired or replaced in time. When the relevant national safety signs change, the safety information signs in the laboratory should also be changed accordingly. It is hoped that the visual management method proposed in this paper can optimize the environment of the national laboratory, ensure the safety of the laboratory, and provide a positive reference for the humanized service of the laboratory.

Reference

1. Fosberg, K., Muz, H., Cotman, H.: Visual project management - practical for business and technology success model. In: Liu, J., Xu, J., Yu, J., p. 2. Publishing House of Electronics Industry, Beijing (2002)

Correction to: Scaling Productivity and Innovation on the Path to Exascale with a "Team of Teams" Approach

Elaine M. Raybourn, J. David Moulton, and Aimee Hungerford

Correction to:
Chapter "Scaling Productivity and Innovation on the Path to Exascale with a "Team of Teams" Approach" in: F. F.-H. Nah and K. Siau (Eds.): *HCI in Business, Government and Organizations*, LNCS 11589, https://doi.org/10.1007/978-3-030-22338-0_33

The chapter starting on p. 408 was inadvertently published with an incorrect copyright holder name. The correct copyright holder name for this chapter is: © National Technology & Engineering Solutions of Sandia, LLC. Under the terms of Contract DE-NA0003525, there is a non-exclusive license for use of this work by or on behalf of the U.S. Government. The original version of the chapter has been corrected.

The updated version of this chapter can be found at
https://doi.org/10.1007/978-3-030-22338-0_33

© Springer Nature Switzerland AG 2019
F. F.-H. Nah and K. Siau (Eds.): HCII 2019, LNCS 11589, p. C1, 2019.
https://doi.org/10.1007/978-3-030-22338-0_39

Correction to: Understanding User Engagement Mechanisms on a Live Streaming Platform

Xinwei Wang and Dezhi Wu

Correction to:
Chapter "Understanding User Engagement Mechanisms
on a Live Streaming Platform"
in: F. F.-H. Nah and K. Siau (Eds.):
HCI in Business, Government and Organizations, **LNCS 11589,**
https://doi.org/10.1007/978-3-030-22338-0_22

In the version of this chapter that was originally published, the word "conversion" was erroneously written as "conversation" in two places. This has now been corrected.

The updated version of this chapter can be found at
https://doi.org/10.1007/978-3-030-22338-0_22

Author Index

Printed in the United States
By Bookmasters